MAKING HARVARD MODERN

By Morton Keller

*In Defense of Yesterday*
*The Life Insurance Enterprise, 1885–1910*
*The Art and Politics of Thomas Nast*
*Affairs of State*
*Regulating a New Economy*
*Regulating a New Society*


By Phyllis Keller

*States of Belonging*
*Getting at the Core*

# MAKING
# HARVARD
# MODERN

*The Rise of America's University*

UPDATED EDITION

MORTON AND PHYLLIS KELLER

Somebody needs to know everything
about each college and university,
but only about Harvard does everybody
need to know something.

—Clark Kerr

OXFORD
UNIVERSITY PRESS

# OXFORD
UNIVERSITY PRESS

Oxford University Press, Inc., publishes works that further
Oxford University's objective of excellence
in research, scholarship, and education.

Oxford  New York
Auckland   Cape Town   Dar es Salaam   Hong Kong   Karachi
Kuala Lumpur   Madrid   Melbourne   Mexico City   Nairobi
New Delhi   Shanghai   Taipei   Toronto

With offices in
Argentina  Austria  Brazil  Chile  Czech Republic  France  Greece
Guatemala  Hungary  Italy  Japan  Poland  Portugal  Singapore
South Korea  Switzerland  Thailand  Turkey  Ukraine  Vietnam

First published by Oxford University Press, Inc., 2001
198 Madison Avenue, New York, NY 10016
www.oup.com

First issued as an Oxford University Press paperback, 2007
ISBN 978-0-19-532515-7

Oxford is a registered trademark of Oxford University Press

The Library of Congress has cataloged the hardcover edition as follows:
Keller, Morton.
Making Harvard modern : the rise of America's university
/ Morton and Phyllis Keller
p. cm.
Includes bibliographical references and index.
ISBN 978-0-19-514457-4
1. Harvard University—History—20th century.
I. Keller, Phyllis, 1930– .  II. Title
LD2135.K45    2001    378.744'4—dc21    2001039093

1 3 5 7 9 8 6 4 2
Printed in the United States of America
on acid-free paper

*To our
Harvard and Brandeis colleagues,
past and present*

# CONTENTS

# PREFACE

Early each Cambridge spring, visiting families and tour groups crop up like crocuses in Harvard Yard. As the weather warms, their numbers mount. Year by year they are more numerous, more polyglot, more like dutiful pilgrims to a shrine. Their guides take them to old familiar places:

To Daniel Chester French's statue of John Harvard, gazing down from his pedestal in front of Charles Bulfinch's University Hall. There they are fed threadworn factoids: that the statue bears no likeness to its subject (no picture of John Harvard exists), that the scant details provided on the pedestal are wrong (he was not the University's founder; the College began not in 1638, but 1636).

Next, to a circuit of the surrounding serene Old Yard: a cyclorama of eighteenth- and nineteenth-century American architecture, starting with prerevolutionary Massachusetts, Harvard, and Hollis Halls and Holden Chapel, proceeding past Federal-era Stoughton, Holworthy, and University Halls, and ending with the ever more assertedly Victorian Thayer, Weld, Boylston, Grays, and Matthews.

Then on to the neighboring New Yard, dominated by the massive Roman front of Widener Library, there to be told the well-worn tale of young Harry Widener '07, precocious collector of incunabula, lost with the *Titanic* and commemorated for eternity by this building, the gift of his grieving mother. Facing Widener is capacious Memorial Church, built to remember Harvard's fallen in World War I, a squat base dominated by ample hollow wooden columns, topped by a classic Congregational spire: "all Emily Dickinson up above, all Mae West down below." Then on to the famous glass flowers housed in the Museum of Comparative Zoology....

What are they looking for? What do they see?

The Old Yard is one of America's architectural treasures. Indeed, there is more physical denotation of the distant past at Harvard than at any other American university save Virginia. "Oldest" is an alluring label in the Land of the New, and Harvard is America's oldest university. "Richest" is another adjective intimately linked to Harvard, and this, too, has its attractions in a country given over to superlatives. Then there is Harvard the "greatest" university in the United States—indeed, the world. This is more arguable. But at least in popular belief, Harvard has a secure claim to primacy in the pecking order of higher education.

What draws its visitors—ambitious parents, casual tourists, ever larger numbers of Europeans and Asians—is the sense that Harvard is the *Ur*-university: the world's leading repository of the higher learning, and the social and economic power that comes with it. Harvard's students and faculty are in common (and their own) belief the best of all; not having gone to Harvard, thought an alum in the 1950s, was like not having gone to Europe. And the College has the glamor that is so essential to contemporary public réclame. It is, after all, the school of FDR and JFK.

Harvard's preeminence in fact has been challenged by other universities: Oxford and Cambridge always; Johns Hopkins in the late nineteenth century; Chicago, Columbia, Berkeley, and now Stanford in the twentieth. During the early 1900s Yale had a stronger grasp on the media's (and hence the public's) idea of the prototypical college. The same was true of Scott Fitzgerald's Princeton in the 1920s. But certainly since World War II, Harvard has been on top of the heap (though Stanford is breathing hard and closing fast). The United States pavilion at the 1958 Brussels World's Fair entertained its visitors by asking them "Where would you like to send your boy to college?" Harvard was the choice of more than 32,000 respondents. Massachusetts Institute of Technology (MIT), with less than half as many, was second; Chicago, Columbia, California, Yale, and Princeton lagged (from a Harvard point of view) deliciously behind.

H. L. Mencken had his own view of what Harvard's standing was all about. In 1937 he advised the son of publisher Alfred Knopf on choosing a college:

> My guess is you'd have more fun at Yale than at Princeton, but my real choice is Harvard. I don't think Harvard is a better university than the other two, but it seems that Americans set a higher value on its A.B. If I had a son I'd take him to Cambridge and chain him to the campus pump to remain there until he had acquired a sound Harvard accent. It's worth money in this great free Republic.

Harvard's idolators and detractors alike dwell on its age, its wealth, its preeminent position in American intellectual, political, and social life. Whether or not Harvard is as potent a force (for good or bad) as they proclaim is difficult to measure. In any event, that is not what this book is about. Rather, it sets out to do what has been attempted for only a handful of major American universities: to explore in depth its evolution as an institution of higher learning over the last two-thirds of the twentieth century.

How did Harvard get to where it is today, the university with arguably the best students, faculty, and libraries, and the greatest impact on America's intellectual and public life? And how does one go about telling the story of so substantial and complex an institution? We do not pretend to examine every facet of modern Harvard. The mysterious processes of scholarly and scientific discovery, the character of courses that excite or fail to excite their students, the complex human relationships that are so much a part of any institution's life: these are beyond our reach. Nor have we tried to review the intellectual achievements of Harvard's faculty, or the prominence in public and private life of its graduates. These are indeed rich and impressive stories. But they belong more to the general history of American cultural, scientific, and political life than to Harvard per se.

Rest assured that this leaves plenty to talk about. The history of Harvard is an evocative and fascinating one. And it is extraordinarily well-documented: a measure, perhaps, of its members' self-regard. Much of the tale we have to tell draws on the rich resources of the University's archives and on interviews with scores of Harvardians. One of us (Phyllis Keller) was a member of the Harvard administration from 1973 to 1997, and we have been able to supplement abundant outside sources with substantial inside knowledge.

Ours is a story of two periods of institutional change. The first occurred during the presidencies of James Bryant Conant (1933–53) and Nathan Marsh Pusey (1953–71). It consisted of the transformation of Harvard from a *Brahmin* university—regional, parochial, dominated by Boston's elite, resistant in varying degrees to Jews, women, and new developments in the academic disciplines—into a *meritocratic* university, with faculty selected primarily on the basis of their scholarly reputations, a student body chosen primarily for its intellectual horsepower, and a campus culture in which national and international academic standing was the measure of all things.

The second great shift in Harvard's modern history followed on the campus unrest of the Vietnam War era. Out of this came a new institutional culture, gradually overriding (though hardly replacing) the meritocratic university of the midcentury decades. We call this most recent Harvard a *worldly* university. By this we mean an expanding international presence, a socially driven pursuit of racial and gender diversity, scientists ever more involved in commercial ventures, students and faculty caught up in politics and public policy, a growing bureaucracy, incessant fund-raising, a swelling institutional hubris: Harvard in the world's service. This change in academic culture became evident during the administration of Derek Bok (1971–91) and came into its full maturity under his successor Neil Rudenstine (1991–2000).

This book, in short, is the story of how Harvard became modern. It is a tale of achievement: by any reasonable measure, Harvard is one of the great success stories of modern American history. It is also a story of discontents. These include not only the grousings of conservative alumni over Harvard radicalism or of radicals over Harvard conservatism, but the follies and misjudgments, the unfulfilled hopes and unexpected events, and the sheer weight of contingency that dogs the heels of a large, ambitious institution. We have tried to demystify the Harvard of idolators and iconoclasts alike by seeing it as what it is: the oldest, richest, and most intellectually influential of American universities, but because of these qualities subject to greater than ordinary expectations and demands. Even wealth and tradition, and brains and power, do not guarantee immunity from the ills to which institutions, like flesh, are prone.

MAKING HARVARD MODERN

# PROLOGUE

# FETE ACCOMPLI, 1936

Like ripples from a stone tossed into a tranquil pond, awareness spread among Harvard's movers and shakers that the university would be celebrating its 300th anniversary in 1936. As befitted a school so rich in tradition and sense of self, President A. Lawrence Lowell in 1924 appointed the Tercentenary Historian: Harvard's gifted professor of colonial history, Samuel Eliot Morison. Lowell retired in 1933, and his successor, James Bryant Conant, emerged as "the true genius of that now famous celebration." According to his secretary, Jerome Greene, "the Tercentenary celebration was really his inauguration."[1]

Serious planning for the Tercentenary began in the fall of 1930, several years before Conant became president, at a meeting of directors of the Alumni Association. According to one of the participants, the "prevailing opinion" even among these Harvard fat cats was "that the dominant note of the Celebration should be intellectual and not material, and that at the Tercentenary should be gathered, if possible, a notable representation of the great scholars of the world." Soon other grand themes emerged: "the present and future of the University rather than ... its past," "putting the university on view as a great modern, academic workshop."[2]

A Tercentenary committee chaired by anthropologist Alfred Tozzer was formed in 1932. It pottered about, planning to do something or other in the summer of 1936 and to have a concluding ceremony that fall in Harvard Stadium (with some vague thought of keeping a tent in reserve if it should rain). Clearly a stronger hand was needed. That turned out to be Jerome Greene, who had been Harvard president Charles W. Eliot's secretary during the early years of the century (and was said to have been Eliot's choice as his successor). Greene left Harvard when Abbott Lawrence Lowell took over in 1909. He made a career for himself in New York, first in the Rockefeller Foundation and then in the Lee, Higginson brokerage house. But he was dragged down by the collapse of that firm in the Depression and (in a genteel way) was on his uppers when Conant in the spring of 1934 asked him to come back to be secretary to the President and Fellows of Harvard College ("the Corporation"), Harvard's board of trustees, and run the 300th. Greene accepted with alacrity. Born to missionary parents and raised in China, he knew a noble cause when he saw it. He gave the celebration a new, more elevated tone: "It shall be a great *festa* and what will make it great will be its simplicity, dignity and beauty." It should be "an expression of what Harvard is as well as of what Harvard has been."[3]

By 1936 even more ambitious and evocative plans took form. The first two weeks of September would be given over to a grand academic convocation of dozens of the world's most eminent scholars. As word of this notion spread, suggestions for topics poured in (including a proposal from the editor of *Beauty Shop News* for a conference on "The Relation of Beauty to Human Behavior").[4]

Eighty-six academic luminaries, "with no regard to national, geographical, racial, or university connections," were invited to give papers and (if they didn't already have one) get a Harvard honorary degree. Seventy-one (including eleven Nobel Prize winners) accepted. More than half were from Europe, all but a handful of the rest from the United States. But no women: as Greene put it, "the Harvard tradition of reserving such honors for men was not broken." Historian Mary Beard took acid note: "What Mme. de Staël would have thought if she could have sat in on Harvard's pretentious symposium remains for the imagination to discover.... Evidently men had gone ... far beyond the seventeenth century ridiculing of women to the utter ignoring of women, not one of whom was invited to read a paper [or] express an opinion."[5]

Harvard's Jewish alumni also had grounds for unhappiness. The culminating ceremony was set for September 18 on the rather tenuous ground that, after adjusting for the later introduction of the Gregorian calendar, it marked the 300th anniversary of the convening of the Massachusetts General Court (the colony's legislature) to adopt the charter that established Harvard College. As soon as this schedule became known, Jewish alumni pointed out that it conflicted with the High Holiday of Rosh Hashanah.

What to do? Change the date, as some of the objectors wanted? Unsurprisingly the Corporation decided not to do that. True, the historical significance of the date was questionable: the 200th anniversary had been celebrated on September 8, 1836. And the Jewish alumni could not be brushed aside as just another pesky interest group. Greene admitted to one protesting rabbi, "There has unquestionably been a lag in Harvard's recognition of the growing number and importance of its Jewish members."

Philosophy professor Harry Wolfson, the most distinguished (and almost the only publicly identified) Jew on Harvard's Arts and Sciences faculty, offered to organize an early morning service on September 18, after which (in his view) it would be proper for observant Jews to attend the ceremonies. But this would not do for the Orthodox, who vexed Greene with their "illiberality." Plaintively he observed that the day's ceremonies would be drenched in religion: an invocation, a benediction, the singing of hymns. He failed to note that all of that was irredeemably Christian.[6]

Despite these premonitory rumblings, the Tercentenary's two-week Conference of Arts and Sciences matched its pretensions. It consisted of panels in which scholars brought their audiences up-to-date on the doings of their fields, along with capstone lectures by especially distinguished men.

The scientific hand of Conant the chemist (and the fact that this was the seedtime of modern physics and biology) is evident. The audiences heard not only informed surveys of the current state of these fields, but previsions of the scientific future. There were reports on a new mathematics that linked relativity theory and quantum mechanics. Astronomer Arthur Eddington described the current state of understanding of the composition of the stars; Eugene Wigner, Robert Oppenheimer, and I. I. Rabi discussed new insights in nuclear physics. Princeton astronomer Henry Russell speculated on the possibility that a Big Bang—he called it a "cosmic New Deal"—occurred between one and two billion years ago, and that "just afterward matter was distributed more widely but more thinly through space to settle down into stars."

Then came biological science, only a step behind physics in its modern transformation. There was talk of a DNAish cell "sculptor." The applications of physical chemistry to "various aspects of biology" came in for examination. There was even an ecological prevision of sorts when Norwegian marine biologist Johan Hjort lectured on "The Biology of Whales."[7]

The second week of the conference took up the less clearly advancing realms of the social sciences and the humanities. The strategy here was to field large symposia, "with a view to breaking down traditionally specialized lines of approach to an important and timely problem and to make its solution the object of a common attack." In short, the approach to social and humanistic topics was to be ... scientific. Here, too, Conant's hand could be seen. As he put it to a Tercentenary audience,

"The origin of the Constitution, ... the functioning of the three branches of the federal Government, the forces of modern capitalism, must be dissected as fearlessly as the geologist examines the origin of rocks."[8]

"Factors Determining Human Behavior" conjoined psychology (represented by Carl Jung, Pierre Janet, and Jean Piaget), biochemistry (James Collip on hormones), and philosophy (Rudolf Carnap on logic). Anthropologist Bronislaw Malinowski provided an overview of his field with a public lecture, "Culture as a Determinant of Behavior." Full of foreboding over what was to come, he spoke of war as a "disease of culture" and of contemporary civilization suffering through a severe stage of maladjustment.

The presentation of the policy sciences, "Authority and the Individual," was no less forward-looking, taking on themes that would absorb them in coming decades: "The State and Economic Enterprise," "Stability and Social Change," "The Place and Functions of Authority." The humanities (not prominent in Conant's intellectual worldview) came in for less attention, with a symposium on "Independence, Convergence and Borrowing in Institutions, Thought, and Art." Man of letters Bernard DeVoto groused that, "as is invariable when Harvard acts officially," the humanities were slighted. But he had to admit that the Tercentenary convocation was "unparalleled on this continent, if indeed it has been matched anywhere."[9]

One purpose of this gathering was to show, in Conant's words, "that it is because of specialization that knowledge advances, not in spite of it; and that cross fertilization of ideas is possible only when new ideas arise through the intense cultivation of special fields." This was his academic philosophy in a nutshell: the university as a place of specialized disciplines and world-class scholars, dedicated to the pursuit of truth.[10]

After this orgy of thought letting there followed three days of Tercentenarial pomp and circumstance: celebration more than cerebration. Robert Frost was supposed to write a Tercentenary ode, but at the last moment begged off. His replacement, Harvard graduate and Theodore Roosevelt idolator Hermann Hagedorn, came up with a competent but uninspired effort, backstopped by an uninspired but competent contribution by England's poet laureate, John Masefield. Then President Conant received representatives of 502 universities and learned societies in Harvard's Sanders Theater. The academic hoods and gowns were colorful; the proceedings were interminable, and so purely ceremonial that there was even room for a sprinkling of women in the audience.[11]

On the following day the alumni celebrated, looking back to the comfortable past rather than at the troubling present or the uncertain future. Much was made of nineteen-year-old Peter Harvard, direct descendant of John Harvard, imported from England for the occasion. A Harvard alumni flag furled at the 1836 Bicentennial was unfurled now, with appropriate ruffles and flourishes. Conant opened and read a packet of letters left by celebrants a century before, reporting that there were only "letters from the alumni of Harvard [including one from Emerson] and, unfortunately, nothing else." A new package was interred for unveiling in 2036. That night the citizenry of Boston and Cambridge were treated to two hours of fireworks, set off from a barge on the Charles. And the undergraduates caroused in Memorial Hall.[12]

On the final day of the ceremonies, the tone abruptly altered. President Franklin D. Roosevelt '04 was scheduled to speak. With the New Deal in full swing and the national election less than two months off, predictable alumni protests surfaced. "There are a great many Harvard men who feel very bitterly towards Roosevelt, and I think having him speak would mar the pleasure of a great many important Harvard graduates," warned one of them. Another told Conant that he would not attend "as I shall be campaigning against Roosevelt. I put my country's good above Harvard College."[13]

Ex-president Lowell, who presided over the ceremony, did not conceal his displeasure over FDR's attendance. Even after some judicious revising by Conant, Lowell's letter of invitation was less than warm: "[W]e hope you will choose for your theme for a brief address something connected with Harvard and the tercentenary of higher education in this country, and feel that you would welcome this opportunity to divorce yourself from the arduous demands of politics and political speechmaking. Do you not think it would be well to limit all the speeches that afternoon to about ten minutes? Does this express your idea?" FDR had a high boiling point, but Lowell's language built up a sufficient head of steam to reach it. In reply, he reminded Lowell that he had been invited to speak as president of the United States, not as a Harvard alumnus: "I am sure you will approve my thought that you did not expect me to do otherwise than to be true to the requirements of the office which I shall represent on that occasion."[14]

As if FDR wasn't enough, a hurricane sweeping up the East Coast raised the threat of a washout of the final day's proceedings. Anxious, minute-by-minute consultation with weather experts held out the prospect of drizzle, but no more, in the morning. Then the downpour came, and the afternoon alumni meeting had to switch to Sanders Theater ("like moving day in the Ark," said a participant). Yale president James R. Angell, a prominent critic of New Deal tax policies, told the afternoon audience (which included FDR): "I was told when leaving the deluge this morning that this was President Conant's method of soaking the rich. So long as they are Harvard's rich, I don't care. But the endowed institutions of the United States cannot long survive under the threat of unjust taxation."

FDR's speech was a vintage display of his wily charm (though he pointedly ignored Lowell in his opening remarks). He echoed what had come to be a recurring Tercentenary theme: "In this day of modern witch-burning, when freedom of thought has been exiled from many lands which were once its home, it is the part of Harvard and America to stand for the freedom of the human mind and to carry the torch of truth." And, famously, he dealt with the subject of his own discomforting presence:

> It is pleasant to remember today that this meeting is being held in pursuance of an adjournment expressly taken one hundred years ago on motion of Josiah Quincy. At that time many of the alumni of Harvard were sorely troubled concerning the state of the nation. Andrew Jackson was President. On the two hundred and fiftieth anniversary of the founding of Harvard College, alumni again were sorely troubled. Grover Cleveland was President. Now [this in a near-whisper], on the three hundredth anniversary, I am President.[15]

Along with the fun and games, something more substantial was afoot. The cloud of totalitarianism hung over the Tercentenary: Japan was on the march in China, as was Mussolini's Italy in Ethiopia, and Hitler was using the Spanish civil war to hone his war machine. Conant later recalled that the celebration "constantly emphasized the fundamental clash between totalitarian ideas and those of free men."[16]

Biologist Hans Spemann of Freiburg was the only official delegate from a German university to show up at the Tercentenary. The star turn from the Third Reich was to have been physicist Werner Heisenberg, scheduled to appear on a panel on cosmology with Niels Bohr—and Albert Einstein. Heisenberg pulled out shortly before the proceedings began; the Nazi government reportedly ordered him to stay home and serve eight weeks in the German army. It may well have been that a coappearance with Einstein was too much for Heisenberg's Nazi handlers. Bohr declined to come too, probably because of demands on his time at his institute in Copenhagen. In any event, Greene and Harvard astronomer Harlow Shapley decided that it was appropriate to let Einstein off the hook after Heisenberg and Bohr withdrew.[17]

Alexander Lindsay, the master of Balliol and Oxford's vice-chancellor, injected a touch of Old World pessimism into the proceedings. He thought it unlikely that there would be such a ceremony a century hence: America and Europe might well be in darkness then, their civilizations destroyed by war. Lowell, presiding over the afternoon's proceedings, could not let that go unanswered. "What I have learned from history," he responded, "is that very few human institutions are killed while they are still alive." And when Conant moved that the alumni gathering be adjourned for another century, Lowell interjected: "All those who believe that the world will still be in existence 100 years hence, and that the universities will still be free, say AYE." And so the audience unanimously did.

Philosopher Étienne Gilson saw in the Tercentenary "a public recognition of the fact that the fate of European culture and Western civilization ultimately rests with what the United States will make of it in the next 100 years." Europe had inherited that tradition from Greece and Rome; now it was moving west. "The very presence of so many European scholars at Harvard," he assured his listeners, "is a safe indication that America is ready to sponsor it." French literary historian Paul Hazard, reporting on the Tercentenary in the *Revue des deux mondes*, enviously regarded the event as the product of a young, strong nation, remote from war and revolution, rich in means and avid for progress.[18]

After the fete was over, Allegheny College president William P. Tolley wrote an account, "The Tercentenary of the Mother of American Colleges." The conclave, "perhaps the most distinguished group of learned men ever to assemble in one place," made clear two truths: "first, that in the quest for knowledge the world is one and men are brothers; and second, that in the achievements of our scholars and scientists and in the flowering of our colleges and universities America has come of age." These were hardly fresh or startling aperçus. But insofar as they reflected the awareness that America in general, American universities most notably, and Harvard in particular promised to be "a new center for the world's culture," they justified the $240,000 or so that the Tercentenary cost.[19]

For decades Harvard and other large American universities had been accumulating the wealth, the faculties and students, the libraries and laboratories, and the research commitment and expertise necessary for major academic institutions. The Tercentenary, because of its timing and character, was one of those moments when a seismic shift in institutional weight and presence can be felt. Three centuries of history, the ability of Harvard to bring together so many of the world's leading scientists and scholars, and perhaps above all the context of the moment-the dramatic contrast between American academic freedom (however qualified by class, race, and gender) and the tyranny spreading over Europe and Asia-made the point that an endangered instrument of civilization was passing from the Old World to the New and that the now certifiably venerable institution on the Charles was an appropriate venue.

During the runup to the Tercentenary, Conant wondered: Would private universities in the future be able to win "that popular admiration and respect which alone can guarantee their survival?" Universities like Harvard now were

> startlingly large and complex; their buildings and equipment are great beyond the imagination of our ancestors; their faculties and students alike have facilities never before at the disposal of any body of scholars. What will be the fate of these institutions thus suddenly developed to such dimensions? Can they escape the curse which has so often plagued large human enterprises well established by a significant history—the curse of complacent mediocrity? What will be written and said about the role of the university, particularly the privately endowed university, when the four hundredth celebration draws near in the winter of 2036?

He was not optimistic about the future. The Great Depression had called a halt to the growth of American universities. If "the present frozen condition continues for a generation," he warned, "we shall have entered a new phase in our educational history, a static phase which might readily become a period of stagnation."[20]

As things turned out, it was not necessary to wait until 2036 to answer Conant's questions. The two-thirds of a century after 1936 saw an explosion in the wealth, variety, and social importance of American universities that dwarfed the experience of the past. The future would not be "static," but dynamic and expansive beyond anyone's expectation.

# PART I

## "HERE AT HARVARD":

The Meritocratic University

*1933–1953*

## ❦ 1 ❧

# JAMES BRYANT CONANT
# AND THE MERITOCRATIC UNIVERSITY

The Harvard that James Bryant Conant inherited when he became president in 1933 was the creation of his Boston Brahmin predecessors Charles W. Eliot (1867–1908) and Abbott Lawrence Lowell (1908–33). Under Eliot, Harvard became a university, and not just a college with some ancillary professional education. As he said of the various fields of higher education in his inaugural: "We shall have them all, and at their best." The Law and Medical schools became world-class. Major scholars began to be more than an occasional fluke in the faculty lineup. And Eliot was the first American university president to become a significant public figure.

No less revolutionary was what he did with undergraduate education. His elective system replaced the former tightly regulated curriculum, a laissez-faire approach to education in full accord with the prevailing beliefs of the Gilded Age. It was also a brilliant piece of educational politics. At one stroke it freed students and teachers from the tyranny of each other's presence. It lulled the undergraduates into thinking that they were free to choose their curriculum when in fact most of them rushed, lemminglike, into a few massively popular courses taught by faculty crowd pleasers dubbed "bow-wows." This freed research-minded professors to pursue their work relatively unencumbered by undergraduate obligations.[1]

At the same time the social character of Harvard College became increasingly "Brahmin," in the sense of domination by Boston's social and economic elite rather than by Unitarian or Congregational ministers. Much of Eliot's Harvard was seriously intellectual; more of it was socially snobbish. Its faculty consisted of a few major figures such as the Law School's Christopher Columbus Langdell and Philosophy's William James and Josiah Royce, and a majority who were gentlemen first, teachers second, scholars (perhaps) third. Its student body, overwhelmingly from New England and New York, stretched from earnest Jewish commuters (whom Eliot welcomed) to good-family swells who dwelt on Harvard's "gold coast" of posh dormitories. But the latter set the social tone of undergraduate life.[2]

Lowell was a strong-minded Brahmin, with little use for the anything-goes tenor of Eliot's free elective system. But he was no less a reformer. If Eliot reflected the values of the Gilded Age, then Lowell may be accounted a Progressive. He came into office as Theodore Roosevelt's presidency ended and, in the spirit of the time, was committed to system, regulation, and order. When he left in 1933, the Eliot-Lowell sequence seemed to the *Alumni Bulletin* "not unlike the transition from *laissez-faire* to 'planning and control' in the economic world."

Lowell put in concentration and distribution requirements, tutorials (based on the Oxbridge model) to guide students in their work, and comprehensive exams to make sure that in fact they had done it. And he oversaw the construction of residential houses, an American version of the colleges in England's ancient universities. He had a Progressive's belief in free inquiry—he was a champion of academic freedom—and a TR-like academic machismo: he opposed graduate student scholarships because they would attract "the docile and studious youth who has not the vigor and aggressiveness to attack the world without aid." Lowell also had a distaste for radicalism and the "lesser breeds" shared by many Progressives. He was one of the three-man review committee that upheld the death sentences meted out to Sacco and Vanzetti, and he attempted in the 1920s to restrict the number of Jewish undergraduates and keep black freshmen out of the Harvard dorms.[3]

Lowell had what Jerome Greene called an "antipathetic obsession" with his predecessor (warmly reciprocated: Eliot warned Harvard's Governing Boards to "keep incessant watch against [Lowell's] defects of judgment and good feeling"). Nevertheless he turned Eliot's dream of a great university into a bricks-and-mortar reality. Widener Library, the Law School's Langdell Hall, the campuses of the Medical and Business Schools, the river houses were his work. These were Roman in grandeur (if mainly Georgian in design), but lacked the architectural originality of Henry Hobson Richardson's Sever (1880) and Austin (1883) Halls, products of the Age of Eliot. That difference was emblematic of the two presidencies.

Lowell was the material implementer of Eliot's intellectual vision. Looking back over the past quarter of a century in 1933, the *Alumni Bulletin* reported: "Many people are of the opinion that the University will never again go through so great a physical expansion in such a short period." But that sequence would recur when in the 1950s and 1960s Nathan Marsh Pusey raised the money, hired the faculty, and put up the buildings that fulfilled James Bryant Conant's dream of a more meritocratic university.[4]

## The Coming of Conant

The seventy-five-year-old Lowell announced his intention to retire in November 1932. There followed a ritual of selection comparable to the choice of a new pope. Faculty of Arts and Sciences dean Kenneth Murdock, the son of a Boston banker, was in the general (and certainly in his own) view the leading candidate. But doubts about his character and intellectual capacity were fatal to his candidacy. Conant publicly supported Murdock, who had been best man at his wedding. But when the names of forty possibles were read off at a meeting and Conant's was not one of them, he recalled: "I must admit to being somewhat piqued— I couldn't help feeling it was a bit hard to be considered beyond the pale of discussion!"

Corporation member Charles Curtis came to consult him on possible candidates (and to look him over). Conant insisted that the new president be a faculty member, and dwelt on "the importance of keeping alive the idea of a university as a center for scholarship and research." At the same time he tempered his expectations to satisfy the less elevated standard of the Brahmin trustees. Thomas N. Perkins, another member of the Corporation, had to be wooed: "We talked about the scholar-teacher problem and I expressed my belie[f] that all the faculty should be scholars. On [my] citing R. B. Merriman ["Frisky" Merriman, whose once-over-lightly History 1 was a longtime favorite of Harvard undergraduates] as a good enough scholar to meet my definition, T.N.P. withdrew his contention for non-scholarly teachers."

One question facing the Corporation: just what kind of a Conant was he? Biochemist L. J. Henderson, Conant's uncle-in-law, was deputed to call on him for information on his family and upbringing ("an envoy," said Conant, "much disgusted with his task!"). True, he bore the name of one of the oldest Brahmin families. But he came from its Plymouth, not its Boston, branch: the one that for long stayed close to where Roger Conant got off the *Ann* in 1623 and over the generations were farmers and artisans rather than merchants and men of affairs. (As he put it, he was a "native" but not a "proper" Bostonian.) Conant's father was a photoengraver and part-time building contractor of a middling sort; his family lived in unfashionable Dorchester; he was its first member to go to college. He quickly showed brilliance as a chemist, got a doctorate and joined the Harvard Chemistry department, married the boss's daughter (her father, Chemistry chairman Theodore W. Richards, was Harvard's first and for some years only Nobelist), and displayed gifts of leadership and intellectual power that ultimately led the Corporation to make him Harvard's president.

The Board of Overseers, Harvard's other governing body, had another question to ask. What was his religion? "Deist," answered Conant, who was not noticeably burdened by religious belief. This seems to have been satisfactory. (He was not asked about his politics, so he did not have to confess to having voted for FDR in 1932.) Another problem: a cold fish named Abbott Lawrence Lowell, whose enthusiasm for Conant could be measured by a micrometer. As chairman of the Chemistry department, Conant had refused to set up a tutorial program—Lowell's fondest cause—for concentrators. Under much pressure from the president, he finally came up with a halfhearted tutorial plan, dependent on a substantial increase in his department's budget. The Depression year of 1933 was no time to ask for more of anything, and Lowell reacted "very harshly" to a proposal that included no provision for a general examination. "I cannot believe that Chemistry is the one field in which there are no general principles," he coldly observed. But Lowell came around to Conant when several Corporation members told him that otherwise they would support their colleague, lawyer Grenville Clark. Conant heard that while Lowell "had very little belief in me, as Presidential timber," he "was inclined to take a long gamble as he regarded Clark as a very second-rate man for this position."

Monday, April 21, was The Day. Conant waited for the call at home and later in his office. At 3:00 in the afternoon he heard that Lowell was on his way to see him. "I tried to continue the calculations connected with the paper I had been pretending to write all day." Lowell came in, sat down, and told him, "simply and rather coldly," that he was the Corporation's choice. Conant responded in kind: "Well." Lowell then unhelpfully observed that it was "a great honor, but a very great responsibility." Conant thought that it was like being ordered over the top in the Great War. This passing of two personalities in the night ended with Lowell saying "a few words about the finances, the balanced budget, the surplus and without a trace of warmth, enthusiasm, or friendliness, that it was to me that he was turning over these assets."[5]

Once the die was cast, things improved. A long talk with Lowell a few days later, initially "very, very chilly," ended "quite remarkably warm." He told Conant: "I hope you will strike out [on] a new path unlike that of your predecessors." And he provided a revealing summary of his own "method of administration." Lowell at first tried to copy Eliot by being "practically the general administrator of the Faculty of Arts and Sciences [FAS], deciding in the first instance on the proposals of the departments for appointments and promotions." But this did not work out, "for I did not study enough the individual cases." Since World War I the dean of FAS had taken over. So now administrative detail came before him only when there was a controversy to be decided. In what may well be a claim unique in the annals of university (or any other) administration, Lowell declared: "When I came here there were two men as secretaries in this office; there is now hardly enough work to fill the time of one."[6]

In May Conant gave his last lecture in Chemistry 5, returned to his office, and (he said) wept. He then took himself and his family off to Europe. He told his sister Marjorie Bush-Brown that he had "few illusions" about the job. He expected it to be "interesting and I hope fascinating but on the whole unpleasant and trying—a very, very lonely job.... until I retire, it will be very hard to find anyone who will speak absolutely frankly and fully to me about any Harvard matter." His dour expectation was that "if the President does the right thing he can count on an almost unanimous howl of disapproval from alumni and others." But still he hoped that "even in the most collegiate and football-mad of our alumni there is a spark of intellectual interest and I shall try my best to fan and *not* water this spark! You notice, I begin to preach already."

Conant proposed to be a strong president in the Eliot-Lowell tradition. He quoted Lowell on Harvard administration as "tyranny tempered by assassination"; he might well have quoted Eliot on the attribute most necessary for the success of a college president: "The capacity to inflict pain." He shared his predecessors' paternal stance toward the institution they led: the proprietary phrase "here at Harvard" frequently crops up in his correspondence. The ways in which Conant put his stamp on the University—and the ways in which he failed to do so—are at the core of Harvard's history in the 1930s and 1940s.[7]

## The President and the Governing Boards

Conant inherited a system of Harvard governance as steeped in tradition as it was fluid in practice. The University was a chartered corporation—the country's oldest—with two Governing Boards. One was the President and Fellows of Harvard College, commonly called the Corporation. It consisted of the president, the treasurer, and five fellows, who served without limit of time. The other was the thirty-member Board of Overseers, elected by the alumni. In theory the overseers were supposed to pass on the Corporation's decisions; in practice their chief function was to run visiting committees to Harvard's faculties, departments, and museums.

Governing Harvard in practice depended as much on its president's personality and purpose as on its venerable institutional structure. The *New York Times Magazine* spoke of Conant's first six months as devoted to the creation of a "new Harvard," in which he was "not to be builder [as was Lowell] but operator; to see that the best material and the best workmanship go into the educational product." Conant, who admired Oliver Cromwell, appreciated this "sympathetic treatment of the new Dictator at Harvard" and confided to the article's author: "I have an idea that I should like to go into politics in the future."[8]

The Corporation that chose Conant consisted of Treasurer Henry L. Shattuck, "a Brahmin of Brahmins," the most influential Corporation member during the early Conant years; physician Roger Lee; Wall Street lawyer Grenville Clark; and Boston attorneys Charles P. Curtis, Thomas Nelson Perkins, and Jeremiah Smith. Smith soon gave way to Robert Homans, yet another Boston lawyer, who in turn was succeeded in 1936 by New York business executive and Eliot biographer Henry James, son of the philosopher William. All were Harvard College graduates, all were part of or (in the cases of New Yorkers Clark and James) had close ties to the Boston Brahmin elite.

The Corporation's power was not what it once had been. During the early nineteenth century it evolved from a combine of clerics to representatives of Boston's socioeconomic elite, out to make Harvard the special preserve of their caste. But during the long, strong administrations of Eliot and Lowell, leadership had shifted to the president.[9]

Conant-Corporation conflict, when it occurred, usually consisted of contretemps over appointments and between personalities, rarely over the course of policy. In 1935 senior fellow Charles P. Curtis became involved in a messy divorce, and asked that his status be discussed by the Corporation. Conant did so—and was "sorry to say that the opinion of the Corporation is that you should submit your resignation as a member of that board, which they are prepared to accept." Curtis duly departed, to be replaced by Brahmin attorney Charles A. Coolidge.[10]

Conant was firmer in matters that involved his presidential prerogatives. In 1945 the sixty-six-year-old Henry James pointed out that he and his colleagues were getting long in the tooth. James put his money where his mouth was and offered his resignation. Conant thanked James for his "fine spirit," but wanted to think about it before responding one way or another. A year and a half later James still was waiting to hear. Finally in 1947 James, afflicted by cancer, retired. Conant wanted no faculty member on the Corporation: "it tends to confuse what should be a clear separation of powers." The president's role was to be the channel of communication between the faculty and the Corporation; the fellows "should confine themselves to matters of general policy of a very broad sort and a review of the budgetary and appointment policy of the president and the various deans." Their part in faculty selection was "only to see to it that an adequate canvass has been made of the situation and the best men appointed to the various posts."[11]

James hoped that his colleagues would look further afield than they usually did when they selected his successor. Were Conant to be "bumped off" and replaced by someone narrowly identified with Harvard, it would be harmful to have a Corporation whose "spheres of influence appeared to be confined to Mt. Auburn Street, State Street, Milton and Boston." The strongest non-Boston candidate was forty-six-year-old attorney William L. Marbury, and Conant proposed him in March 1947. Marbury had two major drawbacks: he came from distant Baltimore and (more importantly) had gone only to Harvard Law School, not the College. James saw the advantage of a fellow coming from a professional school; Baltimore, close to the South, might be a helpful venue for fund-raising. After a boomlet for thoroughly Bostonian Ralph Lowell petered out, Fellows Clark, Shattuck, and Lee were ready to take Marbury, although Fellow Charles Coolidge and, most especially, Treasurer William Claflin were not.[12]

In December 1947 the Corporation, by a 5–2 vote (Claflin and Coolidge against), approved the Marbury nomination, and it went to the Overseers for confirmation. Key overseers met with Corporation grandee Henry Shattuck in January 1948. They asked him flat out: "Is this a battle between Conant and the Treasurer, would the President regard it as a lack of confidence if they voted against it—would it lead to his resignation?" Shattuck "wouldn't put it quite as strongly as that." Conant would: "If this election is not confirmed, it will be apparent to the Treasurer and the President that a majority of the Overseers think that the Treasurer and not the President ought to run the University." Faced with that, the Overseers concurred. Coolidge made his peace with Conant: "I think Baltimore's prompt and enthusiastic acceptance augurs well for the future.... Now that the die has been cast, my doubts are buried, and the same is true with Bill [Claflin]." But Claflin (apparently at Conant's urging) resigned as treasurer (and thus from the Corporation) in April.[13]

Claflin's departure continued the process of Corporation self-renewal. The leading candidates to succeed him were Boston investment banker Paul Cabot and New York investment banker Thomas Lamont, both class of 1921, both J. P. Morgan directors. Grenville Clark wanted a treasurer with more than investment skills. In any event, he thought, it was essential not to appoint Claflin's (and Coolidge's) candidate, Deputy Treasurer Henry Wood. It was important that in the future the Corporation "be really free from the united Claflin-Coolidge influence."

The Corporation chose Paul Cabot in October 1949. This strengthened Harvard's already close links to "State Street," the generic term for Boston financial circles. Cabot headed the State Street Investment Corporation and continued to do so after he became treasurer. The University contracted for portfolio analysis and investment advice from State Street Research and Management Company, a spinoff of the Investment Corporation.[14]

The coming on board of Marbury and Cabot significantly affected the post–World War II development of Harvard. Treasurer Cabot brought a new professionalism and expertise to managing the University's endowment, skills that contributed mightily to its postwar takeoff. Marbury had a national rather than a Boston perspective, and in him the professional schools—the source of over half the University's alumni—had a spokesman without strong ties to the College. The out-of-Boston trend continued with the replacement of Grenville Clark by New York attorney Keith Kane in 1950 and by Thomas Lamont, who replaced Henry Shattuck in 1952.

Members of the Board of Overseers, with good reason, believed they were subordinate to the Corporation—a sentiment most likely to arise when they had to pass (as in Marbury's case) on a Corporation nominee chosen, they thought, without sufficient consultation. Conant tried without notable success to modernize the Board. In 1933 he proposed to reduce its cumbersome and time-consuming visiting committees to academic departments from thirty to four; but they were too popular with the Overseers. Faculty of Arts and Sciences dean Paul Buck sounded out the faculty's opinion on fewer but stronger visiting committees in 1944. He reported the result to Conant: "complete indifference. Visiting Committees are looked upon as a more or less innocuous pastime of the Overseers. The function has sunk to so low a repute that few believe anything can be done with the device ... , and therefore no one seems interested in an effort to reform."[15]

Overseer restlessness flared up in the postwar years. Controversy over economist John Kenneth Galbraith's tenure led to reconsideration of the role that they played in faculty appointments. A committee headed by Johns Hopkins president Isaiah Bowman looked into the matter, and its draft report feistily recommended that the Board "maintain its broad view of the interests of society and of the University without placing too great reliance upon ... preceding inquiries." Conant did not welcome this assertion of authority. Boards, he pointed out, rarely took direct responsibility for appointments in other universities; it was historical accident that gave the overseers their statutory veto power. He recalled that in Eliot's day the president picked the faculty—"After all, this is the way you run a business"—and was supported, or fired, on the basis of the job he did. The overseers should content themselves with making sure that proper procedure was followed.[16]

In 1944 Conant appointed Dean Paul Buck of the Faculty of Arts and Sciences to the newly created post of provost. That meant that in the future the president would not—as Lowell had—directly oversee the Arts and Sciences departments. "For the first time in Harvard history," Conant declared, "we have a sound and workable organization, and whatever happens I trust this will not be weakened; rather it should be strengthened by emphasizing the importance of the position of the provost." (As things worked out, neither the deans nor Conant's successors Pusey and Bok wanted a provost between them. The office lapsed, not to be restored until 1992.)

Conant thought that the primary task of the president's office in the coming decade would be to raise a large sum—perhaps $40 million—for the University. But not much had come in as unrestricted funds "or for the areas where money was really needed." How to get what was wanted? Either by finding a person who could do the necessary selling job to donors or (like other universities) rely on the president for fundraising. "With regret," he concluded, "the writer has come to the latter view, but would be glad to be proved wrong."[17]

There are two things to say about this assessment. One is how accurate a picture (the provost and close coordination among the deans aside) it was of the Harvard presidency during the decades to come. The other is that this is a rendering of the presidency as Conant least wanted it, as an office defined primarily by fund-raising. It reflects the degree to which Conant had detached himself from the position he would hold—or at least occupy—for seven more years. This was not a blueprint for his remaining years in office, but a testament for his successor.

## Conant and Meritocracy

When Conant was chosen for the presidency, he asked Lowell what his salary would be. Lowell's reported reply was that he had no idea, since he had always turned his compensation back to the University. He supposed that Conant should tell the Corporation what he needed. But the new president was not well off, and the job was at times a financial burden. A gossipy alum reported in 1937: "They tell me that young Conant out there at Harvard is having a hell of a time trying to fill with furniture that big mansion that Prexy Lowell built. [The Lowells supposedly left only a lamp and two tables.] Conant is only a poor kid and I guess he has only about 3 rooms fitted out to date."[18]

The slight, youthful-looking, forty-year-old chemist had the demeanor of a mild-mannered academic. But it quickly became clear that in his own way Conant was as tough, and as cold a fish, as Lowell. His biographer dwells on his role in American nuclear and cold war policy making. And indeed there is something chilling about a public career that began with work on poison gas in World War I, went on to bring together the scientists who made the atomic bomb, and ended with a stint as high commissioner to Germany during the height of the cold war. Conant had a personality to match. He seemed at times to combine Eliot's aloof intellectuality with Lowell's chilly remove. He once raked a former student over the coals for his deficiencies of charac-ter, then rather lamely concluded: "I hope that nothing I have said in this letter will be at all discouraging to you."[19]

This is not to say that Conant lacked capacity for human warmth. By all signs his was a serenely successful marriage. His poignant efforts to deal with problems that afflicted his two sons, and his relations with his secretaries Jerome Greene and Calvert Smith, suggest something more than the cold-blooded careerist. But what matters most for Harvard's history is what he sought to do as president. He was not so much a scientist-turned-administrator as a man of unusual ability and ambition who applied his talents first to chemistry, then to university governance, and then to the affairs of the nation and the world. Advising a former student on whether or not to take up a career in university administration, he warned: "There would be more responsibility as an administrator and less responsibility of 'making good' to satisfy your own conscience. No one knows better than I do what weight such responsibility imposes on an individual. Some people like to take up challenges and some do not." He, most certainly, did.[20]

Conant's major contribution to the history of Harvard was his vision—and that is the right word—of what the University might be. Though he tried to be discreet about it, he had a strong sense of Harvard's academic and intellectual deficiencies. No sooner was he in office than he began to formulate a program of his own. This was not one of preservation and survival, the goal of most American college and university presidents during the 1930s. Rather, he sought to build a university given over as never before to *meritocracy*, that is, attracting students and faculty whose distinction lay not in their social origins but in their intellect and character.

Conant's commitment to a more meritocratic Harvard obviously reflected his own career, the product not of background and status but of talent, hard work, and results. It had deeper roots as well. One of these was his commitment to the American values of individualism and self-reliance. Another was his belief that talent was evenly distributed across the socioeconomic spectrum and that to let the accident of birth shape the process by which Harvard (and America) chose its leaders was both irrational and socially harmful. His goal was to eliminate "artificial barriers—geographical or financial—in our educational system."[21]

Nowadays it is customary to dismiss meritocracy as a notion blind to its social and intellectual narrowness. It is true that in his way Conant was no less a snob than his Brahmin critics, though his was an elitism based on intellectual rather than social or economic superiority. But he raised questions that would be important at Harvard and in American university life for the rest of the twentieth century. What *was* intellectual superiority; or more to the point, how was it to be measured? How could meritocratic values be more fully realized in faculty and student selection, and in the curriculum? His efforts to come up with viable answers defined his presidency.

Conant believed that the faculty's primary task was not so much to *preserve* as to *advance* learning. "If we have in each department of the university the most distinguished faculty which it is possible to obtain," he thought, "we need have little worry about the future." He estimated that about half the Harvard staff consisted of scholars and half "of men who are frankly not active or interested in the advancement of knowledge in the widest possible sense of the term." That led him to try to get rid of unpromising junior faculty and to uplift the senior level by the appointment of new "University Professors."

His hopes for Harvard's undergraduates were strikingly similar. "We should attract to our student body," he declared, "the most promising young men throughout the whole nation." This meant that "a path to the top should be open to all of exceptional talent" and that Harvard had to "keep the way clear for the gifted youth of limited means." He planned to do this through a program of Harvard National Scholarships.[22]

Conant's belief in equal opportunity and social mobility coexisted with more than a trace of red-in-tooth-and-claw academic social Darwinism. Though he had an active interest in the social sciences and the humanities, the chemist in him doubted the intellectual rigor of these softer fields. And he drew a sharp line between artistic or literary ability and scholarly aptitude. The world outside was the best place for writers, artists, and performers to learn their crafts. His ideal was a university in which research, professional education, the liberal arts, and undergraduate college life were conjoined.[23]

During the two decades of his presidency, Conant tenaciously pursued these academic goals. He faced a problem that devils most heads of universities: the difficulty of imposing one's will on a substantially autonomous faculty. (Harry Truman understood this and pitied Dwight Eisenhower, going to head Columbia where he would give orders in his accustomed way, but nobody would obey them.) When push came to shove in his dealings with deans or departments, Conant was likely to lose. But in disputes with his supposed overlords, the Corporation and the Board of Overseers, he always won. Power at Harvard—such as it was—flowed up from below.[24]

Conant's desire to strengthen Harvard's faculty was intense and omnipresent. He told a Physics professor during his first month in office: "I am sure you know that I feel as strongly as anyone about the desire of filling this institution with brilliant and productive young men." Nothing, he said, should "interfere in any way with our aim of making the Faculty of Arts and Sciences the most distinguished body of creative scholars it is possible to attain." In 1934 the American Council on Education ranked American universities on their capacity to prepare doctoral students. Harvard narrowly led the list, but Conant thought its showing was "nothing to brag about. It seems clear that there are four universities in this country [Harvard, Columbia, California, Chicago] which are running a neck and neck race and we have very little margin, which fact will probably bring me gray hairs before very long!" He set up committees of leading faculty members in the social sciences, the humanities, the physical sciences, and the biological sciences to advise on appointments, honorary degree recipients, and research support. (The only professors asked who chose not to participate in this very American exercise in self-improvement were Joseph Schumpeter, Alfred North Whitehead, and Serge Elisséeff—all foreign-born.)[25]

Universities, Conant thought, were subject to the play of three forces. The first of these, which he deeply opposed, was "the non-research dogmatic view" of the university as "a place of teaching universal knowledge" rather than advancing it. Equally unattractive was the utilitarian-vocational approach, that universities should train professionals and apply knowledge to social problems. And then there was the view of the university as a place for advancing knowledge, the one to which he subscribed. Valid or not, Conant's optimistic belief in an important role for the university (not unlike FDR's hopes for America's future) was corrective to the tired pessimism so common in the 1930s.[26]

He got caught up in a continuing debate with alumni and others unhappy over his emphasis on meritocracy. One prominent alum could not see why Harvard should raise money to raid other universities for faculty. Complaints came in that Conant was "ousting all the good old tutors just because they have not their Ph.D's or did no research work in Tasmanian Archaeology or some such thing." Conant defended himself by arguing that when he came into office the weight of preference lay in teaching over research and that it was his goal to create "a proper balance between these two factors."[27]

Similar doubts arose over his hopes for a more broadly recruited student body. Grenville Clark, the Corporation's most liberal-minded member, was Conant's strongest supporter: "As time goes on, I think you are developing and refining your philosophy about selecting the talent from all economic levels and giving it a show." But even Clark feared that another group might be at risk: "This is the middle crowd of boys of good but not extraordinary intellectual ability but with exceptional ability to get on with others and possibly to be harmonizers and stabilizers in society." Clark's model freshman class: about half up to Harvard National Scholarship standards (with somewhat more emphasis on physique and all-around personality); fifty to sixty foreign students; the rest from "the traditional sources, picked out on the basis of intellectual qualities only to the extent that they would have no difficulty in passing reasonably well with a reasonable amount of work and with the emphasis primarily on their stability and human qualities." Conant diplomatically agreed. (After all, why not? Fifty percent of a Harvard class chosen by National Scholarship standards was beyond his wildest dreams.)[28]

Conant's meritocratic vision unsettled some Brahmin sensibilities. But he remained unshaken in his belief that the talent Harvard should be looking for was distributed across the population without regard to socioeconomic status. He found confirmation in intelligence testing, which showed that the great majority of gifted children came from families with modest incomes. But that did not imply a general equality of ability in the population. In what would eventually become a culture war between "believers in selection" and "believers in the unlimited power of education irrespective of inherent ability," Conant was firmly in the ranks of the selection camp. He was, he said, "an educational Calvinist. I have but little faith in salvation by good works and a large measure of belief in predestination if not at birth at least at the college entrance age!"[29]

He counted on testing to find and measure talent. (A poignant instance: he asked Columbia's Bureau of Collegiate Educational Research to determine whether his son Ted was of college caliber.) He actively supported the all but universal adoption of standardized multiple-choice testing as a primary means of selecting college students. Since then, the iron law of unintended consequences has, in the view of its critics, turned Conant's source of equal opportunity from an open sesame into a stone wall. Whatever the merits of the current skepticism, it should be kept in mind how unequivocal was Conant's belief in testing as a way to replace Brahminism with meritocracy at Harvard.[30]

## Conant and American Education

Conant was well positioned to be a prominent public spokesman for higher education. Lowell had had little interest in the affairs of the American Council on Education, the voice of the nation's universities; Conant played a much more active role. He proposed to award Harvard honorary degrees to the presidents of western (that is, west of the Appalachians) state universities in order to improve Harvard's relations with Out There. And he tried (unsuccessfully) to get a group of leading universities to join in a campaign to improve their public relations.[31]

His contacts with the presidents of the other major eastern universities—what would later be called the Ivy League—were sparse (except for that perennial bone of contention, intercollegiate football). His most substantial dialogue on educational policy was with Robert Maynard Hutchins of Chicago. This was hardly because they had similar views:

Hutchins's Aristotelian/Thomist beliefs were at polar removes from Conant's relativist skepticism. When Hutchins set forth his ideas about the undergraduate curriculum in the *Yale Review*, Conant responded:

> I have just read with extreme annoyance your very able article.... I cannot refrain from expressing strongly my hearty disapproval of almost all that you say.... When you attempt to fortify the liberal arts tradition in a college I am all for you as I am, also, in your attacks on the vocationalists and the people who would drown the university with all sorts of knick-knacks; but I do wish you would throw your ideas of a "pervasive" philosophy into Lake Michigan!

There developed a joking, mutually disrespectful relationship between the two. Hutchins sent Conant a newspaper headline from a story on Harvard's Entomology collection—"Harvard Has Insects 60 Million Years Old"—with the comment: "We retire ours at 65." In 1938 he offered Conant the chairmanship of the Chicago Chemistry department. The not usually fun-loving Conant responded: "Am framing your wire of the 24th as testimonial. Regret inability to accept flattering offer. Present employers appear to desire continuation my services for indefinite period. If I should leave commercial work for pure science would consider it a privilege to serve under your provocative but inspiring leadership."[32]

This relationship was strained by their opposing positions on America's relationship to World War II. Hutchins was an isolationist, Conant an ardent interventionist. And when Hutchins in 1946 declared that the use of the atom bomb had been unnecessary and that the United States had thereby lost its moral standing, Conant publicly denounced him. In 1948 Hutchins called for disclosure of America's nuclear secrets. Conant told Corporation member Thomas W. Lamont, "there is an enormous gap which separates Mr. Hutchins and myself, and I have not the slightest desire to close it!"[33]

In the late 1930s Conant's restless ambition led him to turn his attention from Harvard to larger concerns. He sought advice from associates on how to deal with controversial issues in his 1937 Commencement address. With manifest regret he conceded: "I take it that it would be agreed in advance that the questions of radicalism and academic freedom were not possible subjects to consider on this Commencement Day.... On the whole, it would seem to me that most of the interesting matters fall in the category 'The less said on that subject the better.'"[34]

He continued to draw a firm line between public engagement and the life of the mind. In 1937 poet Archibald MacLeish read a Phi Beta Kappa poem at Columbia that called on scholars to join in the fight against fascism:

> Rise from your labor now! Enlist
> For warfare in this fighting age!
> No longer may your learning wear
> The neutral truth's dispassionate peace;
> . . . .
> Arise O scholars from your peace!
> Arise! Enlist! Take arms and fight!

Conant wrote "to say how much I dislike" the poem: "your call to arms is a call to the betrayal of what is important in the life of a university."[35]

But this hardly meant that he was neutral on the question of American support for the Allies against Hitler. Indeed, his commitment to American intervention gave his views on education and meritocracy a more assertive, even radical edge. In a May 1940 *Atlantic Monthly* article he called for "education for a classless society." Class lines had hardened during the late nineteenth and early twentieth centuries; upward mobility withered further in the Depression. Educational opportunity was the best way to reverse the pattern. He decried the fact that "the most accidental and unfair circumstances determine to a large extent what boys go to those colleges which give a person somewhat of a leg up on the first ladder of success." Poor boys from big cities like New York and Chicago had access to higher education almost without regard to financial need. But in small towns and the countryside the situation was very different. He added: "There are certain racial results of this, by the way, which may not always be desirable"—a rare lapse into overt anti-Semitism. Still, measured ability remained the sine qua non for entry into higher education. When a donor wished to endow a scholarship not based on academic merit, Conant objected: "If one starts awarding financial aid to the members of the lower half of the class, it is very difficult indeed to establish criteria by which one worthy candidate can be distinguished from another."[36]

When the United States entered the war, debate over the colleges' role in officer training, and then how to deal with veterans at the war's end, made it clear that nagging contradictions and inconsistencies dogged Conant's quest to link meritocracy to democracy. He gave Harvard's alumni, a number of them already pawing the ground over his maverick tendencies, even greater cause for concern with a 1943 *Atlantic Monthly* article provocatively entitled "Wanted: American Radicals." Conant spoke of the need for "an American radical of the 1940s, ... a fanatic believer in equality" who will "be lusty in wielding the axe against the root of inherited privilege" through "his demand to confiscate (by constitutional methods) all property once a generation. He will demand really effective inheritance and gift taxes and the breaking up of trust funds and estates."

These words called for a lot of explaining by Harvard's president. Conant later said that he "was describing at this point the radical in his most extreme mood" and that what he really wanted was "very high inheritance taxes in all brackets but leaving enough property to take care of widows and orphans." He touted the virtue of stiff inheritance taxes designed to liquidate inherited wealth as completely as possible, certainly after the second generation, though "I recognize that there is a lot of dynamite in a president of Harvard talking about this social but also economic complication."[37]

Government-supported officer training in the universities made up for the precipitous fall in tuition caused by the conscription of Harvard's normal student constituency. But what really excited Conant was the grist it provided for his meritocratic mill. "Until the Government undertakes to finance the college education of the future officers of the Army and Navy," he told Walter Lippmann, "we shall be recruiting our officer class largely from one economic group which to me seems very dangerous from many points of view." He wanted the selective service system to choose 50,000 high school graduates each year on the basis of their physical, intellectual, and leadership capacity, and to send them to college for a year or so at government expense.[38]

Conant flogged his plan to FDR and Harry Hopkins, appealing to their New Deal instincts. "I am sure," he told Hopkins, "I do not have to emphasize the importance of such a proposal from the point of view of providing mobility in our social structure." But FDR objected to Conant that his scheme raised serious problems of cost and selection. So most of the officers-in-training came from the usual college-going cohort, though at Harvard from much more diverse social and geographic sources than before the war.[39]

As the war drew to an end, attention turned to the education of veterans. Conant continued to balance meritocracy with equality (for the nation, if not for Harvard): "For some years I have been a fanatic about the importance of keeping alive the American tradition of three generations from shirtsleeves to shirtsleeves. To my mind the really unique contribution of this country to the world has been the implicit idea of a nation without classes." The frontier, he thought, may have protected equality of opportunity from the restoration of hereditary privilege. But now that that bulwark was gone, "it seems to me of the utmost importance that we seek other ways to revitalize the tradition."[40]

The education of returning veterans was a unique opportunity to do just that. The G.I. Bill of 1944 gave every returning serviceman the right to a government-paid education. But Conant wanted the government to finance the education of a "carefully selected number" of veterans. He criticized the G.I. bill because it was based on length of service rather than "demonstrated ability.... Unless high standards of performance can be maintained in spite of sentimental pressures and financial temptation we may find the least capable among the war generation instead of the capable flooding the facilities for advanced education in the United States."[41]

These observations were picked up by the army newspaper *Stars and Stripes* (not ordinarily on the qui vive for Harvard presidents' annual reports). Angry soldiers let Conant know what they thought of his views. One told him: "The general consensus seems to be that you are perfectly willing to make the smart people smarter, and of course those that are so unfortunate as not to be equipped with an ample amount of that grey matter might just as well stay that way." Here was an early instance of the tension between a meritocratic and an egalitarian model of higher education that would explode a quarter of a century later.[42]

As things turned out, postwar Harvard in many respects fulfilled Conant's ideal of a meritocratic university. Ironically this was due in good part to the G.I. Bill of which he disapproved. He responded in character by putting his weight behind the faculty committee that produced, in *General Education in a Free Society* (1945), the blueprint for a curriculum designed to extend the advantages of elite culture to a suddenly nonelite Harvard student body.[43]

Conant spent the World War II years deeply involved in the National Defense Research Committee in Washington. It was hard for him to return to the quotidian Harvard life after the war, and he continued to dwell on national issues. In his January 1947 annual report he called for a greatly expanded system of local, federal-supported but state-run two-year colleges to meet the demand for postsecondary education. And Conant found himself embroiled in sectarian controversy. In a spring 1952 speech to private school administrators, he criticized private and parochial schools for weakening the comprehensive public high schools and attacked public support for church-related schools. The reaction of the St. Grottlesex private school crowd was muted, though hardly favorable; the reaction of the Catholic church—in particular, of Boston's Cardinal Cushing—was not muted (or favorable) at all.[44]

Conant's Harvard years came to an end in January 1953, when he accepted the incoming Eisenhower administration's invitation to become American high commissioner in Germany. Giving three weeks' notice, he resigned his presidency. He was eager to leave Cambridge for a headier challenge: his diary entry for December 22, 1952, when Ike and Secretary of State-designate John Foster Dulles made him the offer, was festooned with "The Day!" and "Oh Boy." Shaken Corporation member Roger Lee asked him where he would be four years hence; Conant responded (to his diary): "Heaven knows, but at least not on *this* job."[45]

Why the sour note of departure? After all, Harvard's faculty and student body had steadily improved; by 1952 meritocratic Harvard seemed well on the way to displacing Lowell's Brahmin school. But there were grounds for discontent: Conant's failure (as he put it) "to bring about a greater integration" of Harvard's schools and faculties; a painful confrontation with the senior faculty in the late 1930s over the status of the junior staff; his undistinguished fundraising record. The bold, bright, energetic young man who took the helm of Harvard in 1933 had learned a painful lesson: that external events such as depression and war, combined with the institutional inertia and faculty autonomy of a great modern university, can—indeed, will—frustrate the most determined and resourceful of leaders.[46]

$\backsim$ 2 $\backsim$

# THE COLLEGE

A t the heart of Harvard lay the College. Half of the University's students were there, as was most of the history that fueled the Harvard mystique. Undergraduate tuition and the contributions of well-heeled College alumni provided much of the income on which the University depended. But the elitist, inbred College culture posed a substantial obstacle to Conant's goal of a more meritocratic Harvard.

## Getting In

Admission was the first step in the student life cycle, and admissions policy went far to set the tone of the College. Eliot did not pay much attention to the matter. But his successor Lowell wanted students who would be a social elite. Catholic students were quite acceptable to him: in comportment and values they passed his entry test for the leadership class. So, too—more doubtfully—did wealthy, assimilated German Jews, though assuredly not their Russian-Jewish brethren.[1]

Anne MacDonald, executive secretary of the admissions office since the beginning of the century, was one of those women then (and now) essential to the smooth functioning of Harvard. In a 1934 memorandum to Conant, she explained the workings of her bailiwick. She and her opposite numbers at Yale (a Miss Elliot), Princeton (a Miss Williams), and the College Entrance Examination Board (a Miss McLaughlin) met yearly "to compare notes on all matters concerning admission, and the different ways in which they are treated at the three universities." Some of her work required special handling: "The interviews with rejected Hebrews or their relatives are particularly precarious, and one needs to be constantly on the alert.... For the past ten years, or since the restriction [Harvard's unofficial Jewish quota] we have been particularly fortunate in settling these cases."

But there were snakes in this admissions Garden of Eden. A substantial portion of each entering class failed to meet the academic standards of the College: 30 to 40 percent of freshmen had unsatisfactory records in the early 1930s. And the student body was too parochial: in 1931 Harvard had the highest portion (40 percent) of students from its home state among the nation's major colleges.[2]

Conant sought to reshape admissions standards. He thought the freshman attrition rate was too high and the number of honors degree candidates (about a third of each class in the early 1930s) was too low. The Depression foreclosed any hope of increasing the 1,000-student class size. More than half of Harvard's freshmen in the 1930s came from private schools, about a third of these from Phillips Exeter, Milton Academy, Phillips Andover, and St. Paul's. Conant wanted more scholarship students and a wider geographical input. He peppered Dean of the College A. Chester Hanford with questions: How handicapped by the progressive education now prevalent in western high schools were the top-level men coming to Harvard? Would (that is to say, wouldn't) Hanford agree that in intrinsic ability the distribution of students at Milton and at a western high school in a moderate-sized city were similar?[3]

Most of all, Conant set himself to raise the undergraduate level by his National Scholarships program. He hoped it would attract talented boys from regions (the South and the West), and with backgrounds (small towns, low or middling incomes), not before represented at Harvard. His plan raised old grad anxieties and hackles. The *Alumni Bulletin* assured its readers that most Harvard students of the future, like the past, will be "men of average ability.... Because Harvard wishes to render a special service to some talented individuals who might otherwise lose the opportunity which they are most capable of improving, it does not follow that President Conant seeks to convert Harvard College into a group of prodigies sustained at public expense." Conant (cold-) comforted an anxious father: "I see no reason why the bottom level might not be kept the same as now."[4]

Of the 161 National Scholars admitted from 1934 to 1940, 24 were the children of teachers or school superintendents; 53 came from business or professional families; 10 were farmers' sons. The only working-class recruits were 2 sons of truck drivers. Fifty-four percent came from towns and small cities, a third from families with incomes under $2,000. For all its symbolic importance, the National Scholarships program was too small to significantly alter the social and geographical makeup of the Harvard student body. And in 1944 Harvard suspended it for the war's duration.[5]

Conant fretted that Harvard would have to do a great deal to reestablish itself outside the Northeast, and the National Scholarships program resumed in 1946. He needn't have worried. In the ten months from August 1945 to June 1946, about 20,000 veterans applied to the College. Accustomed to admitting one of every 1.2 to 1.5 applicants, Harvard now had to pick one out of 15. And the G.I. Bill enlarged the geographical and social range of its pool far more than all of Conant's prewar efforts. By the fall of 1946, enrollment in the College had gone from a prewar 3,500 to 5,500.[6]

After 1947 the postwar tide ebbed. Applications to the College went down to 2,000 to 3,000 a year in the early 1950s, and two out of three were accepted. Three quarters of the students still came from New England and the mid-Atlantic states; in 1948, 30 percent hailed from within twenty miles of Harvard Yard. But the prewar private school preponderance was gone. Fifty-five percent of the freshmen entering in 1952 came from public high schools (though a mere forty schools provided 30 percent of the applicants, 34 percent of the admits, and 41 percent of the matriculants).[7]

Provost Paul Buck worried about the balance between "democratic selection" and "aristocratic achievement." He estimated that "95 percent of the applicants for Harvard from the large metropolitan high schools of New York and New Jersey are of one category—bright, precocious, intellectually overstimulated boys." To make matters worse, the Harvard draw from the top private schools in those states was "weighted with the delicate, literary types of boys who don't make the grade socially with their better balanced classmates who, in turn, head for Yale or Princeton." The result: "a paucity of applicants of the kind we most desire."[8]

Dean of Admissions Richard Gummere did not seem up to the pressures of the postwar admissions scramble. But plans for his successor were well in place. Wilbur J. Bender was one of a number of able young men from the Midwest, of poor or middling origins, who came to Harvard College and later joined the administration as "baby" deans. In 1944 he became assistant to the dean and counsellor for veterans, slated to succeed Gummere when he resigned. Buck assured Conant that Bender "subscribes to the ideals and objectives of what you and I are attempting in the way of educational policy." But after

Bender became dean of admissions in 1952, it was not so clear that that was the case. Though many faculty members regarded the veterans as the best students Harvard ever had, Bender found their purposefulness offsetting: "There is a kind of unhealthy determination to get ahead, a grim competitive spirit, an emphasis on individual careerism which is disturbing." He wanted a student body that was a gathering of all the talents, not just the intellectuals that Conant so highly prized.[9]

Bender worried that because of Harvard's intellectual hothouse reputation Yale and Princeton had more applicants per slot, a "loss of ground" that "has come about in the last few years." But he found no basis for the belief that Harvard was losing its appeal in the most prestigious preparatory schools. The intake from those places could be readily cut with no loss of talent; indeed, quite the contrary. The problem was that the elite prep schools provided "a considerable share of our paying customers." The alternatives were unattractive: expensive recruiting campaigns in private day schools and upper-income high schools across the country—or more admits of you-know-who from New York City high schools.

When alumni spoke of Harvard losing its appeal, Bender observed, they meant to "the well-dressed, polite, Nordic blonde from a family with an income of $20,000 a year and up, living in a swanky suburb." "Frankly," he said,

> this is all right with me. We will win out in any competition for the able boys with strong intellectual and aesthetic interests, the boys who are the real individuals with other interests than college life and "contacts." Our problem ... is to keep some kind of balance among the diverse groups needed to make a healthy student body. ... in the present anti-intellectual and McCarthyite climate of opinion, Harvard, as long as she stands for academic freedom is not going to be as popular among the inhabitants of Westchester, Winetka, etc., as Williams and Princeton which seem so much safer.[10]

When Conant departed in 1953, the student body was measurably closer to his meritocratic ideal than when he came. But it remained overwhelmingly of upper-class and upper-middle-class origins. Admission still was far from need-blind, and established application patterns (favored prep schools, unfavored New York Jews) still had considerable force.

# College Days

Harvard College's 3,500 students in 1933 fell into distinct social groups. About 10 percent inhabited Harvard's nine Final Clubs, the most prestigious fraternities; a larger student elite dominated the houses and most extracurricular activities. The biggest component was an amorphous "middle class" consisting of graduates of the better public high schools and lesser prep schools. And then there was a proletariat-like lower order of commuters (over 20 percent of the undergraduates in 1938), heavily Jewish, often academically prominent, occasionally on sports teams, but not otherwise part of the undergraduate social scene.[11]

The student body reflected the American population—in mirror image. A comparison of major national family income groups with their Harvard student representation in 1936 shows the degree of social skew:

| Income | National % | Harvard % |
|---|---|---|
| $0–2,500 | 88.0 | 16.3 |
| $2,500–7,500 | 10.5 | 36.3 |
| $7,500–50,000 + | 1.5 | 47.3 |

The cost of a Harvard education fed this discrepancy. Dean of the Faculty Kenneth Murdock observed in 1933: "Unless a boy is sure of at least $900 or $1,000, or unless he has some employment in sight, he should hesitate about entering the freshman class"—this at a time when average per capita income was $374, and Depression unemployment was at its peak.[12]

Coexisting with ethnic and class distinctions was a more general differentiation between the "serious" student, intellectuals and aesthetes of the sort portrayed in George Santayana's *The Last Puritan* (1935), and the more frivolous, clubby, "gentleman's C" type that figures in J. P. Marquand's *The Late George Apley* (1937). Both, of course, were stereotypes, but they were models that influenced the self-image of many undergraduates.

The most visible students were the private school elite. They fed the image of snobbery and devil-may-care indulgence that was the prevailing public perception of college life. Lowell had hoped that the new residence houses, which opened in the early 1930s, would reduce student class distinctions. Each house took on its own social but not, as Lowell hoped, academic tone. Eliot House drew many Final Club undergraduates; Dunster was "the last stronghold of Harvard conservatism, informality, and indifference"; Kirkland was noted for its athletes and its theatrical productions; Leverett initially had a "pronounced racial [that is, Jewish] strain."[13]

Gradually the houses eroded the social power of the Final Clubs and the Gold Coast student elite. But the frivolity level of late adolescents—so often decried, so difficult to alter—changed little. The student impulse to challenge authority, as much glandular as sociological, flourished even in the depressed 1930s. The *Lampoon*, the student humor magazine, did a version of *Esquire* in April 1934 so obscene that it was banned from the mails, the Cambridge police threatened to close down the magazine, its building was shut for the rest of the term, and its trustees launched an inquiry. And on March 3, 1939, a few clubby Harvard men, led by Lothrop Withington, Jr., '42, won national attention for their pioneering work in live-goldfish swallowing, while Conant had to deal with an irate Animal Rescue League.[14]

For the gilded undergraduates, college life during the Depression proceeded in its accustomed way. Social—and socializing—events for freshmen such as Jubilee (noted for bringing in name bands) and the Smoker (a gaudy variety show, sobered by a Lowell speech on Harvard traditions delivered each year from 1921 to 1936) continued. So did the established rite of springtime riots in Harvard Square. Still, all was not what it had been. "Sad it is," lamented the class of 1935 album, "that the impact of economic depression has eliminated from the life of the Harvard man many of the luxuries he used to enjoy, and that the Class of 1935 has, as a result, missed the 'Dance of the Millions,' when debutante parties at the Copley-Plaza were graced with squabs and champagne *ad nauseum*." And when FDR closed the banks in March 1933, a Dunster House tutor called in his student charges and tried to ease their anxiety: "I say, fellows, if anyone is short I have a thousand dollars in gold in my room."[15]

But the Depression crimped the already straitened lives of commuters and boardinghouse dwellers. A faculty member sympathetically discussed the plight of commuter "untouchables" in 1932. By the mid-1930s almost a quarter of the undergraduates lived at home, and their numbers were growing. If anything, the house system deepened their isolation from the rest of the College. They had no building they could call their own; the Freshman Union was open to them, but its meals were too expensive. Dean of the College Hanford favored the construction of a commuters' center, "a simple building, where the day students may eat lunch, leave their belongings, and make their headquarters." But there was a difficulty. Hanford met a number of times with the leaders of the Harvard Commuters' Association, and "one objection which I see to this organization is that it is entirely made up of students of one particular race and religion. It is clear that the commuters' building will be managed and used almost wholly by students of this group and that the others will stay away." He supposed "there is no way out of it. Several Christians have been to see me and have stated that all they want is a place to eat their own lunches, that they are not interested in an organization, etc." Despite this obstacle, Dudley Hall opened as a commuters' haven in the fall of 1935.[16]

Most of the silent majority, the student middle class, appears to have been at reasonable peace with itself and engaged in the life of the College. During the early 1930s, 1,000 to 1,200 of the 3,500 undergraduates attended Sunday services in Memorial Church. But there was—there always had been—another type of student, numbers unknown by the nature of the case.

Wall Street lawyer Spier Whitaker wrote in 1937 of his regret that his son had been readmitted after having freshman year troubles. Because of his own experience as a student he had not wanted his son to go to Harvard, and his impression was that little had changed. "Whether the cold impersonal sink [or] swim attitude that governed the Harvard of my day, and apparently governs the Harvard of today, is right or wrong, is not for me to say." He made few friends, knew no member of the faculty well enough to speak to him outside of the classroom. "Had I taken sick and died, no one in particular would have known or cared until the stench became a nuisance. In fact, during my Freshman year, this very thing came close to happening." That experience probably did as much as his academic work to assure his worldly success by hardening him to life. But "the mental scar that my six years at Cambridge left, has never healed." His son, too, got only pro forma counseling and succumbed. "Would it not be better," he asked, "to warn parents that unless their sons are prepared to stand on their own feet, unassisted, they had better keep them home or send them elsewhere?"[17]

It is hard to measure anomie, indifference, alienation. They are as much a part of student life as high-toned revelry or grade-grinding application. Certainly the infrastructure available for students who came without the support system of prep school classmates—houses and their tutors, health care, freshman advising, a flock of assistant deans—grew in the 1930s. Conant observed to a classmate in 1942: "The College does a remarkable amount to help the individual student as compared with the 'sink or swim' policy prevalent in our day."[18]

The most deeply felt cause on campus during the 1930s was opposition to American involvement in another European war. The conservative *Crimson* and most of the student Left were of one mind on this issue. There were ugly town-gown reverberations after some antiwar (or just rambunctious) students acted in various disrespectful ways during a Cambridge veterans' commemoration of Memorial Day 1939.

An essay in the 1939 class album, "Out of the Bell Glass: The Rise of Social Realism at Harvard, 1935–1939," detailed the growing political and social consciousness of undergraduates. A December 1938 mass meeting of fifteen hundred students gathered to raise money for scholarships for refugees from Nazi Germany: in effect "a grand wake for an ancient and much-touted institution, Harvard indifference." New student publications—the *Monthly*, the *Guardian*, the *Progressive*—gave voice to a heightened political and social radicalism. Course taking reflected this change. English long was the most popular major; by 1939 Economics and Government surpassed it. Forty percent of the class of 1939 majored in History, Government, or Economics, a clear sign of change: "Harvard has turned away from the pastel twilight of romanticism."[19]

America's entry into World War II disrupted every aspect of college life, from admissions to graduation. While most of the 1941 freshmen returned as sophomores in the fall of 1942, fewer than a quarter were still there by the spring of 1943. A year later the College had only about 650 civilian students; the University at large, some 1,500. Military programs enrolled four times as many.

All was topsy-turvy, upside down. The Yard and many of the houses were given over to Army and Navy training programs. A depleted staff stopped publishing the *Crimson* in May 1943, offering instead a stripped-down *Harvard Service News*. The Administrative Board, devoted in its prewar years to students with academic and behavior problems, now dealt primarily with men "who want to do all sorts of irregular things in order to get on towards their degrees."[20]

Traumatic change continued after the war, when a flood of veterans came under the G.I. Bill: "Harvard Men by Act of Congress." The transformation was cultural as well as quantitative. By two to one, postwar students planned on graduate study; by almost as large a margin they wanted to go into the professions rather than business. For the first time the College had a number of married undergraduates, and officials had to concern themselves with seeking out and, in extremis, providing housing for these couples. (One alumnus helpfully suggested that Radcliffe students be "farmed out" to ease the servant problem in the far suburbs and their vacated dorm rooms be turned over to married students.)[21]

The veterans invigorated student cultural life. The University's Sanders Theater had been dark four or five nights a week before the war; by 1948 it was in constant use for concerts, plays, lectures, and debates. And they brought a more democratic social style—more informal dress, a preference for beer over wine. A member of the class of 1950 recalled the immediate postwar years:

> The very mood of the college was unique. The veterans, older and more mature, tended to replace college spirit, never a very high-priced commodity at Harvard, with an intense enthusiasm in specific individual enterprises. They poured their energy and ability into the newly flourishing extracurricular activities, atrophied by the war years, and into many of the new areas of the College curriculum. They knew what they wanted as had no other generation in the recent past, and they approached College life with intensity and decisiveness.

Other signs of change: attendance taking in upper-level courses disappeared; ashtrays—and women—were allowed into the reading room of Widener Library.[22]

As the flood of veterans ebbed, and younger, less worldly undergraduates returned, sophomoric exuberance resurfaced. The first student riot in ten years, on the night before the fall 1949 football game with Princeton, marked the passing of the more sober wartime and postwar years. Two large outbursts swirled around the Yale game in 1950, and in the spring of 1952 an appearance by Walt Kelly, creator of the students' favorite cartoon strip "Pogo," led to a roiling clash between students and police reminiscent of earlier days.[23]

Conant, Buck, and most of the faculty were more interested in the substance of a Harvard education than in the culture of the College. When the Korean War in the early 1950s reraised the specter of disrupted college careers and returning veterans, Conant proposed to make the B.A. program a three- instead of a four-year affair. Buck liked the idea. The real difficulty lay in the realm of sentiment:

> The concepts we are facing here are that "college is the time and place to make friends," that "activities like the Crimson give experience more valuable than the classroom," that "football builds

character," that "the class loyalty of Harvard men is a cherished thing," that "the Houses are communities in which values are developed," that "you must not hurry the educational process—it takes time and exposure to let ideas seep in," etc., *ad infinitum*, and that *all these things take four years.*

He thought that a rational, persuasive case for the change could be made. But the faculty had more pressing matters (appointments, resources, research, promotion) to worry about.[24]

## Stadium and Classroom

Two highly organized activities, at opposite ends of the spectrum of student experience, were major components of Harvard undergraduate life. One was intercollegiate football, the other was the curriculum. For all their differences of character and purpose, stadium and classroom had one thing in common: they were locales that drew students together across the social and economic lines that otherwise divided them.

At Harvard as in most other American colleges, the football team was for many students, and more alumni, a major source of institutional identification. Stirring pageantry, tribal loyalty, and vicarious violence made the football season, and in particular the Big Three games— Harvard-Yale and the less momentous encounter with Princeton—an aspect of College life that for many Harvard men was more compelling than the aura of academic distinction.[25]

Football gate receipts during the 1920s were large enough to pay for Harvard's athletic program and more besides. The Harvard Athletic Association, flush with money, was an autonomous entity, plumping for a larger stadium. But Lowell believed that intercollegiate contests should be reduced to the smallest number necessary to maintain student interest and had "long urged that one contest in each sport would be sufficient for the purpose and was the ultimate ideal to be attained. I should like, if possible, to see only one intercollegiate football contest a year, and that with Yale."[26]

Football did not escape the Great Depression. As the 1930s dragged along, the sport changed from a cash cow to a significant drain on the University's financial resources. Conant set out to cut the athletic budget, eliminate minor sports, and bring football under tighter control. A new policy in 1935 had "as its ultimate aim the placing of intercollegiate and intramural athletics on an endowed basis so that the present unfortunate connection between athletic activities and football gate receipts will be eliminated." Athletics would sit on its own financial bottom.[27]

World War II put intercollegiate football on hold. In 1945, to fend off pressure for the resumption of big-time football, the Ivy League of eight schools was created "to maintain the value of the game while keeping it in fitting proportion to the main purposes of academic life." But disastrous seasons in 1949 and 1950 intensified the debate over Harvard football. Critics wanted intercollegiate games dropped entirely; advocates wanted Harvard to take the sport more seriously. Conant expected that "the enraged alumni after the end of the [1950] season (unless by some miracle we beat Yale)" would be snapping at his heels. The age of miracles was past: Harvard lost. But the rise of the meritocratic University inexorably resolved the issue on the side of small-time football. In 1951 the Harvard Athletic Association, its budget already under the control of the Faculty of Arts and Sciences, became the Department of Athletics. While Conant regarded athletic costs as a proper charge on the FAS budget; like the library or the laboratories, football was low on his priorities list. He told Yale president Whitney Griswold in 1951 that William Buckley's conservative screed *God and Man at Yale* "is more likely to make my hair fall out than whether to abolish the two-platoon system."[28]

Nothing in the College more consistently concerned the faculty, or less consistently engaged the students, than the curriculum. "The important thing," explained Dean of Faculty Kenneth Murdock in 1933, "is to stir up the marginal group of 15 to 20 percent who are capable of achieving something more than a gentleman's grade of C." Conant set out to do with undergraduates what he wanted to do with the faculty: make them more scholarly, more serious, more socially useful. His initial concern was with the tutorial system: its cost and the corps staffing it, who by the 1930s were a major obstacle to his desire for a stronger faculty. In 1937 new rules were adopted, reducing tutorial requirements for about a third of the students. During the 1930s, 75 percent of undergraduates had faculty tutors; by 1950, three out of four were tutored by graduate students.[29]

Conant's desire to make the education of undergraduates more meaningful led finally to the Program in General Education, one of Harvard's major contributions to higher education in the twentieth century. In 1939 an intellectually power-packed undergraduate committee, including

James Tobin (later a Yale Nobelist in Economics), R. W. B. Lewis (later a Yale literature professor), and Philip Neal (later a University of Chicago law professor) called for the creation of five introductory courses covering major fields of knowledge. That this might make life tougher for "gentleman's C" students bothered them not a whit.[30]

While these flights of curricular fancy soared overhead, undergraduate foot soldiers slogged along much as in the past, the bulk of them clustered in popular and/or "gut" courses and in a few fields of concentration: more social science (Economics and Government in particular), less Literature and Romance Languages than in the 1920s. Conant was not distressed by this shift from the humanities to the social sciences. But he did want to make available some form of general education for a student body increasingly varied in its social and educational backgrounds. One proposal was "to make Harvard the home of an intellectual elite where only Honors students will be welcome." This was unrealistic in 1938, or indeed at any time.

Then World War II opened the door to a new approach to general education for Harvard's undergraduates. In 1941, as American entry loomed and it seemed likely that the "number of male students studying arts and letters will be enormously reduced," Conant set up a committee, chaired by Provost Paul Buck, to consider "the objectives of a general education in a free society." In the fall of 1943 Conant got the Corporation to allocate the substantial sum of $60,000 to help the Committee come up with a postwar program for Harvard undergraduates.[31]

With the war against fascism reaching a crescendo, the committee's work came to be seen as a statement by America's leading university as to what the war was all about and what curricular legacy it might bequeath to postwar higher education. It sought information and advice from a wide range of sources, both in and out of Harvard. A subcommittee on the education of women sent a questionnaire to all Radcliffe students and 1,000 alumnae (more than half of whom thought that theirs had not been a well-rounded education), and fielded conferences for leaders in women's secondary and higher education. The conclusion was that the need for general education was the same for both genders (though in gender-separated courses).[32]

No one person could take credit for the Program in General Education. Its most conspicuous champions were Provost Paul Buck, classicist John H. Finley, and political scientist Benjamin Wright. Most of all, it reflected Conant's belief in a curriculum that brought a high level of shared knowledge and understanding to a student body of diverse backgrounds: a curriculum suited to a meritocratic university.

It was also designed to instruct students in the ethos of a free society. Finley thought that "if many courses should set forth our view of life as rooted in a humane tradition, it seems only fair that some should set it forth as rooted in a religious tradition." Conant doubted "if a secular university today can take the step necessary to put its argument on the plane of absolute values." But the secular, meritocratic chemist could agree with the religious minded classicist that while "[t]here is no such thing as democratic science ... there is very definitely such a thing as the democratic scientist!"[33]

The committee's report, *General Education in a Free Society*, prescribed a stiff dose of curriculum reform not only for Harvard, but for American education at large. Some wondered if this was presumptuous. But those most involved knew what they were about. Conant said that the study's importance for American public education interested him "quite as much" as its importance for Harvard. He wanted school leavers and college goers alike to have "a common ... understanding of the society which they will possess in common." Buck more parochially thought "[t]he fact is clear that a first rate report based upon a program put into effect in Harvard College would be a very great factor indeed in the future leadership of Harvard. In fact I think that outcome is essential to prevent Harvard from slipping backwards."[34]

*General Education in a Free Society*, published in 1945, came to be known as the Redbook, a reference to its crimson cover. Its larger message was clear: American secondary and higher education had to provide a common ground of knowledge and ideas to a diverse population. By 1950 the Redbook had sold more than 40,000 copies. The higher education community seized on it as the definitive statement of postwar curriculum reform, though Columbia historian Jacques Barzun not unreasonably complained that his university (and Chicago as well) had had General Education programs for decades. But Columbia's program, and most certainly Chicago's under Hutchins, were based on Great Ideas and a venerable tradition of humanistic education. Harvard's scheme was imbued with Conant's very different educational goals of good citizenship and social utility.[35]

Congratulated on having restored Harvard to a leadership role in American higher education, Conant claimed not to have done anything except pick the committee, occasionally "cheer it on," and see to it that it was well funded. In truth he was not totally pleased with the report. He liked its first three chapters, which dealt with the deficiencies of secondary education in the United States. But he thought it could have done more to relate education to larger social forces in the nation, a task he himself soon took on. And he wished that a separate General Education faculty had been proposed. He appears to have doubted whether discipline-bound professors were up to the task.

Still, he thought that the committee had done something rare and valuable, especially in the message it sent to the nation's secondary schools: "it is the first time in history that a group of essentially laymen have expressed judgment on problems of secondary education after examining the facts in considerable detail and after listening to a good deal of evidence. To my mind, the significance of the Harvard report rests primarily on that fact." The Faculty of Arts and Sciences held seven meetings to discuss the report and then approved it by a 135–10 vote.[36]

The General Education Program was under way by the fall of 1946, at the height of the postwar onslaught of veterans: precisely the kind of students for whom it was designed. Conant himself cotaught a course, "The Growth of Experimental Science," in the fall of 1947: the first time in thirty years that a Harvard president had done so. Some Gen. Ed. courses attained quick and lasting popularity: Humanities 2 (John Finley on "The Epic"), Natural Sciences 1 ("Principles of Physical Science"), Social Sciences 2 (Samuel Beer and Louis Hartz on "Western Thought and Institutions"), Edward Reischauer and John K. Fairbanks's "History of Far Eastern Civilization" (immediately student-dubbed "Rice Paddies").

In 1950, after a three-year trial, General Education became a required part of the Harvard curriculum. It goes without saying that as faculty satisfaction rose, so did student discontent. The Undergraduate Council in 1952 took a poll of students' attitudes toward the new program. They regarded its essay requirements much less warmly than did the faculty. And they thought that the program did more to provide useful background for their fields of concentration than to meet the more elevated pedagogical goals of its creators.[37]

The program had other consequences, neither expected nor much remarked upon. Insofar as Gen. Ed. played the synthesizing role that Lowell's tutorial system had been designed to do, it legitimated the downgrading of that pesky intruder on the faculty's research time. In December 1946 the departments were allowed to decide whether or not they would continue to offer tutorials. Astronomy, Biology, Economics, and Geology voted to withdraw.

And since General Education took up a quarter of the undergraduate course load, it fed the faculty's taste for ever more specialization in the rest of the curriculum. By 1947–48 most departments offered two to three times as many courses as they had forty years before. Inevitably this affected class size, that hardy perennial of administration-faculty contention. Conant could see no justification, financial or pedagogical, for courses with less than five students. Presented with a list of offerings that included 169 (primarily graduate) courses with four or fewer enrollees, his marginal comments were feeling: "This is ridiculous"; "My God!" And so the modern university curriculum came to Harvard.[38]

## ∽ 3 ∾

## "LESSER BREEDS"

When Conant became president, Harvard College students were male, almost all white, primarily Unitarian, Congregationalist, or Episcopalian in religion, predominantly from New England. Brahmin Harvard sought to restrict the number of Jewish students and faculty; indeed, that issue often was the outlet for opposition to the effort to make Harvard a more meritocratic university. Even more pervasive was the desire to shield Harvard men and Radcliffe women from the perils of co-education. Catholics were scant, but for different reasons: hostility to god-less Harvard in Catholic churches and schools kept their numbers small during the 1920s and 1930s. As for African Americans, there were so few that it was safe to accept (if not to welcome) them—if they met academic standards for admission and had the money to pay for their education.[1]

### The Jewish Question

Under Eliot's benign lead, turn-of-the-century Harvard was more receptive to Jewish students than were other Eastern universities. Undergraduates from well-off German-Jewish families combined with a growing number of commuters from the Boston area to become a substantial presence. By the early 1920s, an estimated 20 to 25 percent of the undergraduate student body was Jewish. This was cause for concern by alumni, faculty, and not least President Lowell. In 1922 he proposed a formal Jewish quota of 12 percent. This was the limiting device tradi-tionally used in European universities, now much in the American public mind because of the movement for quota-based immigration restriction laws. Harvard historian Samuel Eliot Morison, looking back on the controversy fifty years later, ascribed the emotional strength of the Jewish reaction to the fact that Lowell's 12 percent quota was the same as the *numerus clausus* of the Russian imperial universities.[2]

Lowell's biography, published in 1948, rather laboriously tried to exonerate him: "the poor, hard-working student, native-born or immigrant, Gentile or Jew, white or black, never had a warmer friend, although many excellent persons criticized at times his way of showing friendship." But it is clear that Lowell shared in full measure the prejudices of his caste. Jews, he thought, lowered the moral tone of the College. When data from the office of the dean of the College failed to uphold that belief, he was not happy: "You have basely gone back on me. Somebody told me that of the fourteen men dismissed last year for cheating and lying about it, thirteen were Jews. Now you make out that there were twelve of them, of whom only five were Jews. Please produce at once six more!"[3]

A series of faculty meetings on the "Jewish question" considered Lowell's quota proposal. By a solid margin the faculty rejected an explicit quota for any group "which is not easily assimilated into the common life of the College." (Conant was among the small number who backed a quota.) But it instructed the admissions committee to take into account the proportionate distribution of racial and national groups, and called for a faculty committee to look further into the matter. Lowell coldly warned the faculty that "there can be no doubt that the primary object in appointing a special Committee was to consider the question of the Jews."[4]

The faculty committee unanimously rejected a formal quota. Lowell accepted that decision, whereupon he and the Governing Boards quietly instituted an unofficial admissions cap, reinforced in 1924 by a 1,000-freshman limit. The effect of the new system was dramatic. A (probably low) estimate was that 10 percent of the freshmen who entered in 1930 were Jewish, compared to around 25 percent in 1924. The religious affiliations of Harvard alumni during the 1920s reveals a concordance between a decline in those who identified themselves as Jews and an increase in those who gave no affiliation or ignored the question.

| Class | Jewish (%) | None or Not stated (%) |
|-------|-----------|------------------------|
| 1921  | 10.3      | 20.6                   |
| 1926  | 15.0      | 20.0                   |
| 1927  | 6.4       | 42.7                   |
| 1928  | 6.8       | 37.6                   |
| 1929  | 7.9       | 40.0                   |

When Conant came into office, Lowell gave him his view of the matter, unchanged from a decade before: "The time has not come for any theoretical solution of the Jewish question. I tried, as you know, to find an open, fair and practical solution, but was howled down by the preference of most people to profess one principle and act upon another. Any educational institution that admits an unlimited number of Jews will soon have no one else."[5]

Conant's pro-quota position in the early 1920s, his preference for more students from small towns and cities and the South and West, and his cool response to the plight of Jewish academic refugees from Hitler suggest that he shared the mild anti-Semitism common to his social group and time. But his commitment to meritocracy made him more ready to accept able Jews as students and faculty.

Others in the Harvard community were more overtly hostile to the Jewish presence. An alumnus warned Conant that "the Jews withstood the rigors of the New England climate better than other nationalities" and thus the Jewish proportion "might considerably increase when the class graduated." His conclusion: "Harvard plans to be a National University. The Jews in the United States are less than 6 percent, I believe. Over 25 percent getting degrees at Harvard is certainly out of proportion." Lawrence Berenson '13, a cousin of Bernard Berenson and a Roxbury Latin classmate of Conant, agreed. He regretted that "too many of my people (and I refer particularly to the intellectuals among them)" wanted to raise "the so-called Jewish question." Without limits, he feared, the College would soon become preponderantly Jewish. That would be disastrous: "speaking as a Jew, more good can come to my people from Anglo-Saxon influence than from making a ghetto out of Harvard." Conant circumspectly replied that Berenson's "seems a most dispassionate and clear presentation of some of the complex issues which confront all our educational institutions. I am sure that fundamentally we do not disagree on any of the issues which you mention."[6]

A system of notation (* = Jewish) enabled the masters of the residential houses to share the burden of Jewish students ("a racial group for which the supply exceeds the House Masters' demand"). Julian Coolidge, high Brahmin professor of Mathematics and master of Lowell House, remained ill at ease and unburdened himself to Conant in 1939: "I want to lay before you in all seriousness the vexing question of the number of Jews in Harvard College." The issue had weighed on him ever since Lowell raised it with the faculty, and they voted against a quota. Then the Overseers "gave orders on the quiet to keep down the numbers on any pretext, a not very honorable proceeding." His major concern was with the persisting discrepancy between the unwritten admissions ceiling of 12 percent, and the apparent fact that every Harvard house was at least 15 percent Jewish, even though the nonhouse "commuters were notoriously largely Semitic." This was "curious, especially in light of 'the gentlemen's agreement' of seven years ago that each House would take at least ten per cent."

When he confronted Miss MacDonald of admissions with these figures, she argued that Jewish admissions were indeed limited to 12 percent, but that the house percentages were based "on those who survived a year, and all Jews survive." Coolidge asked her how many Jews were in the current freshman class, and she estimated 120 to 125: about 12 percent. Triumphantly, he displayed the dean of the College's list of "supposed" Jews in the freshman class: 16 percent of the total. Gamely she responded that the dean's estimate included "a number of persons she would not put in that category." While Coolidge was "not in a position to judge between these experts in Semitism," he knew from experience that "it turns out more frequently that a man is a Jew when we thought he wasn't than the contrary."[7]

Jewish students who did get in entered a complex environment. H. R. Glodt, a student in Professor Alfred Tozzer's Anthropology 12 class, wrote a paper on "The Jew at Harvard" that Tozzer thought interesting enough to send on to Conant. Glodt lived in Eliot House for three years and did an ethnographic study of his fellow Jewish students there: thirty-five of them, 11.7 percent of the total. He found that they divided into three groups: a relatively small "isolation" segment, who strongly sustained their Jewishness and separated themselves socially from the rest of the House; a "break from the minority" cadre, who concealed their Jewish origins; and by far the largest portion: those who had casual non-Jewish acquaintances but were widely regarded—and treated accordingly—as Jews. The non-Jewish majority response was similarly divided: small groups of philo-Semites and anti-Semites, and a large majority who coexisted with Jewish students casually and at a distance.[8]

By the late 1930s, full-throated, unapologetic anti-Semitism at Harvard was in retreat. Some house masters were "disturbed by the number of good *'s who are being left out of the Houses." Prodded by Conant, the College administration began in 1940–41 to assure that all upperclassmen who desired to could live in them. During and after World War II, concern over Jews at Harvard all but disappears from the record. By 1944 over 30 percent of the students in the remaining civilian student houses were Jewish. In calculating the proper size of the wartime class of 1946, the "quota for a certain type" was dropped. The result: about 19 percent of the class was Jewish, the highest percentage since the early 1920s.[9]

By now many Jewish applicants were the sons of Harvard alumni, and/or came from a more prosperous and educated American Jewish community. The proportion of Jewish students in the College ranged from a fifth to a quarter during the 1950s (compared to Yale's quota-bound 13 percent). The Hillel Society, founded in 1944 by three students who sought "a feeling of home within the school," continued in the post-war decades as a place of reference (and, for some, of refuge). But most Jewish students in postwar Harvard sought assimilation more than the retention of a separate identity. Acceptance presumably was easier, given the meritocratic tone now so firmly entrenched in Harvard life.[10]

Still, old demons lurked in the background. After the war ended, the house masters resumed their prewar screening and sharing practices. Not until May 1950 did they agree to take every house applicant and relegate the * designation to history's dustbin. And a recruiting pitch made in 1951 to private school headmasters in the New York City area backfired when it emerged that the general belief of the audience was that Harvard sought to reduce, not add to, its New York intake. Corporation member Keith Kane was at the meeting and advised Conant: "To attract a fair share of the 'good [that is, non-Jewish] boys' from this area I submit that the college should try to avoid giving the impression that it aims to reduce the number of New Yorkers." But new Dean of Admissions Wilbur Bender warned: "the last thing we want to do, it seems to me, is to stimulate more applications from New York City. One of the major justifications for an expanded admissions program is that it will help bring us more 'good boys' from other parts of the country, to counterbalance legitimately the snowballing New York contingent."[11]

## No Women Allowed . . .

The prevailing assumption in pre-World War II Harvard was that women had no real place in the University, that it was a male institution doing men's work. Radcliffe College, as its (and Harvard's) officials never tired of pointing out, was a separate corporate entity, awarding its own degrees, although Harvard faculty taught its courses. Harvard's Law, Medical, and Business Schools were all but unique in being for men only. As of 1933, women could attend the Graduate School of Arts and Sciences, the Schools of Public Health and Education, the Bussey

Institution for Botany, and the Ph.D. Program in Medical Sciences. But they could only get Radcliffe degrees.[12]

In 1928 a group of Radcliffe alumnae, backed by President Ada Comstock, asked the Corporation to grant Harvard degrees to Radcliffe graduates and proposed that their school, while keeping its separate identity, become a part of the University. Lowell's response was to *strengthen* gender apartheid. With Corporation members Bishop William Lawrence and Thomas Nelson Perkins present, he told Comstock that Harvard during the next few years would separate itself even more fully from Radcliffe. This was news to her—and to Lawrence and Perkins. She later said: "If anyone asked me who caused the greatest emotional disturbance of my life, I should say Abbott Lawrence Lowell.... President Lowell was determined to cut Radcliffe off from Harvard."[13]

Conant shared more than a little of Lowell's attitude toward the sexes. Besides the normal patriarchal views of the time, special considerations may have influenced him. He had no daughters, and there were very few women in the worlds of business, science, and the professions that his meritocratic Harvard was supposed to supply. When William T. Brewster, a longtime Barnard faculty member, asked him to speak at the college's fiftieth anniversary celebration in 1939, Conant replied frankly to "Uncle Dick": "I have a good many doubts and qualms about education in general, but when it comes to the education of the fairer sex, I throw up my hands in complete despair and consternation.... it is very much like asking a Christian Scientist to speak at the celebration of the fiftieth anniversary of a medical school."[14]

Keeping Harvard College *frauleinrein* involved rules and understandings reminiscent of those governing racial segregation in the South. Repeating a course or two—or three or four—at Radcliffe was a popular salary supplement for Harvard faculty members; advanced courses for one or two students were not uncommon. Radcliffe paid Harvard $1,000 for the right to use Widener Library. But its students were confined to a small reading room set aside for their use (though Radcliffe graduate students had access to the stacks). Radcliffe had its own chemistry and physics laboratories, but used Harvard's biology labs on the basis of a complex system of proportional costs. Radcliffe degrees continued to be signed by the presidents of the two institutions (though in what seems very like a gesture of contempt, the secretary of the Faculty of Arts and Sciences was authorized in 1937 to sign Radcliffe diplomas). Charles Eliot had attended Radcliffe graduations, but by the 1930s they conflicted regularly with the pre-Commencement Corporation meeting, so Conant was a dependable no-show. Comstock gently told him that she "shall never cease to cherish the hope that some day you may be able to renew the custom."[15]

Radcliffe was a struggling institution. It had 750 to 800 undergraduates during the 1930s, about half of them commuters. Some two-thirds of its students came from Massachusetts. Its graduate school dropped from 360 students in 1929–30 to 222 in 1934–35. The college sought in the late 1930s to become more national and to "raise the level of capacity and personality" of its students: a reference to its relatively late discovery that, like its big brother across the Cambridge Common, it had a "Jewish problem."[16]

Radcliffe president Ada Comstock was as anxious as Conant to avoid coeducation. (Her reaction to merger plans in the late 1960s: "I lay awake last night trying to compose a letter to the then [current Radcliffe president] Polly Bunting, to tell her what a mistake I think she is making.") When Vassar president Henry Noble MacCracken asked her to support a petition to open Harvard's new Graduate School of Public Administration to women, she dutifully turned to Conant for advice. "From what I have read of the plans for the School," she told him, "I can imagine some good reasons for not including women at the outset."[17]

Mixed music making was another source of danger. Harvard music professor Archibald T. ("Doc") Davison wanted in 1938 to form a Harvard-Radcliffe chorus. Conant told Comstock: "I know that you are as anxious as I am to avoid the relation of the two institutions drifting into a scheme of coeducation. For that reason I am not particularly enthusiastic about this proposal." Comstock agreed that a large-scale chorus might well smack of coeducation: "Into that, as you say, we certainly do not wish to drift." But a small chorus performing every now and then was acceptable to her—though "[i]f even that concession seems to you like the camel's nose under the tent, I shall be glad to be guided by your judgment." Conant talked to Davison, and it emerged that this was indeed a serious matter, involving weekly practice by some eighty members. So the idea was dropped.[18]

Even in those benighted days, pressure for some less rigid academic separation of the sexes began to build. Conant's belief in meritocratic values had resonance for the education of women, even if it didn't advance the gender education of Conant. The Corporation in 1933 acceded to a request from the Mathematics department that a couple of its advanced courses be open to qualified Radcliffe students, and in 1934 authorized the President to do this more generally. We are still light years away from later challenges to the male monopoly at Harvard. (An old grad lamented that he was "somewhat out of touch with the problems of the University ... because my boys are all girls.") But the Tercentenary stirred questions about old ways, old beliefs. In the wake of that event, Sedgwick Mead '34 chided Conant on the lack of sex equality at Harvard: "So Harvard begat Radcliffe and was content. But what is Radcliffe? An architectural excrescence on the northwest corner of the University, a satellite Yard where earnest young women in flat-heeled shoes and horn-rimmed spectacles scurry busily about trying to appear as masculine as possible. A sort of morganatic wife whose degrees must be apologetically countersigned as being unable to stand on their own feet." Conant's secretary Stephen Stackpole replied that admitting women raised a multitude of questions beyond "merely that of equality." Harvard, he assured Mead, did not regard women as a separate race; it was merely that "the University considers it does its best work on the present basis and is not in a position to expand along these lines."[19]

The Harvard-Radcliffe relationship was substantially affected by World War II. In the fall of 1942 Comstock, Provost and FAS dean Paul Buck, Harvard treasurer Claflin, and Radcliffe treasurer Francis Grey met to find a way to improve the Harvard-Radcliffe relationship. They knew each other well and shared a desire to reach a solution. They proposed that the Faculty of Arts and Sciences assume complete responsibility for Radcliffe instruction and degrees. Almost 85 percent of Radcliffe's tuition income would be turned over to Harvard. The faculty would be expected to teach an additional half course at Radcliffe and would get up to a 20 percent increase in their salary scale. And Radcliffe graduate students might be Harvard tutors—though, as it turned out, at double the former Harvard tutorial load.

After they came to an agreement, Buck went down to New York City and rode back on the train to Boston with Conant, who was already deep in war work and badly pressed for time. He asked only one question: did Treasurer Claflin approve? "Wholeheartedly," said Buck; and Conant gave the go-ahead. Buck assured the Corporation that "safeguards shall be taken to prevent coeducation from spreading to the lower classes. I think myself that no Radcliffe freshmen and sophomores should ever be admitted to Harvard classes and that upperclass students should be admitted only to advanced courses with small enrollments." Radcliffe would get greater security and dignity; "[i]t would also be a recognition which I do not think we can properly escape in the future that Harvard assumes an interest in the education of women." The faculty (not unmindful of the boost to its salaries) unanimously approved the agreement, the Overseers approved in a "surprisingly favorable action," and on April 16, 1943, the new Harvard-Radcliffe treaty was signed.[20]

Once instituted, the new policy could not readily be reversed. When the war ended, Comstock resignedly said to Conant: "I suppose now we must segregate these classes." Conant replied: "Oh no, the professors like this too much." In October 1947 the Harvard-Radcliffe teaching agreement became permanent. Radcliffe continued to offer separate courses (taught by Harvard faculty) for first-year students, except when small enrollments made this unfeasible. Otherwise, Harvard College courses were open to both men and women. Within a few years the last separate introductory courses were gone as well, and coeducation reigned—in the classroom. In 1952 Conant confessed to the Overseers that while he never would have predicted the coming of joint instruction of Harvard and Radcliffe students, "no revolution ever proceeded more smoothly and with so few reactionaries left protesting." But the Chinese wall of institutional separation remained inviolate, as Radcliffe student Dorothy Billings—"simply an average midwesterner raised on public school coeducation, completely without experience with the power of this 'tradition' thing"—found out when she sought, unsuccessfully, to participate in morning services at Memorial Church.[21]

The Harvard-Radcliffe pas de deux went on, like the mating dance of two exotic, undersexed birds. When Music professor G. Wallace Woodworth made a plea to Conant for the continuation of a coed choir in Memorial Church for Sunday services (a wartime innovation), he hit a stone wall. Conant discussed the matter with Provost Buck, who wanted to return to a men-only choir: "it would be a good thing at this time to make this gesture to masculinity at Harvard.... there are gripes that Harvard is going co-ed. It would not hurt us to have a counter criticism that we are excluding women from something." Conant agreed. The postwar construction of Lamont Library for Harvard undergraduates raised another problem of access. Asked to explain why no women were allowed in Lamont, Conant admitted that it was hard to understand—"unless you have had the experience of trying to run an institution which is dedicated to the principle of coordinated education but not coeducation." While instruction was joint, facilities were not.[22]

The conflict between Brahmin tradition and the meritocratic impulse over women's education might have seemed more readily resolvable on the graduate and professional level. But here, too, old habits of thought died hard.

The Graduate School of Education was the first (and for a long time the only) Harvard professional school to admit women. By the late 1920s they made up more than half of the school's students. The next to break the gender line was Public Health. Dean David Edsall of the Medical School told Conant in 1934 that while he had "no particular interest in their getting degrees in the Medical School, though I have no particular objection to it," in public health "there are perfectly clear careers for women that cannot be as well filled by men and it has always seemed to me to be a directly wrong thing that they should not be trained, as it is a matter of public interest to some degree." Martha Eliot, assistant chief of the United States Children's Bureau, pointed out that state public health departments granted leave to women on their staff to take courses in schools of public health. Was Harvard inclined to open its doors? The School of Public Health's faculty unanimously voted that women with M.D.s be allowed to work for Public Health degrees, and finally in 1936 the Governing Boards agreed.[23]

The mass departure of male students after America entered World War II, and the comradely wartime mood, lowered more professional school barriers. The Corporation allowed the Graduate School of Public Administration to admit "a limited number of women with administrative experience." And the School of Design was authorized to take in female students currently enrolled in Smith College's Cambridge-based Graduate School of Architecture and Landscape Architecture. In 1943 Design had 23 male students, "supplemented by sixty girl students." When applications from veterans flooded into the school after the war, female students became an endangered species. Of the 200 (twice the normal number) enrolled in the Graduate School of Design in 1946, 155 were veterans and 15 were women. And after the veterans' crunch passed? The view of the faculty was "that while preference will undoubtedly be given to well-qualified men, the admission of a few women of unusual promise will be of advantage both to the School and to the profession."[24]

The Medical School faculty, too, began to think about the (previously) unthinkable: the admission of women. This change of heart was the product not of a social conversion experience, but of the remorseless logic of the Medical School's commitment to high standards. Most wartime students did not meet those standards: they were in training to be armed forces medics, many had only two years of college work, and their average age was 19.5 years. In April 1943 the faculty by a 66–11 vote recommended the admission of women; the Corporation turned it down. The proposal came up again in May 1944 and was reendorsed 56–3. Pathologist S. Burt Wolbach, who chaired the committee looking into the issue, originally opposed coed admission on the ground that women doctors tended to get married and leave their practice. But he made further inquiries and found that female M.D.s were no more likely to drop out of the profession than male graduates were to work for insurance companies (apparently, comparable career choices to his way of thinking). Now he was ready to support the admission of women— and to argue that the issue was "intimately bound to the problem of human rights."

This time the Corporation agreed to the admission of women "of superior ability and in limited numbers." In September 1945 the first twelve women (only one from Radcliffe) entered the Medical School. There is some irony in the fact that medicine, the most male-dominated of professions, was the first major Harvard professional school to admit women. There is comparable irony in Divinity's being next to last (followed only by the Business School.)[25]

The Law School, despite a severe shortage of students, was more obdurate than Medicine. In May 1944, Pauli Murray, a black Howard Law School graduate, recipient of a Julius Rosenwald Fund Fellowship for graduate study, and later a prominent figure in the civil rights movement, asked constitutional lawyer Thomas Reed Powell, who ran the Law School's graduate program, for an application form. She was interested in labor law and hoped to work with Powell. After she filled it out and sent it in, Powell told her that as a woman she could not apply: "I assumed that you were a member of the sex entitled to be a student at the Harvard Law School."

Murray was no naïf: she had gotten Eleanor Roosevelt to intercede when she tried (unsuccessfully) to enter the law school of the University of North Carolina. A letter on her latest problem came to Conant from none other than Franklin Delano Roosevelt. FDR enclosed a letter from Murray "that I really do not know how to answer. Wholly aside from Radcliffe College, I always had an idea that women were admitted to many courses. Or perhaps this young colored lady wants to become an undergraduate freshman. I do not want to start you on a new dormitory program but perhaps you might ask one of your Deans to drop me a line."

Dean of Faculty George Chase quickly responded that Murray would be welcome as a Radcliffe graduate student and that the necessary application form had been sent to her. There was a problem in that the Rosenwald program specified that she attend Harvard. But Radcliffe degrees were in effect Harvard ones, and a Rosenwald Fellowship holder was currently studying at Radcliffe and living in the women's graduate dorm.[26]

Murray appealed the ruling, sending copies to FDR, Felix Frankfurter, and African American federal judge William Hastie. But Powell told her that no exception could be made to the Law School's men-only policy and suggested that she take up the matter with the Corporation. She duly sent a brieflike document making her case: "There is a campus tradition, that Howard is a miniature edition in sepia of Harvard, and I have been caught between the tradition of Howard and the tradition of Harvard not to admit women. . . . Very recent medical examination," she reassured the fellows, "reveals me to be a functionally normal woman with perhaps a 'male slant' on things, which may account for my insistence upon getting into Harvard." She noted the nearly invisible wartime enrollment in the Law School and argued that by continuing to close the doors to women, Harvard was robbing a generation of her sex of the chance to make a contribution to the nation.

The Corporation told Murray that her proper recourse was to get the faculty to change its mind and make an appropriate recommendation to the Governing Boards. "One of the assets of being a brown American is patience," she replied. "I must admit the Harvard institution is drawing heavily on such asset." The Law School had told her to appeal to the Corporation; now she was being told to appeal to the Law School faculty. "In my country, they would label such procedure 'passing the buck.'"

She tried again. No other law school could offer what she wanted: "It looks like Harvard, or nothing." Harvard as well as she would benefit from her coming: "Wherever new opportunities are opened to a class of persons hitherto denied such opportunities, such persons extend themselves to prove themselves worthy. You are not denying a mere woman an opportunity. You are denying a promising and potential legal scholar the right to use 550,000 volumes in your library and the opportunity, perhaps, to make a contribution to legal thought." So she sent her argument for herself to the faculty—with an addendum: "Humorously, gentlemen, I would gladly change my sex to meet your requirements but since the way to such change has not been revealed to me, I have no recourse but to appeal to you to change your minds on this subject. Are you to tell me that one is as difficult as the other?" Corporation Secretary Calvert Smith assured her: "You are proceeding through the proper channels in addressing yourself to the faculty of the Law School." But her appeal fell on stony ground, and she went off to Berkeley's Boalt Hall instead.[27]

In 1949 a committee on the admission of women, chaired by legal historian Mark Howe, reported to the faculty. Law, Business, and Divinity were the last of Harvard's professional schools to exclude women; the committee could see no grounds for continuing to do so. It proposed, and the faculty and then the Corporation agreed, that the "selective"

admission of women begin with the fall 1950 term. To Dean Erwin Griswold's "considerable surprise," only one alumnus wrote to complain.
(Not many more wrote to commend; apparently the move was "more or
less regarded as inevitable.") By October 1949 about twenty women had
requested application forms. "On the whole," Griswold conceded, "I
should say that it looks as though we would be able to survive the
shock."[28]

## A Different Faith

Catholics occupied yet another niche in the Harvard scheme of things,
one dictated by group preference more than institutional policy.
Through the nineteenth and well into the twentieth centuries, the
number of Catholic students in the University was small. They were
more visible in the professional schools than in the College. In the early
1920s, when Jews were thought to be approaching a quarter of the
student body, Catholics made up only about 7 percent of the total. Not
until the late fifties and sixties did they approach their national proportion of one-fifth of the American population.

This was due in part to the cost of a Harvard education. More important was the sentiment in the Church, and in many Catholic families,
that to send a son to Harvard was to give a hostage to apostasy. Boston's
William Cardinal O'Connell was on good terms with Lowell and got an
honorary degree from Harvard in 1936. But he viewed the University as
a sink of secularism and disapproved of Catholics going there. In 1930
he asked the parish priest of nearby St. Paul's to look into the effects of
a Harvard education on its Catholic students and was treated to a satis-
factorily morose and pessimistic reply.

In fact, Harvard student converts to Catholicism were more conspicuous than those who fell away from the Church. Catholic student life
(according to John LaFarge '01) consisted of a tripartite division very like
that among Jewish students: "some Catholic students gave up the practice of their religion, others simply fell back upon their household faith
and passed through Harvard anonymously, while a third group
attempted to establish some kind of presence and recognition for their
co-religionists."

Low numbers, popularity through sports stardom, and claims to
social acceptability may have made anti-Catholicism a more or less
nonbarking dog on the Harvard scene. But Harvard *did* have a
Catholic—or more accurately an Irish—problem. Cambridge, apart

from its Harvard enclave, was a heavily Irish city. Its inhabitants' relationships with Harvard were troubled. Clement Norton, a perky Irish alumnus who served on the Boston School Board and peppered Conant for years with gossip and advice, counseled him on town-gown relations. "Think over that matter of better public relations with the Cambridge Irish," he told Conant in 1936. "You unbend, you be the magnanimous, forgiving one. You're educated.... When I talk with the Cambridge politicians I don't want to hear such bitterness against Harvard.... Your problem is the hardest in the land because you have a red hot Irish-American political group to fight and they know how to fight politically better than any other group in these parts." In recognition of the strongly Irish Catholic character of the community, Corporation fellow Henry Shattuck underwrote a faculty position in Celtic studies. The appointment of its first incumbent, assistant professor John Kelleher, was announced on St. Patrick's Day 1947.[29]

## Racial (In)difference

Marginality assumed yet another form in the case of African Americans, who had a long (though lightly populated) history at Harvard. The pioneering black students, like Harvard's early Catholics, were in the Medical School; none graduated from the College until 1870. A trickle continued to pass through in ensuing decades, and by the mid-twentieth century a number of distinguished African Americans had Harvard degrees: most notably W. E. B. Du Bois '90; journalist W. Monroe Trotter '95; poet Alain Locke '08; Lyndon B. Johnson's Secretary of Housing and Urban Development, Robert C. Weaver '29 (the first black Cabinet member); Clifton Wharton, Jr., '47, who headed Michigan State and the State University of New York; and Secretary of the Army Clifford Alexander, Jr., '55.

The prevailing pattern: low numbers, even lower visibility. Du Bois later said "I was in Harvard, not of it." Lowell overstepped himself when in 1922 (ostensibly to ease racial tension) he called for excluding blacks from the freshman dormitories. But just as the refusal to institute an official Jewish quota did not block its de facto implementation, so were black students contained in practice. Robert Weaver recalled the situation in the mid-1920s: "it was general knowledge among the Negroes that they were not welcome in the freshman dormitories.... it was my impression that there was de facto exclusion regardless of any action which may have been taken by the Board of Overseers."[30]

The official view was that African Americans who had the grades and money to come to Harvard were welcome, but that there was no call to do anything more. Lowell assured Du Bois in 1931: "the negro presents no problem peculiar to Harvard. The numbers coming here are not large, and as their object is to get an education they do not seek to be publicly conspicuous. No rules concerning them have been made for the Houses." But of course exclusionary custom had more to it than that. Foreign Policy Association president Raymond L. Buell proposed to Conant in 1935 that the poet-philosopher Alain Locke, a 1918 Harvard Ph.D. and the only black Rhodes scholar before the 1960s, might be invited to come for a term as visiting lecturer. Philosophy professor Ernest Hocking, a friend of Locke, was asked to rate him and did so—not highly: Locke was intelligent and an able critic, and had done a good job with the Howard philosophy department, but was not among the country's top twenty philosophers. Even before this, Conant told Buell that he didn't see how Locke could be called to Harvard "even for a few lectures." He would, he promised, bear it in mind "over a period of years."[31]

Blacks registered on the Harvard consciousness primarily when inquiries were made as to their numbers and place in the University. The party line was that Harvard "has no 'Negro policy,'" has "never refused admission to a Negro who could meet our entrance requirements," kept no separate count of its few black students. As for taking race into account in room applications: "This is in order to facilitate assignments of dormitory accommodations.... however, there is no color line in our recitation halls or dining halls."[32]

William A. Hinton, longtime (since 1918) instructor in the Medical School and the School of Public Health, was the sole black faculty member. A survey of Harvard's professional schools in 1940 revealed that the Business School's 1,008 students included precisely no African Americans, though one had been admitted for the coming year. The Dental School reported that its occasional black students were carefully selected and well-received, and that only once in a while did difficulties arise with white patients at the Dental School clinic.[33]

The most notable prewar racial controversy arose in the spring of 1941, when the Harvard lacrosse team played Navy at Annapolis. The Harvard team had an African American member, and Academy commandant Rear Admiral Russell Willson asked it not to field him. Navy had not played a team with a black on it at Annapolis for fifty-seven years, and he feared the reaction from the stands. Harvard athletic director William Bingham agreed: "We were guests of the Naval Academy.... I had no choice in the matter. Had the game been played in

Cambridge, I would have insisted that he be allowed to participate."A public outcry ensued. With after-the-fact resoluteness the Corporation proclaimed: "In the future, athletic committees shall make it plain to other institutions with whom we are competing that it is Harvard's principle that there should be no racial discrimination among our students." Conant was away when the incident occurred, but he reacted circumspectly. He apologized to Admiral Willson and assured him of his hope "that the good relationships between Harvard and Annapolis will continue unimpaired, in spite of certain directions which Press comment has taken."[34]

As in the case of Jews and women, World War II initiated a sea change in racial attitudes and perceptions (though less so in policy and practice). By the 1940s the modern civil rights movement was taking form. Conant still fended off requests that he join in efforts to improve race relations and the condition of blacks in the United States. But when Smith College president William A. Neilson asked him to sign a petition deploring the Detroit race riot of 1943, he broke his usual rule against participating in such ventures and agreed to be counted in (as he did in reaction to the Nazis' 1938 *Kristallnacht* pogrom).[35]

Harvard's distinction, and its liberal tradition, made African American equality and opportunity a campus issue. An Urban League official suggested in 1945 that the University set up an institute to study race relations. Conant might have brusquely dismissed such a proposal a few years earlier. But now he sent it on to the deans of FAS and the School of Public Administration and assured his correspondent: "We are all deeply interested in this problem."[36]

The Oregon mother of a liberal-minded Harvard graduate who had been killed in the war proposed to fund a scholarship for a black student. Conant declared himself to be very "interested in this racial problem," but thought that such a scholarship was not in the best interest of the University, "and perhaps would not be the solution of the problem which your son had in mind." Why? "If we were to establish, particularly now, a scholarship designated exclusively or primarily for a colored boy, it would imply that colored people did not have an equal chance in the competition for regular scholarships." Harvard was asked at times to accept scholarships designated for white Anglo-Saxon students, but was "unwilling to do so because of the obvious bias which, from our point of view, represents an intolerant attitude much to be deprecated." Instead, he suggested a graduate scholarship to support research on "some aspect of the colored problem." (Yet in 1952, after much discussion, the Corporation accepted a scholarship for boys of "white Christian American descent.")[37]

Slowly, slowly, the place of blacks at Harvard and white sensitivity to the civil rights issue grew in the postwar years. In 1949 Harvard's sole African American faculty member, William Hinton, was elevated from instructor to (clinical) professor—just before his retirement after thirty years of service. In the same year Ralph Bunche of the United Nations became the first African American recipient of an honorary degree since Booker T. Washington in 1896. This international civil servant, who earned a Harvard Ph.D. in Government in 1934, was a perfect candidate for go-slow, moderate integration. In 1950 he was asked to come to Harvard as professor of Government—again, a first. (The invitation came from department chair William Yandell Elliott, who in the late 1930s supposedly objected to a black undergraduate living in Lowell House, but finally capitulated with a grudging: "All right, but don't expect me to sit next to him.") Bunche resigned his professorship in 1952 to take up a high United Nations post, without having taught at Harvard. Provost Buck hoped that the Corporation would make clear to Bunche its desire that at some future time he return: "I do think the type of person he is would be very useful to Harvard, would mean much to our students, and would also contribute greatly to our public relations."[38]

By the end of the Conant years it seemed to Harvard's leadership that, as Corporation Secretary Bailey put it, "we just don't have any minority racial or religious group problems" of the sort that characterized other schools. The lack of national fraternities, the nonexistence of (explicit) racial or religious qualifications for admission or residence, even the lack of official records on race and religion (soon to be a source of some difficulty, when antidiscrimination laws began to require this information): all lent weight to that self-estimation. To some degree, in the context of the time, it was justified. Whether Harvard's Jewish, female, Catholic, and African American students would have agreed is another matter.[39]

## ～ 4 ～

# THE FACULTY OF ARTS AND SCIENCES

It was in his dealings with the Faculty of Arts and Sciences (FAS) that Conant's attempt to create a more meritocratic Harvard met its severest test. Out of this often tumultuous relationship came one of Harvard's most influential academic innovations: a system for the appointment of tenured faculty that became standard practice in American universities.

## Conant Takes Command

Conant inherited a faculty that was not necessarily the nation's best. Because of Lowell's stress on undergraduate instruction, the number and proportion of tutors and instructors steadily increased during the 1920s. At the same time, many of the best known Harvard professors during the Lowell years—Charles Townsend "Copey" Copeland and LeBaron Russell Briggs of the English Department, Roger B. "Frisky" Merriman in History—were not world-class scholars but charismatic classroom performers. Harvard had only one Nobelist, Conant's chemist father-in-law, Theodore W. Richards, before 1934; Chicago had three. Nor did its social scientists compare to those at Chicago or Columbia. The rather small stable of Harvard's scholarly stars included historian Frederick Jackson Turner and philosopher Alfred North Whitehead, whose major accomplishments, done elsewhere, were long behind them. Carnegie Corporation president Frederick Keppel reported the prevailing view in 1934: "Harvard is still princeps but no longer facile princeps; and the story is current that at one of America's great universities [no doubt Chicago] it is considered the height of academic distinction to receive an invitation from Harvard and to decline it." Conant warned early on that the growing appeal of other universities and Harvard's standardized salary, teaching, and research scales made it "increasingly difficult to attract from other universities and research institutes the outstanding men whom we desire."[1]

The dean of the Faculty of Arts and Sciences was English professor Kenneth Murdock. Though he resented Conant for having gotten the Harvard presidency, Murdock was "quite willing" to continue to be dean if Conant wanted him. Conant did not. He appointed the less assertive George D. Birkhoff (among his qualities were exceptional mathematical ability and a keen anti-Semitism), who stayed in the job until 1939, when he was succeeded by the even more unassertive historian William S. Ferguson. Weak deans meant that Conant was in effect his own dean, deeply engaged in curriculum, student recruitment, and above all the selection of faculty.[2]

He thought it "mistaken philanthropy to keep a mediocre man in a university"; turnover was essential "so that the very best may rise to the top." And he had high hopes for his innovation, University Professors, outstanding scholars or public figures free from departmental constraints, who would bring a new élan to the faculty. However, this ambitious scheme was undercut by straitened resources, institutional inertia, and the growing disciplinary professionalism of Harvard in the 1930s.[3]

Conant initially thought that he and the Corporation had no obligation to defer to the departments on appointments: "in the opinion of the Corporation the procedure of a faculty nominating its own members is not desirable but . . . they will be very glad to have suggestions and advice on appointments from the members of each faculty." At the same time, he tried to reassure the alumni that their favorite tutors from college days were not necessarily headed for the chopping block: "The majority of the senior positions will probably always be filled by the gradual promotion of the brilliant young instructors who have demonstrated their worth in this University."[4]

Despite this display of a decent respect for the opinions of Harvard-kind, a new and explosive issue was taking form: the clash between Conant's meritocratic ambitions and the fiscal exigencies of the time. Faculty of Arts and Sciences professorships were not solidly funded. Of 102 tenured members in 1935, only 9 had salaries more than half covered by endowments; 71 were supported entirely out of general funds, a shaky source in the 1930s. Conant tried to close the door to easy reappointments in order to free up funds for stronger replacements. The basis for promotion, he told Dean Murdock, "should be exceptional ability as a productive scholar, using this phrase in its widest sense." While outstanding teaching ability was important, in and of itself this no longer was sufficient ground for retention or promotion. Grim realities of faculty size and character fueled his concern. From 1924–25 to 1934–35 the proportion of nontenured members of the Arts and Sciences Faculty went from a third to more than half. Instructors alone came to be 60 percent or more of the members of most of the humanities and social science departments. Economics had seven annual instructors who had been there for six years, one for nine years, one for ten. English had an eighteen-year veteran; Germanic Languages, a twenty-seven-year man. As Conant put it, "we have changed from a guild of masters to a guild of masters overshadowed by a group of apprentices for whom there is clearly no hope in this institution."[5]

This led him to a sweeping conclusion:

> We have come to a period in the history of this institution, and perhaps in the development of all American education, where we cannot make commitments against unknown future assets, as has been done to a remarkable extent in the past. In other words, we have to assume the worst, namely, that the budget of the Faculty of Arts and Sciences will remain essentially stationary during the next decade or two.

So he made what seemed to him the only possible move: a frontal assault on Harvard's long-term instructors. There were predictable alumni complaints. But the real conflict was with the protective inclinations of the faculty itself.[6]

The Economics department was the battleground that gave birth to a new system of faculty review. The *causus belli* was the reappointment of two instructors, John Walsh and Alan Sweezy. The ensuing conflict was not, as many thought then (and since), an academic freedom issue, but rather a milestone in Conant's quest for a faculty selected on meritocratic standards.

In early 1934, Economics recommended that a number of its tutors be promoted to the more elevated rank of faculty instructor. Walsh and Sweezy got three-year terms, continued to be popular teachers, but remained unproductive scholars. By 1936 the situation in the department, from Conant's point of view, had become critical. It had seven instructors on three-year appointments, with uncertain future prospects: a threat to the pressing need to keep "our 'turnover' policy working steadily." The department proposed that three of them, including Walsh and Sweezy, be reappointed to new three-year terms, with the possibility of promotion to tenure. The administration rejected this in place of terminal two-year appointments, a hardline policy that it pursued in other instructor-overstocked departments such as English.[7]

Economics chairman Harold Burbank asked Conant if Walsh and Sweezy's radical views, and their involvement in the left-wing Teachers' Union, should be taken into account. Conant of course said not at all. He told columnist Walter Lippmann, who headed the Overseers' visiting committee to Economics: "I have no bias in regard to these men whose views, as a matter of fact from what little I have heard, do not seem to me to be particularly radical." The problem was that their publication records (one academic article by Walsh, two by Sweezy) left them below even the lax standard of the time.

Conant's decision became public in April 1937. The popularity of Walsh and Sweezy as teachers, and their prominence in radical politics, ensured that theirs would become a cause célèbre. A group of junior faculty members asked nine senior professors—Edmund M. Morgan, Felix Frankfurter, and E. Merrick Dodd, Jr., from the Law School; Samuel Eliot Morison and Arthur Schlesinger (History); Ralph Barton Perry (Philosophy); Harlow Shapley (Astronomy); Elmer P. Kohler (Chemistry); and Kenneth Murdock (English)—to look into the case. These eminences thought it proper that Conant create a review committee, and he appointed them. Kohler died in May 1938, at the time of the committee's first report, and was not replaced: hence the body came to be known as the Committee of Eight. It concluded that no political bias was involved. But it thought that the promotion limits imposed on the department in effect deprived Walsh and Sweezy of a fair review. The committee concluded that the two should be given the three-year renewals and open future that the department recommended.[8]

Conant refused to agree to the Committee of Eight's conclusions, brusquely replying that his decision was sound and necessary. There was little alumni reaction (although the *Alumni Bulletin* took Conant to task for stressing scholarship over teaching). Corporation fellow Grenville Clark reported that the prevailing view among the alums was that "the committee has absolved the University of political and economic prejudice. The other phases are too complicated for them to pay much attention to." Kenneth Murdock, who had his own score to settle with Conant, did much to keep the kettle boiling. He called the decision "a grave error of judgment" that cost Harvard "the services of two men who have made a brilliant record in teaching, one of whom, at least, shows great promise as a scholar." A number of senior faculty members (including Paul Buck, his later dean and provost), found Conant's response unsatisfactory: it "simply answers reason with authority." But Conant persevered, and Walsh and Sweezy resigned: Sweezy curtly; Walsh gracefully.[9]

In the spring of 1938 Conant asked the Committee of Eight to consider the larger issue of promotion proceedure. He told committee member Ralph Barton Perry:

the whole point of view of the faculty in these matters has to be revolutionized. I believe the revolution is half complete and the grief will reach a maximum next winter. All this is nothing short of an academic revolution. I once believed it could be accomplished quietly. Due to tactical errors on my part, it cannot.... But I see no solution to the problems of Harvard College except to press on with this line of reform as rapidly as possible.[10]

In March 1939 the Committee of Eight proposed that the normal nontenured run be a maximum of eight years. Then: up or out, based on a formal review and vote by the department. An ad hoc committee with outside experts would review department promotion recommendations, which then would go to the president and the Governing Boards. And the criteria for judging the junior faculty? The central issue was the balance between teaching and scholarship. The committee hedged its bets by proposing that these should be equally valued.

Conant had a tougher-minded view. He further divided the faculty into three groups: those engaged in the "progressive advance in knowledge" (the sciences and social sciences, history, archaeology), where tenured positions should go "only to men of outstanding research ability"); "poetry" (by which he meant the various language and literature departments); and "philosophy" (by which he meant Philosophy). The appointment criteria for the latter two were different: "The word research can hardly be used to cover the activities and writings of a philosopher, let alone a man of letters." They, like the Law faculty, should be "judged quite as much by their effectiveness as teachers ... as by the quality of their writings."[11]

Committee of Eight member Felix Frankfurter, on the verge of leaving Harvard for the Supreme Court, preened himself on having been part of "an inquiry fundamental to the future not only of Harvard but of higher education in the United States." Conant himself welcomed the report: "I am sure that the document will mark an important step forward not only in Harvard history but in the thinking of all who are concerned with problems of this type." The Committee of Eight had set out what became, with modifications, the normal procedure for liberal arts faculties in universities throughout the nation. It was, arguably, Harvard's major contribution to American higher education between Lowell's tutorial system and the General Education Program of the late 1940s. As committee member Harlow Shapley grandly put it: "Harvard has now again resumed its role in American college and university life."[12]

For all this, there is something puzzling about the Walsh-Sweezy imbroglio and the Committee of Eight report. A faculty group initially critical of Conant for forcing out worthy but not outstanding juniors, had come up with a proposal for a promotion procedure that all but assured rough times indeed for future Walshes and Sweezys. Left-wing English instructor Granville Hicks accurately observed that the report "beautifully serves the needs of the administration." In the fall of 1939, when the faculty was poised to create a committee to investigate the governance of the University (that is, the president), Conant offered a mild apology for his reaction to the first Committee of Eight report. And that was that.[13]

Conant quickly got the new system going. Up-or-out in eight years became the norm. ("This is an iron-clad principle and adherence to it is the essence of the scheme," he told the faculty.) By the fall of 1939, twenty-eight of fifty-six assistant professors, ranging in age from twenty-seven to fifty-two, had been promoted to tenure, fourteen had not been renewed, and fourteen still awaited action.

Conant explained the new appointment system—so different from the *ad personem* approach of the past—to the faculty in 1940. Disingenuously he assured them: "It is expected that normally . . . vacancies will be filled by promotion from the temporary ranks of faculty instructors, and in every case it is expected that there will be at least two contenders on the spot for the vacant position, and these men will have to consider themselves in competition with outsiders." More threatening were his warnings that "[p]ermanent positions which become vacant due to death or resignation several years before retiring age will be filled by calls from the outside," and that "except in very unusual cases" no one would be promoted to associate professor "who is not likely to be worthy of promotion eventually to professorial rank." Friends-and-neighbors preferment had due notice.[14]

Conant at first tried to rely on members of other Harvard departments to review tenure candidates. But this was not satisfactory; the ever more specialized standards of each discipline required that the reviewers come from the candidate's own field—and from other universities. He announced in 1942 that "because of the war situation I am using a new procedure to pass judgment" and set up the first outsider-dominated ad hoc committees. Four met in 1942–43, seven in 1944–45. By the end of the war the system was well-established and accepted by the faculty, its inclination to object dulled by the small number of promotions during the war years. Ninety candidates had passed through the ad hoc mill by 1950; sixty-eight were approved, ranging from all proposed by Economics and History, to one of four from Philosophy. New School economist Alvin Johnson told Conant in 1945: "I regard your invention of the ad hoc committee as the most important step forward in university education of the last generation. Generally applied to the great universities, it would put an end to the evils of inbreeding and clique formation, and open wide the door to scholarly merit, wherever it emerges."[15]

But the new procedure also spurred what would come to be a common feature of the late-twentieth-century university scene: complaints that scholar-professors short-changed undergraduates with scant and indifferent teaching, and that "good teachers" were not kept on. An early instance arose in 1939, when assistant professor of Fine Arts Robert Feild was not renewed. He was a popular teacher: ahead of his time, he lectured on the work of Walt Disney. The *Crimson* took up his cause, and the Student Council appointed a committee to look into the matter, predictably without changing the decision, any more than did David Rockefeller's distress when his favorite tutor from his undergraduate days fell before the up-or-out scythe.[16]

In 1953, when he and Conant were about to leave their offices, Buck looked back at what had been accomplished under the ad hoc system. He rank-ordered twenty-four appointees into four categories: distinguished, successful, mediocre, and failed. Thirteen—more than half—were distinguished; six were successful; four were mediocre. The cause of the single failure was "essentially medical in origin," and he was eased out in 1952. It was the "mediocre" group that most concerned Buck: the argument of need to fill a particular field "is the Trojan horse whereby mediocrity creeps in and spreads among a faculty."[17]

All in all, Buck concluded, theirs was "a record of achievement which … has been outstanding among American universities." But problems remained: perhaps most of all, the persisting tendency to appoint "the 'young man on the scene' … as against the competitor away from Harvard." Happily the Society of Fellows, a Lowell-financed hothouse for brilliant young scholars and a fecund source of Harvard faculty, recruited ever more widely. None of the eight new junior fellows in 1950 had a Harvard B.A.[18]

One nonbarking dog in Buck's *tour d'horizon*: tenured women on the Faculty of Arts and Sciences. Before 1947 there were none. Then a wealthy businessman, Samuel Zemurray, endowed a professorship limited to a female appointee. Money talked, and Cambridge medievalist Helen Maude Cam became the first Radcliffe-Zemurray professor. She was one of three distinguished finalists (psychiatrist Anna Freud and Cambridge economist Joan Robinson were the others). Cam was no token appointee: many thought her the ablest medievalist in the Anglo-American world.

Conant admitted that he had pursued his up-or-out faculty review policy "with perhaps more vigor than finesse." But he was convinced that "except in a period of great expansion there is little hope of building a distinguished faculty unless there is a long-range plan for continual recruitment of the most promising young men." Of course, a substantial increase in endowment would allow growth. This hadn't happened, and it was "quite clear" to him "that it is unlikely to occur in the immediate future." Here as elsewhere, his crystal ball was cloudy. A changing national economy and Harvard fund-raising environment in the years to come would provide the wherewithal for the fulfillment of Conant's meritocratic vision on a scale beyond his highest hopes.[19]

## The Humanities

Harvard's humanities made up an academic subculture sharply differentiated by subject matter and status. The old established departments—English, Classics, Philosophy—had prestige comparable to History, Government, and Economics in the social sciences, and Physics, Chemistry, and Biology in the natural sciences. Then there were the foreign language departments—Romance, German, Slavic—less secure in the Harvard pecking order. Music and Fine Arts constituted yet a third subset: small, self-contained.

When Conant became president, he turned to philosopher Alfred North Whitehead, Harvard's most distinguished humanist, for advice. Whitehead called for a balanced humanities program, composed in equal parts of scholarship, enhancing students' aesthetic appreciation, and fostering new values and taste. Each was necessary; each depended on the others to avoid their respective pitfalls of triviality, routine, and charlatanry. Although the department structure encouraged scholarship and aesthetic refinement, it squelched innovation. "Scholarship," Whitehead warned, "should be restrained from its favorite sport of slaughtering novelty." Soon enough change did come to Harvard's humanities, driven by new intellectual currents and the meritocratic ethos.[20]

Philosophy in the 1930s still basked in the glow of past luminaries: William James, Josiah Royce, George Santayana. These men gave the University its first internationally distinguished academic department. Pragmatism was regarded as a Harvard contribution to the history of thought: "The Harvard elective system applied to the universe." The senior figures in Philosophy during the 1920s and 1930s were of a distinctly secondary order. In an effort to restore its past glory, Philosophy brought Alfred North Whitehead in 1924 after he retired from London and had Étienne Gilson as a half-time professor for a couple of years before he went off to Toronto in 1929. Its major homegrown figures were Ralph Barton Perry, Harry Wolfson, and C. I. Lewis, Wolfson the most distinguished.[21]

Conant sought to foster tougher standards in Philosophy, as he did elsewhere. Chairman William Ernest Hocking told him in 1935 of then-assistant professor Raphael Demos's sense "that the atmosphere of Harvard is pressing him to a rate of production about which he feels somewhat uncomfortable." Hocking assured Demos that nobody was demanding that he do more than what came naturally; would Conant similarly comfort him? Conant would not: "We need excellent teachers certainly, but they will not be excellent in my opinion unless they are something of creative scholars in their own right." Nevertheless in due course Demos got tenure, and in 1945 Provost Paul Buck recommended that he be promoted to professor. "He has not given evidence of his great ability in any formal scholarly work," Buck admitted. But he was regarded as the department's best teacher.[22]

A good example of the change that Conant sought was the appearance of Willard Van Orman Quine, Harvard's (and arguably America's) leading philosopher in the decades to come. Quine arrived as a graduate student in 1930. Married and with little money, he needed a teaching assistantship as soon as possible. Told that he could get one if he passed his preliminary examinations in a year, he did so—though it subjected him to what he later called the indignity of having to plow through the history of philosophy, metaphysics, epistemology, and psychology. A year later he had his doctorate, at the age of twenty-three. Conant's meritocratic Harvard was made for Quine, and he for it. Though few in the department had much interest in Quine's work, he was promoted in 1941 and by the late 1940s was a world figure, as analytic philosophy assumed a leading place in the discipline.[23]

Quine sought to expand the presence of his school of philosophy in the department. He urged the appointment of his mentor Rudolf Carnap, and his colleagues went along. But an ad hoc committee surveyed the field of modern philosophers in the United States and Europe, and declined to endorse Carnap (Isaiah Berlin thought his best work was done) or indeed anyone else. Buck confessed to Conant: "We are in a quandary! The only clear picture I get is that I personally should not be willing to recommend Carnap for the vacancy. . . . If we really had the power many people believe we possess, we would move in and capture this vacancy, on the reasonable grounds that it cannot be wisely spent in Philosophy and hence should be spent where it can be spent wisely. But we don't have the power—or is it lack of courage?" Conant leaped at this: "My conclusions are exactly yours. Why not have the courage and move not to take this vacancy, but to create a roving professorship?" Physicist J. Robert Oppenheimer was the sort of person Conant had in mind, but Oppenheimer had no desire to leave the cushy Princeton Institute for Advanced Study.[24]

Nevertheless by the 1950s the department had a very strong professional reputation, with Quine the first world figure since James and Whitehead. Offers from other universities, increasingly frequent in the postwar years, worked to bump up ranks and salaries in Philosophy as elsewhere. Quine was attracted by the Chicago proffer of a lighter teaching load. Harvard kept him by offering to count his interchanges with colleagues as the equivalent of a course. Berkeley, Buck told Conant in 1952, was ready "to shoot the works" to get him.[25]

Quine's intellectual distinction may explain in part why the Philosophy department was not more deeply riven between its analytic and more traditional wings. (This, at least, is how Quine remembered it. His student and later colleague Burton Dreben recalled bitter fights between Quine and C. I. Lewis over appointments in the 1940s and 1950s. Harvard chair Donald Williams, according to Quine, once said, obscurely, that the new analytic philosophy played into the hands of the Communists.) Older schools—realism, idealism—continued to have a significant place in a department with a continuing obligation to teach undergraduates.[26]

Classics also had a venerable tradition of attention to undergraduate teaching, dating from the time when Greek and Latin were required subjects. John H. Finley, a member of the faculty from 1933 to 1976 and master of Eliot House from 1941 to 1968, was "the embodiment of Harvard" to generations of undergraduates who took his courses in

Greek history. Finley, Roman historian Mason Hammond, and Greek historian Sterling Dow—all members of the Harvard class of 1925, all intensely conscious of the fact that Hammond was a summa graduate, Finley a magna, Dow a cum laude—dominated the department through the Conant years.[27]

The appointments of refugee Werner Jaeger as University Professor in 1939 and of the soon-to-be-eminent Herbert Bloch as a junior faculty member in Roman history in 1947 brought major scholars to Classics. But the hermetic character of the department (and of its subject matter) persisted. When Conant wrote in behalf of a junior faculty member, a talented teacher who failed to get tenure at Harvard, he spoke of him as having "an unusually wide point of view (for Classicists)."[28]

Tradition and self-satisfaction flourished with special luxuriance in the Department of English. George Lyman Kittridge, who started to teach in 1888 and stopped in 1936, was the dominant figure in what the comparatively broad-minded critic Irving Babbitt called the "philological syndicate" that controlled Harvard's English graduate instruction. Requirements in the 1930s had changed little from the 1890s: linguistics, philology, at least six courses in Old and Middle English languages, Old French, Gothic, and "some acquaintance" with modern English and American literature and modern foreign languages. Smith College president William A. Neilson, Ph.D. '98, feelingly observed that "the Egyptians took only five weeks to make a mummy, but the Harvard English Department took five years."[29]

Conant appointed I. A. Richards, a distinguished pioneer in the New Criticism and prominent advocate of Basic English, to a University Professorship. But the department kept its distance from him. Aside from Richards and Douglas Bush, who came in 1936 to teach seventeenth-century literature, the most distinguished appointments in the late 1930s came in the previously marginal area of American literature. F. O. Matthiessen and Perry Miller gave Harvard unchallenged supremacy in the subject. More contentious was the appointment of Americanist Howard Mumford Jones, who came from the University of Michigan. The word on the grapevine was that he was "difficult to get along with, highly controversial in point of view, and not always as profound in his scholarship as one could wish." Nevertheless in Jones came and quickly became a breath of fresh (if not always balmy) air.[30]

By the late 1940s the English department was in healthy intellectual ferment. A younger generation led by Matthiessen, Miller, and Harry

Levin was caught up in the New Criticism, the history of ideas, American studies, and comparative literature. The English visiting committee observed in 1949 that a new department was taking shape, more sensitive to literature's aesthetic and social contexts.[31]

As the department became more pluralist in its interests, it became more receptive to the at times unsettling presence of creative writers. In the fall of 1939, Robert Frost came as Emerson Fellow in Poetry. He warned Conant that his teaching over the past quarter of a century consisted of "no more than a sequence of philosophical positions taken and rather sketchily acted out.... I haven't enough going on for three classes a week forty weeks in the year, or half that. I am a peculiarly advanced case of what I am, good or bad." His preference: to visit an occasional English class and give an occasional public lecture, "or for sitting it out and talking it out in young society in Adams House ... when I am prompted with anything to say. In that way I could feel natural and my thinking would be more nearly at one with my teaching." Frost continued on annual appointments until 1943.[32]

World War II saw marked changes in the personnel, style, and culture of literary studies at Harvard. An early sign of change was the promotion of Harry Levin in 1943. The first Jewish senior professor in English, Levin also pioneered in offering a more modern critical approach to comparative literature. In 1946 Conant (as he had done with Whitehead over a decade before) asked Levin for his views on the future of the humanities at Harvard. Levin pointed to his most illustrious predecessors, George Lyman Kittridge and Irving Babbitt, as the embodiments of now outmoded humanities types: "old-fashioned Gelehrten [scholars]" (Kittridge) and "cultural reactionaries" (Babbitt). But Levin thought that new currents of thought were flowing. Future humanistic study, he predicted, would be more horizontal than vertical, preferring a wide interest in cultural expression to intensive study of a single subject.[33]

Especially important for the future was the appointment of literary biographer Walter Jackson Bate in 1949. He quickly became the department's academic and intellectual leader. And new appointment opportunities arose during the expansive postwar years. Offers went out in 1951 to two Columbia professors, Lionel Trilling and Alfred Harbage. Conant tipped off acting Columbia president Grayson Kirk: "I am not always able to notify the opposite number when I proceed on a raiding expedition, but I feel you should have this warning." Harbage came, Trilling did not (and would be approached again—without success—

a decade later). In vivid contrast to its pokey visage in earlier decades, English had become a lively, intensely professional department, a major player in the fierce struggles for primacy of place in the American university jungle of the 1950s and 1960s.[34]

If Philosophy, Classics, and English were the jewels in Harvard's humanities crown, then the other language and literature departments— Germanic, Romance, Slavic—were more like zircons, diminished in value by their often marginal status and the hard-to-assimilate foreignness of their faculties.

World War I had dealt a severe blow to undergraduate interest in German, from which it never recovered. Hitler's destruction of the nation's academic and intellectual life further lessened the standing of German as a necessary tool of educated men and women. In 1935 the department's visiting committee spoke dispiritedly of its lack of prestige or drawing power and its internal divisions. No promotions from instructor to assistant professor had been made for seven years, none from assistant to associate professor for six years, none to full professor for fourteen years. In 1939–40 the Busch-Reisinger Museum bowed to the prevalent anti-Germanism of the time, turning to research rather than public exhibitions.

Things did not noticeably improve in the postwar years. German language and literature now felt in full force the low esteem to which the Nazi period had brought it. And the department's desire to bring in top people (usually Germans, berthed in German universities) clashed with their inclination to stay in their native land. During the early 1950s two senior European scholars were approached. Both refused to come: the postwar shortage of major academics in Germany and Switzerland made the leading professorships in those countries irresistibly attractive.[35]

The traditional raison d'être of the Romance Languages department was not cutting-edge critical scholarship, but undergraduate and graduate instruction in French, Spanish, and Italian (quaintly called "Neo-Latin" in the 1920s) language and literature. Provost Paul Buck observed in 1944 that "vital contact with living trends in the field ... is something the Department has been utterly without during the last decade."

Tension between the American and foreign-born members of Romance Languages surfaced when the appointment of Francis M. Rogers, a Portuguese literature scholar and junior fellow, as faculty instructor came up in 1945. Rogers was a homegrown product, had a distinguished war record, and won rare praise from Buck: "He not only is unusually outstanding in his own field, but he is one of the very best young men who have been in the University in recent years." Rogers in fact had a thin publication record, which did not markedly thicken in years to come. Foreign-born professor Louis Solano protested to American-born department chair Arthur Whittem against the hurried, backdoor way in which the Rogers appointment had been handled: no department meeting, only a circular letter from the chair stressing that time was of the essence because Rogers had other offers and asking for a quick, written yes or no.[36]

Getting and keeping major scholars was difficult. Buck questioned whether the department's senior members were "as competent to initiate the wisest recommendations for ... appointments as would ideally be possible." He wanted to bring in outside advisers, which Conant encouraged. But then Buck had to report that the consultant plan "has collapsed because I am unable to find really competent advisers. This is an illustration of the deplorable situation in this field where the few older men are no longer very reliable in their judgements and the few good middle-aged men would themselves be competitors for the position."[37]

There were still further reaches in the teeming world of modern languages and literatures. The great philologist Roman Jakobson came from Columbia to the newly created Department of Slavic Languages and Literatures in 1949. With the comparativist Renato Poggioli, appointed in 1947, and Albert Lord (whose work on the Balkan folk-tale/epic tradition, and its resonance with the world of Homer, Harry Levin called "the most striking project now under way in the humanities at Harvard"), the core of an excellent department had been created.[38]

Less happy—then and since—was the Sanskrit department, with a prestige derived from the great tradition of German philology. Walter E. Clark, Harvard's longtime professor in the field, resigned as master of Kirkland House in 1945 because he and his department had not been consulted in the administration of research funds. "If the University has so little regard for my department I can see no reason for devoting time, thought, energy, and money to the administration of one of the houses," he huffed. Injured sensibilities would remain a part of Harvard's tiny Sanskrit scene.[39]

Music and Fine Arts were yet another humanities subculture, as notable for their cozy snugness as English and Philosophy were for their sense of centrality or Modern Languages for showing how close was the link between cultural diversity and academic adversity. The Music department was small: four professors before World War II, including prominent composer Walter Piston. Its strengths were composition, vocal and instrumental performance, and teaching music appreciation to undergraduates. After the war Piston was joined by composer Randall Thompson. But personality clashes and the tensions inherent in the musicologist-composer/performer relationship made for recurrent departmental disharmony.[40]

At the core of the Fine Arts department was a strong program of undergraduate teaching created in the late nineteenth century by the celebrated critic and art historian Charles Eliot Norton, whose reign lasted from 1874 to 1898. No one comparable to Norton succeeded him. Instead, two wealthy art lovers, Edward Waldo Forbes '95 and Paul J. Sachs '00, part connoisseurs, part academic professionals, became the dominant figures. Forbes took over as director of the Fogg Art Museum in 1909, Sachs (of the Goldman, Sachs financial family) joined him as associate director in 1915. They made the Fogg the leading trainer of museum administrators and art scholars.

Along with their connoisseurship, Forbes and Sachs had a financial acumen uncommon among academics. Forbes did much to secure the riverfront land on which Harvard's new houses were built in the early 1930s, and Sachs was an adviser on fund-raising to Lowell and Conant. These "heavenly twins" enriched the Fogg with their own gifts and effectively solicited well-heeled friends. In 1927 a new, grand Fogg Art Museum replaced an older structure. By 1941 the Fogg endowment produced a revenue of $100,000 a year, up from $3,000 when Sachs joined in 1915.[41]

Forbes and Sachs retired on December 1, 1944. ("This is a joint venture. When Edward retires, so do I," said Sachs.) The departure of the Fogg's moneymen and the inflation of the wartime and postwar years eroded the museum's cosseted position. Buck explored cost-cutting possibilities, but without success: "It is hard to cut the leg off an elephant. It may even be that when the friends of the elephant find that we are thinking of such an operation they will save the animal by finding the money necessary to save it." Into the early 1950s the Corporation pressed for a balanced Fogg budget and for the museum to be devoted more to the teaching of undergraduates than to serving as a public museum.[42]

The ability of Harvard departments to control the appointments process despite the ad hoc system was evident in a 1947 search for a professor of Classical Art. After losing its first choice to the Princeton Institute for Advanced Study, the department proposed to promote assistant professor George Hanfmann. Outside advisers doubted that he would develop into a leader in the field. But the department unanimously reiterated its choice. "This rather worries me," Buck told Conant, "because I sense a department's rallying to the support of someone it has on the scene." A new ad hoc committee was convened, in a divided vote reendorsed Hanfmann, and Conant and Buck went along. Departmental desire won out over decanal doubt. And Hanfmann, as it turned out, became a distinguished figure in his field.[43]

By the end of Conant's presidency it appeared that despite its academic prestige, the humanities at Harvard were losing ground to the natural and social sciences. Harry Levin complained that while Conant had scientific and Buck social scientific expertise, they lacked a comparable knowledge of or interest in the humanities. The relegation to subordinate status of what once had been the Queen of the Curriculum would become a leitmotif of Harvard's humanists in years to come.

## The Social Sciences

Prewar Harvard's social sciences had neither the venerable status of the humanities nor the intellectual vitality of the natural sciences. The intellectual trailblazers were elsewhere: at Columbia, Chicago, and Wisconsin, not at Harvard. For some years a Harvard Committee on Research in the Social Sciences distributed an ongoing Rockefeller grant but in the mid-1930s the foundation decided to end the program.

Much social science at Harvard reflected the still half-formed state of the field. Notable work in Psychology went on in, of all places, the Business School's Fatigue Laboratory. It began in 1927 as the venue for inquiries into industrial efficiency by social psychologist Elton Mayo. Another anomaly was the Bureau for Street Traffic Research. Berthed in Widener but under the auspices of the Business School, the bureau had pursued its peculiar career since 1926. Sustained by gifts from the automobile industry, it explored the Sisyphean problems of urban traffic and offered scholarships for the quixotic purpose of attracting "especially brilliant and competent young men into the field of traffic control." Conant told its director in 1936 that he "had considerable doubt as to the advisability of having this Bureau connected with the University," and it drove off to Yale in 1940.[44]

Conant confided in 1936 to Business School dean Wallace Donham that he had made progress in seeking research funds for the humanities and the natural sciences, but found the task conceptually more difficult for the social sciences. "I am particularly troubled," he said, "about the social sciences becoming too 'applied,' too vocational, and our spending too much money in efforts which are not really within the scope of the University." He hoped that a large group of social scientists might work out and approve a scheme of research support, "even if it were on a pork barrel basis." In his bolder moments he envisioned a social science axis stretching from the Business School south of the Charles River, through Widener Library and the Arts and Sciences departments in the Yard, to the Public Administration and Law Schools to the north: a physical interconnectedness that, he hoped, would foster collaborative research and teaching. But this flew in the face of the schools' and departments' tendency to march to their own disciplinary drummers.[45]

In 1938 Conant read Harvard historian Crane Brinton's *The Anatomy of Revolution*, which found a similar pattern of origins, climax, and retreat in the British, French, American, and Russian revolutions. This seemed to him a model work of social science. "[W]ould it be sufficient," he wondered, "to include in the university, if possible, only social scientists who had more or less this point of view?" A University of Minnesota political scientist chastised him for seeing social science through History-tinged spectacles. Social scientists, he warned, regarded Harvard in general and its president in particular as hostile to them. Conant mildly replied that his views on social science were in a state of flux. In fact, as he confessed to Walter Lippmann, "The real question which I keep turning over and over in my mind is whether ... the social sciences are the modern equivalents of astrology or of medicine."[46]

Economics, not least in the eyes of its practitioners, was the most intellectually rigorous of the social sciences, the most scientific in its reliance on quantitative data and analysis and in the close links of theory to empirical work. But the Harvard department raised the ire of the wealthy, conservative men who figured so largely among the alumni and on the University's Governing Boards. The result was conflict between a department that regarded itself as quintessentially professional and scientific, and prominent alumni who saw in the department's Keynesianism, and its ever more arcane subject matter, threats to the proper instruction of undergraduates.

When Conant came into office in 1933, the most distinguished member of the Economics faculty was Joseph Schumpeter, who had arrived from Austria the year before. Conant was told "that we need ... brilliant scholars who have a somewhat radical social outlook. Whether this is true or not, I do not know; but I have a feeling myself that to some extent we might profit by some innovations along this line." He asked Wesley C. Mitchell, head of the National Bureau of Economic Research, for the names of able scholars of a more or less radical persuasion: "I am anxious to bring in social scientists who are somewhat on the left but who have their feet somewhere near the ground."[47]

In 1934 the department recommended the appointment of Columbia labor economist Leo Wolman, widely regarded as the best in a not overtalented field. Wolman was Jewish, but here was a case of need over creed. Though eyebrows went up in old-grad circles, Wolman got an offer. But he had become chairman of the auto industry's labor board under the National Recovery Act and decided not to go to Harvard and a life of scholarship. Conant professed to be greatly distressed by this turn of events: "Our losing him will be a very serious blow to the University and to the department of Economics." Journalist Walter Lippmann, a member of the visiting committee to the department, thought that while Wolman was "about the best in a very poor field," he was not really a first-rate economist.[48]

Meanwhile the department was getting steadily stronger. A clutch of foreign appointees—Wassily Leontief in 1931, Schumpeter in 1932, Gottfried Haberler in 1936—added to its reputation, as did the appearance in 1933 of Edward Chamberlin's *Theory of Monopolistic Competition*. Other new faces in the 1930s put Harvard in the front rank of the Keynesian revolution. These were Alvin Hansen, Keynes's leading American apostle, and Seymour Harris, "of Jewish origins," as the phrase of the time had it, who had to wait eighteen years for tenure and had a nervous breakdown when he got it.[49]

Hand in hand with Keynesianism came modern econometrics: literally so in the figure of Paul Samuelson, who arrived as a graduate student in 1935. A Chicago undergraduate, Samuelson might have stayed on there. However—and this was very much part of the new university scene—he won a Social Science Research Council fellowship, which required that he attend another school. His Chicago teachers advised him to go to Columbia, but he admired the work of Chamberlin. And the Old New England patina of Harvard attracted him, as it did so many other young would-be academics. Yet anti-Semitism blunted Samuelson's prospects. Although he was elected to the prestigious Society of Fellows, he was not allowed to teach in Economics 1, the major course for Harvard undergraduates, and instead was shunted off with other Jewish graduate students to statistics and/or accounting, generally thought of as "Jewish courses." Samuelson went off to an appointment at MIT in 1940.[50]

The fact that Harvard was the most Keynesian Economics department in the country guaranteed trouble with anti-New Deal alumni.

Add to this potent brew the increasingly mathematical and theoretical bent of the new economics, and the prospect for conflict was rich indeed. In 1948 two senior slots were vacant. This was a crucial moment: "The distinction and reputation of the Department for many years to come is at stake." The top prospects were Arthur Smithies, a junior member of the department, and MIT's Samuelson. To appoint the two of them would be a mistake, an Economics committee decided: both were theoreticians, "concerned with the logical and mathematical inter-relations of the elements of their systems." Which one, then? Smithies had some interest in institutional development and public policy, as well as extensive experience in government service. So appoint Smithies and hold off on the other senior appointment. "While recognizing that Samuelson has in his field of activity a better record than anyone near his age in any field," Burbank reported, "the Committee was heavily influenced by the probability that Smithies' contribution to the needs of the Department would be substantially greater." In an act of folly, his colleagues unanimously agreed.[51]

Some did not want to let Samuelson slip away. "With two professors to be appointed at Harvard this year," they warned, "scholars all over the world will ask why Harvard did not offer *one* of the two professorships to Samuelson." But an ad hoc committee including economists I. L. Sharfman of Michigan and Simon Kuznets of Pennsylvania met and, with one dissent (Sharfman, who preferred Samuelson), approved the Smithies recommendation. The committee went on to take note of the department's "relative weakness in empirical research" and suggested that it "explore this situation with the view of correcting it when making future appointments": in effect, a death sentence for theorist Samuelson.[52]

The failure to appoint Samuelson became legendary as the most destructive consequence of Harvard anti-Semitism and the source of MIT's decades-long preeminence in Economics. That prejudice played some role seems clear. Schumpeter is supposed to have told Buck and Conant that he could understand not appointing Samuelson because he was Jewish; if it was because his colleagues questioned Samuelson's quality as an economist, *that* he could not understand. But contingency, too, kept Samuelson from getting an offer. There was a continuing tension between hiring "the best mind" regardless of field and hiring the "body" that most closely met the department's needs. And the presence on ad hoc committees of economists from other universities who were inclined to give their Harvard colleagues the benefit of the doubt (especially, perhaps, when those colleagues were on the wrong track) may have played a part as well.[53]

Revealing, too, was the unsuccessful effort by prominent overseers to block tenure for John Kenneth Galbraith on ideological and character grounds, and to secure the appointments of men who were "sound" in their economics and/or interested in teaching undergraduates. Galbraith came up for promotion for 1948. His field of expertise was agricultural economics, and here the mind-body tension had unexpected results. A 1946 attempt to replace John D. Black, the department's expert in that field, had failed. Most of the senior members favored Galbraith as the agricultural economics "body" that the department needed. What they got instead was a world-class gadfly, Shavian in his unalloyed self-regard, a marvelous writer whose sense of irony and elegance of style coexisted with a taste for command economics and a tendency to skate lightly over the surface of his discipline.

Provost Buck thought the appointment would not be a distinguished one. "But academic economics is in a strange state these days, and I see no one in the field upon whom any real unanimity of opinion can be reached.... The field [of agricultural economics] has to be kept alive." The Corporation approved Galbraith's appointment in April 1949, and it went to the Board of Overseers. Several of them wanted to take a close look at his character, academic qualifications, and policy views. No doubt this was due to Galbraith's special mix of leftist economics and prickly personality. But it appears to have been fed as well by the general redefinition of institutional roles in the wake of a massively destabilizing war, at a time when Conant's mind (if not yet his body) were, primarily, elsewhere.

Conant forcefully warned Economics visiting committee chair Clarence Randall, who headed Inland Steel, of the dangerous implications of an Overseers' rebellion:

> As you know, I feel strongly that ... matters of professional competence must be left to a suitable administrative machinery, and that is a responsibility of the President. On the matter of political beliefs I am sure you will agree with me and with the Harvard tradition that objections on this point would be out of order, and I trust if there is any bias in the minds of the members of the Board arising from such considerations they will either refrain from voting on the issue or do their best to counteract their prejudices!

He warned Randall that a negative recommendation would be the first such in his years as Harvard's president and implied that he would take it as a vote of non confidence. Faced with this not-so-veiled ultimatum, the Overseers acceded, and in November 1949 Galbraith's appointment was announced. He thanked Conant for his support: "Clearly I now face the formidable task of meriting it—and, more generally, of insuring that I was worth the trouble." Conant percipiently replied: "I am certain that you have a long and distinguished career ahead of you as a professor here at Harvard."[54]

But the war between Brahmin Harvard (the Overseers) and merito-cratic Harvard (Conant and the Economics department) went on. In December 1949, the ink scarcely dry on the Galbraith appointment, visiting committee chair Randall raised "the question of balance of social viewpoint within the Department." His view was that it was awash with followers of Keynes, who advocated deficit financing, price controls, and other unsound and dangerous notions. And it had too many foreigners, who couldn't understand the American economic system. Other over-seers agreed. David Rockefeller wanted someone "of proven scholarship whose viewpoint would be less to the left than that of a number of the members of the staff." Thomas Lamont was sympathetic, though he warned against "getting new men in the Department who might be so far to the right as to be unaware of a changing world. . . . What we need is teachers to expound all theories, not propagandists for any." Randall fed Conant likely names: Milton Friedman of Chicago, Arthur Burns of Columbia, Herbert Stein of Carnegie-Mellon, Abraham Kaplan of Brookings. All Jews, it should be noted: Left-Right meant more to Randall than Jew-Gentile.[55]

Conant did what he could to mediate between dissatisfied overseers and prerogative-sensitive professors. He told Randall that the real tension in the department was not over ideology but method: between the applied/institutional and the theoretical/mathematical approaches. He asked John Lintner, an assistant professor of Finance at the Business School, to prepare an ideological comparison of the Harvard department with those of other universities. Lintner found that Harvard was a little more skewed to both the right and the left than the other departments, but in no dramatic fashion.[56]

Besides their ideological concerns, the Overseers worried about the department's ability (and desire) to teach undergraduates. Randall fret-ted that research-obsessed professors were away too much; senior professors avoided teaching lowerclassmen. And he agreed with Conant that the field "has reached a point of ethereal content which is as lifeless to me as much . . . modern poetry. It just doesn't seem to matter." Conant conceded that the department "has not faced up to the problem of making a real effort to improve the instruction in the introductory courses in Economics." Feeling the pressure, chairman Smithies proposed an extensive plan to strengthen undergraduate teaching. Randall appreciated Conant's response to his criticisms. He left the visiting committee in the fall of 1952, but not without a final disappointment. He heard that when he asked the chairman for a copy of the Economics A reading list, Smithies tore off the first page because he thought that Randall would disapprove of many of the authors (as in all likelihood he would have). "I bear no animosity about that," Randall told Conant, "but it does make me a little heartsick. I am always shocked when I find amongst either professors or preachers ethical practices below the standard prevailing in business."[57]

During the 1930s History became one of Harvard's strongest departments. In William Langer and Crane Brinton it had arguably the country's two best younger European historians; in Arthur Schlesinger, Sr., Samuel Eliot Morison, and Frederick Merk (Morison was the only Harvard-grown product of the three) it had the outstanding American social, colonial, and western historians. Paul Buck was a Pulitzer Prize-winning historian of the American South and a rising star in University administration. By all accounts the department was placid and clubby. Visiting committees spoke of its being "harmonious within itself" and praised the "notable personnel, the completeness of the curriculum, and the admirable administration of this Department." History neither grew nor looked to recruit from outside. FAS dean Kenneth Murdock observed of the historians' endogamous appointment practices: "I have sometimes felt that the policy of the History Department at times erred in regarding an assistant professorship as the normal status for any good man who served faithfully, instead of regarding it . . . as something given only to those young men for whom we can reasonably see a clear future."[58]

Solid and self-confident, History flourished under the new promotion rules of the 1940s. The great events of the time fostered a widespread desire to understand their historical underpinnings, and the department entered into a golden age of quality and relevance. History won a heady reputation for blending scholarly excellence with a high order of teaching. It made a flock of first-rate appointments—almost all Harvard Ph.D.s and Harvard junior faculty members—among them Richard Pipes, John K. Fairbank, and Edwin O. Reischauer in Russian, Chinese, and Japanese history. So powerful was this experience that it locked the historians into hiring policies that would have baleful consequences in later decades.

The appointments of Arthur M. Schlesinger, Jr., and Oscar Handlin, two rising young stars in American history, exemplify this bountiful time. Chairman Frederick Merk told Paul Buck in the fall of 1945: "The Department considers Schlesinger and Handlin ... to be men of brilliant achievement and promise and that both ought to be retained if possible on the staff of the university." The younger Schlesinger had a career without parallel in American historical scholarship. A former junior fellow, now twenty-nine years old, he had finished *The Age of Jackson* in evenings and spare moments while working for the Office of Strategic Services (forerunner to the CIA) in Washington. The book was thought certain to win the Pulitzer Prize in History, and indeed it did. Since Schlesinger's father was a senior professor in the department, AMS Jr.'s ad hoc committee consisted of nonHarvard historians, to avoid "any charge of internal favoritism or bias." It readily agreed that he was the best American historian under the age of fifty.[59]

Three years later it was Oscar Handlin's turn. Handlin had published three major books by 1950, when he was thirty-five; the last of these, *The Uprooted*, a brilliantly written rumination on the immigrant experience, won the Pulitzer Prize. But he had neither the pedigree nor the dash of Arthur Schlesinger, Jr. Unspoken (or at least unwritten), but present, was the fact of Handlin's being Jewish. Conant put three questions to the ad hoc committee: did they think the department should delay an appointment? No. Should they prefer Columbia's Richard Hofstadter to Handlin? Only one thought so. Should the department's proposal of Handlin be endorsed? Unanimously, yes. So an appointment that would have been difficult to imagine in 1939 went through ten years later, with scarcely a whiff of anti-Semitism attached to it. And as the department began to plan for a successor to Samuel Eliot Morison in American colonial history—the Brahmin Holy of Holies—interest grew in Harvard Ph.D. Bernard Bailyn as his successor.[60]

Even after they were detached from History and became the separate Department of Government in 1911, Harvard's political scientists retained their traditional institutional-historical orientation. The major figures in the 1930s were Arthur N. Holcombe in American politics, the great scholar of medieval political thought Charles McIlwain, comparative government expert Carl Friedrich, and political theorist William Yandell Elliott. None engaged in the new interest group and qualitative analysis taking hold at Columbia, Chicago, and elsewhere. If the department was premodern social science in its subject matter, in its governance it was positively feudal. Friedrich and Elliott were its "eagles," each with a satrapy peopled by "sparrows."

The New Deal and the rise of totalitarianism strengthened Government's appeal to undergraduates. The number of concentrators in 1937–38 was three times what it had been a decade before. Friedrich saw Government 1, the department's core course, preparing students to deal with the great conflict between constitutionalism and authoritarianism.[61]

After the war, Government, like History, tapped a pool of able young scholars attracted by the manifest importance of the subject. Yale, Michigan, and other schools with stronger empirical social science traditions appointed political scientists committed to the quantitative analysis of elections, government, and political attitudes. But Harvard continued in its traditional way. Its notable postwar appointments included Samuel Beer, a brilliant teacher and comparative politics expert, and political theorist Louis Hartz, a 1940 Harvard summa graduate and 1946 Ph.D., "clearly a man who will in due course of time be a serious contender for a permanency at Harvard." Both got tenure, and turned out to be good bets. Conant said of the Hartz ad hoc committee: "I was both pleased and somewhat surprised to find that those from outside knew Mr. Hartz's work so well and were so enthusiastic about his unusual qualifications." Hartz was the department's first Jewish senior appointment.

The social contrast with the prewar past was even more sharply drawn when political scientist Ralph Bunche became Harvard's first African American appointee to a tenured position (though he never actually joined the department). Yale graduate and Harvard junior fellow McGeorge Bundy became a lecturer in 1949 and got tenure in 1950. This wunderkind, who could teach international relations and American foreign policy, was appointed not because he was a great teacher or a major figure in his field but because he was "endowed with a strikingly clear, imaginative, and incisive mind." Three years later he became dean of the faculty.[62]

Anthropology, Psychology, and Sociology were a trinity of disciplines comparable to History, Government, and Economics. But they differed in the relative shakiness of their disciplinary coherence and their place in the Harvard pecking order. Their experience in the 1930s and 1940s was as much a search for institutional standing as a saga of disciplinary development.

Anthropology divided into two areas, physical and social. The former was the dominant one at Harvard: social and cultural anthropology had only a quarter as many research projects as the physical wing. And there were tensions between the physical anthropologists in the department and the curators in the Peabody Museum, the repository of the University's vast archeological and ethnographic collections: department people looked down on museum people.

The major figures in early-twentieth-century American anthropology—Columbia's Franz Boas, Berkeley's Alfred Kroeber, California's Robert Lowie, Yale's Edward Sapir—were not at Harvard. Conant, well aware of this, asked for a report on who was who among younger people of merit in the field. Lowie stood out, he was told: "He is a Jew, I believe from the East Side of New York but isn't an objectionable one like Sapir of Yale. I suppose he is one of the best social anthropologists in the United States." Kroeber also offered advice. He warned against upsetting the current primacy of physical anthropology. W. Lloyd Warner, Harvard's only senior social anthropologist, whose work on Newburyport made a splash in the 1930s, lacked balance and self-discipline, and his research did not lend itself to program building. "Whatever you do," Kroeber counseled, with an anthropologist's strong feeling for folkways, "don't change the *pattern* of the Department."[63]

Harvard Anthropology's out-of-the-mainstream image was hardly diminished by the work of Ernest A. Hooton. He sought to establish correlations between skull and skeletal measurements and social characteristics: somotyping, he called it. This titillated the popular press and made him one of Harvard's best known social scientists. Hooton's work had its own peculiar problems. When he complained that his skeletons were of unknown origins, and thus made difficult the connections he sought between physiology and culture, the eccentric Boston publisher Porter Sargent rose to the challenge. He offered the skeleton of his son, dead from a hiking accident, for a $1,000 fee, and was ready to encourage others with access to their relatives' remains to do the same. Hooton wanted to accept and sought permission from the administration. Conant passed this hot potato on to Corporation fellow (and physician) Roger Lee, who approved the scheme as long as there was no publicity: the University did not want to be seen soliciting skeletons. Presumably it already had enough in its closet.

Another Hooton hoot was the use he made of a collection of nude photographs of Harvard students from 1880 to 1940, relics of an earlier search for social meaning in physiognomy. He matched these student images with their later careers and concluded that government officials were lean and muscular, scientists were moderately thin with a better-than-average supply of muscles, and theologians were lean, unmuscular, and lightly built (though he conceded the existence of a significant minority of muscular Christian, "fighting parson" types).[64]

Harvard Anthropology became more mainstream after World War II. Ethnologist Carleton Coon, whose work (and ideas) on race were as peculiar as Hooton's ruminations on skeletons, went off to the University of Pennsylvania in 1948. Buck had no regrets: "Pennsylvania seems to think they are getting a good man. Coon thinks it is the place he would like to be. Professors Scott and Hooton of our Department seem relieved that Coon is going. So everyone seems happy." But a substantial Anthropology department was difficult to craft. Clyde Kluckhohn, its only senior social anthropologist, was deeply involved in Social Relations and the Russian Research Center during the postwar years. There was talk of attracting a distinguished outsider: English social anthropologist Raymond Firth, say, or France's Claude Levi-Strauss. But nothing came of this.[65]

Psychology's experimental and social-clinical wings paralleled Anthropology's physical/social-cultural division. Like Political Science, the field took root and developed at Harvard in forced cohabitation with a senior discipline, Philosophy. Not until 1934, long after Psychology was an independent department in every other major American university, did Harvard's psychologists get a departmental identity of their own.

Harvard was the university of William James, which gave it an honored place in the history of experimental psychology. But there was a more ambiguous side to that inheritance. James's strong interest in abnormal psychology took him from the trailblazing analysis of religious experience to an interest in psychic research and the establishment of research funds to support these inquiries. By the 1930s psychic research had become something of an embarrassment. Still, the money was there. Chairman Edwin Boring tried to make psychic research respectable by defining it as the study of unconscious perception and behavior, the effects of attitudes on belief and thought, and the application of probability theory to psychological events. The Corporation readily accepted this definitional cleansing.[66]

Psychology in the 1930s divided into experimentalist "biotropes" and social or clinical "sociotropes." The experimentalists dominated the Harvard department. Karl Lashley, who had a large reputation in physiological psychology, came in 1935 and strengthened the primacy of the experimentalists. Their venue was the department's Psychological Laboratory, headed by Boring for twenty-five years. During the 1930s the independently wealthy clinical psychologist Henry Murray set up parallel Psychological Clinic for his wing of the department, with a staff that came from Anthropology, Philosophy, and Physiology as well as Psychology. Experimentalist Lashley bitterly opposed Murray's presence in the department and sought a title change to professor of neuropsychology, or to physiological psychology, to distinguish himself from what he regarded as his less scientific clinical colleagues.

The energetic, ecumenical Edwin Boring ("perhaps the last great universalist of his profession") brought what coherence there was to a department that lagged behind its peers in the training of graduate students. Its departmental persona as well as its disciplinary character remained unsettled. When Boring asked for a separate Overseers' visiting committee for Psychology, Conant put him off with the vague explanation: "As you know, I am trying to emphasize the general scope of the aspects of the whole University more than the departmentalized work."[67]

At the end of the war, Conant asked a group of outside experts, headed by Alan Gregg of the Rockefeller Foundation, to advise him on the future of Psychology at Harvard. The problem, as he saw it, was whether or not experimental psychology led to anything beyond further research: "I imagine the answer is definitely no." He doubted that the animal research of the experimentalists carried over to human behavior. Similarly, in the realms of personality, public opinion, group psychology, and human relations, "the laws of psychology are only occasionally relevant." He offered up a rather spacey comparison:

> Would the analogy be too far fetched if one compared the situation in regard to the art of brewing beer, at least as it was a generation ago, and the status then of chemistry and microbiology? After all, if one wanted to train a man to make beer, one would have done best in those days at least by establishing schools of brewing, as was done in England and in this country. Biochemical phenomena were only just creeping in and knowledge of them alone would not have made a man a master brewer.[68]

In April 1947, the Gregg Commission produced its report, "The Place of Psychology in an Ideal University." It called for a large, ecumenical department in which social and experimental psychologists cohabited. But by then social psychology was firmly ensconced in the new Department of Social Relations. Conant delicately told Gregg: "Circumstances over which neither of us had control have changed a good deal the setting of the report, and the actions of Harvard may have been such as to lead you and some of the members of the Committee to wonder if we were in earnest in our first invitation."[69]

The psychology department was stripped down to its experimentalist core. Behaviorist B. F. Skinner, the dominant figure in the field during the postwar era, was appointed in 1948. For all his brilliance, Skinner sustained the quirky strain in Harvard's prewar behavioral sciences. During World War II he worked on a scheme for having guided missiles controlled by signals to conditioned pigeons encased within them—and, said Buck, "was having considerable success when other more precise methods were perfected." (One problem: when a pigeon was asked to do "A," or "B," often it didn't. Skinner's solution: put in a troika of pigeons and let the majority rule.) Henry Murray, another original who left Harvard to pursue some erotic Jungian will-o'-the-wisps, returned as a half-time lecturer on Clinical Psychology. For all their eccentricities, these were productive, stimulating, charismatic teachers and scholars. Harvard Psychology was gaining a position in the field that it had not had since the days of William James.[70]

Prewar Harvard Sociology had a clouded past and an uncertain present. It descended from a Department of Social Ethics that began in 1906. By the late 1920s strong departments of Sociology flourished at Columbia, Chicago, and other major universities. Harvard's Social Ethics, whose primary function was to train social workers, had become an anomaly. In 1931 it turned into a full-fledged Department of Sociology, though staffed primarily by part-time members from other disciplines.

The dominant figure during the early and mid-1930s was Pitirim Sorokin, a Russian émigré recruited by Lowell to be the University's first professor of Sociology. Sorokin embodied the eclecticism of the field: his work stretched from rural sociology through the study of social mobility to grand social theory. His colleagues included the outstandingly undistinguished Carle Zimmerman, whom he brought with him from Minnesota, and the barely functioning James Ford, a holdover from the Social Ethics days who managed the not inconsiderable feat of offering a seminar on public welfare in 1935—the year of the enactment of Social Security—for which there was no student registration.[71]

Then things picked up. Despite its limitations, Harvard Sociology attracted a number of graduate students who became leaders in the field. Talcott Parsons was one of them, and he rose to tenure in 1936. His *The Structure of Social Action*, the bible of structural-functional sociology, appeared in 1936, and made his professional reputation. Sorokin's chef d'oeuvre in historical sociology, *Social and Cultural Dynamics*, came out at about the same time—and did much to lose him his standing in the discipline. Parsons' work, although (or because) it was written in a convoluted prose that bore only occasional resemblance to English, was the voice of Sociology present and (near) future; Sorokin's grand but vaporous theorizing was the voice of Sociology past. The two fought it out for control of the department, but it was clear who would win. In alliance with anthropologist Clyde Kluckhohn and psychologists Gordon Allport and Henry Murray, Parsons set out to reshape the social sciences at Harvard. By the 1940s he was more than ready to look to a departmental merger with like-minded social psychologists and social anthropologists.[72]

In 1944 Parsons went to discuss a tempting offer from Northwestern. He and provost Paul Buck found themselves on the same train to Chicago, and in the course of the trip worked out a reordering that created a new Harvard department. Parsons believed that the social sciences were becoming "one of the really great movements of modern scientific thought." He convinced Buck and Conant (who didn't need much prodding) to make him chairman of the Sociology Department, and to seek faculty approval (duly granted in 1946) that allowed him and his Sociology allies to merge with social psychologists Allport and Murray and social anthropologist Clyde Kluckhohn into a new Department of Social Relations.[73]

Sociology was the major beneficiary of the new department. It had two vacancies in 1946. Predictable infighting between Parsons and Sorokin ensued. When the smoke cleared, George C. Homans—old family, on the scene, who did notable work on social structure and historical sociology—and Samuel Stouffer, a leading empirical sociologist from the University of Chicago, were the choices. Buck regarded Stouffer's appointment as indispensable to the development of the social sciences at Harvard. Stouffer would direct the new Laboratory of Social Relations, designed to put social research on a footing comparable to the Psychological Laboratory or Anthropology's Peabody Museum.

Pitirim Sorokin couldn't have been less impressed by the new dispensation. He told Conant that the reorganization was "largely superficial and futile, and partly unfortunate.... It does not change anything seriously in the theories, courses, teaching and so on." Radical sociologist Alvin Gouldner more darkly theorized that "the clinical remove of the Parsonian [structural-functional] approach appeals to Harvard's Olympus complex."[74]

Sorokin, odd man out, turned to directing his Research Center in Creative Altruism, supported by the Eli Lilly Foundation. He told Conant of his desire to study systematically "the energy of all-transcending love." Conant coldly replied that Sorokin's enterprise "adds confusion to an already sufficiently confused world." When Buck proposed that the Corporation give Sorokin a formal appointment as director of the center, that body saw "no need to emphasize the importance of this project by making it the excuse for an additional academic title." Sorokin and his ideas would get a new hearing in the 1960s. But now, in the postwar years, a harder social science reigned supreme.[75]

Conant was asked in 1945 if he thought that the behavioral social sciences were beginning to take on the quality of true science. He had his doubts. Advances in statistics, demography, psychological testing were empirical, not theoretical. Stouffer conceded that there were not yet social science principles for social engineering comparable to physical science theory. So it was Harvard's task to concentrate on research in "pure" social science. Conant did not fully agree. He thought that Stouffer had too idealistic a view of scientific method, which was not much more than sophisticated common sense and benefited greatly from a continuing interplay with its practical application. "[O]nly from practical problems," he cautioned, "can material come that will advance your science."[76]

One new venue in which to test that hypothesis was the area studies center. The first of these (in 1947) was the Russian Research Center, with similar units for China and the Middle East on the drafting table. It is common, and not inaccurate, to link the centers to the rise of the United States as a world power during World War II and the cold war that followed. But as in so much of university life, contingency also played an important part.

The wartime marriage of social science and national policy set the stage. Provost Paul Buck observed that the war "ushered in a new age in ... cooperative research and especially centers and institutes and that sort of thing." Conant was drawn to the idea of an integrated approach by a group of disciplines and by the need to produce men "broadly trained in international affairs." A postwar Committee on International and Regional Studies got faculty approval for Chinese and Russian area studies centers. Conant initially sought research and library support for Chinese studies from the Carnegie Corporation and for Russian studies from the Rockefeller Foundation. But Carnegie president Devereaux Josephs told him that he wanted to develop "a really productive research program on Russia" at Harvard. Carnegie's important postwar policy makers, psychologist John Gardner and lawyer Charles Dollard, hoped to see at Harvard and elsewhere a number of social science disciplines focus on a particular area, as had been done in OSS during the war. The obvious postwar candidate, as the cold war began to take form, was the Soviet Union.

In December 1947 Harvard got a $100,000 Carnegie grant to support research into postwar Russian society and culture. Buck and Conant designed a Russian Research Center (RRC), instead of the more common "Institute," because "center" had a less permanent ring to it. They stipulated that the center's work be entirely independent of the government and that all of its findings be made public.[77]

Over the next decade some $1.5 million in grants came from Carnegie to the RRC. The staff agreed early on to avoid taking public policy positions on Soviet-American relations. But soon enough the political and ideological pressures of the cold war left their mark. The RRC got $450,000 from the Air Force for a large-scale Refugee Interview Project, which made possible Merle Fainsod's trailblazing *How Russia Is Ruled* (1953). And it worked with the New York Public Library to secure Russian and Polish books for the Library of Congress, which feared that if it sought them directly, hostile questions would be asked in Congress.

The center's first political contretemps involved H. Stuart Hughes, its assistant director and a part-time assistant professor of History. Hughes actively supported Henry Wallace in the 1948 election, which embarrassed the Carnegie Corporation. Gardner and Dollard raised the matter with Buck, who suggested to Hughes that he stick to History and create a solid academic reputation before throwing himself into political activism. (According to Buck, Hughes later told him that this was the best advice he had ever gotten.) Carnegie picked up the cost of making Hughes a full-time assistant professor in the History department, and he left the center. Buck regretted "the action of the Carnegie people in precipitating it, but I must confess it makes sense."[78]

Conant was concerned not on the "conservative or hysterical front" but over the administrative style of some RRC staff. Buck for his part fretted about "the apparent costliness of this new type of research the sociologists, psychologists, and anthropologists have developed." There was another worry: the degree to which the centers, with their research-money clout, could erode departmental strength. Pressure rose in 1950 for appointments in Sociology for Barrington Moore and Alexander Inkeles, who were senior research fellows at the Russian Research Center. Conant accepted the necessity of occasional, exceptional "administrative or technical appointments without limit of time, despite the fact that salaries attached to such appointments may be paid from temporary funds." But not for cases like these, or for candidates so young. Why couldn't they be considered in the normal way, with an ad hoc committee? After much to-and-froing, the Corporation "with extreme reluctance" approved the appointments. Both turned out to be distinguished additions to the Harvard faculty.[79]

In 1952 a committee chaired by Overseer Judge Charles Wyzanski reviewed the work of the center's first five years. Was it an appropriate enterprise for Harvard? Very much so: scholars coming together from a variety of fields to study a single region could do so only in a large university. But the committee found that the hermetic, grant-driven ambience of the RRC fostered too-facile research and publication, nor was it clear that the center had a truly interdisciplinary character. Junior people were intensely aware that their career prospects lay more in their departments than in the RRC. Still, area studies centers would become an increasingly important part of late-twentieth-century Harvard. Their effect on established departments and disciplines remained to be seen.[80]

## The Natural Sciences

Meritocracy should have flourished most luxuriantly in Harvard's science departments; in no other area were rank orders of quality more firmly fixed. But inherited department weaknesses, anti-Semitism, and the fiscal constraints of the 1930s slowed improvement. Much of this began to wash away in the late 1930s: first with the new developments in organic chemistry and nuclear physics, then with the wartime spur to scientific work and the fall of religious barriers.

Conant's commitment to scientific research was personal as well as institutional. His *On Understanding Science* (1951) echoed his wartime colleague Vannevar Bush's *Science: The Endless Frontier* (1945) as a paean to the intellectual worth of the scientific enterprise. Physicist-philosopher Thomas Kuhn assisted Conant in teaching a course on the history of science in Harvard's General Education Program, and Kuhn dedicated his *Structure of Scientific Revolutions* (1962) "to James B. Conant, who started it." That book became the bible of those who questioned the intellectual autonomy of science, a view to which Conant most emphatically did not subscribe. But then he always valued intellectual vitality over consensus.[81]

Chemistry was Conant's own department. He might have been expected to give it special attention and indeed he did. Early on he wrote to a number of senior chemists at other universities, asking them to rate the best men in their fields who were between thirty and forty years old. He was after "a composite evaluation with scholarship ranked about 60 percent and teaching ability about 40 percent. Personality is such a difficult problem that I think it best to leave it out altogether."[82]

Like so many other prewar Harvard departments, Chemistry was small, tight, insular. Senior professors staked proprietary claims to the basic courses in their fields. The department was not very hospitable to undergraduates and had a strict rule against directly hiring its own Ph.D.s. But by the mid-1930s organic chemists Paul Bartlett and Louis Fieser and physical chemists George Kistiakowsky and E. Bright Wilson had been added, a strong-to-distinguished array.

A number of able young Jewish chemists were around in the 1930s. But the department was not a very welcoming place. Saul Cohen, a Harvard College summa graduate who had commuted his way through the College, began Chemistry graduate work in 1937. Neither Elmer Kohler nor Feiser, the senior figures in organic Chemistry, would take him on. Instead he and the two other Jewish students who entered that year were assigned to Paul Bartlett, away on sick leave (and hence "it" in departmental tag). Bartlett left behind a sheaf of projects, and Cohen was told to select one. In the folder he found a copy of a letter from Bartlett to the chair: "I hope I will not become the rabbi of the department."[83]

As World War II drew to an end, Conant tried to imagine what postwar science at Harvard would look like. He expected biochemistry to figure prominently, as well as electronics. But he believed "that the field of nuclear chemistry was going to be of the utmost importance in the future." Just what Conant thought nuclear chemistry consisted of is unclear, but he put his money where his mind was. A committee on nuclear physics and chemistry, headed by Provost Paul Buck, got $425,000 to spend over the next five years to support research in "chemical-physics."

Alas, two impediments arose. One was that nuclear chemistry turned out to be a nonstarter compared to organic chemistry and biochemistry. The other was that in a meritocratic university departments pretty much decided for themselves whom they wished to appoint. The ability of Harvard's president to influence that process, even in his own field, was scant. There was a man at Los Alamos who Conant and Kistiakowsky sought to hire, and Conant asked Buck to set up an ad hoc committee. But he warned: "There will be a big row in the department about whether the next permanent appointment should be an organic chemist or the kind that George wants.... Of course," Conant lamely added, "under the present procedure my views are merely to be taken as those of an interested party and in no way binding on you, the department, or [a] possible candidate."[84]

By the early 1950s the department had assumed the character that it would have for the rest of the twentieth century. It was large, research driven, sharply subfield-divided. It had a take-no-prisoners approach to excellence in appointments, in synch with the hard-nosed foundation and government grant sources on which it depended for research sustenance. Louis Fieser, a doyen of the department in the 1930s and 1940s, had his Rockefeller grant cut off in 1951. He had gotten $20,000 a year for six years, but his reports revealed a notable paucity of work. So off with his head.

Top-of-the-field professors, big foundation or government grants, well-supported labs doing hard-driving work: that was the ticket. Not coincidentally, as the department became more competitively meritocratic it became less clublike, less mindful of the ethnic or other pedigrees of its members. In an act with symbolic meaning, the Merck pharmaceutical firm in 1951 gave a fund to establish the Max Tishler Lectures in Chemistry, honoring a Jewish 1934 Harvard Chemistry Ph.D. who of necessity had gone into industry and rose to head Merck's research laboratories. The department's first self-identified Jewish professors, biochemists Konrad Bloch and Frank Westheimer, came in 1954.[85]

Important work in theoretical and quantum physics was done in pre-World War II Harvard: John Van Vleck produced the first thesis on quantum theory by an American and got a Nobel Prize in 1977. The department's prewar star was experimentalist Percy Bridgman, on the faculty from 1910 to 1954 and a Nobelist in 1946 for his work in high-pressure physics. This "tough-minded apostle of ruthless logic" created waves when he decided in 1939 to close his lab to citizens of Germany, Japan, Russia, and Italy. (He soon modified his diktat to make room for talented refugee physicists.) But Harvard Physics played a smaller role than Columbia, Chicago, and Berkeley in the conceptual and applied breakthroughs of nuclear physics. And its aging laboratories were outstripped by those of Yale, Princeton, Columbia, and Michigan.[86]

Prewar Physics, like Chemistry, was a genteel, cosy department. Bonding went on in a weekly colloquium that dated from the late nineteenth century, supplemented in the 1930s by tea and crackers with peanut butter and ketchup, apparently a boon to hungry graduate students in the Depression years. The department was a ripe target for Conant's meritocratic ambitions. In 1935 its chairman, Frederick Saunders, argued for the retention of longtime instructor Martin Grabau on the ground that he was a gifted teacher of undergraduates. Conant coldly responded that he and Saunders were in basic disagreement on faculty policy:

> If you are right, the Corporation made a great error in electing me president; if I am right, the only thing I can do is stick to my course through thick and thin.... It would be only fair for me to state frankly that you undoubtedly realize the Physics Department is one of the two or three in this University which have not at present a good reputation,—quite the contrary.... Your record of calling people to this University and of holding the best people you have had here has been very unsatisfactory. The standing of the Physics Department in the country has sunk very low.[87]

But the effervescence of the field soon enabled Harvard Physics to snap out of its doldrums. Promising new men—Kenneth Bainbridge, Wendell Furry—came in. Furry, quantum mechanics pioneer Edwin Kemble, and John Van Vleck were theoreticians, which gave Harvard an unusually large number for an American university at the time. Between them, Kemble and Van Vleck had trained a third or more of the country's theoretical physicists by the mid-thirties.

Always with a weather eye on where the science action was, Conant appointed (and chaired) committees in 1936 to build a cyclotron and develop solid-state physics. The cyclotron was the brainchild of the department's younger experimentalists. But how to get the wherewithal to build it? Much help was, literally, material: the Navy contributed a large radio transmitter; the American Rolling Mill Company came up with a magnet; six big companies provided sixteen tons of copper. Building the cyclotron cost $55,000, $20,000 of it from donors organized as the Associates of Physical Science at Harvard University. Big science still was small potatoes, at least at Harvard.[88]

World War II opened up new vistas of research support. A number of Harvard physicists went off (not far) to MIT's Radiation Laboratory for wartime work. But the department as such did not play a large part in the development of the atom bomb. Its jerry-built cyclotron won it only a small contract for the preparation of radioactive materials. Indeed, the cyclotron's wartime function was a matter of some dispute. Department chair Kemble floated the idea of having it operated by conscientious objectors, who would participate in non-war-related medical research as distinct from "offensive war work." Conant sharply replied: "If these peoples' consciences are so sensitive that they demand guarantees from the government about the nature of the research to be done with the products of the cyclotron, then clearly the whole scheme is out the window." Finally in 1943 the cyclotron was taken away by the Army for use at Los Alamos.[89]

In the wake of the war (and the atom bomb), Conant got the Corporation to provide $425,000 and set up a University Committee on Research in Nuclear Physics. And in October 1945 the postwar age of Harvard Physics officially began: the tenured appointments of twenty-nine-year-old Julian Schwinger, thirty-one-year-old Edward Purcell, and thirty-one-year-old Robert Wilson were announced. Norman Ramsey, who did not make this first cut, came from Columbia in 1947. All would win Nobel Prizes in later years. Harvard's new appointees, Buck boasted, "are recognized as the best young physicists in the nation." But in the postwar age of the imperial professoriate, supremacy was anything but a solid state. Wilson went off to Cornell in 1947, and there was great danger of losing Schwinger, the best theoretician of them all. Schwinger soon became Harvard's youngest full professor.[90]

Meanwhile the prewar generation departed. One of the last was old-family Theodore Lyman, director of the department's Jefferson Laboratory since 1910. He sent in his resignation yearly, lest he suffer the humiliation of being asked to leave. In the spring of 1947 he was rather curtly informed that the game was up on July 1. The tone as well as the content of this dismissal upset Lyman: understandably so, given his years of faithful and financially supportive service to the department. Amends of a sort were made by naming one of the laboratory buildings after him. So did the Brahmin university give way to its meritocratic successor.[91]

Conant set his sights on new blood in Biology as he did in the other sciences. But the department had a heavy weight of less-than-distinguished members, and their tendency to promote insiders was hard to stop. Between 1930 and 1938 no non-Harvard man got a permanent appointment. Physiologist Alfred C. Redfield, who came in 1934 from the Medical School to chair the department and the Biological Laboratory, complained that to rely on outsiders' judgments when reviewing the tenure prospects of junior faculty "must inevitably encourage our younger men to work with an eye on the grandstand and to tempt them toward charlatanism." He thought it desirable to continue useful people even if they did not deserve promotion. Soon after this, Redfield asked to be relieved from his chairmanship: "I have found it increasingly difficult to interpret certain of your policies in a sympathetic way to my colleagues."[92]

In 1939 Conant summoned assistant professor of Biology Edward S. Castle to give him the bad news that his future at Harvard was past. Castle responded that FAS dean George Birkhoff had assured him of a permanent appointment. (Birkhoff in fact wrote to Castle that he would be considered for promotion, "and it seems to us entirely likely that such a promotion will be advisable.") Conant, who appears to have forgotten about the Birkhoff letter, lamely replied that he was aware of it, but that in his view it still left Castle's case suspended in midair, "like Mohammed's coffin." Castle understood Conant to say that his case was like "a half-nailed coffin," which hardly lessened his sense of grievance. The case went to the Corporation in the fall of 1939, with the recommendation that if the fellows decided that a commitment had in fact been made, Castle would be given a "frozen associate professorship." And that is what he got.[93]

Biology did not reap the financial and research rewards from World War II that came to Harvard's chemists and physicists. And it remained a troubled, troublesome department. Conant thought in 1942 that the biologists' fissiparous tendencies raised the question "[w]hether or not the distribution of their research funds should be done by an outside committee responsible to the President of the University. I should take the line that perhaps they would be delighted to be relieved from this arduous and difficult responsibility." In 1950 he thought it hopeless to try to get first-rate senior men; the cost, and the jealousy of the existing faculty, saw to that. "Sometime in a moment of gloomy leisure," he darkly observed, "I may do an account of the history of the Department of Biology at Harvard from 1925–1950 as a 'case history' of how the University traditions and resources may be dissipated under the pressure of charming people with mediocre standards of academic excellence."[94]

Conant told a Biology ad hoc committee in June 1951 that new money made possible the appointment of three additional professors in the field. The only requirement was that they be outstanding. The department pored over available biologists like discriminating diners, and recommended animal geneticist Tracy Sonneborn of Indiana, biochemist Hans Krebs of Sheffield, and cellular physiologist Alan Hodgkin of Trinity College Cambridge. These were (as a waiter would say) excellent choices: Krebs and Hodgkin later won Nobel Prizes. But alas, all three declined to come. Buck sought advice outside and was told that Joshua Lederberg of Wisconsin was the country's most promising young geneticist. He approached his quarry, "one of those rough diamonds, who flouts every academic convention (such as not wearing a necktie)." Lederberg's wants were no less unsettling: a full professorship (though he was not yet twenty-seven), a paid position for his wife, several additional genetics appointments, ample space and research funds, no teaching except of graduate students. Buck concluded: "He may be a genius. He would have to be to justify such treatment. But so far I have seen no evidence for him as convincing as that presented for [physicist Julian] Schwinger." Conant's response: "I agree completely!" So Lederberg didn't come. He won a Nobel Prize in 1958.[95]

Another stone on Harvard Biology's rocky road was the Museum of Comparative Zoology (MCZ). It housed vast collections of zoological specimens, employed a substantial number of professors and curators, and sponsored frequent scientific expeditions abroad. The MCZ was Harvard's Smithsonian, a great center for taxonomic, evolutionary, and organismic biology in the nineteenth-century tradition. Ernst Mayr, who became head of the museum in 1953, knew of it in Berlin in the 1920s before he had heard of Harvard. (Just after World War II, novelist and dedicated lepidopterist Vladimir Nabokov had a modest staff position at the MCZ. He worked six hours a day, seven days a week, conserving a backlog of specimens and permanently impairing his eyesight. His salary was incorrectly set at $1,200, when it should have been all of $1,250. The necessary adjustment was charged to the Museum's Special Publication Receipts budget line: an incident positively Nabokovian.)[96]

The MCZ's director from 1927 to 1946 was Curator of Reptiles Thomas Barbour, who in the Brahmin Harvard tradition drew on his own ample funds to help the museum along. His passion was to venture to the Caribbean, Latin America, and the East Indies in search of his scaly friends. Alfred S. Romer, a distinguished zoologist who had been on the MCZ faculty since 1934, succeeded him, in accord with the Buck-Conant preference for professionalism over amateurism. The postwar museum ran an annual deficit of about $25,000, and needed an additional $40,000 a year to be on a sound basis. Its rich, devoted following and unique place in the Harvard firmament made this a reasonable goal. But the MCZ's size and financial independence fed an increasingly troubled relationship with the Department of Biology. The two had been administratively divorced in 1939, and Conant in 1944 worried about the future relationship of the "museum people" to the department: a problem "at least as difficult and controversial as that of the future of theology!" Adopting another metaphor, the Biology visiting committee observed: "a preliminary course in the elementary principles of astronomy would be needed to understand properly the relationship of the Department and its related institutions."[97]

That cosmology included Harvard's "Botanical Empire," separate bodies that did with plants what the MCZ did with animals. These included the Arnold Arboretum, the Botanic Garden, the Gray Herbarium, the Harvard Forest, the Farlow Herbarium, the Atkins Institution (a Cuban plantation), and the Bussey Institution. By the eve of World War II, their combined endowment was $6,775,000, and they held more than 3 million specimens.

The Arnold Arboretum resembled the Museum of Comparative Zoology in its autonomy and the devotion of its supporters. Charles Sprague Sargent, its first director, was full of entrepreneurial bounce, a skilled public advocate of conservation more than a scientist. He was also a world-class hater, in a state of near-war with the adjoining Bussey Institution. Corporation fellow Roger Lee remembered how the Bussey's Professor W. Morton Wheeler (no mean adversary himself) would walk on the boundary dividing his institution from the arboretum, shotgun in hand, "and try by terrible epithets to get Professor Sargent to come over ... and get shot." (The study of plant life appears to have fostered a Darwinian struggle for the survival of the fittest.) By the early twentieth century the arboretum had become a hybrid of high horticultural science and urban *plaisance*—an American Kew Gardens. It had close ties with, and much appeal to, a large swathe of Brahmin Boston. It appeared by 1929 that "no department of the University [possesses] wider publicity or greater powers of attracting favorable attention to its needs."[98]

After World War II a committee headed by Bussey Professor of Plant Anatomy Irving W. Bailey proposed a major reorganization of Botany at Harvard. Its most explosive recommendation was that the arboretum's library and herbarium be moved to a new Botany building on Harvard's Cambridge campus, and that most of the arboretum's income be diverted to support the new setup. This meant that the botanical institutions—especially the arboretum—would come fully under the sway of the Biology department.

What followed was a decade and a half of infighting and promiscuous ill will. On the face of it, the Arnold Arboretum controversy amply supports the adage that academic politics is so fierce because it is so insignificant. But a larger issue lurked behind the din of battle. The arboretum's supporters in effect challenged Conant's meritocratic University. They championed an older, less professional conception of what Harvard should be.

Longtime Corporation fellow and Conant supporter Grenville Clark led the in-house opposition to the administration. To move the collections to Cambridge, Clark believed, was a breach of trust. (And his wife was prominent among the arboretum's defenders.) Conant and the Corporation responded that scientific research on the taxonomy of trees required sophisticated lab equipment and expertise in genetics and physiology, not just growing specimens in an arboretum. This could be better carried out in a new building in Cambridge, in close proximity to biologists, chemists, and physicists. If it was not linked to the vast resources of the University, Corporation fellow Charles Coolidge warned, the arboretum "will gradually become little more than a pretty garden."[99]

As the 1950s wore on, so did the Great Arboretum War. The conflict moved to the state's supreme judicial court, which finally in 1966 held that the University did, after all, have the right to transfer the arboretum's books and specimens to Cambridge. Personal resentments festered (Clark broke irretrievably with Conant and Harvard, and—the ultimate rejection—left his papers to Dartmouth): a bitterness assuaged, one might hope, by springtime visits to the Arboretum, whose beauty could speak without favor to committed professionals and dedicated amateurs.

No such tensions existed in the intensely professional, meritocratic field of Biochemistry. As early as 1933 Conant presciently reminded Chemistry's chairman: "I am still to hear from the Chemistry department as to the possibility of their developing biochemistry." But when he tried to get a reading on it in 1935, he came "to the somewhat discouraging conclusion that the field of biochemistry is about like that of economics and that there is no clear consensus of opinion as to the leaders."

After the war Conant sought a department of biochemistry in the Faculty of Arts and Sciences, which duly authorized one in February 1946. But finding appropriately distinguished biochemists to staff it was no easy matter. In 1948 Conant sought start-up money from the American Cancer Society. That depended on the appointment of Carl and Gerty Cori, a Nobel Prize-winning husband-and-wife team at Washington University in St. Louis. But the Coris wouldn't come. Another source of Harvard's relatively slow development in biochemistry was Edwin J. Cohn of the Medical School. Cohn's work on blood fractionation made him one of the University's most notable scientists, but he had a personality that grated on his colleagues. At an October 1952 meeting, shortly before his departure from the presidency, Conant "lost my temper with E. J. more than I intended but 'broke' with him I hope forever. Corporation will have to handle his megalomania from here out." Eventually, though, he agreed with Medical School dean John Edsall to ignore Cohn's "madness."[100]

The need persisted to do more in this burgeoning field. But two large, self-interested obstacles stood in the way: the departments of Chemistry and Biology. Organic chemist George Kistiakowsky confessed to a modest interest in biochemistry, but feared "that its present status indicates a dim future." If Harvard wanted a cutting-edge biochemistry department, it should look to the intersection of Chemistry with the life sciences. Powerful new tools and experimental approaches taken from physics promised to yield insights into the nature of biological systems comparable to those attained into the structure of matter. Alas, "practically none of this work is going on at Harvard, although it is setting the pace in the borderland between physical and life sciences." Why? The big baronies—the Medical School, Chemistry, Physics, Biology—were too strong. They could not—or would not—offer sufficient inducements to attract the stars of the field and they were too set in their ways to seek out trailblazing juniors.[101]

By 1953, the year of Conant's departure, and the year when Francis Crick and James Watson's double helix became public, biochemistry at Harvard still was kept within the confines of the established science departments. But this did not mean that the subject was ignored. Biology gave tenure to biochemist George Wald in 1944; Chemistry's breakthrough came in 1955 with the appointments of Konrad Bloch and Frank Westheimer. (That all of these men were Jews suggests that new, not yet well-settled fields strongly attracted, and were more readily open to, members of a socially marginal group. Early-twentieth-century Anthropology played a similar role for both Jews and women.) It took the emergence of the molecular revolution, and the institutional loosening brought on by the turmoil of the late sixties, to open the door to a Harvard department of Biochemistry.

Engineering had been taught at Harvard since the nineteenth century. By the 1930s the School of Engineering had both undergraduate and graduate degree programs, and benefited from recurring injections of money from the estate of Gordon McKay, who left what turned out to be a very large sum indeed for this purpose. The relationship between pure and applied science interested Conant; the McKay Bequest, even more so. He set out to bring the School of Engineering—and the McKay money—into the more uplifting atmosphere of the Faculty of Arts and Sciences.

But his hopes for change ran head-on into hoary, vested interests in Engineering. Old grads feared that solid, practical engineering would be put at risk by the airy-fairy pure science dominant in FAS. In early 1936

Conant invited Ernest O. Lawrence, who headed Berkeley's Radiation Laboratory, to come to Harvard as dean of the Graduate School of Engineering. He told Lawrence: "[Y]ou are one of the very few men who could do here at Harvard what I wish to have accomplished in the Graduate School of Engineering. An energetic young leader who is thoroughly imbued with the ideals of scientific research and has an interest in the application of science could transform the School, I believe." But Berkeley substantially increased its support for the Radiation Laboratory, and Lawrence stayed where he was. Besides, his work in nuclear physics required outlays well beyond what Harvard was ready to spend. Conant wryly responded: "My sadness at your refusal is tempered by the thought that perhaps we have been of some assistance to you in the future development of your own research activities at the University of California."[102]

World War II strengthened the case for close links between pure and applied science. And if Conant needed further encouragement, the McKay millions kept pouring in, raising the toothsome prospect of strengthening not just Engineering but Harvard science in general. He proposed that research and graduate work in engineering, applied mathematics, and applied physics be consolidated into an FAS department of applied science, offering both undergraduate and graduate instruction. The faculty response split along predictable lines. FAS scientists, savoring the McKay money, were all for it; senior professors in the Engineering School were all against it.[103]

In early 1949 the Corporation approved a plan to merge the faculty of Engineering into FAS. Greasing the wheels was another $8,626,000 from the McKay Bequest, which brought the total from that source to $15.8 million. Conant called on his wartime associate Vannevar Bush to head a committee charged to come up with guidelines for the new arrangement. All winks and nudges, Conant asked Bush to review "the present status of mechanical engineering in its most comprehensive sense," and proceed "not from the standpoint of the curriculum common in engineering schools" but "start with mechanical engineering and work up towards the various peripheries in the field of applied physical sciences." Hint: "I have quite a lot of difficulty with the alumni who want us to continue to train the kind of civil engineers, mechanical engineers, electrical engineers which are regularly turned out by the engineering schools on a four-year basis." Bush's panel dutifully called for training "a new type of engineer, who is known for his grasp and versatility in many fields." Conant creatively interpreted this as an open sesame to applied physics and chemistry, and an invitation to leave geology and traditional mining, mechanical, and electrical engineering to MIT.[104]

In the fall of 1950 the new Division of Engineering and Applied Science came into being. Conant and Buck insisted that the division not resemble "the more ordinary 'earthy' engineering school, and that within applied science we should select a relatively small field in which we can excel." Buck wanted to get rid of electrical engineering (including electronics): all its glory, he spectacularly misthought, was in the past. The most strongly supported programs would be mechanical engineering, solid-state physics, and applied mathematics. Searches for appointments in the chosen fields got under way. Buck wrote to Conant in an elegiac tone: "You and I know that we could not have moved ahead with our program without at the same time quite firmly drowning a few cats. But henceforth we should be positive and confident."[105]

Prewar Mathematics, like Chemistry, was small and clubby. George Birkhoff, its dominant prewar figure, was strongly hostile to Jews, and none were appointed in the department until after his death in 1944. In the wake of the war, Buck and Conant sought to add panache to Mathematics as elsewhere. They tried, and failed, to attract the great theoretician John von Neumann of the Princeton Institute for Advanced Study.[106]

Mathematics was one of the oldest Harvard sciences; computer science was the newest. The Harvard pioneer in the field was applied physicist Howard Aiken, who during the late 1930s worked out much of the basic theory for a large-scale sequence calculator. World War II was a great agent for developing this instrument. Out of it came Harvard's Automatic Sequence Controlled Calculator, Mark I, built and paid for by IBM, given (along with a $100,000 endowment) to Harvard to be used by the Navy for the war's duration. It was unveiled in August 1944, the world's largest calculating machine: revolutionary in principle, expected to solve almost any known problem in applied mathematics. No laptop, this five-ton "mathematical brain" or "robot calculator" was 50 feet long and 8 feet high. It had 760,000 parts, 530 miles of wire, and two million connections.[107]

Harvard faculty members got some exposure to the future potential of the new tool at a fall 1944 meeting. Economist Wassily Leontieff divulged his "considerable dream" of "the possibility of a New Economics developing out of our forthcoming ability to handle multiple correlations in an efficient and grand manner." Astronomer Harlow Shapley told Conant that "the building of these big calculators is something analogous (in a small way) to the building of the first printing presses. We are opening up new fields for exploration." He warned that

Norbert Wiener, "who is perhaps the wildest and perhaps best dreamer on the future of calculators," was talking up the future of the new machine at MIT and the major foundations. After the war Harvard put up a computation laboratory to house its calculator. It was paid for by a contract with the Navy giving it use of the machine in coming years, except for four hours a day when the Harvard staff could work on their own projects.[108]

Like the botanical institutions, the Harvard College Observatory (HCO) was the pet of wealthy benefactors, drawn by the romance of the subject and the éclat of a small, prestigious enterprise. The observatory flourished under Harlow Shapley's direction, which began in 1921. Shapley was a notably effective publicist and fund-raiser. He was also a notably authoritarian director (which may explain in part his empathy with Stalin's Soviet Union).

The observatory's isolation from Harvard pedagogy, and perhaps the assumption that the painstaking work of astronomical mapping was appropriate to them, made it one of the few places on the campus where women could have serious academic careers. Annie Jump Cannon was the longtime curator of astronomical photographs, and Cecilia Payne was Phillips Astronomer (and later a professor) there: Harvard's first significant senior appointment of a woman. (She married astronomer Sergei Gaposchkin in 1936 and, ahead of her time, assumed the married name of Payne-Gaposchkin. Radcliffe President Ada Comstock reported that she was "going domestic" and "would rock the cradle with one hand and calculate the movements of the stars with another.")[109]

By 1952 the observatory's senior staff was getting long in the tooth; it had its share, and then some, of the discord common to Harvard's ancillary institutions; and Shapley's time to retire had come. An ad hoc committee chaired by physicist J. Robert Oppenheimer looked into the state of Astronomy at Harvard and found it less than stellar. The senior members of the staff had not fulfilled their early promise, were not up to the demands of modern astronomy. "[A]re you suggesting we are stuck with three second-rate people for 15 years with high salaries?" asked an appalled Conant. No, it was not that bad, replied Oppenheimer. Unhelpfully he added: "With good direction and the kind of supervision which Physics has had, the astronomers who have been here for 10 to 15 years might have been very different people."

But this was an exciting, evolving branch of science in which Harvard had a strong tradition. There was only one course to follow: put more money into the HCO. Conant told Oppenheimer of his "amazement" that that was what the Corporation chose to do. Oppenheimer's committee recommended three distinguished outsiders as a new director, none of whom came. Buck and Conant proposed that the observatory be governed by a council made up of its tenured professors, with senior astronomer Donald Menzel as ... what? Menzel and his supporters wanted him to be the observatory's director, if only for a year; otherwise, the outside world would assume that Shapley still was running things. Shapley ("for reasons too complex to understand," said Buck; but the reasons seem obvious enough) wanted Menzel's title to be the more limited one of chairman. The Great Compromise: acting director. Soon Menzel had the title he wanted.[110]

The Department of Geology and Geography was a marriage of convenience dating from the nineteenth century. Conant wondered: "Why is it that this is the weakest of our [science] departments judged by outside standards?" (His yardstick: it was the only one with no member in the National Academy of Science.) The electrical, chemical, and metallurgical industries supported their fields in Harvard Engineering, but the oil companies had done nothing for Geology. He concluded, "As far as the Harvard Department is concerned, ... it would seem to me like throwing money down a rat hole to give the money that they request.... I am all for betting on winning horses, but ... they look to me like a bunch of second-raters."[111]

Geology survived on half rations; Geography met a grimmer end. The field was fair game in the Darwinian meritocratic world of postwar Harvard. Edward Ackerman, the sole junior geographer, came up for tenure in the fall of 1947. The department's Geology majority had their eyes on that slot. And they wanted Geography detached because the two were "fundamentally incommensurable disciplines." Conant asked the ad hoc committee whether Geography should be continued as a subject or be allowed to fade out with the retirement of its only tenured professor. The committee recommended that Geography be kept. But Conant was not persuaded "that the subject was a science in any proper sense of the word." He told the chair of the Geology-Geography department: "[I]t is time now to make a policy decision by saying that Geography is one of the things which we will not develop at Harvard."[112]

Geography's place in the University was further weakened by one of the most peculiar of Harvard's ancillary bodies, the Institute of Geographical Exploration. Opened in 1930, it was the creature of Alexander Hamilton Rice, an amateur explorer who married the widowed Eleanor Elkins Widener, the donor of Harvard's Widener

Library. The lure of more millions led Lowell to accept the institute, let Rice direct it, and make him professor of Geographical Exploration. For similar reasons the Geology-Geography department welcomed him.

Rice ran the institute as a private club. He swept up (when he deigned to appear) in his chauffeur-driven blue Rolls Royce at a properly clublike late morning hour and appointed its staff without benefit of FAS or Corporation review. Scandal clung to the institute like a stubborn morning fog. One instructor had to resign in 1935 because of his incarceration in the Billerica House of Correction. Another Rice appointee, dismissed out of hand (which Rice had the power to do), "created a disturbance" in the institute. Finally in 1951 the seventy-six-year-old Rice announced that he could no longer support the institute, and it was discontinued. Thus did Geography, dedicated to the study of where things are, fade from the Harvard scene.[113]

While fringe Geography disappeared, fringe History of Science gradually secured a shaky foothold on the Harvard academic ladder. The subject was taught primarily during the 1920s and 1930s by Belgian scholar George Sarton, who came to lecture as a refugee from the University of Louvain during World War I and stayed on. Sarton edited *Isis*, the field's leading journal. The Carnegie Institution supported him during the 1930s, until it discovered with some dismay that for years he also received salaries from Harvard and Radcliffe.

What most distinguished History of Science at Harvard was James Bryant Conant's strong and continuing interest in it. This was a good test of his capacity to shape the destiny of a department—and a revealing instance of the limits on that capacity. Conant improved Sarton's salary, but could do little more than offer moral and intellectual support to a one-man academic enterprise. He told Harold Laski, "If this were the gay 20s instead of the depressing 30s, I should be in a position, I suppose, to flow a sum of money into this area." Finally in 1940 he found the wherewithal to make Sarton a professor after twenty-five years of annual lectureship appointments.[114]

Conant's interest in the history of science persisted, stoked by the atom bomb and the other scientific achievements of World War II. But the department itself would have to wait for flusher times before it could become a more substantial presence at Harvard.[115]

## ~ 5 ~

# THE PROFESSIONAL SCHOOLS

Harvard's nine professional schools were on the cutting edge of its evolution from a Brahmin to a meritocratic university. Custom, tradition, and the evergreen memory of the alumni weighed less heavily on them than on the College. And the professions they served were more interested in their current quality than their past glory. True, major differences of size, standing, wealth, and academic clout separated Harvard's Brobdingnagian professional faculties—the Graduate School of Arts and Sciences and the Schools of Medicine, Law, and Business— from the smaller, weaker Lilliputs—Public Health and Dentistry, Divinity, Education, Design, Public Administration. But these schools had a shared goal of professional training that ultimately gave them more in common with one another than with the College and made them the closest approximation of Conant's meritocratic ideal.

## The Graduate School

Harvard's doctoral programs in the Graduate School of Arts and Sciences (GSAS) were a major source of its claim to academic preeminence. As the Faculty of Arts and Sciences became more research and discipline minded, so grew the importance of graduate education. A 1937 ranking of graduate programs in twenty-eight fields—the lower the total score, the higher the overall standing—provided a satisfying measure of Harvard's place in the American university pecking order:

| | | | |
|------|-----|---------------|-----|
| Harvard | 63 | Johns Hopkins | 199 |
| Chicago | 121 | Cornell | 234 |
| Columbia | 126 | Princeton | 242 |
| Yale | 157 | Michigan | 245 |
| California | 189 | Wisconsin | 250 |

But there were problems. Money was short, and while graduate student enrollment held up during the Depression years of the early 1930s (what else was there for a young college graduate to do?), academic jobs became rare indeed. Between 1926–27 and 1935–36, Yale appointed no Harvard Ph.D. to a junior position.[1]

The Graduate School itself was little more than a degree-granting instrument, with no power to appoint faculty, no building, no endowment, and no budget beyond one for its modest administrative costs. Graduate students identified with their departments, not the Graduate School. Needless to say, the GSAS deanship did not attract the University's ablest men. Conant in 1941 appointed a committee to look into graduate education, and historian Arthur M. Schlesinger, Sr., "called for a thoroughgoing study without blinders. I do not believe Dean [Arthur B.] Lamb has the disposition, the temperament or the imagination to do the kind of job that needs to be done." Conant coldly replied: "Some day I hope we can discuss the educational problems involved ex-personalities."[2]

Lamb resigned in 1942 for health reasons, and in 1943 Conant appointed feisty American Literature professor Howard Mumford Jones as his replacement. Jones came in full of beans, bent on more forceful supervision of the departments' graduate programs and a large-scale study of the Graduate School. But he was quickly sobered by the realities of GSAS's administrative weakness. His notes for a meeting with Conant suggest the frustrations inherent in his job: "Impotence of dean ... Fellowships and scholarships—go to [FAS dean Paul] Buck ... Research Fellows—go to Buck ... New humanities degree program or any other must be approved by Buck/Buck more generous in attitude than any other Faculty Dean ... Impossible to invite anybody here."[3] Buck was "rather disturbed" by Jones's attempts to deal directly with Conant rather than through him and with "the fact that he is flying around with a lot of new ideas instead of ... getting down to brass tacks on his major report" on the Graduate School. He hoped that Conant would "politely" call Jones to order.

In April 1944 Jones produced a "preliminary report" on the present state and future prospects of the Graduate School. It consisted of an extended cri de coeur over the subordination of his office to Buck. He dwelt on his need to be supreme in graduate student matters and to report directly to the president.

The response: a Conant-Buck proposal that the Graduate School be divided into three separate units (natural science, social science, humanities), thus assuring that it would be even less of a presence on the Harvard scene. An infuriated Jones told "Mr. Conant": "As I cannot acquiesce in the doctrine that the university is a body to be governed under the military metaphor of a chain of command, I submit my resignation ..., to take immediate effect." Adeptly twisting the knife, Conant responded to "Dean Jones" that before he submitted Jones's resignation to the Corporation, he would ask Provost Buck to recommend a proper response. Not yet quite bereft of the power of speech, Jones replied: "In the meantime, in order to avoid even the shadow of misunderstanding, let me say that I am confining my activities solely to the routine duties of this office." Finally, on June 6, Conant told "Professor Jones" that the Corporation had accepted his resignation and greatly appreciated the time and energy he had put into his task. So ended the short, unhappy deanship of Howard Mumford Jones.[4]

The Graduate School benefited perhaps more than any other Harvard unit from the postwar flood of G.I. Bill-supported veterans. Before the war about 800 applied each year and 400 were admitted; in 1946–47, 2,600 applied for 900 places. Architect Walter Gropius's Graduate Commons and its surrounding dormitories opened in the fall of 1950 on the northern edge of the Harvard campus: a symbolic event for a Graduate School now come of age. It also was testimony to GSAS's feeble fund-raising capacity: its newly established Harvard Foundation for Advanced Study and Research sought unsuccessfully to meet the modest goal of $1.3 million from Graduate School alums for the Gropius project. Fortunately the Law School was also involved in the effort and secured the necessary funds.[5]

## Law

The Harvard Law School (HLS) had no such baggage of diffuse character and tight money. Its widely imitated case method of instruction, and the sheer number and quality of its students (it was the largest major law school), made it a national force in the legal profession. The HLS library had perhaps the best legal collection in the world, and many of its faculty were the leading men in their fields. The school developed a culture all its own: fiercely professional; focused on training its students for important careers in private law and public life.

But many thought that the school had lost its earlier edge, had grown complacent and lax. Almost all students who applied were admitted; about one in three flunked out or left after the first year. Columbia and especially Yale were centers of Legal Realism, an approach to the law that had considerable réclame in the 1930s. Later Supreme Court Justice

Abe Fortas, who taught at Yale then, recalled: "Harvard people tended to look upon us as unsound maniacs, and we in turn looked upon them as sort of antiques who time had passed by."[6]

The faculty tried to improve the quality of its student body: the common view was that Yale was getting the best students. From 1937 on, students were admitted with more regard for their academic records and prospects for success. Less than 20 percent of the 1937 entering class failed, compared to a previous average of around 30 percent. But grade-driven academic rigor persisted. A distraught mother wrote to Conant about her son, who flunked out and had a nervous breakdown, "appealing to you to see if something can't be done to save our boys." Conant managed to contain his sympathy. The school provided severe training, which an occasional student "was not fitted to undertake.... I do not believe, in view of the exacting study required for a law education and of the infrequent illnesses of its students, that the Harvard Law School is unnecessarily difficult."[7]

The most important HLS event during the 1930s was the retirement of Dean Roscoe Pound and the selection of his successor. Pound had been dean since 1916. In 1933 he was sixty-three years old: cantankerous, opinionated, unable—or disinclined—to bring his faculty along by suasion. When Conant took office, the air was thick with talk about replacing Pound. One faculty member told him that Pound's failure as dean was such that "everyone who works in this building is suffering from a sort of progressive shell shock. Each September we are all a shade less fit for our several duties than we were the September before." Conant complained of Pound's "complete inability ... to carry out any sort of decent administration. I really think his situation may be almost pathological."[8]

Two names emerged as the most likely prospects to replace Pound: James M. Landis, a former faculty member who headed the Securities Exchange Commission, and—surprisingly—Henry Wolf Biklé, once on the Penn Law School faculty and now general counsel of the Pennsylvania Railroad. Corporation fellow Grenville Clark reported that Biklé was a "liberal-minded" Democrat, though "[m]y guess is that the General Counsel of the Pennsylvania Railroad isn't a wild radical." Conant convinced himself that Biklé was just the leader the Law School needed. Biklé presumably might assuage alumni who worried about a New Dealer dean, radicals on the faculty (namely, Felix Frankfurter, who in fact favored Biklé), and a reputation that, said one of them, led Harvard undergraduates to prefer Yale, and CCNY students (a euphemism for you-know-who) to come to Harvard.[9]

The candidate himself harbored doubts as to his appropriateness for the job. He may also have concluded that recent heart trouble made him unsuitable. In March 1936 Biklé declined Conant's offer, likening the HLS faculty to a hypothetical West Point staff of men who had never been in active military service and regarded it with contempt. He saw no way to change the Law School's culture, and so decided not to come.[10]

Now Landis took center stage. But his New Deal ties and support of FDR's Supreme Court-packing proposal worried many. Grenville Clark, who admired Landis's ideas about legal education but considered him "certainly a most extreme and really intemperate partisan on current questions," hoped that a Supreme Court appointment would waft him out of Harvard's reach. Conant scolded Clark for not displaying his usual tolerance, and Clark conceded that as "a heretic a good deal of the time myself," he couldn't afford to be a "hater of heresies." At the end of 1936 Conant proposed Landis, and the Corporation accepted him. The Law School settled down with a new dean whose vigor and administrative ability offered a refreshing contrast to the recent past. A mildly modernized curriculum and better students also lifted the faculty's spirits. Strong new appointments were made. In 1940 alone, James Casner, Milton Katz, Lon Fuller, and Paul Freund were appointed; all would have notable careers.[11]

Then came America's entry into World War II. Of Harvard's major professional schools, Law was the hardest hit. Attorneys could serve the needs of military justice with relatively little retooling, and the number of law students shrank to the vanishing point. The faculty began to think about its postwar makeup. It saw a golden opportunity to snap up first-class men whose normal career paths had been upset by the war, were acclimated to a reduced income by their wartime service, and might be disinclined to return to the banality of normal law practice. But it was important to strike before they formed firm—law firm—attachments.[12]

Conant proposed a mechanism to do this: a standing appointments committee, nominally chaired by him but in fact run by the dean. Balanced equally between the faculty and distinguished judges and practitioners, it would be charged to come up with a list of candidates. But the faculty took exception to the idea of a committee surveying the field and giving them names from whom to choose. Instead, it drew up a list of its own graduates over the past fifteen years who had A averages. One strong candidate: Harry Shulman, Sterling Professor of Law at Yale and a leading figure in labor law. "I wish to add one further comment on Shulman that I think is not without relevance," Dean Landis told Conant.

He is, of course, Jewish. In discussion the other day in Washington with the Ad Hoc Committee in regard to Shulman I raised this issue in order to get the reaction of men outside the School on adding another person of Jewish extraction to our faculty. The answer came quickly from a source that set my own fears at rest. The source was Colonel George A. Brownell, who is quite conscious of this problem. He said in substance that in calling Shulman we were calling a person of known capacity and known distinction and that hence the fact that he was a Jew did not disturb him and would not disturb others, and that he for one would not be concerned with that aspect of the case. The other members of the [outside ad hoc] Committee echoed his views. Because of that we all went ahead in our consideration of Shulman without any reference to that issue.

Shulman was duly asked—and stayed at Yale.[13]

Concern over the number of Jews on the faculty rapidly diminished as (or because) the number of Jews on the faculty rapidly increased. Even the gender wall showed a tiny crack. In 1946 Soia Mentschikoff of Chicago came as a visiting professor to teach commercial law. The only dissenter was James McLaughlin, "his opposition being based," the dean reassured Conant, "on the fact that Miss Mentschikoff was a woman and not in terms of her intellectual fitness to teach."[14]

The need to appoint a new dean arose again in 1946. The war had given Landis an excuse for taking leave from a job that had already palled for this intense, high-strung man. By the end of the conflict he had a drinking problem, and his family life was in disarray. Corporation fellow Charles Coolidge complained that Landis was "neurotic." Conant defended his dean: "As to his being neurotic,—as professors go, I should say that ... this charge is questionable." But in 1946 Landis resigned to become chairman of the Civil Aeronautics Board.[15]

A poll of the faculty revealed that their colleague Erwin Griswold commanded the greatest measure of support, with Milton Katz the next strongest. Landis told Conant: "I was ... delighted and very proud with the attitude of the faculty with regard to the Jewish problem. It became clear that the suggestion of a Jew like Katz for the deanship would create no internal problem whatever." Active alumnus Harrison Tweed heard otherwise. He understood that "there is one contingent which supports Griswold because he is a Christian and a conservative and another faction which supports Katz because he is Jewish, young and liberal." It is evident that Katz's Jewishness mattered far more in alumniland than in the faculty—not because Law School professors were freer from prejudice, but because the sense of belonging to a *brüderbund,* defined by the mysterious science of the law and the ties of HLS faculty membership, was so powerful.[16]

As the chaos of the immediate postwar years receded, the Law School focused on more traditional concerns: size, curriculum, research, and of course money. Griswold dwelt on the need to make the Law School a "laboratory" in which law and social science were conjoined. The Ford Foundation supported a program in international taxation and Sheldon and Eleanor Glueck's work on juvenile delinquency. Planning began for a separate annual Harvard Law School Fund; campaigns to build new student housing and raise a $7 million endowment for an Institute of International Legal Studies were launched in the late 1940s.[17]

But not all was smooth sailing. Conant in 1947 asked the Harvard deans for estimates of their development needs and combined them into a $90 million dollar package—more a vague wish list than a fundraising objective. As against $18 million for Business, $19 million for Medicine, and $19 million for Arts and Sciences, only a modest $2 million was assigned to Law. Griswold—who lightly started off his response with "You will probably smile when you read this letter"— objected that the Law School's needs in fact added up to $17 million. He blamed his inexperience as a new dean and the multitude of other concerns weighing upon him for not making the school's case more strongly.

Conant replied: "I hope you will smile when you read this letter, for although I am writing vigorously, I can assure you it is in no unfriendly spirit." Vigorous he was. Griswold's letter touched him

on a very personal point. The 90 million dollar program which I circulated to the deans at the last meeting is *my* program.... If after sixteen years of experience, and fairly intimate contact with the budget and educational problems of various parts of the University, the President of Harvard has not the right, and indeed the duty, to state publicly what he thinks are 90 million dollars' worth of the needs, then I don't know what you have a president for. I submit that if the president of a modern university is merely to be a compromiser between various pressure groups, whether they arise as deans or committees of extra-faculty organizations, then you may as well have, as some universities do, politicians as the heads of your organizations!

In his view "the dire needs of the University lie in those areas which are essentially deficit departments [the Schools of Public Health and Education, the Medical School] and which cannot be other than that by nature of the society in which we live. It is therefore the question of urgency and not of need for expansion that is reflected in this budget." This was Conant's "own prejudiced, or should we say jaundiced, view of the way the first 90 million dollars should come in. I leave it to you to argue with my successor where the second comes and I have no doubt you will be able to convince him of a much larger share!"[18]

# Medicine

Some thought that, like the Law School, the Harvard Medical School (HMS) had lost its edge by the time Conant took over from Lowell in 1933. Certainly he considered Eliot's decision to locate the school in Boston, not Cambridge, the "Great Error" of Harvard planning. The Medical School's separation from the rest of the University was "a real handicap to our development"; its quality was high in spite of, not because of, its remoteness from Arts and Sciences.[19]

Conant's first opportunity to put his stamp on the Medical School came in 1934, when David Edsall, its dean since 1918, retired. He chose HMS faculty member C. Sidney Burwell as Edsall's successor. Conant expected Burwell to continue his clinical research on pulmonary diseases: "I do not want the next Dean of the Harvard Medical School to be a full-time administrative officer." He was "convinced that if one outstanding school can show that a scientific clinical man can act as a leader of the school and at the same time stay in close touch with his own profession, an important task will have been accomplished. To my mind, all education today suffers from the heavy hand of the professional administrator." He wanted to see the Medical School more closely integrated with the rest of the University: "my idea of running this university is to try to bring together as much as possible the different activities which are so far-flung." (Conant would not be the last Harvard president to pursue that particular will-o'-the-wisp.) Burwell, a kindly, quiet man, was not a strong dean. Conant confided to his diary in 1940: "Staged a little public row with Burwell over appointment of a faculty committee on educational policy. Hope the demonstration will convince some people that [he] is a real Dean & running his own show."[20]

The major postwar problems of the Medical School were a mounting budget deficit and its perennially vexed relations with its affiliated but independent teaching hospitals. (Harvard was unique among major medical schools in not running its own hospital.) In the past, informal arrangements between the school and the hospitals worked well enough: "As long as there was more money than ambition, this situation ran along fairly smoothly" was the way Conant put it. But the medical breakthroughs of the war years—sulfa and penicillin, the first antibiotics—"greatly whetted [the appetites of] all concerned for more research funds."[21]

Conant recognized that "medical faculties are the most independent of any in our university, and being so tightly connected to the medical profession as a whole, university Presidents have a relatively small leverage on their activities." He could do little to assuage HMS's growing money hunger and thought it unwise for medical schools to get deeply into fund-raising: that was not good either for public relations or staff morale. And he opposed direct federal support for medical school education because it threatened "a degree of federal control, which, I am sure, this university would never accept." But government-funded tuition scholarships were fine and so was the creation of the National Science Foundation to support research.

A committee including Conant, HMS barons, and hospital heads met thirty-six times to clarify the relationship between the Medical School and the affiliated hospitals, and came up with a "statement of general policies" at the end of 1948, policies that would prevail for the rest of the century. Conant sought to make sure that the Medical School retained primary responsibility for teaching and for research in the basic medical sciences. And he wanted an end to the practice of Medical School professorships going to prominent researchers who were full-time staff members in the hospitals. There were to be three grades of Harvard-hospital appointments: Group A, designations made by Harvard (for luminaries such as the department heads of Massachusetts General, the Brigham, and Children's Hospital); Group B, in specific fields (such as pathology and surgery) made by the hospitals; and, by far the largest, Group C, temporary part-time appointments made jointly by Harvard and the hospitals, with the major part of the appointees' income coming from their private work.

Conant was no less concerned to assure the quality of the HMS faculty. The school's permanent staff would be divided (in ascending order) into preclinical and clinical teaching groups, appointments with limited terms set by their endowments, preclinical investigators focused on research and the training of other researchers, and at the top of the heap, distinguished clinical investigators charged to advance medical science. A system such as this, Burwell and the ever-meritocratic Conant agreed, "might have avoided some of the mistakes which have been made by local pressures ... to keep a good [but not top-notch] man at the school by giving him a permanent position."[22]

George P. Berry, who headed the University of Rochester's medical school, succeeded Burwell as dean in the fall of 1949 after the usual exhaustive search. He turned out to be a strong-minded, effective leader, fully in accord with Conant's desire to emphasize basic medical science research. That would cost money. The Corporation approved a spending increase of $1 million a year, which required $25 million more in endowment. And Conant sought to enlighten Surgeon General of the United States Leonard Scheele, and through him the Public Health Service, regarding the true scale of the indirect costs of sponsored research. It was only fair that the government should bear its proper share. But Scheele replied discouragingly that while indirect costs might well be around 20 percent, the present 8 percent allowance would not be increased. Why? Because the Public Health Service did not want to divert money that might otherwise directly support research projects. It was just as well that incrementalism was the keynote of Dean Berry's administrative strategy. Not until the 1960s did a large-scale fund campaign and ballooning federal research money dramatically raise the Medical School's capacity for big-time medical research.[23]

## Business

By the time Conant became president in 1933, business was slow at the Harvard Business School (HBS). The Depression discouraged enrollment, and in the mid-1930s dormitory rooms on HBS's new campus were being let to students studying elsewhere at Harvard. About one in three M.B.A. candidates failed to return for their second year: either because of economic conditions, an inability to do the work, or (for many) out of the belief that the curriculum was not worth another year of one's life. Student interests also changed. In 1928, 110 (40 percent) of the school's 274 graduates went into investment banking and finance, only 52 (19 percent) into manufacturing. Ten years later less than 10 percent entered the bare ruined choirs of finance, over a third went to work in the slowly recovering manufacturing sector, more than half did who knew what.[24]

Conant confessed to some sympathy with those who had doubts about business administration as a subject of academic study. Nevertheless he regarded the Business School as an important part of the University, not only because of its links to big money but because it could be integral to instruction and research in the social sciences. With Conant's backing, Wallace B. Donham, HBS dean since 1919, sought a role for HBS as a training ground for public as well as private administrators. To their disappointment, benefactor Lucius Littauer insisted that his $2.5 million gift be used to establish a separate school of public administration.[25]

World War II, which Donham expected to be "the most critical period in the history of the Business School," was a major opportunity for HBS to make its mark. It did so in grand style, much more so than Law or Medicine. Donham set up the Industrial Administrator Program to retool business executives for defense industry work; he secured an Army Quartermaster ROTC Unit; he arranged with the Navy to train Supply Corps officers. He even fielded a conference, "Labor in National Defense," which Conant flogged to labor leader Sidney Hillman: "our colleges and universities have a major responsibility to work closely with Labor, which they have not exercised to the extent of their capacities." Donham also tried to keep the Business School's civilian M.B.A. program going. (By 1942 the institution was widely known as "Camp Bergdoll," the name of a prominent draft evader).[26]

Donham left the deanship in that year, to be succeeded by Donald David, a former faculty member and businessman: hard-driving, energetic, wholly appropriate to his job. David announced that HBS had "to stop being a Business School and become a military training school." Under him it turned into an educational beehive, running full blast and accumulating a financial surplus of more than $800,000. The Engineering, Science, and Management War Training Program brought "retreads"—older executives—to the Business School campus and was the seedbed of the school's later Advanced Management Training Program. The Army Air Forces Statistical School at HBS trained more than 3,000 officers in the blossoming art of applying statistical controls to complex operations. Among those teaching in the program was Assistant Professor Robert McNamara. Out of this experience came the numbers-based management system that McNamara and his associates—the "Whiz Kids"—applied (with very controversial consequences) to the Ford Motor Company and then to the Vietnam War.[27]

As the war neared its end, thoughts turned at HBS as elsewhere to the peacetime future. Asked by Conant for his reconversion plans, David argued against taking on new programs until his overworked faculty recuperated. They needed time (he had the money) to redo the case studies that were the backbone of the HBS curriculum. In February 1945 the faculty rescinded all previous course authorizations and unanimously adopted a more tightly integrated first-year program of basic courses, with less varied teaching responsibilities for the junior faculty so that they might better develop their research expertise. The postwar Business School, like the rest of the University, committed itself to professionalism and meritocracy.[28]

And like everyone else, it had to cope with a flood of returning veterans. The school responded with a souped-up M.B.A. program that ran for sixteen straight months. By January 1946 Conant thought the situation was "really desperate": some 8,000 veterans sought the 300 places in that month's entering class, compared to the 7,757 degrees given by the school in its thirty-seven-year history up to then.

The postwar crunch soon eased. And by the very nature of who and what it taught, the Business School was better situated than its Law and Medicine counterparts to set out after large donations. It got the Corporation's go-ahead for a $20 million campaign, which purred smoothly to success. By the early 1950s the Business School had fewer financial worries than any other Harvard faculty.[29]

## Public Health and Dentistry

From its origin in 1922 the Harvard School of Public Health (SPH) faculty was subordinate to the Medical School; David Edsall was the dean of both HMS and SPH. Not until 1935, after Edsall retired, did Public Health get a dean of its own, Cecil K. Drinker, who had been assistant dean for a decade. This dependent relationship, and the stringencies of the 1930s, prevented the school from securing a place in its profession comparable to Harvard's other graduate faculties. Its students were few, its staff for the most part undistinguished. But there were signs of quickening institutional life in the 1930s. The Social Securities Act of 1935 included a $12 million appropriation for public health education and increasing numbers of SPH students came with "Social Security money" as well as on Rockefeller grants. In 1936–37, for the first time in the school's history, enrollment was "practically to full capacity."[30]

Nevertheless, a review of SPH in the 1940s concluded that it continued to suffer from its subordination to the Medical School. Much instruction and many appointments were medical rather than public health related. The departments that had developed without HMS oversight—Industrial Hygiene, Maternal and Child Health, Physiology,

Vital Statistics—were the strongest ones. When the United States entered World War II, the faculty turned overwhelmingly to war-related research; Drinker resigned his deanship in 1942 to do so. By then there were only nineteen students: war-straitened state departments of health could no longer send people for training.[31]

Conant told the Corporation in September 1944 that the School of Public Health was "the number one problem" in the University. This seemed like an ideal time to plan for the future, and Medical School dean Sidney Burwell came up with the customary instrument for doing so: a committee. One duly met, and concluded that SPH needed a strong dean, more money, and greater autonomy from the Medical School. Failing that, it might be best "to dissolve the School of Public Health" and transfer its departments to the Medical School.[32]

That, it was generally agreed, was a nonstarter. Pending the arrival of a new dean, Conant set himself "to keep the School from going to pieces completely" and sought $2 million from the Rockefeller Foundation to bolster its endowment. The foundation's officials convinced him that the full separation of Public Health from the Medical School was essential to its future. HMS Dean Burwell agreed that SPH had to be autonomous. But it also needed a larger setting, which membership in a faculty of medicine that included the Medical and Dental Schools would provide. By the end of 1945, things were settled. The deanship went to James S. Simmons, a take-charge graduate of SPH who had been a brigadier general during the war. The postwar School of Public Health would be part of the Faculty of Medicine and would consist of a small group of well-supported departments. The Rockefeller Foundation gave $1 million to be spent over ten years, and the Corporation kicked in $750,000.[33]

But old habits (and problems) died hard. There was some difficulty over the Department of Tropical Medicine, transferred to the Medical School, which SPH wanted back. Another sensitive matter was the alcoholism of the former dean. But his Brahmin sensibility eased the situation. He readily owned up to his illness: after learning "from my friends that I have become an unpleasant spectacle around the School of Public Health," he quietly resigned from the faculty.[34]

Finances remained SPH's heaviest albatross. In the fall of 1946 it faced an annual deficit of $40,000. Either its officials had miscalculated, Conant speculated, "or else Simmons is too great an expansionist," or "perhaps he just thinks the Corporation is a gold mine and he should work it for all it is worth." By 1952–53 SPH's faculty, staff, and student body had more than doubled since its 1946 reorganization. But 72 percent of the school's budget came from short-term research grants and other soft money, only 18 percent from endowment income. Not until the rise of government and Ford Foundation interest in public health in the late 1950s and the 1960s did significant new money become available.[35]

The third, and shakiest, leg of the medical area faculty tripod was the Harvard Dental School. The Depression drastically worsened the school's always precarious financial condition. Conant was concerned enough to make a $3.4 million Dental School endowment appeal part of his Tercentenary campaign. But the Carnegie Corporation, the school's primary benefactor, gave only a tenth of that sum, and little else came in.

In 1939 Conant appointed a committee to look into "the many questions which have been raised in regard to a closer connection between the Dental School and the Medical faculty." It recommended that all future Dental School graduates take the Medical School's preclinical program and after five years of study get a combined M.D.S./M.D. degree. HMS Dean Burwell backed the proposal—turf-building evidently outweighed interschool snobbery—though there was considerable opposition from the Dental school faculty. Conant thought, grandiosely, that the plan's impact on dental education would be comparable to Langdell's case method at the Law school. The new plan went into effect in September 1941, and in 1944 the School's name was changed from the prosaic Harvard Dental School to the more resonant Harvard School of Dental Medicine (SDM).[36]

Leroy Miner, the school's dean since 1924, feared that the rigors of the new approach made it difficult to meet the military's growing demand for dentists. But Conant held that the University was morally and legally obligated to get it started. Besides, an upgraded conception of dental education fit his larger educational goals. He planned to dwell on new departures in the professional schools in his 1941 Annual Report:

> The Dental School is the major theme and it can be made more interesting and a more effective rebuttal to our enemies by discussing the whole problem of providing adequate medical and dental care to a mass of people.... Organization, mass public health, research the answer to medicine *pro bono publico* instead of physicians to the well-to-do. The subject is full of dynamite but would like to take a crack at it.[37]

The new program began with nine students taking the same first-year work as their Medical School counterparts. But HMS dean Burwell reported that a troubling division within the Dental School faculty had appeared between the clinical and the laboratory men. The clinicians wanted to retain the more orthodox, traditional way of teaching the subject. And the Council of the American Dental Association was reluctant to reaccredit SDM until its new curriculum could be more fully evaluated. This led the Army to refuse to certify the school as a fit place to train military dentists, a severe blow to its finances and prestige.

But the Navy gave its stamp of approval in 1943, and SDM and its new program had an easier time of it in the postwar years. Conant thought there had been a substantial payoff in "scholarly gains for dentistry." Meanwhile another, less publicized problem emerged: students used admission to the Dental School to take the joint degree program, then switched over to the Medical School and thus become Harvard M.D.s. Half of the school's forty graduates from 1947 to 1950 took this path. In 1951 that option ended: after their second year, Dental School students could continue on only for a D.M.D. degree.[38]

## Divinity and Education

Conant's view on religious instruction in the College could not have been of much comfort to longtime Harvard Divinity School (HDS) dean Willard Sperry: "[T]he more criticism and pure reason can stick knives into the orthodox dogmas the better.... I still think the answer would be to give up all formal instruction in this emotional area and have an optional get together for a week on an extracurricular basis."[39]

The Divinity School's endowment by 1930 had not grown much since 1890; its faculty, students, and budget were a quarter to a fifth the size of competitors Yale, Chicago, and Union Theological Seminary. Then came the added Depression burdens of diminished enrollment and finances. Conant confided to Wisconsin Law School dean Lloyd K. Garrison, the liberal-minded chairman of the Overseers' visiting committee to the school, that its annual deficit made HDS "one of the problem children from a financial point of view." He could not justify the University's subsidy to the school: "There are many other projects ... which would be more important in the eyes of any impartial group," and inclined to the view "that perhaps the best thing to do was to put the School on a liquidating basis." He toyed with the idea of a ten-year plan of faculty nonreplacement and student attrition or even more drastically, "shutting the School up and simply carrying the present professors as a research group of specialists giving instruction in the Faculty of Arts and Sciences until their appointments shall expire." But he did not tell HDS dean Sperry, or anyone else, "that I am thinking such devastating thoughts." Returning to the planet Earth, Conant conceded that none of this could happen without due process, "which in a University means endless talk and discussion."[40]

The Divinity School saga illustrates with special clarity the limits that Harvard's institutional inertia and the weight of its past imposed on even so forceful a president as Conant. In 1941 he came up with the idea of bringing philosopher-theologian Reinhold Niebuhr to Harvard with a joint appointment in Philosophy and the Divinity School. Dean Sperry welcomed Niebuhr's coming—to Philosophy. He told Conant that Niebuhr was put off by the Divinity School's close identification with liberal Protestantism. Niebuhr himself told a different story: of hearing through the grapevine that Sperry, and in particular *Mrs.* Sperry, did not look forward to someone so non-Unitarian in his theology joining the HDS faculty. In any event, Niebuhr decided not come. He told Conant: "I would in fact have accepted if Harvard did not have a divinity school."[41]

Still, HDS was too venerable a part of Harvard to be lightly discarded. In 1943 the school's visiting committee recommended that the Corporation authorize a commission to look into the future of HDS, and Conant agreed. First he asked John D. Rockefeller, Jr., to head the group, posing questions that revealed his skepticism about the school's future. Was it important for the country that Harvard continue to train ministers? Was there a larger sense in which HDS might play an important role in American Protestantism? If not, was there any reason to continue it? Rockefeller declined to take on the job. Determined to have a lay chairman, Conant finally got Washington lawyer and Harvard overseer John Lord O'Brian to head the commission. "Is there," he asked O'Brian, "a place for a nondenominational Divinity School in Harvard University and, if so, what are the reasons for its existence?"[42]

O'Brian's report, completed in the summer of 1946, did not tell Conant what he wanted to hear. It strongly urged that the Divinity School continue as a center of religious learning and instruction, with a $100,000 increase in the annual budget and $4 to $5 million in additional endowment. Conant's response to these specifics: "No". Given the low quality of the student body and faculty, and the small endowment of "the weakest of Harvard's professional components," he found the report far too optimistic. Harvard produced a handful of ministers and scholars at appalling cost. There had to be a clean break with the past. But he could not ignore the pro-HDS sentiment in the Governing Boards and elsewhere, and though he was "frankly skeptical about the possibilities," asked O'Brian to head a fund-raising committee charged to raise $6 million. The Corporation pledged to contribute a million dollars if there was a reasonable chance—and it soon appeared that there was one—of raising the other $5 million. Conant had underestimated the degree to which God and Mammon occupied common ground.[43]

He accepted the fact that closing down the Divinity School was not in the cards. So he adopted another strategy. This was to engineer a merger with another theological school, spin off the training of ministers to the new partner, and keep advanced instruction and research in Cambridge. He soon had his candidate: the Graduate School of Theology at Oberlin College in Ohio. Conant wrote in January 1950 to Oberlin president William E. Stevenson, telling him in confidence of "the impossibility of raising any such sum of money as is required to do an over-all expansion and renovation of our Divinity School." He wanted to discuss with Stevenson "our mutual problems in this area of training ministers." Conant went out to see him, and in May proposed an HDS-Oberlin merger plan to the Corporation.

But he "found practically no support for my radical ideas." He couldn't even win over Reinhold Niebuhr, who held that it was better "to let history work itself out as a choice between these two alternatives [raising the money or closing the school] than to introduce a third alternative which doesn't have sufficient attractions for any of the parties involved." Conant conceded that his scheme "has become academic in every sense of the word." In this test of wills between school and president, the final score was: HDS 1, Conant 0.[44]

The Graduate School of Education (GSE), like the Divinity School, was often pulled between the competing goals of training practitioners and devoting itself to more rarified levels of instruction and research. And like Divinity, it did not at first stand high on Conant's priority list. But Conant's interest in primary and secondary education grew in pace with his commitment to equal opportunity in American life. In 1939 he admitted "to a conversion ... in my own point of view since I took over the presidency of this University. I suppose I came to this position as much prejudiced against schools of education, including our own, as any member of the faculty of arts and sciences." Now he had come to think that GSE could be the torchbearer of his belief that "the prime aim of our educational system should be to provide support for talented people of all types." Under his urging the school in 1935 adopted a new degree, Master of Arts in Teaching (M.A.T.), aimed at (primarily female) graduates of leading liberal arts colleges. M.A.T. candidates did a substantial amount of their work in the Faculty of Arts and Sciences, a synergy dear to Conant's heart.[45]

On the eve of World War II, faculty member Francis T. Spaulding got an attractive offer from Chicago and to keep him Conant made him dean. Spaulding wanted to train not only teachers but administrators, educational statesmen, and university-level scholars. Conant agreed that this was vital "to the role that Harvard will play in American education in the coming generation." But GSE needed a bigger budget and an additional $1 million of endowment: impossible unless the school became a more effective institution. He asked the Corporation, "at this ominous period in its financial history," if it would be willing to let the school run an annual deficit of $20,000 to $25,000 a year, as it had the Divinity and Dental Schools and the Museum of Comparative Zoology. The alternative was "to agree essentially to the slow liquidation of the School of Education." The Corporation went along.[46]

All thoughts of improvement were sidetracked by America's entry into the war. Spaulding went off to the War Department. The wartime school was administered by the faculty acting as a committee of the whole, with a Corporation-designated chairman. (Not that there was all that much to administer. Along with the usual wartime falloff in enrollment, softened for GSE by its high intake of women, the Corporation ended its commitment to pick up the school's deficit. The faculty was encouraged to go off to war-related jobs or into retirement.) GSE's experiment in participatory bureaucracy was predictably dysfunctional, and Philip Rulon of the faculty became acting dean on September 1, 1943. He was considerably less than a success: his way of dealing with the faculty was not to seek their opinions but to tell them what he wanted done.[47]

The school's wartime experience compounded prewar difficulties over a persistent and growing deficit: "much more so," Conant told the Corporation, "than either of us foresaw." The "aggressive but exceedingly tactless" Rulon had turned the school into a bearpit; "it would be hard to exaggerate the hostility" with which faculty and administrators regarded him. Serious curricular problems abounded as well, with the M.A.T. program suffering from the indifference of the Arts and Sciences faculty. Among the choices open to the school: merging with the Faculty of Arts and Sciences; becoming an M.A. factory like Columbia Teachers College; turning into a research institute; drifting along in its present state; or trying to implement the prewar program under which Spaulding came. Conant preferred the last. But this would cost money.[48]

He entreated Spaulding to return and continue the rebuilding job he had started in 1940: "it seems to me that you have led an unsuspecting chemist out on the end of a very long limb and anything short of continuing a fairly orthodox School of Education here with yourself as the head looks like sawing off the limb! Please think all this over. The more I think about it the deeper into difficulties do I get." Spaulding balanced the pros and cons of returning to Cambridge or becoming New York State's Commissioner of Education. When it became clear that the financing necessary for the kind of school he wanted was not to be had, he went to New York. Corporation members and the GSE faculty met in December 1945 to weigh the future of the school. They agreed on a slimmed-down core of about 100 primarily male students, as distinct from the primarily female M.A.T.s destined to be foot soldiers in the public schools. This elite would be trained for leadership positions in American education by a new and reduced faculty, composed of first-rate social scientists closely tied to FAS.[49]

In June 1946 Conant appointed a committee, balanced between GSE and FAS faculty, to search for a new dean. Their charge: to come up with someone who was as much a social scientist as an educator. Finally, in the spring of 1948, two years and several turndowns later, a dark horse emerged: thirty-two-year-old Frank Keppel, the son of former Carnegie Corporation president Frederick Keppel, a 1938 Harvard B.A., an assistant to Provost Paul Buck, still writing his doctoral thesis. Keppel had worked with Spaulding during the war, where his administrative talents attracted attention. Conant thought that Keppel could work closely with the Social Relations department "and forward our general plans."[50]

Keppel turned with youthful zest to the school's intellectual and financial rejuvenation. He added strong social scientists to the faculty. New programs—in educational administration, a nursery and pre-school "laboratory"—strengthened GSE's role in social science research. Its budget doubled between 1948 and 1950. Most of this came from time-limited foundation grants, not from endowment or tuition. By the time Conant left Harvard in 1953, Keppel had been authorized to raise $6 million in endowment and was hot on the spoor of the big foundations. But it was no easy matter to change GSE's institutional spots. The Overseers' visiting committee to the school complained in 1947 that the faculty was "more interested in training educational technicians and 'petit fonctionnaires' of school administration than in training enthusiastic and stimulating teachers and educational leaders."[51]

# Design and Public Administration

Harvard had long-standing programs in Architecture and Landscape Planning, and in the late 1920s added an innovative set of courses in City Planning. These units were loosely organized under the rubric of the faculty of Architecture. While the Architecture program was by far the dominant one, the other, smaller programs had a fiercely defended autonomy, rich soil for internecine strife. In the spring of 1933, on the eve of Conant's arrival, the Architecture faculty bowed with a flourish to the new esthetic currents of the time. A dramatic curriculum reorganization abandoned the beaux arts tradition (pretty drawings, derivative styles) for a stress on function, the economics of building, new technology, the neighborhood surround—full acceptance of architectural modernism.[52]

But the school was weak in funding and personnel, and Conant by early 1935 was ready "to enter into a complete investigation of our School of Architecture and its related activities." This included a search for a new dean. He soon had his man: Joseph Hudnut, from Columbia's School of Architecture. One of Hudnut's earliest acts was to bring Walter Gropius, a founder of the German modernist Bauhaus School, to chair the Architecture program. Gropius in turn recruited Marcel Breuer, another giant of architectural modernism. They would attract as students a number of architectural luminaries-to-be: Philip Johnson, I. M. Pei, Edward L. Barnes, Paul Rudolph, Benjamin Thompson among them. The school was repackaged as the Graduate School of Design (GSD) to reflect the close relationship of architecture to city and landscape planning, a step welcomed by Conant as "one more indication of a widespread feeling that the separatist spirit of the past quarter of a century has proceeded too far, and that a period of coordination and amalgamation must be the next step in university education."[53]

After the war Hudnut sought to maintain the school as a stronghold of architectural modernism. When the press reported that Harvard planned to build a new undergraduate library "clothed in a romantic architecture reminiscent of the eighteenth century," Hudnut was quick to take this as an affront to his school. He and Gropius were due to retire in 1949; Conant, not one to break up a successful team, extended them to 1953. But the two men had a falling out. Hudnut warned Conant: "Mr. Gropius will continue to run his sword through the corpse of the Beaux-Arts. This is a good show and will probably fill our halls for four more years. We should make a serious mistake, however, if we appointed another Gropius at the end of this period. What is needed is a sound practitioner who thinks more about architecture than about ideas related to architecture."

The surface issue was a new two-year course in design fundamentals that Gropius and his younger architect colleagues thought essential. Hudnut (backed by some of the always-aggrieved regional planners and landscape architects) "thinks it largely nonsense." Conant urged the Corporation to underwrite it for the two years remaining before Gropius left and a new dean came. Hudnut rather coldly told Conant to feel free to set his own retirement in 1950; the next two years, with Gropius around, would be hard ones for him. Conant not too warmly asked him to stay on until his successor was chosen.[54]

The search for a successor to Hudnut came to a head in the summer of 1952. Gropius resigned in June ("in a bit of a huff," said Conant). Before he left he convinced the president that the outstanding candidate to succeed him—and to be GSD dean—was the noted Spanish architect José Luis Sert. That appointment was announced on January 14, 1953, coterminous with Conant's departure. Urban planning and landscape architecture would continue in a small way as the Department of City and Landscape Planning. But it was clear that architecture—and architectural modernism—would reign supreme in the late-twentieth-century School of Design.[55]

In March 1934, when the New Deal was in full flower, the Government department's Carl Friedrich proposed that Harvard establish an institute of public administration to meet the need for a "higher type of public official, especially in the Civil Service." The Corporation approved the general idea, but wanted a more modest program, a Committee on Public Service Training. "There is a strong objection," Conant told Friedrich, "to setting up any more institutes around this University." Times were hard, endowment money was short, and the Corporation wanted no more ill-funded permanent bodies. By the spring of 1935 the committee was up and running, and University of Minnesota professor Morris R. Lambie came to head the program.[56]

Then in November 1935 ("quite out of a clear sky" according to Conant), former Republican congressman and sometime glove manufacturer Lucius Littauer, of the class of 1878, offered to give $2 million for a graduate school of public administration. This, he thought, was "the best hope of avoiding disasters arising from untried experiments in government and administration"—a thinly veiled slap at the New Deal. Conant and the Corporation quickly accepted Littauer's gift. They had no desire for a separate school, but that was what the donor wanted.

Conant intended to draw on existing faculty to make up the staff: "it will be, therefore, less of a separate school than any other department of the University." Felix Frankfurter chimed in with some grandiose thoughts on the future school. He wanted it to field a graduate program not limited to the "civil service problem," but taking on as well public law, relevant history and economics, regulation, labor organization, colonial administration, science in the modern world, social welfare, criminology, public opinion.[57]

Conant set up a committee to advise him on how to train people for government service. One of its members, Dean Wallace Donham of the Business School, offered his thoughts on the subject—not surprisingly, thoughts suffused with the Business School approach to management. Conant asked President Robert M. Hutchins of the University of Chicago to comment, telling him: "We are confronted with the problem of whether indeed administration can be and should be made part of the University curriculum." Hutchins's reaction was "long and violent." He proclaimed: "We deny that apart from economic theory any body of systematic knowledge about social phenomena exists to be taught." What Harvard should do, Hutchins mischievously proposed, was leave it to Chicago and other parvenu institutions to turn out minor officials, and limit itself to the training of statesmen—perhaps through an institute of administration that focused on classical texts of moral and political philosophy.[58]

Conant feared that Hutchins was "all too right." But he was not ready to plunge into the dreamy world of Great Ideas. His preference was that the proposed school train students from Harvard's other professional schools in the art of government. Chicago's down-to-earth administrative law expert Leonard White emerged as the most promising prospect to head it. When Conant sounded out White, Hutchins (who probably thought of White as too grounded in practicalities) posed no objection: "I hope you appreciate my generosity. How about letting me have John Williams for Chairman of my Economics Department in return?" White accepted, but a day later changed his mind: "Further reflection convinces me [it is] impossible to leave my life work [in] Chicago".

The obvious next choice was Morris Lambie, recently brought to the Government department to train public servants. Littauer, "stunned" by White's refusal, regarded Lambie as "a substitute or second choice who does not arouse my enthusiasm." Conant agreed. Who, then? Someone not too practical or undistinguished but, on the other hand, not too theoretical. Finally John Williams, the Harvard economist whom Hutchins wanted in a trade for White, was the choice. This satisfied

Littauer, who thought that "the enormous results of the [1936] national election must result in a growing invasion of government into every aspect of our nation's life," thus making it more important than ever that there be well-trained bureaucrats. Conant diplomatically agreed on the need for superior civil servants, though he was not so certain that the future would see a big increase in "the heavy hand of government descending upon us."[59]

And so the Graduate School of Public Administration (GSPA)—Harvard's last new professional school of the twentieth century, if one thinks of the Kennedy School of Government as its offspring—got under way in 1937. From the first, GSPA struggled to develop an identity separate from the departments of Government and Economics and the Law and Business Schools, the sources of its faculty. But it could not develop a professional persona comparable to medicine, law, or even business.

HBS deans David and Donham of course wanted to see GSPA run on Business School principles. The Law School's Erwin Griswold and Henry Hart resigned from the GSPA faculty in 1942 on the ground that the school's program was "drastically deficient" in offering adequate training in public administration. It was, they thought, "an ineffectual enlargement of the Departments of Government and Economics rather than an effective and vital School of Public Administration." Hart was deeply skeptical of GSPA's emphasis on "policy." Instead, he thought, it should school its students in "patterns of administration." He came up with no less than thirty-three teachable categories—adjudication, rule making, office organization, delegation of authority, relationships with the legislature, publicity, budgeting, and, most basic of all, decision making according to law—the whole tied together by the case method of teaching. In short: why couldn't GSPA be more like the Law School? It couldn't because its strongest disciplinary ties were with the departments of Government and Economics. So the lawyers left.[60]

Nor did the initial expectation of a student body composed primarily of midlevel career bureaucrats pan out. Instead the thirty-five or so incoming students each year included a larger-than-desired number of newly minted college graduates, many working for joint Ph.D.s in Government or Economics, and a growing presence of foreign students.[61]

Harvard Treasurer William Claflin observed in 1944: "I suppose it isn't much of an exaggeration to say that the School of Public Administration is not really a separate school at all except in name." Overseer Charles Wyzanski, a member of the visiting committee to the school, worried about its raison d'être and the way it pursued its elusive goals. GSPA's reliance on invited lecturers like himself produced "a pleasant cross between a Chautauqua lecturer and a chat among the male dinner guests at a Washington party after the ladies have withdrawn," but little more than that. The school, he thought, should offer core courses on the philosophy and methods of public administration. Its goal should be "not less than to train the intellectual leaders of the permanent branch of that government which has now become the most powerful in the world." The rumor quickly spread that the overseers were investigating the school, and Conant had to calm down an overheated Dean Williams.[62]

Williams gave up the GSPA deanship and returned to the Economics department in 1947. Asked by Conant to describe the state of the school, he gave a picture conspicuously at odds with its initial goals. Almost all its faculty—"quite different from Mr. Littauer's original conception"—came from the Government and Economics departments. Very few of the predominantly American student body of sixty-three had previous government experience and many planned on teaching careers rather than government work. "We have faced the peculiarly difficult problem," Williams observed, "of giving to the school a sufficiently separate identity to meet the terms of Mr. Littauer's bequest and at the same time of providing a form of organization which would assure a strong faculty and enable us to carry on the kind of program we wished to undertake." How well had things gone? Williams thought the school's greatest contribution had been to make the Government and Economics graduate programs pay more attention to public policy, hardly a triumph.[63]

Government professor Edward S. Mason succeeded Williams as dean. He set out to make the school stronger, more independent. But the basic problems remained: small size; lack of a separate faculty (feeding the complaint that "the Littauer School is merely a rather luxurious convenience for some social scientists"); and the continuing dilemma of how to prepare students to enter a field which, unlike law or medicine, had no agreed-upon professional standards. When he left the presidency, Conant thought GSPA a "complete failure as an experiment in inter-faculty cooperation." Not until the very different world of the 1960s and 1970s did a full-fledged school of government get a new lease on life.[64]

# MANAGING HARVARD

Harvard's evolution from a Brahmin to a meritocratic university involved alterations in its governance as well as the makeup of its students and faculty. The cozy, we-happy-few atmosphere of the past began to give way to more professional administration. As a chemist accustomed to overseeing a laboratory and working systematically on problems, Conant rejected Eliot's and Lowell's style of running the University "largely 'under their hats.'" His close associate Calvert Smith recalled that he devoted the pre-World War II years to seeking "a modus operandi adaptable to the present size and complexity of the institution, which at the same time still fitted in with the traditional precedents."

But the embedded culture of a venerable, decentralized university made change difficult. Looking back in 1952, Conant concluded that administration at Harvard was not very different from what it had been in Lowell's day. He saw the central administration "as a sort of holding company responsible for the activities of some 20-odd operating companies." There were occasional ineffective attempts to draw up a Harvard organizational chart, but as Corporation Secretary David Bailey conceded, "the difficulties of setting down complex relationships in black and white have always prevented their being cast in final form." The University, he thought, "is suffering from acute decentralization."[1]

## Changing the Guard

For all his commitment to institutional change, Conant relied as did his predecessors on graduates of the College with strong institutional loyalties. When he assumed office in 1933, he brought in Jerome Greene to be both his and the Corporation's secretary. Until his retirement in 1943, this consummate civil servant was Conant's closest counselor on alumni and other matters. Greene's successor was A. Calvert Smith, a classmate of Conant. Smith had strong public relations skills, honed by several decades in the wilds of New York's investment and banking world, not unlike Greene's background.

Soon after he came into office Conant made John W. Lowes, the son of Higginson Professor of English John Livingston Lowes, his financial vice president. But it was not easy to work this new position into the existing Harvard structure, especially with power-seeking Treasurer William Claflin on the scene. When Lowes left for military service in September 1941, Conant told him his position would not exist when he returned.

The dean of Harvard University, created at the end of 1938 by the Corporation with the grand charge "to assist the President in exercising a general superintendence over all concerns of the University and to act for the President in such matters as from time to time the President may entrust to his care," was a no more successful attempt to modernize (that is, expand) the bureaucracy. Conant more succinctly saw the new officer as "a sort of deputy president." The first (and last) incumbent (1939–45) was George H. Chase, an amiable classical archeologist who welcomed important visitors, chaired an occasional faculty meeting when Conant couldn't make it, did scattered faculty consulting and opinion gathering: "altogether I am kind of a handy man."[2]

Legal representation was another growth sector by the eve of the war. Ropes and Gray was Harvard's traditional law firm; Oscar M. (Ott) Shaw handled most of the University's legal business. Ammi Cutter of Palmer and Dodge advised on labor relations policy and practice; George Rublee of Washington's Covington and Burling kept an eye on national legislation of interest to Harvard.[3]

By 1941 the president's office had "a loose form of staff organization." The "headquarters staff"—Conant, Greene, Lowes, and Chase, along with a dozen assistant deans—had moved in 1939 from University Hall (home to the president and his staff since 1815) to the lower two floors of Massachusetts Hall. The *Harvard Lampoon* described the building as "now filled with filing cabinets, Venetian blinds, Dodge McKnight water colors, unanswered letters"—a description that Conant thought had much truth. But while the administration had grown, it was not very bureaucratic. After all, this was a *brüderbund* of Harvard College graduates.[4]

What changed Harvard governance more than anything else was not managerial theory or practice but World War II. Conant threw himself into the work of running the government's Office of Scientific Research and Development. Harvard took a distinctly subordinate place in his life, though he dutifully commuted back and forth between Cambridge and Washington and kept involved in significant University matters. His true frame of mind is reflected in his diary entry for November 28, 1940, upon arriving in the capital after a long weekend of Harvard business in Cambridge: "WASHINGTON!"[5]

Enmeshed as Conant was in the world outside, he needed on-campus deputies. After Pearl Harbor, Secretary to the Corporation Calvert Smith kept an eye on many University activities, down to the level of campus mail delivery ("By common consent, the service is lousy"). A heart attack killed Smith in September 1945. A shaken Conant told a friend: "It is quite impossible for me to find anyone to replace him. . . . he fulfilled a function that was absolutely unique."Otherwise, Harvard's wartime housekeeping needs were met by the "Herculean labors and great skill" (and inordinate ambition) of Treasurer William Claflin." Conant did not, as he delicately put it, expect Claflin to continue to bear this burden after the war. He thought at first that the answer was to get a capable businessman as executive vice president, in charge of budgets and housekeeping and possibly fund-raising as well, reporting directly to the Corporation (and thus sparing the president the details). The treasurer would then be free to concentrate on Harvard's investments.

Conant came to agree with Corporation fellow Roger Lee that what was needed was "the appointment of a very top-flight fellow to be essentially a deputy president." To some degree Paul Buck assumed that role during the war. Conant got the Corporation to create the post of provost, which went to Buck as dean of the Faculty of Arts and Sciences (the original legislation required that the provost be the dean of FAS). His charge was to oversee the Arts and Sciences departments, the Graduate School, and the ancillary museums and research institutes, but not the professional schools. The able, forceful Buck was only too happy to relieve Conant of direct concern with Arts and Sciences. But there was a cost: Conant thought at the end of his presidency that he had become too remote from the faculty.[6]

## Housekeeping

Governing Harvard included the more humble but necessary business of managing what was in fact a large enterprise. Much of this had been in the hands of the faculty in earlier days. But growing size and complexity made more systematic administration a necessity. A small scandal erupted with the appearance in 1941 of an *Atlantic Monthly* article and then a book, *Pardon My Harvard Accent*, by William G. Morse '99, who had been a Purchasing Agent for the University since 1923. Morse portrayed a carnival of mismanagement. Biology chairman W. J. Crozier, he reported, bought five machine calculators, one for each floor, at $550 each so that he wouldn't have to climb the stairs. Crozier threatened a libel suit, and Secretary Smith suggested that Morse be fired.[7]

Meanwhile the number of managers—and bureaucratic turf wars—grew. John Baker of the Business School, the first (and last) associate dean of the University, took on some managerial responsibilities; Treasurer Claflin kept an eye on the bursar and the auditor; Business Manager Aldrich Durant (appointed in 1941) was responsible for the "housekeeping" side of the University and reported directly to Conant. Gladys McCafferty, director of personnel relations and the most highly placed woman in the administration, was up in arms over Durant deciding on secretarial wage rates in the president's office. Conant assured her that he had only asked Durant "to keep in touch with you in your work" and that "[n]eedless to say, I shall always be glad to see you personally and talk over any of your problems." But it was clear that (male) bureaucracy was taking command.[8]

By the end of World War II the need for professional management of the University's business operations seemed greater than ever. In 1946 Edward Reynolds, onetime president of Columbia Gas and Electric, became administrative vice president. He supervised the comptroller and the business manager, the personnel office and the Harvard University Press, and oversaw buildings and grounds, contracts, and other business operations of the University. Provost Buck warned Conant that he "would not ever want Harvard to forget that the ideal scholar is more important to the University than the ideal administrator" and that top administrators should not have salaries out of line with those of leading professors. But 1946 salaries stretched in fact from a professorial ceiling of $12–15,000 to Reynolds's and Claflin's $20,000 and Conant's $25,000.[9]

In the wake of the National Labor Relations Act of 1935, Harvard became the first university to enter into a contract with a national labor union, an AFL affiliate representing dining hall employees. But Harvard's workers (maids, maintenance men, and the like) voted overwhelmingly to stay in the Harvard University Employees' Representative Association, which the AFL (with some reason) dismissed as a company union.

Labor relations were relatively quiet during the 1930s. A largely docile, largely Irish workforce was disinclined to make trouble in hard times. But as the employment picture brightened from 1939 on, things got more tense. The cost of living kept rising, and unsettling rumors drifted up from Yale of difficult negotiations with John L. Lewis's brother—a "tough baby"—who led the CIO union there. "Lewis and his union," personnel director McCafferty reported, "are particularly sore at Harvard and the fact that an independent group is functioning here." Finally in late 1941 the Corporation voted a less than munificent dollar per week increase.[10]

Postwar inflation led to new labor trouble. Harvard's janitors and maids sought a wage increase in 1947. A raise of five cents an hour (the union wanted ten cents) required an unstaggering $35,000 a year for a workforce of 205 men and 437 women. But Reynolds held that hourly rates for janitors were among the highest in the Boston area. As for the maids' wage rate, he "cannot say it is the top," but there was little turnover or difficulty in hiring replacements. Not for some decades would changes in the composition and culture of the workforce significantly erode the almost feudal relationship between Harvard and those who worked for her.[11]

The University's pension policy also became more of an issue, as Social Security came into being during the 1930s and inflation and interuniversity competition raised the stakes after the war. In 1936 the Corporation changed the existing, rather penurious faculty pension plan to a Teachers' Insurance and Annuity Association (TIAA)-run system in which the University and the faculty member each contributed 5 percent of the latter's yearly salary. In 1950 a new pension plan reduced the faculty's contribution and raised the University's ante. And the Corporation took over from TIAA responsibility for investing retirement funds. The University Council, a rarely convened faculty body (its last meeting had been in 1919, when "it also argued inconclusively about pension plans"), was asked to consider the revised pension scheme. "The debate on this occasion," Corporation Secretary Bailey recalled, "was desultory, contradictory, and inconclusive, and the council adjourned without having established itself as a cogent means of canvassing academic opinion." Then as since, the tree of university bureaucracy was watered by faculty indifference.

Nonfaculty employees did not fare as well. The Social Security Act allowed universities to exempt employees from its unemployment insurance provisions, which Harvard readily did. But Treasurer Claflin warned in 1945 that there was much employee resentment over Harvard's noninclusion policy: "It may be difficult for universities to retain public good-will if they refuse to be progressive employers.... Social Security is here to stay. It seems only proper that universities should treat their employees as well as industry."[12]

Patents on faculty research and the overhead costs of burgeoning government contracts were other new items on the agenda of Harvard governance. In December 1933 the Medical School administrative board asked the University to prohibit its faculty from securing patents for discoveries in public health. The Corporation made this University policy in 1934–35, Conant noting that "we have on our faculty men whose sense of duty is so high that they will not neglect their university work and the advancement of true scientific knowledge for their own private gain." Professors were free to treat a patentable discovery as their own property. If it was the product of work done by arrangement with an outside company, the patent was a matter for negotiation between the faculty member and the firm. But if it had public health or therapeutic purposes, its patents must be dedicated to the public interest.

To accomplish this end, public health patents were placed in the hands of the Research Corporation, a non-Harvard, nonprofit organization established in 1912 to hold them and use their royalties to support scientific research. "[S]o far as I know," said Conant in 1935, "the University itself has never taken out a patent and I hope that it never will." But the growth of externally supported research during the war made patenting an important issue—and an increasingly tempting source of revenue. Dean Sidney Burwell of the Medical School thought that perhaps the time had come to regard patents "not only as a means of control but as a source of income for the University, and consider also the special case of products of therapeutic value in this connection."[13]

The most notable test of Harvard's patent policy involved the brilliant young chemist Robert Woodward. He got a Ph.D. from MIT in 1937 at the age of twenty and in 1941 became an instructor in Chemistry at Harvard. In 1942 the Polaroid Corporation took him on as a consultant: all in all, New Academic Man. With graduate student William Doering, another wünderkind, Woodward synthesized quinine in the breathtakingly short time of fourteen months. Polaroid did not intend to manufacture the new product: the military preferred the far less expensive substitute atabrine. But Woodward assigned several patentable applications to Polaroid, under which it could extend licenses to manufacturers. High-mindedly, Polaroid declared that at least half of the proceeds would go to further scientific research.

All well and good, but quinine clearly came under the Harvard rule against patenting public health discoveries for profit. Woodward claimed—and Chemistry chair Paul Baxter confirmed—that he had not been informed of that rule. The Corporation saw no alternative but to take Woodward at his word and to make sure that from then on a copy of the University's patent policy was sent to, and its receipt attested by, every Harvard appointee.[14]

In 1944, computer pioneer Howard Aiken recommended that the University's health-related patents policy be applied to all patentable discoveries by faculty members. The implicit academic social contract, he argued, should be made explicit: university-supported research time in return for giving up private profit. Those who found this unacceptable were at liberty to pursue their careers in private industry. Conant aide Calvert Smith had reservations: "Can you get good men on this basis? Isn't this the crux of the question?"[15]

Overhead costs on government contracts raised similar issues. The amounts involved in the first wartime contracts were so small that Harvard money advanced to meet operating expenses was insignificant. But by 1943–44 this added up to some $3 million. Harvard adopted the practice of crediting itself with 3½ percent interest on money advanced to meet the running expenses of government contracts and to charge this as "overhead." Any balance remaining at the end of the contract term would be returned to the government. The executive secretary of the Office of Scientific Research and Development, Irwin Stewart, suggested that Harvard ask for government money up front to cover its start-up costs, and arrangements to do so were soon worked out.

After the war, research overhead began its steady climb to the sunny uplands of today. By 1950 the overhead on government contracts met the costs of the office that handled them, 10 percent of the costs of the administrative vice president's office, small shares of the expenses of the personnel and comptroller's offices, and "space charges" ranging up to 12 percent for buildings and operations. In most cases a 15 percent overhead rate was in effect; on October 1, 1951, the great majority of contracts would be operating under a new 25 percent rate. Even so, "Navy cost inspectors have expressed the opinion that Harvard could justify a considerably higher overhead rate if it sought to recover all allowable expenses under the Navy's theory of overhead." Soon enough, Harvard took the hint.[16]

Harvard like other universities had a large research library (though one of unique size and quality). And like other schools it had a university press. Both sat in a no-man's-land between the academic and nonacademic realms: in function, close to the faculty and Harvard's intellectual life, but subject to the same budgetary and operations oversight as the rest of the University's housekeeping responsibilities.

The greatest of university book collections, housed primarily in imposing Widener Library, the Harvard College Library (HCL) was at the core of Harvard's claim to academic preeminence. Reinforcing it were dozens of more particular collections belonging to the professional schools and museums, crowned by the spectacular holdings of the Law, Medicine, and Business Schools. During World War II the Harvard College Library surpassed the New York Public Library to become the second largest in the nation, behind the Library of Congress. It was a measure of the library's importance that two of the most notable Harvard buildings erected during Conant's twenty-year presidency were Houghton (to house rare books and manuscripts) and Lamont (a library for Harvard College's undergraduates).[17]

For some time the librarians of Harvard College had been journeyman professionals, reporting to vigorous faculty directors of the University library. Conant went out after a man who could take on both positions. He found him in Keyes Metcalf of the New York Public Library, who ran HCL from 1937 to 1955. Conant initially saw Metcalf as equivalent to the dean of a Harvard school. But Arts and Sciences soon reasserted its special interest in the library. In 1949 HCL lost its status as an independent operating department and became an FAS budgetary unit.[18]

A nagging library problem, then and since, was to find room for its ever larger holdings. In the late 1940s and early 1950s the librarians of the major northeastern universities came up with a scheme for a regional deposit library. Conant wanted it to be in Stamford, Connecticut, not the more distant and expensive New York City; to be primarily for the deposit of older materials; and to cost far less than was proposed. But the plan, as would be the case with similar proposals for interlibrary cooperation in in later decades, fell victim to the sense of turf that appears to be part of the mystique of the book.[19]

Like so much of the University that Conant inherited, the Harvard University Press (HUP), founded in 1913, was not all it could be. It plodded along under Director Harold Murdock from 1920 to 1934, a reliable outlet for the faculty's publications but not much more than that. In 1935 Jefferson scholar-editor Dumas Malone became director of the Press. He published more important books, but ignored HUP's financial position (always shaky, especially so in a decade of depression and war).

Conant described Malone's performance with a candor unusual even for him: "Frankly, Mr. Malone has not made an outstanding success of his work.... [He] completely lacks the instincts which make for success in commerce. He has shown no ability to adjust his point of view to that of a practical publisher."[20]

Malone went off to the University of Virginia in 1943 to edit the Jefferson papers. It had been apparent to him for some time "that ... the Press was becoming increasingly a business rather than an academic organization," and he had no desire "to be the administrative head of a publishing house which approximated a commercial establishment." Little, Brown vice president Roger Scaife was induced in 1944 to take on the job for a stopgap three years. Meanwhile, Conant and the Corporation mulled over HUP's future. "Much as I feel if we were honest and brave, we would give up the press," he told Corporation member Henry James, "we cannot undertake the gruesome slaughter. The death agonies would drag out for many years because of the nature of our contracts and many commitments." So resignedly he proposed a $40,000-a-year subsidy for the publication of scholarly books: "It is at least honest academic bookkeeping, whereas running the Press in the red is an indirect subvention of different areas of scholarship without people knowing who does in fact get a free ride."[21]

That turned out to be a wise decision. Thomas J. Wilson, a recruit from the hermetic world of university presses, succeeded Scaife in 1947, and the Press flourished in the academic boom years of the 1950s and 1960s. The Corporation tried to assure better business management by creating a new board of directors responsible for that side of the Press, and Wilson settled in for a term that lasted until 1967—Conant assuring him in 1951 that any doubts as to the place of the Press in the life of the University were long since gone.[22]

Governance during the Conant years was at the gate, but not fully within the world, of the modern American university. It was not yet solidly bureaucratic, just as the faculty and the student body were not yet solidly meritocratic. But the one, like the others, had come steadily closer to that next stage.

## Spending: Finance and Budgets

Fiscally prudent Boston, like brash New York and provincial Philadelphia, is an American urban stereotype. And it is true that cautious investment and tight reins on spending were conspicuous parts of

Harvard's early twentieth-century history. Lowell was asked in 1931 how he had contrived to increase the salaries of full professors by 50 percent over the course of his presidency. His magic formula, he replied, was not to spend all that came in, "reserving something for extras." The result of this "constant trickle" was an increase in endowment from 18 to over 125 million dollars. "It was in this way," he explained—vividly revealing his order of priorities—"that Harvard was enabled to introduce the tutorial system without raising any money for the purpose, to buy land that has proved of great value, to construct tunnels for the supply of steam heat to all our buildings, and finally to raise the salaries of professors."[23]

In some respects Harvard's finances rode lightly over the Depression. On June 30, 1934, its stock holdings, a quarter of the endowment in 1929, were only 12 percent under book value. The endowment, which fell marginally from $128.5 million in 1933 to $126 million in 1935, rose to $143 million by 1940 and produced just under half of the University's income, a percentage not matched since. Harvard's relative financial well-being rested also on good management and reduced costs. An audit of the University's books in 1934 gave it generally high marks for its bookkeeping practices. College tuition, raised from $300 to $400 in 1928–29, remained unchanged despite the massive deflation of the Depression years. There was no falloff in the size of the undergraduate student body since Harvard drew overwhelmingly from the thin upper stratum of American life able to pay the full tuition freight. This was not accident but policy: the Corporation declared in 1935 that it did not "wish to have an undue proportion of scholarship holders." The result: tuition income rose from $1.1 million in 1927–28 to $1.6 million in 1933–34.

While employees' wages were slashed during the Depression, very different conditions prevailed for the faculty. The salary scale for full professors, $8,000 to $12,000 in 1931, stayed there until after World War II. For the tenured faculty the 1930s were a golden age of secure and substantial income and low-cost housing, food, travel, and servants. Nor did nontenured instructors get fired during the worst of the Depression.[24]

The full impact of the Depression on Harvard's finances came at the end of the 1930s and in the early 1940s. Diminished alumni giving and endowment yield pinched when the general price level began to rise, and America's entry into World War II led to a substantial (if short-term) reduction in tuition income. A million dollar deficit was predicted for 1944–45. But increased payments from the military, more civilian tuition because of a three-term schedule, and savings on faculty off to war work averted that horror.[25]

During the war, Treasurer William Claflin gave voice to an attitude that would become common in the postwar years: "It is my opinion that the financial security of Harvard University no longer is assured through its large Endowment.... Aren't we on the threshold of a return to fundamentals where the university must depend much more upon payments for services currently rendered than upon receipts from accumulated wealth?" He sought to increase the security of Harvard's investments, rather than search for large returns or substantial capital gains. Claflin told Conant in 1944 that 31 percent of Harvard's endowment in equities was about right: "It seems to me we should continue to keep a vital interest in American business. Possibly, this much talked of event, inflation, may become a real factor in our lives and our holdings of [common stock] ... may take on a rosier complexion. Regardless of market prices, when you look at the analysis of Income you will see that our equities have done well by us." At the same time, the University accepted a civic duty to buy government bonds regardless of income sacrificed.[26]

Paul Cabot's selection as treasurer in 1949 put Harvard's finances in the hands of an exceptionally skillful, classically prudent Boston financial man. Under his tutelage, and with the advantage of the research expertise of his State Street Investment firm, Harvard prospered during the 1950s and 1960s. It was in these years that the University's endowment pulled well ahead of its competitors. A highly conservative distribution policy contributed to Cabot's success: Conant constantly sought a larger distribution rate, and with equal consistency failed to get it.

Harvard's modern affluence was not yet evident in the immediate postwar years. Inflation and stagnant fund-raising made it clear that the school could not continue to rely on income from fixed tuition and slowly increasing endowment. An operating deficit of $800,000 ($300,000 in FAS), the largest ever, appeared in 1946–47. Tuition finally went up from its prewar $400 to $525 in 1948, $600 in 1949, and $800 in 1953.[27]

A triple squeeze hit hard at the University's resources. Costs escalated: even after adjusting for inflation, expenditures in 1951–52 were more than 50 percent greater than in 1940. Endowment covered a declining proportion of expenditures: 25 percent by 1950, half of what it had been before the war. And only about 8 percent of income came from the government, compared to more than 50 percent at MIT and other schools.

True, the College had loyal alums, and Law and Business were beginning to run successful annual fund appeals. But Harvard's central administration, the "holding company," suffered. The balance on its books shrank from $1.3 million on July 1, 1945, to $148,931 five years later. As the *Alumni Bulletin* dolefully put it, "The parent has apparently dissipated his substance in caring for the needs of his less fortunate children; if these cannot quickly secure the additional sources of income they require, or radically reduce their activities, something will have to be done to keep father in funds."[28]

Yet fund-raising languished. Conant had other interests; and Depression-era parsimony was still in the air. Over half the value of capital gifts received in 1950–51 came from three benefactors, one of whom (Gordon McKay) had died half a century before. Pressure mounted for deficit financing to maintain the level of the University's operations. Another option was to rely more on nonrecurring grants from foundations and the government. But to do so would threaten Harvard's vaunted independence.

Of course the University could stop expanding, could even shrink in size: have a smaller staff, offer fewer courses, close buildings. The new treasurer, Paul Cabot, chose instead to expand the University's endowment base and its earning power. By the end of 1951, 54 percent of the endowment was in equities; real estate, once a fifth of the endowment, was down to 1 percent. And a large cash reserve was on hand to enable the University to buy more stock when the time seemed right. But endowment growth depended most of all on new gifts, and that meant private donors, in particular, the alumni.[29]

## Getting: Fund-raising

When Conant entered office in 1933, there were about 64,000 Harvard alumni, clustered geographically in New England and New York and occupationally in business, finance, and law. This was the core group of donors to the University. But they felt neither flush nor generous during the 1930s. In 1936 novelist John R. Tunis analyzed the twenty-fifth anniversary report of his class of 1911: "Twenty-five years after graduation, one in six of us is trying to tell the rest how to invest money the other five haven't got!"[30]

Gift and bequest income dropped from $15.6 million in 1931 to a low of $2.6 million in 1935. In 1933–34 the largest donations were one for $2,000 and two for $1,000. Gifts for general purposes added up to a minuscule $4,556.96. Conant later recalled a Washington bureaucrat who, asked in 1933 what he thought about the future of privately endowed colleges, replied: "I didn't know they had a future."[31]

Conant warned in February 1934: "I don't propose to be in the money-raising business directly as I fear it is 'infra dig' [at] the present and also too time-consuming." But his desire for better students and faculty, and the approach in 1936 of Harvard's 300th anniversary, led him to seek new funds "[t]o strengthen the life of the university and increase the national scope of its effectiveness." He asked the departments and schools for estimates of their needs. The total wish list (with the Law School and the Arnold Arboretum not heard from) added up to a spectacularly unrealistic $81 million. On top of that were Conant's own preferences: $15 million endowments each for University Professorships and for National Scholarships. He decided to scrap everything except his own agenda: to focus, as he put it with unconscious irony, "entirely upon men." In his October 1934 "Proposal for a Three Hundredth Anniversary Fund," Conant sought $30 million for 40 University Professorships (a 15 percent increase in the tenured faculty) and 400 to 500 National Scholarships (totaling 20 to 25 percent of the undergraduates). This turned out to be a farcically unrealistic goal.[32]

Conant relied on a policy committee that included Paul Sachs of the Fogg Museum and Dean Wallace Donham of the Business School. Problems abounded. There was no great on-campus enthusiasm for fund-raising that served Conant's broad educational agenda but did little to meet what he called the "pork barrel" wants of Harvard's schools and departments. And he had somehow to engage an alumni body many of whom worried more about Harvard's supposed radicalism than its academic quality. (He wrote an admonitory memo to himself before giving a pep talk to the New York Harvard Club: "Confine yourself to exposition almost entirely.... *Don't mention*: Free speech; composition of Harvard College; justification of research; faculty.")[33]

Most harmful was the difficulty of fund-raising during the Depression, and the lingering Harvard sentiment that too overt solicitation just wasn't done. Conant told a prospective volunteer: "We do not intend to indulge in the usual drive with its attendant publicity, quotas, etc.... We all realize that these are desperate times to attempt to raise money, but a Tercentenary Anniversary is an occasion which we can not overlook." By June 1936 the campaign was in trouble. Corporation fellow Grenville Clark complained: "we have had going on a sort of campaign, but not a very well-organized one and without the usual features of a campaign, viz., a fixed date and fixed amount of money to be sought." Clark tried to tap rich New York alums and found that many who gave $10,000 to $25,000 in the 1920s could be counted on now only for $500 or $1,000.

And they "treated it from the point of view of a complimentary or sentimental gesture rather than a very serious enterprise."[34]

When Conant told Lowell of the problem of preparing appropriate remarks to the Alumni Association, his predecessor sympathized: "It is difficult to combine the collection and the benediction." But Lowell, who in the 1920s concluded that Harvard "needed no more money, and probably never would," was not helpful in tapping the Governing Boards. Conant's secretary Jerome Greene asked Lowell to exclude two sentences from the published version of his remarks to a Corporation-Overseers dinner celebrating his eightieth birthday: "Yet a reduction in large gifts would not be fatal to us now. We have enough for a great university if wisely used."[35]

After the Tercentenary celebration in the fall of 1936, the 300th Anniversary Fund drive desultorily dragged on. By the end of the year a generously based calculation was that $5.5 million—18 percent of the $30 million goal—had been raised. But only about 30 percent of this diminished amount met the campaign's objectives. One University Professorship was endowed by banker Thomas Lamont, who wanted someone to bring proper probusiness values to the teaching of economics at Harvard. About $1 million came in for ten National Scholarships, along with such welcome but by-the-way benefices as $350,000 from the Carnegie Corporation for the Dental School, $250,000 from the wife of Corporation fellow Roger Lee for research on law and medicine, and Nathan Littauer's multimillion dollar gift for a school of public administration. The failed Tercentenary campaign behind him, Conant sought to reshape Harvard fund-raising. He was "very anxious that we should increase the art of dignified publicity" and hired Arthur Wild, a Chicago newspaperman, as secretary of the University for information, charged to shake up the news office (a fixture since 1919). He also was on the lookout for someone "who knows something about the country west of the Alleghanies and also a little about the Eastern coast" to oversee alumni relations.[36]

Persisting amateurism plagued Harvard fund-raising. Annielouise Bliss Warren, wife of Harvard graduate and lawyer-scholar Charles Warren, wrote to Conant in December 1940 of their desire to leave a considerable sum to Harvard (eventually, $7.5 million for American history). A badly briefed Calvert Smith responded to "Mrs. Charles Beecher Warren" that Conant would like to meet with her. Mrs. Warren was "greatly taken aback at the way you addressed your letter to me. I really should have returned it—as it was not directed to me—but to another person—had I not seen that it was my address.... How in the world you thought that my husband was Charles Beecher Warren," whom she identified as "a bad Republican politician of the mid-west and a graduate of Michigan University," she "cannot imagine."[37]

In 1939 the Corporation's Committee on University Resources asked writer Archibald MacLeish to prepare a statement on the recent development and future plans of the University. As MacLeish understood it, the Fellows wanted "a kind of magnificent *Fortune* article in which ALL should be told beginning with the history of the University and ending with a check for twenty-five millions." That, he thought, was too grandiose a concept. What was needed was a more pointed appeal to potential donors, offering them a fresh reason for giving to Harvard. In September 1939, when World War II erupted, he found the theme he was looking for: the cultural and economic crisis of the West. "The Next Harvard," he quite inaccurately predicted, would be in the business of synthesizing knowledge: "The swing toward specialization and isolation of knowledge seems to have come to a temporary stop in our generation and the thrust is now in the opposite direction.... the present period in the history of the university is a period of integration. The perpetual frontier, the continuous expansion, are slogans of the past not of the present."

Conant called the essay a "masterpiece" that "caught exactly the spirit of what I hope is modern Harvard" (though he cautiously wanted to call it "The Next Harvard As Seen by Archibald MacLeish"). But as the war went on, MacLeish's words came to seem outdated and irrelevant. Conant was vexed over what to do with this "excellent but perhaps untimely presentation," and finally it was distributed only to the Corporation and the Overseers, not to the alumni at large.[38]

Discussions on postwar fund-raising began in 1943. They dwelt on a more unified approach, with the Corporation vetting the proposals of the faculties. Files were compiled on potential corporate and foundation givers, and on individual donors with special interests. Conant's office in September 1946 prepared a list of donors of $500 or more since 1933: 467 of them, a surprisingly high 52 percent, were not alumni. Long-standing bequests and unexpected benefices remained the most conspicuous features of the postwar fund-raising scene. In 1949 the final $8.25 million from the Gordon McKay Bequest for engineering became available. The bequest added up to $15 million, Harvard's largest gift up to then. Thomas W. Lamont died in 1948, leaving $5 million, blessedly unrestricted, to the University. This was the biggest single gift to date from an alumnus, an act of fealty rather than a donation for a particular purpose.[39]

Most promising of all were the large foundations: old standbys Carnegie and Rockefeller, and Ford, the new member of the club. Rockefeller traditionally supported science and education; Carnegie, the social sciences. Now they were inclined to fund promising research projects, or establish new ventures such as the Russian Research Center, rather than endow professorships and existing programs. Attention turned in the late 1940s to the newly formed and very flush Ford Foundation. Conant sought the advice and assistance of Corporation member Charles Coolidge, whose brother-in-law was a Ford trustee.[40]

In 1950 Ford gave Harvard $300,000 for "Research in Individual Behavior and Human Relations," to be allocated as the president saw fit. Conant asked the faculties for proposals. The Design School's dean proposed to explore human behavior and the science of urban growth. Divinity developed a sudden interest in the psychological fitness of men for the ministry. The Dental School sought to study the relationship of dental problems to the behavior and social relationships of patients, covering a "wide range of adverse behavior patterns all the way from incorrect muscle habits to major psychological aberrations [which] may appear as causative factors of dental difficulties." (This was serious business since, the school warned, a dental extraction could trigger not only pain, fear, shame, and guilt, but also "the profound response to loss of any part of the body which the psychiatrists call 'Castration Neurosis.'") Conant finally decided to allocate the money to the Business School, to be spent in two parts. One was a long-range program "to increase our scientific knowledge" of the impact of the newly isolated drug cortisone on personality, involving biochemists, clinicians, psychiatrists, and social psychologists and sociologists drawn from Business, Medicine, and Arts and Sciences. The other supported the Business School's research and training program in human relations.[41]

The quickening activity of the competition concentrated the Harvard fund-raising mind. Princeton launched a $57 million campaign in late 1946. Treasurer Claflin mused: "Princeton is certainly going to town"; Conant wanly enthused: "Quite a sum!" Yale (which would come up with an $80 million, ten-year plan in 1950), Columbia, Chicago, and Northwestern also were making noises. Conant said that Harvard was being forced by the competition "into a rather aggressive campaign."[42]

Meanwhile he sought to get the fund-raising reins more firmly in hand. In October 1947 he quietly made Wall Street lawyer R. Keith Kane his part-time special assistant (or, as Kane would have it, special advisor) to coordinate fund-raising. Kane and Conant quickly got down to business; said Conant: "Considering how intimately we are going to work, I suggest we go on a first-name basis at once and avoid formality!" Soon "Jim", at "Keith's" behest, went on the boards of the Sloan Foundation and the Sloan-Kettering Foundation for Cancer Research, "as this may be to the best interests of the things you and I have in mind," and dutifully addressed a New York Community Service Society banquet on Kane's suggestion because some twelve hundred to fifteen hundred influentials were present.[43]

In the summer of 1947 the faculties were asked to set down their most essential needs for the next ten years. The Arts and Sciences list alone added up to $55 million; the total was almost $110 million. Conant pared this down to $90 million, a sum he made public at the 1948 Commencement, but dared not set as a campaign goal: it was an amount that "we have no expectation of completing for a long time to come." Instead of a general campaign, he planned to support existing or soon-to-begin fund-raising efforts by the various Harvard faculties. The problem, he thought, was how to convince donors that the University really needed what it said it needed. It was easier for Princeton, in a financial hole, to plead poverty: "When you are running a $600,000 deficit out of an $8,000,000 budget, no one needs to be fussy about how the figures are laid down!"[44]

Kane planned to get the $90 million by an increase in yearly fund-raising from $7 to $16 million. In 1950 he optimistically calculated that half of the desired total had been raised; the other half should come by 1953. But the Korean War impeded fund-raising; by late 1951, $55 million had still to be gathered. And since this was not so much a campaign as a pastiche of faculty programs, there were large imbalances. The Business School was well on its way to meeting its $19 million goal. Not so Education ($300,000 of $7 million in hand), the Fogg Art Museum ($12,000 of $1 million), the Medical School ($6.1 of $19 million), the School of Public Health ($1.25 of $12 million), or Arts and Sciences ($4 of $19 million).[45]

The faculties varied widely in their fund-raising sophistication, from the well-organized Business School to the nonorganized Medical School. But their learning curve was climbing. The Corporation authorized a committee on research and development to oversee things in November 1948, and a month later the Harvard Foundation for Advanced Study and Research was created to seek funds for the Graduate School. Professional consultants Booz, Allen and Hamilton did a preliminary report on long-range plans for the Medical School; Kersting and Brown helped to draw up alumni lists and explore their giving potential for the Law School's new student dormitories; the John Price

Jones Corporation was engaged by the Divinity School. By 1949 Kane had a busy office of the special advisor in Cambridge, coordinating the campaigns of the Law and Business Schools and the Harvard Foundation, helping other faculties to gear up. Research and grant development sections hummed along, publications and gift development units were in the offing, charts and tables and reports flowed.[46]

As night follows day, Kane's bureaucratic power play created problems. In his scheme of things, Assistant to the President James R. Reynolds would report to James Conant's special adviser—that is, to Kane. Reynolds did not agree. Corporation fellow Charles Coolidge warned Kane against going too far too fast: "Except for out-and-out drives for specific objectives, the traditional method of raising any substantial sums for Harvard has been so personal that standard money-raising tactics must be applied with extreme care and much variation." Even Conant doubted the worth of the expensive reports and development plans that Kane brought in from consulting firms: "The chief value seems to be to instill confidence in outsiders that there has been some check on our administrative methods and a review of a very complex situation which confronts us in this area. Their recommendations are, I think, of very little value."[47]

Still, $26 million, the largest annual sum ever, came in from gifts and bequests in 1950. Giving to the major professional schools went up sharply. Of some concern was the fact that 87 percent of Harvard's bequests and gifts income between 1939 and 1949 came from 196 large donations, the other 13 percent from 145,513 smaller ones. But the scale of alumni giving would expand exponentially with good times and better-organized efforts in years to come.

In 1950 Kane resigned his advisory job to join the Harvard Corporation; a year later, on the advice of the Committee on University Resources, public talk of the Ninety Million Dollar Program ended. By 1953 it was only "of interest historically." A more effective assault on the Harvard fund-raising problem would come with a new president, and a new approach.[48]

## ～ 7 ～

# HARVARD AND THE REAL WORLD

Conant liked to recall that he became president of Harvard in the same year that Franklin D. Roosevelt became president of the United States and Adolf Hitler became chancellor of Germany. The University would feel the impact of what those others wrought. More than ever before in its long history, Harvard during the 1930s and 1940s found itself enmeshed in the affairs of the world outside.

## The New Deal, Refugees, and Nazism

Harvard had a presence in the early New Deal: but aside from alumnus FDR and Felix Frankfurter, not a very conspicuous one. The *Alumni Bulletin* took note of the absence of Harvard faculty in FDR's early Brains Trust, and in 1936 Conant estimated that only five or six out of a staff of eighteen hundred had been granted leaves of absence since 1930 to work for the federal government. A member of the Economics department, asked about Harvard's lack of visibility in Washington, replied: "We are standing by for the next New Deal!" Nor was the New Deal popular with a preponderantly Republican faculty and student body. In a *Crimson* poll in the fall of 1934, undergraduates opposed Roosevelt's policies by 1,149–704, the faculty by 141–50.[1]

Though Conant voted for FDR, he was careful to preserve the outward forms of political neutrality. But conservative alums soon had a Harvard New Dealer they loved to hate: Law Professor Felix Frankfurter, ace recruiter for the New Deal, eminence grise to FDR, Vienna-born Jew. A fund-raiser reported trouble with donors over Frankfurter in the spring of 1934, and Mrs. Charles Francis Adams, the wife of Harvard's former treasurer, "quizzed" Conant "heavily on whether or not Felix Frankfurter was a dangerous communist."

Conant had ample opportunity to polish up what became his standard response to radicalism-at-Harvard complaints: indignant denial that students were taught sedition and appeals to "the glorious tradition of freedom which is our heritage." When an alumnus wanted to know what the University was doing about indoctrination by New Dealish professors, Conant quickly changed the subject to academic freedom: "democracy is made safe only to the extent that a reasonably tolerant point of view is engendered in the people at large. The present witch-hunting attitude of the Hearst papers and, I regret to say, of some merchants and manufacturers of prominence does more harm to democracy than perhaps some of the worst conceived of the New Deal measures." Academic freedom was "no mere question of vested academic right" but "the most important thing ... that the universities can do for the country."[2]

Controversy flared when Harvard awarded an honorary degree in 1935 to Secretary of Agriculture Henry Wallace: not for his political views, Conant stressed, but for "his integrity of character and his unselfish devotion to the public good." Corporation secretary Jerome Greene optimistically hoped that "a pat on the shoulder to an honest idealist in the Cabinet" would not "be mistaken for a comment on the New Deal." After he was invited, Wallace gave a speech lambasting New England manufacturers, and the fat was in the fire. But he got his degree. And then there was That Man in the White House. FDR dutifully played the role of loyal son of Harvard, inviting his class of 1904 to celebrate their thirtieth reunion at the Executive Mansion. (A skeptical journalist noted: "They are going to get more food out of him than he got votes out of them.") It was both appropriate and unavoidable to invite Roosevelt to speak at the Tercentenary celebration in 1936. As we have seen, ex-president Lowell did what he could to tamp down FDR's speech—and FDR turned the manifest hostility of conservative Harvard to his own purposes.[3]

The real world's most poignant impact on Harvard in the 1930s came with Hitler's creation of thousands of displaced scholars. The curator of Harvard's Germanic Museum told Lowell in the spring of 1933 that he had been approached by the Schurz Memorial Foundation, which (with money provided by prominent New York German Jews) would pay for the salary of a refugee brought in as a visiting curator. Lowell's answer: "I told him that this seemed to me an attempt at using Harvard for purposes of propaganda, to which we would not want to lend ourselves; that if we invited anyone it would be trumpeted all over the country by

Jewish organizations that Harvard was calling one of these expelled Jews, and that other places ought to do the same." He responded in a similar manner when asked to sign a condemnation of the Nazis' anti-Jewish policies, already subscribed to by a hundred college presidents. He took it up with the Corporation and reported that their (and his) view was that while Harvard was committed to academic freedom, a protest against the acts of other institutions or governments posed problems: "We know only in part the actual conditions in Germany, and recognizing that we should not welcome criticism from German universities on the race question in America, we may well hesitate before making what will be taken as an official University protest against the acts of that country."[4]

An emergency committee sought to provide temporary aid to refugee German scholars. Fifteen major American universities were asked to invite displaced scholars: the committee and the Rockefeller Foundation would contribute $2,000 toward each man's salary. The requests went out in May 1933; almost every university joined; Harvard was conspicuously absent. Lowell brought the matter before the Corporation, which took no action. After he assumed office in September, Conant and the Corporation decided that Harvard would not participate in the aid program in the foreseeable future. And when Harold Laski asked about the appointment prospects of international lawyer Albert Mendelssohn-Bartholdy, Conant replied: "I feel that any temporary measures in such a case can lead only to misunderstandings and do more harm than good. We are therefore not following the lead of other universities in this regard."[5]

Conant explained to Corporation member Grenville Clark, who favored taking in a few refugee scholars, that the problem was one of both morality and money. It would be improper to pay a noted scholar less than Harvard's going rate of $8,000, or to keep him for only two years, the time span covered by the aid program: "A university employing a distinguished man enters into a moral commitment if not a legal one." Of course, if a department recommended a refugee scholar as a normal appointment, this would be quite acceptable. Indeed, two such recommendations were on his desk at that moment, "although they are not Jews." There was a larger issue as well: "the best chance of a brilliant, intellectual future in America is to give every opportunity for our young men to develop. If we fill the important positions in our universities with imported people of middle age, we are striking a blow at the prospects of every young man in that branch of academic life."[6]

But the refugee issue would not go away. DuPont's chemical director asked Conant about Max Bergmann of the Kaiser Wilhelm Institute of Leather Research: "our London representative states that he is decidedly of the Jewish type and raises the point that his appearance might react against favorable reception in many circles in the United States.... I would like to know how his personality impressed you and whether he is of the objectionable type." Conant had met Bergmann and knew his work well, but was "rather against bringing him over. I have fortunately had no occasion to make any official ruling in this matter, but my own personal feeling is that we shall not help the cause of American science any by filling up the good positions in this country by imported foreigners.... I think a deluge of medium and good men of the Jewish race in scientific positions ... would do a lot of harm. Needless to say, don't quote me too widely on any of this."

By the fall of 1933 Bergmann was in New York, a jobless refugee. Conant called him to the attention of the Chemistry department, but reported to Columbia chemist Hans Clarke (with whom Bergmann stayed on his arrival): "I doubt if we can use him." Clarke prodded Conant to lend his prestige to an effort to get Bergmann a post at the Rockefeller Institute: "the outcome of the ... plan ... lies almost entirely in your hands." Bergmann did wind up at Rockefeller, where this modest, generous man did much to vitalize research in his field.[7]

Viewed through the lens of history, these are chilling words and deeds. Even in the context of their time, they exude if not *schadenfreude* at least an indifference to what was happening in Germany. Lowell's response was of a piece with his general attitude toward Jews. Conant's was a more complicated reaction: a product of his strong scientific ties to Germany, a certain coldness of character, and his fixation on the self-improvement of American education in general and of Harvard in particular. Of course, it may be argued that the single best thing he could have done to strengthen Harvard in the 1930s would have been to seek out major refugee scholars, as Chicago and other universities did. And that is right; Conant was wrong. By 1935, 1,684 faculty members had been dismissed from German universities, including 5 Nobel Prize winners. Harvard eventually appointed some of them, but only after they had been vetted by a stay at another American university. And many of Harvard's émigré scholars—Walter Gropius, Marcel Breuer, Karl Vietor, Heinrich Bruening, Gottfried Haberler, Werner Jaeger, Richard von Mises, Sergei Gaposchkin—were not Jewish.

This is not to say that Conant had any use for the Nazi regime.

Harvard Law School dean Roscoe Pound was sympathetic to the Third Reich, and in 1934 he accepted an honorary degree from the University of Berlin, bestowed on him at the Law School with Nazi officials in attendance. Conant was present at the event, but refused to be photographed and was quoted by the press as saying: "I'm not in it. I'm not in it. It's strictly a matter between these two gentlemen. I'm not in it."

Much national notice attended an offer by alumnus and Hitler associate Ernst ("Putzi") Hanfstaengl of scholarships for Harvard students to study in Germany. A demonstration against Hanfstaengl took place at the 1934 Commencement. Criminal charges against two young women—Communist Party members who (shades of days to come!) interrupted Conant's Commencement address—were dropped after he interceded on their behalf. In September Conant and the Corporation turned down Hanfstaengl's transparently political offer. Conant told the would-be donor, "We are unwilling to accept a gift from one who has been so closely associated with the leadership of a political party which has inflicted damage on the universities of Germany through measures which have struck at principles we believe to be fundamental to universities throughout the world."[8]

Little was lost, much was gained by this step. Favorable reactions flooded in. But Conant responded more problematically when Harvard was invited to send delegates to Heidelberg University's 550th anniversary celebration in 1936. Heidelberg was thoroughly Nazified by now, and a number of English, French, and Belgian universities refused to participate. Conant thought they took "an unwise step in breaking diplomatic relations with the German universities. . . . If one allows political, racial, or religious matters to enter into a question of continuing academic and scientific relations one is headed down the path which leads to the terrible prejudices and absurd actions taken by scientists and universities during the World War." So "in spite of all that we feel about the terrible actions of the Nazi government," Harvard would be represented by Dean of Faculty George Birkhoff, who would be traveling in Europe at the time.[9]

Conant, Columbia president Nicholas Murray Butler, and Yale President James Angell initially planned to use the occasion to protest what the Nazis had done to academic freedom. Butler composed the text of a greeting to Heidelberg that pointedly took note of great Jewish figures in German culture such as Heine, Mendelssohn, and Spinoza (in fact, Dutch). Conant responded that he and Angell thought the draft "perhaps too gentle to accomplish the purpose that you and I had in mind." He wanted more stress on the fact that academic freedom was under siege in many countries. And he thought that three identical letters would be discourteous. Instead, he favored a joint statement deploring the Nazis to be released if the Heidelberg event became a celebration of Nazism; if it was strictly academic, then not.[10]

After the celebration, Angell wanted to publish their statement on the ground that the speeches of Science Minister Bernhard Rust and philosophy professor Ernest Kreick were particularly obnoxious. The *New York Times* damagingly reported that the foreign guests (including Harvard representative Birkhoff) were in accord with what was said. And indeed Birkhof ebulliently reported to Conant that he had sat at the head table between Rust and the rector of the University of Rome; that while Rust had made it clear that this was "a political affair with him," otherwise his remarks were in good taste; and that Hitler's propaganda minister, Joseph Goebbels, "spoke briefly and gracefully and appropriately." Conant conceded that Rust and Kreick "pronounced a lot of nonsense." But nothing, he thought, had been said that justified the publication of the joint statement, especially since Harvard was in the midst of its Tercentennial celebration and expected to host delegates and scholars from German universities. "I hope," he said, "that our celebration here may do a little something toward binding together the broken fragments of the world of learning." (As things turned out, all but one of the invited German scholars failed to show.)[11]

When Goettingen celebrated its 200th anniversary in 1937, Harvard initially agreed to send a delegate if one was available. Princeton president Harold Dodd suggested, on the basis of the Heidelberg experience, that Harvard, Yale, and Princeton collectively decline. Conant stubbornly insisted that there were two sides to the question, that he wanted to maintain contacts with the German universities "even if we dislike what they are doing," and acidly added: "you will undoubtedly receive paeans of praise from certain sections of the press and particularly from our Jewish friends in New York!" But Grenville Clark and others advised him not to accept, and finally Harvard joined with Yale and other leading universities in snubbing the ceremony (after its designated delegate found it inconvenient to attend).[12]

Conant's accommodationist stance eventually gave way in the face of the Nazi descent into ever greater barbarism. He joined with other university presidents in November 1938 to denounce the Kristallnacht assault on Jews. And the Corporation established twenty $500 scholarships for refugee students, provided that the recently formed Under-graduate Committee on Refugee Students raised matching stipends. The students set out to meet their $10,000 goal with a rally at Sanders Theater, with football captain Robert Green presiding and appearances by Massachusetts Governor-elect Leverett Saltonstall and singer Eddie Cantor (who promised to match the $1,500 pledged). They had their money by January 1939, and the first two recipients (one of them Karl Deutsch, later a prominent Harvard political scientist) were named. By the fall of 1939 there were fourteen refugee students, and by 1944 Dean of the College Chester Hanford was telling Conant how well they had turned out.[13]

The Corporation in December 1938 was still "unwilling to appoint refugees or to approve their engagement through the use of departmental appropriations or otherwise until a [national university policy toward refugees] has been formulated and adopted." And it still was Harvard policy in 1940 that no refugee would be appointed unless his department or school was ready to support him to the end of his working life. Despite this, the refugee presence steadily grew. Conant's responses to refugee issues became more empathetic. When a friend in industry asked if something could be done to admit the two children of an Austrian Jewish employee of his company, he saw to it that the College was accommodating.[14]

## Academic Freedom and Dissent

Academic freedom, most agreed, was one principle that Harvard honored more in the observance than in the breach. Radicals and dissenters—religious, political, cultural—were an honored part of the University's history. In 1936 American Civil Liberties Union head Roger Baldwin and the iconoclastic Corliss Lamont celebrated Harvard's "Heretics and Rebels" in the *Nation*, conceding: "If Harvard has been careful in selecting teachers with not too unconventional views, it has also adhered to high standards of academic freedom."[15]

Conant fended off old-grad squawks about New Dealers, Socialists, and Worse on the Harvard faculty:

It is my belief that the young students obtain their radical ideas not from their instruction but from the general source of contact throughout the country,—books, articles, and talk.... I feel there is more danger in having the students feel that the university is taking a closed door attitude and that our professors are reactionary old men who refuse even to discuss current problems than there is in the possibility of our disseminating radical doctrines.

Corporation members Grenville Clark and Henry James, and Overseer Thomas S. Lamont (whose brother was fellow-traveling Corliss Lamont) shared his disinclination to indulge in red-baiting.[16]

Free speech issues on the Harvard campus flared most brightly not during the depths of the Depression, or over the New Deal, but in the late 1930s and early 1940s. It was then, during the time of the Popular Front and the great debate over American intervention in World War II, that students and faculty became embroiled in controversy over the nature and extent of free speech.

Conant was not indifferent to radicalism on the campus. An aide of his quizzed Dean of the College Hanford on the National Student League: "is it a predominantly radical or communist body, and what sort of leadership does it enjoy from among our own students?" Hanford didn't know much about the League, "although it has been something of a trouble maker since its appearance at Harvard." Its primary cause was hostility to militarism. Otherwise it championed innocuous causes such as student aid, freedom of speech, lower tuition, and opening the library at night. As for its membership: "Brown, in spite of his name, I am certain belongs to the chosen race, as his mother's name was Cohen. . . . Robbins, Marks, Pavlo, Weiner, and Bronstein all belong to the particular racial group which in the past has more or less dominated this organization." On the other hand: Brown had gone to the Peddie School and was a good student; Robbins was one of the top scholars in the College, "a very able and interesting boy, who has had a hard struggle financially." In sum, "I cannot believe that the organization is doing any harm at Harvard. I do not believe that they are any more radical than the Liberal Club was in the early days of its history."[17]

A brouhaha erupted in the fall of 1939 over a request by the John Reed Society to use Sanders Theater for a speech by American Communist Party head Earl Browder. Permission initially was granted. But then Browder was indicted by a federal grand jury. The administration urged the John Reed Society to withdraw the invitation, on the ground that someone under indictment should not be able to use the University as a sounding board. Predictably the society refused; predictably, Corporation Secretary Jerome Greene rescinded the authorization to use Sanders.

Predictably, protest followed. Five hundred students signed a petition demanding that Browder be allowed to speak, and senior faculty members criticized the administration. The Corporation upheld the decision "until the basis of Harvard's practice in granting free use of its buildings for meetings has been further explored by a special committee of the Corporation meeting with members of the Faculties." Grenville Clark headed the committee, and he was ready to let Browder speak. But Conant was adamant, and of course the Corporation backed him. It issued a statement reiterating Harvard's policy "to favor free expression within wide limits and not to restrict or interfere with such expression, however unorthodox, controversial or unpopular." As for Browder, he would have to wait until his trial was over.

ACLU head Roger Baldwin mildly chastised Conant. Harvard, he said, was expected to be more liberal on free speech issues than other universities. Conant conceded that he might have been wrong, though it was a time when such decisions were hard: "Whether or not Father Coughlin should speak on anti-Semitism is more debatable. Probably even there we should let him in, though I should hate to do it." Perhaps some new mechanism—a joint faculty-student committee to pass on such matters, say—would emerge, and the administration and the Corporation "can then wash their hands of the affair."[18]

In October 1940 the *New York Times* titillated its readers by reporting; "Harvard Descends on Student Communists; Burns Five Thousand Soviet-Hitler Pamphlets." What really happened was that a watchman stopped a student who was distributing circulars headed "Keep America Out of Imperialist War," the Communist Party line of the Nazi-Soviet Pact era. It was against the University's rules to distribute handbills in the dormitories outside of the regular mail delivery system. No disciplinary action was taken against the student; indeed, the chief effect of the incident was to liberalize the rules for the distribution of material in the dormitories. Patrick O'Dea, state secretary of the Massachusetts Young Communist League, regretted that "an over-zealous individual should have infringed upon the regulations of the University" and praised Harvard for seeking to maintain academic freedom.[19]

Harvard had another chance to preen its free speech feathers when the Philosophy department invited Bertrand Russell to give the William James lectures in 1940–41. Russell had been asked a decade before and refused; now (perhaps because he was anxious to get away from wartime England) he accepted. He had a record of trouble with American colleges and public officials over his penchant for appearing with women not his wife. Boston politico Thomas Dorgan, whom Conant called "an anti-Harvard fanatic," threatened a public suit over this affront to the morals of the community. Pressed on whether or not to withdraw the invitation to Russell, the Corporation showed a half-profile in courage: three members favored rescinding, three were for no action. Conant, the seventh member, held that the appointment should go ahead. He saw the issue more as the independence of the University than freedom of speech. (Besides, he had made discreet inquiries, and there was no likelihood that Russell would withdraw.) So the Corporation supported him, Russell came, and Harvard and the Commonwealth survived.[20]

## Harvard Goes to War

After war broke out in Europe in September 1939, Harvard like other American universities was caught up first in the great debate between isolationists and interventionists, and then in a war effort that led to a new scale of government-sponsored research and loyalty-security issues. In this sense, Conant's abrupt transformation from harried educational leader to powerful and confident science statesman exemplified the larger story of Harvard's changing relationship to American society.[21]

The war's first major impact on Harvard life was the debate over whether or not the United States should aid the Allies. In this Conant took a major part. His relative indifference to the Nazis' Kulturkampf against German Jewish academics melted away when the issue became that of England's—and Western civilization's—survival. He gave up his fixed policy "never to join any group or movement not connected with education or Harvard and never to sign a petition or associate myself with a committee." At one point he toyed with the idea of leaving the Harvard presidency so that he might more freely speak up for American involvement.

Conant was an early and conspicuous member of the Committee to Aid America by Defending the Allies, the chief interventionist counterfoil to the isolationist America First Committee. Like-minded faculty led by philosopher Ralph Barton Perry formed American Defense: Harvard Group, an interventionist organization that included historian Arthur Schlesinger, Law School dean James Landis, and Radcliffe president Ada Comstock. Harvard College librarian Keyes Metcalf gave the organization a vacant Widener room to use as its headquarters. Challenged by Corporation member Henry L. Shattuck on the propriety of this arrangement, Conant conceded that normally it would not be allowed. But "I submit that this group is *sui generis*. . . . While it is definitely a propaganda organization, its aims have been endorsed publicly by the President of the University and at least one member of the Corporation. If and when a similarly distinguished group can show a similar record, we might be worried about the precedent involved." Shattuck went along.[22]

Harvard had its share of isolationists, cutting across the Right-Left dividing line of the 1930s. Left-wing faculty members Harlow Shapley and F. O. Matthiessen adopted the Soviet line in the wake of the Nazi-Soviet Pact favoring neutrality. In this they were joined by conservative colleagues such as philosopher William E. Hocking and political scientist Arthur N. Holcombe, still smarting over America's entanglement in World War I. But the collapse of France and the Battle of Britain decisively shifted the weight of Harvard opinion to the interventionist side. Math A—mathematics was required for most military-related course work—leapfrogged over History 1, Government 1, and Economics A to become the most popular undergraduate course.[23]

In 1940 Conant began to go regularly to Washington as a member of the National Defense Research Committee (NDRC), which oversaw the government's burgeoning support of scientific research for military purposes. Soon he was in Washington two to three days a week, "avoiding Cambridge as a whole." Then he was asked by Vannevar Bush to play a major role in recruitment for the greatest scientific effort of the war: the Manhattan Project, to construct the atomic bomb. He talked at first of resigning the Harvard presidency, but found that the prestige of his Harvard position was a good security screen for his ultrasecret work. There was some grumbling in the Corporation over Conant's absence. But Fellow Henry James assured him that he was in fact doing more for Harvard by being in Washington: "As head of the University, you ought to be in close touch with what is going on in these rapidly moving times, and your Washington connections very much help you to do that."[24]

By the winter of 1943–44 Conant was deep into expediting the Manhattan Project. Corporation fellow Henry L. Shattuck gathered "that there are reasons why ... it is most important that for some months to come you give as much time as at present to affairs in Washington." Perhaps the Corporation should "examine our organization with a view to determining whether something more might be done, through further delegation of authority or otherwise, to hold things together, and to take a look ahead?" (In other words, should Conant step aside?) But Conant continued as president, and after Paul Buck became provost as well as dean of faculty, presidential governance at a distance became easier, though never easy.

After the war, Buck concluded that despite his "playing 'hooky' on such an extensive scale," Conant had kept on top of major Harvard matters. "There were times when you lost track of the complex details of our war calendar or wondered without knowing the reason why so many Radcliffe girls were sitting on the steps of Harvard Hall." But "[o]n the matters that really counted you somehow kept yourself informed and in some manner found the time to exert leadership." Buck confessed that

> there were moments during the past four years when I doubted this and I fretted and grew impatient with a restlessness that was emotional rather than intelligent. That was a failing on my part for which I now offer apology. There was never a time when I did not understand perfectly and accept the conditions on which I had to operate during the war years.... My reason has always been loyal to you, but I make my confession that emotionally I have on occasion been quite a fretter.[25]

Becoming deeply enmeshed in wartime efforts had long-term institutional consequences. World War II did much to heighten major American universities' sense of their importance. Opportunities for Harvard's faculty to serve in government abounded, far more than in New Deal days. Harvard scientists got $31 million in NDRC grants during the course of the war; only MIT and Cal Tech got more. Conant met in June 1941 with "Wild Bill" Donovan, the flamboyant lawyer who "appears to be organizing some kind of a super-intelligence service for the government," the Office of Strategic Services (OSS). Donovan asked him to help find people "with penetrating intelligence and a wide point of view and some historical background" to assist in the enterprise. Conant thought that members of the prointerventionist American Defense: Harvard Group "would be just the people they were looking for," and a clutch of his colleagues were recruited by Harvard historian William Langer, who ran the OSS research division.[26]

Much of the research activity of the University, particularly in the natural and social sciences, was given over to the war effort. Among Harvard's major contributions:

> Howard Aiken and his Computation Lab developed data-gathering techniques that enabled the Navy and the Air Force to conduct operations over vast areas.

The Underwater Sound Laboratory, run by professor of Applied Physics Frederick V. Hunt, adapted radar to submarine warfare and developed a torpedo that did much to eliminate German submarines from the Atlantic in 1943.

The Radio Research Laboratory had over six hundred scientists working on defenses against radar detection, and with the even larger MIT Radiation Lab made Cambridge the center of radar research.

The Psycho-Acoustical Laboratory was home to groups headed by Leo Baranek and S. Smith Stevens, who worked on the improvement of communications under noisy conditions (in warplanes, on battlefields).

Psychologist Harry Murray developed methods, widely used by the military, for evaluating people through personality testing.

A Chemistry group headed by Louis Fieser developed the petroleum jelly (napalm) used in the devastating firebomb raids on Japanese cities.

Anthropologist Clyde Kluckhohn did work on Japanese psychology that was reputed to be an important factor in the decision to drop the atomic bomb.

Conant, as well as Harvard scientists George Kistiakowsky and E. Bright Wilson, played important parts in the making of the atomic bomb.

This is, from a later perspective, in some respects a chilling record. But to the Harvard generation of that time, some seven hundred of whose students, alumni, faculty, and staff died in service, it was an important contribution to the winning of a war that had to be won. A young soldier alumnus wrote to Corporation Secretary Smith in September 1945, after Conant's role in the Manhattan Project became public: "Thank Jim for bringing us back to our homes."[27]

On December 8, 1941, the day after Pearl Harbor, a crowd of six thousand gathered in Harvard Yard to hear Conant and others commit Harvard to victory. What followed was a flurry of change so extensive that it came to be known as "The Hundred Days," Harvard's equivalent of FDR's First New Deal in 1933. Wartime Harvard was dominated by Army and Navy personnel taking intensive programs run not by the University, as Conant had wanted, but by the military. Formations marched to class, martial music wafted over the Yard. While the freshman class entering in September 1942 was the largest ever, some 1,400, most of its members expected to have only a brief spell at the College before going to war. The College in 1943 had 500 freshmen and 582 upperclassmen, well under a third of its prewar level. Hard hit, too, were the Graduate School (down from 1,034 to 172), Law (from 1,248 to 72), and Medicine (from 527 to 68). All but the Law and Graduate Schools made up for the deficiency by military enrollees: a more than compensatory 6,000 to 7,000 in sum.[28]

Conant readied the Corporation to expect wartime deficits and thought it prudent to expect that the war would last through the 1944–45 academic year. Since he expected the postwar years to be "hardly likely to prove a favorable environment for privately endowed institutions," perhaps the war would help in the necessary effort "to lower the standard of living here at Harvard." Most of all, Conant feared that the wartime dispersion of the faculty into other lines of work would heighten the temptation to fill permanent positions with available but inferior men: "The present low state of Yale (and I do not refer to her athletic record) and relatively high state of Princeton can be directly traced to the policies in force at the two institutions when the [1918] armistice was declared—I have personal knowledge of the departments of physics, chemistry, and mathematics in this regard."[29]

As things turned out, government compensation for housing and training military personnel eased the University's financial crunch. And in a multitude of other ways this complex, time-encrusted institution adapted to the exigencies of war. About 400 faculty members—20 percent of the total—were in full-or part-time war service by the fall of 1942. Those remaining voted unanimously to go on a year-round schedule, with no increase in salary. This meant a twelve-week summer term and the admission of freshmen in June and February as well as September. The professional schools were authorized for the duration to admit students who did not have their B.A.s. Conant thought in 1942 that "the real educational job for the next two or three years" would be to teach science and math, and wondered how Buck "will succeed in making professors of humanities into instructors in mathematics." Asked in 1944–45 to list the year's contributions to knowledge of the History and Literature program's faculty, chair Elliott Perkins disarmingly reported: "Nobody made any, certainly not the chairman."[30]

## Postwar

Gearing up for the war's end was in many respects a replay of the wartime effort, driven by a similar sense of mission, of normal ways set aside to meet a national need. From 1943 on, attention turned to how to deal with a flood of returning veterans. "For the moment," Conant declared, "I think we had better concentrate all our thoughts on this transitional period, as it may well last until 1950; and what the world will be like in the 1950s ... God only knows!"[31]

By the fall of 1944 the end of the war seemed imminent. Conant in a lengthy report to the Corporation laid out a program of postwar demobilization and return to normal University operations in 1949. What might be expected in the wake of the war were not hard and straitened times, as once seemed likely, but "a period of great activity and prosperity for Harvard and every other so-called educational institution." Money and students should be in good supply. The challenge was to select the best students and educate them quickly, all the while recruiting the necessary staff without mortgaging the future "by unwise commitments." On schedule, the Japanese war ended in time for the fall 1945 semester. Harvard's postwar enrollment peaked at 12,500 in 1947, 50 percent over its prewar attendance level. Veterans were 75 percent of the total, 30 percent of the students were married—a new student body, indeed.[32]

The rapidly changing character of American society, and the coming of the cold war, gave an unexpected turn to the postwar history of Harvard. There was no return to prewar normalcy after a reconversion hiatus, but instead a continuing evolution of Harvard (and American universities at large) from prewar parochialism to the nationally, indeed internationally, engaged multiversities of the late twentieth century.

Portents abounded. The number of foreign visitors to Harvard in 1945–46 was markedly higher than before the war. Harvard continued in the nation's service after the end of hostilities, as the cold war and the growing welfare state ensured a continuing flow of government-sponsored research. In 1949 the Faculty of Arts and Sciences approved a new sponsored-research policy. Government contracts were welcome, though not for classified (secret) work. And as much as possible, the University's "core activities" should not depend on transient government subventions.[33]

Academic freedom became a more contentious issue as the cold war burgeoned. Conant predicted in 1946, "I think we are in for a period of witch-hunting and red-baiting, and I shall be very glad to do what I can to help in bringing sanity into the situation." Soviet sympathizer Harlow Shapley came in for much alumni criticism, with no discernible effect on his Harvard standing. And Conant staunchly defended his wartime colleague J. Robert Oppenheimer from suggestions that he had Communist sympathies: "a more loyal and sound American citizen can not be found in the whole United States."[34]

In 1948 the *Chicago Tribune* ran a series of articles with provocative headlines ("Red Poison Tinges Ivy of Harvard," "Harvard Pupils Get Red Poison in Subtle Doses.)" When Massachusetts attorney general Clarence A. Barnes proposed a bill banning Communists from employment in the state's public and private schools, Conant, Corporation fellow Henry L. Shattuck and Harvard Law professor Zachariah Chafee forcefully (though unsuccessfully) opposed it. Roger Baldwin of the ACLU called Conant's statement to the state legislative committee considering the bill "magnificent.... It was in the best Harvard tradition, and in what I have come to know also as yours." In his January 1948 annual report, Conant warned of the need to protect universities from outside interference with academic freedom at a time of "armed truce." And in June he spoke of the "Hebraic-Christian tradition" and the need for a nation of immigrants to tolerate diversity. As if to underline the point, the 1949 Commencement honorary degree list included black political scientist Ralph Bunche and Robert E. Lee's biographer Douglas Southall Freeman.[35]

All very Harvard, and commendable. But World War II had significantly altered Conant's—and the University's—relationship to public affairs. As the tensions of the cold war rose, Conant did not hesitate to cast Harvard's lot on the side of anticommunism. He became a member of the National Council of the Committee for the Marshall Plan—"in joining I am thus making one exception to a standing rule not to sponsor anything!" And in 1950 he joined the Committee on the Present Danger, the cold war counterpart of the 1940–41 Committee to Defend America by Aiding the Allies. He may well have had in mind the Heidelberg incident of 1935 when he and the presidents of Yale, Princeton, Columbia, and Cornell recalled their delegates to the 600th anniversary celebration of Czechoslovakia's Charles University after the Communist takeover of that country: this despite assurances from literary scholar F. O. Matthiessen, back from a visiting lectureship there, that the Communists were not interfering with academic freedom at the university.[36]

As the cold war deepened and red-baiting grew, Conant's response reflected his immersion in the security-obsessed wartime scientific effort. Asked in 1949 what he would do if a prominent member of his faculty walked in and announced that he was a Communist, Conant replied: "I would send for a psychiatrist." He publicly stated that a Communist Party member should not belong to a University faculty. (A *Crimson* survey revealed that students by two to one did not object to Communist faculty members; the faculty by a similar margin did.) Conant's position on this matter was strongly criticized then and since, and he appears to have regretted it later in his life. In any event it was all but a moot issue at Harvard: no member of the faculty was publicly identified as a Party member, and Conant had no desire to find out if any in fact belonged. The worst of times was yet to come: particularly in the spring of 1953, when Joseph McCarthy and his subcommittee descended on Cambridge. Conant's hostility to faculty members who took the Fifth Amendment to avoid self-incrimination suggests that it was just as well that not he but his successor Nathan Pusey faced that onslaught.[37]

These policy tempests arose in a University many of whose members believed that their institution had a uniquely important part to play in matters of national, indeed international, importance; in short, the Harvard hubris so evident in the latter half of the twentieth century. When Conant appeared on *Time*'s cover in September 1946, the *Alumni Bulletin* thought it "might be taken as public recognition of Harvard's new position of responsibility in the community of the world.... Together, University and war-wrought scholar are coming out of the tower to meet the world face to face."

World War II in fact enormously strengthened Harvard's standing. "America's Great University Now Leads the World," *Life* magazine proclaimed in May 1941. That image was fed during the war by events such as the secrecy-enshrouded appearance of Winston Churchill ("Mr. X") to receive an honorary degree in early 1944. FDR, who during a Harvard visit in 1941 was honored by Oxford emissaries, wrote to Conant: "It is rather a nice thought that he received his Harvard degree in the same place that I received my Oxford degree."

Harvard's postwar commencements confirmed its sense of institutional manifest destiny. Its honorees in 1946 included the commandants of America's triumphant armed forces: Dwight Eisenhower of the Army, Chester Nimitz of the Navy, H. H. Arnold of the Air Force, Alexander Vandergrift of the Marines. Douglas MacArthur, now the American procurator in Japan, was also on the list. He couldn't attend that year, but assured Conant that when he got back to the States, "one of my most immediate obligations and one of my most pleasant will be to report at Cambridge to you for honorary enrollment at that great seat of learning and culture." (He never made it.)[38]

A year later nuclear physicists Enrico Fermi and J. Robert Oppenheimer were recognized for their contribution to the Allied triumph, as was General Omar Bradley. Poet T. S. Eliot represented an Anglo-American high culture that in its way was also one of the victors of the war. Honored, too, was Secretary of State George Marshall, who declined to deliver a formal address "but would be pleased to make a few remarks in appreciation of the honor and perhaps a little more": remarks that in effect launched the Marshall Plan for the reconstruction of postwar Europe. By the time Conant left and Pusey came in 1953, the culture of the University had shifted decisively from the snug Brahmin insularity of "here at Harvard" to the prideful self-regard of an institution that saw itself as "an engine of power and responsibility."[39]

# PART II
## "An Engine of Power and Responsibility":
### *1953–1971*

## ∽ 8 ∾

# NATHAN MARSH PUSEY
# AND THE AFFLUENT UNIVERSITY

On New Year's Day 1953, James Bryant Conant made known his intention to resign, effective January 23—all of three weeks later. In June the Corporation announced his successor: forty-six-year-old Nathan Marsh Pusey, the president of Lawrence College in Appleton, Wisconsin. Why this wholly unexpected choice? Who was Pusey, and what did he offer Harvard?

## Pusey

He came from an old New England family transplanted to Iowa, graduated from Harvard College in the class of 1928, earned a Harvard Ph.D. in Classics in 1935, went off to stints of college teaching at Lawrence, Scripps, and Wesleyan, and in 1944 returned to Lawrence to become its president. This was a small, highly regarded college in Wisconsin, founded in 1847, with strong New England roots. Pusey did well there, recruiting able faculty and taking a public stand against Appleton native Joseph McCarthy when that sinister figure began to hack his way through American politics. All respectable enough; and, it appears, sufficient to secure Pusey a place on the short list of candidates. But enough to make him Harvard's twenty-fourth president?[1]

Lawrence board chairman William Buchanan reported that Pusey had done little fund-raising for the college, and noted his cool personality and lack of popularity with students despite his manifest skill as a teacher. Another member of the Lawrence board doubted that Pusey had the administrative ability required by the Harvard presidency: "He is stubborn and uncompromising." More weighty was Carnegie Corporation vice president (and Harvard president wannabe) John Gardner's "serious doubts that he would have the particular leathery quality required to take on the great administrative job which Harvard is."

But positive views substantially outweighed these reservations. An Episcopal church source reported: "Pusey is stubborn at times but it is always a stubbornness on matters of principle and not with respect to his biases." Another who knew him well said: "He is all mind, character, and perception. He is no promoter.... He is as firm as iron. He always succeeds in getting what he wants done.... His religion is top flight 100 percent all wool and a yard wide Episcopalian." Reassuring, too, was Provost Paul Buck's swing from doubt to endorsement: "I still think he may have a problem in handling the robust deans of our professional faculties. But he is unquestionably able, resourceful, and strong."[2]

No other widely supported candidate emerged. Buck was an obvious alternative, and certainly was available. But his lack of a Harvard B.A. and too close identification with Conant counted against him. (Conant tried unsuccessfully to talk Buck out of his candidacy, resignedly reporting in his diary: "Paul Buck will run. Got nowhere. 20 years of failure on this front!") And it is part of Harvard lore that wunderkind McGeorge Bundy (he was thirty-four in 1953) would have gotten the job if he had gone to Harvard College.[3]

But the qualities that the Corporation saw in Pusey made him its favorite early on and led to an uncontentious—though typically helter-skelter—decision. (Fellow Roger Lee said later: "I am sure our procedure was as disorganized as possible.") Diplomat and Overseer Joseph C. Grew told Pusey that reading his Lawrence reports was "like hearing a symphony because you brought out in them the themes which many of us older alumni realize are so terribly important, and often so terribly lacking, in school and college and the universities today, including the welding of individual personality and character, intellectual curiosity, religion, sane athletics, and all the rest of it." Corporation fellow Keith Kane was drawn by the fact that Pusey's "primary concern is college education and he can be counted upon to concentrate on trying to improve the place. His preoccupation is with teaching and not with pure scholarship."

Thomas Lamont later told Pusey: "It may have appeared to you that the Corporation acted with almost indecent haste but we have seen you and liked you and we have checked you out rather exhaustively.... we felt we couldn't do any better for Harvard by further investigations." Pusey started with a great fund of good will, Lamont said, "and the added help of the drama implicit in choosing a Harvard man, born in the Midwest, the head of a small Wisconsin college, a man especially interested in college education and in the liberal arts tradition, and a Classicist. But we didn't choose you for these particular qualifications.... We chose you because you were the best man."[4]

In a nutshell: Pusey wasn't Conant. The most conspicuous dynamic in the Harvard presidential selection process—get someone as unlike his predecessor as possible—had once again kicked into gear. This was true of the choice of Eliot in 1869, of Lowell in 1909, of Conant in 1934; it was true of Pusey in 1953.

Pusey's predecessor may have come from a marginal strand of the family, but at least he was a Conant and had gone to Roxbury Latin School. Pusey went to Cedar Rapids High School. (He reported that when he told a Boston matron of his secondary education, she rolled her eyes heavenward and sighed: "Oh, well. God is everywhere.") He had little interest in a public life: no dashing off to Washington or immersion in grand national policy for him. He was a classicist, a humanist, far indeed from Conant's high-powered world of Big Science. He was strongly religious, a devout and active Episcopalian layman; Conant had little taste for religion. Pusey was an able teacher and effective administrator rather than a scholar: he published no book before his Harvard presidency. A friend said, "Nate made it the hard way, on points"; Corporation fellow William Marbury once told him: "Nate, you're the last of the small college presidents." If Conant's presidency reflected the assertive, meritocratic spirit of FDR's New Deal, then Pusey's embodied the affluent, confident mood of the Eisenhower and Kennedy years.[5]

So in the fall of 1953, "without a line of any kind on his face," Pusey took the helm of one of the world's leading universities. In sharp contrast to Conant's "hundred days" rush to put his stamp on Harvard, Pusey had little in the way of immediate plans for the future, other than to strengthen the Education and Divinity Schools. Indeed, he spent his first six months as president getting to know the large and complex institution—in particular the major professional schools—now in his charge.[6]

Who he was, and what he said, deeply pleased many alumni. A "sturdy Bostonian of the old school" told Corporation secretary David Bailey: "Mr. Pusey believes in God and he goes to football games. This is progress enough for the present." The first material expression of this regard was John D. Rockefeller's gift of a million dollars to the lagging Divinity School fund campaign. He told Pusey: "Your profound belief in the underlying importance of the spiritual life promises to have far-reaching influence on education in this country."[7]

Pusey's religiosity would come to be a major source of vexed relations with the faculty. He set himself "to try at least to do more to promote interest in religion here than seems to have been done in recent years. It will be a source of considerable satisfaction to me if Harvard can make a helpful contribution in this area, to meet what seems to me to be a very widespread and urgent need." One of his earliest public pronouncements decried the low state of religion at Harvard, a declaration that led to some faculty and alumni unease. Pusey found it necessary to assure one correspondent, "we have no intention of lessening our devotion to 'the discovery, preservation, and dissemination of learning' in any field. The aim is simply to do this a little more successfully in the field of religion than has recently been the case." When a (Jewish) alum told Pusey that his Harvard College years were marred by the lack of some larger purpose, the president replied: "Your account of your experience at Harvard and the subsequent misgivings you had concerning it so exactly parallels my own that yours might have been a letter that I had written. I hope very much that in time my influence here will enable the University to make gains in the direction you have indicated."[8]

In the midst of the highly secular Harvard of the fifties, with an expanding Jewish component of both students and faculty, stood Memorial Church: an oversized version of the classic New England Congregational place of worship. It began to be used for weddings in 1932, and two were conducted by rabbis in 1945 and 1949. But Willard Sperry, chairman of the Board of Preachers and dean of the Divinity School, wanted Jewish weddings stopped, ostensibly on the starkly nontheological ground that the ritual wine glasses stepped on by the grooms left the church carpet cut and stained. When a Jewish undergraduate sought permission for a wedding in 1953, Sperry suggested that a Unitarian minister conduct the (presumably glass-free) ceremony.[9]

In April 1958 the *Crimson* editorialized against restrictions on Jewish weddings. Pusey replied that the University's policy had been consistent for years, broken only by an occasional unauthorized deviation. What had been accepted, or ignored, before ("don't ask, don't tell"?) now flared to white heat. Many of the faculty's heavyweights petitioned to open the church to all faiths. Pusey at first hoped that "a judicious committee can examine the role of the Memorial Church, making sure its Protestant character is preserved but by some means providing a more appropriate place for the observance of the private services of non-Christians." Feeling the pressure of faculty outrage, the Corporation quickly agreed to allow "private services" of any denomination, and Pusey concurred. But this did not mean that he approved.[10]

Pusey's religiosity and the Memorial Church incident is a major source of the view of him as a president monumentally out of synch with faculty and students. Indeed, his faith was at the core of his character: in his baccalaureate address at the 1958 Commencement he spoke of "the enlightenment and joy of belief." But it hardly defined his presidency. The Memorial Church episode made it clear that the faculty was too secular (and too Jewish) for creedal Christianity to be University policy. And despite the expectations of the Corporation and traditionalist alumni, Pusey did not reverse but rather facilitated Harvard's evolution into the meritocratic University of Conant's dreams. Like Conant he believed that "developing an educational elite" was "just what we have to do!" He would later say that "liberal education had become a god for me"—linked to, but not identical with, the Christian God in which he believed.[11]

Harvard's modernization showed no sign of being impeded by its religious-minded president; quite the contrary. No architectural traditionalist, Pusey presided over a building program that sprinkled the campus with modernist works. Nor did he romanticize small town America. Recommending a family friend for admission to Smith, he said of her: "She is completely free from any of the bad effects, the cheapness and crudeness, which teenage life in small towns can impart to people." And on academic freedom in the cold war-McCarthy era and the education of women (Lawrence was 40 percent female; Pusey, unlike Conant, had a daughter), he was markedly more enlightened than his predecessor.[12]

Pusey's presidency was dominated not by his devotion to the College, the humanities, or the church, but by the headlong growth and ever more meritocratic culture of Harvard's faculty and students. In one sense what happened was an ironic gloss on the expectations of those who chose him and perhaps of Pusey's initial expectations as well. Another view—and Pusey himself confirms this—is that he arrived, took a long, hard look at what had happened to the University during the sixteen years he had been away from it, and came to the eminently rational conclusion that his task was not to return Harvard to an idyllic past, but to make it an academically stronger University by making it a more affluent one.[13]

In 1963 Pusey prepared a volume of speeches and writings drawn from his first ten years as president. He borrowed from Emerson to call it *The Age of the Scholar*—hardly a call for a return to a traditional student-focused liberal arts college. His book complemented rather than took issue with *The Uses of the University*, by the University of California's

Clark Kerr, delivered first as the Godkin Lectures at Harvard and which popularized the concept of the "multiversity." (Kerr said that Harvard was the model he had in mind.) Pusey was not overly impressed by Kerr as an educator, but he had no argument with the other's view of the modern American university. A *Crimson* article, "The First Ten Years," summed up Pusey's tenure as of September 1963: growth and prosperity; success.[14]

This would not be the case in later years. The Harvard dynamic during the 1950s and 1960s was that the triumphs of the meritocratic, affluent University inexorably bred adversarial antibodies. Success created its own discontents. An institutional drama of hubris (in part justified, to be sure) followed by nemesis (severely limited, to be sure) would be played out on the banks of the Charles in the late sixties. When Pusey departed from the Harvard presidency in 1971, his sense of disappointment to some degree echoed Conant's mood in 1953. But its source was different: not an inability to attain his goals, but rejection by his institution. Conant left because he was bored and frustrated; Pusey left because he had lost the confidence of faculty and students.

## Fund-raising

Harvard's most notable feature during the 1950s and 1960s was its growing affluence: relative, in comparison to other universities and even to its own not exactly straitened past; absolute, in the scale of the money it raised. Getting—acquiring the unprecedented funds that came to the University during those decades—and spending—deciding how to manage and use that money—was at the core of the Pusey presidency. Meritocracy and money conjoined to produce the University that approached Conant's ideal.

It is no small irony that Conant, a man defined by his educational ambitions, never found the resources for more than their token implementation, while Pusey, whose academic goals were more modest, oversaw the fund-raising, hiring, student aid, higher faculty salaries, and new buildings, labs, and books that kept Harvard at the forefront of American higher education. While its age and prestige made Harvard America's richest university, it was by no means clear when Pusey came in that this would continue to be the case. Smaller Yale raised $13.6 million in 1951–52, as against Harvard's $11.7 million. In 1958, 50 percent of Yale's alumni gave $22.7 million; 36 percent of Harvard's graduates gave $14.9 million. "More significant than the differences between Yale and Harvard, however," warned fund-raising head James R. Reynolds, "is the evidence of recent competition from other universities": MIT, Chicago, Cornell, and Columbia in particular. He could have added the top state universities—Michigan, California—and Stanford, casting a shadow as yet no larger than an outstretched palm.[15]

Pusey at first concentrated on meeting the $6 million goal of the Divinity School campaign that had begun (and languished) under Conant's unenthusiastic oversight. Otherwise things went on as they had in the late Conant years: low-keyed, scattershot, unplanned. The deans of the several schools were responsible for designing and carrying out their own campaigns. The Overseers' Committee on Resources met once a year, but did little to define or coordinate Harvard fund-raising.[16]

Government grants began to matter during World War II, and continued to do so after it ended. Between 1940 and 1954 these added up to more than $55 million, some 16 percent of Harvard's operating expenses. But they fell off in the mid-fifties, to only 8 percent of the normal operating budget. Foundations filled some of the gap. Those old standbys Rockefeller and Carnegie were joined now by a lusty new arrival, the Ford Foundation. Proposals to tap this Maecenas poured in from every part of the University. After an Asian trip in 1961, Pusey hoped that Ford would finance Harvard training of Asians: "If there is any one institution in the world today whose name is synonymous with 'university' it is Harvard." Between 1950 and 1958, Ford Foundation gifts to Harvard added up to a not inconsiderable $16 million, 13 percent of the $123 million in capital and current gifts raised by the University from all sources.[17]

Despite these new sources of revenue, it was evident that piecemeal, decentralized campaigns would no longer do. The breakthrough to a new concept, and level, of Harvard fund-raising came with the Program for Harvard College (PHC) of 1957–59. In its scale—$84.5 million, twice as much as any university previously raised in a campaign—and in its concept, putting together a variety of needs (buildings, faculty salaries, scholarships) into a single fund-raising effort, this was something new. Even more innovative was the ingenuity with which the needs of a modern research university were packaged in a form attractive to the alumni.[18]

The Program for Harvard College took shape in late 1955 and early 1956, when the postwar economic boom, which had been dampened by the Korean War, got under way again. FAS dean McGeorge Bundy played a decisive role in the planning that gave form and substance to the campaign. He told the Board of Overseers in the spring of 1954 that the College needed to become 10 to 15 percent larger, with an infrastructure sufficient to at least maintain its quality. He thought that a $40 million campaign would do the job. Corporation fellow Thomas Lamont also wanted a large fund drive: projects such as new undergraduate houses were (literally) concrete ways of engaging alumni interest in the future of the College and could help justify less tangible capital needs. Meanwhile Bundy advised Pusey to assure the faculty that the real priority of the campaign would be higher salaries, not buildings.[19]

Donald David, former dean of the Harvard Business School and an eminence grise in Harvard fund-raising, proposed that the goal be $50 million. One member of the Resources Committee found this amount "quite startling even to this old banker accustomed to astronomical figures." But heavy hitters—New York moneymen Thomas Lamont, Keith Kane, and George Whitney, Clarence Randall of Inland Steel—agreed on a large campaign to meet the needs of the College. Lamont observed that the school had been "badly disrupted first by the effects of war and then by the stresses of the GI bulge." The theme of restoration and upgrading was an appealing one. Pusey disarmingly admitted that it had taken him three years to figure out what Harvard was all about; now he was ready to seek "from the alumni and friends of Harvard by far the largest sum ever asked of private means for the support of undergraduate education."[20]

By the time the Program for Harvard College was formally announced at the June 1957 Commencement, ambitions had soared even higher: to $82.5 million, to be raised by June 1959. Half was earmarked for construction and half for strengthening undergraduate education (including $10 million for a revolving student loan fund): objectives sure to warm old grads' hearts. A flock of new faculty chairs, less loudly trumpeted, also was part of what Bundy called "a great general drive for funds to strengthen the basic financial structure of the College and its Faculty."[21]

Fund-raising went into high gear in the 1957-58 academic year. Pusey spoke on September 19 to more than a thousand campaign workers over a closed-circuit telephone hookup; he traveled 10,000 miles to "kickoff" dinners across the country; he went on the television show *Meet the Press* to try to explain to a national audience why Harvard needed $82.5 million. Getting into the spirit of things, the Harvard Band planned at one football game that fall to form into Pusey's name (with a '$' instead of an 's'), re-form into "$82.5," and then play "Put Another Nickel In— In the Nickelodeon." Advised that the "$" touch was in poor taste, the band (in those halcyon days) agreed not to do it.[22]

"The Case for the College," a Harvard-crafted radio show, was broadcast by CBS during prime time on March 28, 1958. Nielsen ratings indicated that 11.2 million homes tuned in for at least part of it. The popular Ford Foundation-supported television show *Omnibus* did a segment on Harvard (including a four-minute history of the University by Samuel Eliot Morison, a contender for inclusion in the Guinness Book of Records).[23]

Nevertheless by February 1959 the PHC was behind schedule. About $60 million was in hand, but the last $22.5 million would be difficult to secure. Part of the problem was the program's operating head, New York investment broker Alexander M. White, who fell ill in the summer of 1958. There was a paramount need for a successor who could secure the large gifts necessary to put the campaign over the top. By November the program had its man: H. Irving Pratt, heavily moneyed son of a Standard Oil family, a New York money manager, yachtsman, and bon vivant who got along well with the well-heeled and was not reluctant to ask them for money.[24]

P-day—Commencement Day, June 5, 1959, marking the formal end of the Program for Harvard College—came, and the campaign had $67 million in hand: no mean sum, but $15 million shy of its goal. In what would become standard university fund-raising practice, the program was extended. And with considerable drama, the $82.5 million goal was reached in the early days of 1960. Pusey and Pratt convinced alumnus Harold Vanderbilt that the success of the program would raise the fund-raising sights of every major university in the land, including the one that bore his family's name. With a flourish, Vanderbilt wrote to Pratt at 3 P.M. on January 6: "In precisely 1 hour, I will be precisely 75½ years old" and turned over securities sufficient to yield the $2.5 million that took the program over the top.[25]

The Loeb Drama Center, two new residence houses (Mather and Quincy), and a new behavioral sciences building (William James Hall) were the PHC's most significant physical additions to the campus. A substantial increase in undergraduate loan and scholarship money moved Harvard along the way to need-blind admissions. The Program enabled Harvard to take the lead in an across-the-board increase of faculty salaries and made possible an expansion of the faculty that added significantly to the school's academic heft. Between 1954 and 1969, Harvard established more endowed professorships than in all of its previous history.[26]

The PHC left its mark not only on Harvard but on American higher education at large. Between 1956 and the fall of 1958, 134 colleges and universities embarked on campaigns totaling three-quarters of a billion dollars. Princeton raised $58 million in the late fifties, and MIT corralled almost $100 million between 1960 and 1963.

Another legacy: a new, more aggressive approach to fund-raising. The Harvard Alumni Fund had long been the domain of old grads whose emotional ties to the College outweighed their efficient solicitation of gifts. Its chairman, Harvard poetaster-booster David McCord, was popular, sentimental, and not much of a manager. Corporation fellow Thomas Lamont thought that in the wake of the program the time was ripe to do something about Harvard's "deficient and inglorious record" of alumni annual giving. The Alumni fund's supporters spoke of it as "a uniquely Harvard institution"; the only unique thing about it, Lamont snorted, was its ineffectiveness. The more energetic James Rousmaniere replaced McCord, and the Fund raised $1.3 million in 1961–62; it hoped to reach $4 million by 1970.[27]

The ink on the Program for Harvard College checks was barely dry before the next campaign hove into view. The Medical School was anxious to get on with significant fund-raising, after lying low until the PHC ran its course; the Business School was also champing at the bit. A pecking order in the Harvard barnyard had to be established. Medicine had the clear priority, and in 1959 a $58 million Program for Harvard Medicine (PHM) got under way.

When Pusey spoke in 1963 of the need for some $200 million more in endowment and capital expenditures over the next ten years, Overseer Thomas Cabot wondered: Is there any ceiling to the quest for excellence? Was it just a matter of racing other leading universities for supremacy, with no thought to the real needs of the nation? The implicit answers then, and since, were no, there isn't; yes, in part, it is.[28]

During the five years between 1960–61 and 1964–65, Harvard raised $207 million, comfortably outstripping its chief competitors. Its edge came not from large individual or corporate gifts but from bequests, the fund drives of its schools and faculties, and foundation and government support. In October 1964 the Harvard endowment (which stood at $442 million in 1955) passed a billion dollars. This had real news value. But it also smacked of undue affluence, and the University's public relations people made much of the fact that Harvard barely held its own when it came to meeting necessary expenses.[29]

Major new sources of income, the federal government and the big foundations, reached the apex of their munificence in the 1960s. Federal grants provided more than a quarter of annual income: 30 percent of the Faculty of Arts and Science budget, 57 percent in the Medical School.

Ironically, Harvard's decentralization was one reason for its fund-raising success. Its schools and departments—loaded with entrepreneurial adepts, the fittest survivors of the age of meritocracy—proved to be highly successful at securing their share (and more). And the major faculties turned alumni fund-raising into a fine art. The Law School's Dean Griswold crowed over the $865,000 raised from almost a thousand donors in 1963–64 and recalled how hard it had been to induce Conant to let the school establish a separate annual alumni fund. The Harvard College Fund brought in $3.5 million from former undergraduates in 1968–69, and the Business School raised $1 million. Medicine still lagged, but was catching on fast. Education (which raised a risible $14,000) and the ill-fated Harvard Foundation of the Graduate School of Arts and Sciences underscored the truths that there was no money in teaching and little more in professors.[30]

In the spring of 1964 the central administration polled the deans on their needs (or wants). The response, as always, was so outsized that the Corporation dropped any idea of a centralized campaign, and decided to let each faculty go forward on its own—after it got the approval of the center. In the following year Pusey cleared a package of $160 million. This included a $49 million Program for Science in Harvard College, $30 million for the School of Public Health, $15 million each for Education and Law, $11.6 million for Design, $6 million for International Studies, and $12 million to $13 million for a variety of lesser claimants. Some were successful, others were not. But together these programs set the tone for Harvard fund-raising: keyed to the needs of the schools, ambitious in scope, assuring that at any moment some part of the University was in campaign mode.[31]

## Spending

Harvard's affluence rested on managing as well as raising its money. The treasurer had considerable discretionary power in investment and distribution policy. His staff was small: two assistants, a few secretaries. He relied heavily for investment advice on the State Street Research and Management Company. By 1967 about half of State Street's staff of fifty worked full-time on Harvard investments. The New England Merchants' Bank handled the purchase of investment securities. The Harvard Trust Company, one of the two leading Cambridge banks, was the depository for the University's incoming revenue; the other, Cambridge Trust, managed the funds kept on hand to meet expenses.

"The trick," said the *Alumni Bulletin*, "is to keep the Harvard Trust balance large enough to keep the Cambridge Trust balance from getting too small, while skimming off as much as possible to the Merchants Bank."[32]

Paul Cabot, Harvard's treasurer from 1948 to 1965, effectively combined an aggressive investment strategy with conservative money management. In his early years as treasurer he increased Harvard's common-stock portfolio from 36 percent to over 50 percent of the endowment, and sold off real estate, mortgages, preferred stock, and long-term bonds. The biggest stock holdings were blue chips: IBM, Texaco, Gulf Oil, General Motors.

Cabot was also the almost parodic exemplar of the cautious, capital-conserving Boston money manager. Before him, endowment earnings went to the faculties as they were received. Under Cabot they were not committed until the beginning of the next budget year. And his income estimates erred invariably, and solidly, on the side of caution. The result was a reserve fund—"unapportioned income on general investments"—that by 1956–57 had come to equal a year's endowment income. This meant that Harvard, alone among American universities, could make up its annual budgets on the basis of endowment income already at hand. Cabot equated this condition with "that of a commercial corporation, which achieves earnings one year and distributes them in the form of dividends the next." When unapportioned income piled up to $60 million in 1959, it was gradually reduced to $14 million through distributions to the schools and faculties. Conant's view of the central administration as a holding company for the University's faculties continued to prevail.[33]

Fiscal prudence at the center went hand in hand with Harvard's classic each-tub-on-its-own-bottom budgetary rule. Early in his presidency, Pusey questioned the efficacy of that principle. Senior Fellow Charles Coolidge instructed him in its whys and wherefores. The deans had considerable leeway over the allocation of funds, but they were expected to live within their budgetary means. Under this system, the head of each budget unit had an incentive to plan for the future and be economical: what he saved went into his credit balance, not to a general University pool ("I should hate to have the job of convincing Dean Griswold of the Law School that some of his tuition money should be diverted to the Medical School").[34]

As the University grew in size and wealth, budgeting became more complex. By the early 1960s Harvard had 50 departmental and school budgets, with 2,300 subdivisions. Bundy worried in 1958: "we are still in the grip of Parkinson's law, and our staff increases faster than our infantry; we have a widening group of research ventures dependent on annual support from outside—is this the discharge of a clear duty or a somewhat chancy growth based on nothing better than faculty imperialism and the availability of soft money? Are we as frugal as we think, and as efficient, or could we save a lot of money as friendly critics tell us?"[35]

Borrowing—not to be thought of in the time of Brahmin Harvard—began to be touted as an appropriate financing tool in an era of large construction and unstable prices. Treasurer Paul Cabot opposed this for reasons both of prudence and morality. The great majority of alumni, he thought, favored "in no way hocking the future." One form of borrowing justified others, and then off you went down the slippery slope, "robbing the future to take care of the present." None of his predecessors over three centuries had borrowed, and Harvard was in excellent financial shape. As for borrowing at the lower than market rate, made possible by new government programs, and then lending at a higher rate (a common practice by the 1990s): "To my mind that is nothing more than running a margin account."

FAS dean Bundy, driven by the need to meet competition from other universities and respond to the faculty's desire for growth, did not "quite have Paul Cabot's religious opposition to borrowing," though he agreed that 1957 was not the time to do it. Economist Richard Cooper, then a second-year graduate student, took Cabot on in the *Harvard Alumni Bulletin*, arguing that borrowing in an inflationary economy was an acceptable way of shifting part of the financial burden of higher education to the larger community. His, as it turned out, was the voice of the University's fiscal future.[36]

While the market value of the Harvard endowment more than doubled between 1955 and 1965, expenditures went up even faster. The shortfall was covered by government money for research projects—from almost none in 1948 to $47 million (36 percent of the University's expenses) in 1965–66—and by robust tuition increases (from $525 in 1948 to $1,540 in 1962). With its impressive inputs and powerful constraints, Harvard's budget was in balance or better until the late 1960s.[37]

## The Economics of Research

Bigtime research was a notable feature of meritocratic Harvard, and it brought its own financial and fiduciary problems. Disputes over the University's patent policy, an old bone of contention, became more frequent as potentially profitable research grew. Plasma pioneer Edwin J. Cohn and the Corporation agreed in 1953 that some of the patents emerging from his work on blood fractionation would be assigned to the Protein Foundation, which would charge users for the cost of production but not impose royalty or licensing fees. That reflected the established Harvard ban on profit from health-related discoveries. But Financial Vice President Edward R. Reynolds thought that "these agreements which Edwin negotiated failed of their purpose and in fact have proven to be self-defeating," in that they discouraged expensive development work. He warned that the no-profit policy would hamper development for practical use.[38]

In 1960 a faculty committee reviewed the University's patent policy and endorsed the traditional approach. But pressure from increasingly market-minded scientists was on the rise. By the mid-1960s, another review was in order. The increasing interconnections of the University with industry and government and the burgeoning profit potential of scientific research required more detailed conflict-of-interest guidelines. Division of Engineering and Applied Sciences dean Harvey Brooks thought that Harvard's patent policy was "thoroughly unsound and incompatible with its obligations to society." The University needed to see to it that the benefits of its research served the public. If the only way to do that was to allow the faculty (or the University) to benefit from its discoveries, then so be it. But his was an outlier view. Most faculty opinion appeared still to favor the existing policy. Perhaps another committee might consider the matter.

In 1971, on the eve of Pusey's departure from office, Brooks again questioned Harvard's patents policy. Pusey's resigned reaction: "Two or three times during my years as president the Fellows have spent hours, days, weeks—even months, as I recall—on questions of patent policy, and I am not especially eager to indulge again in my final weeks. But someone has to take another look." Perhaps a small committee.... [39]

By the mid-1950s research supported by outside sources had grown enormously, but within a framework and a set of assumptions unchanged from simpler days. The "project" approach that the major foundations relied on in the early 1930s, and then the "contract" approach of the government during World War, II, as Administrative Vice President L. Gard Wiggins noted, were "both essentially the same in providing short term support for rather precisely defined activities." The problem was that they had little to do with the principles or objectives of the University.[40]

In the fall of 1953 Harvard had about a hundred government contracts, sixty-five of them in the Faculty of Arts and Sciences and almost all of the others in the Medical School. "Research," Pusey observed, "used to be a kind of professorial avocation. Now [it is] a major joint enterprise with teaching." Yet compared to other universities, Harvard's dependence on research money was modest: just under 20 percent of total income in 1958–59, compared to Cal Tech's 83.6 percent, MIT's 78.2 percent, Chicago's 55.5 percent, and Princeton's 54.1 percent.[41]

In the mid-fifties Harvard adopted the view that the government should meet all of the overhead costs of funded research. Other schools, it grandly argued, might agree to share overhead as a way of getting more grants. But Harvard had no such need; and besides, the quality of its faculty was sufficient justification for it to be so compensated. In practice the Defense Department and the Atomic Energy Commission already paid almost all indirect as well as direct costs. The problem lay in the medical and biological sciences, where only a small proportion of indirect costs were met by agencies such as the Public Health Service and the National Science Foundation.[42]

Government rules kept changing, a fecund source of conflict and concern. In 1963 the Public Health Service, which ran the National Institutes of Health, tightened the administration of NIH grants, leading to much worry over the greater government control and extra University paperwork that this entailed. Then in 1965 the Bureau of the Budget required that indirect costs be based only on the salaries and wages of the project's participants. Faculty members doing abstract and theoretical work, who used most of their grants for their salaries, could claim a disproportionately high share of indirect costs. This (in Harvard bureaucracy-speak) would "obviously create certain intangible but definite psychological overtones," that is, reduce the appeal of applied research.

The administration told the faculty that it would have to conform to the new rules. By accepting the principle that tenured faculty salaries were part of the University's contribution to cost sharing, Harvard was drawn more deeply into a web of federal regulations. In the spring of 1966 the administration asked that the faculty fill out monthly (for professors, quarterly) "Effort Reports" and that time/attendance records be compiled for staff whether or not their salaries were reimbursed from federal funds.[43]

That breached the always fragile dike containing the faculty's sense of its prerogatives. Mathematics chair George Mackey saw effort reporting as a breach of academic freedom. It smacked of the mind-set of accountants and businessmen, who had no feeling for the psychological needs and special status of scholars. Research was not "services rendered" but "a privilege and is a duty only in the moral sense." It was the center of a scholar's life; it went on all the time; to try to reduce it to a percentage was impossible. Division of Engineering and Applied Physics dean Harvey Brooks shared these concerns. The faculty, he told Pusey, feared that academic freedom was being compromised "in order to secure for the University additional unrestricted funds." Brooks warned that the faculty saw this as a breakdown of the traditional separation of responsibility for academic and fiscal matters: "I believe in this instance we have a decision which was taken for primarily fiscal and administrative reasons without full realization of its implications for the principles of academic freedom and the conditions of work for the tenured faculty."

During the summer of 1966, Harvard lobbied to eliminate effort reporting and won the support of the Budget Bureau and the National Science Foundation. Other universities declined to support a change that benefited rich Harvard but not them. And the sums at stake were substantial. The difference between Harvard's old self-denying 20 percent indirect cost level and the present, effort reporting-encumbered 26 percent was $6.8 million in 1964–65. A failure to comply might cost the University $11 million in 1966–67. This squabble over effort reporting was a revealing episode. It contributed to the increasingly difficult relations between University faculties and the federal government during the 1960s. And it was another bone of contention between Harvard's faculty and its administration.[44]

## ∽ 9 ∽

# GOVERNING

# THE AFFLUENT UNIVERSITY

When Conant left the presidency in 1953, Harvard was still under the sway of its traditional soft-shoe, old boy administrative style. Pusey felt no great obligation to modernize governance. To the end of his presidential days, he relied on an almost ostentatiously small staff. When he came to work each morning, he opened his own mail. Here as elsewhere, older folkways stubbornly endured.

## An Empowered Elite

Pusey's closest associates in the 1950s were two very different breeds of cat. One was personal assistant William Bentinck-Smith '37, an affable, cool-minded former journalist with a facile pen (something the president lacked). Bentinck-Smith was Pusey's amanuensis and a close adviser on a variety of alumni and policy matters, very much as Calvert Smith had been for Conant in the 1940s. "I worked for him for eighteen extraordinary years, in a relationship of mutual trust and intimacy," Bentinck-Smith recalled.[1]

Pusey's (improbable) other close confidant was Faculty of Arts and Sciences dean McGeorge Bundy. If Pusey was as much a product of middle America as a Harvard president was likely to be, Bundy was as close to an aristocrat as America was likely to produce. He was a scion of the Boston Lowells, self-confident enough to have gone not to Harvard but to Yale. Rumor had it that the Corporation put pressure on Pusey to make Bundy dean of the Faculty of Arts and Sciences. Fellow Roger Lee told the president-elect in the summer of 1953: "only if a first-rate administrator is available and thoroughly briefed before the opening of college will you yourself be free to deal with the many policy questions which will naturally arise with a change in the presidency." Pusey himself says that he was attracted by an acerbic Bundy review of William Buckley's assault on the liberal university, *God and Man at Yale*.

Only thirty-four when he became dean in 1953, associate professor of Government Bundy soon showed those who didn't know it already that he had as sharp a mind as anybody in the University. A consummate meritocrat, he handled his faculty with effortless ease, and for the most part they loved it. Pusey devoted himself to raising the money that made possible a significant increase in the faculty's size and salaries, and got precious little thanks for his pains. But as a team—Pusey, Mr. Outside, wooing the alums; Bundy, Mr. Inside, cosseting the faculty—they were unmatched in Harvard's modern history, except perhaps for the Derek Bok-Henry Rosovsky pairing of the 1970s and early 1980s. Each had qualities lacking in the other: dash and imagination in Bundy's case, moral solidity and tough adherence to principle in the case of Pusey.[2]

Pusey's relationship with the Governing Boards, the Corporation and the Overseers, was comparably smooth. How could they not warmly regard a man of high religious and moral principles, dedicated to education, skillful at fund-raising, an able administrator wedded to his job? Meanwhile, time and mortality inexorably changed the Corporation's personnel, if not its persona. The most significant addition was Francis H. ("Hooks") Burr, an impeccably Brahmin-lineaged Ropes and Gray attorney who replaced Roger Lee in 1954. Pusey relied heavily on Burr as a problem solver and confidant. And he freely employed the other fellows to assist him on problems suited to their expertise.

In 1959 William Marbury took note of the fact that he, Keith Kane, and Thomas Lamont were the same age and that if all stayed on the Corporation until they were seventy, their simultaneous departures would leave a big hole to be filled. Marbury thought that he was the logical one to leave earlier: he had served longer than the others and was not as useful. His Baltimore locale and lack of a Harvard B.A. made him something of an outsider in what was still a Brahmin-dominated body. (When Treasurer Paul Cabot and Charles Coolidge retired in 1964, accounts of their lives were circulated. Marbury mused: "I must confess that in reading the biographical material which had been sent to me, I felt almost as if I were reading a Marquand novel.") Nevertheless Marbury became the Corporation's senior fellow in 1964 and did not retire until 1970. That ancient body had a magnetic pull on the loyalty and commitment of its members.[3]

Treasurer Paul Cabot, ready to retire in the mid-1960s, wanted his close associate George Bennett to be his successor. This was hardly looking far afield: Bennett like Cabot (and Burr) was a director of State

Street Investment, which guided Harvard's endowment. Thomas Lamont looked into Bennett's qualifications. While his lineage was impeccable, there was some question as to his ability to make decisions. And how active a role would he play in nonfiscal matters? "I recall," Lamont warned, "that when Paul became Treasurer of Harvard University he swore he would not take any interest in affairs of the University other than investment matters. After a year in office he was the first man to have ideas on every Harvard problem running from real estate matters to future plans of the Divinity School and how bad our teaching of French was." But Cabot had clout, and Bennett it was.[4]

Charles Coolidge retired in 1964 after nearly thirty years on the Corporation, and Socony Mobil chief executive Albert Nickerson replaced him. For the first time the Corporation had a member whose views on how to run Harvard came from a big national corporation rather than from State Street or the law. When Harvard faced its crisis of 1969 and after, Nickerson's inclination to equate the University with a large business corporation would have a significant impact. When Thomas Lamont died after heart surgery in 1967, former Secretary of Defense Robert McNamara and John Gardner of the Carnegie Corporation were sounded out (without success) as replacements. Cleveland attorney Hugh Calkins, the final choice, turned out to be notably responsive to the changing student-academic scene. By 1971, when Pusey left office, no one remained from the Corporation that had welcomed him twenty years before.[5]

As Harvard grew, so did the concerns, and the work, of the Corporation. In 1962, Marbury wondered:

> Apart from financial difficulties, has the time not come when we should put the brakes on the explosive expansion which seems to be taking place in every department of the University? Are the demands for more space, more equipment and more personnel really justified by the accomplishments? May there not be something in Jack [Chase Manhattan executive John J.] McCloy's stricture that the Harvard faculty is spending too much money on a kind of intellectual featherbedding?

Thomas Lamont complained in 1966 that since "the world of universities exploded," Corporation meetings were much longer. Beset by a flood of paper, the fellows found it hard to make informed decisions. Yet costly and complex projects came before them, such as the Kennedy School of Government. With no time and insufficient information, the Corporation had become "a fire engine putting out fires." But Pusey denied the accuracy of the picture Lamont drew, and the remedies (an enlarged Corporation, greater control by the center) that he proposed. The essential task of the fellows was to choose the president and then to help him. If there were serious administrative problems, Harvard didn't need a new Corporation; it needed a new president.[6]

The Board of Overseers was more restive. Members of its Executive Committee paid a call on the new president in May 1954. They complained that they had been marginalized in big decisions such as Pusey's own appointment, and were so now in the selection of Burr to the Corporation. They had no objection to these choices, only to the manner in which they were made. Pusey tried to mollify his visitors by assuring them that he would (unofficially) consult the Overseers when the Corporation considered major appointments. In turn, they assured him that they would favorably recommend Burr's nomination to their fellow-Overseers. But little appeared to change. Following custom, the Overseers' executive committee approved the Nickerson and Bennett appointments in 1965—and, following custom, complained about the lack of prior notice or time for deliberation.[7]

## Keeping House

There was supposed to be, somewhere, a document called "The History of the World," which purported to describe Harvard's administrative structure. When in 1956 Francis Keppel, the newly appointed dean of the School of Education, asked to see it, Corporation secretary David Bailey had to admit that he could not find a copy: a measure of its importance. In practice, Bailey thought, there were three distinct realms of governance at Harvard, each subject to its own system:

*Finance and budgeting:* Here the president and fellows ruled the roost. The lines of authority were clear, precise, downright military. The president was the commanding general; the administrative vice president was the field commander; the deans got general orders and were responsible for the efficient financial management of their bailiwicks.

*Faculty selection:* "Here we have a bureaucratic or oligarchical system. Committees everywhere." The Governing Boards in theory had the ultimate power of review. But in practice they were in thrall to a selection process dominated by the departments and the ad hoc review system. Only four times in the past century had the Overseers challenged a faculty choice, not once successfully.

*Academic policy:* Faculty authority over students, curriculum, and degrees was all but absolute, though the Governing Boards retained a pro forma say on degree and curriculum changes. In practice "nothing is authoritarian. Even bureaucratic interests and pressures are subordinated to what may best be described as a pure parliamentary system of unlimited public debate."[8]

Harvard's central administration in the Pusey years still was lean: by later standards, positively anorexic. The relative size of central administration costs actually declined in the early 1960s, from 4.6 percent to 3.1 percent of the budget. Growth appears to have occurred first within the various schools. Gadfly Thomas Lamont went after the Business School in 1964 when it asked the Corporation to approve seven new administrative appointments. This struck him as "attempting by honest effort to prove Parkinson's law [that work expands to fill the time allowed for its completion] to be the whole truth." HBS dean George Baker explained that these were only new designations for people already working for the school. (Translation: only a little title inflation.)[9]

Meanwhile Harvard inexorably took on the scale and complexity of a modern university. There were 3,164 Corporation appointments, academic and administrative, in 1953–54; by 1966 that figure had grown to 6,100. More people meant more paper. Pusey's secretary asked him in June 1955 if he minded having the wall of the front office of his Massachusetts Hall quarters lined with file cabinets: "There has been a considerable shift in the peak volume of work in Massachusetts Hall in the past year or so and we are in need of desk space in places where we've never needed it before."[10]

An in-house staff of lawyers lay in the future. But Ott Shaw of Harvard's favorite law firm Ropes and Gray dealt with a lengthening laundry list—the Arnold Arboretum imbroglio, complex and dicey dealings over the Kennedy Library and School of Government, sensitive negotiations with city officials over Cambridge street changes—forty items in all. And new concerns called for new administrative posts. In 1958 an assistant to the president for civic affairs was charged to deal with "the manifold problems connected with the University's day-to-day existence in a large urban area."[11]

A rapidly changing communications technology led to pressure for more responsive, and more centralized, management. (That these might be contradictory goals was not yet widely recognized.) Division of Engineering and Applied Sciences dean Harvey Brooks warned that information storage and processing needed "forward planning and technical services" beyond the routine maintenance and plant operation that was the classic function of buildings and grounds. The solution was the office of information technology, which became the largest component of Harvard's central administration in the 1970s.[12]

The bureaucracy found a proper home for itself in Holyoke Center, which opened in 1962. This centrally located, high-rise building was designed to house the offices and some of the departments of the Faculty of Arts and Sciences. But it quickly became Harvard's version of the United Nations Secretariat building in New York: a fit symbol for a proper modern university. By the early 1960s Administrative Vice President L. Gard Wiggins directed, literally, a cast of thousands: some 5,000 nonacademic employees and 6,000 casual workers (3,000 of them students).[13]

The story of the University Health Services (UHS) suggests how the interplay of demand and supply fed the growth of Harvard governance. Conant appointed a committee in 1952 to look into the present state and future prospects of health care. Predictably it called for a more thorough system, with a centrally located clinic and infirmary. In 1954 Dana Farnsworth, MIT's medical director, came to head UHS, with the charge to put these recommendations into practice. He set up a comprehensive student health plan, but soon found himself immersed in administrative tong wars with the Business and Law Schools, who wished to keep their own clinics.

Corporation fellow Charles Coolidge was not entranced by the new, more caring care: "It annoys me to think that if I were now going through college I would be taxed some $65 a year so that Farnsworth's people could gambol around with 'emotionally disturbed students.'" But his was a voice of the past. A new University Health Services Center, one of the goals of the Program for Harvard College, opened in 1962. By 1970 health care was a big player on the Harvard scene. Medical School dean Robert Ebert looked with some concern on a health care program that now cost $6 million a year.[14]

As in the past, the Harvard College Library and the Harvard University Press were the largest academic units run by the central administration. Library director Keyes Metcalf retired in 1954, with a final report that Bundy angrily characterized as "one of the most discouraging and disappointing things I have read in the last two years. It is one long wail," an appeal for funds "in the least attractive possible form." But Bundy was well aware of the library's importance, and of an increasingly assertive faculty's desire for one of their own to run it: "a return to the older system when we had a faculty member as director of the libraries, with a skilled technical librarian under him." He duly asked former Provost Paul Buck to succeed Metcalf, and in 1964 Merle Fainsod of the Government department followed Buck. Metcalf's longtime associate Douglas Bryant, the executive officer of the system, had his title upgraded to University librarian. But Pusey and FAS dean Franklin Ford made it clear that Fainsod and the Faculty Library Committee had the final say over policy and practice.[15]

The major facts of the library's life were the unremitting growth of its collections and the need to find more space to house them. By the mid-1960s Harvard had 7.5 million books and pamphlets; Yale, with the second largest university library, trailed far behind with 4.7 million. Widener Library, its shelves groaning with the weight of 3 million volumes, was full; more space was needed badly, and soon. Countway Medical Library, opened in 1965, absorbed the University's medicine-related collections. Radcliffe's Hilles Library (1966), a separate-but-equal complement to Harvard College's Lamont, and Pusey Library, an underground complex adjacent to Widener (1975), were supposed to meet Harvard's library's needs until the 1980s. But the financial cost of maintaining this growing library infrastructure was heavy and would become a lot weightier in the financially troubled decade of the 1970s.[16]

The Harvard University Press went through shaky times in the 1930s and 1940s, but settled down to a golden age after Thomas J. Wilson became director in 1947. Wilson, a courtly North Carolinian well-schooled in the ways of academe, paid close attention to the Press's relations with an imperial faculty. Ford Foundation grants and benefactions such as the Belknap endowment for publications in American history fed a burgeoning publications list: up from 68 a year in 1947 to 144 two decades later. Staff tripled; receipts went up sevenfold.[17]

In 1967 the Press became embroiled in a controversy with academic freedom overtones. Harvard biochemist James Watson wrote a lively, highly opinionated version of his and his British partner Francis Crick's great discovery. He gave it to the Press, which was delighted to have this plum and prepared to publish it under the provocative title (Watson's own) of *Honest Jim*. Then Crick complained to Pusey that Watson's was a misleading, superficial, self-serving memoir, not a serious account of what they had done: "It is to me almost incredible that the Harvard University press should consider publishing such a mass of tasteless gossip." He threatened Press director Wilson with a libel suit and wrote to Watson: "Should you persist in regarding your work as history I should add that it shows such a naive and egotistical view of the subject as to be scarcely credible.... Your view of history is that found in the lower class of women's magazines."

The faculty Board of Syndics, which decided on what the Press published, got their backs up and stuck by their acceptance of Watson's manuscript. But Harvard's legal advisors warned against publishing. The syndics pulled back a little, conceding that the book should not appear in its present form. Pusey and the Corporation finally decided that the Press should pull out, on the ground that it would involve the University in a bitter scientific quarrel. So the book, retitled *The Double Helix*, went to a commercial publisher—and to best-sellerdom. Some faculty members, convinced that Harvard had buckled under, found yet another cause for discontent with the administration.[18]

## Icons and Iconography

Harvard's iconic status among American universities required care and feeding. The traditional Harvard attitude toward publicity was not unlike its view of debt: this was not something that well-bred people did. Lowell never gave a newspaper interview, Conant only rarely. "In general," observed the University's press officer, "it might be said that Mr. Conant was cooperative but inaccessible, and, when occasion required, cordial but uncommunicative." Pusey, who hardly seemed the type, was far readier to make public appearances. After his appearance on the television show *Omnibus* in 1956, Corporation fellow Thomas Lamont effused: "I think that it was probably the best piece of Harvard propaganda of any form, shape or description that has been presented to the American public in my lifetime." He commended Pusey for his courage and thought (no doubt correctly) that neither Lowell or Conant would have done it.[19]

In an age of large-scale money raising, dealings with the alumni took on ever more importance. An inherited sticking point was the rivalry between the Associated Harvard Clubs and the more broadly based (plebeian just isn't the right word) Alumni Association. Corporation fellow Hooks Burr thought that the complexity of alumni affairs, "with the Harvard Alumni Association on the one hand and the Associated

Harvard Clubs on the other and a mass of bewildered alumni in the middle," was a major disincentive to most graduates. Finally in 1964 the two alumni associations merged into an Associated Harvard Alumni. But some things persisted, among them, old grad eccentricity. The chairman of the fiftieth reunion of the class of 1913 was afire to see the affair turn its attention to three hot ticket issues: "something along the public relationship angle of Harvard as slanted to Communism"; a better football scoreboard; and adequate restroom facilities for women at Harvard Stadium. Pusey's aide Bentinck-Smith feared that the reunion chair "sounds as if he should be put out to pasture. Should we head him off before he tramples the corn?"[20]

Honorary degrees to the great, the good, and the well-heeled are the customary way for universities to demonstrate their public-spiritedness, feed their amour propre, and add to their fund-raising clout. Almost all schools play the game; Harvard did so with special flair. It sought to keep its honorary degree choices secret until Commencement, thereby giving the *Crimson* a toothsome annual challenge. Between 1921 and 1945 about 330 (male) people were honored, 122 of them in public service, 92 in science, 57 in social studies, and 55 in the humanities.

Honorary degree giving (or withholding) could be contentious. FAS dean Kenneth Murdock never got one, Bundy thought, "at least in part because of his unhappy falling out with Mr. Conant." Novelist William Faulkner declined to be so honored in 1952, on the ground that to give it to someone who had not even finished grammar school "would violate and outrage the entire establishment of education, of which degrees are the symbol and the accolade. That is, I would defend the chastity of Harvard, the mother of American education, even if Harvard herself would not." With more genuine modesty, Harvard Nobel physicist Edward Purcell removed himself from the list in 1956. He had already gotten adequate recognition for his work, and "I am unwilling to be singled out further within my own university from my colleagues, many of whom have received less public recognition for their work than I although they have earned as much or more."[21]

Pusey expanded the annual number of degrees to as many as eighteen, and opened up the process in other ways. Besides the usual list of white Protestant males he added conspicuous Catholics (John F. Kennedy in 1956, Cardinal Cushing in 1959), the first woman (Helen Keller in 1955), and more than occasional Jews. Robert Weaver, soon-to-be secretary of the Department of Housing and Urban Development, was chosen as a 1964 recipient, Corporation fellow Charles Coolidge noting that Weaver had a white wife and "probably looks more like a Latin American than an American Negro."[22]

In 1959 faculty members John Kenneth Galbraith and Arthur M. Schlesinger did a study of Harvard honorary degrees designed to show that liberals and labor leaders were under-recognized. Only four prominent Democrats, as compared with eighteen to twenty-three Republicans, had gotten degrees since 1945. The charge had validity: a few overseers objected to Adlai Stevenson in 1962, and the Corporation withdrew his name to avoid a row. Not until 1965 did Stevenson get a degree. (But then a similar study of the last quarter of the twentieth century would reveal a comparable dearth of conservatives.)[23]

After decades of stasis, the physical face of Harvard changed dramatically during the Pusey years. Its new buildings were uncompromisingly modern. The International School architectural creed of School of Design deans Walter Gropius and José Sert superseded the mega-Georgian traditionalism of Coolidge, Shepley, Bulfinch and Abbott, Harvard's longtime architects of choice. Gropius set the tone when he defended his stark, constructivist Graduate Center in 1950: "the student needs the *real* thing, not buildings in disguise. So long as we do not ask him to go about in period clothes, it seems absurd to build College buildings in pseudo-period design. How can we expect our students to become bold and fearless in thought and action if we encase them in sentimental shrines feigning a culture which has long since disappeared?" Architecture, he declared, should not be confused with applied archaeology.[24]

Pusey favored modern architecture: it was less costly and better suited an urban university's need for tall buildings. In 1956 he made Sert his consultant on planning, development, and design. Thirty-three new buildings and eighty-six major renovations got under way during his first decade as president. Harvard became a showcase of the works of leading contemporary architects. The results were (and are) frequently criticized as ugly, dehumanized, at war with instead of building on Harvard's architectural past. But the contemporaneity, style, and spirit of the new buildings also won them wide acceptance.[25]

Corbusier's Carpenter Center for Visual Studies, his only American structure, was completed in 1963, after customary dithering by the great man. (Pusey in 1961 informed donor Alfred Carpenter of the receipt of the first plans: "they are unfortunately not much more than designs and need a great deal more work by Sert before they can be submitted to the Corporation for practical consideration.... 'Le Corbu' is certainly not winning any prizes for speed! But we shall press ahead with the task of perfecting and 'Americanizing' the drawings as fast as we can.") The stark concrete structure attracted predictable criticism. But the visiting committee on Fine Arts and some thirty faculty members commended Pusey for having had it built.

Other new Harvard buildings have not gained luster over time. Among these was Minoru Yamasaki's William James Hall (1964), a technologically challenged sixteen floors for the behavioral sciences. (Pusey nervously bet on it: "I can only hope that in terms of the total development of this part of Cambridge posterity will prove us right." Most would say he lost.) Other less architecturally notable but more workable buildings included Hugh Stubbins's Loeb Drama Center (1959) and Countway Medical Library (1965), and Sert's massive Holyoke Center (1961–66) and Peabody Terrace (1963), riverside housing for graduate students. Even Harvard's old architectural standbys Coolidge, Shepley, Bulfinch, and Abbott got into the spirit of the age with their halfheartedly modernist Quincy House (1959), Leverett House Towers (1960), and high-rise Mather House (1970). The last and largest of the new structures begun in this period was Sert's undergraduate Science Center (1972), made possible by an $11 million gift from Polaroid founder Edwin Land. Lamont and other fellows complained that the building's appointments were too lush, and deficiencies in oversight led to costly engineering errors. But in general, modernity and affluence comfortably coexisted.[26]

The assertive modernism of the new buildings at Harvard (and other universities) celebrated the booming present and the promising future, not the storied past. To look back meant, for many, to fix their gaze on Memorial Hall. This monumental Ruskinian commemoration of Harvard's Civil War dead was regarded by many as the largest blot (and by a few as the finest adornment) on the Harvard architectural landscape. By the end of World War II, Memorial Hall badly showed its age, and a project began in 1946 to restore it to its former glory, appropriate for a building commemorating what had been up to then the nation's greatest military victory. But on September 6, 1956, its ornate tower was consumed by fire. The prevailing attitude was that the fire was a welcome act of God (or of man). There was talk of tearing down Memorial Hall, but sparing its attached Sanders Theatre—like Ste.-Chapelle on the Ile de la Cité, said one official: a notable instance of Harvard hubris.

Pusey hopefully observed that "the failure, through fire, of the recent efforts to rehabilitate Memorial Hall points unmistakably to a time not too distant when we may have to find an appropriate replacement for this important historic building which would still preserve its memorial quality." University counsel Ott Shaw warned that this posed testamentary difficulties. Since Memorial Hall honored Harvard's Civil War dead, it would be hard to argue that the building had become an "impracticable" instrument of its original purpose. *But* suppose one argued that Memorial Hall was designed to be the focal point of the University's life; that it had failed to do this; and that to replace it would be, in a sense, not to violate the trust but to carry it out? (Tastes change. Forty years later the interior of Memorial Hall was restored beyond its original grandeur. And by 2000 the stunted tower had been rebuilt, to general acclaim.)[27]

As Harvard expanded (displacing residents and businesses, reducing the tax rolls), so did community resistance. The Shady Hill estate of Fogg codirector Paul Sachs, adjacent to the homes of well-heeled Harvard faculty on Francis Avenue, came into the University's hands during the 1950s. Pusey and his aides saw this as an opportunity to keep more faculty in Cambridge by building housing for them on the site. Unneighborly neighbors had a bad attack of NIMBYism and managed to preserve the parklike parcel in its pristine state.[28]

More significant was the acquisition of the Bennett Street Yard of the Metropolitan Transit Authority (MTA), which eventually became the site of the Kennedy School of Government. Harvard had long been interested in this large, choicely located property. Although the Cambridge Planning Board opposed Harvard's purchase of the parcel (priced at $6 million), the University was the only serious bidder. Things got more complicated after John F. Kennedy's assassination: his family and former associates saw the location as ideal for the Kennedy Library. The site was parcelled out in the 1970s to the Kennedy School of Government, a commercial hotel-apartment house complex, and a locals-assuaging riverside park.[29]

The old class and ethnic tensions between rich Harvard and poor or working-class Irish (and, increasingly, black) neighbors continued to affect the University's relations with its Cambridge-Boston surround. Cambridge councilman Alfred Vellucci was the leading impresario of town versus gown street theatre. He enlivened City Council meetings with proposals to pave over Harvard Yard and turn it into a parking lot, or require Harvard to fix its Memorial Hall clock tower so that "students and residents of Cambridge will know what time of day it is."

Urban environmentalists were another group to reckon with. Pusey agreed with one of them in 1955 that "there has to be a community movement for urban renewal and planning in Cambridge." Charles Whitlock, in charge of Harvard's community relations, peppered Pusey with progress (or, more often, stalemate) reports on zoning problems. (He reported that the League of Women Voters, a visible presence in community issues, "feel[s] that Cambridge should be a pastoral village.") When a state highway plan threatened to cut a wide swath through Cambridge, Harvard joined in the general outcry, and it died aborning.[30]

Especially serious was a clash with residents and their supporters over the Houghton Urban Renewal Area, a section east of the campus that had seen a large influx of black residents. Harvard had future development plans there and sought to secure a large tract through the city's urban renewal program. Growing public opposition put an end to that idea, and Harvard turned to its traditional practice of buying up real estate parcels as they became available. But the incident only fed the inclination of local activists to see Harvard as The Enemy.

Suspicion spilled over to ancillary areas such as fluoridation of the water system. "The paranoid Irish," Whitlock told Pusey, "feel that someone at this end of town is trying to poison them." On the other side of town (geographically, economically, and ethnoculturally), "our hysterical friends on Brattle Street" mobilized against Harvard plans for an underpass that threatened the sycamores lining Memorial Drive along the bank of the Charles River. The battle raged on into the 1970s, ending with the John F. Kennedy Library and its tourist hordes consigned to the edge of Boston Harbor, and the sycamores preserved. (The antifluoridation cause was less successful.) By the end of the 1960s, Harvard like other large urban universities was enmeshed in town-gown relationships far more complex and difficult than in the simpler past.[31]

## The Crimson and the Reds

The Harvard faculty faced almost no internal constraints on its academic freedom, that is, on what they taught or wrote, or whom they appointed or promoted. But during the Pusey years issues whose loci were outside the academy—conflict over American domestic and foreign policy, culminating in the civil rights revolution and the Vietnam War—reached new levels of intensity. From this perspective the Pusey years were bounded by McCarthyism and the Red Scare at their beginning, and Vietnam at their end.

Harvard's administration was not so willing a partner in red-baiting as some of its critics allege. But it was hardly immune to the prevailing temper of the time. Even civil libertarian Harvard Law professors Zechariah Chafee and Arthur Sutherland urged faculty members called before a congressional committee to testify fully and frankly about their

Communist connections. When cold war anxieties reached a boiling point during the Korean War years, the University's leaders worked with the FBI and bent to public opinion on a scale unequaled until then in Harvard's modern history.[32]

In 1953, during the interregnum between Conant's departure and Pusey's arrival, the House Un-American Activities Committee and the Senate Internal Security Subcommittee turned their attention to a number of Harvard-connected suspects, including associate professor of Physics Wendell Furry and Social Relations teaching fellow Leon Kamin. Both pled the Fifth Amendment, refusing to talk about their radical pasts. Furry had kept his Communist Party affiliation to himself when he was a research associate at the MIT Radiation Lab during the war, and he concealed his knowledge of the Party membership of two job applicants to the atom bomb project at Alamogordo. The general view in the Corporation was that a serious question existed as to whether Furry should remain a member of the faculty or be dismissed for "grave misconduct." Conant and Treasurer Paul Cabot wanted to strip Furry of tenure and give him a term appointment. But Harvard counsel Ott Shaw thought he should either be discharged or receive a severe reprimand.

Most of the overseers and the faculty, as well as Provost Paul Buck, opposed firing Furry. McGeorge Bundy, not yet dean, weighed in with an influential letter to his colleagues arguing against dismissal. Journalist Joseph Alsop warned that he would resign from the Overseers and take Harvard to task in his newspaper column if Furry was fired. Corporation fellow Thomas Lamont suspected that Furry still was a Communist, possibly was a perjurer, certainly was very foolish. But he recalled that back in the 1840s, when Medical School professor John W. Webster murdered his colleague George Parkman, the Governing Boards took no action against him. (Though the state did: it tried and hanged Webster.)[33]

A Corporation committee interviewed Furry and discussed his case with a faculty advisory committee. His teaching was excellent and betrayed no Communist slant (in any event not easy, given his field). Pleading the Fifth Amendment was misconduct, but not necessarily *grave* misconduct. More serious was Furry's giving misleading information to the government. But the interest of the University would not be served by removing him. So the committee suggested, and the Corporation agreed, that Furry stay on, with a finding of grave misconduct on the books for three years. If he committed further improprieties, or more information about his past behavior arose, then he would be fired. Provost Buck steered this proposal through the faculty.

The Corporation found no basis for accusing Social Relations teaching fellow Leon Kamin of misconduct, grave or otherwise. But Buck did not recommend him for reappointment. The department's chairman employed him during the 1953–54 academic year on a research project without teaching duties or any other potentially contaminating contact with students. Kamin left Harvard in 1954 and eventually became a professor at the University of California at San Diego.

In August 1953 the United States Senate voted contempt citations against Furry and Kamin. The faculty advisory committee on academic freedom and tenure urged that Furry not be suspended even if he was indicted. The Corporation agreed to make no further statement while Furry's case was pending. A number of prominent faculty members raised funds for Furry's defense, and in 1957 the charges against him were dismissed. But the "grave misconduct" finding stopped his promotion chances for some years. Finally, in 1962, he became a full professor; he had been an associate professor since 1940.[34]

Pusey took office in the fall of 1953, when McCarthyism was approaching its climacteric. He had tangled with the Wisconsin senator in his Lawrence College days. Not involved in government work during World War II, as were Conant and Bundy, he appears to have been less keyed up over loyalty-security concerns. He assured a worried alumnus: "I don't know why anyone goes on talking about such an unsubstantial phantom as 'Communism at Harvard.'" And he told Agnes Meyer, the journalist wife of *Washington Post* publisher Eugene Meyer: "[Y]ou can count on us here to continue to fight against the obscurantism now rife in our society as best we can. Some day I am sure we shall all look back on the hateful irrationality of the present with incredulity, but in the meantime it is not exactly amusing."[35]

When McCarthy hectored Harvard to do something about Furry, Pusey coolly replied: "Harvard is unalterably opposed to Communism. It is dedicated to free inquiry by free men." Massachusetts governor (and Harvard overseer) Christian Herter called for the dismissal of any faculty member who pled the Fifth Amendment. Pusey firmly rejected the idea and won the faculty's commendation: "Stubborn in the right, strong in his convictions as an administrator and as a man. . . . he has made himself President of Harvard in name and deed." But Pusey also had to compromise with a society widely (if temporarily) obsessed with fear of communism. He agreed with the Conant-Corporation view that a Party member should not be on the faculty. And while he did not regard the Fifth Amendment as a confession of guilt, he deplored its use.[36]

At Commencement time in 1956, when it seemed that the anti-communist furor was subsiding, the Fellows asked Bundy to review cases of Corporation appointees to the Faculty of Arts and Sciences where the issue of present or former Communist affiliation had arisen. There were five: Robert Bellah, Sigmund Diamond, Sydney James, Everett Mendelsohn, and Alan Westin.

Bellah, a graduate student in Sociology, told Social Relations chairman Talcott Parsons that he left the Party in the spring of 1950, his senior year in college, and had had no connection since. He was ready to talk about his own past, but not about the involvement of others. Bundy said he "seemed to us an ex-Communist of good conscience and sound character, with unusually high qualifications professionally." If Social Relations decided that his academic qualifications were outstanding and that he had overcome his past Communist involvement and was "in respect to this matter a 'well-balanced' person," and if it chose to nominate him for an instructorship, Bundy would support the appointment. The department did so recommend, and the Corporation approved the (one-year) instructorship. It added the proviso that if in the course of his appointment Bellah was called before an investigating body and refused to speak about his Communist past, it "would not look with favor on the renewal of his appointment." Pusey urged Bundy to make sure that Bellah understood this. So informed, Bellah declined the appointment and went off to a research post at McGill. In time he returned to Harvard, got tenure, and then went to a professorship at Berkeley.

Diamond, a new History Ph.D., was up for appointment as counselor for foreign students and dean of special students. When Bundy learned that Diamond was disinclined to testify fully to congressional investigators, he recommended that the appointment be withdrawn: "It seems wholly clear that no man holding Mr. Diamond's position should be appointed to the particular office of Counsellor for Foreign Students." Diamond went to Columbia, where he rose to be professor of History and Sociology.

James, also a History graduate student, was interviewed by the FBI and told Bundy that he had been less than forthcoming on some particulars. According to James, Bundy warned him that if he did not fully cooperate he would have no future in American higher education. Nevertheless his appointment to a fourth year as a teaching fellow was approved. In June 1955 he left the University to teach at Brown and eventually became professor of history at Iowa.

Mendelsohn, a teaching fellow in History of Science, persuaded Bundy and History of Science chair I. Bernard Cohen that he had never been a communist or under Party discipline. His appointment was renewed; in time he became a professor of the History of Science at Harvard.

Westin, also a teaching fellow, convinced Bundy that he had broken with the Party and was prepared to respond to all questions from legitimate bodies. He was reappointed, but moved to a research position at Yale Law School, and wound up a distinguished professor of law at Columbia.

The experiences of these young men were, to varying degrees, traumatic, though something other than a litany of lives shattered, careers destroyed. But their later success was a tribute more to their abilities, the rapid decline of McCarthyism, and the expansion of higher education than to Harvard policy. Diamond in particular nursed a grievance for decades. He finally went public in 1977 with an attack on Bundy for his readiness to cooperate with the FBI and pressure Corporation appointees who were former Communist to name names. Bundy defended himself as doing what was best for Harvard at the height of the McCarthy furor.

That tough-minded man had limited empathy for those who were caught up in communism. He once told Pusey that while he did not know whether one object of their inquiry "is a real Commie or not, ... he has certainly been a fellow-traveler for a long time, and I think we ought to use a pretty long pole in dealing with him." His harshness cannot be justified. But then the faculty members who came to the aid of their embattled colleagues and students did not have to deal with the same calculus of outside pressures and institutional responsibility that Bundy and Pusey did.[37]

When Harvard itself came under assault from alumni or the outside world, its leaders took a more principled stand. *Boston Post* publisher John Fox '29 and other agents of the anticommunist conspiracy exhorted alums to contribute to a separate fund, Free Harvard, which would hold their gifts until Communists and their ilk were driven from the University. They also had plans to run their own candidates for the Board of Overseers, foreshadowing a similar effort by the Left in later years. Under pressure, Pusey met with Fox, who proposed that a number of left-wing professors be removed. En passant he spoke of his desire for a preemptive nuclear strike on the Soviet Union. Pusey's comment on this encounter: "clearly a sincere zealot, not a fellow cynically trying to sell papers. McCarthy, Buckley, Pegler's kind of 'mind'—convinced of their rightness, other people's blindness and pusillanimity."[38]

The last redoubt of the communism-at-Harvard critics was the Veritas Foundation, created by a few right-wing alumni. Year after year it leveled charges that fair Harvard was corrupted by subversion most foul. The foundation widely (but to little effect) distributed a pamphlet exposing "Keynesism-Marxism at Harvard."[39]

As the Korean War wound down, cold war tensions eased. When in

October 1955 McCarthy accused Pusey of harboring Communists at Harvard, most saw this not as fascism but as farce. J. Robert Oppenheimer, stripped of his AEC security clearance for concealing his association with radicals, was asked to give the William James Lectures in Philosophy and Psychology in 1957. A few protests arose, but the administration brushed these aside.[40]

There remained a heritage of what might be called prudence, or could be called timidity. Visiting and exchange scholars from the Soviet Union and its satellites began to appear in the late fifties, and in 1963 FAS dean Franklin Ford reminded department chairmen that the Corporation wanted to "be given some indication of the nominee's political orientation and the purpose of his visit to Harvard." The Physics chairman took exception to Ford's "political orientation" phrase, and it turned out that those words had not been used by the Corporation. What that body did do in 1961 was modify its 1958 rule that no member of the Communist Party would be knowingly appointed, thus allowing short-term appointments of Soviet scholars.[41]

There was much controversy over Pusey's response to the loyalty-security provisions of the National Defense Education Act (NDEA) of 1958. This honey pot of federal aid for graduate students was sullied by the requirements that recipients sign an oath of allegiance and an affidavit disavowing membership in subversive organizations. Pusey joined with other university presidents to object to the provision, though he believed that more could be done through quiet protest than by confrontation. He wrote to Massachusetts senator and Harvard alumnus John F. Kennedy: "There are indications of mounting uneasiness among the Faculty here regarding the government's position toward federal aid to education. I must say my confidence that future aid may be forthcoming in an atmosphere of non-interference, with complete understanding of the purposes of higher education, has been rudely shaken by the record of the debate of the Senate." Universities, he thought, "ought seriously to reexamine their relationship to the federal Government lest we all start in a direction from which there is no easy return."[42]

Most administration sentiment was for a freeze on accepting NDEA funds until the oath-affidavit issue was resolved. Kennedy warned Pusey against Harvard indefinitely suspending its participation: that would turn the controversy into a harmful morality play. Harvard joined other schools in opting out of the NDEA student loan program in the fall of 1959, at the cost of $358,000 in foregone aid. President Eisenhower asked for repeal of the affidavit requirement in his January 1960 budget message; Vice President Richard Nixon favored repeal "under the circumstances." Finally in 1962 a unanimous Congress eliminated the disclaimer affidavit, and Harvard rejoined the program.[43]

During the 1960s the cold war's impact on Harvard shifted from external assaults on the loyalty of faculty and students to on-campus protest against American foreign policy and the University's involvement in it. Increased political activism on campus, and the administration's responses, weakened the links between Pusey and his faculty. When H. Stuart Hughes of the History department ran for the U.S. Senate as a radical third-party candidate in 1962, the administration looked into how other universities dealt with faculty political activism, but did nothing more than that. There was some concern over the fact that sociologist David Riesman used his office to run the Council for Correspondence, an antinuclear group, which meant that Harvard was subsidizing the rent for the operation. In the wake of the Bay of Pigs fiasco of 1961, seventy-five academics—forty-four of them from Harvard—signed an ad critical of American policy toward Castro's Cuba. Predictable alumni protests rolled in over their use of the Harvard name, and Pusey aide Bentinck-Smith had a quiet talk with an FBI agent who warned of substantial Communist influence in the "Fair Play for Cuba" movement: all with no apparent effect.[44]

There was more of a fuss over the administration's refusal to let folk singer Pete Seeger, under indictment for contempt of Congress and free on bail, appear at a Student Council-sponsored concert. Pusey reversed himself after still-respectful students assured him that it would be a purely musical evening. The result, of course, was much favorable publicity for Seeger and a concert that in itself was a political statement. Pusey held that while student organizations had broad latitude in selecting speakers, the final decision had to rest with the administration: "In my view it is not a question of academic freedom but rather a question of propriety, public order, decorum, good taste. These involve questions of observance upon which only the administration has the right to insist." That view further widened the gulf in perception between the generations during the sixties.[45]

## The Crimson and the Red, White, and Blue

The University's relationship with the federal government had greater long-term impact than the alarms of the McCarthy era. It ranged from hidden ties with the CIA to the federal grants and contracts that became the mother's milk of much faculty research. Ruth Fischer, the sister of

Communist spy Gerhard Eisler, had been connected with the Harvard Library since 1944. In that capacity she wrote *Stalin and German Communism* and was working on a second volume. In the mid-1950s librarian Keyes Metcalf arranged for her to be paid from CIA funds. Buck and new library head Douglas Bryant brought this up with Pusey, who asked himself, "Should we be a party to this kind of operation? . . . should we be a blind for C.I.A. agents?" The obvious answer was no, and Fischer was given a lower-paying but properly vetted appointment as a specialist in book collection.[46]

A fertile source of trouble was Harvard's growing financial dependence on federally sponsored research. An ever larger infrastructure of government grants, area studies centers reliant on government contracts, and a dense web of federal regulations came to be part of the life of the University. It was Harvard policy, adopted by Conant at the end of World War II, not to approve of classified research projects. But there were other ways—favored subject matter, reporting requirements—in which the government could influence the style and substance of academic research.[47]

The Corporation began to worry about Harvard's ever larger dependence on federal government support. The portion of the University's budget coming from that source increased from 1.5 percent in 1941 to about 20 percent in 1959, most of it for medical research. A study of the effect of federal funds was launched in 1960 and appeared a year later as "The Impact of Federal Programs on Harvard University." Relatively little of this money went to the social sciences, almost none to the humanities. Pusey wanted Congress to spread the money more widely among fields, but not more widely among universities. His not disinterested view was that support should be concentrated on the major schools, where it would do the most good. The students benefiting would then fan out to less-favored areas of the country, spreading the gospel of academic excellence.[48]

More contentious was Harvard's Reserve Officer Training Corps (ROTC). In the 1950s Harvard had Army, Navy, and Air Force ROTC units, and the program was an established (though small, about a dozen ROTC graduates in 1957) part of campus life. Meritocracy began to put strains on the Harvard-ROTC relationship well before Vietnam. A controversy blew up in the midfifties over a "Harvard Plan" to enrich the ROTC curriculum and put in a summer training course. The Army resisted this, and Bundy warned that its response "will be received with misgivings by the faculty." A compromise was reached in which Harvard offered courses on civil-military and government-military relations.[49]

Yet another source of future trouble was the widespread sense that Harvard had moved to the center of the American Establishment. Old Harvard was intimately identified with Brahmin Boston, but Yale and Princeton had competitive claims to national influence. Now, in the 1960s, Harvard pulled ahead: not only in money and academic standing but in the corridors of power.

The most visible sign of this development was what followed on the 1960 election of John F. Kennedy '40 as president of the United States. Harvard's relations with the Kennedy family were not always easy. Patriarch Joseph P. Kennedy harbored class, religious, and ideological resentments against his alma mater. In 1956, when Joe's youngest son Edward graduated from the College, Boston's archbishop Richard Cushing wrote to Pusey that the young man "has focused his ambition on Harvard Law School." But despite being on the dean's list, he had not done well on his law aptitude test. Could anything be done? Alas no, said Pusey: "his score on the admissions test failed to bring him up sufficiently so that the factors of his good character and family interest in Harvard might have entered into the final decision." So Ted went off to study law at the University of Virginia. (When in 1962 an alum asked if it were true that the student who took a Spanish test for Ted had been expelled, but not Kennedy, he was informed that both were readmitted: an application of the old Harvard/Puritan belief in salvation through works.)[50]

But JFK was a loyal son of Harvard: an overseer, the family's most generous donor, and now the University's most eminent living graduate. Far more than FDR, Kennedy brought numbers of Harvard faculty and graduates into his administration. McGeorge Bundy left the FAS deanship in early 1961 to be Kennedy's national security advisor. David Bell of the School of Public Administration became director of the budget; Archibald Cox of the Law School, solicitor general; Arthur M. Schlesinger, Jr., a special assistant (and resident historian) in the White House. Overseer Douglas Dillon became secretary of the treasury; Law School graduate James E. Day, postmaster general; onetime Business School faculty member Robert McNamara, secretary of defense; School of Education dean Frank Keppel, commissioner of education. Professors John Kenneth Galbraith, John K. Fairbank, and Edwin O. Reischauer went off to be the ambassadors to India, China, and Japan. (With his customary distaste for self-effacement, Galbraith explained to Pusey: "My appointment as Ambassador is obviously related to the work in economic development which I led in initiating in 1952 and which is now a leading field of teaching and research at Harvard. I have hopes, as a result of this service, to make myself uniquely the master of the economic and social problems of the Asian subcontinent.")

The media commented on this hegira in news stories, cartoons (Bill Mauldin offered an encounter between two old pols festooned in raccoon skin coats and carrying Harvard banners: "Why, Joe, I didn't know you was a Harvard man, too"), and commentary (James Reston: "There is nothing left at Harvard except Radcliffe"). JFK told a Harvard student reporter: "We are starting up a university of our own of Harvard in Washington. As you know, we have Dean Bundy as our dean, and we're getting enough professors to have a good faculty." Arthur Schlesinger lip-smackingly reported that as of August 21, 1961, Harvard graduates had been president of the United States for a third of the twentieth century. Pusey aide Bentinck-Smith's mock-horrified response: "What an appalling thought! How long can we keep this up?" (The answer: not much longer.)[51]

All of this strengthened the belief of the Radical Right that Harvard, Kennedy, the Democrats, and communism were joined in shadowy conspiracy. Of more significance to the University, the Kennedy connection reinforced an already substantial Harvard self-regard. Even modest-minded Nathan Pusey could not but respond warmly when National Security Advisor Bundy wrote soon after arriving in Washington: "We would like our first party to be a little gathering of the President, the President, and the professors they are sharing. Will you come?" Bundy (not quite accurately) told Pusey: "The president ... notes that you are more successful in managing the *Crimson* than he is in managing the national press. Perhaps he can get some advice from you on this art at Cambridge!"

In 1963, JFK (who remained a member of the Board of Overseers after his 1960 election) invited the Governing Boards to meet in Washington and have their annual dinner at the White House. "There is much to see of Harvard here in Washington," he told Pusey, "—not only Dumbarton Oaks and the Hellenic Institute, but Harvard men actively serving their country at every level." Duly the overseers came, met, dined, posed. Heady stuff. When troubles came in the late sixties, this sense of Harvard's preeminence went far to define the character of the revolt, the response of the administration and then of the public, and its ultimate resolution.[52]

$\backsim$ **10** $\backsim$

# THE ASCENDANT FACULTY

The most substantial legatee of Harvard's new affluence was the Faculty of Arts and Sciences. These were years of heady growth in that body's numbers, salary, perks, and power. It is not surprising that many professors later looked back wistfully to a Golden Age stretching from the late 1940s to the late 1960s.

When Pusey arrived in 1953, nearly half of the 448 members of the Faculty of Arts and Sciences had Harvard Ph.D.s. But the old Harvard habit of promoting from within was declining. Of 68 senior appointments between 1953 and 1957, more than half came from other schools; only six had come up through the College, the Harvard Graduate School, and the junior faculty. Harvard College graduates, 25 to 30 percent of the faculty in the Conant era, dropped to 5 to 10 percent in the Pusey years. Meritocracy had come into its own.[1]

## The Faculty Triumphant

Dean of the Faculty McGeorge Bundy, in office from 1953 until 1961, presided over the ascendancy of the professoriat. He was deeply committed to the meritocratic ideal of a faculty made up of the best and the brightest. He closely tracked the present state and future prospects of the Arts and Sciences departments. Biology worried him: it was a large department dominated by men in their fifties and sixties, "whose center of gravity is toward traditional taxonomy and the fulfillment of the great nineteenth century prospects of biology, rather than toward the new and growing subjects of a biochemical and biophysical character." It divided into "the traditionalists, the neutralists, and a small fighting group of modernists.... The modernists are outnumbered, but it is my strong impression that they are our most promising and significant contributors to biological science.... I don't think we ought to let ourselves be outweighed by entrenched voting power in this field full of growing new edges."

As for Physics: he would like to appoint a senior professor of great eminence and had MIT's Victor Weisskopf in mind. Another potential MIT target: economist Paul Samuelson. Here all that held Bundy back was the likelihood that Samuelson would want a University Professorship—in Bundy's view, a bit above his station in academic life. True, there was a gentleman's agreement that the two schools did not raid each other's faculty. But with vintage Bundy arrogance he suggested that recruiting its stars would in fact help MIT by conveying the message that one might go there with the hope of making it to Harvard.[2]

The size, character, and ultimately the culture of the professoriat substantially changed during the Pusey-Bundy years. In 1953 the University had 132 endowed chairs; ten years later it had 212, a 61 percent increase. Research slots went from 107 (5.4 percent) of 1,984 Corporation appointments in 1939–40 to 815 (19.4 percent) of 4,206 in 1958–59. Visiting professors increased seven- to eightfold during the period, as the University became more of a national, indeed international, institution. Nobel Prize winners accumulated: one a year, on average, between 1961 and 1965. And the postwar decline of anti-Semitism, along with the rush of Jews into the academic profession, made this the time when the Jewish Harvard professor evolved from a rarity to a cliché. In these bounteous years, it did not seem outsized for Law School professor Barton Leach to suggest to Pusey that he bring Winston Churchill to Harvard for a few years as Franklin D. Roosevelt Professor of Anglo-American Relations. But Pusey thought it unlikely that Winston (then eighty-one years old) would care to take on even the modest responsibilities of such an appointment or play an active part in Harvard academic life.[3]

Women fared far less well. None held a professorship in the Faculty of Arts and Sciences before World War II. By the time Conant departed in 1953, about 150 women had academic appointments at the University, all but a few at lower or off-ladder levels.[4]

Conant originally conceived of his University Professorship program as "roving professorships" given to extraordinary outsiders. A few were used instead to attract distinguished appointees who met specific program needs. Arabist Hamilton A. R. Gibb was brought in to get the new Middle East Studies Center off to a decent start and theologian Paul Tillich gave the Divinity School some badly needed prestige. But most University Professorships went to in-house scholars: a perk for the stars of an imperial faculty. A 1956 FAS committee warned against regarding them "as an upper class to which we should all aspire."[5]

The purchasing power of faculty salaries had declined by 50 percent during the years of war and postwar inflation. But the growth of competition among top-drawer universities and the success of Harvard fund-raising turned things around. The FAS salary ceiling went from $18,000 in 1956 to $22,000 in 1960. Bundy wanted it to rise to $25,000: "We have run like the dickens, but we have only just caught up with 1930, and we are well behind 1940." Things slowed down a bit under his successor, Franklin Ford, who told a questioner what the maximum salary was, but added (with, one suspects, some satisfaction) that no one on the faculty was making it.[6]

Professors normally had to quit when they were sixty-six, unless the president (usually dropping by the man's office) asked him to continue on to sixty-eight or seventy—or, once in a while, even beyond that. With a strong taste for new faculty blood, Bundy initially took a tough line on extensions. Five FAS professors reached the age of sixty-five in 1954–55, and he recommended that all of them be retired the following year. But the trend was for more extensions. Corporation secretary David Bailey thought that longer life expectancy made mandatory retirement at sixty-six unreasonable. Well over half of those who reached that age between 1956 and 1965 continued for at least a couple of years. A suggestion by the American Association of University Professors that left-leaning professors were not kept on was easy to refute. Of five such—Karl Sax, Zechariah Chafee, Harlow Shapley, Archibald MacLeish, and Arthur Schlesinger, Sr.—only Sax was involuntarily retired at sixty-six.[7]

Pensions were so important that they hardly counted as a fringe benefit. A professor retiring in 1966 after a forty-year career could expect a modest annual pension of $7,200. The problem was that pensions were based on accumulated reserves with a fixed dollar value. If they had been invested in a good retirement trust, a typical retiree's nest egg would have been $325,000, instead of the $58,900 credited to it. Pusey wanted to maintain the system of letting accumulated reserves fund Harvard pensions. But the pressures of inflation and interuniversity competition could not be ignored. A 1956 compensation committee recommended that the University's retirement plan be wholly noncontributory, with Harvard picking up the faculty's 5-percent-of-salary contribution.[8]

A still more impressive display of the faculty's new clout was the growth of research leave-taking. Conant had worried over how to spur his professors to greater scholarly effort; now the problem was how to keep them down on the Harvard College farm when so many think tanks and research grants beckoned. Leaves of absence multiplied (though, as Corporation Secretary Bailey wryly observed, "the stated purposes of some special leaves currently granted sound rather more exotic than would have been tolerable in the consulship of Calvin Coolidge").[9]

The Corporation began to worry about the number of faculty members (about four a year) going off to that "rest home," the Center for the Behavioral Sciences at Palo Alto. Bailey suggested that those who went there be asked to prepare reports on what they did during their sojourns. Corporation fellow Thomas Lamont feared that the faculty was coming to assume that it had the right to take off every third year. He suggested that sabbaticals be granted only once a decade, with a semester's unpaid leave in between. Bundy's (understated) response: "I do not like this idea at all." Frequent leaves, Bundy thought, kept the faculty intellectually sharp, and gave Harvard the benefit of a steady flow of visitors.[10]

When a *Reporter* magazine article, "The Affluent Professors," took a critical look at a professoriat fat with grants and other perks, Bundy leapt to the defense. The fact was that "exceedingly few men of the first quality have escaped the attention of [government] granting agencies whose first greed is for the credit of backing first-rate men." That able scientists and autonomous universities had grown in numbers and influence was all to the good, though he had to admit that neglected graduate students and more complex administrative demands were part of the cost.[11]

A more sensitive issue was the rise of paid work outside the University. High on the Corporation's worry list: chemist Robert Woodward's Swiss laboratory, political scientist Charles Cherington's employment as special counsel to the New Haven Railroad, the Business School's Donald David serving as chairman of the board of Standard Brands, two Law School faculty members who were also of counsel to Ropes and Gray. Even School of Education dean Francis Keppel carved out a lucrative niche for himself as a board member of Science Research Associates, which published and sold educational materials to schools. Keppel, in an ideal position to recommend the use of such materials, bought 9,000 shares of the company's stock for $3,700 before its public offering; it was worth $157,500 by the time it went on the market. Lamont admiringly observed: "Maybe we ought to elect him Dean of the Business School!"

But Bundy knew of only one senior FAS faculty member who devoted himself more to outside than to Harvard work, and he was not regarded highly by his colleagues. In 1965 the Faculty of Arts and Sciences adopted a statement on conflict of interest which laid down general guidelines regarding royalties, contracts, and consultancies, primarily (said Pusey) "to avoid the necessity for Government agencies to draft some unacceptable code of ethics."[12]

Before he departed for Washington in early 1961, Bundy looked upon the state of the Faculty of Arts and Sciences and found it good. He wryly apologized for "my inability to produce a deficit at a time when this difficulty does not arise in most other colleges." Year after year, conservative deficit projections turned into surpluses: $400,000 in 1959–60, $220,000 in 1960–61. In 1961–62 an anticipated deficit of $688,681 (all of it due to the heavy cost of athletics) was transmuted by the magic of overcautious budgeting into a $100,000 overage.[13]

Pusey did not exaggerate when he said that Bundy had been "an extraordinarily able, energetic and forceful leader of the Faculty . . . , and has served Harvard with great distinction." Pending the selection of a replacement, Pusey assumed the Arts and Sciences deanship as an ancillary task: not, it appeared, an overly onerous responsibility when all was so sunny and serene. In the spring of 1962 he settled on Bundy's successor: German historian Franklin Ford, who was spending the 1961–62 year at (where else?) the Behavioral Sciences Center in Palo Alto. Ford warned the president that he was no clone of Bundy: he would not be so social or political and would remain an active teaching member of the faculty. It may be assumed that Pusey did not regret a diminution of the hectic Bundy pace. Besides, he found in Ford a kindred spirit: a fellow Midwesterner (Ford was a Minnesotan who, like Paul Buck, came to Harvard as a graduate student); low-keyed and easygoing in contrast to the intense Bundy; but withal, Pusey told the Corporation, possessed of a first-rate mind, high integrity, mature judgment, personal courage, and a saving sense of humor.[14]

As the 1960s progressed, this sunny age of the imperial faculty began to darken. Ford conceded that there was grumbling over salaries. Yet only about 10 permanent FAS professors left between 1963 to 1965: no great bite out of a faculty of 375. The problem lay in other universities adopting a "politics of frank discrimination" in trying to get and keep faculty stars. Chicago's average salaries were below Harvard's, but its chemists and mathematicians were more highly paid.[15]

In 1967 an FAS committee on recruitment and retention of the faculty got to work. Labor economist (soon to be FAS dean) John Dunlop chaired the committee, whose membership included some of the major figures in the meritocratic revolution that had swept over Harvard during the past quarter of a century: historian Oscar Handlin, political scientist Merle Fainsod, chemist George Kistiakowsky, economist Edward Mason, physicist J. Curry Street.

Pusey summed up the problem confronting them: "We face the need to make as much sense as we can out of the increasing heterogeneity of our community, without losing all sense of structure in the ordering of designations, privileges, and compensation." Not surprisingly, the committee's solutions were modest ones: start young Ph.D.s as assistant professors rather than instructors, improve Cambridge schools and housing. The faculty's barons were not about to upset the cart that had borne them this far.[16]

A very different concern bubbled up in the Governing Boards: how loyal to Harvard, how dedicated to teaching, was the new faculty breed? Lamont darkened Dean Franklin Ford's day by sending him "The Flight from Teaching," an article by Carnegie Corporation head John Gardner. Lamont reassuringly observed that Gardner's bleak view of nonteaching research professors did not yet apply to Harvard, where most of the faculty subscribed to the view that teaching and research went together. But there was a "real threat" that "institutional loyalty may be disrupted through dependence on outside funding, so that teaching, whether formal or informal, could come to be viewed as a costly distraction from productive research." The administration, Lamont thought, should be more concerned over the danger that the faculty was tilting more to research, less to undergraduate teaching. As the explosion of knowledge went on, the pressure to be on its cutting edge could outweigh the obligation to train young minds.[17]

Other, more subtle tensions built up as well, eroding the traditional Harvard faculty-administration relationship. Ford lacked Bundy's touch with the faculty, and the times they were a-changing. Humanists sensed—and resented—the growing status of research-fat scientists. Notable faculty members often regarded themselves more as scholarly entrepreneurs than as members of a collegial body. Two prime examples: historian Arthur M. Schlesinger, Jr., and economist John Kenneth Galbraith. Schlesinger later recalled his blithe disregard of the rule (adopted in January 1964) that Corporation approval was necessary for brief leaves of absence in term time.

He was hardly alone in this. In 1966 Dean Ford chastised Galbraith for a three-week absence from Cambridge during Harvard's reading and examination period. Galbraith had been authorized to attend the funeral of the Indian prime minister, but no one expected that the trip would include a skiing vacation with Jacqueline Kennedy at Gstaad. Galbraith responded with his customary adversarial zest. He had "considerable difficulty in imagining myself in the role of an indolent professor; ... the suggestion of a three-week vacation amazes me." But Ford stubbornly insisted that only the Corporation could give permission for an extended leave of absence in term time; and that, manifestly, had not been done. A year later Galbraith, pleading ill health, requested blanket permission to be absent during reading/exam periods. Ford and Pusey thought it best to respond to particular, year-by-year requests; to do more would, in effect, authorize a part-time professorship. It is hard to imagine that these exchanges did not hang in the middle distance when Galbraith confronted Pusey and Ford during the student protests of the late sixties.[18]

## The Social Sciences

It was during the 1950s and 1960s that a meritocratic faculty took command at Harvard. But it did so as members of particular departments and disciplines, not as a corporate body. The social sciences were especially conspicuous in this disciplinary efflorescence. The widespread belief (not least among themselves) that they were uniquely qualified to plumb the depths of the human personality, society, and the economy greatly enhanced their prestige. The most charismatic, intellectually stimulating pre-World War II Harvard teachers tended to be in the humanities; now they were more likely to be in the behavioral and policy sciences and in History.

The appearance in 1954 of a massive faculty committee report, *The Behavioral Sciences at Harvard*, signaled the institutional coming-of-age of these disciplines. It reviewed their past condition (nothing special), their present state (full of vitality and promise), and their future needs (to appoint more senior faculty, concentrate on theory, and leave applied research to the professional schools). The triad of Sociology, Psychology, and Anthropology threw off their prewar marginality. The new Department of Social Relations and the older departments of Psychology and Anthropology made a flock of strong appointments, bringing Harvard to the forefront in one social science field after another. Large-scale research projects, centers, and laboratories flourished, well watered by grants from the National Institutes of Mental Health (NIMH) and other Croesian founts.[19]

Social Relations, created in 1946 by Harvard's social anthropologists, social psychologists, and sociologists, personified the ebullient self-confidence of the postwar social sciences. The new department rapidly expanded, with nine senior appointments in 1965–66 alone. True to its origins, Social Relations was receptive to appointments that went beyond traditional disciplinary confines. Laurence Wylie came from Haverford in 1959 as Clarence Dillon Professor of French Civilization, a chair whose perks included a yearly case of wine from Dillon-owned Chateau Haut-Brion. He taught French literature, but his *Village in the Vaucluse* (1957), the book that made his reputation, was popular social anthropology. Social Relations was glad to have him, Romance Languages (Wylie's was a joint appointment) less so—"which," Dean Bundy observed, "seems to suggest that languages and literatures are not necessarily the central method of inquiry into French civilization." Bundy himself took the lead in bringing lay analyst Erik Erikson as professor of Human Development in 1959. Again, Social Relations welcomed this out-of-the-ordinary appointment.[20]

As befitted a serious social science department, Social Relations had a laboratory, which housed enterprises such as Henry Murray's Center for Research in Personality and George Miller and Jerome Bruner's Center for Cognitive Studies. But success was an evanescent thing, even in so hospitable a clime as the 1950s and the 1960s. The deaths in the summer of 1960 of Social Relations Laboratory director Samuel Stouffer and anthropologist Clyde Kluckhohn hit the department hard. And of nineteen senior offers between 1957 and 1967, only ten were accepted. Chairman Talcott Parsons thought the no-shows were put off by the "Harvard rat race": the pressure of hordes of undergraduate and graduate students, examinations and theses, department and committee meetings.

Most of all, the continuing appeal of autonomous disciplines, so strong in every field, gradually dimmed the aura of Social Relations. As anthropologist John Whiting aptly noted, the new department "contained several tribes whose identities were not interchangeable and could not be merged." The sociologists in Social Relations reconstituted themselves as a separate Department of Sociology in 1970. The remaining members divided into three groups: social anthropologists, social psychologists, and personality and developmental psychologists. Each ran its own graduate program and controlled its faculty appointments, a halfway house before the full restoration of Anthropology and Psychology and the disappearance of Social Relations in the early 1970s.[21]

Sociology, always loose limbed in its disciplinary boundaries, flourished during the 1960s as social theory and race relations assumed a more conspicuous place on the Harvard (and national) academic scene. Invigorated by its new lease on academic life, the sociologists dropped their statistical methods requirement for the Ph.D. on the ground that their subject had become so diverse that it was best to leave it up to students to meet their methodological needs. Besides, the flourishing antinomian sentiment against rules and requirements found in Sociology rich soil indeed. When Soviet expert Alex Inkeles left for Stanford in 1970, the new department preferred a theorist to an empiricist and made an unsuccessful reach for Berkeley's Neil Smelser. Public intellectuals Daniel Bell (who was also a leading social theorist) and Nathan Glazer reinforced the prevailing nonquantitative emphasis.[22]

Psychology continued to be divided between its experimentalists, who dominated the department, and its social-clinical wing, which in the 1960s resided in Social Relations. The problem, Pusey thought, was "[h]ow to build back a strong unified department of psychology?" That would not be easy. Social psychologist David McClelland, who became the chair of Social Relations in 1962, complained of how hard it was to deal with Stanley Smith Stevens, the director of the Psychological Laboratory. Stevens was a severe, traditional experimentalist, uninterested in undergraduates. But the standing of Harvard's experimental psychologists was not to be sneezed at. Stevens's colleague Georg von Békésy won a Nobel Prize in Medicine in 1961 for his work on the inner ear. And the Psychological Lab was the home of the brilliant (and controversial) B. F. Skinner's work on conditioning.[23]

Relations among the experimentalists themselves were troubled. A bitter feud raged between Psychological Lab director Stevens and lecturer Edwin B. Newman. Pusey decided in the fall of 1962 to remove Stevens as director. Stevens agreed—so long as Newman was not his successor; otherwise, he would have to be forced out. After some huffing and puffing, Stevens relented, assuaged by a change in the title of his professorship and his laboratory from Psychoacoustics to the more prestigious Psychophysics. Soon after this, "Smitty" Stevens married Geraldine Stone, his assistant for more than 30 years, and underwent a personality change, from dour and sour to open and pleasant, that left Pusey awestruck. "How amazing," Pusey observed, "that it should turn out this way!" But perhaps not so amazing, psychologically speaking.[24]

Anthropology's strong disciplinary ties to exotic, remote times and places—to ethnology and archaeology—kept it a relatively marginal player in the brave new world of behavioral science. Harvard's department found it difficult to gain a standing in its discipline comparable to its fellow social scientists. It benefited, however, from growing student interest in the Third World. And the national demand for anthropology Ph.D.s gave a boost to its doctoral program.[25]

Anthropology, like the other behavioral disciplines, was sharply divided into wings: archaeological, social, and biological. The Peabody Museum, where traditional, genteel archaeology and ethnography peacefully prevailed, was most resistant to change. Longtime museum director John Otis ("Jo") Brew set the tone. By the 1960s the museum was badly short of money, its important ethnological collections were deteriorating, its storage space was scarce, little new money was coming in. Finally in 1967 Pusey told Brew that the Anthropology faculty and the Peabody staff had lost confidence in his leadership and that Stephen Williams, the new Anthropology chair, would be better able to raise the money that the Peabody needed.[26]

Williams took over a museum in financial and procedural disarray. Oldtimers grumbled that the Peabody in effect was being "turned over to the Department of Anthropology for the study and teaching of that science." Then the widow of longtime Anthropology professor Alfred Tozzer gave the department a million dollars for a library in her husband's name. The power of Harvard's disciplines to shape the destiny of their affiliated institutions was too great, too much a part of the established University culture, to be seriously challenged.[27]

The behavioral sciences made great strides during the 1950s and the 1960s; but then they had so very far to go. Even in this high noon of scientific social science, the loopy (though occasionally brilliant) style of investigation evident before World War II persisted. Sociologist Pitirim Sorokin retired in 1955, and the Lilly Foundation wanted to continue its support of his inquiries into what he called creative altruism. Bundy discussed the matter with Talcott Parsons and Samuel Stouffer of Social Relations and found them quite ready "to see the old boy get research funds from those who believe in his work," but Sorokin's intellectual irrelevance to his Sociology colleagues was evident. As Parsons carefully put it when Sorokin retired: "Perhaps no major figure in this country has been so drastically critical of the work of almost all his colleagues at Harvard and everywhere else, as Professor Sorokin has." By opposing the creation of the Department of Social Relations he had, said Parsons, failed to see that "something of great importance was happening in American science and that we at Harvard could have a vital part in it."[28]

On a more contemporary note, psychiatrist John Spiegel, a research associate in the Social Relations Laboratory, was threatened with an obscenity prosecution because he had in his possession a number of photographs of nudes in sexually suggestive positions. Bundy assured Pusey that Spiegel was using them for the respectably scientific purpose of studying how emotionally disturbing attitudes were communicated by adults to children, and he thought that Harvard should be ready to come to Spiegel's aid if necessary. So it did, and Spiegel was cleared.[29]

And then there was the widely noted case of lecturer on Clinical Psychology Timothy Leary and his associate Richard Alpert (soon to be known more euphoniously as Baba Ram Das). Leary got a term appointment in 1959, Social Relations chair Robert White assuring Bundy that he was fully trained to teach the theory and practice of psychotherapy "and to fit in several other ways with the Department's program in clinical psychology and personality research." Fit Leary did—like a knife in a glove. He and Alpert set up a project for research into (and proselytizing for) the "consciousness-expansion" potential of the drug psilocybin. Their research subjects: Harvard undergraduates.

Concern grew over the scientific, moral, and legal liability of what became a half-experimental, half-communal search for a higher consciousness. In a parodic self-portrayal of the dedicated researcher stifled by conventionality, Leary complained to Social Relations Laboratory director Robert Bales: "My own notions about the university hold that consciousness-expansion should be its central concern and primary mission." Surely much of the faculty should be "out on the uncharted frontiers stirring up new and disturbing ideas. If a goodly percent of parents aren't disturbed by what their sons are experiencing and discovering at the university then I would question whether the university is doing its job. If a goodly percent of its faculty are not unpopular with conventional policy-makers then I suggest the university administration re-examine its mission and their motives."

Leary recognized that "[d]ramatic advances in human knowledge have usually had to develop outside the academy." So he did not contest the decision to separate his project from Harvard in late 1962. He already had his own, independent venue: the International Federation for Internal Freedom, encased in a nonprofit corporation. In the spring of 1963 Leary's and Alpert's University appointments lapsed, amid charges of neglect of teaching and absence from Cambridge (and in Alpert's case grave misconduct in continuing to give drugs to undergraduates after being told not to). Leary took his crusade for "informal self-exploration" by the young into the larger history of the decade.[30]

Harvard's Department of Economics threw off its history of internal divisions and external threats during the 1950s and 1960s. It came now into heady days as the Queen of the Social Sciences, the discipline most highly regarded (not least by its own members) as the most scientific, the most predictive, of them all. In the 1960s the department's visiting committee, reflecting a general change in business sentiment, became less worried that the economists bore the mark of Keynes. More important was the persistent tension in the department between the desire for the best minds and the need to fill slots. Chairman Arthur Smithies warned in 1953: "While the Department's basic policy in proposing new appointments is to strengthen itself generally, it must pay attention to its requirements in particular fields."[31]

Meanwhile a new economics came of age: highly mathematical, self-confident, and intellectually compelling. The visiting committee, for years a fount of criticism, reported in 1958 that the Economics faculty was in excellent shape. It detected a new interest in undergraduate teaching; Chairman Seymour Harris was energetic; an apolitical ambience prevailed. Harris playfully told the visiting committee: "You can assure the Overseers that there is only one dangerous man left in the Department and that is the Chairman himself!" Galbraith came to be regarded by his alumni critics not as a threat to the Republic but as a stimulating (if annoying) gadfly in the Harvard tradition. Bundy summed up his unsettling colleague:

> I myself think that Kenneth Galbraith has one of the most imaginative and powerful minds in the Faculty of Arts and Sciences. I also think he shares this view. He is not a man distinguished by modesty, and in his map of the world is quite near himself. I wish these defects did not exist, because I am more and more persuaded that generosity is a cardinal virtue in university life. But intellectual distinction, energy, industry, and creative imagination are rare, and he has them all."[32]

The department moved from strength to strength. Simon Kuznets, arguably the leading American economist of his generation, was appointed in 1959, an ad hoc committee waived because of his eminence. During the 1960s Harvard Economics added appointees involved in sexy new areas of policy: the economics of defense, health, education, science, and the arts; of human resources, water, the city, and development. Cooperation with the professional schools, so much desired by Conant but impeded by the ideological divisions of the past, now blossomed under the warming sun of shared disciplinary professionalism. Economist Richard Musgrave joined the Law School faculty, statistician Howard Raiffa belonged to both the Economics department and the Business School.

In 1968 Kenneth Arrow, Kuznets's successor at the top of the theoretician pecking order, came from Stanford. Martin Feldstein became director of the National Bureau of Economic Research, which was transported from New York to Cambridge. Otto Eckstein took over Economics 1 and made it the undergraduate supercourse that overseer critics had so long sought. The department's staff, a substantial 55 in 1959–60, grew to a distended 118 in 1966–67. Most of the bulge consisted of an expanded helotry: teaching fellows and junior faculty, hewers of undergraduate wood who helped free the senior faculty to pursue their research. Some \$600,000 a year came in for the members' projects: 50 percent from foundations, 40 percent from government, a modest and uncorrupting 10 percent from business.[33]

As the department rose in eminence, so did a nervous concern over what it would take to stay on top. Bundy was aware of "the growing strength and financial exuberance of more than one Department elsewhere." Harvard Economics lagged behind MIT in most rankings and often lost out in competition for junior faculty and graduate students to that institution as well as to Yale, Princeton, Chicago, Stanford, and Berkeley. In the new world of high-powered interuniversity competition, secure standing was a will-o'-the-wisp.[34]

Few departments in postwar Harvard matched History's prestige. In 1954 Dean Paul Buck recommended that Oscar Handlin and Arthur Schlesinger, Jr., be made full professors. They were leaders of their generation of American historians, "should guarantee Harvard distinction for many years," and internal friction would be avoided if they moved up in tandem. In a close decision, the department chose its own Ph.D. Franklin Ford over its own Ph.D. Carl Schorske for a professorship in German history. Harvard Ph.D. and assistant professor Bernard Bailyn succeeded Samuel Eliot Morison as the senior colonial American historian in 1958, everyone involved convinced that he was the best of his generation. The same was true of Richard Pipes in Russian history.[35]

By the end of the 1950s, History at Harvard was widely thought to be at the pinnacle of its profession (though Columbia, Yale, and Berkeley pressed hard). But the department came to be dogged by what Bernard Bailyn called "the Harvard problem": a "ridiculously inflated" reputation and a self-esteem that fed a hobbling fear of making less than superlative appointments. In 1954 it sought a replacement for Paul Buck in American history. The Americanists defined the position as one in which undergraduate teaching—particularly the American history survey course—was a sine qua non. This had the effect of eliminating Richard

Hofstadter and C. Vann Woodward, arguably the two best non-Harvard American historians, from serious consideration. The final preference: Frank Freidel of Stanford. Oscar Handlin explained why. In "innate intellectual ability" Freidel was ahead of his competitors. He was a dedicated and effective undergraduate teacher. Perhaps most of all, his appointment "would do Harvard a lot of good in the country." Freidel went to national historical association meetings, was well-known and well-liked, was a Westerner and not a Harvard product:

> So long as the University considers itself a national institution and so long as the Department strives to preserve its role as a great center for the graduate training of scholars, it is vital that appointments command the respect of the whole profession and also further our associations with scholarship throughout the country. Only thus will we continue to attract the best graduate students, place them in desirable jobs, and diffuse our influence nationally, as we have in the past.[36]

In the mid-1960s Annielouise Bliss Warren, the widow of former assistant attorney general and constitutional scholar Charles Warren, left $7.5 million in her husband's memory to further American History at Harvard. Much of it endowed chairs in Arts and Sciences, Law, Education, and Divinity. The rest went to establish the Charles Warren Center for Studies in American History, a research center designed by the senior American historians to further strengthen the record of that field at Harvard, "measurable within the University by the prominence of American history in undergraduate instruction and outside it by the number and distinction of its Ph.D.'s who have entered the academic life of the nation."

Now, they warned, this jewel in Harvard's crown faced a moment of choice. The graduate program in American history "will either be established in a sound institutional structure or, responsive to the uncontrollable, expansive forces in American education, it will be swept away." The rise of new universities, and the promiscuous distribution of federal support, had led to the multiplication of well-heeled but, they thought, inferior programs in other universities. With the Charles Warren money, Harvard's American historians would be able to meet their responsibility by bringing in promising young Ph.D.s from elsewhere to benefit from a postdoctoral year at Harvard. And it would give the faculty annual research supplements allowing them to pursue their scholarship without the need to seek outside aid. Finally, the Warren

Center in some unspecified way would "benefit the Department as a whole as well as the Americanists."[37]

The Warren Center had some harmful consequences. It led the senior American historians to pay less attention to the history profession and to be less inclined to add to the roster of tenured historians of the United States. Indeed, during the 1960s the department at large appeared to lose its appointments touch of previous years. Though some strong appointments were made in the European wing, most notably economic historian David Landes and Reformation historian William Bouwsma, major foreign historians declined to come because they did not want to leave their homelands, and turndowns increased from American scholars comfortably ensconced in ever more prosperous research universities.[38]

In 1967 Judge Henry Friendly, who headed the Overseers' visiting committee to the department, took note of its growing disarray. Seven of twenty-one permanent slots were empty, as were ten of thirteen assistant professorships. He urged the historians to do more to identify the best young men at an earlier age and offer them either tenured positions or a reasonable assurance of promotion. And he suggested that "it might be wise to adopt a slightly more benevolent attitude in the selection of men from other universities." Meanwhile the department's annual reports to the dean, never noted for detailed treatment of internal developments, became (uniquely among the major FAS departments) nothing more than a list of the faculty's publications and honors. The curtains as well as the wagons were drawn. Perhaps nowhere else at Harvard were the costs of success so heavy.[39]

When Nathan Pusey became president it was time—past time—for the department of Government to snap out of its doldrums. William Yandell Elliott and Carl Friedrich, its most powerful prewar barons, lasted until 1962 and 1971. Comparative Government scholar Samuel Huntington recalls that he was denied tenure in the late 1950s because the clubby types who ran the department were put off by his (then relatively liberal) political views and even more by "the smell of the lamp"—the odor of the déclassé scholar—that clung to him. Off Huntington went to Siberian exile: to Columbia. A more quality-driven department brought him back in 1962.[40]

Change came first in American politics, which fell between the baronies of comparative politics expert Friedrich and international relations specialist Elliott. The promotion of theorist Louis Hartz and the arrival of voting analyst V. O. Key from Yale in 1953 were signs of a new vitality (though Key had only a decade more to live). In 1959 a divided department proposed Stanley Hoffmann and Henry Kissinger for permanencies in comparative politics and international relations, and brought in urban politics expert Edward Banfield from Chicago. Bundy reported that even those opposed to Kissinger agreed that he had "one of the most powerful minds currently at work in the area of international affairs." But he had "a certain rigidity of mind which is disconcerting in a field as subtle and full of nuances as international politics" and "a certain Germanic cast of temperament which makes him not always an easy colleague." More serious: Kissinger spent much time as a general public sage and advisor to politicians. Still in sum his appointment was "a thoroughly worthy gamble, of the sort which it would be timid not to make."[41]

The "body" needs of a department, in healthy tension with the value placed on "mind," shaped the course of appointments. As in Economics, a more rigorously theory-driven Political Science was displacing the old institutional approach. William Yandell Elliott warned that behaviorists who wrote about politics and government without participating in them contributed to "the sterility of a tremendous part of what has been termed 'political science' in this country." Thankfully, Harvard's department still had a considerable attachment to the pursuit of political theory. He hoped "that the time may not come when the tradition may disappear from Harvard in favor of incantations in the jargon of the sociologues."[42]

It is true that the department lagged in quantitative and behavioral political science. In this sense it did not keep pace with Yale, Chicago, or MIT. But in other respects it flourished. After Elliott and Friedrich left, its internal governance became more democratic. And the department began to recruit junior faculty from outside, instead of relying exclusively on its own students.

Strong new appointees kept arriving. Banfield's Chicago protégé James Q. Wilson came as a junior faculty member in 1961, got tenure two years later, and quickly became a major political scientist and Harvard citizen. The 1965–66 academic year—high noon of the meritocratic University—saw the appointment (jointly with Social Relations) of political sociologist Seymour Martin Lipset, up-and-coming political theorists Michael Walzer and Harvey Mansfield (one leaning left, the other right, products of a deal appropriate to a department of government), and Karl Deutsch in International Relations (to occupy a new chair endowed by the Ford Foundation). One of the earliest and best of Harvard's senior women faculty was Judith Shklar. When foot-dragging in the department suggested that tenure would be a problem, she successfully proposed that she be made a permanent lecturer, which converted in 1972 to a full professorship.[43]

While the old disciplines wrestled with the consequences of meritocracy and affluence, Harvard's area centers—Russian, East Asian, Middle East, International Affairs, Urban Studies—claimed an increasing share of faculty time and commitment, financial assets, and the University's intellectual life. They were in Bundy's view the most striking development in postwar Harvard. He sought to maintain the principle that all of the centers' appointees belonged to and came from academic departments. But some feared that the centers "tend to ... lead to aggrandizement of individual scholars or special interest groups on the periphery of the University's logical areas of concern."[44]

Another source of anxiety was the danger that foundation and government grants would wag the research tails of the center dogs. Curmudgeon columnist Joseph Alsop resigned in 1961 from the Overseers' visiting committee to the East Asian Center over this issue. He decried the decline of classical Chinese studies in favor of contemporary concerns. The study of Communist China, he thought, was better left to the CIA. As for Robert Bowie's Center for International Affairs and the Russian Research Center: "In the diminishing community of serious American scholars, both Dr. Bowie's boondoggle and the Russian boondoggle are established laughing stocks and with good reason." Pusey rejected Alsop's criticism, and East Asian Center director John K. Fairbank gave assurances that there was no intention of abandoning classical scholarship. Russian Research Center director Merle Fainsod admitted that Alsop's skeptical view of the center's work might have been valid in its early days, when it was dependent on the Air Force for its funds, but claimed that this was no longer the case.[45]

The Harvard-MIT Joint Center for Urban Studies got under way in 1959. It came into its palmiest days when James Q. Wilson took over in 1963 and America's urban crisis assumed center stage in domestic affairs. In 1965 the center turned to the Ford Foundation for large-scale support. Wilson pushed hard for professorships, not research money. When the application smoke cleared, Harvard had five Ford-endowed chairs in urban studies. But for all its topicality, and despite directors of the caliber of Wilson and Daniel Patrick Moynihan, who ran it from 1966 to 1969, the Joint Center did not become a permanent fixture on the Harvard scene. Why? In part because cosponsorship with MIT posed all but insurmountable jurisdictional problems. And in part because faculty who were interested in urban studies found more compelling reasons (rooted in their disciplinary identities and access to research funds) to work in their own departments or professional schools.[46]

The Center for International Affairs (CFIA) was another story. It got under way in 1957–58 as an adjunct of the Graduate School of Public Administration. CFIA's first director was professor of International Affairs Robert Bowie and Henry Kissinger was its associate director: ambitious men with big plans. In 1960 the University asked the Ford Foundation for a hefty $17.2 million to pay for a building, a flock of new chairs, research grants, and books. Harvard finally wound up with $5.5 million for the support of international studies programs and $4.5 million for the endowment of professorships in the field. Dividing this cake called for an allocation committee, run by Pusey, to avoid (in FAS dean Franklin Ford's words) "turning individual departments into self-ish, parochial little institutes, trying to do what departments of instruction are not really designed for."[47]

From its start, CFIA was deeply and often controversially involved in politics and public policy. Its initial areas of concern were a what's what of potentially troublemaking topics: arms control, foreign aid, development. Being so much in the world had its risks. The Center's development projects stirred up enough criticism to lead CFIA to try to shift its role from advice and management to teaching and research. But Ford and other foundations wanted more hands-on training. Soon plans were under way for the Development Advisory Service—established in 1962, later renamed the Harvard Institute for International Development (HIID)—to do this sort of work, in association with but separate from CFIA.[48]

The tensions between teaching departments and research centers, the problems of balancing scholarship and activism, and of dividing grant money among a flock of clamoring claimants, paled beside the hubris of "Harvard in the World." Inevitably the richest and most powerful of America's universities zestfully took on the challenge of area and international studies. No less inevitably, CFIA, the chosen instrument of this imperial reach, became a prime target of radicals in the late 1960s.

## The Natural Sciences

Science at Harvard, as everywhere else, flourished in the 1950s and 1960s, boosted by its vastly enhanced prestige in World War II and kept aloft by the theoretical and applied triumphs of quantum physics and the molecular revolution in biology. This was the age of Big Science: big in its breakthroughs, in its cultural, social and economic effects, in its scale and cost. The place of science in Harvard's curriculum and intellectual life steadily grew in importance. In 1958 a committee headed by psychologist Jerome Bruner called for a new tack in General Education science courses, one designed to expose students to the workings of the scientific method. A supporter of the more historical Great Ideas approach that Conant had championed called this a "surrender to specialization." Bruner responded: "It was our feeling simply that it was of the essence that a student get some firm grasp on what science is."[49]

Envision Harvard science as a complex system of autonomous departments, large (Chemistry, Physics, Biology, the Division of Engineering and Applied Physics) and small (Mathematics, Astronomy and the Harvard College Observatory, Geology). Wheeling around these bodies are moonlike affiliates: the Botanical Institutions, the museums, Harvard Forest, the Blue Hill weather observatory. Holding it all together (insofar as it *did* hold together) are the academic equivalents of gravity: innovation and intellectual horsepower, status, money.

Money most definitely. The Higgins Trust, a $15 million benefaction that appeared out of nowhere in the early 1950s, enabled the presidents of Harvard, Yale, Princeton, and Columbia to make large annual distributions for scientific projects. FAS dean McGeorge Bundy, scrambling to satisfy his hungry scientists, tried hard to increase the size of the pie. He wanted to urge upon the fund's trustees "a more rake-hell policy— and damn the consequences." But the money was conservatively invested, its largess limited.[50]

The Gordon McKay Bequest for Engineering and Applied Physics fully matured (as fund-raisers put it) in the 1950s when the last family legatee died. And the richly laden Maria Moors Cabot Foundation for Botanical Research enabled that wing of Biology to live in a manner to which their colleagues would have loved to become accustomed. Most of all, the growth of Harvard science was sustained by rising foundation and especially federal support.[51]

An ambitious fund-raiser, the Program for Science in Harvard College, got under way in the mid-sixties. The centerpiece of this effort was a massive new science center to provide the labs and lecture halls required to teach science more effectively to Harvard undergraduates. Harvard's biologists, and in particular its biochemists, who saw little place for themselves in so undergraduate-centered a structure, thought it a waste of money. The center, they complained, would separate undergraduates even further from the faculty. What was really needed were better and more abundant research laboratories. But Polaroid head Edwin Land, who had been given Harvard laboratory space to work in after he dropped out of the College, donated $11 million to make the building a reality.[52]

Physics may have had more glamor during the 1940s, but Chemistry still was regarded (at least by the chemists) as the best and best managed of Harvard's science departments. Its towering figure was Nobelist Robert Woodward. He and his senior colleagues, observed Corporation Secretary David Bailey, shared "a fierce individualism which sometimes generates a good deal of personal heat." The sun of Harvard meritocracy blazed nowhere more strongly than in Chemistry hiring: a ceaseless effort (usually successful) to appoint The Best.[53]

Major appointments changed the face of the Harvard Chemistry faculty during the Pusey years. Konrad Bloch and Frank Westheimer came as its first biochemists in 1954, organic chemist E. J. Corey and physical chemists William Lipscomb and Dudley Herschbach were added in the 1960s. All of them except Westheimer had done their graduate work in other universities, all were teaching elsewhere when they were appointed. Woodward, Bloch, Lipscomb, Herschbach, and Corey would win Nobel Prizes. Harvard Chemistry had a reasonable claim to be the best in the world.[54]

Meritocracy had its costs, not least in undergraduate teaching. Famous, busy scientists often had more compelling things to do. Woodward refused to teach elementary courses (and in time *any* scheduled course); another member of the department taught physical chemistry so carelessly that he was excused from that chore. A Harvard chemist observed in the mid-1950s: "As my colleagues gain in prestige, they almost automatically lose drastically in the amount of time they can spend on teaching and research. Even the number of days which Woodward had to take to go and get his honorary degrees and prizes adds up to a formidable total."

And the passage of time had an erosive effect. By the early 1970s biochemists Bloch, Westheimer, Lipscomb, and Paul Doty were near retirement or had transferred to the newly established Department of Biochemistry. The very fact of the department's long preeminence in organic and physical chemistry may have contributed to the failure to make on offer to inorganic chemist (and soon-to-be Nobelist) Geoffrey Wilkinson. The competitive pressures that helped make Harvard Chemistry so good also ensured that success would remain an unstable compound.[55]

* * *

Harvard Physics professors won Nobels at an ego-gratifying rate: Percy Bridgman in 1946, Edward Purcell in 1952, Julian Schwinger in 1965, John Van Vleck in 1977. The popularity of the subject made it the fourth largest undergraduate concentration in 1957–58. But as in Chemistry, the department had to navigate between the competitive desire for the best of the best, and the more quotidian need to maintain departmental balance. The stiff standards of a high-achieving field, and the competitive pressure of other universities, left their marks. Serving on an ad hoc committee, J. Robert Oppenheimer opposed the appointment of physicist Richard Feynman in 1955 for several reasons, including age: he thought the thirty-seven-year-old Feynman was a bit long in the tooth for the position. When in 1964 the department, on the hunt for an outstanding theorist, decided (with some reservations) to invite Murray Gell-Mann, the thirty-four-year old accepted—then backed away when confronted by even more delectable goodies: university professorships at Berkeley or MIT. Future Nobelists Sheldon Glashow and Steven Weinberg eventually filled the gap.[56]

High energy physics, the most glamorous area of the time, required lots of space and money, so Harvard and MIT opened the Cambridge Electron Accelerator (CEA) in 1962, the most powerful of its kind until 1970. Its direction was in the hands of an executive committee composed of the major users. But the group proved to be unable to work together amicably, to make hard choices, or to build needed equipment. Then a 1965 fire crippled the CEA, and federal support ended in 1967.[57]

Physics was a discipline international in its culture, much of it dependent on the big machines of Big Science. Quantum physics came to focus on the hunt for ever smaller particles of matter, which required ever larger accelerators. Harvard had neither the people, the space, nor the big government financing to be a major player in that game. The comings, and especially the goings, of particle physicist Carlo Rubbia exemplified the problems this raised. Rubbia's work led him to spend much of his time at CERN, the accelerator center straddling Switzerland and France. Soon he was known as the Swissair professor: rarely around and unavailable to teach the elementary course in particle physics.

Old-timers regretted the loss of a once strong sense of community. The weekly department lunch, in prewar years an effective bonding device for the faculty, came to be limited to senior faculty every other week, and the juniors complained. Criticism mounted, too, over the dominance of the theoreticians, once a source of shared pride. Experimentalists complained in 1970 that Harvard Physics had become in effect an institute for theoreticians, its Lyman Hall laboratories converted into blackboard-lined offices. The department, all agreed, was well run. But it did not assert itself as well as aggressive Chemistry in the eternal struggle to get more financial support from the dean. Its great men—Julian Schwinger, Norman Ramsey, Edward Purcell—were temperamentally disinclined to fight for resources, nor was it clear to them that big and good were the same thing.[58]

In 1970 the department got only a handful of the graduate applicants it accepted that year, apparently because of limited financial aid and its lack of strength in high-energy physics. And in 1971 Julian Schwinger, past his prime but still a luminary, went off to California. A senior member thought that Harvard for some time had slipped from the forefront in both theoretical and experimental physics. Meanwhile other places—Princeton, Cal. Tech., Berkeley, Illinois, Cornell—moved ahead. In physics as in chemistry, the successes of Harvard past, and the money and talent of Harvard present, did not in and of themselves assure supremacy in fields where past strengths could so quickly become current impediments.[59]

Biology's vexed relations with the University's botanical institutions eased after the Twenty Years' War over the Arnold Arboretum sputtered to its close. But tensions continued between the department's biologists and appointees of the Museum of Comparative Zoology (MCZ), heightened by infighting among Biology's organismic/evolutionary, cellular, and molecular wings.

Prospects for a more fruitful relationship between the department and the museum improved in pace with the MCZ's greater financial well-being. But the old Brahmin curatorial tradition continued to fight a losing battle against professional-academic Biology. In 1955 the MCZ recommended that Curator of Mammals Charles Lyman get tenure. President Pusey turned him down. Other priorities in the field were more important, and it was not clear that Lyman was the best person available. Lyman was shuffled to an off-ladder appointment, and promotion went instead to Curator of Reptiles and Amphibians Ernest Williams, who did work more closely linked to the museum's major research interests.[60]

A larger issue was the relevance to modern biology of the museum's chief reason for being, the collection and classification of species—systematics, in the lingo of the field. When the distinguished paleontologist George Gaylord Simpson was under consideration to be

Alexander Agassiz Professor at the MCZ, Bundy sought the opinions of a few knowledgeable people. One of these was James Bryant Conant, whose unsettling response was that he had never heard of Simpson and that "[a]s an ex-laboratory scientist I take a dim view of all museum scientists whose period of importance closed with the 19th century!" But Simpson came, and when MCZ director Alfred Romer retired in 1960 he was succeeded by the noted evolutionist Ernst Mayr. Thereafter the MCZ-department relationship focused on questions of teaching and governance more than on scientific standards.[61]

Biology itself was riven by the rise of its molecular and cellular wings. The New Biology came to the fore with the breathtaking discovery of DNA, as dramatic as the triumphs of nuclear physics a generation before. At the heart of the molecular-organismic conflict were the outsized personages of James D. Watson and Edward O. Wilson. Both had been assistant professors since 1956. Bundy observed that Watson's "outspoken disapproval of many of the practices of our Department of Biology has not been made more palatable by the fact that he is usually right." Wilson was a comparably *wünderkindlich* comer in evolutionary zoology and animal behavior, who rose from a close-to-dysfunctional Alabama family to become a Harvard junior fellow. He came up for tenure in 1958. His unusual qualifications, Bundy explained, "have brought the department to an abandonment of its usual strong insistence upon a governing concern for specific subjects, rather than individuals. In my judgment, this shift in emphasis is highly desirable." Mind over body.

The ad hoc committee cautioned that Wilson's appointment should not block Watson, "a young man of even greater brilliance and research promise." Bundy guaranteed that room would be made for a permanent appointment in the molecular field. He used a Wisconsin offer to the thirty-year-old Watson to prod the department into action. The vote was a resounding 16–1. Although Bundy regretted "that the enthusiasm of the Department is not equal to the size of the majority," he feared "that this lack of enthusiasm reflects more on the Department than on Watson," who was "one of the most remarkable young men in American biology, and as one man [on the ad hoc committee] put it, if there were no place for him here, then there must be something radically wrong with the study of biology at Harvard." Bundy delicately added that Watson was also "a young man whose brilliance and judgment in scientific matters are not matched by remarkable personal tact or administrative tidiness." Nevertheless, "it is quite unthinkable that we should fail to promote a young man of such extraordinary abilities."[62]

Here, crystalline in its clarity, is the culture of meritocratic Harvard at high noon. Watson appears to have come as close as anyone could to test the degree to which mind mattered not only over body but above collegiality. Mincing no words, Wilson in his memoir called him "the most unpleasant human being I had ever met, the Caligula of biology." Utterly convinced that the discipline had to focus on molecules and cells and use the language of physics and mathematics—the kind of commitment that made him a great scientist—Watson dismissed traditional, taxonomic biology as little better than stamp collecting.

While the organismic-molecular division in the department was abrasive, it had positive scientific consequences. Wilson later claimed that the competitive stimulus of the revolution in molecular biology and his "brilliant enemy" Watson "was part of the motivation for my own attempt in the 1970s to bring biology into the social sciences through a systematization of the new discipline of sociobiology."[63]

The molecular biologists grew in numbers and clout during the 1960s, much as the quantum physicists did in the 1930s and the 1940s. Thirty-year-old Matthew Meselson came from Cal. Tech. in 1960, like Watson with the very highest promise "in the great new field of study which connects understanding of the molecule with the basic processes of life." Four years later FAS Dean Ford recommended Meselson for a full professorship, noting that he "has thrown himself and his high abilities unreservedly into the campaign to make this University one of the world's leading centers in the rapidly expanding and proliferating field of molecular biology." Edward O. Wilson was promoted too: "At a time when much of the 'noise' in Biology is inspired by new developments in the molecular field, it seems important for Harvard to maintain some balance by showing its interest in the study of whole organisms as well."[64]

The Old Guard, as Old Guards do, viewed these changes with alarm. Former MCZ director Alfred Romer thought that the rise of molecularism was all to the bad. It dealt with a narrow segment of the discipline; the new men showed little interest in teaching; they sought not breadth of coverage but only the hot man in the hot field of the moment. Endocrinologist Carroll Williams bitterly complained that the "Biochemical Mafia," and especially its "hatchet man" Meselson, were "afflicted with intellectual glaucoma for all aspects of Biology outside his own narrow specialty of microbial genetics. In terms of Biology as a whole he is utterly naive and impoverished, and much of our present difficulties in the Department of Biology channels straight back to this man and the tightly-knit group that he represents."

The Darwinian Empire struck back through the new subfield of sociobiology and a greater emphasis on ecological issues. The MCZ's Ernst Mayr thought that the glory days of molecular biology were nearing their end; organismic biology, left for dead, had come alive again through its relevance to population, environmental, and behavioral concerns. In 1967 the department established the Center for Environmental and Behavioral Biology, an alliance of evolutionary biology with marine biology, animal behavior, population genetics, and circadian rhythm.[65]

Another consequence of the molecular revolution was the growing disciplinary identity of Biochemistry. Strong research groups formed around Watson and Meselson; Walter Gilbert came into the field from Physics; junior fellow Mark Ptashne began to attract notice. George Wald's Natural Sciences 5 (eventually most noted for the frequency of the instructor's references to his Nobel Prize) was for years a major stimulant to student interest in Biochemistry. Undergraduate courses in that subject flowered, and the Board of Tutors in Biochemical Science enabled students to concentrate in the subject.[66]

But Biochemistry's separate identity had to make its way in the face of strong resistance from the existing science disciplines. A case in point: the biochemists put a high priority on appointments in nucleic acid and protein chemistry. Their first choice for a nucleic acid position was Har Gobind Khorana of Wisconsin. But when his name came before the Chemistry department, the two leading organic chemists did not support him. Why? They judged him by the standards of organic chemistry. Ford observed: "The goals of biochemistry have now become so clear that other disciplines such as organic chemistry have simply become tools and hence the context in which we judge a man is quite different. Yet this distinction cannot be conveyed to chemists who do not feel the main thrust of biochemistry and molecular biology."

Biology in 1965 had eight unfilled positions, but "the museum-botany axis" blocked further biochemistry or molecular appointments. The logical way out, biochemist Paul Doty thought, was to adopt the example of the separation of the MCZ people from the Biology department proper and engineer yet another fission, so that ultimately there would be three separate Biology departments: organismic, centered in the MCZ; cellular; and molecular. There was in fact no single Biology department but only a congeries of groups, each wanting "to insure his own afterlife allowing no room for new developments." Finally, (academic) human nature prevailed; the Department of Biochemistry and Molecular Biology came into being on July 1, 1967.[67]

The Biology visiting committee bravely declared in 1968: "Among its many distinctions the Department of Biology has a ruling distinction: it is, for the present at least, a department of biology." Its chair piously hoped that Biology at Harvard "can be formed into relatively small, well-knit, cooperative groups rather than remaining as a sprawling, sometimes argumentative and amorphous entity." But this was whistling in the wind. The department's organismic and cellular wings were reorganized into separate divisions in 1970, each with its own budgetary, appointment, and promotion powers: a weaker version (if such can be imagined) of the Austro-Hungarian Dual Monarchy.[68]

The Division of Applied Science (DAS) flourished during the academic bull market of the 1950s and the 1960s. But it continued to suffer from its place in the Harvard academic pecking order, where engineering and applied science were lower on the scale than more theoretical endeavors. If the DAS people got too practical and hands-on, they faced the scorn of their colleagues in the Big Science disciplines. But if they strayed too deeply into the tempting groves of the theoretical, they heard from their Engineering alumni. Like Biology's botanists, the DASers had the consolation of money: the ever-fructifying Gordon McKay Bequest. By 1956–57 the division had an endowment of about $17.7 million, $16.3 million of it McKay money. This brought not only professorships but a new Gordon McKay Laboratory, which opened in 1954.[69]

Pusey eased some of the Engineers' resentment over Conant's manifest hostility to them. One alum hoped that Pusey's bringing theology back to the Divinity School meant that "engineering may again be taught in the Engineering School." By a 19–2 vote the division chose to change its name to Engineering and Applied Physics (DEAP). Bundy advised Pusey to approve: the feeling among Engineering alumni was that the previous title "does not adequately indicate Harvard's interest in and resources for the study of engineering," that "it implies a slight against a distinguished profession." Several of the division's Engineering programs, so weakened under Conant that they lost their accreditation, were restored to respectability: electrical and sanitary engineering and engineering physics in 1954, mechanical engineering in 1957.[70]

Under energetic solid-state physicist Harvey Brooks, who was its dean from 1958 to 1975, the division shared in the general efflorescence of science in that time. The coming of the computer was the DEAP equivalent to large accelerators in experimental Physics, the molecular revolution in Biochemistry and Biology, and radio astronomy in Astronomy. But the division's ability to reap full benefit from the computer revolution was limited by the Harvard culture of which it was a part.

In 1954 Harvard established the first program leading to a Master of Science in Data Processing degree, and in 1957 hosted a major conference on the computer. Some 800 attendees heard physicist John Van Vleck ruminate on the beginnings of an information revolution comparable to the industrial revolution. Linguist Anthony Oettinger became director of Harvard's computer program in 1961. When Oettinger suggested to Pusey that the computer's usefulness to the faculty would be hardly less than that of the library, the humanities-minded president was skeptical to hostile. Nevertheless computer use was growing, and in May 1962 the new Harvard Computation Center replaced the old Statistical Laboratory. By the mid-1960s, demand for computer time was doubling yearly. For budgeting purposes the center was a subdepartment of the Faculty of Arts and Sciences. But when DEAP dean Harvey Brooks proposed that it be treated as a University facility, with a Widener-Library-like arrangement in which the central administration picked up a good portion of the cost, Pusey's response was an unequivocal "no!"[71]

The Computation Center was expected to operate as a business, without a subsidy. But the lack of University support punished the numerous faculty members who did not have the funds to pay for computer time. By the late 1960s the center had accumulated a deficit of more than a million dollars, twice the liquidation price of its assets. Brooks threatened to have nothing more to do with computer management at Harvard if the problem was not resolved. The Overseers' visiting committee to the center agreed that the administration appeared not to recognize how completely the computer was altering the basic ways of academic life. It called for a massive diversion of funds and long-range planning. Harvard once had a leading role in the development and use of the computer. To regain its place, it needed a strong computer science faculty and major in-house facilities.

Pusey conceded that "[FAS Dean] Dunlop is himself desperate about what can be done." The answer? Set up a committee, of course. The Committee on Computing Services recommended that the central administration establish an Office for Information Technology. Computing at Harvard had become another source of tension between faculty and administrators, leading to a solution which gave a larger role to the central bureaucracy.[72]

Small, secure Mathematics posed a dramatic contrast to the size, complexity, and turmoil of the larger science departments. Without much controversy over either the substance or the rank order of their discipline, the mathematicians were in a sense free to let their often vivid personalities determine the course of departmental affairs. One administrative emollient was their all-but-unique policy that every full professor had to serve a term as chairman, regardless of his (sometimes spectacular) incapacity to do so.

Under the longtime oversight of George Birkhoff, the most distinguished of Harvard's prewar mathematicians, the department had not been open to Jewish members. But as elsewhere, this broke down in the wake of the war. Algebraic geometrist Oscar Zariski, who got tenure in 1947, was the pioneer. Like many of his generation, Zariski kept his Jewish origins to himself. When Orthodox Jew Schlomo Sternberg came as a junior faculty member in 1958, then-chair Zariski sent him a letter of welcome—and of warning. He understood that Sternberg's beliefs would not allow him to teach on Saturdays; a Monday-Wednesday-Friday schedule could be arranged for him, though with some awkwardness. But did he follow other rules of observance that might cause problems? "Assistant professors participate regularly (and vote) in our departmental luncheon-meetings. I do hope that you will be able to find something special which you can eat. If not, you will attend the business meeting after luncheon," though "something intangible but nevertheless important will be lost through your inability to be present at the informal phase of our departmental meetings."

Zariski had another concern: Sternberg had "started wearing a hat even in your classes." He warned: "in the interests of your future career, and also as a matter of common sense, you might well try to draw somewhere a line between the purely mechanical aspects of your religious observance rules and the intrinsic necessities inherent in the participation in the life of an American University." Zariski needn't have worried. Without modifying his religious practices, Sternberg got tenure in 1962.[73]

Mathematics like the other Harvard sciences faced stiff competition from other universities, Princeton and Chicago in particular. Harvard's mathematicians were stretched by their large undergraduate and graduate teaching responsibilities (ninety-five graduate students and fourteen research fellows in 1961–62) and limited numbers (nine senior faculty in the late 1950s). But the department's small size and coherent character helped it retain its excellence. Raoul Bott, the leading topologist of his generation, came from Michigan in 1959. In good part because of Bott's arrival, number theorist John Tate decided to turn down an attractive

Princeton offer. Bundy thought a turning point in the department's history had been reached: it had clearly (if not permanently) pulled ahead of its Princeton and Chicago competition.[74]

Though larger than Mathematics, the Department of Astronomy and its affiliated Harvard College Observatory (HCO) was a relatively small body in the University's science solar system. Nevertheless HCO director Harlow Shapley, a talented publicist and entrepreneur, made Astronomy perhaps the best-known of Harvard's sciences. At the same time, Shapley's scattershot administrative style had its costs. And until the advent of radio astronomy, the computer, and astrophysics, the HCO was hobbled by its location: distant from the clear skies and high mountains necessary for visual or photographic stargazing, much as Physics was affected by the physical constraints that kept it from being a major player in the high-energy field.

To compensate, Astronomy had links with distant field locations. But their cost was a source of mounting concern. Responsibility for the High Altitude Observatory in Climax, Colorado, was transferred to the University of Colorado in 1954. And Harvard's arrangement with the Boyden Observatory in South Africa came into question, in part because of its relationship with the segregated Bloemfontein University. In 1966 that tie was cut.[75]

Shapley retired in 1952. Conant advised Provost Paul Buck to resist the quick appointment of a successor or committing the University to continued HCO growth. "I see no harm," he counseled, "in letting the world know that this University is not sufficiently wealthy to do all things for all professions!" After approaching a couple of distinguished outsiders without success, Pusey chose acting HCO director Donald Menzel. The latter and his colleague Fred Whipple shared Shapley's imperial impulses. In 1955 they proposed that Harvard take over the faltering astrophysical program of the Smithsonian Institution. Harvard's work in solar astrophysics and meteors focused on the upper atmosphere and relied on astronomical geophysics: a good fit with the Smithsonian's space-related government programs. A skeptical Bundy permitted Whipple "to proceed with this dear dream." In the spring of 1955 the details of the deal were worked out, and the Corporation approved. Whipple became director of the Smithsonian Astrophysical Observatory, while Menzel continued to head the HCO.[76]

Then Sputnik went into orbit in 1957, the space race lifted off, and HCO entered a Golden Age. Satellites, radio astronomy, and computer-aided astrophysics became the new order of the day. The "wealthy amateurs" who had bankrolled Harvard Astronomy in the past could not meet HCO's financial needs. The future lay, of course, in government support. By 1960 federal money provided more than three-quarters of HCO's revenue.

Astronomy, Menzel excitedly told Pusey, was in a takeoff mode of the sort that Physics experienced before and during the war. Would Pusey and the Corporation please give early approval to Menzel's proposal to double the present available space? NASA doubtless would pay for the building. Pusey permitted Menzel to approach NASA, but warned him not to count on matching funds from Harvard. By 1964 Menzel had NASA money for an expanded Smithsonian building and asked the Corporation for $500,000, which it refused to give him. It did not authorize the addition until 1968, and then HCO-administration conflict erupted over who would cover skyrocketing construction costs.[77]

The University's reluctance to extend full support to HCO, limitations of space and scale, and internal dissension kept Harvard Astronomy from cashing in on the space race as much as it might have. Nor did personnel problems help. Astrophysicist Thomas Gold came in 1957, but left for Cornell two years later, a major loss. In 1960 Leo Goldberg arrived from the University of Michigan. A leading figure in modern astronomy, "[h]e will," Bundy predicted, "bring to the observatory a style and sensitivity which it greatly needs." In 1966 Goldberg replaced the ailing Menzel as director of the observatory.

But in a few years he was ready to leave. Why? Because, he said, he had not been given the resources, nor did he have the authority, to raise the level of the department. His inability to ride herd on Smithsonian appointments meant that the permanent staff there fell below the overall Harvard standard. A committee headed by S. Dillon Ripley, secretary of the Smithsonian Institution in Washington, reviewed the Harvard Astronomy situation. In February 1971 it not very helpfully recommended that a joint advisory committee try to smooth things out between the department and the Smithsonian unit. But it could not agree on whether a closer relationship between the two wings was feasible, or even desirable. Meanwhile Goldberg went off to head the Kitt Peak National Observatory in Tucson. Once again, the powerful forces of past precedent, current resources and priorities, and the University's academic culture shaped the course and character of a Harvard science department.[78]

## The Humanities

The humanities' relative standing in postwar Harvard slid a bit because of the growing popular appeal and intellectual vitality of the social and natural sciences. But their problems had internal sources as well. The heavy weight of their Harvard past slowed their adaptation to a changing academic climate. They were not quite as ready as the natural and social sciences to tap into the rich academic vein of Jewish scholars after World War II. And when it came to hiring the second sex, they manfully suppressed what few impulses led them in that direction. Not until the postmodernist/cultural studies upheavals of the 1970s and after did the humanities undergo a change comparable in scale (though perhaps not in substance) to the transformation of the natural and social sciences that went on from the 1930s to the 1960s.

English was the most notable of Harvard's humanities departments. Between 1945 and 1958, nine senior professors turned out 250 Ph.D.s. The department's recent history, thought its doyen, Walter Jackson Bate, had been an upward ascent from the stolidity and dullness of the 1920s and early 1930s to a high plateau in the 1950s. The causes: unusually talented professors, student interest in Western culture revivified by the triumph over Hitler, and the attractions and challenges of the New Criticism. Bate, who chaired the department most of the time from 1956 to 1968, feelingly recalled a past when it "huddled into an arid, self-righteous, and uncreative professionalism." But by the 1950s and early 1960s (Bate's salad days, as it happened), it changed "from one of the most militantly 'closed' and narrow departments in the country into one of the broadest and most imaginative and energetic departments."[79]

Bate feared, though, that the department was sliding back into intellectual stolidity and social complacency. Young Turks of the postwar years hardened into an Old Guard. (And a quarrelsome one: Corporation secretary David Bailey described English in 1962 as "a department in which professors are hopelessly at odds with each other.") Still, the senior professors—Bate, Harry Levin, Perry Miller, Douglas Bush, William Harbage—were at or near the top of their games, strong enough en bloc to give Harvard's English department a firm belief in its national primacy. (The rank order looked different when viewed through the similar smug of New Haven.) In the midsixties English attracted 700 graduate applications yearly and had some 250 students in its program. Undergraduate course enrollments approached 1,000.[80]

As in the case of History, the sense of being on top made for a certain slackness over time. To justify a department decision to promote one of its juniors, Bundy had to reach a bit: "I am not able to dispute the judgment that he is not plainly of the first rank as a scholar, but I am persuaded that he has none of the weakness which will lead him to favor or to encourage less than first-rate or top-notch standards among his colleagues and in all the work of the Department." Besides, "there is a certain truth to the department's own view that it has plenty of stars and not an overwhelming number of hard-working full-time conscientious laborers in the vineyard."[81]

Retirements and deaths during the 1960s began to tear holes in the department that were not easily filled. Major figures such as Northrop Frye and Frank Kermode turned down offers. As in History, that meant that lesser homegrown talent had to be chosen: epigones standing on the shoulders of giants. By 1968 the department, thought its visiting committee, was "at a peril point in the swing between attainment and decline." Yale took a commanding lead in the Top Dog sweepstakes.

An attempt was made in 1969–70 to get deconstructionist pioneer Paul de Man, then at Johns Hopkins. Harvard's tentative approach coincided with Yale's final offer, and off de Man went to New Haven. This annoyed the department's Reuben Brower, who added: "I might point out that the best woman graduate student we have had in seventeen years, by general agreement, Helen Vendler of Boston University, has been invited to go to Yale. [She didn't accept.] This is a story that gets rather tiresome in repeating."[82]

Some of the senior faculty had long regarded women doing graduate work in English as unwelcome interlopers. Vendler (then Helen Hennessy), who would one day be a University Professor and perhaps Harvard's most distinguished humanist, arrived as a graduate student in 1956. She recalls that when she went to have the chairman approve her program, his first words to her were: "You know, we don't want you here, Miss Hennessy. We don't want any women here." Despite her evident star quality, she was allowed only to teach tutorials. She won an instructorship, but when she gave it up to go with her husband to Cornell, where he had a job, a senior member's reaction was to throw a major tantrum, complete with screaming and book throwing. (He later said of the incident: "I was crazy then.") As was the case with a number of Harvard's humanities, it was not until the 1970s and 1980s that the Harvard English department made room for both postmodernism and women.[83]

\* \* \*

Classics was an even more venerable department, its faculty culture even more hermetic. (One member got tenure on the less than overwhelming ground that there was no one "significantly preferable.") Like English it was firmly anchored in the Germanic-philological scholarly tradition, though in the 1930s it began to make room for a more historical-literary approach. Classics suffered from the decline of the ancient languages as a vital part of the Harvard curriculum, and it had little contact with analytic-dominated Philosophy or the New Criticism of the literature departments. But its very insularity (buttressed by an abundance of endowed professorships) kept the department from being too badly buffeted by the winds of change in the postwar decades.[84]

Slowly the department's clubiness ebbed, as deaths, retirements, and departures imposed constant pressure for new blood. Herbert Bloch became the department's first tenured Jewish professor in 1953, Ernst Badian its second in 1971; Emily Vermeule overcame the gender barrier in 1970. But old prejudices died hard. When Latinist Glenn Bowersock came up for tenure in 1967, Greek historian Sterling Dow (who erroneously thought him to be Jewish), testified against him before the ad hoc committee reviewing the case. His argument: Bowersock had an undistinguished undergraduate record. Pusey, leafing through the candidate's folder, noted laconically that Bowersock had been a Harvard summa and a Rhodes scholar, and his appointment went through.[85]

Philosophy was another story. Harvard was at the cutting edge of the triumph of the new school of logic resting on mathematical analysis. By the 1950s Willard Van Orman Quine, the leading American exponent of the analytic approach, was the department's great figure. But the need to strike a balance between the new analytic wing and the department's traditional commitments to the history of philosophy, aesthetics, and metaphysics, was as strong as the organismic-molecular trade-off in Biology. Burton Dreben, a highly regarded young analytic logician and junior fellow, became an assistant professor in 1956. So did the more traditionally grounded Rogers Albritton, in accord with a departmental understanding that appointments would be divided (as chairman Morton White put it) between "the broad areas suggested by the words 'history' and 'metaphysics,'" and "those which are ... suggested by the words 'logic' and 'analysis.'" Dreben and Albritton, White assured Bundy, were "as close to antitheses as we can find on the philosophical scene today while maintaining standards of scholarly excellence." It "might mean a generation of peaceful existence in this department between the hedgehogs and the foxes."[86]

Sustaining this balance had its costs. Albritton was promoted in 1960. His publications were limited, but he had the respect of his colleagues, no small matter when intradisciplinary differences ran so deep. Dreben got tenure a year later under similar conditions. Bundy correctly expected Dreben to be one of the liveliest and most influential members of the faculty: "He is certainly not always wise, and he has some of the intolerance of the very bright young man, but he has the elements of great distinction as a Harvard professor unless my guess is very bad indeed." Dreben in effect (according to Dreben) ran the department from then on.[87]

Tensions between the opposing philosophical camps continued. Ethicist John Wild left in 1960 to chair Philosophy at Northwestern, which he expected to lead along "non-analytic, non-positivistic lines." As things turned out, there followed a renaissance of moral and social philosophy at Harvard. Wild's successor, John Rawls, came from MIT in 1962 and published his greatly influential *A Theory of Justice* in 1971. A year after Rawls's arrival, philosopher of language Stanley Cavell was promoted; a year after *that*, analytic philosopher Hilary Putnam came from MIT to balance off the Rawls-Cavell supplements to the department's "metaphysical" wing. The result would later somewhat hyperbolically be called "the second golden age of Harvard philosophy," comparable to the reign of William James, Josiah Royce, and George Santayana at the turn of the nineteenth and twentieth centuries.[88]

Romance Languages and Literatures continued to be a troubled department: in part because of what member Francis Rogers called "its mixture of Americans and non-Americans, and its mixture of representatives of quite different cultures"; in part because other academic agendas had higher priority in the postwar University. A story of the time suggests the prevailing atmosphere. After a fierce battle at a department meeting, a professor of French literature and a colleague in Spanish passed in the hall. One of them turned his face away; the other erupted: "How dare you not speak to me? I'm not speaking to you!"

An outside observer told Pusey in 1957 that the department was "an open scandal in the eyes of the profession.... A long series of inept departmental chairmen, and presumably deans as well, have not been able to curb the bickering and dissension, even the vicious throat-cutting, of its irresponsible members." Good scholars and teachers departed. What was left was "a heterogeneous assortment of soured, embittered men whose potential productivity has turned into unprofitable strife with their colleagues." Pusey replied: "I am afraid that your comments [are] ... all too true."[89]

In the mid-1950s FAS dean Bundy put the English, Romance, Germanic, and Slavic departments into a Division of Modern Languages, with English professor Harry Levin at its head. Levin was charged to oversee permanent appointments in the area. Bundy distinguished the recommendations of "a large department with a well established pattern, like English," which Levin was to pass along, from those of "a very small department or a joint appointment," which he was to subject to close scrutiny.

The difficulties inherent in this override of departmental autonomy quickly became evident. Bundy asked Levin to take the lead in coming up with a senior appointee who might more closely link Romance Languages with General Education. His choice was Wilbur M. Frohock of Wesleyan, who was vigorously opposed by five of the eight permanent members of Romance Languages. Besides objecting on procedural grounds, they found Frohock's knowledge of French too limited, his interest in French literature too narrow, his teaching less than adequate, his temperament difficult (which if true should have made him right at home in the department). But the ad hoc committee unanimously supported Frohock as one of the most distinguished American-born scholars of French literature, a consideration to which Bundy gave great weight. Frohock was made chairman and was charged to upgrade Romance Languages. Jean Seznec, a distinguished scholar who had fled Harvard to the more placid scene of Oxford's All Souls in 1951, was asked to return. Bundy did not expect him "to re-enter the bear pit of ... Romance Languages and Literatures (although I must say that under Frohock the Department shows many signs of rising civilization)"; indeed Seznec stayed where he was.[90]

But departmental social engineering was difficult in the age of the sovereign faculty. One of the department's most tempestuous members (which is saying quite a lot) was Marcel Françon. He was so obstreperous at a March 1958 meeting that Frohock chastised him for his behavior, called another meeting to get on with the department's business, and pointedly proposed: "Please do not feel yourself under any compulsion to attend if you do not wish to." Frohock was ready to entertain a motion that Françon be excluded from future department meetings and warned him that if necessary he would enforce that policy with the appropriate University officers (presumably not armed). Another handful was Louis Solano, who got more subtle treatment. He was, said Bundy, "one of the very few members of the Faculty whom we would gladly pay to stay away from Harvard." So a deal was struck: an extra $1,000 a year in return for a signed pledge to keep out of the department's regular business. "This is certainly not an ordinary way of handling our affairs," Bundy conceded, "but in the circumstances I think it is a good one." Alas, the bought would not stay bought. After Bundy left office, Solano complained to Pusey of his "segregation," which Pusey coolly pointed out was of his own choosing.[91]

It was a tribute to Harvard's drawing power that despite all this, the quality of the Romance Languages department steadily improved. The Spanish wing flourished with the presence of stars such as Juan Marichal (promoted to professor in 1961, Bundy calling him "the bright image of future possibility, in the Department which has been most troublesome, to itself and to the Administration, since 1953"). Even the French division, the most contentious wing, shared in the general upswing of the sixties. French scholar Paul Benichou visited for a year; got unanimous department backing for an appointment; was, said a wondering Bundy, "not only acceptable, but pleasant." By the late 1960s most of the major combatants in the civil wars of the French division had retired, replaced by promising appointees chosen "with full regard both for scholarly distinction and [the] political health of the Department." A troubled chapter finally came to an end when Solano retired in 1971. This caught the eye (and stirred the memory) of McGeorge Bundy, who now headed the Ford Foundation. Echoing Galileo, he wrote feelingly to Pusey: "*e pur si muove!* [and yet it does move!]"[92]

Other dwellers in Harvard's extensive domain of language and literary studies had problems of their own. The German department appeared to have lost its ability to plan for the future or make strong appointments. FAS dean Franklin Ford was not surprised that the 1969 report of the department's visiting committee "will have to be couched in terms of deep concern, indeed of alarm." In his seven years as dean "I have seen no other relatively small department so plagued by what I should have to call non-academic, highly personal difficulties for many of its members." He and Pusey agreed that a receivership committee should be convened to recommend possible appointees. Such a reversal of the ordinary ad hoc system was rare, Pusey conceded, "but occasionally we have done so, when a department showed signs of needing artificial respiration, so to speak."[93]

Slavic Languages and Literatures had in Roman Jakobson one of Harvard's most distinguished scholars. But Jakobson was deeply involved in the burgeoning discipline of Linguistics, and from the late 1950s to his retirement he spent half his time at MIT, the center of new developments in the field. Bundy thought that having half of Jakobson's time (and paying half his salary) was an eminently desirable arrangement with "a complex and difficult colleague." One problem was Jakobson's sustained unhappiness over the courses in Russian literature taught by his colleague Renato Poggioli, whose command of the language he thought inadequate to the task. For his part, Poggioli identified most closely with Comparative Literature. A major donnybrook may have been averted by the fact that neither Jakobson nor Poggioli was fully invested in the Slavic department.[94]

Comparative Literature and Linguistics were humanities outliers, heavily dependent on the kindness of kindred departments. Of the two, Comparative Literature flourished more in the Harvard of the fifties and sixties. The English department's Harry Levin took charge, and under his forceful direction Comp. Lit. became an influential (and autonomous) presence in literary studies at Harvard.[95]

The Linguistics department was much slower to adjust—insofar as it did adjust—to the intellectual transformation of its field. The postwar decades saw the rise of a new Linguistics. Its herald was an MIT professor whose name, thought the *Harvard Alumni Bulletin*, was "Noamchomsky." The Chomskian revolution moved Linguistics from musty philological inquiry to a cutting-edge association with analytic philosophy and the study of cognition. Joshua Whatmough, Harvard's sole senior man in Linguistics since the late 1920s, was quite sensitive to this transformation. In 1951 he changed the name of the department from Comparative Philology to Linguistics. But a department whose primary orientation still was philological posed no serious challenge to MIT, the heartland of Chomskian linguistics: testimony to the continuing strength of the Harvard tradition of humanistic, philological literary studies.[96]

Fine Arts had deep roots in the Harvard past, with strong traditions of connoisseurship and museum training that worked against a ready adaptation to new trends in art history and criticism. The relationship between the Fine Arts department and the Fogg Art Museum was close and amicable. But the Depression, the war, and Conant's indifference brought about a decline in the museum. The Fogg bought little art, relying instead on gifts, and readily sold off holdings when the money seemed more valuable than the object's pedagogical function. During the postwar decades it lost its primacy as a trainer of museum people to Yale and the NYU Institute of Fine Arts.[97]

Growing numbers of graduate students and an increasingly high-powered disciplinary professionalism left their mark on Fine Arts. But efforts to bring the leading stars of the postwar art history world to Harvard were only occasionally successful. Renaissance scholar Millard Meiss came in the early 1950s, but after four years went off to the student-free environs of the Institute for Advanced Study in Princeton. Superstars Meyer Schapiro of Columbia and Ernst Gombrich of London could not be lured from their high-urban environs. Next best were the young Renaissance art historian Sydney Freedberg, who came from Wellesley in 1955 (with Anglified speech mannerisms that raised an eyebrow or two), and Renaissance architecture historian James Ackerman, wooed from Berkeley in 1960. Dutch art expert Seymour Slive soon joined them, and the department had a first-class core.[98]

Contemporary art, in particular modern American art, traditionally had little place in the hermetic world of the Fogg. This changed under the prodding of John Coolidge, the Fogg's director from 1948 to 1968. Corporation fellow Thomas Lamont distastefully took note of the Fogg's "growing collection of contemporary art." He warned of a flood of gifts of modern art in coming decades, "as the collectors begin to tire of their junk." Despairingly he announced: "I can't bear it. I am resigning from the Friends of the Fogg Museum."[99]

The department, too, had new realities to contend with. In the fall of 1954 the Committee on Visual Arts recommended a $6.5 million development plan, including a design department and a department of art history situated in the Fogg. Bundy found this "in a funny way, a rather naive and unsophisticated document—and unless we can get its tone changed, I fear that its authors may be disappointed in the reaction from within the Faculty." But by the 1960s, making movies and practicing (as distinct from studying) the other creative arts had great and growing appeal to a new student generation. The establishment in 1963 of a full-fledged program in Visual and Environmental Studies (VES), and the opening of Corbusier's Carpenter Center for the Visual Arts (to serve VES as the Fogg did Fine Arts), marked the coming of age of this component in the Harvard College curriculum. The department initially welcomed VES, expecting it to draw off undergraduate would-be artists who majored in Fine Arts *faute de mieux* and with low enthusiasm. But because the new concentration took only a limited number of students, the Fine Arts chairman complained, "we still have the same number of frustrated creators, except that Carpenter Center gets first choice, and may be leaving us a group that is uninteresting as well as uninterested."[100]

\* \* \*

The major irritant in the Music department—then, later, forever—
echoed the art historian-curator-artist tension in Fine Arts. This was the
strained relationship among musicologists, composers, and performers.
The classic expression of this animus: a Harvard musicologist's declaration—supposedly after attending a performance of a composer
colleague's work—that music should be seen and not heard.

There was some dispute in the late fifties over the department's
relationship to the Harvard Glee Club. It wanted to control the appointment of the club's director, but was less ready to assume budgetary
responsibility for the slot. Finally in 1958 Elliott Forbes came from
Princeton to run the Glee Club to everyone's satisfaction: he was Old
Harvard; the club was content; music chairman Randall Thompson
could not but welcome the author of an admiring article on the music of
Randall Thompson. But it was another story when composer Leon
Kirchner came as Walter Piston's replacement in 1961 and four years later
succeeded Thompson as Walter Bigelow Rosen Professor of Music.
Heightened musicologist-composer hostilities, and then, with the 1967
appointment of Earl Kim, composer-composer hostilities, ensured the
department interesting times in years to come.[101]

The construction of the Loeb Drama Center in the early 1960s, and the
evolution of its role in undergraduate education, is a revealing commentary on faculty autonomy and the lure of professionalism in modern
Harvard. The postwar years saw a student-led renaissance in drama. The
intent of the new Loeb theater, and the reason why John Loeb gave the
money for its construction, was clear enough: it would be "an educational
facility," a "student theater in which Harvard and Radcliffe students and
their neighbors in the Cambridge community will produce, direct,
mount and act plays." As plans for the theater were drawn up in the late
1950s, donor Loeb asked that they be reviewed by the College's drama
groups: "It seems to me particularly important that they be happy and
satisfied with the new facilities."[102]

But in 1962 a member of the theater's faculty committee made a pitch
for full faculty control of the Loeb's offerings, with a resident graduate
company as its mainstay. Pusey reacted with unusual vehemence. To the
observation that "student proposals govern the repertoire and student
personnel control the style, manner and quality of the productions," he
responded: "why not?" The faculty committee complained of being
limited to choosing from among student proposals (NMP: "can they not
teach?"); it had no power over the theater in practice ("why should it?");

the Loeb had an obligation to mount excellent, serious productions, not undergraduate efforts ("necessarily exclusive?").[103]

It soon became apparent that to lure undergraduates from their familiar world of house productions to the formidable venue of the Loeb, more hands-on adult supervision was needed. Theater professionals on short-term appointments came in to instruct the undergraduates. But faculty criticism of the Loeb's student productions continued, and when faculty and student desires came into conflict, it was clear whose in the long run would prevail. In 1978 Robert Brustein came from the Yale Drama School to run the Loeb, with ambitions that would leave little room for student fumblings.[104]

At the outermost edges of the University's humanities empire were isolated outposts, hill stations flying the crimson flag of Harvard cultural imperialism. The oldest of these was Washington's Dumbarton Oaks. In operation since 1940, it became a major center of Byzantine studies. Ernst Kitzinger took over as its academic director in 1955, after Bundy firmly rejected "the notion that Kitzinger should be barred because he is of German Jewish origin." Donors Robert and Mildred Bliss strongly agreed: an important matter, since they were very much *there*, and many millions more from them were in the offing. Bundy conceded that most of it would go to Dumbarton Oaks, "but if the atmosphere there is happy, there might be a few millions for the rest of us!"

One problem: Mrs. Bliss very much wanted to field strong programs in garden research and pre-Columbian art. (Dumbarton Oaks had splendid gardens, and the Blisses collected early American objects.) Bundy observed, "A Horticultural Institute and a Byzantine Foundation are natural and harmonious partners, I fear, only in the mind of Mrs. Bliss." The trick was to convince her that while the gardens and the pre-Columbian art should be displayed, Byzantium should be *studied*. Bundy and Pusey did this with impressive skill. In 1962 Robert Bliss's will left some $35 million, most of it for Byzantine studies (alas, all of it to be used in Washington); in 1969 Mrs. Bliss bequeathed another $6 million.[105]

Harvard's Center for Hellenic Studies, also in the nation's capital, in some respects resembled Dumbarton Oaks. Mrs. Marie Beale, the widow of an American diplomat who served in Greece and became enamored of its classical past, gave six acres of prime Washington real estate and $4 to 5 million to the Old Dominion Foundation "for the study of the Hellenic spirit." The foundation shopped around for proposals, and Pusey came up with the idea of a center for postdoctoral

Hellenic study modeled on Harvard's Society of Fellows. The center got under way in 1960, and within a year Yale classicist Bernard Knox began a twenty-five-year run as its distinguished director.[106]

It was in 1960, too, that the Corporation accepted Bernard Berenson's Florence villa I Tatti from the executors of his estate. (Crusty Treasurer Paul Cabot was against taking on this obligation without a sheltering endowment. But Pusey wanted it, and that was good enough for Cabot—though he could not refrain from a worried "Oh, Jesus, Nate. I can see the first busload of fairies arriving now.") If I Tatti was to be an effective center for the study of Italian Renaissance art, a substantial amount of money, $2 million, had to be raised. Its advisory committee—Bundy called it "my comic relief"—proved singularly unable to do so. Kenneth Murdock became I Tatti's first director in 1961, and soon was under fire from the National Gallery's director John Walker for making the operation too academic, something Berenson would not have wanted. But fellowship money gradually began to come in, spurred by an anonymous $500,000 challenge grant from David Rockefeller, and in time I Tatti became an accepted part of Harvard's humanities empire.[107]

## ∽ 11 ∾

# THE PROFESSIONAL SCHOOLS

Meritocracy flourished most luxuriantly in Harvard's professional schools. The Big Four—the Graduate School of Arts and Sciences and the Schools of Law, Medicine, and Business—threw off the constraints of lack of money and student cutbacks imposed by World War II. The smaller professional schools—Public Health and Dentistry, Education, Divinity, Design—shared in the good times, though their old problems of scarce resources and conflicted missions continued to bedevil them. The major alteration in the Harvard postgraduate scene was the establishment of the Kennedy School of Government. By the time Derek Bok—as well disposed to the Kennedy School as Conant was to Education and Pusey to Divinity—became president in 1971, this new boy on the Harvard professional school block was well situated to capitalize on his good favor.

## The Graduate School, Law, and Business

The Graduate School of Arts and Sciences remained, as in the past, rich in renown, poor in fund-raising and administrative autonomy. Between 1952 and 1962, fewer than 5 percent of GSAS alumni donated a total of about $60,000; during the early sixties giving went down to $3,000 a year. Its dean had little or no budgetary or curricular control; its faculty, curriculum, and student admissions were in the hands of the departments. In 1954 Overseer/Judge Charles Wyzanski grandly proposed that admissions to the Graduate School be sharply cut back. The reduction, he thought, would free up the faculty for more creative thought, improve undergraduate education, and upgrade the level of the graduate student body.[1]

But the post–Korean War expansion of American higher education led to boom years for the Graduate School. In 1961, 190 male and 60 female Woodrow Wilson Foundation Fellows, more than a quarter of the national total, chose to go to Harvard or Radcliffe; 80 of 172 National Science Foundation grantees wanted to go to Harvard. A 1969 rating of the nation's graduate programs gave Harvard Chemistry a perfect 5, Mathematics 4.9, Physics, Biochemistry, Molecular Biology, History, and Classics 4.8, Art History and Sociology 4.7, English and Spanish 4.6, Philosophy and Government 4.5. Impressive enough, all in all, to sustain the faculty's elevated impression of itself.

But in the late sixties the Graduate School bubble deflated. Government aid, foundation fellowships, and college jobs declined; student disaffection grew. In March 1969 an FAS committee took note of the widespread sense of isolation and alienation among graduate students, and recommended a 20 percent cutback in GSAS enrollment.[2]

Erwin Griswold later recalled that when he became dean of the Harvard Law School in 1946, it had "a great reputation" and "a superb library," but was "unbelievably poor," with a large mortgage on its major building, Langdell Hall; inadequate dormitory accommodations and no dining facilities; a faculty that once had been distinguished; a student-faculty ratio of more than 50 to 1; and bad-to-nonexistent alumni relations. Like his contemporaries George Berry in Medicine and Donald David in Business, Griswold turned out to be an effective school builder. He had suffered, as did many of his colleagues, during the twenty-year reign of Roscoe Pound and was determined not to repeat that unhappy experience. Pound, he observed, "never willingly delegated anything," and Griswold sought to avoid that by setting up an administrative staff "many times as great as had ever been used at the School." (All things are relative. Harvard Business School dean David thought Griswold was a poor administrator because he did not do more delegating.)[3]

In the fall of 1953, when Pusey came in, the Law School had a faculty of sixty-eight, two-thirds of them appointed since 1945. Thirty more were added by 1966. The preferred appointee was a young man fresh out of law school (more precisely, The Law School: less than a third had gone Elsewhere) or an established academic legal scholar. When the faculty proposed to appoint Stanford constitutional law expert Charles Fairman, members of the school's advisory committee of distinguished lawyers and judges had their doubts about this choice. But the faculty wanted him, and in he came.[4]

The student body became more select, readier to stay the course. Competition with Yale in particular was bracing: more than a third of HLS's best admittees did not accept, and it appeared that for the most part they went to New Haven. Other leading law schools became more competitive on faculty salaries and fund-raising. Griswold noted in 1960 that Yale Law, a third the size of Harvard, had a $5 million campaign under way; ipso facto, HLS should go for $15 million. The Committee on Planning and Development went to work, and in the fall of 1964 came up with that $15 million goal—half the $30 million that the faculty thought the school needed. The Law School's Sesquicentennial in 1967 seemed like a good peg on which to hang the campaign, and it ended successfully in 1969.[5]

During the 1960s the feeling grew that the school was stagnating. Part of the problem was that Legal Realism, the dominant intellectual paradigm in postwar legal education, had lost its edge. But no compelling new way of thinking about the law had yet replaced it. And competing professorial models—pure legal scholarship and devotion to teaching, engagement in the glittery outside world of money and power—divided the school's faculty. Legal philosopher Lon Fuller argued that more attention should be paid to the scholarly output of appointees before they got tenure and that there should be less pressure on them to publish thereafter. But Griswold thought that easing off the pressure to publish might lull all too many into nonproductive somnolence.[6]

By the late 1960s a number of HLS appointees had backgrounds in other disciplines as well as (and occasionally in place of) the law. A former faculty member feared that such goings-on would turn the Law School into "a sort of second-rate petitversity." Ideologically, too, the new appointees differed from their predecessors: most leaned to the Left. But when in the 1970s Critical Legal Studies posed an institutional and intellectual challenge to the most fundamental postulates of the law and of legal education, the bulk of the faculty adhered to the meritocratic legal academic culture to which they belonged.[7]

Faculty sentiment grew during the 1960s that Griswold had passed his peak, and he left in 1967 to be Lyndon Johnson's solicitor general. Pusey quickly chose HLS labor lawyer Derek Bok, who was supported by more than two-thirds of the faculty, to be Griswold's successor. Bok's concern for students, and his interest in bringing the law into closer relation with the liberal arts, made him in Pusey's eyes the proper man for the job. And there was more. Pusey told the Corporation: "One of the more vocal younger members of the Faculty mentioned Mr. Bok's thoughtful skepticism and caution as a possible sign that he might not be a bold and vigorous leader in matters of public concern." Skepticism and caution, he thought, were virtues in a dean.[8]

Before he got the job, Bok told Pusey that all in all the school was in fine shape: "There is no factionalism to contend with, no strong resistance to change, and no dearth of new ideas and initiatives from individual professors." That judgment soon was obsolete. Responding to post-1969 student pressure, the faculty eased its grading standards, thus at a stroke turning the student body into a clone of the student population of fictional Lake Woebegone, where everybody was above average. (But it was also true that the students were far more select than in the past.) And in tune with the new academic morality, the publication of class rankings ended.[9]

Bok became president of Harvard in 1971, and after only four years the Law School had to select a new dean again. Corporation fellow William Marbury wanted an outstanding appointee "who would break the Law School out of its present self-infatuation." But he could not come up with a name. The choice of most of the faculty (and then of Pusey) was HLS faculty member Albert Sacks, whose amiable persona outweighed a marginal scholarly output and a less than decisive administrative style. Students showed some displeasure with a new dean who said that their call for pass-fail demonstrated their laziness. Activists wanted someone who was "not part of the unspoken and powerful institutional politics whose informal existence is acknowledged by all." But it was precisely those qualities that appealed in a time of troubles, and Sacks was appointed.[10]

By the time of its fiftieth anniversary in 1958, the Harvard Business School was a flourishing part of the University and an important presence in the new corporate culture of postwar America. The school's student body of 1,675 was twice what it had been in the mid-1930s; its faculty had increased from fifty to eighty-six. Dean Donald David, whose energetic assertiveness echoed that of Berry in Medicine and Griswold in Law, retired in 1954. Corporation fellow Thomas Lamont wanted a successor who would get the school to explore ethical and social issues: the obligations of directors, the treatment of workers and the like. He pushed Pusey to consider people in the real rather than the academic world: CEOs Mark Cresap of Westinghouse or Frank Stanton of CBS, economists Gabriel Hauge or William McChesney Martin, or Paul Mazur of Lehman Brothers (though "Mazur of course is Jewish"). Pusey sounded out David Rockefeller for the job, with no success. And it was clear that the faculty preferred one of its own. David's longtime associate dean Stanley Teele duly succeeded him in 1955. But Teele was not up to the job and in 1962 faculty member George Baker took over, running things to general satisfaction until 1969.[11]

The Business School modestly shared in the general academic expansiveness of the time. Its Trade Union Program, in which rising labor leaders came for a year of courses (much as the Nieman Fellows program brought journalists to the University), had been in operation since 1942. By 1960 the program had neither grown nor attracted much labor union (or any other) support, and its impact was slight. But by the middle of the decade it had a more secure place, with an endowment of $400,000 and about 25 fellows, half from overseas, in each thirteen-week session.

Women, too, inched their way into HBS's confines. In 1960 Henrietta Larson, a lecturer in Business History since 1929, got late-career recognition with a professorship. To placate critics of its ban on female students, the school helped to develop a one-year Radcliffe Management Training Program, for the most part taught by HBS faculty. In 1959 women who completed that program were allowed to apply for admission as second-year students at the Business School, the first breach in the wall of Harvard's last all-male professional school. A faculty committee recommended that first-year women be admitted in 1963, assuring queasy colleagues that there was no reason to think that their presence would impair the effectiveness of instruction. Besides, there would be only six to eight skirted intruders a year. (By 2000, women were over half of the student body.)[12]

The primary challenge facing HBS during the fifties and sixties was to make its curriculum more meaningful both to business and the University at large, and to make sure that it led the field. The faculty put more emphasis on preparing the Harvard case studies—teaching materials that were the distinctive HBS contribution to business school pedagogy—to be used nationally and internationally. And the school strengthened its quantitative and social science capacity during the 1950s, appointing economist Raymond Vernon, statistician Howard Raiffa, and psychoanalyst Abraham Zaleznik.[13]

All of this whetted the faculty's taste for academic respectability. It more carefully spelled out its promotion standards. Greater weight would be given to opinions from outside: the Harvard case studies had been adopted widely enough to make it conceivable that Out There were at least a few business school professors capable of passing judgment on HBS appointees.

In 1963 Dean Baker suggested that the Business School offer a Ph.D. in Business Administration. Over 80 percent of its advanced students went into teaching and that degree would help their careers. But Pusey—backed by FAS dean Ford and HMS dean Berry—firmly responded that Ph.D.s should remain in the Faculty of Arts and

Sciences alone; Berry hoped that the Corporation "will stick to its guns." From the other side, as it were, no-nonsense Thomas Lamont found the *Harvard Business Review*'s jargon-laden articles "full of the usual hogwash about how to make good 'organization' men out of the raw material of a corporation's staff, all expressed in the usual gobbledy-gook of business school sociology." Heretically he thought that the school did not try hard enough to reveal to its students "some of the faults of our corporate institutions and of the so-called free enterprise system, which need attention if the system is to be preserved. The Harvard Business School would be more worth its salt if it could produce just a few more cynics and skeptics."[14]

Not surprisingly, HBS was less caught up than other parts of the University in the upheaval of the late sixties. (After all, its very reason for being was under attack by the radicals.) In May 1969 the head of the school's Afro-American Student Union told Pusey how much progress had been made by reasoned discussion with a responsive Dean Baker and hoped politely that the new dean would be equally sympathetic to this mode of working for constructive change. The school did worry about, and look into, a widespread (though, as it turned out, fleeting) student disenchantment with business careers.[15]

In the troubled Harvard spring of 1969, George Baker made ready to retire, and a search got under way for his successor. It went on in a remarkable state of remove from the excitations on the other side of the Charles. As usual, the faculty was polled on whom it wanted for its new leader. Attention focused on two of its members, Kenneth Andrews and Lawrence Fouraker. Andrews was supported (and opposed) as a leader of the HBS establishment. Pusey chose Fouraker, primarily because Fouraker seemed likely to be more attentive to problems of race relations and a new student culture that even the Business School could not escape.

## Medicine, Public Health, and Dentistry

The Harvard Medical School was old, distinguished, and in the early 1950s afflicted by a financial crisis: the result of decades of fund-raising stagnation during a time when the scale and cost of medical research steeply rose. George Packer Berry, who became dean in 1949—Conant considered this his best appointment—set out to do something about the school's financial condition. (His was no simple task. Conant wrote to Berry after he became American high commissioner in Germany: "It may comfort you to know that as compared to the finances of the Harvard Medical School, the complexities of European politics are nothing.") Endowment grew during the 1950s from $20 million to $32 million, alumni giving escalated, and the budget was balanced. But more was needed, given the takeoff in medical science.[16]

Traditional ways of raising money for the Medical School no longer sufficed. Researchers came to rely on project grants from the government and large foundations. That money was welcome but unpredictable: short-term project grants played havoc with long-term budgeting and financing. In January 1956 Berry proposed an $83.6 million fund-raising campaign in collaboration with Harvard's affiliated hospitals. He, Pusey, and the Corporation finally agreed on a $58 million decade-long Campaign for Harvard Medicine alone; the hospitals would seek their own funds. More than half of the $58 million goal was in hand by the end of 1962, divided equally between individual and foundation or corporate contributions, almost all of it from Boston and New York. By 1970 the HMS endowment stood at $72 million, well more than double what it had been ten years before.[17]

Berry was a force for change in medical education and patient care as well as fund-raising. During the early fifties he sought help from the Commonwealth Fund to explore ways "to focus the teaching of medicine on the student rather than on the subject, to focus the physician's efforts to help on the patient, rather than on his disorder." And in the course of his deanship HMS underwent changes similar to those going on elsewhere at Harvard: abler (or at least higher-scoring) students; fewer restrictions on (and hence more) Jewish students and faculty; the admission of women. Applications stabilized in the mid-fifties at about 1,300 contenders for a little over a hundred places.[18]

Alone among Harvard's professional faculties, HMS had a close relationship with other institutions: its seven (eventually seventeen) affiliated hospitals. An agreement between Harvard and the hospitals during Conant's presidency covered joint appointments and other touchy issues. But new strains arose. While the hospitals also shared in the postwar boom in medical science, they were far more ready to plunge into the research rain forest on the basis of "soft" money (short-term government or foundation grants). The transient character of this support, and the appointments that came with them, created a potentially menacing fiscal overhang.[19]

In 1963 Berry announced his intention to retire. Pusey sounded out the HMS faculty and uncapped (as always at the end of a strong deanship) accumulated discontents. One complaint: the school's curriculum and administrative structure were not up to the demands of modern American medicine; in particular, the need to incorporate the social and behavioral sciences. At the same time a significant minority of the faculty thought there was too much emphasis on research. A recurring note was the desire for more communication between the dean and the staff. Berry's authoritarian approach, effective as it was, had diminishing appeal as a more participatory style gained favor in the sixties. Faculty meetings were big and unwieldy, and Pusey thought the prevailing seating arrangement—department heads around a central table, younger and less privileged faculty on the room's periphery—smacked of nineteenth-century German academicism. In earlier days the faculty ran the HMS show; under Berry it had a sharply diminished role.[20]

Berry's successor, Robert Ebert, saw himself not as "an autocratic figure exercising a rigid leadership" but an arbitrator, an encourager and expediter, able to tap the creative possibilities of the HMS tradition of semiautonomous departments. And he was more committed to social medicine and the delivery of health care. He set out to improve the strained relations with the faculty and the affiliated hospitals that had accumulated over the two decades of the tough-minded Berry's deanship.

Ebert launched a curriculum review designed to foster all sorts of good things: increased electives and a first-year core curriculum integrating the biological, behavioral, and clinical sciences; encouraging independent thinking and reducing the amount of factual information; earlier student exposure to patients, and more emphasis on the emotional and socioeconomic aspects of illness. Clinical training shifted entirely to the hospitals, accompanied by a twelve-week reduction in the basic science curriculum and a significant increase in the size of the student body.[21]

When in the late sixties radical students attacked Harvard for its relations with the community, HMS was relatively well situated to respond. The Medical School and the School of Public Health set up the Harvard Center for Community Health and Medical Care in 1967. In 1970 the research-oriented David Rutstein stepped down from the chairmanship of the Department of Preventive Medicine, and a committee took a fresh look at what that department might do to become more relevant. It concluded that the traditional focus on epidemiology and public health should shift to the major health problems of the community: infectious disease, schizophrenia, automobile accidents, alcoholism. These called for community medicine, not the traditional system of medical care delivery. To make clear its new mission, the department's name should be changed to Preventive and Social Medicine. One dissenter warned that defined this way, it would be open to political indoctrination. But that was a minority view.[22]

The 1970 Committee on the Future of the Harvard Medical School, chaired by clinical psychiatrist Leon Eisenberg, reflected the academic mood of the day. This manifesto of the New Egalitarianism proposed the removal of examinations and grades for first-year students, the school's honors society, and honors degrees. It called for wide student and faculty involvement in HMS policy making. And it wanted HMS to help meet the national need for more doctors by increasing the size of its entering class from 165 to 200. More controversially, Eisenberg's committee proposed that the admissions committee be instructed to set a minimum goal of a 20 percent female intake in the coming year, rising to 35 percent within five years. Other favored classes: African Americans, Hispanics, and (what struck some as a mite self-serving) HMS faculty children.

One seeming consequence of the new order was that the mean score of the class of 1971 on the 1970 National Boards fell substantially, dropping it from first to third in the national ranking. Critics dwelt on the limited time allowed in the curriculum for the study of any subject in depth. Students, it appeared, relied heavily on compendia ("camels" in their jargon) prepared for each course, which gave them a false sense of security. Still, things could have been worse: that year Yale went from second to fortieth in the boards' ranking. And while the shift in student interest to areas such as psychiatry, family medicine, and public health correlated at least in time with their lower National Boards scores, it was not unreasonable to hope that out of it all might come a better balance between scientific rigor and social concern.[23]

During the postwar years, the faculty of the School of Public Health became an autonomous body distinct from the Medical School. With a vigorous dean, James S. Simmons, in charge, it took on an identity that was more than a paper change. But the school's finances remained shaky, heavily dependent on Simmons's personal contacts. Members of the SPH faculty advised Pusey to keep Simmons on to 1960, well beyond his normal retirement age, but he died in the summer of 1954. Fresh from the funeral, professor of Microbiology John C. Snyder assured Pusey that he had no desire to be dean and then went on to offer deanly advice. His core message: the effectiveness of the school rested on its administrative and financial independence from HMS. Soon after, Pusey offered the SPH deanship to Snyder; sooner after, Snyder accepted.[24]

Although Public Health and the Medical School were administratively separate, their curricular and research interests converged. The SPH faculty found both higher status and more funding in medical research; at the same time the Medical School faculty became more responsive to such concerns as the doctor-patient relationship and the delivery of health care. SPH was flush during this prosperous time in academic medicine. During Snyder's deanship (1954–1971), its tenured faculty went from nine to twenty-five, its endowment quadrupled, its annual budget increased from $1.3 to $8.5 million. The school got its first endowed professorship in 1954; by 1970 eleven more had been added. It even had a female professor, Martha Eliot, in the uncontroversial field of Maternal and Child Care, for the last years of her career.[25]

A husky Ford Foundation grant made possible the Center for Population Studies in 1953 with an endowment of more than $2 million and five professorships. Roger Revelle was recruited from the University of California at San Diego to be the center's director. Population Sciences became a new SPH department in 1962, as did Behavioral Sciences in 1965. But for all this institutional muscle flexing, relations with the Medical School continued to be sensitive. Tropical Medicine professor Thomas Weller complained that HMS dean Berry did not expect SPH to long survive on its sparse endowment, and that its only recourse was to rejoin the Medical School. This, he groused, was typical of the condescending, derogatory attitude of most medical men toward public health doctors.[26]

Public Health's tender financial condition made it highly dependent on federal research support. That source provided a whopping 74 percent of the school's income at its 1967 peak; only 11 to 12 percent of the School's expenses were met by endowment. The SPH visiting committee wondered if it should not be remerged into HMS. But Pusey backed autonomy, tempered by greater cooperation. With the bloom off the SPH rose, and he himself getting long in the tooth, Snyder left the deanship in June 1971. As elsewhere in this time of turmoil and transition, choosing a new dean had to take account of students' expectation that they would have a large voice in the selection. Medical School Dean Ebert's candidate was traditional public-health-type David Senser, head of the Centers for Disease Control. But new president Derek Bok chose Howard Hiatt, a doctor with the more socially engaged perspective now in vogue.[27]

The School of Dental Medicine also did well in the postwar decades. It had a balanced budget and a flock of new professorships (including the fuzzy but fashionable field of Ecological Dentistry). But old problems persisted: hostility in the profession to the school's relatively high-flown approach to dental education, and difficulty in recruiting and holding able students. Tension between SDM and the Medical School continued over the merged preclinical training in place since 1940. Unhappiness flowed in both directions. HMS professor Oliver Cope blamed Dental School discontent on the insecurity of a professional group with a lower educational background, threatened "when the older and more securely established profession of medicine moved in and took over." And while HMS students steadily improved in quality, SDM students if anything were getting worse. Cope's answer: hold dentistry students to the highest preclinical standards and make the SDM curriculum measure up to that mark: "Dentistry is a technical skill; dental medicine is a part of medicine." The final solution, he thought, was absorption into HMS.[28]

The Dental School marked its 100th year in 1967, small in size (it admitted only sixteen students a year), shaky in standing, in need of a new building. HMS dean Ebert dangled the prospect of fostering strong clinical departments of dentistry in the teaching hospitals, dropping the D.M.D. degree, and bringing dental education more fully into the warm embrace of Mother Medicine. Meanwhile he proposed SDM faculty member Paul Goldhaber for the Dental School deanship. Goldhaber was tough, stubborn, smart: in short, just what the dentists ordered. He took the job in the spring of 1968, buoyed by Corporation approval of a $15 million endowment drive.[29]

## Education, Divinity, and Design

The Graduate School of Education stood second only to Divinity in Nathan Marsh Pusey's rank order of Harvard faculties requiring tender, loving care. Presidential favor reinforced other hopeful signs for a school with a shaky past. Frank Keppel, its new dean, was young, full of bounce, a little league Mac Bundy. And the 1950s were a propitious time for GSE. The postwar baby boomers were pouring into the nation's schools, and social scientists were increasingly involved in (and confident of solving) the problems of education. Keppel set out on a large-scale expansion of research and instruction. But this rested on foundation and government grants: soft, insecure money. The school's endowment in 1954 was about $3 million, not much more than its initial 1920 funding of $2 million. And it had run large yearly deficits—the ultimate Harvard no-no—since 1946.

Like Divinity, Education had a fund-raising goal of $6 million for buildings and endowment; unlike Divinity, it had no organized campaign. When John D. Rockefeller gave $1 million to the Divinity School, Keppel told Pusey that it "aroused the cupidity of this lean Dean." (He said of a smudge on his signature: "Though it might seem so, the blot above is not a tear!") Could Rockefeller be induced to give $2.5 million, to be matched by a similar amount to be raised by the school? With what they already had, that would get them to their $6 million goal. But like so many of Keppel's hopes and plans, this was not to be.[30]

The goals of the School of Education were clear enough: faculty appointments more attuned to the relevant Arts and Sciences disciplines; a coherent, professional curriculum as in Law and Medicine; a better student body; national leadership in educational policy making. There were promising signs: applications rose from 430 in 1950 to 1,965 in 1960 and three-quarters of the graduates went to "leading school systems." By 1961 GSE had four times as many students as a decade before.[31]

The ambitious Keppel threw himself into the heady business of faculty recruitment and fund-raising. He sought out people who had standing in Arts and Sciences disciplines. GSE relocated from Lawrence Hall, its venerable but outmoded lair on the northern fringe of the campus, to the more centrally located Appian Way, next to Radcliffe and within hailing distance of Harvard Yard. A new classroom and office building was planned, but its all-but-windowless, warehouselike design aroused much criticism. The Corporation, already unhappy with the school's financial condition, indicated that it had no objection to a slowdown in the building's construction. Mollifying changes and a gift from *Time* publisher Roy Larsen solved the problem, and GSE had its new Larsen Hall in 1963. The Gutman Library next door, added in 1969, completed the new GSE campus.[32]

But the dangers of short-term funding threatened the school. Its professorships were not fully endowed, and much of its staff subsisted on limited foundation grants. The Sisyphean task of rolling the GSE stone uphill sapped Keppel's enthusiasm for his job, and John F. Kennedy's Washington enticingly beckoned. He stayed at Harvard until December 1962, and then went off to be federal commissioner of education. He left behind a school that for all its advances was overcommitted in research programs, had too small a faculty and endowment, and ran a teaching program badly in need of rejuvenation. And an old division— between traditionalists still committed to professional training in education, and advocates (including Pusey) of "the prime importance of close working relationships with the arts and sciences faculty"—contin-ued to be a source of discord.[33]

The search for Keppel's successor finally ended in January 1964 with the selection of assistant professor Theodore Sizer, director of GSE's Master of Arts in Teaching program: another young man, with higher professional credentials than Keppel and an equally strong desire to see Education closely tied to Arts and Sciences. Sizer came in at a time when the financial handwriting on the wall could no longer be ignored. Unless the school came up with additional income of $300,000 a year, cutbacks on the order of 10 percent of the budget would be necessary. GSE was at the bottom of Harvard's professional faculties in the portion of its income (15.5 percent) derived from endowment and alumni gifts.[34]

However shaky its financial underpinnings, the School of Education was a lively place in the mid-1960s. A massive 1965 report, "The Graduate Study of Education," called (of course) for more advanced graduate study in the relatively rarified and hence prestigious areas of administration and curriculum development. But it firmly rejected the view that there was a science of education to be taught by a faculty made up of specialists. It proposed instead that GSE be a meeting place for people in the arts and sciences disciplines who wanted to work on educational problems. Faculty appointments in the 1960s reflected that bent. The most notable were made jointly with FAS departments: Daniel Patrick Moynihan in Educa-tion and Government, Berkeley emigré Nathan Glazer in Education and Sociology. And a new source of funds arose: the federal government, via Lyndon Johnson's Great Society. At their peak in 1968, GSE research projects got $4.7 million in federal funding, about 60 percent of the school's budget (compared to 5 percent in 1956).[35]

But the school's basic problems remained. The number of its entering students declined from 433 in 1967 to 194 in 1968, when it ceased to serve as a sanctuary from the draft. By 1970, GSE faced an annual deficit of $500,000 and was "broke on a grander scale than ever before." Sizer called on Pusey to remedy the "inequities" in National Defense Educa-tion Act (NDEA) and other funds that favored "the older faculties"; Pusey warned him that "a budget in such a serious situation as yours must be a subject of continuous concern" to the Corporation.[36]

Sizer became as discouraged as Keppel had been before him and gave notice in 1969 that he wanted out as dean (though he did not leave until 1972). A decade before, he observed, few doubted the soundness of the American public school or the standard liberal curriculum. But "the overriding mood today is cautious, contentious, unsure.... We now envision education as something children *use*, rather than as something that is *done* to children." But that raised even larger doubts about the mission of the school. True, the faculty was more committed to advanced research and to instruction designed to produce leading scholars and administrators, not "practitioners." But GSE's training programs still were too trade-school oriented. And the low status of teaching as a profession compared to law or medicine, and of education as a subject compared to physics or history, continued to retard the school's search for a more conspicuous place in the Harvard firmament.[37]

GSE responded with alacrity to the new issues coming to the fore in the late 1960s: a greater voice for students, civil rights, urban poverty. These had obvious relevance to education and offered a way out from the school's less than fully developed professional sense of itself. In particular, GSE took on the challenge of race and urban education. By 1969 African Americans—only a handful a few years before—were 10 percent of the student body. Their demands escalated in pace with the faculty's receptivity. Student unrest continued to be visible and acute. The Overseers' visiting committee concluded in December 1969: "The School of Education presents an unusual combination of high morale and creative malaise." And it appeared that GSE had a critical need for financial support from the University.[38]

The financial and academic well-being of the Harvard Divinity School was at the top of Pusey's priorities list. And HDS needed all the help it could get. Students were sparse; the faculty was depleted, undistinguished, in even greater thrall to FAS than the School of Education. In 1953, ailing Dean Willard Sperry retired after thirty-one years in office. (The *Boston Herald* spoke of the school seeking a "brilliant new dean capable of raising the once great institution from its slump of recent years": an observation that did not speed Sperry's recovery.) In April 1955 Douglas Horton, an amiably ecumenical, sixty-three-year-old Congregationalist, took the deanship pending a more durable successor. Five years later, still unreplaced, Horton retired. Pusey then appointed professor of Pastoral Theology Samuel H. Miller, whose lack of standing as a scholar was compensated for by his successful parish ministry in the Old Cambridge Baptist Church. Pusey saw in him a counterpoise to an increasingly intellectual, scholarly faculty who threatened the school's pastoral role, much as their counterparts in GSE did the training of teachers.[39]

Ironically, that faculty was in part the product of a $6 million fund campaign whose success owed much to Pusey's support. The school's 1960–61 budget of $737,224 was over four times what it had been in

1954–55. Plans were under way for institutes to study the relationship of religion to business, medicine, law, and the arts. A new Ph.D. program in the Study of Religion, offered jointly with the Faculty of Arts and Sciences, began in the late fifties.[40]

The old HDS problem of being a sectarian school in a secular university did not go away. The ecumenical tone of postwar America led Jewish scholars and potential donors to propose that Jewish theology be included in the school's curriculum. Fund-raiser John Lord O'Brian liked the prospect of getting "some of our Hebrew friends" to give by dangling treats such as a chair in Old Testament history before them. But he feared that to do so would be to open HDS "to domination by Jews more interested in pushing the interests of their sect than in the scholarly relationships between Judaism and other religions." Pusey, too, was loath to see the school "develop in such a latitudinarian fashion that it became a 'true center of religious learning' only by virtue of losing its own religious commitment." Still, "as long as our basic Christian position is made crystal clear," he could "see no reason why in the University there should not be considerable interest in Semitic studies nor why Jewish graduates of the College and other Jews should not contribute a chair or chairs in this area, including a chair of Old Testament studies."[41]

Outreach to Roman Catholicism was less problematical. Pusey responded warmly to a Harvard Catholic Club proposal that a professorship be established for the interpretation of Catholic doctrine. Alumnus Chauncey Stillman provided the funds for the first chair of Roman Catholic studies in a Protestant divinity school. In 1958 English Catholic scholar Christopher Dawson came for a year as a guest professor: it was thought better to bring Rome into the picture via visitors rather than by a permanent appointee.[42]

A nagging problem of purpose afflicted the teaching of religion (as it did the teaching of education) at Harvard. Should HDS train the kinds of ministers that churches wanted or those that, in the view of the faculty, they needed? Was the school's principal role the propagation of faith or fostering a religion-colored approach to social issues? What were the unifying themes of a curriculum ever more prolix and heterogeneous?

The school tried to deal with these issues by a new Bachelor of Divinity program designed to integrate its traditional meat-and-potatoes Bible, theology, and church history curriculum with the new social sciences. And the faculty sought constantly to strengthen its ties to the rest of the University, through joint appointments with FAS and proposed links with the School of Public Health's Population Studies program and an IBM-endowed study of technology and society. But FAS dean McGeorge Bundy doubted that the Divinity School was in fact the proper venue for scholarly inquiry into religion. He told Pusey: "[T]he experience of Harvard should be enough to show that the standards and objectives of the Divinity School are too fluctuating to furnish any solid basis for long-term academic achievement."[43]

In the 1960s the thrust of the Divinity School, like Education, shifted from its traditional subject matter to social problems. But in sharp contrast with GSE, HDS sought not to teach the teachers of practitioners but the practitioners themselves. A new Department of the Church offered field training for students who planned to serve in the ministry. And in 1967 the school created a Master of Theological Studies degree, designed for religiously minded candidates who planned careers in other fields such as journalism. The doyen of the new worldliness was Harvey Cox, who became professor of Church and Society in 1965. His *The Secular City* (1966) became the bible (perhaps not quite the right word) of church-in-the-world advocates.[44]

Social activism turned out to be as pricey as theologizing. In the mid-sixties Dean Miller grandly proposed a capital investment of $12.6 million in buildings, professorships, scholarships, and Centers for Research on Contemporary Life and Advanced Thought. As in Education, expansion outpaced capital growth; soft money and shortfalls went hand in hand. Budget woes mounted; Miller bewailed "the critical financial story" of the school despite the University's "generous and providential" assistance.

Miller died in March 1968. His successor, the faculty's Krister Stendahl, was more of a scholar, but shared his predecessor's pastoral and social concerns. By now the Divinity School was deeply absorbed in the great issues of the day: race, Vietnam, poverty. In the wake of Martin Luther King's assassination, Stendahl asked Pusey if the new Rockefeller Hall could be renamed after the slain civil rights leader. (The answer was no.) The faculty refused to take action against students involved in the April 1969 occupation of University Hall, and severely criticized the administration's response. John Lord O'Brian, who had run the HDS fund drive of the 1950s, was deeply distressed by all of this. But Pusey, strong in his faith, told him that he had confidence in Stendahl and in the school's long-range prospects.[45]

José Luis Sert became dean of the Graduate School of Design in 1953, at a low point in its turbulent history. Walter Gropius, the brightest star in the GSD firmament, was gone; faculty morale was abysmal; student enrollment was low and falling; GSD finances were in such disarray that

City Planning, one of the school's major programs, had to be suspended. The Corporation gave Design $350,000 to help the new dean get started, and things began to pick up. Seven new faculty members came in Sert's first year. And with the end of the Korean War, the market for the school's graduates was poised for rapid growth.[46]

City Planning and Landscape Architecture, the two Cinderellas in a school dominated by its Architecture program, had been merged because they were so small and weak. Now they attracted enough students to be separated again. City Planning in particular drew on the new interest in urban conditions. But old GSD problems persisted: a shortage of money; a faculty most of whom were part-timers with extensive private practices; the infighting to be expected of a gathering of artistic temperaments. Other architecture schools—Berkeley, Columbia, Pennsylvania, Yale—paid higher salaries and were thought to be outstripping Harvard.[47]

Dean Sert was part of the problem. There wasn't much space between his architectural firm (which provided several members of GSD's part-time faculty) and the Architecture department (which he headed in addition to his deanship). And he failed to provide crisp, decisive, ambitious leadership in the preferred Harvard decanal style. In 1959 he proposed an exceptionally modest $3.75 million campaign, stretching over an exceptionally lengthy twenty-five-year period. In May 1965 a more properly ambitious $11.6 million campaign for a new building, higher salaries, new professorships, and more scholarships got under way. The Gund family (Cleveland banker-businessman George Gund and his architect son, Gordon) came up with a $7 million gift in 1968. By November 1968, about $11 million had been raised, but inflation made it necessary to increase the fund-raising goal to $12.6 million.[48]

The school's new Gund Hall opened in 1972, preceded by controversy of the sort one might expect of an architecture school's building. Harvard's customary way of doing things was for the president to select the architect, but Sert and much of the GSD faculty wanted an open competition. Pusey opposed that idea, as well as the suggestion that students and faculty help design the new building. He finally chose GSD alumnus John Andrews (Sert wanted Gropius), who came up with a Ziggurat-like structure, its sloping glass roof covering a single, massive drafting space designed to express the school's ideal of architecture, urban planning, and landscape design working as an integrated whole. In the unsettling way that architectural metaphors have of striking back at their creators, the roof leaked, and the solar heat it generated could not be controlled.[49]

Like its fellow Lilliputian faculties, Education and Divinity, Design was highly vulnerable, institutionally and ideologically, to student unrest. City and Regional Planning became a major battleground in 1968, as student complaints mounted over the quality of its program. In 1969 that department got 80 applications to MIT's 425; of the 7 students accepted by both, all went to MIT. Criticism focused on what students called "the Oligarchy": professors William Nash, François Vigier, and Reginald Isaacs. They were attacked as an aesthetics-obsessed Old Guard, insufficiently attuned to the larger and more radical implications of urban design in an age of social upheaval.[50]

Sert was due to retire in 1969. It was not easy to attract an outsider of distinction to replace him at that tumultuous time. Pusey finally appointed Maurice Kilbridge, an applied mathematician and economist at the Business School who had worked closely on urban planning matters with GSD people, to be acting dean. He was regarded as a tough man for a tough job: no Harvard faculty was at peace with itself in the late sixties. Kilbridge assured Pusey that the *Crimson* got it wrong when it reported that the GSD Forum, a trendy gathering of faculty, students, and staff, was running the school. And a donnybrook broke out over the school's failure to give tenure to Chester Hartman, a charismatic, radical assistant professor of city planning.[51]

Kilbridge initially won high marks from his colleagues, and in January 1970 went from acting to regular dean. But troubles old and new continued to afflict the school. The cost of completing Gund Hall threatened GSD's finances. Kilbridge warned Pusey: "If you hear unusual grunts and groans from this corner of the Yard ... , they quite likely will be associated with my efforts to do something about this." And sure enough, before the school year was over, the chairs of the GSD departments and a preponderance of faculty and students were at odds with the dean.[52]

## The Kennedy School

The Graduate School of Public Administration, Conant's only addition to the University, limped along in the 1950s much like the other Lilliputians: small, underfunded, unclear as to its mission in life. In 1958–59 the GSPA endowment was only 13 percent larger than at the time of its founding in 1937, compared to a growth of 133 percent for the University as a whole. Edward Mason of the Economics department, who became dean in 1947, began to enliven the school. Alert to growing foundation interest in international relations and overseas development, he worked hard to tap Ford Foundation money.[53]

But a twentieth anniversary retrospect in 1956–57 revealed that the School of Public Administration's inability to establish a distinct persona was alive and well. Its faculty, borrowed primarily from the Economics and Government departments, not surprisingly was more interested in public policy than in the techniques of public administration, an approach not readily distinguishable from what went on in their home disciplines. The biggest change was in the makeup of the students. In the postwar years about half of them had little or no previous government experience, and most sought Ph.D.s in Economics or Political Science rather than the M.A. and Ph.D. in Public Administration offered by the school. But by 1956–57 all but eight of the sixty entering students had been in government, and the vast majority wanted only a master's degree in Public Administration.

Don K. Price, a professor of Government and onetime vice president of the Ford Foundation, became dean in 1958. In order to get him to take the job, the Corporation ended the school's subordinate position in the Faculty of Arts and Sciences and put its dean on a par with his counterparts in the other professional schools. In his first annual report, Price observed that the United States was the only country without professional civil servants. America's leaders were not schooled to be bureaucrats, but studied law or a special field of expertise. The need was great, he argued, for training based on the assumption that public administration was a profession.[54]

Then the election of John F. Kennedy in 1960 put a gloss on government service not seen since the New Deal. Dean Price compared himself to "a general who claimed that the war was ruining the Regular Army. The drafting of our faculty members by the new administration has not only interfered with the teaching of public administration but even more with the administration of the School." Those heady days encouraged GSPA (like Harvard's other professional schools) to raise its sights: "not to give preliminary training to specialists in the housekeeping functions of government, but to give education to those who are expected to rise to positions of responsibility for the general direction of governmental programs, and to contribute through research to the guidance of future policies"—to be, in short, an engine of power and responsibility.[55]

During the 1960s the school began to hire an occasional faculty member of its own: most notably, in 1964, the stellar Albert O. Hirschman as professor of Political Economy. There was Camelot-like talk of the State and the universities coming closer together than at any time since the seventeenth and eighteenth centuries. In June 1963 Price invited Secretary of Defense Robert McNamara to give a series of lectures, in the belief "that the experience that you have had in the Department of Defense is the best illustration in many years how the handling of great policy issues, and even the maintenance of a proper constitutional balance within our system of government, depends on the quality of administration and its use of the most advanced techniques." (The armamentarium of the new science of public policy did not include a crystal ball.)[56]

With tragic irony, it was not John F. Kennedy's presidency but his death that did most to transform the School of Public Administration. Discussions had gotten under way in the early days of Kennedy's term in office over the future location of the Kennedy Presidential Library. The participants agreed on two possible sites near the Harvard campus, both on the Boston side of the Charles River. Then contingency intervened. The assassination of the president in November 1963 gave the library project great emotional (and political) urgency. At the same time the Metropolitan Transit Authority (MTA) car yard, a choice parcel of land close to Harvard Square long coveted by the University, became available. Robert Kennedy, who represented the family in these dealings, fixed upon the succulent MTA yard. Brother Edward Kennedy and Governor John Volpe weighed in with a successful effort to get the Commonwealth to buy it as a memorial to John Kennedy, and put the JFK Presidential Library Corporation in charge of its disposition.[57]

Harvard faculty members Arthur M. Schlesinger, John Kenneth Galbraith, and Samuel Beer had something else in mind: a research and training center as a JFK memorial. This, they thought, would keep the legacy of the martyred president evergreen in a more creative and substantive way than a library-museum. Deans Ford of FAS and Price of GSPA duly proposed a Kennedy Center for the Politics of Democracy. Pusey met with Robert Kennedy in June 1964 and suggested that the center (its name changed to the Institute of Politics) be lodged within GSPA, which would then be renamed the John F. Kennedy Graduate School of Public Administration in Harvard University. That was fine with Kennedy. But a few details needed clarification. What would be the role of the family and/or its representatives in the choice of the director of the Institute of Politics? Pusey replied that of course the director would be formally appointed by the Governing Boards. But it was understood that the first appointee "would be an individual jointly acceptable to the Kennedy family and to Harvard" and that the family would be consulted on successors during Robert and Jacqueline Kennedy's lifetimes. (This pleased—and surprised—RFK).[58]

Robert Kennedy wanted an institute of the sort that his brother might have headed, had he lived. That meant a closer connection to politics and public affairs than to the academic study of government. He had no objection to the institute being part of the Kennedy School of Public Administration. Then Kennedy (prodded by McGeorge Bundy) had second thoughts. Couldn't Pusey see to it that the name of the school was altered from "Public Administration" to the more inclusive (and less academic) "Government?" Pusey could.[59]

There was another problem: the existence of the Littauer bequest of the 1930s. How completely could the Littauer name be effaced from the school that his gift had created? University counsel Ott Shaw thought it best to get a reading from the Massachusetts attorney general, and perhaps talk it over with the Littauer family as well. Littauer Foundation president Harry Starr made his unhappiness known. When he gave the money in the 1930s, Littauer asked Harvard to attach his name to the school. He was told that ironclad University policy forbade naming a school for an individual. "To apply the Kennedy name now," Starr complained, was "a breach of moral commitment." But the administration argued that it would meet its obligation by attaching the Littauer name to the main Kennedy School building (as well as leaving it on the Littauer Center, which once housed GSPA and now was given over entirely to the Government and Economics departments). The Massachusetts Supreme Judicial Court and the state legislature agreed. In June 1966 the Corporation formally authorized the creation of the Institute of Politics and renamed GSPA the John F. Kennedy School of Government (KSG). With masterful disingenuousness, it said that in doing so it was furthering the purpose of Lucius Littauer's gift.[60]

High institutional ambitions, and the toothsome parcel of land provided by the Commonwealth, fed a grandiose building scheme. Kennedy court architect I. M. Pei proposed a Big Plan (as it came to be called) for a complex that included the Kennedy Presidential Library, the Institute of Politics, a new Littauer Center of Public Administration to house the Kennedy School, and an international studies building (hopefully paid for by the Ford Foundation).

The Kennedy Library Corporation agreed to provide a $10 million endowment and a building for the Institute of Politics. Paul Mellon anonymously donated $500,000 to give the institute endowment a proper send-off, and in 1966 the Ford Foundation gave $2 million more. But by September 1967 the projected cost of the Big Plan had risen to $24.6 million. Pusey found this "quite unacceptable" and demanded cuts. Meanwhile the Kennedys kept pushing Harvard to get on with the Big

Plan. Their discontent grew when in 1970 fund-raising for the Lyndon B. Johnson Library pulled ahead of the JFK project. Even more dismaying: site plans for a Richard M. Nixon Library were under way.[61]

By 1971 the estimated cost of the Library-School of Government complex was over $70 million, with $33.2 million expected from Harvard ($7.5 million raised to date), $20.9 million from the Kennedy Library Corporation (of which $17.3 million had been raised), and $16.5 million from other foundation and government sources (almost none yet in hand). Harvard agreed to commit its $7.5 million to buy 2.2 acres of the site from the trustees of the Kennedy Library and go ahead with a $2.5 million structure paid for by the Ford Foundation, "presently designated" an international studies building. Ultimately the building became the first unit of the Kennedy School of Government, a change to which Ford (headed by the supportive McGeorge Bundy) readily agreed.[62]

Thus did the Kennedy School of Government become a Harvard reality. A grand dinner in the fall of 1966, attended by the Kennedy clan, celebrated its launching. Jacqueline Kennedy told Pusey how moved she was by his speech, and by the event:

> When I saw the people at that dinner—so many part of his administration, when I thought of the ones still in the administration who will at great effort come to Harvard this year for him, and when I saw the young people everywhere who seem so interested—well I cannot say all the things I really felt—there is a kind of wild irony to it—the irreverent student [—] that quizzical laugh—as you describe him, forever young—should now have a school at Harvard named after him. I know it would touch him so much—more than anything we could do for him—and I know the school will foster in all the young people who will pass through it—that same questioning spirit that made it possible for John Kennedy to be what he was—and what he always will be for the young.[63]

Powerful national emotions and a strong-minded family helped to shape the beginnings of the Kennedy School of Government. Jacqueline Kennedy, now remarried to Aristotle Onassis, appears to have been troubled by its increasingly academic tenor. Dean Price wondered in the fall of 1968:

> What happens now? I think I will consult the oracle [possibly a reference to British statesman Lord Harlech, who briefed Jacqueline Kennedy on the school and tried to ease her concerns], or else

go back to my Bullfinch to recall how Persephone behaved after *her* marriage. I can't think of any more recent experience to base my prediction on, though [Institute of Politics director] Dick Neustadt insists there are some lessons in Voltaire's book on the Court of Louis XIV.[64]

In April 1969 the Kennedys (remaining brother Edward in particular) and the school's faculty clashed over a proposed program in public policy. This, rather than the Institute of Politics, was to be the intellectual heart of the school. But Ted Kennedy had reservations. Would it, he asked Neustadt, in fact further the goal of a living memorial to JFK's memory? Was it not merely an updating of GSPA's original purpose, a "modernized Littauer?" He feared that the cost of the Public Policy Program would reduce the resources available to bring practitioners of politics and government to the campus. He wanted something "far freer and [more] risky than the regularized largely academic approach."

Neustadt told Kennedy that he was "astonished" by the letter. As he understood it, Robert Kennedy in effect had accepted a change in the fundamental character of the enterprise when he agreed to Pusey's offer to place the Institute of Politics within a school of government named after JFK: "From that point on the memorial could only be the Harvard School which bore the President's name.... The great stake was the School as a first-class, educational enterprise within the University." He came from Columbia to head the institute on the assumption that it was to be an energizing and innovative force within a School of Government whose broader purpose was teaching and scholarship. From this perspective, a new graduate program was essential.

For all their clout, the Kennedys were no more able to impose their will on the academic development of the KSG than were those overseers bothered by the department of Economics. The essence of the meritocratic University was faculty autonomy; the essence of an autonomous school was its own staff and curriculum. And over time the Kennedy School of Government evolved in accord with its faculty's vision, not that of America's most prominent political family.[65]

In 1971 a new player entered the game: Harvard president-elect Derek Bok. Dean Price set forth his plans for the school. While the Institute of Politics would focus on "the political as opposed to the scientific aspects of policy making," the Public Policy Program rested "heavily on quantitative and scientific method." Price was politic enough (he was, after all, a political scientist) to be aware that the new president, in post-1969 Harvard, expected something more than this: "I am eager to push a bit further in the direction of a systematic consideration of the way in which conceptions of basic values (moral, ethical, political, theological) affect attitudes toward public policy."

The Kennedy School of Government, like its GSPA predecessor, could not claim to prepare its graduates for careers in an established profession, or to be part of a major scholarly discipline. Then wherein lay its special contribution? The amateur generalists of the British civil service, the highly trained products of France's *École Nationale d'Administration*, would not do in the United States. The Kennedy School sought to produce a new kind of American Public Man by combining a "strong professional or specialized education with a command of the intellectual skills most useful in analyzing specific programs or projects, weighing them, in the light of general political purposes, and synthesizing them into a responsible national policy." Harvard hubris took quick and deep root in its newest school.[66]

## ∽ 12 ∾

# A PLURALITY OF MINORITIES

The triumph of meritocracy at Harvard had social as well as academic and intellectual consequences. It changed the ethnocultural and class structures of both the faculty and the student body. Jews in particular became a substantial, accepted part of the Harvard scene. And in more complex and ambivalent ways, Catholics, women, and African Americans gained in numbers, impact, and visibility.

## " ... loves the Irish and the Jews ... "

After World War II, meritocratic principles substantially overrode anti-Semitism in the admission of students and the appointment and promotion of faculty. An inquiry into the religious identification of Harvard College students in the mid-1950s revealed that 52 percent identified themselves as Protestants (about 15 percent of these Episcopalian), 12 percent as Catholics, 15 percent as Jews; 20 percent claimed no religious affiliation. Residual discrimination against Jewish applicants arguably lurked within an admissions policy that sought a Harvard class as diverse as possible in geographical origin, social background, and nonacademic talents. But the 1956 admission rate to Harvard from strongly Jewish feeder schools was (with the glaring exceptions of New York City's Stuyvesant and Erasmus high schools) not too far below the overall Harvard acceptance rate of 43.3 percent of applicants. (Though it may be assumed that the academic record of these candidates was well above the norm.)[1]

After World War II, anti-Catholicism like anti-Semitism retreated to the margins of respectability. The religiously inclined Pusey had an ecumenical sympathy for Catholics, substantially reciprocated. And Catholics themselves became more ready to send their sons to Harvard.

JFK's election to the presidency in particular gave the University a cachet among them that all but obliterated the suspicion-ridden past.[2]

Catholic undergraduates, substantially greater in numbers than in the prewar years, felt more at home by the 1950s. In 1960 a Catholic Student Center opened adjacent to the campus, with Cardinal Cushing's encouragement and assistance. *The Current*, a Catholic student magazine, concluded in the spring of 1963: "we are convinced that Catholics belong at Harvard." A poll of 175 Catholic students revealed that 67 had had their faith strengthened by their Harvard experience (admittedly an ambiguous result: was it due to acceptance or adversity?); 27 thought that their Catholicism had been weakened; the rest reported little effect one way or the other.[3]

## In the Company of Women

During the 1960s women substantially replaced Jews as a major issue at Harvard. Nathan Pusey was more responsive to their educational needs and desires than Conant had been. The president of the Radcliffe Club of New York welcomed him soon after his arrival: "Rumors have been floating down from Cambridge that you have a certain fondness for Radcliffe and have even on occasion, crossed the Square and Common to visit the College"—an indirect reference to the very different ways of his predecessor. Pusey saw the Harvard-Radcliffe relationship as a successful exercise in "coordinated education." And he seemed to be open to the prospect of something more. He was confident "that there will be a rapid shift in the next decade as our whole American educational effort begins to grow."[4]

But the inclination to regard women as marginal was deeply ingrained in Harvard. The graduates of the leading women's colleges were viewed not as potential graduate students but as fodder for secretarial and clerical jobs: a recruiting folder in 1955 sought "to stimulate an interest in employment at Harvard among the girls who will be graduating in June." At the same time Harvard's long coexistence with Radcliffe made it difficult to summarily dismiss women as alien beings in the Harvard world. Corporation secretary David Bailey noted in 1963 that more than a quarter of Radcliffe graduates were married to Harvard men and that 18.3 percent of Radcliffe's undergraduates were the daughters of alums. "Obviously," he concluded, "when the Overseers talk about Radcliffe girls they are raising not an abstract problem but a problem which in many cases falls within our family circles."[5]

Some 400 women who earned Radcliffe Ph.D.s between 1902 and 1951 were asked about their life experience. Of the 321 who replied, 175 had married; 136 did some college teaching; only 32 held full-time jobs. Yet when Jill Ker Conway, later president of Smith, came to Radcliffe Graduate School from Australia in the fall of 1960 to study history, she found "one of the world's great concentrations of international women," of diverse origins and serious, powerful scholarly drives. It may be that her foreignness gave her status and access denied her domestic counterparts (something experienced by non-American black students as well). In retrospect she recalled a reasonably serious scholarly treatment from her teachers, but exclusion from the conduits of a serious faculty career: no access to a resident tutorship, no serious thought of her as a candidate for jobs other than in women's colleges.[6]

Despite these obstacles, the second sex gradually found a place in Harvard academic life. Poet Archibald MacLeish, then master of Eliot House, excitedly told Pusey in 1955 that the English writer Barbara Ward might be induced to come as a visiting lecturer. Her preference was to be asked by Harvard, not Radcliffe. So successful was her appearance that in 1957 Ward (even more appealing now as Lady Jackson) became the first woman to speak at a Harvard commencement.

But women with Corporation appointments in 1959–60 overwhelmingly held minor, impermanent ones.

| Position | Total | Women |
|---|---|---|
| Professor | 427 | 4 (.9 %) |
| Associate professor | 118 | 8 (6.8 %) |
| Assistant professor | 299 | 8 (2.7 %) |
| Instructor | 529 | 52 (9.8 %) |
| Lecturer | 196 | 28 (14.3 %) |
| Research staff | 769 | 107 (14.7 %) |
| Teaching fellows | 597 | 76 (12.7 %) |
| Clinical (HMS) | 236 | 8 (3.4 %)[7] |

In the mid-1950s the only tenured women in Arts and Sciences were anthropologist Cora Du Bois, the (restricted-to-females) Radcliffe-Zemurray Professor, and Astronomy professor Cecilia Payne-Gaposchkin, the first of her sex to rise from the ranks. More representative was Tilly Edinger, research paleontologist at the Museum of

Comparative Zoology. A refugee who had run the vertebrate paleontology division at a major German university, she was a—perhaps *the*—world authority on brain evolution in fossils. She came and stayed on annual appointments until 1954, when she got a bit more security with a five-year contract at a modest annual salary of $5,000.[8]

Under Pusey's prodding, the Corporation took on the weighty task of selecting Harvard's first female honorary degree recipients in 1955. Exceptionally unexceptionable Helen Keller was its first choice, safe as houses. Her actually showing up at Commencement was iffy, and Pusey pushed poet Marianne Moore as a backup. Resistance rose in the Corporation on the ground that Moore was less than a first-class candidate. Pusey sent the fellows copies of Moore's "Poetry": "Marianne Moore has this to say about poetry. If you read her to the end, I think you will find she is not so bad after all!" Finally the Corporation voted for both Keller and Moore, with the stipulation that if Keller could not attend, no degree would be offered to Moore: both or none. As things turned out, Helen Keller came and was honored, Marianne Moore did not and was not—until 1969. Liberal New York corporation lawyer Charles C. Burlingham overoptimistically declared: "Harvard has now put an end to anti-feminism." He recalled the dark, misogynistic past: "I have sometimes wondered whether Mr. Lowell's extraordinary prejudice came from his dislike of some of the performances of his sister [the flamboyant poet] Amy."[9]

Piece by piece, institutional barriers began to come down: not unlike the slow erosion of racial segregation. By the early 1960s, all of the University's classrooms were open to women. They made up over 2,000 of the University's 13,000 students, though 80 percent were in Radcliffe and the Graduate School of Arts and Sciences. In 1955 the daily service in the Appleton Chapel of the University's Memorial Church was desegregated. Before this, women sat in the church auditorium, separated from the chapel by the chancel and a substantial screen: "a kind of 'court of the women'" was Divinity School dean Willard Sperry's unfortunate metaphor. The first chink in this unisex theological armor came in 1948 when Helen Cam, the first Radcliffe-Zemurray professor, gained access to the services by the unsubtle tactic of showing up at them. Minister George Buttrick came to the conclusion that "none should be barred from services in a Christian church because of sex, rank or race." Predictably, attendance (male as well as female) rose, and Buttrick soon was thinking of moving to a larger space.[10]

As the female faculty and staff presence grew, so did the need for a maternity leave policy. "It seems hard to believe," Corporation secretary

Bailey warned, "that the 554 women listed as Corporation appointees in the University Catalogue for 1960–61 are all going to remain childless." The rule in the Medical School was that the incipient motherhood of a staff member required her resignation. Women there asked for a half-time alternative. "[I]t would seem likely," Bailey observed, "that social pressures in the future might suggest this would be a possible expedient." The solution: unpaid leave of absence.[11]

Harvard's schools and departments relied for their administration on capable, long-tenured, self-effacing female secretaries and assistants. In 1955 Pusey proposed that a new class of Corporation appointees be created: "a small group of women in administrative positions whose responsibilities include confidential participation in the implementation of University policy at a relatively high level." Six names immediately surfaced. Law School dean Griswold wanted four more female staffers added to the list in 1959. Corporation secretary David Bailey was annoyed: "I have often heard it said that the Law School Faculty, like the Mexican Army, consists only of generals. It would seem to me that the logical outcome of Dean Griswold's present proposals might be to make all the present noncoms into second lieutenants." But the Business School had three new names of its own, with dozens more to come if the bars were lowered. It appeared that Harvard's invisible government was more extensive than anyone thought.[12]

But it was the Harvard-Radcliffe relationship that lay at the heart of gender relationships in the University. An early sign of change appeared in 1960, when Radcliffe's new president, Mary (Polly) Bunting, was named a lecturer in Biology with the unanimous approval of that department. It was highly desirable, said Pusey, that Radcliffe "should have a genuine membership in the Faculty of Arts and Sciences." (And besides, it was only for the term of her presidency.) But that there still were many miles to go was evident when "Mrs. Carl J. Gilbert"—Helen Homans Gilbert, chair of the Radcliffe Trustees—invited Pusey to the inauguration of "Mrs. Henry I. Bunting" as Radcliffe's sixth president.

Polly Bunting proved to be a skillful political infighter. She understood that the way to a Harvard dean's heart was through his pocketbook. Bundy contentedly told Pusey in June 1960 that "Radcliffe continues to raise its basic percentage of tuition contributed just as fast as it can, and I have found Polly anything but sticky about the rights and wrongs of small transactions." At the same time she sought to make Radcliffe more a part of the throbbing Harvard world around her. She established the Radcliffe Institute in 1960 as a place "for highly educated women who wish to continue their scholarly activities during or after taking time out to raise a family," an instance of the truism that all educational policy is autobiography.[13]

Nourished by the heady, can-do academic atmosphere of the sixties, the integration snail inched along. Radcliffe undergraduates had had access to almost all Harvard College classes since the 1940s, and Conant thought (wrongly) that the University was coeducational in practice if not theory. Radcliffe had a jealously protected separate corporate identity, and its leaders were as anxious as the most hidebound Harvardian to keep the wolf of coeducation (that is, women getting Harvard, not Radcliffe, undergraduate and graduate degrees) from the schoolhouse door.

Pusey thought it not "likely or advisable that Radcliffe should ever become completely absorbed by Harvard. It is appropriate that the women students of the University have their own social and cultural life and live apart as a group in much the same way that Harvard undergraduates enjoy 'the collegiate way of living' in the Houses." But pressure mounted for full female membership in Harvard student organizations. The Harvard-Radcliffe Affiliation Committee polled thirty-three Harvard student groups and found that only nine opposed merger, though ten out of fifteen Radcliffe groups were against it. By 1960 a Radcliffe student was president of the Harvard Liberal Club, and coeds were on the *Crimson*, the college radio station WHRB, and the executive board of the Young Democrats. As late as February 1966, Harvard students petitioned against letting women use Lamont, the College's undergraduate library. Then Radcliffe's new Hilles Library opened. Male readers (or at least viewers) were welcome, and in unsettling numbers they accepted the invitation. This put a new face on things, and the Harvard College Library Committee unanimously decided to admit women to Lamont. In 1970 eight Radcliffe students were admitted into the Signet Society, the first Harvard club (admittedly not one of the most exclusive, and with literary pretensions) to admit women. The *Lampoon*, the College humor magazine—blue in two senses of that word—soon followed. Radcliffe's class of 1970 declared that it wanted to graduate as part of the Harvard commencement rather than separately; and the deed was done.[14]

Integrated housing was the most sensitive issue in the Harvard-Radcliffe social relationship. Radcliffe president Bunting held that "merger does not necessarily mean coed dormitories." Pusey thought that even an experiment along those lines was out of the question as long as Radcliffe was not in fact a part of Harvard and its students a responsibility of the Faculty of Arts and Sciences. On this he and the

Corporation were adamant. But all things were possible after the student uprising in the spring of 1969. The Committee on Coresidential Housing came up with a complicated plan for gradual integration, complicated because it sought to take account both of the desire of all Harvard houses for women residents and the wish of Radcliffe students not to be small islands in a sea of maleness. By most measures (save athletics), the all-male Harvard game was over.[15]

Administrative merger of Radcliffe and Harvard turned out to be more problematical than academic and social integration, which on the face of it entailed more substantive change. This was due as much to Radcliffe's reluctance to lose its individuality as to Harvard's intransigence.

In April 1961 Pusey asked Radcliffe President Bunting if she and her trustees "would be interested in exploring the possibility of becoming fully a part of Harvard University," though he himself was "not clear that such an arrangement is either possible or desirable." There were formidable legal and financial obstacles. But a journey of a thousand miles ... By the summer of 1965 Bunting was keen to talk to Pusey about some "rather basic policy decisions." She agreed that "the time has ... come, far sooner than I had once anticipated, to consider incorporating Radcliffe formally within the University structure." In her scenario Radcliffe's president would become a Harvard dean, its board of trustees a visiting committee. She could of course do nothing until Harvard approved; and then she would have to get the okay of Radcliffe's trustees. If they said no, then Bunting "would conclude that the timing was wrong."[16]

In late November 1965 Bunting reported to Pusey that her trustees had reexamined the Harvard-Radcliffe relationship, with (as she delicately put it) somewhat more vigor than she anticipated. Some worried that opening up the merger issue would hurt fund-raising. Nevertheless she continued to believe that "Radcliffe's special mission will be accomplished when it is incorporated *as a distinctive unit* within Harvard University or, to say it the other way, when Harvard cares enough about the education of women to want to see it carried forward as effectively as possible." Pusey, however, now thought that no attempt should be made "until those to whom Radcliffe's governance is entrusted are fully persuaded that union will be a good thing, actively press for it, and wish fully to entrust their responsibility to Harvard." The reluctance of Radcliffe's board members suggested that perhaps the time had not yet come. So it would be best for the two of them to continue to talk informally, "looking for a more propitious time or waiting until we are confronted with an urgent occasion to move ahead."

The reality of coeducation and an ever more integrated undergraduate life kept merger on the two schools' agendas. In late 1968 Pusey and Bunting agreed on a draft memorandum of understanding. It declared that the purposes of Radcliffe could best be carried out by transferring its funds and property to Harvard; Harvard would assist in the fundraising for a $10 million campaign, the Program for Radcliffe College. Harvard's Corporation and Radcliffe's trustees agreed to merger talks, aiming at its implementation in the fall of 1970.[17]

Pusey put the proposed merger before the Faculty of Arts and Sciences. Should Harvard College become a coeducational institution? He thought it more or less bound to happen: the curricular and extracurricular lives of the two undergraduate groups were so entwined that separate entities no longer made sense. But the turmoil accompanying the student occupation of University Hall in April 1969 delayed things. Not until the summer did Pusey appoint faculty groups to look into the complexities of admissions and financial aid, budget and personnel, extracurricular activities and student services, and housing.[18]

By the fall of 1969 merger was unraveling. The delay enabled Radcliffe trustees and alumnae and Harvard faculty, staff, and alumni who opposed it to regroup. Radcliffe grandee Mary Bundy and other Boston Brahmin ladies strongly opposed the step: Radcliffe, after all, was a college of their own. Robert Lee Wolff of the History department, a tower of standpattism and a Radcliffe trustee, warned Bunting and the Harvard leaders that hope of immediate merger was chimerical. There were complex legal and financial problems to be sorted out and wide opposition within the faculty. Many did not want to see Radcliffe women competing for Harvard scholarships. And the pressure to add women so as to lessen the present one to four female-male ratio could be met only by adding to the total (thus overloading libraries, laboratories, and so forth) or by reducing the number of men admitted to the College (unthinkable). The ever realistic Polly Bunting now hoped that whatever was agreed upon would be seen as the best compromise available, rather than a final decision one way or the other. She remained convinced that "Radcliffe is now so much part of Harvard that it should be recognized and run as such."[19]

The opposition tide swelled during the 1969–70 academic year. Corporation fellow Henry Shattuck opposed merger and was assured by Pusey that "it does not appear that [it] . . . will take place without further study." A faculty committee looking into admissions and financial aid strongly advised against legal merger: it would lead inevitably to an "undesirable" increase in the size of the student body with adverse effects on its quality, the transformation of Harvard into a megaversity, and a loss for women of institutional concern for their special problems. (Pusey's marginal responses: "!", "?"). Radcliffe board chairwoman Helen Gilbert finally exploded to Corporation fellow Hugh Calkins in August:

> I am at the end of my patience and I think I speak for a collective Radcliffe patience. Radcliffe has had the decency to agree to discuss "merger" and has waited, at Nate's request, until the Faculty agreed to equality for women at Harvard. We were assured that the summer of 1970 would see a top committee of Harvard Corporation members and Radcliffe trustees get to the details and work out a new Harvard-Radcliffe agreement.

But she had had only one brief, unsatisfactory meeting with Calkins; otherwise, there had been no communication.[20]

Merger, once seemingly inevitable, now was a rapidly receding possibility. Strong feminists and women in the Graduate School were among the few still unequivocally in favor. A group of them complained that while Radcliffe students became ever more integrated into Harvard academic and social life, the College tried ever more staunchly to preserve its separate identity. The fact of the matter, they argued, was that Radcliffe, with no faculty, was not really a college at all. Separate but equal—which ultimately served both Harvard and Radcliffe interests— was no more desirable for women than it was for blacks. If the cost of integration was fewer men, or a larger class, or—horror of horrors— sex-blind admissions: so what? But this was whistling in the wind. In early 1971 the Corporation approved a "nonmerger" agreement. Radcliffe continued to be responsible for admissions and financial aid; Harvard would be in full charge of female students' curricular and extracurricular life. Polly Bunting resigned the Radcliffe presidency in June, possibly under pressure from antimerger alumnae: with what emotions, it is difficult to say.[21]

## The African American Presence

African American students during the 1930s and 1940s were a not unwelcome sign of Harvard tolerance, as long as they were small in numbers and of acceptable demeanor. By the mid-1950s, genteel liberal integrationism was the norm. The dormitories were integrated, Harvard teams did not play against segregated colleges. When an NAACP leader asked if Harvard had any courses on segregation in the wake of the Supreme Court's 1954 *Brown* decision, Bentinck-Smith thought that "[i]t does not seem to me that this question particularly pertains here." School spokesmen concentrated on prejudice and discrimination outside, such as Cambridge landlords who excluded black and Jewish graduate students. In 1960 an antidiscrimination pledge was required for all rentals listed with Harvard.[22]

In 1954 Oscar De Priest III, whose grandfather was the first black northern Congressman, came up for membership in the Harvard Club of Boston. He was "an honorable negro, a gentleman, and an exceptional scholar," said one member, who threatened to resign from the club if De Priest was kept out. The candidate was elected by acclamation, though a couple of members—quickly "hooted down"—spoke against his being allowed in the ladies' dining room. ("[I]magine!," wrote an indignant Bentinck-Smith to Pusey.) When a southern Law School alumnus took Pusey to task for a prointegration statement on TV's *Meet the Press*, the president responded: "I simply wish to express my sorrow that you as a Harvard man feel as you do."[23]

As black demands for equality and inclusion grew, feel-good tokenism came under pressure. When in 1981 the NAACP planned an investigation of institutional hiring practices in the Boston area, a Harvard official observed that Harvard's record was "by and large ... excellent as regards negroes—with two exceptions. Apparently it is departmental policy not to hire negroes in Buildings and Grounds, and in the Comptroller's office." He thought it wise to urge them "to find at least one qualified negro each to forestall possible public criticism."

In 1963 about 7 percent of Harvard's unskilled employees were African American; when it came to clerical, administrative, and faculty appointees, approximately none. Pressure on the University went up a notch when the federal Equal Employment Opportunity Commission required a compliance report from government contractors (including Harvard) providing "in effect, a head count of all employees for the purpose of listing Negroes and certain other minority groups." University officials contested "the notion of recording the racial origin of its employees, a notion repugnant to our idea of the dignity of the individual." But the University had to comply. And the number of black students in the College became a sensitive issue. It had 50 to 70 American-born blacks (out of 4,600 undergraduates) in the spring of 1964. The Law School, which ordinarily had two or three black students in each class, accepted fifteen that year.[24]

Liberal outreach began to enter into its painful, frustrating interaction with black separatism. One instance: a 1963 proposal for a Harvard African and Afro-American Club, apparently to be restricted to blacks. What in a few years might be widely regarded as an acceptable instance of group self-expression offended the sensibilities of white and black integrationists alike. By a two-to-one margin the students' Council for Undergraduate Affairs refused to approve the new organization. William M. Brewer, Harvard alumnus and editor of the *Journal of Negro History*, was eloquently indignant:

> At a time when America and much of the world are searching consciences and hearts about civil and human rights, the colored Harvard and Radcliffe students are asking you to sanction "self-jimcrowism and self-segregation" by desecrating Fair Harvard's *glorious and sacred traditions as well as name*! As a colored alumnus twice of Harvard, I beseech you not to veer from your long-established policy by approval of this.... The colored students should be ashamed of themselves.

But Dean of the College John Monro defended the students and their proposal. White citizens of African countries (except South Africa) would be able to join; "Europeans or North American whites would not be eligible, for the reason that they have no ties to Africa." He agreed "that we do not want a segregated Negro club at Harvard," but was "not yet certain that such is what our Negro students have in mind." (He would soon be disabused of that uncertainty.)[25]

The administration's efforts to recruit black students, faculty, and employees fed on a steady diet of white guilt and black pressure. The score by the spring of 1968, in the wake of Martin Luther King's assassination and the ensuing urban riots: African American employees had more than doubled over the past four years to about 400. Some gains (a few painters, carpenters, plumbers, one house superintendent) had been made in that Irish preserve, buildings and grounds. Harvard had about forty black faculty members, almost all of them in the lower ranks. Only one was in Arts and Sciences: assistant professor of Government Martin Kilson. "I believe," Pusey said, "we are making 'unusual' efforts to improve this really inexcusable situation throughout the country."[26]

The protests of 1969 ratcheted up assumptions as to what should (and could) be done to bring more black students to Harvard. That fall 174 black applicants were admitted to the College. About 270—6 percent of the student body—were expected in 1970. A bolder approach had its advocates: "the university will be performing its proper function when it will take a chance on black students or poor whites.... Students with disadvantaged backgrounds will in the long run bring to the university an air of reality and more honestly reflect the varied backgrounds of people in our society at large." Integration versus separatism, meritocracy versus diversity—issues that in decades to come would define race relations at Harvard and other universities—were alive and growing by the end of the sixties.[27]

The creation of an Afro-American Studies department became the chief cause of blacks at Harvard. A faculty committee headed by Economics department chairman Henry Rosovsky proposed in the spring of 1969 that a degree-granting program rather than a full-fledged department of Afro-American Studies be launched. Rosovsky assured his colleagues that this was in the Harvard tradition of adapting its curriculum to new areas of study. But the committee's recommendation that the program be headed by "a distinguished scholar deeply concerned with Afro-American Studies and identified with the black American experience and community" seemed to some "racism in reverse."

The Faculty of Arts and Sciences met to decide on the proposal on April 22, 1969, in an atmosphere heated up by the University Hall occupation a couple of weeks before. The meeting was held in the Loeb Drama Center: necessary because of the turnout and appropriate because of the high level of histrionics. Faculty hawks warned of the fall of Harvard, and even civilization, as they knew it. Radical whites and blacks threw themselves into this opportunity for agitprop: one black militant paraded outside the meeting sporting a meat cleaver. White liberals and moderates supported a parliamentary maneuver that scuttled the Rosovsky Committee's proposal for a program and replaced it with the militants' demand for a department. Unsettling, too, was the proposal that ten or more faculty appointments be made, and that they be proposed by a faculty-student committee.

Rosovsky called the faculty vote "an academic Munich," a triumph of confrontation over rational debate. But professor of Astronomy Charles Whitney announced that it was "time for revolution in the College" and welcomed the students' role in faculty and course selection in the new department as the dawn of a fresh approach to higher education: "If ... students in my department insisted on the appointment of an astrologer, I would assume that we could argue the matter rationally and both sides would benefit from the argument."[28]

So in the fall of 1969 the African and Afro-American Studies department got under way. The distinguished historian John Hope Franklin was asked to head it. But the department's problematic origins and structure dissuaded him and other prominent black scholars from getting involved. Afro wound up finally with Ewart Guinier, a lawyer, 1949 candidate of the left-wing American Labor Party for Manhattan Borough president, most recently the associate director of Columbia's Urban Center: a fresh approach, indeed, to a Harvard academic appointment. Some black nationalist students at Columbia warned of Guinier's indifference to the cause of black advancement, his laziness, and a record of misuse of funds. But an administration fearful of trouble put pressure on the faculty ad hoc committee to go along, and so it did.[29]

Increased hiring of African American workers on Harvard construction sites was one of the few issues on which black and white activists found common ground. In the fall of 1969 the Organization for Black Unity (OBU), a black campus group, called for 20 percent minority worker representation on Harvard projects. An attention-grabbing occupation of University Hall led to hiring commitments for specific projects. But the administration would not agree to a flat 20 percent black workforce. More building occupations occurred, with white radicals trying to get into the action. Rhetoric heated up. The OBU declared: "The black nation has come to our support ... the only legitimate purpose African students have on this white campus is to study and push for the liberation of all African peoples ... judgment has come to the house of scholars."[30]

An association of black faculty and administrators called for the appointment of a vice president on race relations with real authority and expected the University to "seek our counsel and approval regarding the structure of this office and the individual who would be appointed to head it." Pusey chose instead to appoint a personal assistant to coordinate minority policies and programs. Clifford Alexander, Jr., '55, who had been special assistant for civil rights to Lyndon Johnson and chaired the Equal Economic Opportunity Commission from 1967 to 1969, took on the job in January 1970. Pusey told the dean of each school to appoint a representative for minority employment.[31]

These efforts led to no visible improvement in campus race relations. Nor did the new Afro-American Studies department get off to a salubrious start. FAS dean John Dunlop took exception to a statement by Chairman Guinier that the department had a "black perspective to serve the interest of the black community and thereby the interest of all." A difficulty arose when the instructor of an Afro-American Studies course

excluded a white student. In the first tenure vote of the new department's standing committee, four white faculty members and black
Medical School microbiologist Harold Amos opposed the candidate;
Chairman Guinier and the student members favored him (Amos found
the whole business quite distressing). In an intensely compressed couple
of years, major changes in policy, experience, institutions, and attitudes
swept over black-white relations at Harvard. As in the case of women,
much of the infrastructure, and most of the tensions, that would define
those relations in decades to come were in place by the time of Pusey's
departure in 1971.[32]

## ～ 13 ～

## THE COLLEGE

E ven in the age of the imperial faculty and powerful professional schools, the College was at the center of Harvard's sense of itself. This was evident in the two most significant events of the Pusey years: the great fund-raising effort of the late 1950s, pointedly called the Program for Harvard College; and the upheaval of 1969, in which the largest source of attention (and concern) was the degree to which Harvard undergraduates were involved.

### College Life

After the postwar rush of veterans, Harvard College during the 1950s appeared in many ways to return to its prewar state. Only about a quarter of the students in 1958 were on financial aid. The typical graduate five years out in the mid-fifties lived in a large northeastern city, was married with one child, was a Republican who went to church once a month. Most undergraduates sought to live up to their national billing as the elite of the elite. The dress-down clothing style of the postwar vets gave way to resurgent preppy attire: casually (that is, purposefully) dirtied white buckskin shoes, tweed jackets, green book bags, alpine parkas. "At a distance and even from quite close up," said one observer, "everyone looks alike." The prevailing social style was "polite arrogance—spare, dry, cautious, and angular." Too cool by half, thought a critic: "Even in the unregimented student life of the Yard, there has been a certain failure of nerve, a hint of the youthful generation's prudence."[1]

The psychological downer of the Depression and the more mature post–World War II veterans temporarily squelched the venerable Harvard tradition of spring student riots. When there was talk of resurrecting that custom, a Radcliffe girl "sniffed scornfully: 'What sort of riot is it when it has to be planned?'" Springtime hijinks returned in the 1950s with a younger, more affluent student body. These had a satirical, self-conscious edge, appropriate to a more intellectual student generation. The first rumpus came in May 1952 when students gathered to welcome cartoonist Walt Kelley, creator of the popular cartoon strip "Pogo." Confusion and delay turned to streetcar disabling and fights with the police. In April 1961, protests raged through two unruly nights against the administration's decision to switch to less costly printed diplomas—most inexcusably in English, not Latin. The chief target was president Pusey and his decision to make the change. But this was much more good-natured than what was to come. A week after the diploma fracas, students taking a bartending course offered by the Harvard Student Agency demanded that their certificates be in Latin—which, they charmingly claimed, would help them in their search for employment.[2]

Professors bored by undergraduate normality (and restless in the Age of Eisenhower) urged students to be less risk averse. The response: your generation was more adventurous; look at the world now. After years of depression and war, Harvard undergraduates of the fifties like the rest of their peers welcomed a respite from ideology and engagement: "Nobody feels like going out with a billboard saying, 'Adam Smith Saves.'" The thrust of their class work, most notably the General Education program, was toward synthesis, not destruction or decon-struction. Literature, Philosophy, and History got more popular, Government less so. Only about 10 percent of the 5,000 undergraduates belonged to political organizations.

A 1956 Student Council report, "Religion at Harvard," found a level of commitment and interest that surprised its authors. *Newsweek* took note and concluded that religion was on the upswing on the campus. The determinedly secular *Crimson* disagreed. But who really knew? In any event, this hardly signified a Great Awakening. When an under-graduate asked Pusey why classes could not be suspended on Good Friday, that far from secular-minded president explained that Harvard did not plan its schedule around religious holidays.[3]

Harvard football settled down in the 1950s to the half-parodic style of the Ivy League. Pusey's attitude was much like Conant's: "We believe the most sensible way to keep football a game is to have the athletic poli-cies and the sports programming in the hands of academic authorities who have power to control admissions and financial aids." In any event, an increasingly meritocratic College was not fertile soil for football prowess. The 1957 season, when Harvard was routed by Princeton and Yale, was grim enough to satisfy the most dedicated academic athletiphobe. In the wake of that disastrous year John Yovicsin became coach, Harvard football improved, and football prowess within the limited confines of the Ivy League gradually became another brick in the rising tower of Harvard self-esteem.[4]

But the carapace of old ways was misleading. When professor of English William Alfred reminisced about the 1950s two tumultuous decades later, he thought it was then that "the old Harvard, the eastern school, prep school center with an emphasis on final clubs" had "gone underground." Small but cumulatively significant changes altered the lives of undergraduates. Meals served at table were a casualty of World War II. And beginning in the fall of 1954, students were required to make (or, more accurately, not make) their own beds, as mechanized room cleaning by (male) crews replaced the traditional daily maid service.[5]

The dual triumph of meritocracy and affluence changed the face of Harvard's undergraduates as it did the faculty. Foreign students gradually became a more significant presence on the campus. There were 800 of them in the fall of 1957, 128 in the College. Commuters—"black-shoes" in the derogatory argot of the time—were a diminishing breed. By 1956 only 285 were in the three postfreshman classes. And most had very different social origins than their prewar working-class counterparts. Now commuters lived off-campus because no dormitory rooms were available or because they were married. Almost 40 percent had gone to private secondary schools. Three 1956–57 commuters had car accidents while driving to school—in their Jaguars.[6]

Two new undergraduate houses opened in the late fifties and early sixties, uncontroversially honoring former Harvard presidents Increase Mather (d. 1723) and Josiah Quincy (d. 1864). A suggestion that one of them be named Roosevelt House—without specifying TR or FDR—fell on stony ground. Corporation Secretary Bailey explained, "Our governing boards are bulging with people who never liked Franklin and Eleanor." The next addition to undergraduate housing came in the late sixties, when Radcliffe built Currier House. By now the voice of the student was heard in the land. Currier was carefully crafted to respond to student criticism of the inhuman, soulless rooms-and-corridors layout of the older dormitories. The new house consisted instead of a few cuddly suites on each floor of a podlike set of buildings. The paint was scarcely dry when Currier's denizens began to complain that it was all an administration plot to isolate the undergraduates into politically manageable groupuscules, and that what they really wanted was the rich, informal street life of the old-fashioned dormitories. . . . [7]

# Admissions

Who got into Harvard, rather than how they behaved once they were there, was the flash point in conflicts over the character of the College. The prewar days, when 80 to 90 percent of those who applied were admitted, were gone, never to return. In 1953, the year Pusey became president, the College took slightly more than half of its 3,400 applicants. A decade later the applicant pool had risen to 4,155, and about 38 percent were accepted. Admissions officers fretted over the declining percentage of alumni children taken by the College: nine out of ten in 1951, two out of three in 1956.

One problem: Harvard sons had grades and test scores well below the average applicant. It wasn't that some sort of intergenerational decay made for dumber alumni children, but that the general level of the pool was rising so much. The able, competitive postwar veterans, it turned out, were not an aberration but a foreshadowing. To add to the crunch, the Harvard matriculation level kept rising, from 60 percent or so of the acceptees coming in the early 1950s into the stratosphere of 80-percent-plus a decade later. More and more were from families who could afford Harvard or had outside aid such as National Merit Scholarships. The able sons or grandsons of immigrants who came to Harvard a generation ago now were successful doctors or lawyers, sending their sons to private or good suburban public schools and expecting them to go to dad's alma mater.[8]

Wilbur Bender, Harvard's dean of admissions from 1952 to 1960, had tough sledding when it came to mollifying influential alums alarmed by the rising rejection of Their Sort. And the Campaign for Harvard College loomed in the late fifties. Bender asked in 1957: "Should we, frankly, during the next three years of intensive fund-raising effort among alumni, for Harvard College, swallow hard and admit every Harvard son who looks as if he might survive?" (That, more or less, is what was done.)[9]

Corporation fellow Thomas Lamont fretted that Princeton and Yale were better able to attract "good men." He told Bender that nine out of ten Harvard alumni

> would want just the kind of boy at Harvard whom you yourself want.... Of course, there are a lot of rich Cafe Society families in this country who want to send their dumb kids to college, and of course there are a hell of a lot of families who are "on the make" and want to send their boys to college because they think it will

give them a bench mark of social standing. But it is just plain good boys from whatever background that Harvard wants and Exeter wants and Yale and Princeton want.

When Lamont warned that the old Harvard families might not continue to send their sons to a larger College, FAS Dean McGeorge Bundy took him on. Only through expansion would character, promise, athletic ability, and the rest have a look-in. He rebuked Lamont for implying that there should be room in the College for young men of strong background and good character whose commitment to hard work and large careers was less than complete: "Harvard is too great an engine of power and responsibility ... to be merely a place for the later adolescent years of nice young men." The current student body, Bundy held, "is not only more intelligent, but more mature and less given to cheap snobbery, intellectual or social, than it was before the Second War."[10]

Meanwhile Bender developed an elaborate rationale for placing greater weight on nonacademic factors. He told Pusey that "the myth to be combated is the notion that we are just a grind factory full of goggle-eyed bifocal geniuses or precious effeminate types none of whom speak to each other, have any juice in their veins or give a damn about normal, healthy aspects of life." Given the size and quality of the applicant pool, he needed reasons to admit more than reasons to reject, such as "strength of character, creative ability of various sorts, attractiveness of personality, capacity for leadership, geographic distribution, rural or small-town origin, athletic ability, Harvard parentage, energy and enthusiasm, strength of motivation, intellectual curiosity, interest in a particular field of study." In short: a constellation of qualities, interests, talents, and backgrounds so varied (and so resistant to precise measurement) that selection would rest securely in the hands of the admissions professionals who had mastered the mysterious science of winnowing the applicant wheat from the chaff.[11]

And a mystery (in the dictionary sense of "a secret religious rite") admissions was. Bender's associate Delmar Leighton tried to explain it to the alumni in 1956. Harvard parentage and place of origin did not readily lend themselves to numerical ratings. (Why? Not explained.) But the relative importance of academic ability, personal attributes, and school reports *could* be measured. Candidate interviews placed a weight of 52 percent on personal attributes, 33 percent on academic ability, 14 percent on the secondary school principal's report. If no interview took place, then personality slid to 28 percent, academic ability rose to 51 percent, and the principal's report to 20 percent. Athletic or other talent, he said, had a (suspiciously low) 1 percent value. But not all was numbers. One academically top-drawer applicant was turned down on the "somewhat intuitive ground" that because he was small, weak in build, and stuttered badly, he could not stand up to the rigors of Harvard undergraduate life. (Harvard had no hammerlock on such standards. A *New Yorker* article, "How an Ivy League College (Yale) Decides on Admissions," told of one candidate taken because he was "more of a guy.")[12]

Bender resigned from the admissions deanship in October 1959. Rumor had it that Bundy (one with the faculty in his preference for brainy students) forced him out—after the Program for Harvard College was safely done. Bundy himself claimed that Bender left because he had reshaped the admissions office and sought new worlds to conquer. Yet Bender's final report was hardly an exercise in satisfaction over a job well and fully done. The key question, he thought, was whether or not the College would be "simply a pre-professional school whose students are expected to absorb as rapidly as possible the material deemed necessary for entrance to the next phase of professional training? Will the College become just a kind of anteroom for the future Ph.D.?" "The top high school student," he warned, "is often, frankly, a pretty dull and bloodless, or peculiar fellow." Originality and creativity had only a casual relation to school and college records. But if current patterns went on, the likes of the current bottom half of the class would be gone. With them would go the loyal alumni who did the hard work of fund-raising, and the so-so students who then rose to society's heights: TR, FDR, (soon) JFK.... Harvard could avoid that Orwellian future "provided we don't raise the present academic level too much and do maintain our relationships with the private schools and the Harvard family." In memorable words Bender envisioned "a college with some snobs and some Scandinavian farm boys who skate beautifully and some bright Bronx pre-meds."[13]

Meanwhile applications kept rising, as did the applicants' qualifications. To ease the crunch, the Corporation in January 1964 formally ended the 1,000-freshman ceiling. About 1,500 were admitted in 1965—out of 6,700 applications from some three thousand secondary schools. For the first time, fewer than half of the alumni children who applied got in. "We don't really see how we can turn down a really first-rate candidate in order to take an average Harvard son," new admissions dean Fred Glimp declared. The scale and sensitivity of admissions made it an ever more elaborate process. By the early sixties more than a hundred school and scholarship committees and 1,400 alumni worked on recruiting and interviewing. They not only found and vetted candidates, but often helped mollify traditional feeder secondary schools whose graduates had been rejected.[14]

In the early 1960s financial aid began to be topped up by FAS general funds, enabling Harvard to move closer to the goal of need-blind admissions. "Gamble-fund" scholarships allowed for the acceptance of about 200 high-risk students between 1957 and 1966. They had very low College Board scores and came from city slums, unaccredited black southern high schools, migrant labor camps. Only a few admissions people knew who they were. They spent a year or so in a New England preparatory school before coming to Harvard. Generally, admissions thought, they did well; one of them became a Rhodes scholar. (Focusing on successes—representative or not—was (and is) the accepted way of evaluating admissions experiments.)[15]

As the civil rights movement took hold, interest grew in recruiting black students from the South. A Birmingham, Alabama, alumnus was distressed that a black applicant from his state who won a National Merit Scholarship did not get in. But when a Louisiana grad complained that three of the twenty-seven accepted applicants from his state came from the same black high school, Pusey's aide William Bentinck-Smith looked into the matter, and reported: "Incredible though it may seem, the three Negro students were superior to the 22 remaining white students in the applicant list, with the possible exception of one [of the whites] whom the committee felt was too dependent on his parents and rejected for that reason."[16]

The fact that so many applicants had SAT scores in the highest (750–800) group added to the weight of other, nonacademic considerations. Almost all of the readings of applicants' folders was done by admissions staff members. They were confirmed in their judgment of their judgment when a study of the class of 1962 found a mild but clear correlation between the ratings of applicants and their success at Harvard. The conclusion: "what seems 'right' for a humane college that has a broad educational mission also seems to work out well for the students and the College."[17]

In the fall of 1968 the American Council on Education polled thousands of entering students in hundreds of American colleges and universities. The result: a statistical profile that showed how incoming Harvard students resembled, and differed from, their counterparts elsewhere. They came, of course, from much better educated and richer families. The religious backgrounds of Harvard freshmen were above the Protestant and Jewish and below the Catholic national distribution. The students' own religious preferences, across the board, were significantly weaker: apparently many were agnostics before they got to Godless Harvard. Needless to say, their grade averages, high school leadership, and plans for postgraduate study were far above national norms. So, too, were the numbers who planned to major in the social sciences and become college teachers or research scientists. They were far less likely to want to become rich. Sixty percent of the national sample saw monetary benefits in going to college; 16.4 percent of Harvard freshmen did. Many more than the national norm expected to participate in demonstrations while in college (17.1 percent as against 4.6 percent), favored the legalization of marijuana, cared about air pollution, planned to engage in political activity.[18]

## The Culture of Student Discontent

The message of these findings for Harvard's guardians of tradition and order, in short and in sum: trouble. This was not immediately evident during the high noon of meritocracy. A 1958 study concluded that "student culture at Harvard is primarily middle class and work oriented. There is, to be sure, an overlay of upper-class customs and stylistic features, but these are merely the overlay and not the core." Compared to the past, this was a "new order." Certainly it was a high-achieving one. The ability of Harvard graduates to win society's glittering prizes took on a life of its own. The class of 1960 was a milestone. For the first time more than half of the graduates got honors degrees; 82 percent planned on graduate study. Only 134, 13 percent, went directly to work: most of them (26) in engineering, 18 into teaching, a risible 11 into banking and 10 into sales. The class of 1966 corralled 25 percent of all Rhodes and Marshall Scholarships awarded in the country that year, as well as 40 National Science Foundation and 45 Woodrow Wilson Fellowships. More than two-thirds graduated with honors.[19]

Most undergraduates in the fifties and early sixties appear to have reveled in the heady mix of high status and social and intellectual vitality available to them. Wherein, then, lay the sources of discontent? One was the curriculum. A highly professional, highly specialized faculty not surprisingly offered highly professional, specialized courses. The 1961–62 catalogue had 1,614 offerings, more than one for every four undergraduates. A *Crimson* editorial in 1958 attacked overacademization in the College: too much emphasis on grades, too much stress on preparation for academic careers. A 1964 report by the students' Council for Undergraduate Affairs found a deep well of cynicism, with two schools of course coping: "bull" (analysis without facts) and "cow" (facts without analysis). As in the past, students protected themselves from academic rigor by flocking into a few popular courses. Crane Brinton's offering in European intellectual history, "one of the most mercifully graded courses at Harvard," had some 800 attendees.[20]

Another source of strain: what happened when freshmen came face-to-face with their supercharged peers. Half of those who arrived in 1959 said they intended to concentrate in the natural sciences; 28 percent of them wound up doing so. Forty-three percent majored in the more user-friendly social sciences. The College set up the Bureau of Study Counsel in the 1950s, which quickly evolved from a body charged to deal with problem students to one that dealt with students' problems.[21]

In late 1964 Dean of the College John Monro took note of a growing sophomore slump: fewer students on the dean's list, more with unsatisfactory records, pulling out voluntarily, or being expelled. Pusey aide Bentinck-Smith, "very apprehensive" (NMP: "et moi aussi!") about a forthcoming *Life* magazine article on the emotional problems of Harvard students, unsuccessfully tried to block it. "Crack-ups on the Campus" came out in January 1965. The piece led one old grad to chastize Pusey:

> it seems to many of us that you are engaged in transforming the College from its former unique role as the foremost agency for training a wide spectrum of leaders in all walks of life to a factory dedicated solely to the development of scholars, professors and research scientists.... This is not a plea for mediocrity, but for pragmatism and moderation. It is basically wrong to subject the student of modest scholarly potential to the standards which are easily met by the scholarly eagles.[22]

At the same time Conant's General Education Program came under increasing faculty criticism: in part because of the entropy endemic to curricular reform, in part because the faculty was more interested in its areas of expertise than in general instruction. A faculty committee in 1964 found Gen. Ed.'s administrative structure inadequate, its requirements too inflexible, its courses too limited in number, its content flawed in that it emphasized historical and critical modes of analysis while slighting natural and social science theory and practical instruction in the arts. (Otherwise, all was well.) But these concerns did not engage the undergraduates; their response to proposed changes ran the emotional gamut from boredom to indifference. In 1966 the remaining Gen. Ed.

introductory course requirements were ended; with it, the "last remnants of a core curriculum will have yielded to the demand for flexibility."[23]

Tension between teachers and the taught is as old as Harvard—or college—history. But now something else was at play as well. A fast-changing American society forged a culturally unsettling new breed of undergraduates. A 1959 *Crimson* poll suggested that the religiosity of the fifties was on its way out. A fifth of the Catholic, a quarter of the Jewish, almost 40 percent of the Protestant students in the sample said that they had "apostasized" during the course of their College experience. Along with this secularism emerged a leitmotif of discontent with an administrative (and to a lesser but increasing degree, academic) infrastructure seen as repressive and constraining. A fall 1962 report, *The Long Reach, A Report on Harvard Today*—one of those recurrent pickings at the scab of student sentiment that were in themselves a sign of the times—asked undergraduates to describe the most interesting thing they had done on a given day. One response: "My whole day evolved in complete independence from any authoritarian word from the University. My time was for me alone." This may be dismissed as late adolescent *angst*. But there were signs that a more consequential change in student attitudes was under way.[24]

One was the appearance of a student drug culture different in style and substance from the alcohol-laden club and house life of the past. It was in the early 1960s that those purveyors of better living through chemistry, Timothy Leary and Richard Alpert, made their cameo appearances. Leary and Company were gone from the campus by 1963, but drug use by then was an established part of the Harvard social scene. College and Health Service authorities began to warn undergraduates of its dangers. In December 1964 the *New York Times* reported that a fifth to a half of Harvard undergraduates had tried pot. On the assumption that one guesstimate is as good as another, Dean of the College John Monro thought 10 percent was closer to the mark. Pusey thought even that too much.[25]

What soon would be called the counterculture had its origins in the late fifties. A 1956 issue of the student magazine *Cambridge Review* attacked Harvard's intellectual and cultural rigidities, with much trendy reference to the ideas of Wilhelm Reich and Henry Miller. A live folk music "orgy" was a twice-a-year feature of the College radio station by 1958. One old grad saw the end of (Harvard) civilization as he knew it as early as 1961. The photo on the cover of a presidential report drew his ire: "many of the people in the picture are lounging and they all look unkempt. The individual who is declaiming cannot be clearly identified as definitely a short haired woman or a long haired man." Several of those identifiably male wore beards: a sure sign of cynicism or—worse—nihilism. Pusey sympathized with his correspondent's concern over beards and beatniks. But he had to point out that in fact the hirsute students were the made-up cast of *Troilus and Cressida*.[26]

A more significant source of unease was Harvard's undergraduate newspaper the *Crimson*. While occasionally an object of official displeasure, the newspaper in decades past was a relatively tame animal in the Harvard menagerie: soundly Republican until the late thirties, fashionably anti-Semitic in its recruitment until after the war. Relations between Pusey and the *Crimson* were strained after its reportage (Pusey thought unfair) of the 1958 ruckus over Jewish weddings in Memorial Church. His aide Bentinck-Smith, a former journalist, complained of slanted headlines, distorted stories, inaccuracies, fabrications.[27]

Then things got uglier. In April 1962, a series of six *Crimson* editorials sharply attacked the president: "Mr. Pusey's view of Harvard remains essentially conservative.... If the President continues to look for sanction in history and tradition, he might remember that powerful and imaginative executive leadership is of all Harvard's traditions one of the strongest." There was, the paper said, "a growing feeling among the Faculty that the President does not understand his University.... The Faculty's suspicion that Mr. Pusey's Harvard is not their Harvard is dangerous; it is also disastrously close to true."

This was unprecedented and unsettling, a precursor of the *Crimson* to come. The assault attracted the attention of *Time, Newsweek*, and even President John F. Kennedy, who wrote consolingly to Pusey: "I have been reading recently some comments in the Harvard Crimson that are not favorable to you. As a fellow President I hope these comments do not disturb you too much. I write to you as one who is daily attacked in the papers that unfortunately have much larger circulation than the Harvard Crimson. I am sure you will maintain your perspective in this matter, because all of us who are familiar with your work are wholeheartedly in support of you."[28]

Another instance of generational ships passing in the night: It appeared that members of WHRB, the student radio station, paid nocturnal visits to the Gordon McKay Laboratory, where they helped themselves to engineering equipment. WHRB president Michael Rice was told to look into the matter. He airily reported that the thefts were minor, the parts taken not for personal use but for the station. Besides, they belonged not to individuals but only to the laboratory, so nothing really criminal had happened. But now that the cat was out of the bag, he reluctantly supposed that some restitution was called for. In response, Dean Monro gave him hell. Rice's response was "morally muddled and wrong"; his handling of the matter showed "a remarkable insensitivity to the central ethical issue involved in the stealing, to the rights and expectations of the University, and to the moral obligations of WHRB." Indeed, serious thought had been given to punishing *him* as well as the malefactors. "I am far less worried by the thefts themselves," Monro observed, "than by the moral confusion and obliqueness with which you and your associates have met your resulting problems."[29]

Perhaps the most revealing expression of the rise of a new student culture, and of a widening intergenerational gap, was the issue of parietals, the rules that governed women's visits to Harvard undergraduates' rooms. Discontent with these restrictions was hardly unknown in the past, and the veterans of World War II found them infantile. But the student body soon became younger, and presumably less worldly, so the old rules remained in place.

In 1953, after years of student agitation, they were mildly loosened, and in the fall of 1956 a faculty committee extended upperclassmen's visitation rights from 11 P.M. to midnight on Saturday nights. Freshman innocence was protected by an 8 P.M. cutoff. In 1959 the freshmen stirred themselves, seeking to extend their Saturday night rights from 8 to 11:30, temptation to sin checked by chaperones and "normal lighting." A call went out for a demonstration in the Yard. Neither Paris 1789 nor St. Petersburg 1918 was the model in mind: after dark there would be a sing-along in front of John Harvard's statue, followed by a return to the dormitories and a mass turn-on of radios and hi-fis to bathe the Yard in musical entertainment. Anyone still there after 10:15 would be subject to assault by water bombs. But the faculty said no to the proposed changes.[30]

Meanwhile the looser sexual mores of a student generation liberated by the pill took hold. A *Crimson* editorial in October 1963 declared that "as long as a student adheres to certain necessary rules of order, his moral code is his own business." Dean of the College Monro heatedly criticized the paper's "flagrant separation of private morality and public order," and charged that "what was once considered to be a pleasant privilege has come to be considered a license to use the college rooms for wild parties and sexual intercourse."

The national press had a field day with Monro's vivid language. He explained to Corporation fellow Thomas Lamont what led to it: "We have created a situation at Harvard in which a sizeable number of our students now think . . . that the College intends to, and should, provide a 'dry, warm

place' for sexual intimacy. These students are furious to learn otherwise."
Monro was convinced that "[t]here has been an awesome slippage the past
ten years in the standards and attitudes of College women. I begin to
think this may be the most difficult part of our problem." Fellow William
L. Marbury naïvely suggested that perhaps constructing a student center
would solve the problem, and Pusey thought that "eventually we can make
the majority of the student body believe that the administration's case
stands on firm practical and ethical ground."[31]

This optimism was shaken by a revealing incident involving two
tutors. They were graduate students in Biology and Music, and resident
tutors in Dunster House. Acting on a tip, campus police raided their
rooms early one morning in September 1963, before classes began. They
found a Radcliffe student in each suite, one of them a tutee of her
consort, who had been living there for weeks.

When news of this came to Monro and FAS dean Franklin Ford,
their first inclination was to recommend the tutors' immediate severance
from the University. But then.... As Monro put it: "What distressed us
more than anything else in that case was the attitudes we found on every
side." Ford interviewed the two men, both terrified, genuinely bewildered by the scale of the reaction: "At the risk of having the same
adjective applied to myself, I can only say that they both seemed uncom-
prehendingly 'innocent.'" Their defense was that they were never told
that they shouldn't do what they did. Monro's conclusion: "We are looking at a wide and potentially dangerous difference in fundamental
attitude between the bulk of our undergraduates and the bulk of adults."

As unexpected was the reaction from the two young men's professors,
the master of Dunster House, and the president of Radcliffe College.
All counseled that nothing be done beyond removing them from their
resident tutorships. To do more would unfairly blight the careers of
promising young academics. Ford concluded that the real issue "is the
collegiate culture which led both men—and both women—to assume
that this was safe, smart, adult behavior. One way to address ourselves to
that culture is to fire the teaching fellows and thus punctuate our statement. Another would be to hit hard at the masters and others who ought
to be helping such youngsters define their responsibilities to our
community, but especially to themselves." He could not recommend the
culprits' dismissal without the sense of "having pounced on scapegoats
who can't even measure in their own terms the extent of the problem."
So he proposed that their house affiliation be ended, and that alone. The
Corporation, after some bluster about totally unacceptable behavior,
went along.[32]

Pusey reacted to the incident with unusual passion:

> There is ... a permissiveness and easy tolerance in American life which does not exclude Harvard.... the moral-religious position has never been an easy one to take, and particularly so in these times. I simply have faith that there is a subdued desire on the part of most people to have the position stated as clearly as possible, and again and again. So long as I am President of Harvard I do not propose to let the University strangle itself in an amoral morass of knowledge without wisdom and facts without conviction.

He asked the house masters and University Health Services director Dana Farnsworth for data on just what—and how much—was going on. The masters tended to downplay the problem. But Farnsworth reported twenty-two known abortions, all but one illegal, during the past year, about thirty-six pregnancies (one student had two young women pregnant at the same time), and a dozen instances of intense promiscuity. According to him over a hundred Radcliffe students reported having regular sexual intercourse in their rooms. Peer pressure to go along was strong. Postperformance parties at the Loeb Theater—heterosexual and homosexual, the participants high on drugs—were a special problem.

Student perceptions were very different. Most freshmen thought that the dean of the College had no right to interfere in their emotional lives. The Student Council's Parietals Committee argued that the issue was not excessive sexual activity, but how the loneliness and uncertainty of student life might be lessened. It proposed a bracing schedule of visiting hours from 2 to 7 P.M. Monday through Thursday, 2 P.M. to midnight on Friday, noon to 1 A.M. on Saturday, and 2 to 8 P.M. on Sunday. As "[f]or those dislocated by a roommate with a date, all the library facilities of the University are open."[33]

By the late sixties the students' antiparietals offensive was in full flower. Monro tried to hold what was left of the old behavioral trenches. On sex: students were expected to act like gentlemen and "take responsible care that your behavior does not injure other people." On drugs: "if a student is stupid enough to misuse his time here fooling around with illegal and dangerous drugs, our view is that he should leave college and make room for people prepared to take good advantage of the college opportunity."

But things were sliding out of control. In the spring of 1968 an FAS committee on parietals with two faculty, one administrator, and three students (Pusey: "?") observed that Harvard now had a student body more varied and skeptical, less conventional than thirty years ago

(Pusey: "?!"), and that the existing rules had to be substantially revised in light of changing attitudes and the more liberal policies of neighboring institutions (Pusey: "?!"). In the fall of 1968 the administration explored Harvard's legal liability under Massachusetts's immoral conduct laws if it lifted parietals. Soon after the uprising of 1969, the rules were gone with the wind.[34]

Ultimately, push came to shove in the late sixties not over the curriculum, or sex, or drugs, but (in the broadest sense) over politics: the politics of Harvard and the community, Harvard and race, Harvard and Vietnam.

The students of the 1950s reflected the political passivity of the time. The graduating class of 1955 was 35 percent Republican, 28 percent Democratic, 31 percent Independent: less conservative than most of the other Ivies or their Harvard predecessors, but hardly a powder keg of incipient revolutionaries. Historian Arthur Schlesinger, Jr., complained: "where questions of public policy are concerned, this is an uncommonly unoriginal, conventional-minded, sloganized, and boring undergraduate generation." Student creativity appeared elsewhere: in analytical philosophy, mathematical economics, quantitative sociology, drama, and music. But changes were under way. Adlai Stevenson's lack of popular support in 1956 stopped at Harvard's edge: he won a student majority in every school but Business (and among the not yet acculturated freshmen). JFK swept all but the Business School in 1960; in 1964 even that last bastion of Republicanism went for Lyndon Johnson.[35]

Foreign policy, civil liberties, and civil rights issues, like waves breaking on a beach, eroded the bulwark of Harvard indifference. A crowd of 10,000 came in 1959 to hear Fidel Castro in Harvard Stadium (the relative draws of curiosity and support difficult to determine). Increasing numbers of Harvard students joined the burgeoning black civil rights movement in the South. Pusey rejected direct involvement: "[t]he University cannot take an official stand in regard to the means; nor can it be expected to aid individual students who, for better or for worse, come to suffer because of their connection with racial activities." He reluctantly accepted a $30,000 gift to support needy students who wished to participate in civil rights projects approved by the College, "but I urge caution in its administration."[36]

The nuclear disarmament movement had particular appeal. Tocsin, a new student group, passed out blue antinuke armbands in the fall of 1961: about 1,000 undergraduates wore them before the day was out. Opponents sporting red armbands staged a rival demonstration. For the first time since the interventionist-isolationist debates of 1940–41, numbers of undergraduates engaged in serious political controversy. In February 1962 some 200 Harvard and Radcliffe students joined in a Washington rally for peace and a nuclear moratorium. The *Crimson*, not yet radicalized, continued to support lobbying and conventional politics: "As a political action, the march is unwise, dangerous, perhaps irresponsible; as a move vital to the effective organization of those who support its political aims, the march justifies itself." A September 1963 summation of politics at Harvard over the course of Pusey's first decade as president saw a shift from the "careful" students of the 1950s to the more "careless" ones of the early 1960s: a new, politically active generation, relatively moderate on foreign policy, strongly integrationist on race, not ideological.[37]

That soon changed. The left-wing May Second Committee appeared in 1964. And in December of that year the Harvard chapter of Students for a Democratic Society (SDS) gave notice of its intention to hold a rally in Harvard Yard in support of the Berkeley student demonstrators. Dean of Students Robert Watson expected that "they will be quiet, will probably have a few placards, and will be accompanied by a policeman." By February 1965 the May Second Committee and SDS were less mindful of procedural niceties, holding unauthorized gatherings on the steps of Memorial Church. (Bentinck-Smith reported to Pusey: "Watson has warned them very severely about the trend and the consequences if disorder occurs. He has been told this is 'probably' the last time they will do this.")[38]

Dean of the College Monro was not unsympathetic to the SDS position. He saw much merit in its attack on the undemocratic character of the selective service system and thought that "in a way, they are right" that the administration should have taken the lead in opening up discussion of a public policy that so deeply affected higher education. But Corporation fellow Thomas Lamont talked to the presidents of Princeton and the universities of Texas and Minnesota in late 1966, who warned him that Harvard should not take SDS and student discontent too lightly.[39]

The 1968 Berkeley student uprising—against limits on campus speech, against the Vietnam War, against the bureaucratic multiversity—made it clear that something more than normal undergraduate hijinks were going on. When Clark Kerr was forced to resign from the presidency of the University of California, Pusey called it "an affront to higher education" and invited him to take refuge at Harvard. But Pusey attributed Berkeley's troubles in good part to "uneasiness about the quality of undergraduate education" there. Bentinck-Smith assured a Berkeley professor that "it is very, very hard for a student to be 'lost' at Harvard. If this ever happens—and I doubt it—something has gone awfully wrong with the system!"

Overseer Henry Friendly, too, thought it "hard to believe that anything of this sort could happen at Harvard." But six months before he would have thought it "equally incredible" at Berkeley and wondered what "standby plans there are to meet any such eruption." Pusey assured him that he read everything he could on the Berkeley events and talked to many of those involved. His conclusion: "I do not believe that the situations at Berkeley and in Cambridge are at all comparable. The events at Berkeley amounted to a real revolution on issues which have largely been resolved here over the years."[40]

As anti-Vietnam sentiment and militant protest grew, the underlying gulf in generational sensibility between the administration and the undergraduates became ever more difficult to bridge. Dean of the College Monro bridled when the Massachusetts American Civil Liberties Union's director suggested that the University ignore the political activity of students. The issue now was not Harvard's long tradition of allowing free speech, but militant students who were shouting down others trying to exercise that right. He coldly suggested: "it may be a legitimate concern for a civil liberties union that student activists themselves have repeatedly insisted on their right to shout down, or intimidate physically, public figures [of] whom they disapprove." Pusey, meanwhile, detected a more general decline of belief in the University as an educational institution: "I have been surprised to observe the guilt feelings of our academic communities—teachers and students, who seem almost ashamed to be educating themselves for those kinds of national service which require the highest intellectual ability." The stage was set for a major challenge to the meritocratic University.[41]

Brahmin Harvard personified: Abbott Lawrence Lowell, professor of Government and president from 1909 to 1933. (Arch [Harvard University Archives])

Lowell's vigorous, meritocratic successor, James Bryant Conant, professor of Chemistry and president from 1933 to 1953, asserting himself in 1937. (Arch)

The panoplied Tercentenary of 1936, under full sail. FDR, not Brahmin Harvard's favorite politician, sits appropriately isolated, appropriately on the left. (Arch)

Kenneth B. Murdock, professor of English literature, Dean of the Faculty of Arts and Sciences from 1931 to 1936, disappointed presidency-seeker, and adversary of Conant. (Arch)

John H. Finley, longtime professor of Classics, master of Eliot House, and favorite of the undergraduates, in 1937. (Arch)

Percy Bridgman, professor of Physics, who received a Nobel Prize in 1946: the new science comes to Harvard. (Arch)

Professor of Sociology Talcott Parsons, a fresh, more professional figure in Harvard's social sciences. (Arch)

Paul Buck, dean of Arts and Sciences from 1942 to 1953 and provost of the University from 1945 to 1953, Conant's right-hand man in his quest for a more meritocratic Harvard. (Arch)

Members of the Corporation and Harvard administrators have dinner with the Cambridge City Council in 1944: a transient attempt to bring Town and Gown closer together. Conant sits in the center; Treasurer William H. Claflin is seated far left; Fellow Roger Lee stands at the far right. (Arch)

Harvard Yard during World War II. (Arch)

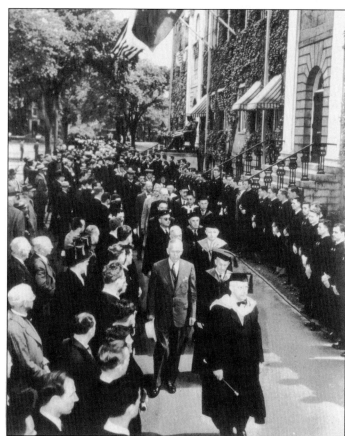

George C. Marshall leads the procession at the 1947 Commencement, preparatory to giving his address that was the scene-setter for the Marshall Plan. (Arch)

Iconographic vistas I: history-drenched Harvard Yard, serenely presided over by John Harvard's statue. (NO [Harvard News Office])

Iconographic vistas II: massive Widener Library, the embodiment of Harvard as a commanding scholarly institution. (NO)

James Bryant Conant, in 1953, delighted to be on his way out. (HM [Harvard Magazine])

Nathan Marsh Pusey, doing what he did so well: raising money. (Arch)

McGeorge Bundy, dean of FAS from 1953 to 1961, an engine of power and responsibility. (Arch)

Mary (Polly) Bunting, the canny president of Radcliffe, who came close to a merger agreement with Harvard in the late sixties. (RA [Radcliffe Archives])

Erwin N. Griswold, dean of the Law School from 1946 to 1967, exuding legal authority. (Arch)

Donald K. David, dean of the Business School from 1942 to 1954, exuding managerial authority. (Arch)

Walter Gropius, professor of Architecture at the School of Design from 1937 to 1952, in front of his Harvard *chef d'oeuvre*, the Graduate Center. (Arch)

George Packer Berry, dean of the Medical School from 1949 to 1965, who with Griswold and David oversaw the postwar rise of Harvard's major professional schools. (HMS [Countway Library, Harvard Medical School])

Professor of Economics John Kenneth Galbraith, world-class gadfly and perhaps Harvard's most conspicuous faculty member during the sixties and after. (Arch)

Willard Van Ormand Quine, Harvard's most distinguished modern philosopher and the exemplar of the meritocratic university. (Arch)

Professor of History Oscar Handlin, one of the long and distinguished roster of Harvard's postwar Jewish faculty. (Arch)

Julian Schwinger,
the brilliant theorist who
helped put postwar
Harvard Physics at or
near the top of the heap.
(Arch)

Robert Woodward,
who had a comparably
dramatic impact on
Harvard Chemistry.
Both he and Schwinger
won Nobel Prizes in 1965.
(Arch)

Professor of English
Walter Jackson Bate,
two-time Pulitzer Prize
winner and the doyen
of Harvard's English
department in the
fifties and sixties.
(Arch)

Nathan Marsh Pusey and his Corporation in 1954. Seated left to right are William L. Marbury, treasurer Paul C. Cabot, Pusey, and senior fellow Charles C. Coolidge. Standing, left to right, are Thomas S. Lamont, Francis ("Hooks") Burr, and R. Keith Kane. (Arch)

The Governing Boards (the Corporation and the Overseers), the President (JFK), and the President (NMP) foregather at the White House in 1963. (Arch)

Paradise Lost I: radical students seize University Hall. (Arch)

Paradise Lost II: hostile police prepare to enter the building. (Arch)

John Dunlop, professor of Economics, Dean of FAS from 1970 to 1973, an architect of post-1969 institutional reconstruction. (Arch)

Henry Rosovsky, professor of Economics and Dean of FAS from 1973 to 1984. (HM)

The undergraduate Science Center: New Modern on the Harvard campus. (NO)

Deans of late-twentieth-century Harvard's Brobdingnagian professional schools:

Daniel Tosteson of Medicine (1977–1997). (HMS)

John MacArthur of Business (1980–1995). (Arch)

Robert Clark of Law (1989–    ). (HLS [Harvard Law School])

Biology's great
adversaries:

Nobelist James
D. Watson and the
DNA double helix that
won him renown.
(Arch)

Edward O. Wilson,
the zoologist whose
*kulturkampf* with
Watson spurred him,
he says, to his work
in Sociobiology.
(Arch)

New faces, new forces:

Helen Vendler, Porter University Professor of the Humanities. (Arch)

Henry Louis ("Skip") Gates, head of Afro-American Studies. (NO)

Presidents Derek Bok of Harvard and Matina Horner of Radcliffe sign a 1977 agreement, a step on the road to the merger of the two institutions. (RA)

Derek Bok, president from 1971 to 1991, who cautiously set modern Harvard on the road to greater worldliness. (Arch)

Neil Rudenstine, president from 1991 to 2001, who continued on that road. (Arch)

Lawrence Summers, whose short and contentious presidential term lasted from 2001 to 2006. (Arch)

## ∽ 14 ∾

# CRISIS AND RECOVERY

Every institution goes through crises produced by a mix of outside stimuli, internal discontent, and administrative failings. In the case of higher education, that happened in the late 1960s: to Berkeley in 1967 and Columbia in 1968, to Paris in the May Days of 1968, to Harvard in the spring of 1969. Critics of those upheavals resorted to the language of world-class disasters: "The Time of Troubles," "The Terror," "World War III." Apologists favored comparably distended metaphors of revolution and rebirth, of a Wordsworthian sense of sheer bliss to be young and alive and involved in a time of institutional re-creation.

The university protests of the late sixties had large-scale demographic, cultural, and political sources: the coming of age of the baby boomers, the rise of the counterculture, the trauma of Vietnam. But the greatest institutional disruption in Harvard's history occurred as well in a more particular context: that of the increasingly meritocratic, affluent, self-satisfied university of the sixties. Of course other schools shared these qualities and experienced similar (or worse) student uprisings. But there appears to have been a special degree of shock on the part of Harvard faculty, administrators, and alumni that so much student disaffection existed in their university: that it could have happened here.

## Issues and Portents

The Vietnam War was the flash point that set off the protests of the late sixties. As American involvement in Vietnam grew, so did on-campus opposition. Initially it proceeded within the prescribed Harvard tradition of civility and open debate. Divinity School dean Samuel Miller wanted "to be sure that all viewpoints are represented" at a faculty meeting on Vietnam in the spring of 1965, and National Security Adviser

McGeorge Bundy participated in the (relatively) polite discussion. Antidraft demonstrations were limited to a handful of students; even the *Crimson* had what a Pusey aide called a "mature" editorial on the topic.[1]

In November 1966, Secretary of Defense Robert McNamara came to discuss the Vietnam War at the invitation of the Kennedy School's Institute of Politics. He emerged from a talk with students in Quincy House to face a crowd, organized by Students for a Democratic Society, which tried to engage him in a "debate." Ultimately he was obliged to escape through Harvard's steam tunnels. The protestors' confrontational style and manifest disdain for the exchange of ideas was something new on the Harvard scene. Pusey profusely apologized to McNamara: "Those young SDS students, while worshiping something they call participatory democracy but adopting tactics of Brown Shirts, must surely be confused. Let us hope that their continued experience in higher education and a growing maturity will clear up this matter for them." McNamara brushed aside the incident. It was appropriate that students be deeply concerned about the war and essential to keep open the channels of dispassionate discussion and safeguard the right of rational dissent. Sixteen hundred Harvard undergraduates had signed an SDS petition before McNamara's visit calling on him to debate the war; more than twenty-six hundred signed a letter apologizing for what happened after he came.[2]

A few months later UN Ambassador Arthur Goldberg paid a visit. Once again SDS raised the question, as Dean of the College John Monro sympathetically put it, "whether the college community should not press for a public debate or confrontation with a senior figure of a national administration which is engaged in a deeply controversial war." SDS was wrong to threaten the use of force, "but I think their instincts about the university community are right and that they should press us hard on this issue." Goldberg agreed to an untelevised meeting limited to University members. So structured, the evening came off reasonably well. But if Harvard learned by experience, so did SDS; not again would it be coopted into an open exchange of views. Jon Wiener, an SDS tactician, wrote: "It should be remembered that this was not an intellectual confrontation, it was a political one.... The political effectiveness of the anti-war arguments, rather than their mere correctness or rationality, should have been the primary consideration. Rational arguments that do not imply or provide a radical critique of the war should have been eliminated."[3]

As protest turned violent at other universities, there was general satisfaction over how much more genteel things were at Harvard. But turbulence increased during the 1967–68 academic year. Fliers and leaflets attacked Harvard for its links with the CIA, for holding stock in Southern Mississippi Power and Light, for abetting highway planning and urban renewal that threatened to displace blacks. FAS dean Ford criticized the *Crimson*'s "unrelieved shrillness."[4]

In the fall of 1967 an SDS-led group barricaded a Dow Chemical recruiter for some hours in the Mallinckrodt Chemistry building. The SDS leader told the recruiter that he could leave if he signed a promise never again to interview students for Dow, which he refused to do. This incident was comparable to the McNamara episode a year before, but the reaction was much more polarized and intense. Sociologist Barrington Moore hurried over to the Center for International Affairs building, "thinking that possibly I might be able to pull a cop off the back of a student." Alas, he found the students unencumbered, gave them a few words of support, and left. SDS, ever improving its operational techniques, collected some three hundred bursar's (student ID) cards from participants and sympathetic onlookers and turned them in to the authorities, along with a demand for amnesty.

Corporation fellow William Marbury reacted with a passion shared by many of his Harvard generation:

> Chinese students rioting on behalf of their government surround a British diplomat whose government they accuse of assisting United States aggression, subjecting him to taunts and trying to force him to sign a humiliating letter. The civilized world ... likens it to the behavior of the young Black Shirts and Brown Shirts in the early days of the Fascist movement in Italy and Germany.
>
> Harvard students, rioting against their government, seize a representative of a chemical manufacturer which they believe to be aiding United States aggression, subject him to taunts and try to force him to sign a humiliating letter.
>
> Aside from the obvious difference that the Chinese students are rioting in support of their government and the Harvard students against their government, what is the difference? Perhaps the editors of *The Crimson* can enlighten us.[5]

Much of the faculty also regarded the event as beyond the academic pale. Government Professor Samuel Beer equated the Dow disrupters with the destructive and irrational forces of the McCarthy period. Harvard had withstood the earlier threat, and it was necessary to do so again as an example to other universities. The Administrative Board of the College recommended that 74 students be put on probation and 171 be admonished for misuse of their bursar's cards in the Dow incident. The *Crimson*, by now the voice of the student radicals, found this unreasonable and arbitrary punishment. But the 478 faculty members attending an October 31 meeting—the largest in FAS history to then—supported its recommendations by a five to one margin.[6]

Harvard's belief in its relative levelheadedness got a boost from the spring 1968 upheaval at Columbia, when students occupied a number of buildings and the police evicted them with some violence and much ensuing bitterness. Law School professor Archibald Cox chaired a commission that looked into the Columbia events. Its report magisterially blamed all parties and observed loftily that the uprising came "at a time when the university was deficient in the cement that binds an institution into a cohesive unit." But some were troubled by the implications of the Columbia experience. David Rockefeller wanted the Overseers to meet for a couple of days to discuss the prospect of something similar happening at Harvard and what might be done to get ready. Pusey asked the deans of Harvard's schools what they were doing to reduce the danger of disturbances, now not just a matter of anti-Vietnam students but of neighborhood (that is, black) protest. Everyone agreed on the need to be prepared; no one seemed to know just what being prepared meant.[7]

As 1968 wore on, antiwar sentiment proliferated. Draft resistance groups sprang up; a surge of undergraduates abandoned their senior theses and asked for term paper extensions. Sentiment grew in the faculty that members of the administration, Pusey in particular, were not responding as they should. In early 1968 chemist Bright Wilson and physicist Edward Purcell, leading lights of Harvard science, asked Pusey to make a public statement on the war. Pusey doubted that "it will serve Harvard well to have me make such comments in the present political atmosphere," but he agreed to sound out his fellow presidents in the Association of American Universities on a joint statement.[8]

When it came to student protesters, he was not so accommodating. His January 1968 annual report spoke of "Walter Mittys of the left" who "play at being revolutionaries." That evoked a number of critical responses (including a predictable *Crimson* reaction: his belligerence was "intemperate and impolitic"; he was "sadly out of touch"). The June 1968 Commencement was a dreary one, marred by a rare siege of rain. On the previous day the class orator spoke of the need for "fundamental changes" in society; an honorary degree to the shah of Iran turned out to be an untimely choice, given the growing criticism of his regime's tyrannical character.[9]

The clash of generational and ideological sensibilities came to a head in the 1968–69 academic year. By now student unrest was a worldwide phenomenon, transcending Vietnam: in Paris and São Paulo as in Berkeley and New York. Harvard was leagues away from its placid past. An undergraduate explained in the *Alumni Bulletin* "Why Harvard Fails." He called for an end to the disciplinary system and proposed a curriculum with no courses allowed "other than those asked for, and deemed significant by, the students."[10]

A Student-Faculty Advisory Committee (SFAC), designed to serve as a semiofficial prod to the administration to be more responsive, appeared in the summer of 1968. Ford and Pusey regarded this exercise in participatory bureaucracy with considerable skepticism. But they were "prepared to let it rock along until such time as virtually everyone has clearly lost interest." There is an evocative photo of Pusey, arms folded, oozing obduracy, being worked over by SDSers who packed an SFAC meeting: an experience, he said with some accuracy, that "seemed to me more of an inquisition than a discussion!"[11]

Students for a Democratic Society led the campus protest against the Vietnam War and the other ills of what it declared to be a sick and corrupt America. The Harvard branch was the nation's largest, with some two hundred members. It directed its fire as much at the University as at Vietnam, racism, and poverty. The radical protestors, and the larger body of students more or less sympathetic to them, were distant enough from the struggles against totalitarianism in the 1940s and 1950s to be untouched by the rhetoric of the cold war; of an age to take affluence and peace, but not racism or segregation, for granted; smart enough to see through the often factitious justifications for America's involvement in Vietnam.[12]

Faculty "conservatives" (they preferred the term "moderates"), whose views closely accorded with those of Pusey, included émigrés from Europe (such as economic historian Alexander Gerschenkron and chemist George Kistiakowsky) who detected more than a trace of the fascist brown or the bolshevik red shirt in the student protests. Political scientist Carl Friedrich proposed that students entering Harvard be asked to pledge, on pain of suspension, not to engage in building takeovers or other disruptive demonstrations; Pusey had to point out that in light of the University's long opposition to oaths and test of belief, this was a nonstarter. He hoped that the point could be made by education and persuasion. Conspicuous, too, were a number of senior professors (such as American historian Oscar Handlin, philosopher Willard Quine, and political scientists Samuel Beer and James Q. Wilson) who saw in the tone and style of the protest movement a threat not only to liberal democracy but to the University as a refuge for scholarly excellence and free thought: values embodied in their careers and reflecting their deepest beliefs. Constitutional law expert Robert McCloskey said of the radical student assault: "I felt as if I had been raped."[13]

A smaller number of senior faculty (most notably biologist George Wald and philosopher Hilary Putnam) supported the radicals, again for reasons as much psychological as ideological: solidarity with the young was to affirm one's own youthfulness. More numerous were those from the social democratic Left (economist John Kenneth Galbraith, Stanley Hoffmann and Michael Walzer of Government) who endorsed the general stance, though not all of the specifics and techniques, of the radicals.

This was the complex dramatis personae as the 1968–69 academic year unfolded. During the summer of 1968, a group of radicals asked the Social Relations department to include a new course, "Social Change in America" (Soc Rel 148), a critique of American institutions and policies, in its fall offering. The department—one in which not everything, but a lot, went—readily agreed. When Pusey saw a flyer announcing the course, he thought it was a hoax. Was it, he incredulously asked Ford, authorized by the faculty? "Is it to be a course of scholarly objectivity and high standard? Is it being given by a member of our faculty and will he have control of the content and grading?" Ford in turn asked these questions of Social Relations department chair Roger Brown. Brown's—and the department's—response was that while they had some concern over Soc Rel 148's procedures, they saw something in the argument that a strong explicit position had pedagogical value and were ready to give it a try. In a University whose curriculum was in the hands of its faculty, that was that.[14]

The course, headed by Jack Stauder, a first-year instructor in Social Anthropology, drew hordes of undergraduates. Stauder proposed a follow-up spring term offering, "The Radical Perspective" (Soc Rel 149), in which the lessons learned in Soc Rel 148 would be treated in greater detail. Enrollment in Soc Rel 149 went over 750. Its numerous sections touched on topics such as Existential Psychology, Marx's *Capital*, Leninism, Psychology and Literature, Imperialism and the University, and The American Maelstrom.

Senior professors in Social Relations began to have second thoughts about a course whose section leaders' competence (they were drawn from other schools as well as Harvard) neither instructor Stauder nor anyone else was in a position to judge. So plans were made to drop the course.

Word leaked to the *Crimson*; student protest erupted. The Social Relations faculty explained to the students what they thought was wrong with the course: no standards, no substantive content, no meaningful evaluation of student performance. Students told the faculty what was right with it: informality, lack of hierarchy and competition—two streams of consciousness that flowed smoothly past each other. One student-teacher in the course warned the faculty: if you don't let us teach *our* course, we won't let you teach *your* courses. And soon *Crimson* president James Fallows and others were engaged in "The Conspiracy Against Harvard Education," an attempt (which did not get very far) to create a student-designed-and-taught countercurriculum.[15]

Stauder proposed that in the next academic year Soc Rel 148 be taught as a yearlong course on radical social change. The department went along, but added an advisory group of three faculty members and specified that undergraduates and graduate students facing disciplinary action for disruptive activities—"persons under political punishment by the University" was the way the course's supporters put it—would not be allowed to teach sections. Stauder protested that this would exclude "many of our most committed people," and in an act of ideological hara-kiri he and the others running the course cancelled it on the ground that they would not be able to staff it properly.[16]

Meanwhile the struggle against the war, against racism, against Harvard went on outside the classroom. The most important effort was an SDS-led campaign against Harvard's Reserve Officers Training Corps (ROTC) program. Here was a palpable on-campus instance of the University's complicity in the American war machine. And ROTC's participants (345 of them, 60 percent from the College, most of the others from the Law and Business Schools) were sufficiently marginal to pose no threat to student solidarity.

The Faculty of Arts and Sciences planned to consider a resolution ending ROTC at a fall 1968 meeting in the Music department's Paine Hall. SDS announced its intention to physically confront the dean and the faculty if they did not abolish ROTC, and a flock of its student supporters hunkered down in the auditorium. The faculty meeting was adjourned; bursar's cards were collected . The Administrative Board proposed that five students who also were veterans of the Dow Chemical incident be suspended, and fifty-two others be put on probation. But now, a year after the Dow Chemical incident, the majority of the faculty was not inclined to support the Administrative Board. John Kenneth Galbraith, who found much that was good in the earlier McNamara incident ("afterward Mr. McNamara may well have had a better view of the University community than he had had before") and little that was bad in the Dow affair (nobody was hurt and "research surely was not badly interrupted"), said of Paine Hall: "This last action seems the most Gandhian of all." That did not mean that he called on the participants to accept punishment in the tradition of Gandhi-style civil disobedience. The faculty voted by a two-to-one margin to reduce the five suspensions to probation.[17]

In February the faculty returned to the question of ROTC. It rejected SDS's ROTC-out-now position by a seven-to-one margin, but then voted two to one to withhold regular College credit for ROTC courses and deprive its instructors of faculty standing: in effect, to turn it into an extracurricular activity. Franklin Ford considered this a "very badly framed, gratuitously unpleasant and basically confused pronouncement." In effect, he thought, it was a vote of lack of confidence in himself as dean. But Pusey and the Corporation, relieved that so large a majority opposed the elimination of ROTC, preferred to try to work things out with the military as the faculty desired. Finally a faculty committee decided that it was not possible to make ROTC an extracurricular activity, and recommended that all ROTC programs be ended in two years.[18]

## University Hall

All of this was prologue to the events of April 1969, when Harvard's elevated self-esteem was dealt its severest blow. The Corporation in January authorized Pusey to take all necessary steps to protect Harvard's buildings, business, and personnel. By early April, rumors were rife that SDS might occupy University Hall, the abode of the dean of the Faculty of Arts and Sciences. Its ostensible reasons for doing so were to protest the faculty's refusal to end ROTC immediately and to try to stop Harvard's building expansion. On April 9 the organization's more radical faction went in and, with some force, evicted the administrators in the building.

Sympathizers and the curious gathered around. General student opinion was more critical than supportive: 613 undergraduates signed a petition condemning the seizure. SDS leader Michael Ansara told a radio reporter that protesting against ROTC was only a pretext: "we are radicals and revolutionaries." They were also from financially comfortable families, even beyond the hefty Harvard undergraduate norm. Only one of those arrested for occupying University Hall had a Harvard scholarship. Dean of Admissions Chase Peterson, asked by a Senate committee investigating campus disorders to send in a list of involved students who were getting federal aid, found only 32 of 175 who did so: "the radical students in the University at least tend to be affluent." (Daniel Patrick Moynihan predicted that most SDS members would end up as civil servants. He was close: many became academics.)[19]

The University Hall occupiers broke into a number of files in the dean's office and extracted what they saw as juicy revelations of administration complicity with the CIA and other government agencies. These were published in an SDS paper, *The Old Mole*. (They also formed the basis of a pamphlet, *How Harvard Rules*, which in its assumption of Harvard's omnipotence in the corridors of power differed more in disapproval than in substance from the hubristic Harvard tone of the Kennedy years.) The occupiers did some physical damage, but even now the weight of the Harvard past made itself felt. When one of them was asked if plans were afoot to desecrate the dean's desk, his response was: "Good God, no. [It] was used by Mr. Eliot."[20]

On April 10, the morning after the takeover, Pusey met with Hugh Calkins, the Corporation fellow most ready to listen and talk to students. Calkins dwelt on the need for Pusey and other Harvard leaders to drop in on classes, make themselves as accessible as possible to undergraduates—and avoid calling in the police. The Corporation planned to invite a group of twenty students at its next meeting. But Pusey and Ford were not inclined by policy or personality to indulge in new-style crisis defusing.

It is also true that they had some reason to think that negotiation with the occupiers would be unproductive. The rifling of files (including confidential personnel records, with a potential for embarrassment and blackmail) was another disincentive to delay. The administration believed—and in this they were reinforced by Archibald Cox's advice, based on his Columbia inquiry—that the occupiers should be cleared by police early or not at all: fast bust or no bust. Pusey and Ford concluded that to allow the seizure to go on would mean more file rifling, more outsiders drifting into the Yard, more disruption of Harvard's normal educational activities, ultimately a more violent confrontation.

Galbraith later spoke for many who had a different view: "twelve hours of patience and it would have been over." Pusey supporter James Q. Wilson also thought that calling in the police was a mistake: "Harvard's Vietnam," he later called it. But *Harvard Alumni Bulletin* editor John Bethell, who occasionally took an unhouse-organly critical stance toward the administration, concluded in June: "A first-hand appraisal of the temper of the University Hall occupation force, and the tactical tendencies of the SDS, reinforces the conclusion that only a police action could get the demonstrators out. The degree of force used by the police was anguishing, yet probably inevitable." At the same time Bethell thought—and many faculty and most students agreed—that Pusey underestimated the bust's emotional impact on the community. Several deans (Bok of the Law School, Sizer of Education, Stendahl of Divinity, perhaps Ebert of Medicine) had reservations about using the police to clear the building. Pusey bitterly recalled that when he told the deans of his decision and asked for objections, none spoke up; their position was that they had made their views clear to him, and it was his decision to make.[21]

At 5 A.M. on April 11, with only a few minutes' warning, 200 state troopers and about the same number of local police removed the University Hall occupiers. This was in part a clash of antagonistic social groups: the police were working class, the occupiers upper middle class. (Students outside of University Hall shouted at the police: "Fascist pigs!" The cops responded: "Long-haired Commies!") Pusey thanked the nine police departments that sent men and equipment for their prompt response to his request for help. He appreciated the speed and efficiency with which they conducted their operation, the rapidity of their withdrawal, and the small number of injuries (in fact, about fifty occupiers were clubbed by the police).[22]

It hardly seemed so antiseptic to the bulk of the Harvard community. Emotions ran high in the wake of the bust. Those caught up in the University Hall drama—the occupiers and their mostly student sympathizers; the administration and its mostly faculty and alumni sympathizers; the media, with its own reasons for fixing on events at Harvard—thought of it as an event of mythic proportions: a projection, in its way, of the Harvard self-regard that was one object of the protest.

Much of the Old Guard found the happenings beyond belief (though not beyond words). Former Treasurer Paul Cabot wrote to his successor George Bennett in the wake of the takeover: "The small hard core group not only lacks discipline but to a greater or lesser degree they are immoral sexually and otherwise, they are extremely rude and ill-mannered, they are intolerant and bigoted, and they are physically and mentally dirty." It was time for the Governing Boards to take back the disciplinary authority that they had vested in the faculty a century ago. Corporation fellow Keith Kane noted that many of the radicals came from well-off, well-educated families—and that, given the history of Germany, they should know better: a reference to the fact that a number of them were Jewish.

Pusey for his part saw in the reaction to the police bust evidence that many members of the faculty lacked a strong commitment to Harvard. Three-quarters of the staff, he noted, had been at the University for less than ten years. Harvard historian Samuel Eliot Morison later observed of the faculty critics that "many of them were foreigners," unaware, apparently, that a number of professors of foreign birth were especially sensitive to what they saw as the totalitarian tint of the protest movement.[23]

Historian Robert Lee Woolf wrote a long, troubled letter to Pusey and the Governing Boards. He belonged to a faculty group that took turns protecting Widener Library after hours in the wake of the University Hall seizure. Drawing on this tactical experience, he thought "that defense of the Library and our other vulnerable buildings may be impossible unless Summer School is cancelled and a summer crisis averted." The fall 1969 term offered little hope of respite, especially from "the blacks, ... who have won from a cringing Faculty every one of their demands." How to get the faculty to take the stern measures required of it? The Governing Boards might declare that the Faculty of Arts and Sciences consisted only of its permanent members and thus disenfranchise junior faculty with little stake in the University. Pusey politely replied that he was in sympathy with much of what his correspondent had to say. In its tone and substance, probably he was; in its strategy and tactics, manifestly not.[24]

Student radicals had no less extreme a view of what had happened. That the rhetoric, attitudes, and actions of the more dedicated revolutionaries had an *Animal Farm* tone is incontestable. One episode suggests how fragile was the revolutionaries' mix of sense and sensibility. A dirt-stained envelope with a letter inside, found on the University of Minnesota campus, was sent anonymously to Pusey. The letter was from Jon Wiener, a Government graduate student and University Hall occupier who processed many of the documents and letters that were "liberated" from the dean's files and published in *The Old Mole*. He escaped arrest at the time of the bust and wrote euphorically to a friend at Minnesota of the heady days of April. Plans were afoot to launch the next stage of the revolution in the fall. And money for him was no problem; an accounting glitch meant that he was continuing to be paid for a job on which he was no longer employed, thus increasing his University stipend by a fortuitous (if illegal) 50 percent.

Wiener learned that his letter was in the hands of the authorities. The furious author accused the administration of "interception" of his correspondence and demanded that it be returned and all copies destroyed.

He would, he threatened, write an *Old Mole* story on how the University used private correspondence for its own purposes. It would have been hard for Pusey's aide William Bentinck-Smith not to have pointed out that the unauthorized use of other people's letters was hardly unknown to the complainant; indeed he succumbed to the temptation. But a sense of irony was not a conspicuous part of the radical mind-set. Wiener got his letter back; but a photocopy in the files preserved the episode for history.[25]

FAS dean Franklin Ford, in the vortex of the storm, offered his resignation the week after the bust, "[w]ith deep sadness, mixed with frustration," not because he thought the use of the police was wrong, but because he had become an encumbrance: "The cynical caricaturing of personal roles is an essential feature of all revolutions, real or artificial. In the present case, I am now neatly cast as a 'repressive' figure.... it is for the moment a political reality encased in apparently unpierceable layers of suspicion and distrust." All would benefit "if this strange new figure, the 'public Ford,' is subtracted from the equation." Pusey refused to accept this offer: "Frank, if you go I go too, and I'm not going." But shortly after, Ford suffered " 'a vascular-cerebral episode' " and economist Edward Mason took over as acting dean.[26]

For all this sturm und drang, when history's lens is turned on the events of April 1969 the result is decidedly miniaturizing. The Great Rebellion looks more like a bench mark, a test of Harvard's strengths and weaknesses, than a historic divide in its history. Almost three decades later, both Pusey and Stanley Hoffmann, one of his strongest faculty antagonists, agreed that the crisis was not the watershed that the radicals sought and the conservatives feared. It is clear that Pusey and his administration were insufficiently sensitive to changes in student and faculty attitudes that had been going on for years before April 1969. Equally certainly, the militants misjudged the transient issues and passions of the late sixties. Looming over, and eventually overriding, both perceptions is a larger, longer story of institutional change and continuity that was affected but hardly defined by the events of 1969.[27]

## After the Fall

"No matter how the present crisis is resolved," *Time* pontificated in May 1969, "the great temple of learning on the Charles will never be quite the same." James Bryant Conant, whose memoir *My Several Lives* had just appeared, echoed that sentiment in 1970: "The rapid changes in the academic world in the last five years have rendered much of what I have written about education—irrelevant! I feel like a cavalry officer who published his memories just as the horse was disappearing from the scene!"[28]

The common expectation was for even more student turbulence. Sociologist Nathan Glazer, one of the so-called White Berkeleyans who, because they were refugees from the chaos of Berkeley 1966, were thought to have special insight into the chaos of Harvard 1969, offered in the fall of 1970 what the *Alumni Bulletin* called "the definitive analysis" of recent events. He spoke of several major sources of the student revolt (among them the expansion of higher education, the youth culture, Vietnam, and a general failure of authority in the West), and concluded: "It is almost a certainty that another year of campus crisis lies ahead."

In January 1971 Glazer admitted: "it just shows you how wrong you can be." The years from 1967 to 1969 had seen rising conflict, culminating in the University Hall takeover and police bust; the next two academic years, from 1969 to 1971, saw a phoenix-like emergence from discord. The shape of events was neither the slide into a revolutionary nirvana that the radicals sought nor the plunge into primeval chaos that the conservatives feared, but that most normal of social configurations, a bell curve.[29]

Like most earthquakes, the University Hall affair had aftershocks. Radical *aktions* continued. A fire broke out in the ROTC building on May 5 to no great effect (a Marine officer observed, "They did such a rotten job you almost feel sorry for them"). A hundred or so protesters marched on the University planning office, shouted down the planning officer, and did some damage to building models. A smaller number descended on Radcliffe president Mary Bunting's house for a *conversazione* and had the satisfaction of drowning her out when she tried to speak. A few enragés struck a blow for the new society by attacking a truck delivering laundry to Dunster House and strewing its white goods on the street.

A September raid on the Center for International Affairs by the breakaway Revolutionary Youth Movement (Weatherman) faction of SDS resulted in some roughing up of staff, physical damage, and obscene slogans on the wall. But it had no visible impact on the hearts and minds of the community except, perhaps, to strengthen the general reaction against such tactics. Government professor Samuel Beer, whose perspective was much influenced by his experience in Germany during the 1930s, observed the episode: "I cannot get out of my mind the sound of a girl screaming and then looking down the street and seeing [CFIA staffer] Ben Brown with the blood beginning to show on the side of his head."[30]

Yet as was often the case at Harvard, street theatre (new style revolutionary action as much as old style student rioting) easily slipped into opera bouffe. The SDS Labor Committee planned a "tour" of CFIA, inviting participants to feel "welcome to bait and trap these animals, and to ride them hard whenever you can." *Crimson* editor and SDS tactician Richard Hyland wanted the CFIA building destroyed—"terrorism against capitalism is always justified"—though he confessed: "the only reason I wouldn't blow up the Center for International Affairs is that I might get caught."

Of greater consequence was the polarization of sentiment in the Harvard community at large. Over the course of the 1968–69 academic year two faculty caucuses emerged, one supportive, one critical of the administration's response to campus troubles. The University Hall police bust ignited an explosion of anger against the administration in general and Pusey in particular. Decades later, Government professor Stanley Hoffmann still had not overcome his anger toward Pusey: "[T]he man was stupid. And arrogant. Arrogant beyond belief." Pusey for his part found it difficult to contain his contempt for his faculty opponents. A transcript of one of the post-bust faculty meetings faithfully recorded Pusey's audible asides: sighs of exasperation and a pronounced "hmph" during radical philosopher Hilary Putnam's remarks; a mutter to himself when those who supported an antiadministration resolution were asked to remain standing for the vote count: "Well, we'll see the boys under Party discipline now."[31]

Nerves were raw, resentment was rife in the wake of the April events. FAS dean Ford charged that members of the Philosophy department allowed the third floor of their building, Emerson Hall, to come under SDS control; Morton White, the chairman, all but called him a liar. Biochemist-turned-political activist George Wald in particular drew the ire of his more conservative colleagues. Wald rather plaintively brought to Pusey's attention a newspaper report that Dean of the College Ernest May had told a group of incoming freshmen that he "had the political intelligence of a 7-year old." Wald called May on this and was assured that his name had not been used: hardly sufficient consolation.[32]

In December 1969 liberal caucus stalwart John Kenneth Galbraith sent a note to conservative caucus stalwart Robert Lee Wolff. He praised Wolff's memorial minute on recently deceased historian Crane Brinton, and then turned to his favorite subject: John Kenneth Galbraith. He recalled how he and Brinton were among the few academics who favored John F. Kennedy for president in the late fifties: "we had by that time concluded the elements of a political alliance." But Wolff was in no mood for civility: "When there falls to me the melancholy duty of preparing a minute on your life and services to Harvard University, I shall not fail to note your early adoption of Brinton's political views."[33]

Faculty emotions ran high at an April 11 meeting two days after the bust. Among the more conspicuous speakers were European émigrés with a visceral fear of revolution not shared by their homegrown colleagues. Wassily Leontieff of Economics and Stanley Hoffmann of Government were men of the Left, sympathetic to the students and highly critical of the administration. But they did not support the seizure of University Hall, and Leontieff called for expelling the occupiers. Economic historian Alexander Gerschenkron told the story of a king who offered his daughter in marriage to the man capable of doing "the most unbelievable thing": an accolade won by a brute who came along and destroyed a beautiful, delicate clock. He equated this with the destruction of a great, free university. But this hardly meant that the faculty supported the administration. Almost unanimously it favored dropping criminal charges against the University Hall occupiers. And it created a Committee of Fifteen to investigate the affair and recommend penalties, which in effect took the disciplinary process out of the hands of the Administrative Board.[34]

Skillfully chaired by labor economist John Dunlop, the committee recommended in early June that sixteen students be "separated" from the University and another hundred be put on "warning," a new category. Its primary yardstick: the degree to which the accused used force against the staff in University Hall. And it proposed a resolution on rights and responsibilities that tried to define more precisely what was acceptable and what was not in student protests. The faculty overwhelmingly approved these recommendations.[35]

Stickier still was what to do about Corporation appointees—junior faculty and graduate teaching fellows—who had been in University Hall. First came a fact-finding committee chaired by the Law School's Paul Freund, a pillar of moral rectitude. It concluded in early June that three junior faculty members (including Jack Stauder of Soc Rel 148 and 149 fame and assistant professor of Economics Arthur McEwen) and ten teaching fellows engaged in acts that called for punishment. During the summer a committee of three members of the faculty and two fellows of the Corporation went to work to decide just what that punishment should be.

The result forcefully underlined the degree to which the shared value system of the faculty transcended its political differences. The committee readily agreed that Stauder was guilty of grave misconduct in his University Hall involvement. Nevertheless the faculty committee members were as one against firing him and told their Corporation colleagues that "leading members of the conservative caucus had advised against both firing and suspension." The committee's final recommendation: a one-year reappointment for 1969–70, conditional on his behaving himself. But the Social Relations department recommended that Stauder be kept on through the 1970–71 academic year as a lecturer in Social Anthropology. The president and the Corporation found this unacceptable. The department held its ground, and Stauder got a second year.[36]

Government chair James Q. Wilson, a major figure in the conservative caucus and a staunch supporter of Pusey, took strong exception to the Corporation's decision not to reappoint teaching fellows Jon Wiener and Alan Gilbert until their involvement in the University Hall takeover was resolved. He wanted them warned that future participation in disruptive activities would lead to disciplinary action. Meanwhile, there were no charges currently against them, no evidence that they used force in the takeover, or were in the building after being warned to leave. And they had excellent academic records. Economics chair Henry Rosovsky and his colleagues adopted a similarly protective stance toward McEwen. FAS dean Ford urged the Corporation not to reduce his appointment from a five-to a one-year term. To reject the department's recommendation would be seen even by "some of the solider members of the community" as a punitive act, ignoring due process. Once again, the faculty had its way.[37]

Sobering in another sense was the Faculty of Arts and Science's less than satisfactory effort to engage in participatory bureaucracy during the 1969–70 academic year. Large numbers gathered for a mind-numbing eighteen faculty meetings in the Loeb or Sanders Theatres: the traditional Faculty Room in University Hall was not ample enough. Some meetings were broadcast, so that the community might share in this experiment in open governance. The impression on the auditors was not all that was hoped for. According to one of them, listening was like "wading through streams of lukewarm chewing gum."[38]

When the Cambodia incursion burst on the campus scene in May 1970, the faculty got more political. Overwhelmingly (218–31, with 57 abstentions) it passed a resolution offered by historian and former ambassador to Japan Edwin Reischauer deploring the expansion of the war. A more contentious proposal by historian of science Everett Mendelsohn called for the immediate withdrawal of American troops from Southeast Asia. This too passed by a three-to-one margin. But the then fashionable idea of a two-week recess of classes before the fall election, during which students could go out and work for peace-minded candidates, was another story. A number of faculty influentials of varying ideological stripes successfully opposed this subordination of the academy to the street.[39]

The faculty's desire to preserve the meritocratic university was strong and growing. In early May 1970 Stanley Hoffmann, Gerald Holton, Jerome Bruner, and Laurence Wylie, a group of professors prominently associated with the liberal caucus, wrote to the *New York Times* to deny that the faculty was deeply divided. They pointed out that it almost unanimously deplored the SDS occupation of University Hall, as it did the administration's calling in the police. When the story circulated that Henry Kissinger would not be welcome if he returned to the Government department, a number of his colleagues vigorously denied this. Government chair Samuel Huntington said in his 1968–69 annual report: "So far as I know ... everyone in the Department is speaking to everyone else. This may well be the most significant accomplishment of the Department this year."

As passions subsided, faculty members across ideological lines called for a return to first (University) principles. Political scientist Adam Ulam argued that Harvard "should mind its own business.... The university's function is to educate and to advance knowledge," not solve social problems. Longtime left-activist historian H. Stuart Hughes agreed: "If you lose the 'ivory tower,' you've lost the university."[40]

In the confrontation between Brahminism and meritocracy during the 1930s and 1940s, meritocracy (inevitably) won. Now the meritocratic faculty faced up to—and ultimately faced down, though not without institutional and attitudinal change—the challenge posed by student radicalism. In the clash between students' desire for a "morally pure community" and the faculty-administration ideal of a "politically neutral community," it was clear which would prevail—at least until the students of the 1960s became the faculty of the 1980s and 1990s.

The events of April 1969 affected student culture more profoundly than it did the faculty. *Sorrows-of-Werther*-like angst and despair, always part of the emotional baggage of sensitive late adolescents, flourished. In 1967 the chief of psychiatry at the University Health Services detected a growing problem of "Loneliness at Harvard." The writer of "The Undergraduate," an *Alumni Bulletin* column that kept old grads up on campus life, said in March 1969 that the typical senior that year was "unhappy with the formal education of Harvard College, loath to go to graduate school, totally uninterested in business, less concerned about a career than about a life, wanting to create and worrying whether I'm capable, wanting to help and wondering how I can." There was a widespread (if transient) reaction against the curriculum and career aspirations fostered by the meritocratic faculty of the fifties and sixties. In the spring of 1971 some 250 seniors still were in "vocational limbo" regarding their future careers, compared to about 90 in 1967. And more than the usual number were on leaves of absence.[41]

Life style as well as values underwent a sea change. Students still had to wear jackets and ties at meals in the houses in 1969; a year or so later, dress codes were gone and some students dined without shirts. By 1971 the sexes swam nude together in the Adams House swimming pool. Freshman parietals came to an end in the fall of 1969 after 1,000 of the 1,200 members of the class of 1973 and 41 of the 47 dormitory proctors so petitioned. A survey found that a third of the class of 1969 had smoked pot more than once and a quarter had tried a variety of hallucinogens. A freshman reported in the spring of 1970 that advisors and proctors ignored rampant drug use and the fact that one of his fellows was selling pot, mescalin, and LSD to high school students. He thought that 5 of the 19 freshmen in his entry were using drugs daily, that 10 or more did so even more frequently. During that period three undergraduates were dismissed for drug trafficking.[42]

Belief in a coherent curriculum was fading fast, and the events of 1969 and after opened the door to proposals for an educational Liberty Hall. Two student members of the newly established Committee on Under-graduate Education got down to the brass tacks of educational utopianism: a three-year B.A. with a flexible course load; no language, expository writing, or General Education requirements; faculty appoint-ment and promotion committees instructed to put greater weight on teaching; students consulted all the time on everything. Only courses in the student's concentration or to meet professional requirements (there was, after all, a world out there) should be graded, though with a pass-fail option. Failing grades were nobody's business but the student's: "We believe that only a success should be recorded permanently; failure should be erased from the transcript upon the satisfactory completion of an additional course." And off with the heads of honors or grading on a curve, relics of "a deliberately competitive academic system."[43]

The faculty loosened up on its own. Final examinations gave way to term papers in a number of courses; pass-fail grading and independent concentrations appeared in the fall of 1970; grade inflation became noticeable. But it soon appeared that pass-fail did not encourage the bolder course taking (humanities majors flocking into Chem 20, say) forecast by its proponents. Journalist-in-training Michael Kinsley, who reported on matters undergraduate for the *Alumni Bulletin*, took a pass-fail flier on Reuben Brower's course "The Augustan Myth." He confessed to having no idea of what it was about after eight weeks of attendance.[44]

Admissions also felt the winds of change. Applications to the entering class of 1971 fell 12.5 percent below the level of the year before. Dean of Admissions Chase Peterson blamed this on higher application fees, rising tuition costs, the financial constraints of a weakening economy, and the competition of other colleges. (Besides, Yale's applicant pool was down by 18.7 percent, so how bad could things be?)[45]

Yet it is clear that just when the student counterculture reached its peak, institutional restoration—or, to use a different vocabulary, cooptation—was under way. Some ten thousand students and staff gathered in Soldiers' Field, the Harvard football stadium, on the Monday afternoon after the bust. They voted to continue a class boycott for another three days, but (very narrowly) rejected an indefinite strike. Some five to six thousand students met again on Saturday, after the faculty voted on ROTC and University expansion. *Crimson* editor David Bruck called on students to refuse to take their finals, a first step in dismantling the existing academic system. But by a two-to-one margin, the gathering voted to suspend the boycott. The prevailing view was that the faculty's stands against ROTC, University expansion, and criminal proceedings for the occupiers were sufficient ground to do so.[46]

The inexorable process of student turnover began to have its erosive effect. Pusey spoke to the incoming freshmen in September 1969 and got two standing ovations from students as yet unaware that they were not supposed to do that. Second thoughts began to surface. Rick Edmonds, who chaired the *Crimson* editorial board in 1968–69 and then went to the *New York Times*, told Pusey in June 1970 that he now thought it proper to have called in the police and was appalled by the sweeping, mindless denunciations of the "administration" that followed. Pusey for his part agreed with Edmonds that there was reason for students' dissatisfaction with their undergraduate experience: "I would hate to think that the American college, which has proved its value and utility over such a long period of time, would be junked for more intensive preprofessional training, but there are, I think, trends in this direction."[47]

The June 1969 Commencement, widely expected to be dominated by postbust anger, instead became a showcase for Harvard's institutional staying power. SDS voted the night before to seize the podium microphone, make a statement, and lead a mass student walkout. Members of the faculty gathered in the Yard early on Commencement day to foil any disruption. When SDS made a last-minute demand to have a speaker at the Commencement ceremony, Pusey initially said no. But two class marshals pled that an SDS spokesman be allowed to say a few words. After hurried consultation with Corporation members, Pusey reluctantly agreed. Senior Bruce C. Allen came up from the crowd armed with a 1,500 word statement. He went on twice as long as his allotted five minutes, plunging ever deeper into the thickets of revolutionary rhetoric (the Commencement was "an obscenity," "an atrocity") and antagonizing the great majority of his audience. Hissing, booing seniors pointed thumbs down; cries of "throw him out!" became general. Overseer Charles Wyzanski finally declared: "Marshals, take that fellow off!" and Allen was led away.

Twenty-five years later Allen misremembered that after he spoke "most of the graduates walked out." In fact about a hundred members of the audience, including a few dozen seniors, shifted to a countercommencement nearby. There they heard philosopher Hilary Putnam announce (on the basis of no visible evidence): "Cambridge may now be the first place to have a true worker-student alliance." Otherwise, calm prevailed. A red-bearded sophomore who helped lead the walkout was one of the first in line for the Noon Spread in the Yard.[48]

A letter in late June from KSG affiliate Robert Bowie who directed the Center for International Affairs to Dean Franklin Ford seemed to that embattled administrator a voice from a past he had thought forever gone. Bowie complained that the letterhead for a new German Research Program substituted the name of the Committee on West European Studies for the Kennedy School: an affront to academic territoriality he found unacceptable. A bemused Ford replied: "It says something (though I am not quite sure what) about this remarkable year at Harvard that among the last pieces of post-Commencement correspondence we have the issue of the letterhead." This was not only the voice of normalcy past; it was the voice of normalcy yet to come.[49]

The Vietnam War dragged on, and its extension into Cambodia in the spring of 1970 produced an outburst of protest even greater than that of the year before. But Harvard weathered the passions of 1970 far better than those of 1969 and by Commencement 1971 it could truly be said that the greatest crisis in the history of Harvard governance was over. How? Why?

For one thing, the leadership learned much from the events of the spring of 1969. The American incursion into Cambodia came when classes were over, so final examinations and semester grades were the most sensitive on-campus issues. With Pusey's encouragement, the faculty quickly and with almost no dissent authorized alternative ways of winding things up, among them, pass-fail grading and delaying final exams until the fall.

Nor was there much division over the larger issues at stake. Some thirty thousand people attended a somber protest rally in Soldiers' Field on May 9, the outpouring of a community as united as at any time since Pearl Harbor. Pusey joined with other university presidents to warn President Nixon that the campus mood was explosive. The faculty overwhelmingly (218 for, 31 against, 57 abstaining) endorsed a resolution urging the speedy withdrawal of American troops from Vietnam. But when Hilary Putnam proposed the usual radical potpourri of unilateral and immediate withdrawal, the end of defense research, and the freeing of Black Panther Bobby Seale, an almost identical vote (215–36) defeated it. And in June the faculty soundly (148–56) rejected a proposal for a two-week preelection recess in the fall.[50]

Changes in leadership also defused discontent. An ailing Franklin Ford resigned from the FAS deanship in November 1969, declaring that he no longer had the heart for a job that had as much to do with politics as with education. Pusey chose economist John Dunlop, a man of notable negotiating talents and personal force, to succeed Ford. The president's 1968–69 *Annual Report* looked back on "a dismal year." He confessed that he had "failed to do justice to the widespread and varied malaise in both student and faculty populations." But he detected "a major adjustment now going on in the University to a fundamental alteration in the intellectual climate of our time." There was "a widening impatience with narrow scholasticism, that kind of scholarship which exists for its own sake. There grows among us, instead, a deeply-held conviction" that it was necessary "to pursue knowledge for moral, social, and political ends. What is wanted is an education which will recognize this and help to make it possible." Soon after, in March 1970, he announced that he would retire in June 1971, two years earlier than he had intended to. His old enemy the *Crimson* now praised him: "Harvard has owed him thanks before, and does now."[51]

Commencement 1970 was a milestone on the long march of institutional healing. Pusey hoped "that we can halt the desire of every political or social splinter group to have a say at Harvard's Commencement. We wouldn't have much of an audience if it becomes a vaudeville protest show." But activists protesting Harvard's impact on the neighboring low-income Riverside area were allowed (on the advice of troubleshooter Archibald Cox) a couple of minutes to convey their message to the audience. They then met offstage with Corporation members, who quickly struck an agreement on a Harvard building moratorium and support for low-income housing.

Student speakers were more anguished and supplicating than angry. For the first time Radcliffe students got their degrees at a Harvard Commencement, and Kirsten Mishkin gave the Latin oration ("Together, let us establish a new society"). *Crimson* editor James Fallows's Class Day address called for a "new kind of American patriotism that this country may not recognize as loyalty": for the time, relatively mild rhetoric.[52]

Cox told the Council of Deans in early September 1970 what they might expect in the coming academic year: continuing disruption by the radical Left, but with declining student and faculty support. In the fall of 1970 a large crowd disrupted a pro–South Vietnam teach-in in Sanders Theatre. Cox, who tried to restore order and was shouted down, thought that "[n]othing more important or sad has happened at Harvard for a long, long time." The Committee on Rights and Responsibilities conducted an inquiry and found that student radicals systematically threatened those who planned the teach-in: "Perhaps the most repugnant aspect of this case is the bland assertion by presumably intelligent students at the hearing that harassment ... was well-known and widely discussed in certain circles during the several week period involved. The Committee finds such callous disregard of the rights of others disgusting." But only about 10 percent of the disrupters were Harvard or Radcliffe students, four of whom were suspended.[53]

Distressing, too, was the tale that Dr. and Mrs. Seymour Rothschild (he was president of New England Nuclear Corporation) had to tell. Their son Joseph came to Harvard in the fall of 1970 with sophomore standing: adept at physics and math and music, but only sixteen years old. SDSers soon befriended him, as did a radical faculty member. At the end of his first semester he gave up Physics to study Philosophy of Science with that professor—and was one of the students charged with disrupting the pro-Vietnam teach-in. At his urging his mother attended a subsequent meeting at which his faculty mentor spoke, praising the disruption, urging its continuance, and pinpointing specific people and places for the engagés in the audience to pursue. Mrs. Rothschild wrote to the professor giving him hell for encouraging her son to become Movement cannon fodder. The boy was suspended until September 1972: his parents were not consulted. Could the University really feel threatened "by a pathetically ignorant and idealistic seventeen-year-old"?[54]

Incidents such as these in fact marked the end of a period of polarization and direct action. With the draft over and the war winding down, politically engaged students were turning to other issues: the environment, feminism, poverty; above all race. True, new attitudes toward education and new social styles had come to define the Harvard student scene. But the meritocratic, research-and-scholarship-driven University culture that took form in the postwar decades was not going to be easily displaced.

## The Challenge to Governance

The crisis of 1969 made a large splash in the Harvard pond, and its ripples unsettled every part of it, including those venerable bodies the Governing Boards. When Corporation fellows William Marbury and Keith Kane decided to retire in 1970, for the first time thousands of letters went out to the faculty and alumni asking for suggestions as to their replacements. The fellows decided that it would be nice to have a scientist or a doctor, or even an academic. Retired Fellow Charles A. Coolidge thought it a bit much to choose a student, but a Jew might well be considered or an African American such as Clifford Alexander or a woman to speed the Radcliffe merger—though perhaps not yet.

According to Pusey, we "[w]ere shocked ourselves when the quest ended in our nominating 2 professors!" These were University of Illinois physicist Charles Slichter, the first Corporation member from west of the Hudson and the son of University Professor Sumner Slichter, to replace Kane, and Yale history professor John M. Blum to succeed Marbury. "Hooks" Burr was the only Boston Brahmin fellow left.[55]

The Board of Overseers, too, bent before the winds of change. They had always been discontented over the Corporation's tendency not to consult them when choosing a president, new fellows, or deans. Now, when authority came into question on all sides, old grievances gained new life. Banker Douglas Dillon, the Overseers' chairman, sought a more significant role for his body. He proposed that as the voice of the alumni they formally review Corporation decisions. Pusey agreed that when the appointment of new Corporation members came up, he would give the overseers "their very fullest opportunity for discussion and decision on these especially important elections." Meanwhile the overseers did some changing themselves. In 1970 the first female and African American members were elected: Radcliffe honcha Helen Homans Gilbert and attorney Clifford Alexander.[56]

In the wake of the University Hall takeover, the Overseers set up a committee chaired by Judge Henry Friendly to study the causes of that event and what might be done to prevent its recurrence. Reflecting the sky-is-falling attitude then fashionable, the committee's draft report called for student participation in faculty appointments and the curriculum, a "socially responsible" investment policy, more democracy and diversity in the selection of the Governing Boards, and Overseer representation at Corporation meetings. Pusey found its analysis of the Harvard situation "not sufficiently searching," its recommendations "much too specific," its tone too negative: "It suggests that a totally unexpected catastrophe befell Harvard revealing glaring weaknesses which we are now seeking frantically to repair."[57]

From a larger perspective, Daniel Patrick Moynihan set the report in a sequence of developments that had all the spontaneity of a Japanese Noh play: "I refer to the *ritual* quality of the Harvard experience. Everything went off exactly as scheduled. . . . after the seizure of the promising issues by this small band of radicals, the building occupation, the bust, the strike, the script calls for the appointment of a Committee 'to undertake a deeper long-range study'." But on one point Moynihan agreed with the Friendly Committee: the need to strengthen the executive branch of the University. It was too small, too limited in its powers. During his term as director of the Joint Center for Urban Studies, he "found the administration at Harvard exquisitely civil, and unfailingly accessible. But also deeply passive." That passivity was purposeful: its goal was to give people like himself the utmost freedom to pursue their academic goals. But it incurs a "great cost when the freedom of the institution itself is under attack."

Corporation member Hugh Calkins also was clear "that we need to strengthen Harvard's central administration." He distinguished between the Harvard that had been—an institution full of shared purpose and self-regard, ready to leave politics and policy making to the administration—and the Harvard that had come to be: hostile to authority, receptive to participatory democracy. The University had to strike a balance between efficiency and democracy. But quick-fix tinkering with the machinery of governance was not the answer: "Surely in the summer of 1969 any judgments on the government of the University in the 1970s are premature.... In May the critics dominated the stage; by January is it possible that the constructive middle will have asserted itself? ... Whether Harvard needs a Provost or a Chancellor or (God forbid) a Chairman of the Board or none of these is a question which surely should be deferred until the next President is chosen."

The Friendly Committee duly went back to the drawing board and came up with a revised report. Pusey found it a vast improvement: primarily, perhaps, because its most substantive proposal was—what else?—another committee: a University-wide committee on governance drawn from the Governing Boards, the faculty, students, and alumni. That body, thirty-five-strong and headed by John Dunlop (soon to be the FAS dean), was quickly formed. Its charge was to look into the major components of Harvard governance: fund-raising and financial management, the office (and selection) of the president, the rights and responsibilities of students and faculty.[58]

Of more immediate concern was the impact of the campus crisis on the bread-and-butter business of fund-raising, finance and budgeting, and admissions. Letters of protest flooded in from the alumni, and familiar Old Grad grievances resurfaced: "Character and background are now neglected for high marks from places like the Bronx High School of Science, a breeding ground of carefully tutored student radicals.... Excessive departmentalization and professionalization have caused faculty members to conceive of themselves as journeymen whose services are for sale to the highest bidder."[59]

The Harvard Fund—annual contributions from alumni—declined in 1969–70 for the first time since the Depression. The depressed stock market could be, and was, blamed: the value of Harvard's endowment had dropped 18 percent. But the decline in giving appeared to be steepest among graduates of the 1950s (who loudly held that Harvard was too responsive to the protesters) and the 1960s (who loudly held that it was too unresponsive). The fund provided only 10 percent of the University's income. But along with the erosive impact of inflation, its shrinkage helped to create an $860,000 budget deficit in 1970–71, the first in fifteen years.

The old Boston Brahmin phobia against dipping into capital kicked into play. Pusey warned that a period of financial stringency had come; the free-spending attitude of the past twenty years would have to change. Treasurer George Bennett saw no likelihood of income growth in the foreseeable future and warned: "The crunch is coming." Still, enough of the old confidence remained to launch, in February and March 1971, an $11.4 million campaign, "To Finish A Job for Harvard," as a going-away present for Pusey. Its goals: $6 million to complete the massive Undergraduate Science Center, $4.3 million for an addition to Widener Library to be named after Pusey, and $1.1 million for a CFIA building in the Kennedy School complex.[60]

A new fiscal issue now came to the fore, very much a product of changing times: the place of social responsibility in Harvard investment policy. In the spring of 1970, Ralph Nader's Project for Corporate Responsibility proposed auto safety and antipollution measures, and a provision for public members on the General Motors Board, to be voted on at that company's stockholders' meeting. A campaign got under way for Harvard to vote its 287,000 shares of GM stock in favor of the Nader proposals. Given the fevered atmosphere of the time, this bid fair to be an explosive campus issue. The Corporation solicited the views of the University community and spoke of a Harvard representative casting the University's vote at the stockholders' meeting. Present and former Treasurers Bennett and Cabot opposed the Nader proposals as a socialistic attempt to insert nonowners between stockholders and management, and insisted that the treasurer should have a proxy to vote the stock as he saw fit. Pusey agreed, but "when larger social and political issues are involved, it seems only reasonable to have the Treasurer consult the members of the Corporation." Unsurprisingly, the Corporation decided to support GM's management. Pusey then created a University Committee on Relations with Corporate Enterprise to look into the general question of Harvard-corporation relations.

The committee recommended that Harvard seek the maximum return on investments, except for those "justifiable on the basis of the University's duty to the more or less immediately surrounding community." Even this rather constrained response bothered those who believed that maximum return was the proper goal of money managers. Supreme Court Justice Abe Fortas (no mean profit maximizer himself) found the committee's report infected by "an unwillingness to resist the fashionable Naderism of our times: namely, that social reform is everybody's responsibility, to be discharged in every possible way, regardless of his own particular mission and role in our society." Pusey thought that Fortas was "quite right in his analysis of the document." But its language was necessary to get all of the committee members to sign it.[61]

Social responsibility reared its head in another context as well. Harvard was a looming presence in the life of Boston and Cambridge. It increased its Cambridge property holdings by a fifth during the 1960s and now occupied 4.5 percent of the city's land. Almost seven thousand Harvard students and staff—a 34 percent increase since 1958—lived off-campus and occupied 10 percent of Cambridge housing. After the Columbia upheaval in the spring of 1968, Pusey asked Government professor James Q. Wilson to head a new Committee on the University and the City. Its task, said member Daniel Patrick Moynihan, was to come up with a strategy to blunt trouble with the community when the "totalitarian radicals" turned to Harvard next.

The University, Wilson urged, should not identify itself with "those natural forces now working to make Cambridge more like Harvard and less like [working-class] Central Square." Moynihan put it more bluntly: "The unremitting scandal of Harvard's relationship to its community has been its relation to this working class. The oldest, deepest ethnic, religious and cultural prejudice of the University is to be encountered here." If anything, the situation was getting worse: fewer students came to Harvard from Cambridge and Boston high schools than a generation ago. "The Catholic middle class has now made its way to Harvard, and in quite impressive numbers. But the group which one might imagine would comprise the first concern of socially conscious administrators and faculty, continues to be consigned to the outer darkness of Central Square and Southie [South Boston]."

The Wilson committee report appeared in January 1969—and, said Moynihan, "The rest was silence, until late in the Spring, when, with Harvard very nearly brought to ruin over the issue of University 'expansion' in Cambridge and Boston," the Faculty of Arts and Sciences all but unanimously adopted its proposals. That experience highlighted what Moynihan took to be the most serious problem afflicting governance at Harvard: "there was no executive branch to report to in any functioning sense."[62]

## Governing the Future

How Harvard should be governed in years to come was the most important policy issue to emerge from the crisis of 1969. John Kenneth Galbraith made "The Case for Constitutional Reform at Harvard" in December 1968. Naughtily he confessed: "There can be few Harvard professors who have more diligently avoided or evaded administrative responsibilities in the University over a longer period than have I. Accordingly, it will be thought that I am a poor person to plead for new faculty responsibilities." But now he made up for his past indifference. He dismissed the Corporation as a group of elitist amateurs, incapable of recognizing and dealing with the needs of a modern university. Their fund-raising and investment policies were too conservative; not they but the faculty should choose the president.

Nathan Pusey responded predictably: this was "a ridiculous and arrogant article, ... notable for its factual inaccuracy and its Galbraithian potshots." Charles Coolidge, who had retired in 1965 after thirty years on the Corporation, took Galbraith on. The selection of presidents by faculties and deans in other universities did not appear to produce superior results. Without some distance between the Corporation and the faculty, favoritism and politicking were sure to flourish. And Coolidge could not conceal his surprise that Galbraith appeared to think that Harvard was deficient in fund-raising; certainly that was not the view of the world at large.[63]

But Coolidge admitted privately that he had talked to faculty barons Walter Jackson Bate in English and George Kistiakowsky in Chemistry and found that, while they were able to contain their admiration for Galbraith, they were not content with the present administrative structure. They felt cut off from an increasingly bureaucratized administration. The Corporation was remote, and suffered from the lack of a scientist member; the Overseers' visiting committees were ineffective. They wanted an advisory committee from all of the faculties to consult with the Corporation on important matters: a proposal, Coolidge feared, that would undercut the deans.[64]

As things developed, change in Harvard's governance went in a very different direction: not to more immediacy and intimacy, but to expanded bureaucracy. The Dunlop Committee on Governance concluded that the office of the president was overburdened and proposed that vice presidents for internal financial management, external relations, and education (a provost) be created. Corporation fellow Albert Nickerson, who headed Socony Mobil, had an agenda of his own. He, key Fellow "Hooks" Burr, former Treasurer Paul Cabot, and current Treasurer George Bennett went sailing off the coast of Maine for three days in the summer of 1968. Out of this came a Nickerson memo, "Thoughts on University Budgeting and Planning." He did not, he confessed, have much knowledge of the inner workings of the University. But he had consulted with some of his Mobil associates and concluded that what Harvard needed was "meaningful expense control, the use of advanced systems and equipment, and an effort to introduce coordinated planning."

Nickerson proposed that the "budgetary units" (departments, professional schools, museums) prepare five-year forecasts of revenues, expenditures, and capital requirements, to be collected by a central systems and analysis group, which would evaluate and implement (or modify or reject) the proposals. He was well aware that his approach cut across the grain of Harvard's traditional soft-shoe administrative system, with its low costs, informal relationships, and autonomous faculties. But that structure had come under pressures it was not designed to bear: ever more complex relations with government, operating costs outstripping income, adversarial students. Communication among administration, faculty, and students was breaking down; the pressures on key people were rising; the president's office in particular felt the strain. The world outside was full of large organizations better organized and managed. There was no reason why the principles that governed them should not govern Harvard.[65]

What might have seemed chillingly Orwellian before was not beyond the pale after the events of 1969. Overseer Douglas Dillon also thought the time had come to do away with archaisms such as each faculty tub on its own bottom. The University as a whole had a stronger gift-attracting potential than its component parts. The result, said Dillon, "would be greatly increased responsibility on the part of the central administration, and in particular the Corporation, for determining where available funds should go." Dean of the Law School Derek Bok, soon to be president, also questioned the decentralized character of Harvard decision making. He did not propose that student grievances and the like be "centrally determined." But what one faculty did impacted on others, and without some common ground student groups "will push for reforms in one faculty and then use that decision as a lever to pass for similar changes elsewhere."[66]

The Corporation got the consulting firm of McKinsey and Company to study Harvard's administration. The McKinsey Report, "Meeting the Challenges of the 1970s" (it might more playfully have been entitled "The Administrative Behavior of the Harvard Male"), appeared in February 1970, all large type, short sentences, and simplistic outlines: a typical professional consultants' product. Exponential growth, increases in government funding and oversight, and the University's need for largely increased funds made it essential that management and capital planning be modernized. A larger and stronger central administration, it concluded, was the answer. By the time of his departure, Pusey had come to agree. He feared that his successor "is going to be faced with a great many organizational situations which would make me rather uncomfortable. Yet the place has grown so much that it seems inevitable that there should be a sensible division of the central power structure."[67]

# The King Is Dead ...

The most conspicuous short-term consequence of the great upheaval of 1969 was the departure of Nathan Marsh Pusey in June 1971. Elegaic notes of sympathy poured in from supporters. A number of correspondents saw Pusey's Harvard presidency bracketed by the McCarthyite challenge of the mid-1950s and the student uprising of the late 1960s, and found a common chord in his response to both. New Corporation fellow John Blum was "furious" over the *Crimson*'s treatment of Pusey: "They have mastered the old McCarthy technique you did so much to defeat and discredit." "I don't in the least blame you" for leaving, said Pat Moynihan. "You were strong when many were weak. And you were true when truth was hard to perceive and harder still to avow." Sociologist David Riesman commended Pusey for his modesty and lack of aloofness, his sense of principle and dedication to scholarship, his concern for the University, the deprived, and the handicapped. And Pusey's successor Derek Bok told him: "Above all, I want you to know how much I have admired the courage you have shown through the events of the past eighteen months. How hard it must have been to endure the lack of reason and understanding that were so evident. Your patience and courage and strength of conviction have taught us a great deal."

He heard, too, from his predecessor Conant:

> I am the last person in the world to question the decision of a Harvard president to leave office. I walked out on the University with only a couple of weeks' notice! Nevertheless, I cannot refrain from saying that I am sorry you have decided to end your term of office in June, 1971. I was hoping you would stay the course until you reached the retiring age, for I believe there will be great difficulty finding anyone who can handle the turbulent scene as effectively and courageously as you have done in the past two years.

Pusey replied that Conant's was the letter that mattered most to him: "Only you can appreciate what went into it and what a sense of relief there is to have it over and done with."[68]

McGeorge Bundy, bloodied by Vietnam and now in the questionable sanctuary of the Ford Foundation presidency, looked back to the years of his deanship under Pusey, a time when the University's real ruling class—not the Corporation or the alumni or the students, but the faculty—was supreme. It was the faculty that ultimately prevented the firing of physicist Wendell Furry for pleading the Fifth Amendment. And though some members of the Board of Overseers tried to block the tenuring of Galbraith, "Professor Galbraith remained, except when on leave." Rich donors were induced to give not only for what they wanted (rare books and music) but for what the faculty wanted (international affairs, undergraduate science). And it was the scholars, not the amateurs, who finally won Harvard's Twenty Years' War over the Arnold Arboretum.

By banning classified contracts and not allowing government grants to underpin the salaries of senior faculty, Harvard retained a critical measure of intellectual and financial independence from the government. And its rigorous selection procedure, arrogant and presumptuous though it may have been in assuming that only the best would be appointed, did produce what was probably the strongest university faculty in America: "it was the one that others claimed to watch. Its own opinion of itself was plain."

The system was not without its faults. The administration, Bundy thought in retrospect, erred in giving departments too much leeway in choosing whom they wanted: "very good in his field" too often trumped high intellectual quality. But students got better each year. This reflected Bender's shrewd admissions policy, which assumed that America's ablest youth were not limited to the most academically talented and thus assured the real distinction of the student body. The gravest failing of the University in that shining time was that neither faculty nor students were quite as good as they thought they were: "We were proud of Harvard; were we perhaps too proud?"[69]

Not all were so sympathetically inclined. Curmudgeon Overseer Joseph Alsop, long on a tear over what he saw as the faculty's "decay into unseriousness," recalled that he and J. Robert Oppenheimer had opposed Pusey's election, "and I am not sorry that I did, to this day. We were both sure that he would be a morally impeccable president; but we were equally sure that he would be unable to enforce the new standards of intellectual rigor, which we thought to be essential. What has happened since, seems to me to have verified our forecast." Another old antagonist—from a very different angle of fire—also was unrelenting. At the last faculty meeting over which Pusey presided, he had a tense clash with John Kenneth Galbraith over the Corporation's stand on voting Harvard's General Motors stock. One faculty member observed: "That's just Ken's way of saying goodbye."[70]

Pusey did not deny the unbending stubbornness most often imputed to him by his opponents. When Union College president Harold C. Martin wrote to Pusey calling him—one assumes sympathetically—"obdurate," his aide Bentinck-Smith observed that that was "not the word I would have picked to describe your character" and gave him the dictionary's several definitions. The third—"Not giving in to persuasion; intractable"—caught Pusey's eye. He underlined "intractable" and wrote in the margin: "that's me!"

His last public remarks as Harvard's president were, appropriately, to his core constituency, the Associated Harvard Alumni, at the June 1971 Commencement. He looked back to that happy time after World War II when a fresh appreciation of the importance of free institutions, and an enlarged sense of the place of America in the world, shaped the culture of the University. Belief in the positive, ameliorating effects of knowledge was pervasive. "It was a great time for all university people to be alive, and especially so here, for Harvard was in the forefront of all this.... Once a New England college, Harvard had finally been transformed into a national university in Mr. Conant's time. In the postwar years it grew steadily in international influence and esteem."

But discontents came with success, and "[t]he effort has not come out exactly as we had hoped." Students were less readily impressed by what their professors offered them; the ideals and goals that animated the postwar generation had lost much of their appeal; confidence in the ability of universities to provide answers had declined. His predecessor Conant—who was in the audience—had had to wrestle with the Great Depression and World War II. "Now, after a period of readjustment and phenomenal growth, there comes for another president an era of radically altered conditions, sharp change, and formidable obstacles.... One Harvard is passing into history and another being born. One is dying while another, burgeoning with new life, is eagerly waiting before. We salute it and welcome it."[71]

# PART III
## "A Buzzing Confusion":
### *1971–2000*

## ∽ 15 ∼

## DEREK CURTIS BOK

## AND THE WORLDLY UNIVERSITY

During the last three decades of the twentieth century, the merito-cratic Harvard of Conant and Pusey evolved into the more worldly university of Derek Bok (1971–91) and Neil Rudenstine (1991–2001). This is not to suggest that Harvard sloughed off its intensely meritocratic character, or even its Brahmin antecedents. And of course Harvard faculty at least since World War II had been conspic-uously engaged in public affairs. But the prevailing culture shifted. Worldliness—Harvard as a participant in, as much as an observer of, the larger society—became the dominant tone in the late twentieth century. To the social elitism of Brahmin Harvard, and the disciplinary emphasis of meritocratic Harvard, there was added the ever-expanding social engagement of worldly Harvard.

### Harvard's Bok

After Nathan Pusey announced his intention to leave the presidency in June 1971, Harvard turned to the heady business of deciding who was to be his successor. Students wanted someone young, accessible, sensitive to their educational wants and needs. Faculty members sought an eminent scholar attentive to the life of the (academic) mind. Nor could politics be ignored in this post-1969 age: one professor called for "a man who conveys a sense of sympathy with values from quite far left to some-what right of center." Corporation fellow Hugh Calkins later recalled that the search committee "saw Harvard as within a forest of perplexing issues, through which no clear path was visible." The most troubling problem was an apparent shift in the prevailing view of the university's purpose. Harvard, he observed, traditionally sought to educate "leaders of high intellectual capacity in scholarly, professional, business and public life." Now there was a widespread sense that "intellectual capacity is suspect as a confederate of inequality and injustice." Given these conditions, Calkins and his colleagues were uncertain whether to look for a leader with a clear vision of Harvard's future or for one without preconceptions.[1]

The selection committee of five Corporation fellows sent out 203,000 letters soliciting suggestions from faculty, students, employees, and alumni. This yielded some 3,500 replies and 900 names. (One alumnus helpfully suggested Pope Paul VI, on the grounds that there had not been an infallible president since Lowell and that a strict bachelor "would get women out of the place.")[2]

After an eleven-month search, the nod went to dean of the Law School Derek Curtis Bok, who by all accounts had been the leading candidate from day one. For the first time since Charles Chauncey (1654–72), Harvard chose a president who had not attended the College. It seemed to one observer that Bok and his non-Bostonian predecessor Pusey "were the one-two punch that took out the Brahmin tradition at Harvard." The Corporation saw in Bok a mediator with the capacity to avoid a reprise of the unpleasantness of 1969. What they got was a president more interested in shaping the Harvard that was to be than in healing the hurts of the Harvard that was. But so it had ever been in the Harvard presidential selection process. Like the French general staff, the Corporation sought constantly to win the war just past; as is so often the case, well-laid plans had unanticipated consequences.[3]

Yet the forty-year-old Bok, who had been on the HLS faculty since 1958, was a known quantity. And he had the "resilience, calmness of temper, tenacity of purpose" thought to be prerequisites for the job. A Stanford B.A. in political science, he graduated from Harvard Law School in 1954 and returned as an assistant professor in 1958. Ten years later his colleagues warmly endorsed him for the deanship. During his first year in office he was startled by student complaints that they had not been consulted about a one-week change in the Law School's academic calendar. It was, he said, his "first intimation that the faculty needs to consult anybody" about such matters. He learned soon enough that all things were up for grabs, that "no authority was left standing." His instinctive reaction was to listen intently to student protests, no matter how shocked he was by their manner of presentation. This lawyerly attentiveness made him an attractive choice for Harvard's president in 1970. As *New York Times* education editor Fred Hechinger observed, "lawyers are much in demand" to deal with an often adversarial campus culture.[4]

Bok had other attractive attributes. He looked presidential: not quite Brahmin, but unmistakably patrician. He had an easy manner (laced with the secure self-confidence of the wellborn) and a dry, often self-deprecating wit. (He later said of the priority he gave to refurbishing Harvard's physical plant: "It's probably a response to some deep need to reassure myself that something had gotten better during my administration.") He drove a Volkswagen to work and was not above playing in a basketball game against the undergraduate women's team.[5]

Beneath this informality lay a deep reserve. Bok was accessible to faculty members and keenly interested in what they were doing. Still, there were those who found him aloof. Mistaking modesty for a lack of substance, some professors initially concluded that he had no idea as to where he might lead Harvard. As it turned out, they were wrong. Bok resolved early on not to scatter his energies, but to concentrate on improving the quality of instruction and enlarging the University's contribution to society. He sometimes grew impatient with the pace of change (or lack of it). But as a former dean he knew better than to issue directives on educational goals or institutional ambitions. He relied instead on persistence and persuasion.

Bok had almost six months to prepare himself for office. He used the time to read background materials, visit departments and graduate schools, talk to faculty, students and alumni, meet with the presidents of other universities. In late September 1971, he made his first speech before the Faculty of Arts and Sciences in the ornately formal Faculty Room, adorned with portraits of Harvard's past presidents and faculty luminaries—the room at the center of the University Hall occupation of April 1969. He alluded to the "turbulence" of the recent past, and noted the decline in the ability of Harvard's president to effect change. But "the power the president has retained is the only kind worth having in a university, and that is the power of ideas developed through careful observation of what is happening in education both here and elsewhere." He already had ideas aplenty; for the moment, he said simply that he would undertake to protect the faculty "from oversight and complacency by insisting upon the very best appointments and by identifying new problems and opportunities" for the faculty to consider. And he was true to his word.

To add to the efficiency (or more accurately, to reduce the inefficiency) of Harvard's administration, Bok thought it necessary to recruit "a slightly larger number of key assistants" who would manage the University's expanding agenda. That would allow him to focus on "the processes of learning and discovery at Harvard. Like you, I did not come to Harvard out of ambition for the administrative life but from a love of teaching and scholarship. It would be a personal loss and a serious reflection on Harvard if the President of this University could no longer dedicate his principal efforts to the process of education in the fullest sense."

According to one faculty member, these remarks took many of his colleagues by surprise. It had been widely assumed that the new president was brought in primarily to repair Harvard's internal management, not to chart a new course for the University. But as Bok's presidency evolved, he became preoccupied with exploring "the proper nature of [Harvard's] social responsibilities." When he departed in 1991, he left behind a more worldly Harvard, responsive to both the needs and the dictates of the outside world. His successor, Neil Rudenstine, accepted and extended this change, much as Pusey had done with Conant's meritocratic University.[6]

## Worldliness

What, in practice, distinguished worldly late-twentieth-century Harvard from the meritocratic midcentury University? Changes in emphasis, tone, nuance. The by now deeply entrenched stress on securing The Best faculty and students and on the primacy of scholarship and research went on as before. If anything, Bok made tenure reviews even tougher than before. But the decades after 1970 were also a time when an egalitarian critique of meritocracy, and a concomitant stress on diversity and social responsibility, gained greater currency.

Between 1979 and 1987 Bok published a number of "open letters," which analyzed the complex and heated campus issues of the day. "Reflections on the Ethical Responsibilities of the University in Society" (1979) set out what had to be taken into account when the University was asked to take a political stand. "Reflections on Divestment of Stock in Companies Doing Business in South Africa" (1979) explored the options on a contentious question, as did his "Open Letter on Issues of Race" (1981) and "Reflections on Free Speech" (1984). These decretals were Bok at his best: tough-minded, balanced, carefully reasoned.

But the quotidian realities of Harvard governance required a more mundane response as well. Student activism was an accepted Harvard extracurricular activity, even though its intensity had declined precipitously from its 1969–70 peak. Race replaced Vietnam as the flash point. In April 1972 a group of black students occupied Massachusetts Hall, the site of Bok's office, to protest the University's failure to divest its Gulf Oil stock. Though Harvard's holdings were a mere .3 percent of the total, the protesters claimed that divestment would put pressure on Gulf to withdraw from Portuguese-run Angola. While Bok was out of town, his lieutenants secured a court injunction to remove the students. But he decided to let the occupiers stay where they were. He would not give in on the substance of the issue, nor would he risk inflaming the situation with a replay of the University Hall police bust.

The divestment of Harvard-owned stock in American companies doing business in South Africa became for a season the most popular campus cause. Bok insisted on making a distinction between companies going along with apartheid and those trying to improve the lot of nonwhite workers. Blanket divestment, he believed, was a "dubious" policy in which the University would "deviate from its proper role, jeopardize its independence, and risk its resources" with "no realistic prospect of success." At the same time he allocated a million dollars for black South Africans to study at Harvard and for Harvard people to do public interest work in South Africa: a worldly response to a worldly issue.

Student activists were not satisfied with these subtleties. Bok mused that sometimes his presidency "seemed like one long, endless argument over divestment." But the principle at stake was an important one. For all his social concern, or perhaps to make sure that it retained some viability, he thought it wrong to take an institutional stand on a political cause—even one so just as the end of apartheid in South Africa—unless Harvard's interests were directly at stake.[7]

One such case was affirmative action. Many advocates saw the policy as just compensation to minority groups for past and present discrimination. But Bok supported it on the ground that "the opportunities for minority students to contribute to the understanding of their fellow students and to the welfare of society" were "sufficiently important to us to justify an effort to enroll a significant number of applicants from these racial groups."[8]

He felt the same about gender. One of his first acts as president was to increase by 50 percent the number of women undergraduates. But when it came to faculty appointments, he rejected quotas in favor of seeking out "qualified" women and minority candidates: a stance that grated on critics who attacked his position as a prime example of "racism disguised as meritocracy." Bok, however, believed that racial and gender preferences should come into play only when academic qualifications were equal, and on the whole his tenure decisions reflected that principle.

Bok assumed the role of gadfly in his dealings with those near-autonomous fiefdoms the College, the Graduate School of Arts and Sciences, and the professional schools. His annual reports, traditionally summings-up of the previous year's Harvard doings, became essays on a particular schools or faculty, in which he sought "to describe the planets from the trackless void of academic administration." Stressing the need for "common standards to hold a diverse society together," Bok advocated courses in applied ethics in the professional schools and efforts in the College to school undergraduates in norms of "honesty, nonviolence, promise keeping, and respect for property."[9]

When it came to the curriculum, his chief concern was not *what* but *how* Harvard students learned. He backed programs to improve the pedagogical skills of graduate students and to discover more effective teaching techniques. (Looking back in 1997, he characterized the faculty's response to these efforts as "a great blob of inertia.") And he insisted on evidence of teaching ability in tenure appointments, though he could be overborne by best-mind pitches from the departments.[10]

Expanding the international character of Harvard was especially close to Bok's heart, and here, perhaps, the gap between his high expectations and earthbound reality was widest. He wanted Harvard students to study abroad, and he wanted the University to prepare more foreign students for leadership roles in their own countries: Harvard in the world's service. Again, he was disappointed by the faculty's disinterest in his ideas. He hired a special assistant for international projects whose job was to get businessmen and government officials in a dozen countries (beginning with Costa Rica, Guatemala, Ecuador, and Mexico) to send students to Harvard and to bring Harvard students to their countries as interns: a private Fulbright program. To finance these exchanges, Harvard entered into "treaties" involving complex debt swaps and matching funds. Between 1989 and 1994, Harvard students from Latin America increased (from a small base) by 40 percent, those from Mexico alone by 100 percent.

But in late 1990 the faculty rejected a plan to expand the size of the College in order to accommodate more foreign students. It responded no more favorably to a major increase in overseas internships ("work abroad is not a substitute for study abroad"), nor did it approve a student major in international studies. Though the enrollment of foreign students in the University at large rose by more than 25 percent between 1989 and 1998, to 17.6 percent of the Harvard student total, they still made up only 7 percent of Harvard undergraduates.[11]

Bok devoted his 1988–89 annual report to a discussion, "What's

Wrong With Our Universities?" While international opinion polls rated the American system of higher education the best in the world, American opinion polls showed a sharp decline of domestic confidence in the system: from 61 percent in 1966 to 33 percent in the mid-1970s. Bok brushed aside charges that the faculty had an airy workload (maintaining, instead, that they "work too hard"), that tuition was too high (it was below the cost of educating students and was substantially reduced by financial aid packages), and that Harvard engaged in perpetual fund-raising (it was necessary to maintain quality in the face of rising costs). The most significant deficiency in American universities, he thought, was that they did much less than they should to "help the country address its formidable array of problems—lagging competitiveness, poverty, inadequate public education, environmental hazards, and many more."

His taste for jeremiads grew as he neared the end of his term in office. He dwelt on the "present dangers" clouding the future of higher education in 1989–90, much as Dwight Eisenhower pointed to the dangers of the military-industrial complex when his presidency drew to a close. One of these threats was politicization: using the university for political purposes and imposing political orthodoxy from inside. Another was overextension: the "proliferation of activities in the University and by the faculty." A third was the "commercialized university," fueled by the incessant and distracting search for more resources. "[I]ronically," he observed, "it is the very success, the visibility, the mounting influence of our universities that has brought about these pressures."

In his final Commencement address (1991), "The Social Mission of American Universities," Bok recalled that when he came to Cambridge in 1951 to study at the Law School, "America and its universities were united in a common resolve to build a system of scientific research preeminent in the world and to expand our colleges to embrace . . . a much larger segment of the nation's youth." By the time he took office as president two decades later, that unity of purpose had all but disappeared:

> Our students were alienated from a society in which they saw their heroes assassinated, their government engaged in a cruel war, their leaders embroiled at the highest level in scandal and deceit. . . Some turned to political protest and cried out loudly for grandiose reforms. . . . Meanwhile, government officials and the general public had very limited patience with the violence and intolerance on university campuses. . . . many Americans even lost confidence in advanced knowledge as a key to progress or in experts as guides to

help resolve our problems. In this demoralized environment, the social purposes of the university seemed very, very much in doubt.

That "angry tumult" soon subsided, but a "common effort toward common goals" was not restored. Instead, "there is a buzzing confusion of complaints about tuition, over financial aid practices, over reading lists, over affirmative action, even over modern literary theory."

Bok paid deference to the "traditional view that great universities should promote discovery and growth of knowledge, not by trying to solve the world's problems but by encouraging scholars to pursue the truth wherever their curiosity leads them." But that was not their only purpose:

> Unless society appreciates the contributions of its universities, it will continue to reduce them to the status of another interest group by gradually stripping away the protections and support they need to stay preeminent in the world. Unless universities take their social responsibilities seriously . . . they will never inspire their students with a purpose large enough to fill their lives with meaning . . . [and] will fail to do everything they can to make this "troubled planet" a better, happier place.

He knew that "no social problem will ever be solved by universities alone." Admittedly, "lawmakers and officials will never solve those problems without new discoveries, the specialized knowledge, the highly educated people that universities can uniquely supply." But at the end of his presidency, Bok concluded that universities did not adequately serve society because they were insufficiently attuned to ethics and social and civic responsibility.

Historian Bernard Bailyn, one of Harvard's most distinguished scholars, admired Bok's "moral center" but not the degree of his emphasis on serving society. Bailyn argued that Harvard had never been a pure ivory tower: it had trained leaders for important social roles from its early seventeenth-century beginnings. The University of the future would have to strike a better balance, "serving society while also devoted to learning for its own sake."[12]

How involved in the outside world, in fact, was Bok's Harvard? An in-the-nation's-service tradition was part of its Brahmin and meritocratic past. But this had taken on an unprecedented scale. Bok himself noted that consulting and other outside activities represented "for many professors a mounting source of excitement, variety, status and income."

(A Princeton quip was that the Harvard faculty was like the Strategic Air Command: a third of its number were airborne at any given time.) He took the faculty to task for trying "to combine the freedom and security of a tenured academic post with the income and visibility traditionally reserved for people who take much greater risks and work at much less elevating tasks."[13]

Something else was new in the University's cultural ambience. During the midcentury years the University's intellectual and academic aspirations had defined the institution. Now, in the century's closing decades, issues with a larger, public resonance—affirmative action, political correctness, the cost of and access to elite colleges—came to the fore.

## Race and Gender

During the decades after 1970, Harvard like much of the nation was caught up in the cause of greater racial and gender equality. By its lights the University already had done much. It substantially expanded its intake of black students from the late 1960s on, and soon after integrated Radcliffe undergraduates as full-fledged members of the College. But a revolution of rising expectations was under way, and yesterday's reform was today's inadequacy. The result was an unsettling mix of a record of progress and continuing accusations of failure.

The relationship of blacks to whites at Harvard continued to be tense, difficult. Demands grew for more black students, faculty, and staff. In 1971 Bok made African American attorney Walter Leonard his special assistant for minority affairs. Leonard sought to compel Harvard's schools to adopt more race-conscious hiring policies. But it was not clear how much the central administration could enforce its writ in so decentralized a university. More effective pressure came from students and a few faculty in each school, and from the growing general sensitivity to matters of race. Active recruitment of minority students and faculty became the norm, with a range of carrots—special scholarships, additional faculty slots—as inducements. Principles of selection became more precise over time: other things roughly equal, a black candidate for a position had priority over a white one, as did an American-born over a West Indian black or a senior over a junior minority appointment.[14]

In 1988, 6.2 percent of Harvard's tenured professors and 11 percent of its entire faculty were black, Hispanic, or Asian American. Harvard Law professor Derrick Bell wanted the tenured figure for blacks alone to rise to 10 percent by 1990. Hispanics, too, began to make themselves heard, but to less effect. When in 1993 the Coalition for Diversity called for the appointment of a tenured Latino professor, some *Crimson* editors thought this an excessive application of affirmative action. The dearth of minority candidates, and the inertial tendency of each faculty to maintain its traditional hiring standards, meant that minority recruitment lagged behind the goals of the most vocal advocates. It became established Harvard policy to keep trying to find black faculty. But accusations that more could be done, and explanations of why more was not being done, persisted.[15]

The admission of black students was a less contentious matter. When *Bakke v. Regents of the University of California* came before the Supreme Court in 1978, Harvard (together with several other universities) filed an amicus brief defending "race sensitive" admissions on the ground that diversity of background enriched the exchange of ideas among students. General counsel Daniel Steiner helped prepare the brief, and HLS professor Archibald Cox of Watergate fame appeared before the Court in its behalf: Harvard in the world.

A couple of faculty members objected to Harvard's intervention as a political statement in the University's name. But Bok held that this was as much an educational as a political issue. He joined in 1998 with another former president, William Bowen of Princeton, to defend both the practice and the results of race-based affirmative action. His successor, Neil Rudenstine, was equally outspoken. At the end of the century affirmative action remained a hotly contested public issue. But it had a secure place in Harvard and other elite universities.[16]

Closely related was the movement for a larger female presence at Harvard. Here controversy focused on sexual harassment and the tenuring of female faculty members. A 1984 survey found that half of the nontenured female faculty, 42 percent of women graduate students, and half the undergraduates had experienced harassment on a scale ranging from verbal teasing to sexual intimidation and abuse. Formal complaints became more frequent (though the number remained small) in the 1980s. In the more serious instances, punishments ranged from frozen salaries to forced resignations. As overt forms of gender discrimination came under surveillance, attention turned to more subtle, elusive considerations. A 1990 survey revealed that the problems of women in science involved both numbers (none at all in small departments such as Mathematics) and an intensely aggressive competitive ambience.[17]

Women undergraduates became full-fledged Harvard students in the early 1970s. In 1977 Harvard College adopted a policy of sex-blind admissions and absorbed Radcliffe's admissions and financial aid offices.

The proportion of women undergraduates steadily rose; by the end of the century it was close to 50 percent. Meanwhile Radcliffe continued as a separate entity, with its own endowment, property, fund-raising, and diminished responsibility for female undergraduates.

Psychologist Matina Horner succeeded Mary Bunting as Radcliffe's president in 1972 and sought to preserve her institution's autonomy. But Radcliffe's role in an age of unisex higher education was unclear. It was no longer involved in undergraduate education, yet it relied on the support of "alumnae who had known Radcliffe as a college that separately admitted, financed, and supervised women undergraduates." Horner sought to turn Radcliffe into a center for the study of women's issues and an advocate for female undergraduates in Harvard College. She rejected the view that Radcliffe could work within Harvard and warned that the historical dominance of men put many psychological pressures on women that made it essential for Radcliffe to maintain a separate identity.[18]

While integrated education and housing moved ahead, the administrative merger of Harvard and Radcliffe bogged down in a welter of clashing interests and personalities. Successive deans of the Faculty of Arts and Sciences viewed the president of Radcliffe as an impediment to the full development of coeducation at Harvard. That was natural enough; but so, too, was the desire of Radcliffe's officers and trustees to retain their voice on the status of women at Harvard, their corporate independence, and their access to alumnae donors.

By the early 1990s only a small share of the Radcliffe budget went for extracurricular programs for female undergraduates, and the Radcliffe presence at Harvard was largely ceremonial. Unkind critics suggested that Radcliffe had come to consist primarily of an administration and a development office, with the Bunting Institute for scholars and the Schlesinger Library for women's history as fronts for an academic Potemkin village.

Linda Wilson, a chemist-administrator from the University of Michigan, replaced Horner as Radcliffe's president in 1989. She, too, sought to strengthen its independent activities. In 1993 she established a Public Policy Institute to focus on issues relating to gender and society. While a Radcliffe fund-raising campaign included undergraduate support as one of its priorities, its primary goal was to support postgraduate programs and research on women. But it was hard to raise money for this purpose from older alumnae (who wondered what was going on in their College) and harder still to capture the loyalty of recent graduates (who regarded themselves as Harvard alumnae).

By the end of the century, Radcliffe had fallen victim to the success of coeducation at Harvard. Its fund-raising campaign lagged, and its administration relied increasingly on deficit financing to pay for the campaign's costs. There were angry protests when FAS dean Jeremy Knowles asked publicly in 1997 what might be done to engage more women as Harvard alumnae leaders and donors. A growing number of Radcliffe graduates were responding favorably to Harvard, not Radcliffe, fund-raising initiatives. Given these conditions, the full merger that Pusey and Bunting sought in the 1960s once again seemed viable.[19]

In April 1999, after two years of private negotiations, Radcliffe was absorbed into Harvard. Its Bunting Institute, Murray Research Center, Schlesinger Library, and Public Policy Institute were merged into an ambitious (though vaguely defined) Radcliffe Institute for Advanced Study, with a dean appointed by Harvard's president. Radcliffe's $150 million endowment was turned over to Harvard, with the understanding that the income from that endowment, and from another $150 million added by the University, would be earmarked for the operating costs of the institute. "To the outside world," said the *Boston Globe*, "the negotiations may have seemed like bickering over seating arrangements at the same elaborate dinner table." At a greater remove, the *Los Angeles Times* saw it "as a burial that took place twenty years after the funeral." In any case, the formal absorption of Radcliffe College brought a long-troubled relationship under the benign dominion of a Pax Harvardiana.[20]

Asian Americans were second only to women as a growing presence on the campus. In academic qualifications and desire to succeed, they resembled Jewish students of earlier decades. There was a perception— vigorously denied by the admissions staff—that the number of Asian American admits was restricted. Some advocates of other minority groups resented counting Asian Americans as a minority group when they were students for whom affirmative action was manifestly superfluous. The suggestion of one department chair that Harvard had a moral obligation to provide special funding for Asian American graduate students "whose recent immigration is the result of U.S. foreign policy during the 60s and 70s" was quietly ignored.

The race and gender makeup of Harvard at 2000 differed markedly from thirty years before. From the perspective of the more vocal advocates of a black and female presence, there still were miles to go, especially in faculty appointments. From the viewpoint of those who had experienced the Harvard of earlier decades, a new world had come into being. No one walking through the Yard could fail to note the degree to which it had become a multicultural environment. Portent seekers might, in the century's waning years, take note of such milestones as the appearance of the Half Asian Persons Association and of a lesbian couple as the co-masters of venerable Lowell House.[21]

Harvard's new multiculturalism did not necessarily lead to a greater diversity of political and social backgrounds. And while racial, ethnic, gender, and gay/lesbian consciousness remained high among some students and faculty, interest in separate academic programs lost much of its strength by the century's end, in good part because so many of those concerns had been absorbed by the traditional disciplines. Postmodernists continued to come up with new gigs—whiteness studies, the cultural meaning of body parts—but in the view of one critic, "permanent revolutions, as the Maoists have demonstrated, never succeed." Indeed, the academic pendulum at century's end seemed to be swinging away "from adding trendy new courses and toward reinstating a humanities core that emphasizes classics."[22]

## Political Correctness

Harvard, like all institutions, has always been in thrall to one or another brand of conventional wisdom. The Unitarian-Republican-Brahmin mind set of the nineteenth and early twentieth centuries; cold war anticommunism in the 1950s: each held sway in its time. Now, in the 1970s, a new generation came into its own. It had strong commitments, forged by the struggles against the Vietnam War and for black civil rights and feminism. But this was an age cohort, influenced by the New Left's disdain for "repressive tolerance" in the 1960s, and the heightened group, race, and gender sensitivities of the ensuing decades, that did not put a high priority on academic freedom and free speech. Charges of a pervasive, cloying political correctness became a common criticism of the late-twentieth-century campus.

Topics resistant to open debate included American policy in Vietnam, racial preferences, and the environment-heredity relationship. Political scientist James Q. Wilson observed in 1972:

> the list of subjects that cannot be publicly discussed [at Harvard] in a free and open forum has grown steadily.... During my adult life I have been part of five institutions—the Catholic Church, the University of Redlands, the United States Navy, the University of

Chicago, and Harvard University. If I were required to rank them by the extent to which free and uninhibited discussion was possible within them, I am very much afraid that the Harvard of 1972 would not rank near the top.[23]

A major cause of Wilson's comment was the experience of his friend and subsequent collaborator, Harvard psychologist Richard Herrnstein. In a 1971 *Atlantic Monthly* article, Herrnstein argued that differences in mental ability were largely inherited and suggested that inequalities of income were attributable in part to this. Although he advocated supplementing I.Q. tests with other measures of performance and did not focus on race, he ran into a storm of obloquy, including death threats, badgering in and out of his classroom, and demands for his dismissal. Bok decried these attacks at a faculty meeting; the Committee on Rights and Responsibilities found that the harassing students had violated the University's rules, but could not agree on disciplinary action.

A decade later a confidential preliminary study of admissions by Kennedy School economist Robert Klitgaard (commissioned by Bok) was leaked to the *Crimson*. One of its findings was that, contrary to popular belief, blacks and (to a lesser degree) women did less well academically than their SAT scores predicted. Even more upsetting was its passing observation that affirmative action at elite schools might have undesirable consequences for minorities. Administrative damage control went into high gear; the study was not released.[24]

But Harvard avoided the trap of speech codes into which schools such as Michigan and Wisconsin fell. In 1990 the Faculty of Arts and Sciences proposed a set of free speech guidelines that for the most part reaffirmed Harvard's traditional commitment to untrammeled speech. It asserted the right of a public speaker to speak over the right of dissenters to shout him down (though it put "racial, sexual, and intense personal harassment" beyond the pale). Some faculty members held that, especially on the subject of race, the University's standard of acceptable speech should be narrower than that set by the First Amendment. Derek Bok strongly disagreed, and the First Amendment continued to be Harvard's free speech standard.

Law School professor Kathleen Sullivan thought it proper that Harvard as a private institution should have, and enforce, political views. Thus General Colin Powell should have been excluded as the 1993 Class Day speaker because he was identified with the government's "don't ask, don't tell" position on gays in the military. Her colleague Duncan Kennedy proposed that universities "enter into a wide variety of political struggles," and imagined "a wonderful university" committed to the support of radical causes and candidates "as its ideological mission." Conservative political theorist Harvey Mansfield, who held that the University's business was the pursuit of truth, grimly replied: "I can imagine it, too."[25]

As in the 1960s, though in muted form, ROTC continued to be a source of contention. After Harvard pulled out of the program in the early 1970s, it paid MIT to take Harvard students into its ROTC unit. But in the early 1990s the status of gays in the military became a prominent national, and campus, issue. Finally in 1995 the University ended its support of Harvard students in the MIT ROTC, and the tab was picked up by an alumni group. ROTC had no officially recognized place in Harvard at the end of the century.

Over time, the political correctness of the 1970s and 1980s lost its confrontational edge. By the end of the century it had become a pervasive liberal orthodoxy. Describing the Harvard Divinity School in 1999, one professor observed:

> You try to take a pro-life position there, boy, you're dead. . . . In the old days, one was required to believe certain theological dogmas: the incarnation of God in Jesus, the Resurrection, and so on. Now the School requires that one subscribe to radical feminism, to inclusive language, to their views on homosexuality and affirmative action—there are probably more things that one has to subscribe to now than there were 50 years ago.[26]

## Internationalism

Perhaps the most distinctive feature of Harvard worldliness in the closing decades of the century was the degree to which it in fact (and not just in rhetoric) came to be an international university. This was an important part of Bok's educational vision, one in which his successor Neil Rudenstine wholeheartedly concurred. Rudenstine spoke of Harvard creating "empires of the mind" in an "increasingly internationalized, competitive, and demanding new world." Global leadership was as alluring a goal as national leadership had been in earlier decades.

Going international took a variety of forms. One was a multinational student body (especially in the professional schools). Another was the faculty and the curriculum. From the 1970s on, a number of foreign states and wealthy nationals endowed professorships in the history and/or culture of their countries, allowing FAS to boast of "unparalled breath and depth in international and area studies."[27] "Globalization" initiatives of one sort or another took hold in the professional schools. In the mid-1980s FAS dean Henry Rosovsky raised funds for a new program to enlarge the national pool of area studies specialists. By the late 1990s, Harvard had more visiting foreign scholars than any other university.

But Harvard's globalism could have unintended consequences. There were risks in honoring foreign heads of state in an unstable world, as the embarrassing honorary degree to the shah of Iran in the sixties showed. In later years Harvard gave honorary degrees to Radcliffe alumna Benazir Bhutto of Pakistan and Mexican presidents Miguel de la Madrid and Carlos Salinas, both Kennedy School graduates: awards soon sullied by the course of the recipients' careers. One China expert strove mightily to keep Overseer (and computer magnate) An Wang from securing an honorary degree for China's premier Deng Xiaoping; it was only Deng's reluctance that prevented it.

In the 1990s a Hong Kong businesswoman gave $7 million to endow a program for high-ranking Chinese military men—almost all of them, it turned out, intelligence officers—to come to the Kennedy School for short courses. The risks of institutional coziness with a state such as China were underlined in 1997 when that nation's president, Jiang Zemin, spoke at Harvard: the only university appearance in the course of the first visit by a Chinese head of state to the United States. Demonstrators put off by his regime's behavior in Tibet, at Tiananmen Square, and toward Taiwan threatened to rain on the hubris parade. Nor did it help that University authorities agreed to a scripted public meeting in which prescreened questions were fed to Jiang by the moderator of the event.

Even more embarrassing was the Harvard Institute for International Development's entanglement in a full-blown bond scandal in Russia, where two senior staff officials were fired in the wake of allegations of conflicts of interest and "activities for personal gain."[28]

## Cost and Quality

Affirmative action and political correctness were the university issues most on the minds of the Harvard community and the media during the late twentieth century. But other concerns had a larger place in the general public perception of Harvard and its peer universities. Two in particular tugged at popular heart (and purse) strings: the cost and the quality of a college education.

In 1996, 92 percent of American college students paid less than $12,000 a year for tuition; 60 percent paid less than $3,000. But in a small number of elite schools, the picture was very different. Harvard's tuition rates loped ahead of inflation, rising from $2,600 in 1970 to $22,699 in 2000–2001—close to $1,000 a week of term time. Why did tuition rise so steeply? In-house explanations dwelt on the usual suspects: escalating labor, material, and fuel costs; growth in faculty and staff; increased fringe benefits and student financial aid; higher administrative expenses, fed by such things as the rapidly rising cost of complying with government regulations: all this with no offsetting gain in productivity.[29]

But according to Duke economist Charles Clotfelter, these explanations still left almost two thirds of Harvard's tuition increases unaccounted for. The most convincing explanation, he thought, was the competitive cost of "top dogism." As in other realms of the economy, the luxury end of the higher education business was dominated by a small number of large firms, among them Harvard, Yale, Princeton, Stanford, Chicago, MIT, Cal. Tech. These elite schools engaged in fierce conflict for the best students and the best faculty, neither an abundant resource. Committed to diversity, they sought with equal fervor not cheap, and not numerous, African American applicants with demonstrated academic ability.

At the same time, the top schools found themselves besieged by a growing number of well-heeled customers. The admission of their sons and daughters to the elite schools, and particularly to Harvard, had come to have a value as outsized as the tulip mania in early seventeenth-century Holland. And they were ready to pay for the scarce good of admission on a comparable scale. This coincidence of demand (rising competitive costs) and supply (ready-to-pay parents) had predictable consequences for tuition charges.[30]

Universities—Harvard not least—also discovered that, properly cultivated, successful alumni could be induced to give on a scale matched only by the rich merchants and aristocrats of medieval and early modern times who had sought eternal absolution for their sins by large donations to Mother Church. This added to the swirl of wealth, worldliness, and self-regard that characterized late-twentieth-century Harvard. A British observer in 1980 found an ambience of competitiveness, mobility, and instability in the elite American universities that he thought differed fundamentally from Oxbridge. Even Harvard, whose "weight of both hereditary and self-made prestige is unique in America" and who "comes closest to being an establishment institution in the

British sense," had stepped up to the pit in the Great American University Barbecue.[31]

The size of Harvard, and the fact that its appeal lay most of all in what it stood for, had consequences for its students. An opinion poll conducted by the Ivy League's student newspapers found that Harvard undergraduates had the highest level of discontent with the quality of their instruction. Exposés that linked rising costs and falling pedagogy at Harvard and elsewhere became common in the early and mid-1990s. One critic took Bok to task for pooh-poohing complaints over tuition, financial aid policy, affirmative action, and modern literary theory in his last speech as Harvard's president. The fact that these matters "dominated the debate over American higher education," Bok thought, "only shows how muddled we have become about why universities truly matter to society." Not so, said his critic: the cost of higher education, how to pay for it, what to study, who was admitted and on what basis, how and what courses are taught—this was the essence of the university and fit matter for general discussion.[32]

Criticism died down in the century's last years. The bull market eased the tuition strain, and cost increases slowed (though not to parity with the cost of living). While the number of freshman slots—1,660—did not change, the number of families for whom Harvard was the summum bonum kept rising. But the tension between the new view of a worldly university as a social force, and the older but tenacious perception of the university as a more narrowly defined, ivory-towerish educational institution, was hardly likely to go away.

Harvard, like that other venerable institution the British monarchy, had an annus horribilis in 1994–95. An Ethiopian undergraduate killed her Vietnamese roommate, and then hanged herself. Several hundred freshmen succumbed to food poisoning. A Medical School professor published a book taking seriously the belief that alien invaders were abducting humans; a "publicity-crazed law professor" joined O. J. Simpson's defense team; still new president Neil Rudenstine had to take several months off to recover from exhaustion. "Is Harvard cracking up?" asked the *Economist*.

Hardly. Its faculty and students were still, all in all, the best around. Harvard's libraries remained one of the world's intellectual treasures; first-class scholarship and scientific research poured forth from its confines; the Harvard mystique continued to defy both competition and reason. "Of course," the *Economist* concluded, "it is not as good as it thinks it is. But that would be impossible."[33]

## ✌ 16 ✌

## GOVERNING

As soon as he became president, Bok set out to modernize
Harvard's central administration. His first move, recruiting a core
of professional administrators, met with universal approval. In principle
the administration simply provided services: financial, legal, health,
information technology, food, real estate, personnel, development,
government relations. But in practice this meant replacing Conant's
and Pusey's low-keyed central "holding company" with a much more
assertive, take-charge body of managers. As the number and agendas
of the new bureaucrats grew, so did the tension between the faculty and
the administration, between the more centralized direction of the University's affairs and the venerable each-tub-on-its-own-bottom
Harvard tradition.

## The Old Guardians

When Bok took office, the Harvard Corporation consisted of two
recently elected academics, Charles Slichter of Illinois and John Morton
Blum of Yale; two lawyers, Bostonian senior fellow Hooks Burr and
Hugh Calkins of Cleveland; Socony-Mobil executive Albert Nickerson
of New York; and Harvard's treasurer, State Street banker George
Bennett. By the time he left in 1991, all of them were gone, replaced by a
heterogeneous mix ranging from Boston-New York businessmen
(Gillette CEO Colman Mockler, *Time* publisher Andrew Heiskell,
venture capitalist Robert G. Stone, Jr.) to Henry Rosovsky, the Corporation's first Jewish fellow and its first Harvard faculty member since
1852, and Washington lawyer Judith Richards Hope, the first female
fellow. Brahmin Boston had no representative on the Corporation that
Bok bequeathed to his successor. During this time, too, three new

treasurers came in quick succession: George Putnam, another State Street banker; Roderick MacDougall, a Bank of New England executive; and Ronald Daniel, a former partner in the conspicuously non-Old Boston consulting firm of McKinsey and Company. Across the board, old boys gave way to non-Brahmin newcomers.

As both Harvard and its bureaucracy grew, the Corporation became more detached from the mundane realities of University governance. Streaming in from points south and west, the fellows met every two weeks on Monday mornings for a heavy schedule of reports, discussions, and meetings with the president and his chief administrative officers. When he was invited to join the Corporation in 1979, *Time*'s Heiskell could scarcely believe its lack of organization. Every other Friday the fellows received "an incredible amount of reading [material] on subjects that had not been thought through or studied or digested in any way.... [Yet] when we arrived in Cambridge for the Monday morning meeting, we were expected to discuss each item intelligently." One day in his second year he blurted out: "I'm sick and tired of being tossed a bowl of untreated sewage to consider for the next meeting." That declaration produced results. The Corporation's agenda was revamped so that it could systematically review Harvard's schools and administrative units. An hour was set aside at each meeting for discussion of more immediate problems.[1]

The Corporation came to resemble a company board of directors. It retained the authority to select presidents, and what McGeorge Bundy called the "Queen's rights to warn, advise, delay, say no." But without direct knowledge of the issues, the fellows found it difficult to evaluate the reports that came before them. They clung tenaciously to their fiduciary authority, especially their control of Harvard's endowment policies. Here as much as anywhere, the traditions of Brahmin Harvard persisted. The fellows consistently favored the interests of future generations over current academic needs; or, as Bundy more pungently put it, "[protected] the Treasurer against the goddam greedy Deans."[2]

The Board of Overseers, Harvard's other governing body, met about five times a year. It groused its way through the pro forma confirmation of Corporation selections of the new president and new fellows, gave advice to Bok (who by no means always took it), and ran visiting committees to Harvard's schools and administrative departments (which by no means always welcomed them). Heiskell had served on the board for six years before joining the Corporation. He found the Overseers dysfunctional in a different way: "They spent a lot of time arguing.... Instead of talking and thinking about what's good for Harvard, they talked and thought about 'the woman issue at Harvard,' or whatever their favorite issue was." Heiskell feared that the board was "underpowered" to raise the money that Harvard would need in the future. He wanted candidates who were more disciplined, preferably "businessmen, first because we needed them for the capital campaign, and second because they were trained to operate in a committee structure. Most of them had been on lots of boards, so they didn't take advantage of being elected to the Overseers by expressing every view in the world."

The Overseers set up a committee in 1975 to consider that body's future—or if it had any. According to Heiskell, "Several members ... seriously questioned whether the Board ... performed useful enough functions to justify its continued existence. Some said their concern came from a sense of lack of purpose in their own service. Others believed that they were not sufficiently involved in active decision making. Others simply thought that they were part of a cumbersome and ineffective group." Acknowledging that "there is no ideal form" of governance, he decided that in principle the Overseers provided an important "check against self-perpetuity and unlimited control" by the Corporation. Besides, any major change in Harvard governance would require either legislation or an amendment to the state constitution. Harvard's leaders were not about to invite the Massachusetts legislature to get its nose inside their tent.[3]

Heiskell's businessman board was not to be; the cultural currents of late-twentieth-century Harvard ran against it. When the overseers dined in the White House with fellow member John F. Kennedy in 1963, theirs was an all-white, all-male body. Seven were financiers, eleven were in business and industry, four were eminent lawyers. Kennedy himself was a new boy in the company of an Adams, a Cabot, a Saltonstall, and a Rockefeller. With the election of Clifford Alexander (the first African American overseer) in 1969 and Radcliffe trustee Helen Gilbert in 1970, the makeup of the board began to change. In 1970, the Committee of Concerned Alumni (CCA) announced that it would run Terry Lenzner, a Washington lawyer and former football captain, as a candidate favoring "socially responsible" investment policies. He was elected. A year later the CCA asked all overseer candidates to say what they hoped to accomplish, and it endorsed three, one of them African American and one a woman, who replied to the query.[4]

By 1977 no overseer came from banking or finance and only three from business. Nine were educators, six were lawyers, four worked in government. There were three blacks, seven women, and four were under the age of forty. No officially nominated woman or black was turned down by the alumni electorate, while prominent business executives and financiers, as well as past presidents of the Alumni Association, frequently failed to place among the top vote getters.

During the late 1980s, the divestment of stock in American companies doing business in South Africa was a rallying cry for politically active alumni as well as undergraduates. Between 1986 and 1991, a cascade of twenty-seven (mainly prodivestment) petition candidates ran for overseer, and four got elected. As Bok struggled to explain his position on divestment to student and alumni critics, communication with the Board of Overseers effectively broke down. According to Heiskell, Bok found the group "unruly and indiscreet." He thought that the president "would happily have disbanded the body" if it had been possible. But with the end of apartheid, the divestment issue subsided, and so did the overseers' agitation.[5]

## Building Up: The Central Administration

John Dunlop, dean of the Faculty of Arts and Sciences from July 1970 to February 1973, thought that the most significant element in Harvard's transition from the 1960s to the 1970s was not the student takeover of University Hall, but the institutional changes unleashed by that event. Dunlop was ideally suited to take charge in the confusing post-bust period. Forceful, self-confident, canny, he became the czar of the interregnum. He sought to restore civil discourse by engaging the faculty in institutional reform. He chaired the University Committee on Governance that Pusey and the Corporation set up in September 1969. From it came a flow of subcommittee reports: on Harvard and money, faculty and student rights and responsibilities, the presidential selection process, the nature and purposes of the University, and the organization and functions of the Governing Boards and the president's office.[6]

The committee found a Corporation and a president overwhelmed by day-to-day problems. It proposed that there be vice presidents of finance, administration, development, and government and community affairs, and that a senior academic officer—a chancellor or provost—foster interfaculty programs and speak for the president on matters of educational policy. The authors knew that "[d]enigration of the administrative function is so pervasive in the University that the sudden assertion of its importance ... may send shock waves through the community and cause particular concern among Deans." But they believed that it was essential "to staff and perform properly the neglected [service] functions" of the University.[7]

Derek Bok decided that to plunge at once into centralized administration was "too much." He agreed on the need for a passel of new vice presidents, but was well aware of the powerful Harvard tradition of autonomous schools and faculties led by baronial deans. (He had been one himself.) While he had favored the appointment of a provost before he took office, now he had second thoughts. The major responsibility of most university provosts was budgetary: deciding how the financial pie should be sliced. That would reduce the authority of the deans. Even less attractive was the notion of having a provost to deal with educational and academic matters; Bok intended to do that himself.

At the same time he was a strong believer in professional expertise. This meant breaking away from Harvard's tradition of administrators whose qualifications consisted in good part of having gone to the College and having close Harvard ties. Bok sought a different type of bureaucrat, of the sort prevalent at other large universities: professionals with outside experience.[8]

Financial Vice President Hale Champion was Bok's most important initial appointee. Champion's background typified the varied, high-powered, conspicuously non-Harvard careers of the new generation of administrators. He started out as a journalist and became California governor Pat Brown's chief of finance in 1960, taking charge of the state's budgets (including that of the University of California), taxes, and personnel. Then he briefly headed the Boston Redevelopment Authority under Mayor Kevin White, and in 1969 went to the University of Minnesota to be vice president for finance and administration. It was there that Bok found him.

Stephen Hall became vice president for administration, with a mandate to streamline the University's service operations and reduce costs. He had worked for thirteen years as an executive at the Sheraton hotel chain, where he was "a whiz at sophisticated management and cost-control procedures." The rationale for Hall's appointment was unassailable: here was someone whose real-world experience was highly relevant to the task at hand.

During Hall's vice presidency the harsh economic environment of high inflation and budget deficits strained his working relations with the faculties. They complained of rising assessments by a central administration that seemed more ready to spend money on buildings and grounds than on teachers. The deans wanted "an atmosphere in which before the fact consultation on major changes of policy and procedure

could take place." To make matters worse, Hall had an abrasive personality and an in-your-face management style. He reinforced his
reputation as a hard-nosed moneyman when he forced out Harvard
University Press director Mark Carroll, whose relaxed oversight had
contributed to a substantial budget deficit. Convinced that Harvard's
standards for constructing new buildings were "stodgy, costly and time
consuming," Hall rejected the "gold-plating" style when it came time to
build an additional freshman dorm in 1973 and instead endorsed a new
"fast-track" construction technique. Predictably, design and construction
flaws appeared in pace with steadily rising building costs. Hall left the
University in June 1976, followed by the more academically politic Joe B.
Wyatt, who had run Harvard's Office of Information Technology (OIT)
and later became chancellor of Vanderbilt University.[9]

Charles Daly joined Bok's staff in the fall of 1971 to take charge of
government and community relations, after five years of doing the same
job at the University of Chicago. Bok was attracted by Daly's tough,
earthy Irish style (barely tempered by a Yale B.A.) and by a richly varied
career in business, journalism, and Democratic politics. Daly set out to
smarten up the University's news and information services, enlarge its
Washington lobbying presence, and mend fences with community
groups opposed to Harvard's constant physical expansion.

But one important project—to build the Kennedy Library and
Museum adjacent to the JFK School of Government—went awry in the
fall of 1975. Construction delays nourished by community concern over
the library's threat to some cherished adjacent sycamores led the
Kennedy family to switch to a site on Boston harbor. Daly, whose
patience with academics was far from limitless, left the University in
June 1976. His successors, recruited for the most part from the world of
Washington politics, continued to be frustrated by the lack of fit
between their aspirations to shape Harvard's public policies and the reality of a decentralized institution with no single voice.

Chase Peterson became vice president for development and alumni
relations in 1972. A graduate of Harvard College and the Medical
School, he had been dean of admissions since 1967 and was a known
quantity with wide contacts among alumni and within the University.
But Peterson chose to be a bigger fish in a smaller pond when the
opportunity arose. He went off to be vice president for health sciences
at the University of Utah in 1978, leaving behind an expanded fund-
raising operation. Peterson's deft successor, Fred Glimp (also a Harvard
B.A. and Ph.D., and a former dean of admissions and dean of
Harvard College), continued the work of making the development

office a top-notch professional organization. It is not surprising that development, one of the more successful units of Harvard's new administrative structure, was led by graduates of the College with close ties to faculty and alumni.

General Counsel Daniel Steiner had been hired by Pusey at the insistence of lawyers on the Corporation who thought that the University needed someone in-house to keep track of its legal problems. Pusey's notion, Steiner recalled, was that "lawyers are like plumbers: when a pipe is broken, you need someone to fix it, but you are not going to ask your plumber to go into your room and design it." Under fellow lawyer Bok, Steiner's role changed. He became for a time the president's closest and most influential administrative colleague, and the crisis manager during much of his term in office. As in the case of the heads of development, Steiner's effectiveness was strengthened by links to Harvard faculty dating back to his undergraduate days in Eliot House.[10]

The professionalization of Harvard's administration did not go smoothly. By 1978 all of Bok's original vice presidents had left, an attrition rate unheard of in pre-1970 days. In the fall of 1974, Assistant Vice President for Public Affairs Robin Schmidt (every vice president quickly had an assistant vice president) warned his boss Charles Daly that the faculty's negative perception of "the Mass. Hall gang" [the vice presidents] was a growing problem. They regarded the administration as "too corporate," too numerous, and responsible for "the shrinking $ for academic pursuits." The professors were put off by the fact that the new managers were "non-College. Worse yet, they are also non-Harvard. What greater sin could one commit in Lilliputia?" It was imperative to find ways to "move the Administration closer to the faculty—particularly in the Faculty of Arts and Sciences."[11]

Bok gave his vice presidents a great deal of independence. They were the experts, and he left it to them to do their jobs as they saw fit. It all made good sense from the vantage point of current managerial ideas. But Harvard was "a confederation of semi-independent baronies, squirearchies, and small farms," with a hoary academic culture that did not take well to modern managerial theory. Harvard U., it appeared, was not quite ready to be run as though it were Harvard, Inc.[12]

## Managing and Making Money

New style or old, Harvard's post-1970 managers had to worry about money management most of all. Over the course of the next quarter of a century, meeting the costs, overseeing the budgets, and raising more money for an expensively expanding University was their top priority.

The Dunlop Committee's 1970 report on *Harvard and Money* warned:

> the new president is likely to face severe financial difficulties. Relative to widely felt needs, money has been scarce all along. It is likely to become a good deal scarcer. In the next decade, Harvard's governing institutions will face hard decisions about what activities are to stand still, or shrink, or even disappear. That will certainly be the case if the University is to undertake new ventures that are not popular enough to finance themselves.

A stagnant stock market in the 1970s, high and persisting inflation, declining federal support, and lackluster alumni giving darkened the Harvard financial picture. But Financial Vice President Hale Champion worried as much about the internal "financial maze" that greeted him on his arrival. Treasurer George F. Bennett wore several hats: he was the University's chief financial officer, a fellow of the Corporation, and a managing partner of State Street Research and Management Company, which invested the Harvard endowment. Apart from the potential for conflicts of interest was the problem that the Treasurer worked out of his Boston office and visited Cambridge only when it was necessary. Like his predecessor Paul Cabot, under whom he served as deputy treasurer from 1948 to 1965, Bennett was "a rugged individualist" and a plain-spoken man. The University changed greatly during his years in office; the same could not be said of him. He believed that corporations (including Harvard) were responsible only to their employees, customers, and shareholders, and he did not share the public-spiritedness of his "more liberal" colleagues. Increasingly out of tune with the new Harvard, he resigned in the fall of 1972. Not all was flux: his successor was Old Bostonian George Putnam, a great-nephew of A. Lawrence Lowell and cousin of McGeorge Bundy.[13]

At the same time there was a major change in the management of Harvard's endowment. The Harvard Management Company (HMC), a wholly owned subsidiary, was created in 1974 to "provide total returns that are competitive with those earned by other leading universities." Bennett in fact recommended this plan, and Putnam endorsed it. The company was charged to invest Harvard's endowment in a manner appropriate to its size and the complexity of modern financial markets. Quartered in the treasurer's offices at 70 Federal Street, HMC employed "a small, balanced team of highly competent investment professionals" to handle the bulk of the endowment. Five outside firms—"satellites" with differing investment approaches—were given modest chunks to manage. (Up-and-coming Boston-based Fidelity Investments was not one of them, which raised an eyebrow or two.) They were expected to feed information and "strategy inputs" to the Harvard Management Company. Financial vice president Champion liked the idea of having complementary but competing players in the Harvard investment game.[14]

But more than the dregs of old Harvard wine remained in the new financial management bottle. Walter M. Cabot, a nephew of former Treasurer Paul Cabot, was chosen to head HMC. He in turn recruited eight other partners for the "team," mostly Harvard M.B.A.s and/or bright lights in Boston investment banks and companies. The company showed no lack of boldness and imagination in its investment policies. By 1995 it was "knee-deep in derivatives," private equity, venture capital funds, and other exotic flora of the investment rain forest, and during its first decade alone it grew from nine to a hundred professionals. Its performance was strong enough to keep Harvard's endowment growth well ahead of inflation, match or better its major university competitors, and (except for an occasional misstep) successfully navigate an ever more complex investment world.[15]

By 2000 Harvard's endowment had reached a staggering $19.2 billion, far beyond that of any other university. Yale Law School professor Henry Hansmann, trying to answer the question "Why Do Universities Have Endowments?" concluded in 1990 that from the "peculiar perspective" of trustees, having a large and growing endowment was an end in itself. Certainly that seemed to be the case at Harvard. The average distribution rate to the faculties between 1971 and 1996 was a super-prudent 4.6 percent, leaving plenty to plow back into endowment. With a few exceptions, the Corporation resisted any significant use of the burgeoning endowment to allow for heavier investment in faculty or other academic needs. Only in the superflush years at the century's end did it loosen up a bit.[16]

The returns of the heady bull market of the 1990s fattened the income of the Harvard Management Company's senior managers, which led to some faculty grousing. Those more familiar with professional money management did not find their compensation out of line. Of more concern was the opacity of HMC's annual reports, and its penchant for leveraging, in particular, borrowing large sums on the basis of Harvard's triple-A credit rating in order to exploit tiny mispricings in bonds and equities. One critic worried that HMC was too "caught up in the short term relative performance game versus its peers."[17]

When he became the University's chief financial manager in 1971, Hale Champion found that while there was a gap between income and expenses in Harvard's overall budget, it was small. He concluded that sophisticated money management was more important than increasing the endowment. And he wanted greater financial transparency, in response to faculty criticism that the treasurer's reports

> are so complicated, and so devoid of any explanation of broad policy, that anyone not regularly a party to the management of Harvard's portfolio would find it exceedingly difficult to evaluate the results. No information is given that would reveal the guidelines that inform choices, the trade-offs made between present and future, among yield and growth and risk and liquidity. Anyone interested in the underlying policies can only guess at them by inference.[18]

A big step forward in managing Harvard's money more efficiently was taken in 1970, when all endowment funds were pooled into a single account, the General Investment Account, and proportionate unit shares were reassigned to the faculties. Of even more significance was the creation in 1973 of the General Operating Account (GOA), Champion's major contribution to Harvard money management. The GOA was essentially a central bank, which had the exclusive right to receive, manage, and set interest rates on deposits (from tuition and other income) made by faculties and other units, invest working capital, make loans, and arrange financing for major capital projects. This was in stark contrast to the previous system, in which each faculty managed its own cash balances.

One estimate is that by the tighter control of cash balances alone Harvard added some $428 million of value to its resources between 1973 and 1996. Beginning at ground zero in 1973, the net assets of the GOA grew to $2.72 billion by 1999. Income that was not turned over to the faculties was set aside for subsequent use by the central administration "for general University purposes." Champion expected that as the bank's balance grew, the president's growing command of resources would enable him "to do things."

Another target of financial opportunity was tax-exempt, government-underwritten money for campus construction, in particular, the Massachusetts Health and Educational Facilities Authority's (HEFA) bonds, established in 1968. Champion shrewdly made the case for financing capital construction without tapping internal funds. (Driven by moral anguish and/or a Brahmin sense of propriety, Treasurer George Bennett is said to have left the Corporation meeting room when Champion outlined his plan.) Bonds for $12.5 million were issued in November 1972 to pay for a couple of campus garages, a refrigeration plant, and a housing facility. That was only the beginning. By 1986 Harvard had issued more than $782 million in HEFA bonds, in large part to meet the escalating costs of its Medical Area Total Energy Plant (MATEP). This provoked Congress to pass a tax reform act that capped at $150 million the amount of tax-exempt debt a private college or university could hold at one time. Nevertheless by 1996 the University's total bond indebtedness reached a high point of $1.25 billion, substantially larger than that of any other university. More than 60 percent of it was in tax-exempt bonds acquired before the congressional restriction.[19]

Innovative money management by itself could not meet the steadily escalating costs of worldly late-twentieth-century Harvard. Constant, large-scale fund-raising became a categorical imperative. That required new levels of organization and solicitation. What made Harvard fund-raising work beyond anyone's expectation were the effectiveness of its development operation, the iconic status of the University, and the bull market of the 1990s.

Harvard's fund-raising apparatus in 1971 consisted primarily of development offices attached to the central administration and to each of the major schools, except for the Faculty of Arts and Sciences, which imposed few restraints on faculty members who sought out gifts for particular activities or programs. Taken together, the number of people and the size of budgets devoted to fund-raising were large. But to one observer, the aggregation seemed like "a collection of retail grocers." The growth rate of annual giving to Harvard declined between 1964 and 1973, and a rash of small, project-oriented minicampaigns from 1973 to 1978 had disappointing results. A consolidated fund-raising operation in the University's development office became an increasingly attractive option. But the venerable each-tub-on-its-own-bottom Harvard tradition was a strong counterweight.

Pressure for a fund drive to aid the Faculty of Arts and Sciences began to build in the mid-1970s. Arts and Sciences was running deficits, and its unrestricted reserves were dwindling. Bok and his aides proceeded methodically through the requisite stages of planning and preparation, but FAS dean Henry Rosovsky barely contained his eagerness to wade into the five-year campaign launched in 1979. As with Pusey's Program for Harvard College twenty years before, the centerpiece would be the College, whose alumni were the biggest potential donors. The main purpose of the campaign was to "halt erosion in faculty salaries" (which declined 17 percent in real terms between 1970 and 1980) "and to ensure that the College remains accessible to students from all economic levels of society." Rosovsky wanted to raise unrestricted funds for his faculty's perennial needs. But many feared that underpinning existing activities was not sufficiently glamorous to attract major gifts. That, plus Bok's natural caution, capped the goal at $250 million—still the most ambitious campaign of any university to that time.[20]

In the past, major gift solicitations were handled directly by the office of the president. Now the work of identifying, rating, tracking, and cultivating major donors was in the hands of professionals in the University's development office. Working with the Harvard Alumni Association, development assembled a volunteer force of some five thousand alumni and friends across the country. The campaign wound up with 385 gifts of $100,000 plus, which accounted for 58 percent of the total raised; eighty-two donors gave $1 million or more.

The campaign met its target in three years—whereupon the goal was lifted to $350 million, to absorb the impact of higher than expected inflation and reductions in federal aid to education. Rosovsky proved to be a powerhouse fund-raiser. His appointment as dean in 1973 was widely celebrated in the Jewish community. In the course of the campaign, he became a bridge to wealthy Jewish alumni: younger real estate developers and financial magnates, as well as older German Jewish graduates.[21]

For all this, inflation and a lackluster stock market reduced endowment income to a low of 18.1 percent of Harvard's total revenue in the mid-1980s. This meant that tuition, the only discretionary source of income, had to fill the breach. Planning for a new campaign began before the previous one was cold. A study showed that despite Harvard's deep donor pool, the growth rate of its gift income lagged behind other institutions. To be sure, Harvard had raised more money than anyone else in eighteen of the twenty years between 1968 and 1987. But its major competitors were closing the gap, and Stanford and Cornell attracted a larger number, and size, of gifts over a million dollars.

Estimates suggested that the University would need to raise more than $3 billion between 1988 and 1997 to keep up endowment income and meet new teaching and research needs. That was a sobering sum. Senior development officers believed they would be lucky to raise half that amount—if fund-raising persisted in its current form. Meanwhile, other Harvard schools sidelined by the FAS campaign strained at their leashes. Three new school-based drives had been authorized; five more were in the making.

What to do?

Development officials Fred Glimp and Thomas Reardon came up with some radical recommendations to the Corporation in the fall of 1988. They argued that Harvard's decentralized mode of fund-raising, based on the principle that each school "owned" its alumni, badly under-utilized the donor pool. Encouraging potential donors to focus on limited school needs rather than on larger and more varied University purposes lowered their sights. Fund-raisers should not ask "who can we get to give the Law building," but "what will motivate Mr. Smith to make a $10 million gift."

Persuaded by this argument, Bok assembled the deans of Business, Medicine, Law, and Arts and Sciences—the schools most likely to believe that they had something to lose from a more centralized mode of fundraising—to discuss the proposed strategy and how it would work in practice. He assured them that they would exercise continuing oversight when it came to identifying and allocating prospective donors. And they could reserve some top donors and key volunteers for themselves. The point of the new strategy was not to take donors away from the schools, but to identify those with philanthropic interests that extended to other parts of the University as well. Business School dean John McArthur, widely viewed as the most ardent practitioner of school autonomy, broke the ice in 1990 by inviting the deans of the smaller schools—Education, Divinity, Public Health, and Design—to lunch with wealthy Business School alumni who had an interest in those areas.

Harvard's first University-wide campaign began to take shape. The scale of preparation, and the intensity of donor involvement, had to be up to a multibillion dollar fund-raising goal. Social mixing among wealthy and well-connected alumni, as well as between these alumni and University officials, was always a vital ingredient in fund-raising. In what came to be called "Bok weekends," selected alumni were invited to campus with their spouses to hear faculty members discuss pressing political, economic, or scientific issues of the day. And the president and a dean or two reported on important Harvard academic or administrative concerns. High-mindedness was tempered by luncheons, dinners, concerts, football games, and general socializing. The (correct) assumption: "whether involvement is formal or informal, whenever people come together to talk about Harvard—whether at a football game, a dinner, or a Bok Weekend—the interests of the University are advanced."[22]

Development officers were eager to get on with the campaign. But some of the deans dragged their feet. Harvard, they thought, should invest more in human and physical resources, and less in the build-up of its endowment. Endowment policy, they complained, placed a higher value on future uncertainty than on immediate good. The departure of FAS dean Michael Spence in 1990 and of Bok himself in 1991 further delayed things, until May 1994. That gave new president Neil Rudenstine time to put his own stamp on the effort. Rudenstine's years as provost at Princeton had schooled him in university-wide fund-raising. He soothed the distrustful deans by getting the Corporation to cover their fund-raising costs with a one-shot increase in endowment payout. And he saw in the campaign an opportunity to foster one of his pet objectives: closer collaboration among Harvard's faculties.

The University Campaign, as it was called, set a target of $2.1 billion. Almost half of this was devoted to the College and the Faculty of Arts and Sciences. The Medical and Business Schools were in for 10 percent each; 12 percent was designated for a first-ever "President's University Fund" to be used at the president's discretion.

One problem: how to justify so large a campaign goal, given Harvard's existing head-of-its-class endowment of $5.8 billion. Campaign literature stressed Harvard's size (more students than Yale, Princeton, and Amherst combined) and the sheer range of its activities. Princeton, Rice, and Cal. Tech. had more endowment per student; endowment income covered less than a fifth of operating expenses, and much of it was committed to existing activities, leaving little for new initiatives.

What no one foresaw was the stock market boom of the late 1990s. Under the chairmanship of Corporation fellow Robert Stone, the campaign raised more than $1 million a day and overshot its goal by $500 million, reaching $2.6 billion when it ended in December 1999. No doubt the strategy and structure of the University Campaign lifted donors' sights. And no doubt the sheer number of successful alumni, the irrepressible stock market, supportive tax laws, the cultivation of new constituencies (women, West Coast, and foreign alumni; young millionaires) and the culture of elite philanthropy so well understood by Harvard's fund-raisers made it all possible.

But less tangible factors mattered too—a lot. "Don't join too many gangs," wrote Robert Frost; "Join few if any. /Join the United States and join the family—/But not much in between unless a college." In 1995 John L. Loeb '24 gave the campaign $70.5 million, the bulk of his remaining assets and the largest gift Harvard had ever received. He said that it was "an easy decision." He had served on more than a dozen

Overseers' visiting committees, worked on or led several fund-raising campaigns, knew four of the University's presidents well enough to "speak of his friendships with them with affection," and "fell in love with Harvard over the years." He supported other charitable causes, but "[i]n my old age it occurred to me that we [he and his wife Frances Lehman Loeb] could make a difference to our country, and do it with an institution that had staying power and that I was familiar with."[23]

Harvard is hardly unique in its ability to tap such sentiments. But it has been in the game longer than anyone else and has the largest alumni body among the nation's elite schools. And because it was relatively more open to Jews, it capitalized on the material success and philanthropic impulses of that group (as Stanford has benefited from its ties to Silicon Valley entrepreneurs). That out of it all came more than two and a half billion dollars was eloquent testimony to Harvard's iconic place in American life at the close of the twentieth century.

## MATEP

When it came to managing and making money, Harvard's new central administration was a smashing success. But in other realms of governance, top-down management could have calamitous consequences. The most ambitious, expensive, and trouble-plagued venture of worldly Harvard's new central administration was the Medical Area Total Energy Plant (MATEP).

An old generating plant had provided steam (for heat) and chilled water (for cooling) to the Medical School and its affiliated hospitals since 1906. By the late 1960s it was sadly inadequate to the demands placed upon it. Then oil prices took off in the early 1970s, raising the threat of a protracted energy shortage. Vice President for Administration Stephen Hall believed that the medical area could cut its energy costs by a third if a new plant incorporated the newly fashionable process of cogeneration: reusing its steam and other exhaust products to produce electricity as well. Financial Vice President Hale Champion asked Boston Edison, the medical area's electricity supplier, to join Harvard in building the new facility. The utility said no; it was too busy constructing a nuclear power plant. But the appeal of cutting costs and finding a long-term solution to the medical area's problems was irresistible. So, too, was the lure of a large project to Champion, who like other vice presidents felt constrained by Harvard's federalist system of autonomous schools.[24]

The initial price tag of $50 million for the new plant was more than Harvard had ever spent on a construction project. But an anticipated annual savings of $2 million was an attractive prospect in the straitened days of the early 1970s. Derek Bok supported it, and the Corporation swung into line. Then the engineering firm advising on the project gave Harvard a cost projection more than twice as much as the original estimate. Champion fumed, argued with Hall, who managed the project, and called for a new team to build the plant. Philadelphia-based United Engineers and Constructors, a Raytheon subsidiary, took over construction. Time passed and costs kept rising. The project, slated to take two years, was to begin in November 1976. In the same month Champion was asked to be undersecretary of Health, Education, and Welfare in the newly elected Carter administration. Before leaving he tried to put a cap on MATEP costs by hiring a firm to supervise the work of the construction company. According to Champion, once he was gone someone decided that the watchdog operation was unnecessary, and "excess costs inevitably followed."[25]

Construction began with all permits in hand save the one certifying that MATEP would not cause pollution. Champion maintained that there "never was a health hazard." But many outsiders believed otherwise. In the fall of 1977 a citizens' group in the affluent adjacent town of Brookline charged that the plant's stack emissions would threaten the public's health. Neighborhood activists followed up with a coalition bearing the snappy acronym NOMATEP: Neighborhood Organizations Mobilized Against the Total Energy Plant. In late 1977 the state Department of Environmental Quality Engineering (DEQE) allowed the project to proceed with its steam and chilled water components, but not electricity cogeneration. A court injunction reinforced that decision. By this time the anticipated cost of MATEP had risen to $130 million.

Further DEQE hearings failed to overturn the initial ruling. Meanwhile additional construction and financing costs pushed MATEP's estimated bill to $180 million, to say nothing of legal and consulting fees. And it wasn't over yet. Overseer Andrew Heiskell later remembered that the "horror" called MATEP "was happening at the same time we were starting a massive capital campaign. If you are in a capital drive, you need a good reputation for handling your finances, because nobody likes to give money to an institution that is financially irresponsible.... While we were raising tons of money for the university, we were trying to drape dark blankets over the cogeneration plant so that nobody could see it."[26]

Joe Wyatt, Stephen Hall's successor as vice president for administration, took over the management of MATEP in the spring of 1979. But the stranglehold of rising costs and diminishing revenue prospects did not loosen. In 1979–80, 39 percent of the University's general operating account was used for temporary advances to finance construction. Though the plant began to produce steam and chilled water in July 1980, it was not fully operational until 1985, by which time its cost had topped $350 million—the same amount raised in Harvard's 1979–84 fund drive.

The University sought to off-load the financing of MATEP through leveraged leasing. It would transfer ownership to a bank or lending company, which would then lease it back to the Medical Area Service Corporation (MASCO), a consortium of MATEP consumers that included the area's hospitals, research centers, and the Harvard schools of Medicine, Public Health, and Dentistry. After negotiations with Citicorp and the Commercial Union Assurance Companies fell through, a subsidiary of Household Finance Corporation showed interest. But the scheme collapsed in the spring of 1980 when spiraling interest rates threatened to add significantly to the cost of financing MATEP. Then George Siguler, a young financial strategist working for the Harvard Management Company, came up with the notion of using the state's HEFA bonds to help pay the MATEP bill. He and Thomas O'Brien, Champion's successor as vice president for finance, worked out a scheme enabling them in 1983 to sell $350 million worth of bonds with a coupon three points below market.[27]

But the end was not yet in sight. When MATEP came on-line, the affiliated hospitals insisted on thirty-five-year contracts guaranteeing that they pay no more for their electricity than they would to the local public utility. This was significantly below MATEP's funding and operating costs. "Internal" users—the University's Schools of Medicine, Public Health, and Dentistry—were no more helpful; they lined up with their hospital colleagues on the rate issue.

MATEP produced revenues above operating costs: over $14 million by 1996–97. But that was not enough to service the project's massive debt; its net cash loss in that year alone was $10.7 million. The saga finally came to an end in 1998, when the plant—by now in need of major repairs—was sold to Commonwealth Energy Systems of Cambridge for $147 million. Taking into account construction, annual outflows, and foregone opportunity costs to other parts of the University incurred by the demands of MATEP financing, the venture appears to have cost Harvard somewhere between $350 and $515 million.

On the plus side, cogeneration did reduce oil consumption. But MATEP had been a risky venture from the beginning. *Harvard Magazine* reported that "in Boston boardrooms, MATEP has been held up as a prize example of academic arrogance and naiveté—a painful lesson for a university that took an unjustified risk." And former Treasurer George Putnam publicly commented (to the fury of Corporation fellow Hooks Burr): "I really didn't believe Harvard should be in the power business. If anyone had asked me, I would have said so. Nobody asked me." For at least a decade, MATEP cast a large shadow over Harvard's finances and administration. The Corporation devoted an inordinate amount of time to the project; Bok at one point thought that his presidency was at risk because of it.[28]

## There Once Was a Union Maid . . .

Harvard's administration faced another unsettling challenge on a very different front. District 65, a small left-wing New York City-based trade union, tried to organize the clerical workers and technicians at the Schools of Medicine and Public Health in the 1970s. But general counsel Daniel Steiner and associate general counsel for labor relations Edward Powers blocked these efforts. They claimed that any union should be University-wide, and in 1984 the National Labor Relations Board upheld that view. The ruling posed seemingly insurmountable obstacles to labor organizers: Harvard had about thirty-four hundred service workers scattered over a wide range of jobs, geographical locations and workplace cultures; 83 percent were women; the turnover rate was 25 percent a year.

Nevertheless Kristine Rondeau, a Medical School lab assistant, got together with a group of like-minded friends to form the Harvard Union of Clerical and Technical Workers (HUCTW). From 1987 on they had significant financial help from the American Federation of State, County, and Municipal Employees. But what really brought HUCTW to its May 1988 election victory was the combination of a tough-minded leader with a clever strategic plan, and a disunited and ineffective management response.

Rondeau's people worked the hallways and offices of Harvard's campus, getting to know the employees and what they did. HUCTW's slogan, "it's not anti-Harvard to be pro-Union," was designed to multiply, not divide, loyalties and to signify that this was unionism with a different voice. Rondeau wanted women to learn "self-representation skills"; her theme was "cooperation, not confrontation." The senior administrators who dealt with the union appear not to have appreciated how appealing to an increasingly well-educated female workforce was its emphasis on issues such as flexible working conditions, day care, less demeaning treatment by supervisors, and careers in lieu of jobs. The union's goals of "dignity, respect, and participation" were difficult to argue with.[29]

The administration's approach was to see to it that employees received sufficient information to make their own "intelligent judgments" about the issues and to rely on devices such as its ninety-seven page "Briefing Book for Managers and Supervisors." Attorney Anne Taylor, recruited from the general counsel's office to develop the campaign against the union, later observed: "Kris [Rondeau] and her folks knew us better than we did. We didn't know our employees in this huge, decentralized place. They organized employees that we didn't know existed."[30]

Sympathetic press coverage, endorsements by public figures, pro-union delegations paying calls on Harvard's president, and student-faculty petitions strengthened the union's hand. The result: a 55-vote victory (1,530 for, 1,485 against) in May 1988: a tribute to the union's organizing skills, the administration's mistakes, and (in its closeness) to the still-strong identification of many employees with the University. Bok vetoed suggestions that the close result be contested in court and recognized the union.

The administration had been so confident of victory that no labor relations professional was on hand to bargain over a labor contract. Bok recruited Economics professor and former FAS dean John Dunlop as the University's negotiator. Both sides wanted "fewer work rules, more involvement and discussion." The meat-and-potatoes terms of the contract—salary increases of 16 percent over three years, improved pensions, and a major hike in Harvard's contribution to health care plans—were sufficient to buy labor peace for years to come.

Dunlop was inclined to be openhanded in part because of his distaste for the escalating number and compensation of Harvard's professional managers. He wanted the white-collar workers that Rondeau represented to have a larger role in Harvard's management. But the bureaucratic clock ticked on. Growth in the number of managers continued to outstrip that of clerical and technical workers. Between 1993 and 1999 the former increased by 36.3 percent, the latter by 4.5 percent.[31]

## The Faculty Provoked

The struggles with MATEP and the union battle only marginally engaged the faculty. But when issues arose that more directly touched on their academic interests and prerogatives, the professors were heard from. One such was Harvard's "gene-splicing affair" in 1980. Until the mid-seventies, the University had a hands-off attitude toward its staff's discoveries, except for requiring that those affecting public health be used only for the public's benefit. But pressure for the speedy transfer of technology to industry led to the appointment of the Committee on Patents and Copyrights to oversee the process. It relied on three broad principles: that "ideas or creative works produced at the University should be used for the greatest possible public benefit"; that "the traditional rights of scholars ... to the products of their intellectual endeavors" should be protected; and that when University money, facilities, or equipment was used "for the development of ideas or the production of works, it is reasonable for the University to participate in the fruits of the enterprise ... if such ideas or works are introduced commercially."[32]

In 1978, when relatively few universities focused on technology transfer, the committee took up the case of biochemistry professor Mark Ptashne, who had found an economical way of using recombinant DNA techniques to extract or synthesize proteins. Ptashne was not initially interested in the commercial potential of his work; the most the committee could do was to get him to file a patent application. Then Business Development Services, General Electric's venture capital unit, approached Ptashne to set up a joint-venture company to support his research and work on commercial applications. Ptashne turned the matter over to Associate Dean Henry Meadow of the Medical School. Meadow and the Harvard Management Company saw the potential economic value of the new technology. Business School dean John McArthur among others warned that the odds were very high against a DNA company striking it rich. And he was disturbed by the likely diversion of time and energy from the University's main tasks of research and teaching.

But HMC officials insisted that their experience in the world of venture capitalism qualified them to participate in ongoing discussions. In the spring of 1980, Bok asked general counsel Daniel Steiner and Harvard Management Company head Walter Cabot to form the Ad Hoc Committee on Recombinant DNA. It proposed that a company based on Ptashne's research be created. The University's partners would provide capital and management capability; the University would have "some voting control, a present or future equity interest, and significant guaranteed research support for Dr. Ptashne." It foresaw no problem with respect to freedom of publication and scholarly communication, nor any other conflict with University policy.

Many FAS scientists were exercised over this new Harvard worldliness. Should the University invest in one faculty member and not another? Would such arrangements affect the appointment process? Would graduate students be encouraged to do research of commercial rather than scientific value or be attracted to work with certain professors because of employment prospects? Would business considerations lead to secrecy, divert professors from academic duties, affect the faculty's ability to speak to public issues as impartial experts? In the face of these concerns, Bok had no choice but to pull back. He took Harvard out of the Ptashne project in the fall of 1980 and returned jurisdiction over technology transfer to Harvard's old in-house patent office. Ptashne joined a group of private investors to found Genetics Institute, which became a successful biotechnology company. In 1983 the Faculty of Arts and Sciences adopted the Guidelines for Research Projects Undertaken in Cooperation with Industry. These were far more stringent (especially regarding the acceptance of confidential information) than those at most other universities.[33]

Bok's central staff was bold and imaginative when it came to making and saving money. But its remoteness from the academic life of the University was a fecund source of faculty-administration discord. One small example: the office that managed Harvard-owned rental properties set salary requirements for the rental of its housing units so high that junior faculty in Arts and Sciences were ineligible. Presidential intervention cooled *that* hot potato, but resentment lingered.

A considerably larger issue arose in 1988. Some FAS faculty members angrily protested a central administration plan to build a hotel on property located near Widener Library. The site had been purchased by the University's real estate office in 1979 "for future University needs, especially those of the FAS." The city of Cambridge was on the verge of imposing tight building restrictions on the parcel, quick action was necessary, and FAS did not have the resources in hand to pay for a new building.

The issue soon became the "absence of significant interaction between the central administration and FAS on the use of such sites." A faculty critic caustically recalled that "when the medical faculties ... needed a new fuel plant for the hospitals, it had been built—at the cost of considerable borrowing." Why, then, was there not some way for the central administration to advance funds to FAS in order to relieve its library and office space problems?

Once again the president worked out an arrangement. Arts and Sciences would buy the property for a price that reimbursed the University for its initial cost, plus a reasonable return on that investment. Dean Michael Spence further eased matters when he decided that a new library building was not FAS's most immediate priority. He elected instead to proceed with the construction of a hotel designed for easy conversion to offices. He (rightly) expected that profits from its operation would enable the faculty to pay for the building and the property before the space became essential for FAS expansion.

Some central administrators persisted in believing that the crux of the affair was the faculty's mismanagement of its space needs. But the faculty involved saw it as an example of the misalignment of academic and administration perspectives. Reflecting on the incident some years later, Spence concluded that "the [central administration] never really viewed itself as a working partner for whom the main event was the College."[34]

Members of the faculty had no wish to spend time on administration. But this did not make them either grateful to or respectful of administrators. Not surprisingly, Harvard's central managers were bewildered by and resentful over the faculty's attitude. General Counsel Daniel Steiner would not soon forget the time he approached a professor at the Law School for advice on a problem in his area of expertise. After considering the matter briefly, the professor replied that his fee was too high for the University to afford, and he was not in a position to make an exception to his standard rate.

Long-simmering faculty distrust of the administration bubbled over in the fall of 1994. A task force on benefits had been appointed to address a cumulative deficit of $50 million in the University's fringe benefits account. Its job was to figure out how to reduce annual outlays by $10 million. It recommended that the University lower its subvention of health-care premiums for those with incomes above $45,000, cap contributions to postretirement health care, and reduce Harvard's subsidy of faculty pensions by 1 percent. At a May 1994 Faculty of Arts and Sciences meeting, President Rudenstine discussed the changes—but did not mention the lower pension contribution. In June the Corporation approved the task force's recommendations, and the decision was announced in the fall.

The plan caught the faculty by surprise. Hackles were raised by the break with a long tradition of faculty consultation on benefits and compensation. A standing committee was set up to "provide an official avenue of communication ... in any future situation where major changes in benefits must be considered by the central administration. It

would help to take us from the situation in which managerial considerations appeared to dominate ... into one in which collegial consultation
plays the role that has traditionally been its due at Harvard." The
committee held that the reduced pension contribution was a grave
mistake, for it would "predispose more than a few faculty members to
delay their retirement dates ... solely for financial reasons." It recommended that the pension cutback be rescinded. But the president and
the Corporation stood firm, citing the sharp rise in faculty benefits
during recent years.[35]

This response was widely viewed as inadequate. One professor
bitterly observed: "they have rather forcefully told us to go back to teaching, that they'll be responsible for this place." At a May 2, 1995, faculty
meeting, the conflict reached a climax. Floor leaders of the benefits
revolt attacked the Corporation's "misleading" suggestion that faculty
benefits played a significant role in the growth of costs. Other critics
charged that faculty pensions had been targeted for reduction by administrators who thought the well-paid faculty did not need the money
accumulating in its pension accounts.

Economic historian David Landes drew more sweeping conclusions.
He saw the benefits controversy as part of a larger and more compre-
hensive problem that "threatens to alter the constitution of this
University":

> Twenty-five years ago, we were an institution devoted primarily
> to teaching and research. We had a President and one vice presi-
> dent. We had an accompanying apparatus of staff whose function
> was to maintain and facilitate.... Since then, there has been a
> proliferation and hypertrophy of these ancillary services.... We
> have hired new people at salaries that reflect the market for expe-
> rienced executive personnel.... These salaries approach those
> prevailing in the business world; but at these higher levels, they
> far surpass the salaries of professors.... whether intended or not,
> this difference conveys a sense of hierarchy ("we are management;
> you are employees") that promotes unfortunate illusions ... [and]
> a need to do things in order to justify this high remuneration and
> these august titles.[36]

Galvanized by these events, the dean created a new faculty body, the
Committee on Resources. Its purpose was to figure out how to ensure
"badly needed transparency and accountability" in the financial and

managerial affairs of the University. But there was no built-in guarantee of consultation between the center and the deans on major fiscal issues. Nor was it clear to the schools just how much they were paying to the central administration as the equivalent of taxes, or whether they were getting fair value. What *was* clear, at the century's end, was that the administration-faculty relationship would be a continuing sore point in worldly Harvard.

## ∽ 17 ∼

# THE FACULTY OF ARTS AND SCIENCES

The changes of style and sensibility in Harvard's governance during the last third of the twentieth century had close parallels in the academic realm. The faculty, like the bureaucracy, became more professional, more specialized, more worldly. Nevertheless, in most respects Harvard's academic fundamentals in the magic year 2000 were pretty much what they had been half a century before. Faculty autonomy, the disciplinary pecking order, the tension between teaching and research, the sheer intellectual quality, range, and vigor of the place: these remained alive and well. Harvard changed more between 1940 and 1970 than it did between 1970 and 2000.

The Faculty of Arts and Sciences traditionally was Harvard's academic core. Medical School administrator Henry Meadow spoke in 1974 of the "religious" feeling that the FAS departments were the heart of the University, their faculty the *real* Harvard professors. By the end of the century that was a less self-evident proposition. The crisis of the late 1960s, the intellectual and career problems afflicting the humanities and the social sciences, and Derek Bok's ideal of a more socially engaged and useful University eroded FAS's privileged place. Yet the College and the Arts and Sciences departments still made the largest claim on the University's assets and on its public reputation.[1]

## Leaders

The FAS deanships of Paul Buck in the 1940s and McGeorge Bundy in the 1950s gave their office a place in Harvard affairs second only to the president. John Dunlop, appointed to stanch the flow of institutional blood after the events of 1969, made way in 1973 for fellow economist Henry Rosovsky, who held the post until 1984 and then came back for a fill-in year in 1990. Rosovsky's was one of the notable deanships in Harvard's history, and he played a major role in the University's glissade from meritocracy to worldliness.

Like his predecessors Buck, Bundy, Ford, and Dunlop, Rosovsky had not gone to Harvard College. Unlike them he was Harvard's first Jewish, and foreign-born, dean. He came to the United States in 1940, a thirteen-year-old refugee from Hitler's Europe, and went to college at William and Mary. As a Harvard graduate student and a member of the Society of Fellows he studied Japanese economic history, laying claim to scholarly expertise of the sort bound to win him respect in the postwar academic world. After a stint at Berkeley, he left that turbulent scene to join the Harvard faculty in 1966.

Rosovsky's success as dean during the difficult years of the seventies stemmed from his sound political instincts and ease in dealing with people. He did much to restore the faculty's self-confidence after the trauma of 1969 and was a prime mover in the creation of the new Core Curriculum in Harvard College. At the same time he supported Derek Bok's efforts to make Harvard a more worldly university. He and Bok formed a diumvirate not unlike the Conant-Buck pairing of the 1940s and early 1950s.

Bundy had been an imperial dean, who conducted the faculty's business through committees (thereby avoiding faculty debate). Rosovsky was the very model of a democratic dean. He artfully managed the elected Faculty Council and passed on as much business to faculty meetings as he thought that body could ingest without choking. He set up a cabinet-like group of faculty to advise him on appointments and other issues. In annual budget letters he explained, in language that even a professor could understand, how and why FAS was in a financial hole during the deficit-ridden 1970s and what he planned to do about it. Characteristically, he came up with a healthy salary increase in 1983–84, his last year as dean, to compensate for most of the fall-off in real income during the preceding years: a sumptuous dessert designed to erase the memory of lesser fare before. Like Buck and Bundy before him, Rosovsky was viewed by many as a likely Harvard president. Age and circumstance in the end kept him from that prize. But he went on to play an important role on the Corporation as one of Harvard's late-twentieth-century movers and shakers.

Rosovsky was succeeded in 1984 by thirty-eight-year-old A. Michael Spence, also of the Economics department, the third in a row. Spence was Canadian-born, a Princeton B.A. and a Rhodes Scholar, a Harvard Ph.D. with the Clark Medal (given for the most distinguished work by an econo-

mist below the age of forty) under his belt. As Rosovsky's FDR-like political skills were ideal for the troubled time of the 1970s, so Spence, a
preternaturally intelligent expert on industrial organization, was eminently
qualified to oversee the institutional reconstruction now at hand. Political
scientist James Q. Wilson characterized the 1980s as a "middle-aged"
decade, in which the impulse to change and criticize gave way to the
impulse to make things work. That is what Spence turned to. He prodded
the departments to appoint stronger, and hence more tenurable, junior
faculty. And he asked the Corporation to decapitalize—that is, spend some
of the money being squirreled into endowment—to improve Harvard's
aging physical plant and pay for more aggressive faculty recruitment.[2]

But when it came to the (essentially political) implementation of
these goals, the going got hard. It was no easy task to break down the
departments' habit of treating junior faculty as transients: the meritocratic fear of not winding up with The Best was too strong. Nor was
Spence able to convince Bok and the Corporation to free up money for
the purposes and on the scale that he desired. It became increasingly
clear to him that his deanship was not what he wanted it to be. When
pressing family considerations intervened, he suddenly and to general
surprise announced in late March 1990 that he was leaving to be dean of
Stanford's Business School.[3]

Spence's successor was Jeremy Knowles, a distinguished chemist who
had turned down an invitation to be dean when Rosovsky left. English-
born and Oxford-educated, a member of the Chemistry department
since 1974, Knowles was a dramatic example of how readily modern
academics could take on new, transnational institutional identities. With
a canniness honed by years in Oxford's senior common rooms, Knowles
ended stubbornly persisting FAS budget deficits without weakening the
faculty's quality or sacrificing its autonomy. Then the returns of
Harvard's multibillion dollar fund drive of the 1990s came pouring in.
Belt-tightening (even in the nonaustere form this took at Harvard)
seemed less in order.

Grand restorations gussied up the campus: a stunning renewal of the
nineteenth-century dormitories in the Old Yard; a magnificently refurbished Memorial Hall; a $25 million conversion of the old Freshman
Union into a sparkling new Center for the Humanities. At the end of
the century, new science facilities and plans for a $100 million-plus
complex of buildings to house the Government department and the area
studies centers were on the drawing board. In a grand retro gesture,
Memorial Hall's tower, gone since a fire in the 1950s, was restored in all
its resplendent Victorian glory.[4]

These were abundant signs of—what? A Golden Age, reflected in Knowles's ambition to create new facilities for "communities of scholars"? Or the workings of Parkinson's Law that an institution's structural grandeur comes to a peak just when its internal substance is eroding?

## The Professoriat

Despite this commotion, much in the character of the Arts and Sciences faculty spoke more of stasis than of change. By 1980 it was considerably older on average than in earlier years. In part this was the product of a sharp decline in faculty growth (especially of nontenured junior appointments) from the mid-1970s on. But an older, more heavily tenured faculty was not necessarily a better one. Other universities had the wherewithal to attract and keep top-rank scholars. And the growing difficulty of getting people to move in the face of spouses' careers meant that the old Harvard belief that all it had to do was ask the best and they would come was less and less valid. Between 1965–66 and 1984–85, about sixty tenure offers to outsiders were turned down in the sciences, thirty-five in the social sciences, twenty-five in the humanities. The rejection rate rose to as much as a third in the early eighties. And informal approaches were often rebuffed before formal offers went out. Rosovsky estimated in 1980 that a department got its real first choice about half the time.[5]

Average professorial salaries remained at the top of the American academic pay scale. But other universities had a star system of appointments, which meant that in particular instances they could do substantially better. Harvard's response in the late 1980s was to increase total compensation packages, including a major housing subsidy program for new senior faculty. This strategy kept Harvard competitive. And while traditional principles of salary equity prevailed within departments and disciplinary areas, there was a growing tendency for the most recent hot properties from outside to be hired at the top of their range. At the junior level, the fixed salary scale came under pressure in the late 1970s, began to crack in the late 1980s, and was gone by 2000.

Spousal or family reasons for not coming increased in number (though divorce and remarriage sometimes gave wheels to previously immovable objects). Scientists were deterred by the delay and inconvenience of setting up a new lab, and at times by the attractions of a more laid-back lifestyle where they were. The quality of Harvard's undergraduates and libraries, and its elevated social standing, meant more to social scientists and especially to humanists—though the sturdy record of turn-downs in History showed the extent to which a dysfunctional departmental culture could lessen Harvard's appeal.

Along with the new problem of not being able to appoint the right person, there remained the old danger of appointing the wrong one. Bok fretted that too many departments had appointment problems: they failed to agree on candidates or were unable to recruit the people they wanted or didn't make a convincing case for their choices. The system worked well enough when it came to vetting world-class scholars. But when other desiderata were at stake—a candidate's leadership qualities, promotions from within, considerations of gender and race—problems arose. Tensions increased between departments who weighed factors other than scholarship and ad hoc committees who did not.

The changing character of the academic disciplines was another source of strain. The old mind-body problem often gave way to a new body-body dilemma: this specialist ... or that one? And the bodies could be specialized indeed. A professor called the president's attention to the "most lamentable deficiency" in the Faculty of Arts and Sciences: the lack of a scholar whose specialty was the language and literature of Catalonia. (By 2000 that gaping void had been filled.) Such concerns did not coexist easily with the demands of affirmative action or the growing pressure—from the president, from students—to pay more heed to teaching undergraduates.

The loudest calls for change were for more internal promotions of junior faculty and the appointment of more women and blacks. Traditional standards—the best disciplinary "minds," the most necessary specialist "bodies"—were joined now by "diversity," defined by gender and race (but not by class, ethnicity, or ideology). Here was a faithful representation of the concerns of the larger society, posing a challenge to the meritocratic model that had shaped the Harvard faculty during the previous twenty-five years.

By the end of the century, the eight tenured black professors in FAS were clustered in Afro-American Studies, Anthropology, English, History, Sociology, and Government. The cohort of women was larger, broader, more like the postwar influx of Jewish academics except for their scarcity in the sciences. Special problems afflicted women at work, including the conflicts of work and motherhood, sexual harassment by colleagues, and campus security. Young male scientists at Harvard defined "security" as the problem of protecting lab equipment from theft; their female counterparts defined it as the ability to make one's way safely to the parking lot late at night.[6]

Because Harvard was so constantly in the media's gaze, and because conflicting definitions of merit were at stake, publicly ventilated tenure disputes over women became a conspicuous part of the late-twentieth-century Harvard scene. The first crop of post-1969 tenured women in FAS were long-term lecturers hurriedly promoted to professorships. But as female junior professors grew in numbers, in the time-honored Harvard way most of them failed to get promoted. A flap arose in 1976 over the promotion of Doris Kearns, whose book about Lyndon Johnson was waiting to be published. Despite the endorsement of the Government department one senior member thought her scholarly output too slim. Then her former editor claimed in effect to have written much of her book himself. Her promotion was put off, to be reviewed after three years. Before that, she went off to what became a notable career as a biographer and television personality.

Theda Skocpol in Sociology had a more tempestuous (and public) time of it. Denied tenure by her department, she filed a gender discrimination complaint, won a three-year deferral, went to Chicago, accepted a Berkeley appointment, and when a Harvard offer finally came returned to Cambridge instead: an academic comet leaving a trail of triumphs (and grievances) in her wake. Also public, and publicized, was the denial of tenure to political theorist Bonnie Honig in 1997. This decision was protested by fifteen of Harvard's tenured female faculty members, though almost none were in her field: a measure of how the issue of diversity was altering the culture of faculty evaluation.

In fact seven of the eight women who came up for tenure at Harvard that year got it. And in relative if not absolute terms, impressive gains were made: 2 tenured women in 1970, 14 in 1980, 35 in 1990, 60 (14 percent of the tenured faculty) in 1999. There were 10 female junior faculty members in 1970, 59 (32 percent of the total) in 1999. Between 1986–91 and 1991–96, outside offers to women went from 13 percent to 24 percent of the annual total; internal promotions from 18 percent to 32 percent.[7]

The rise of discipline-wide pecking orders—not how do you stand at Harvard, but how do you stand in your field?—reversed the situation that Conant had confronted in the 1930s. Insidership was then the most potent factor in appointments. Now a different issue held sway: who— insider or outsider—is the best candidate? By 1983, half of Harvard's tenured social scientists and humanists and about a third of its natural scientists had risen from the ranks, considerably below the earlier norm. During the last two decades of the century, outside offers outstripped inside ones by three to one. Only about a third of the faculty had Harvard Ph.Ds in 1998.

Hiring, or not hiring, your own raised old issues of standards and equity. The English department's Walter Jackson Bate argued that character was as important as reputation, that quality of publication was more important than quantity, and that when it came to a permanent appointment, Harvard should rely on its own, not outsiders', judgments. But political scientist Sidney Verba warned that subjective measures of "character" over hard evaluations of scholarly worth could mean the recrudescence of an old boy network. Dean A. Michael Spence shifted the terms of debate by arguing that the future quality of the senior faculty would depend increasingly on the recruitment and promotion of tenurable junior faculty.[8]

Uncapping the retirement age in 1994 hardly helped, injecting a new factor into the calculus of staffing: when might senior faculty be expected to leave? The very things that made a Harvard appointment so attractive—excellent students, high salaries and good perks, status galore—might encourage many to stay past the previous retirement age of seventy. During the late 1990s more than a third did so: a disproportionate number of them in the natural sciences, where the loss of one's lab could mean the end of one's work. And this was when times were good and pensions fat. No one knew what a market downturn might do to retirement rates in the future.

The *Boston Globe* in 1998 took a skeptical look at internal advancement at Harvard. It noted that History had not promoted any of its junior American historians since 1959. American colonial historian Laurel Ulrich (who came from the University of New Hampshire) declared: "It's vital to change the perception out there that coming to Harvard as a junior faculty member is a dead end. Creating a more flexible tenure system is the wave of the future." But it was a tad early to brace for the undertow. In the late 1990s two new tenured appointments were made in American history; both were from outside. America always was a big country; now it was a big country well accoutered with excellent universities, which made the equation of excellence and insiderhood more iffy than ever.[9]

What Henry Rosovsky called the "classic pathology" of Harvard professors—finding it difficult to consider anyone worthy of joining their ranks, coupled with their ability to manipulate the appointments system so as to get their not-quite-the-best favorites if they wanted them—had its costs. But it should not be forgotten how good Harvard's faculty was, and how it still had a better chance than any other university of getting most of those it wanted. And it is easy to forget that the modern appointments system, with all its drawbacks, was a response to an academic culture where the old boys in a department chose their colleagues at will.

But it would be hard to deny that the faculty's ties to the University, the College, their departments, and the student residential houses had manifestly weakened. Other forms of identification—of "professional entrepreneurs" with their "field" (or subfield) or along lines of gender, race, or politics—became more important. A sampling in 1993 found that only about half the faculty had some involvement in University affairs. It was a sign of the growing importance of the administrative bureaucracy, or of a quieter University, or of faculty indifference, or all of these that in the 1990s the number of scheduled FAS faculty meetings went down, and the number of cancelled meetings went up.

As the mystic bonds of institutional identity lessened, the practical rules of bureaucracy increased. In 1973, many traditional academic procedures and practices survived in the memory of older faculty and in the head of the dean's longtime executive secretary, Verna Johnson. Whether driven by new forms of auditing, fear of litigiousness, or simply the growing complexity of academic business, by the 1980s department chairs found it difficult to function without recourse to a handbook of rules and regulations. A therapeutic administration worried about the dos and don'ts of retirement, parental leave and more flexible teaching schedules, affirmative action and an ever more complicated appointments and promotions procedure, sexual harassment and unprofessional conduct, faculty rights and responsibilities.

With some reason, the Harvard faculty at the end of the century thought itself overburdened. Research and scholarship was what mattered most to most of them. And then there was their teaching: the course "load," as the revealing term had it. But they had as well to conduct searches, tend to academic visitors, prepare grant proposals, run programs, serve on committees, deal with the Harvard bureaucracy, and write student recommendations. Neither junior appointments nor increases in the faculty's size were, in the common view, easing these escalating demands.

Things looked different from the administration's perspective. A more worldly faculty by definition spent more time on conference going, advising, consulting, pontificating, and general entrepreneurship. Bok and the Corporation questioned the degree to which these activities conflicted with the faculty's teaching responsibilities. But an FAS study showed that the senior faculty most engaged in outside activities often were the same people who were academic leaders inside. Nothing further came of the president's enquiry. However altered its character and situation, the faculty still reigned supreme over its own domain.

# The Sciences

The natural sciences took center stage in late-twentieth-century Harvard, securing resources and réclame that the other disciplines could only envy, or (in the case of Economics and the behavioral sciences) try to emulate. But this did not mean that Harvard's scientists were immune to the cultural and intellectual currents that affected their colleagues in other fields. Government and foundation research support for the physical sciences declined in the 1970s, as did student enrollments and academic positions for their graduates. Some scientists were caught up in the political radicalism of the sixties and seventies or the entrepreneurialism of the eighties and nineties.

The strength of Harvard science was more qualitative than quantitative: as Spencer Tracy said of Katharine Hepburn, there wasn't much meat, but what there was was choice. The comparatively small size of Harvard's science faculty hurt it in the university rankings game. Nor was it getting any bigger. There were 143 tenured FAS scientists in 1971 and 163 in 1999, but junior faculty decreased from 67 to 48. The percentage of Harvard scientists in the faculty at large was smaller in 1991 than forty years before.

As in the past, constraints of size and space bent Harvard science in the direction of theoretical more than applied work, and individual and small group projects rather than large-scale Big Science. Despite—or because of—this, Harvard's cache of twenty-six Nobelists between 1945 and 1990 (nine in Physics, five in Chemistry, four in Medicine and Physiology, eight in the Medical School) was in a class by itself. The $60 million a year in contract, grant, and gift money obtained by Harvard's scientists equaled FAS's annual tuition income. The sciences could make a fair case for being the jewel in the academic crown of late-twentieth-century Harvard.[10]

Stiffening competition for research funds heightened (if that was possible) the scramble for the payoffs that came with scientific achievement. The culture of Harvard science was determined by Nobelists, high strivers, and ego-spurred competition. E. J. Corey's organic chemistry lab was arguably the best, and most productive, in the world. But excellence on this level had a price: three graduate/postdoc suicides between 1980 and 1998. A shaken department launched a major effort to combat the isolation and stress of its younger members.[11]

The pressure-cooker world of modern science appears to have led as well to an increase in cases of careless results hurriedly published, with work-harried senior professors exercising inadequate oversight. These cropped up primarily in the medical area, where thousands of researchers worked at the affiliated hospitals and Harvard Medical School. The Medical School adopted new guidelines after several of its faculty wrote recommendations for a young colleague without mentioning that he was convicted of rape. A handful of overeager premeds in the College cooked research results, withdrew fellow students' medical school applications, forged letters of support for their own candidacies.[12]

More troublesome at Harvard was another feature of high-powered science: the lure of profit. Although patents traditionally were the most common way to capitalize on scientific discovery, Harvard's strict rules against profiting from health-related research kept it from being a big player in that game. But in 1986 the Corporation approved a revision of the University's patents policy that allowed more of a return to inventors while securing the bulk of the take to the University. In 1989 Harvard entered into a $10 million, five-year patents-sharing partnership with the Hoffman-LaRoche pharmaceutical company, the first of a series of joint enterprises with commercial firms.[13]

Individual ventures by Harvard's increasingly worldly scientists were another story. The faculty's reaction in 1980 to the University investing in a venture built around the work of biochemist Mark Ptashne showed the strength of the pure science ethos. Nobelist Walter Gilbert went on leave in 1980–81 to be director and chairman of the board of scientific advisors of Biogen, a genetic engineering start-up company. He then asked that the University's rules be waived to allow him a second year off to act as the company's CEO. He was turned down and left the department of Biochemistry. (He later returned to Cellular and Developmental Biology.)

Some graduate students and postdocs complained that the laboratories of Ptashne and others relied on grants from biotech companies, which obligated them to do applied rather than basic research. Ptashne denied this. His lab, he insisted, did no secret or commercially relevant work, and no more than 20 percent of his time was devoted to consulting for his company, Genetics Institute. During the 1980s the FAS Committee on Research Policy was created to be a watchdog over the new issues posed by privately sponsored research.[14]

Biochemist George Wald and organismic/evolutionary biologists Richard Lewontin and Stephen J. Gould were conspicuous spokesmen on issues such as Vietnam and the cold war, race, the environment, and scientific research. Biologist Ruth Hubbard, Wald's wife and one of Harvard's female lecturers awarded a mea culpa professorship in the early 1970s, announced that she would give up scientific research and devote herself to women's studies and social issues in science. She blamed a male-dominated science for the prevailing view of women as creatures confined by their biological constitution and saw a link between the science of women's place in society and the place of women in science. Supporting evidence: the struggle-infused language of male-dominated science, full of wrestling with nature and wresting truth from it, of making war on diseases and conquering them, of privileging hard over soft science. But it was one thing to criticize the social construction of science; it was another to apply political standards to scientific work. To do so was to lose standing as a scientist.[15]

Sometimes radical dissent took an uglier turn. Geneticists Jonathan Beckwith and Larry Miller attacked two Medical School scientists for exploring the physical and behavioral consequences of the XYY chromosomal abnormality. Suppression of that work was justified, they argued, because it spread racial stereotypes. And biologist Richard Lewontin raised a sticky problem of academic ethics (and academic freedom) when he refused to let a white South African visitor work in his lab because the latter was ... a white South African. (This echoed Physicist Percy Bridgman's short-lived ban on German, Italian, and Soviet scientists in 1939.) The academic deans of FAS thought that President Bok should write to the visitor disavowing Lewontin's action and make it clear that his was a personal and not an institutional stance.

Beckwith, Lewontin, and Gould also led an assault on the social implications of their Biology colleague E. O. Wilson's *Sociobiology*, which appeared in 1975. Wilson's "use of suppositional rhetoric," Lewontin charged, "makes things sound as if they are true." More hands-on critics subjected Wilson to personal abuse. The controversy over sociobiology would continue to be a contentious one, characterized by persisting hostility between Wilson and his Harvard detractors, and in public between those who found it an exciting new branch of science and those who thought it was disguised racism. But these clashes barely affected the mainstream of Harvard science.[16]

Chemistry and Physics, Harvard's longtime science powers, took their lumps in an era dominated by the genetics-biochemistry revolution. But they continued to maintain their notably high standing. The two departments ranked first in the number of citations in physics and chemistry papers published between 1981 and 1993.[17]

For all its quality, Chemistry faced a batch of problems in the post-1970 years. Like other Harvard science departments, it had lost its old cohesiveness. Laboratories and research teams were the significant reference groups for most faculty. The mounting pressure of competition also took its toll. Lunch was something to be snatched at the desk, not lingered over in the company of colleagues.

Centrifugal, too, was the effect on Harvard's chemists, who were caught up in the heady, remunerative world of consultancies and entrepreneurship. This hardly fostered a taste for the classroom. Once upon a time, Physics Nobelist Edward Purcell turned to undergraduate teaching when he got older; now Chemistry Nobelist Robert Woodward, in association with a Swiss pharmaceutical firm, devoted himself to the alchemical process of turning Swiss francs into more Swiss francs. One thing did persist: the overwhelming maleness of the department. In 1989 Cynthia Friend became the first (and as of 2000 the only) tenured woman.

In times past Chemistry sent its Ph.D.s to other academic institutions; those who excelled might be asked to return. But the attractions of other schools, and the sparse prospects of promotion within the department, made it increasingly difficult to recruit strong juniors trained at other universities. By the late 1990s, three out of four junior appointments were of new Harvard Ph.D.s. Senior appointments were something else again. Until the department made three promotions in the 1990s, the only post-1945 internal promotions were of organic chemist Robert Woodward in 1946 and physical chemists William Klemperer and Roy Gordon in the 1960s.

The discontent of Chemistry's junior members was up to the customary high Harvard standard. It was not reassuring to be told by the senior professors that while Harvard Chemistry attracted the country's best graduate students, they understandably chose not to work in labs run by junior faculty who soon would be gone. Aging facilities compounded the problem of wooing and holding junior faculty.[18]

By the early 1980s, leading members of the older generation of Harvard chemists—Konrad Bloch, Bright Wilson, Robert Woodward—

had retired or died. New stars, among them Nobel Prize winners William Lipscomb (1976), Dudley Herschbach (1986), and E. J. Corey (1990), sustained the department's stellar reputation. But its relative weakness in physical and inorganic chemistry continued, as the organic chemists battened on the molecular/cellular triumphs of the late twentieth century. To mark that victory, Konrad Bloch proposed in 1989 that the department's name be changed to Chemistry and Chemical Biology. Corey wanted the even more in-your-face title of Chemistry and Biochemistry. Embattled physical chemists offered up Chemistry, Chemical Physics, and Chemical Biology as a distended alternative. In the mid-1990s the Chemists adopted Bloch's formulation—a recognition of the shifting intellectual core of the discipline.

Harvard Physics in the 1970s faced the dual shocks of a decline in appeal to students and the emphasis elsewhere on a Big Physics in which it was ill-situated to compete. The Cambridge Electron Accelerator closed in June 1973, already outclassed by the more powerful installations at Brookhaven on Long Island and Batavia in Illinois (with Stanford's Linear Electron Accelerator and CERN in Switzerland on the way). Harvard's experimental physicists had to do a good deal of their work elsewhere, which led to faculty and graduate student "absenteeism." And as in Chemistry, the department's collegiality broke down as its numbers grew.

Just as the inorganic chemists lagged behind their organic colleagues, so did a gap exist between the experimental and theoretical branches of Physics. But limited access to high energy facilities did not weaken Harvard's already notable strength in theory: Nobelists Steven Weinberg and Sheldon Glashow (1979) succeeded Julian Schwinger.[19]

By the mid-1970s, the old experimentalist generation—Bainbridge, Street, Pound, Purcell, Ramsey—was at or near retirement. Frequent offer turndowns by junior faculty in low-energy Physics made it more difficult to hire top experimentalists. It was not surprising that the experimentalists turned to the Division of Engineering and Applied Physics. DEAP had a solid base in applied physics, and the money to support experimental work. During the 1980s and 1990s DEAP Dean Paul Martin fostered ever closer ties, doubling the Physics faculty through joint appointments. By the end of the century there were more undergraduate Physics majors at Harvard than at MIT or Berkeley, though still well below the palmy postwar years.[20]

Mallinckrodt Professor of Physics David Nelson recalled that he entered the field in the 1970s expecting to play a role "in the creation of fundamental new ideas." But by the 1990s Physics seemed further than ever from attaining the unified "theory of everything" that was Einstein's dream. "There comes a point," Nelson warned, "when conventional 'fundamental' particle physics burrows down to such short length scale and high energies that its conclusions become largely irrelevant to the physics of the world around us. That is why many of my colleagues are not aiming to discover the 'fundamental' laws at the smallest length scale."

By the end of the century the picture had brightened. Cosmology and string theory were attracting younger physicists interested in coming up with big answers to large questions. While much of the pioneering work was done elsewhere, Harvard string theorists Juan Maldacena, Andrew Strominger, and Cumrum Vafa were important figures. But Physics did not find it easy to maintain its disciplinary cohesion in the face of developments that belonged at least as much to Astronomy and Mathematics, not unlike the relation of Chemistry to the molecular/cellular challenge.[21]

Biology has been at the cutting edge of science in the late twentieth century. Harvard's biologists were deeply engaged in the biochemical revolution, full of hearty contention between haughty molecularists and doughty organismicists (James Watson versus E. O. Wilson) and between leftist evolutionists and sociobiologists (Richard Lewontin and Stephen J. Gould versus the feisty Wilson). Big discoveries, exciting Nobels, fierce conflicts between outsized personalities: this was the invigorating environment of late-twentieth-century Harvard Biology and Biochemistry.

Old battlegrounds—between the botanists and the Arnold Arboretum, between the Biology department and the Museum of Comparative Zoology (MCZ)—were fading memories. Arboretum buffs darkly suspected that Harvard wanted to milk that institution's funds to help pay for Biology professors. What was the Arnold Arboretum left with? Curators, gardens, vandalism (Jamaica Plain wasn't getting more affluent), and the satisfaction of being a place of repose in a big city. Despite its weakened role in the life of the University and the deterioration of its physical plant, the arboretum continued to offer an active public education program. By the end of the century it got a fillip from a quickening public and scientific interest in ecology. And it was the principal American institution doing research on Far Eastern flora and the repository of the world's most comprehensive scientific collection of living woody plants.[22]

The MCZ always had been more in the Biology mainstream. Its distinguished director, Ernst Mayr, was succeeded in 1970 by Alfred

"Fuzz" Crompton, who shifted the museum's focus from systematics (anatomy and evolutionary theory) to population genetics, ecology, and comparative physiology. The new position of professor/curator, created in the late seventies to ensure that curators met the standard of Biology professorial appointments, furthered the integration of the MCZ staff into the department. By the time Crompton retired in 1982, MCZ had in effect merged into Biology's organismic and evolutionary wing.[23]

Meanwhile the department continued on its fissiparous way. By the end of the 1970s it was among the nation's best, but was wracked by chronic dissension between its two divisions, Organismic and Evolutionary Biology (OEB) and Cellular and Developmental Biology (CDB). (Biochemistry and Molecular Biology [BMB] had been a separate department since 1967.) Space and facility shortages added to the already rich store of OEB-CDB tension. The Biology chairmanship rotated between the two wings; there had been no department-wide faculty meeting in years.

The cellular and developmental biologists worried that there were only nine of them, compared to OEB's twenty-three, and that they were cut off from their scientific soul mates in Biochemistry. The OEB faculty (many of whom belonged to the Museum of Comparative Zoology) in turn resented the assertiveness of their molecular-cellular colleagues. Exacerbating their concern was the swing of federal research support to health-related projects, which tended to be down CDB's alley. In the fall of 1981 CDB split off to become an independent department. So now the organismic, cellular, and molecular biologists inhabited separate departmental realms: the product of more than thirty years of mutual suspicion and dissension. It would take more than a decade before the increasing overlap of work in these subfields, and the fading away of old animosities, made a reunion possible.[24]

The medical school boom of the 1970s pushed up the number of Biology course takers and concentrators. (One faculty member proposed that the department stanch the flow by the novel step of refusing to improve its undergraduate courses.) While senior professors taught the basic courses, the junior faculty taught most of Biology's 500 majors, which enhanced their sense of second-class citizenship. As elsewhere in Harvard science, promotion chances were scant, salaries not always competitive, laboratory setups slow. Graduate students complained that the senior professors' labs were baronies locked in competition, like so many medieval fiefdoms; that the professors were uninterested in teaching or in their students' careers; that (as in Chemistry) the laboratory and not the department was the most meaningful social unit.[25]

But overriding these difficulties was the shared sense among biologists and biochemists (much like physicists in earlier decades) that they were participants in a major event in the history of science. The department offered one course in Biochemistry in 1954, fourteen in 1983. The molecular-biochemical revolution of the late twentieth century gave Biochemistry and Molecular Biology and Cellular and Developmental Biology great prestige. Matthew Meselson's proof of DNA replication, Mark Ptashne's demonstration of how a virus is turned on and off, Walter Gilbert's technique for cloning genes for medical use signified that Harvard Biology and Biochemistry were in exceptional ferment, in which theoretical and experimental work fruitfully conjoined.[26]

By the 1980s a separate Biochemistry department made less and less sense. The techniques and agendas of biochemists and cellular and developmental biologists overlapped, and Biology like Chemistry had come to terms with the molecular revolution. Biochemistry retirements and departures made for constant recruitment pressure, which was intensified by competition in salaries and facilities from places like MIT and Harvard Medical School, other major universities, or new institutes backed by private foundations (Hughes, Markey, Whitehead).

The message was clear: capture the economies of scale that come with merger. (Business corporations got the same word at the same time.) Bok urged that appointments be coordinated with CDB since there was no sharp discontinuity between the BMB and CDB programs. The biochemists resisted, but declining enrollments and a low yield on graduate students weakened the case for independence. Finally in 1994 BMB and CDB merged into the Department of Molecular and Cellular Biology, which with OEB offered an integrated curriculum in Biological Sciences. It seemed likely that there might be, once again, a single Biology department, much as Zoology, Botany, and Physiology had come together to create the department in the 1930s.

Looking back in 1995, E. O. Wilson concluded that the "Molecular Wars" between the organismic/evolutionary and the molecular/cellular biologists spurred the development of sociobiology and ecological studies. These new lines of inquiry linked OEB to general social concerns, comparable to molecular and cellular Biology's connection with the cure of disease. At the same time there was a steady methodological and substantive convergence between Biology's wings. By the century's end evolutionary biologists regularly relied on molecular data, while molecularists had a growing interest in the whole organism. Wilson forecast "a thematic shift in biology" to the study of groups of organisms by teams drawn from across the discipline. The "expert naturalist" and the "taxonomist" were, he thought, likely to regain leadership in biological research. The Biology of the future would be a pluralist science, not formed by a large, general theory. Like physicist David Nelson, he concluded that "[n]ew general principles, the grail of biology, are becoming ever more elusive." He predicted that "deep expertise in particular groups of organisms (such as ants, his specialty?) if combined with free-wheeling opportunism in the choice of problems, is the wave of the future for biology."[27]

Harvard Mathematics remained strong, close-knit, self-assured. In 1980 it had fourteen full-time tenured professors, compared to twenty-one at Princeton, twenty-six at Chicago and Yale, and over sixty at Berkeley. But three of them (the just retired Lars Ahlfors, David Mumford, and Heisuki Hironaka) had been Fields Medal winners, the top prize for under-forty mathematicians. Junior morale was good, students (and there were a lot of them) enthusiastic. In Deborah Hughes Hallett the department had an exceptionally gifted teacher of numerically challenged undergraduates. And when the Soviet Union bottomed up circa 1990, department chairman Arthur Jaffe was quick off the mark to capitalize on "the demise of one of (if not the) greatest mathematical traditions in the world." This spirit helped the department to expand to thirty-five members by 1995, making it larger than Chemistry.[28]

Geology had no such good fortune. The department did not change much in size between 1940 and the 1970s. It saw the need to expand in Geophysics to complement its strengths in Petrology and Geochemistry, but found appointments hard to make because of its lack of critical mass. Lethargy and complacency, a dearth of research, inability to compete with MIT: these were the problems confronting the department in the mid-1970s.

Things improved in the 1980s, especially in geophysics. In 1986 the department was renamed Earth and Planetary Sciences, combining study of the earth below with the planets above. This set the stage for a broad program in environmental science. Undergraduates were wooed by a worldly new concentration in Environmental Science and Public Policy.[29]

Astronomy did even better. Space exploration and the revolution in cosmology put the field at the forefront of late-twentieth-century science. The Harvard College Observatory (HCO) and the Smithsonian Astrophysical Observatory (SAO) had worked more or less closely together since 1955. These two units formally merged in 1973 into a Center for Astrophysics (CFA). With over 300 researchers, CFA had a

$50 million annual budget and perhaps the world's largest concentration of astronomers: unHarvard-like Big Science. It became a world center for radio, optical, and X-ray astronomy. Science that lives by federal grants can die, or at least be wounded, by grant cutbacks, and in the late 1970s CFA was hard hit by falloffs in NASA and National Science Foundation (NSF) support. But the continuing national interest in space and the quality of the Harvard operation soon remedied that.[30]

For all its strength, Astronomy did not escape problems common elsewhere in Harvard science. A poor academic job market and fragmented research groups fed graduate student discontent. In 1978–79 only 20 percent of accepted Astronomy graduate applicants came to Harvard. Junior faculty, as junior faculty do, thought themselves exploited by their seniors. There were complaints that the department had been absorbed into the Center for Astrophysics, to the detriment of undergraduate instruction. And tensions continued between the Astronomy faculty and the Smithsonian Astrophysical Observatory people, who subsisted on federal research grants. While the observatory contributed less than half as much to the CFA as did the Smithsonian, astronomers in the department had a higher place in the academic pecking order than their Smithsonian colleagues.[31]

The Division of Engineering and Applied Physics occupied yet another niche in the world of Harvard science. Through most of Dean Harvey Brooks's long tenure (1958–75), the division grew and flourished. But it shared in the post-1969 malaise, and by the mid-seventies suffered from a lack of direction and less than stellar appointments.

In 1974 a committee headed by Bell Labs physicist Solomon Buchsbaum considered how the division might change to meet the conditions of the next quarter century. DEAP's resources were impressive: thirty-three tenured positions, compared to fourteen in Physics and twenty-two in Biology. It had a $30 million endowment, courtesy of the massive Gordon McKay Bequest. Even so, the number and diversity of its research and teaching areas—applied mechanics, computer science, applied mathematics, environmental science and engineering, solid-state physics and materials, earth and planetary physics, electromagnetism—stretched its resources and led to complaints (common in Harvard science) that each component was isolated and understaffed.

The Buchsbaum committee recommended that Harvard stick to its definition of "applied science" as a search for basic principles and their practical applications. But it called for more emphasis on student careers in applied areas and closer ties to industry. This did not mean that

Harvard should (re-)create an engineering school. Indeed, the Committee recommended that "Engineering" be dropped from the division's name and that it remain part of the Faculty of Arts and Sciences. But it wanted applied science to be a more substantial part of the Harvard curriculum: worldliness at work.

The committee proposed that "integration, flexibility and versatility" replace "fractionalization and minute specialization." Admirable; how to do it? Not, as some proposed, by breaking up the division into separate departments of Applied Mathematics, Applied Physics, and Engineering. Each would be too small to be effective. By retaining the division form, greater flexibility in making appointments in the unpredictable future was assured. Instead, the committee proposed to combine the seven existing DEAP programs into four research groups: materials science, planetary physics and engineering (the atmosphere and the oceans), applied bioscience (the environment), and applied mathematics (in particular, computer science). As many as a third of the division's new appointments would go to other science departments—outposts of applied science designed to bring the message of utility to heathen theorists.[32]

This met with resounding opposition from a DEAP faculty not disposed to see its research groups merged and its appointments go elsewhere. Nevertheless, physicist Paul Martin, who became the division's new dean in 1977, did much to enact the Buchsbaum committee's goals and confound the belief (dating back to Conant) that Harvard had to choose between Applied Physics and Engineering. He reorganized the DEAP faculty into four units that showed a greater sensitivity to the division's engineering past: Applied Physics, Earth and Environmental Science and Engineering, Mechanical Engineering and Materials Science, and Electrical Engineering and Computer Science. Growing student interest in applied science or engineering careers led to a new concentration in Computer Science, honors programs in Engineering Science, and an interdepartmental Applied Mathematics program.

A similar respect for the opinions of division-kind led to a name change to Engineering and Applied Science (DEAS), instead of the Buchsbaum Committee's more anti-Engineering proposal of Applied Mathematics and Physical Sciences. In a burst of scientific ecumenicism, DEAS in 1977 became the Division of Applied Sciences. But the nagging need to pay due attention to engineering did not go away, and in 1997 back the title went to Engineering and Applied Science.

The biggest single challenge facing the division in the late twentieth century was to strengthen its relatively modest program in computer science. Many believed that Harvard's greatest failure in science was the missed opportunity to build on computer pioneer Howard Aiken's legacy. Microsoft's William J. Gates had been—briefly—a Harvard undergraduate, and Steven Ballmer, Gates's chief assistant, was a full-fledged alumnus. By the century's end this connection had yielded only a $25 million gift (not large compared to computer zillionaire gifts to Stanford and MIT) for a new state-of-the-art computer center.

Science in late-twentieth-century Harvard was distinguished in most of what it did. But it was far from doing everything. It was small in size compared to its counterparts in the major state universities and technical schools, and (as always) stronger in abstract theoretical pursuits than in practical, applied work. Harvard science, like Harvard itself, chose to build richly and with high standards on an established tradition. This was hardly a bad thing. As a Harvard scientist observed, large fortunes were not to be made in proving theorems or explaining the universe. It was, rather, in biomedical and chemical research and in information technology that big payoffs were to be found. But so, too, were the most serious threats to old traditions of disinterested scholarship, the pursuit of truth, and minimal bureaucratic oversight.[33]

## The Social Sciences

The social sciences might have been expected to flourish in post-1970 Harvard. What, after all, was more in and of the world than the study of economics, politics, history, psychology, society, and culture? But with the exception of economics, the social science disciplines labored under substantial constraints. True, they had greatly raised their relative standing in the academy between 1940 and 1970. And many social scientists adopted statistical methods and theoretical constructs which, they fondly thought, gave them the character and the authority of the natural sciences. But they could not by the century's end lay claim to break-throughs in understanding on the order of the nuclear-quantum revolution in physics or the molecular-genetic revolution in chemistry and biology.

Radical critics saw in the scientism of the social sciences a capitulation to major vested interests: government and corporations. In their view quantification and empirical research made social science a hand-maiden of privilege and power. During the late 1960s and the 1970s this critique won considerable support in the academy and the media. But the intellectual prestige of scientific ways of thinking and the rise of the computer ensured that the social sciences would remain in thrall to testable theory and quantitative analysis.

By the end of the century, the god of irony that so evidently runs things in the academic disciplines saw to it that another approach—long devalued because of the dark cloud of racism attached to it—came into prominence. The genetic revolution in biology and biochemistry gave new explanatory power and disciplinary respectability to the view that nature as well as nurture had much say about the sources of social behavior. Sociobiology, scorned by the Left, nevertheless fed on advances in neuroscience to become an increasingly important tool in the study of consciousness and personality. At the same time the theoretical and analytical models of neoclassical economics gained comparable authority in the more policy-oriented social sciences of economics, political science, and law. The outraged response of many sociologists, social anthropologists, and social psychologists to the rise of sociobiology, and of radical economists, political scientists, and law professors to the rise of the market model of analysis, resembled nothing so much as the response of academic traditionalists to the radical triumphs of the 1960s.

Social science at Harvard cautiously made its way between the Scylla of overrelevant policy making and the Charybdis of underrelevant theory making. By the century's end its form and content were not substantially different from what they had been thirty years before. As in the case of the sciences, the story of Harvard's social sciences is one of variations on rather than the transformation of the intensely meritocratic, discipline-minded academic culture that emerged during the midcentury decades.

After the dismantling of the Social Relations department in the early 1970s, social psychologists and social anthropologists returned to their ancestral homes. For the first time in memory, Harvard psychologists were under one departmental roof. The newly reunified department of Psychology housed three programs, experimental psychology, personality and development, and social psychology. But problems remained: keeping the peace between grant- and space-rich experimentalists with their few—mainly graduate—students and underfunded social, developmental, and personality psychologists who did most of the teaching; attracting senior faculty and keeping them; attracting top graduate students and keeping them satisfied; and doing something about the undergraduate concentration that might lessen student hostility. While undergraduates were drawn to social psychology, it had diminishing research appeal as a subfield of the discipline. Many graduate students wanted to work in clinical psychology. But the graduate program in that area, berthed in the School of Education, was discontinued in 1973, a victim of scarce resources. And the department's experimentalist wing, few in numbers, found it difficult to compete with the larger spread down the river at MIT. Seven of eight experimentalist graduate students in the early 1980s said, when asked, that they wished they had gone elsewhere.

By the end of the century Harvard Psychology had settled down. It recruited more effectively and substantially strengthened its cognitive/experimental wing. The earlier stage of the field, in which "anything a researcher found out was new," gave way to a more sober sense of the complexity of human behavior and development. Collaborative research became the order of the day. Evolutionary psychology, fed by neurophysiological advances, came into vogue, though as so often was the case, cutting-edge work went on elsewhere. At Harvard, left-wing evolutionary biologist Steven Jay Gould exuded skepticism and urged caution (Bourbonism has many hats ... ). Still, the dual verdicts of "not proven" for genetics-based explanations of human behavior and of "not enough" for environmental explanations were not authoritatively refuted. Harvard Psychology's hedging had something to be said for it.[34]

Just as late-twentieth-century Psychology benefited from student and public fascination with the Self—a New Age inheritance of the sixties— Anthropology got a lift from the upsurge of interest in indigenous peoples and cultural studies. The department's 175 concentrators in 1974–75 were two-and-a-half times the 1968–69 count.

Like Psychology, Harvard Anthropology's ability to take advantage of its moment in the sun was limited. It, too, had a relatively small faculty, for the most part solid, traditional practitioners of solid, traditional anthropological approaches. Hoary archaeology was well-staffed, and most of the social anthropologists adhered to the established British structural-functional school. More arcane topics such as anthropological linguistics and urban anthropology were taught by transient juniors. Up-and-coming biological anthropology was short on staff and courses.

While Anthropology was a field in intellectual ferment, much of the bubbling took place away from Cambridge. The Harvard department's national standing had gone down. It continued to attract substantial numbers of undergraduate and graduate students, but had only eight senior faculty, who often were away on fieldwork or held part-time administrative appointments. A worsening national job situation made the junior faculty feel "not only temporary but marginal," preoccupied with finding another position and leaving abruptly when they did so.[35]

For all its shrunken state, Harvard Anthropology did not escape the conflicts that divided the discipline. Its unity in the past rested on the fact that archeology and physical and social anthropology had common values: the mystique of fieldwork, a shared concept of culture. Now this was riven by growing criticism of the relationship of the anthropologist in the field to his native subjects and by conflict between the environmental base of social anthropology and the genetic base of biological anthropology.

Social anthropology, the darling of the discipline in the 1960s and 1970s, had identity problems by the 1980s. Its structural-functional foundation was in decline, and while more-or-less Marxist formulations had some appeal, their place in the intellectual pecking order was insecure. More was needed to respond to the intellectual challenges of biological anthropology and sociobiology. The answer: a resurrection of myth-and-symbol cultural anthropology. This approach had been out of fashion since the turn of the century; reformulated by Princeton Institute for Advanced Study anthropologist Clifford Geertz and made politically and ideologically correct by the rise of cultural studies, a postmodernist social anthropology came into national prominence. But not at Harvard. Its relatively small size, slow turnover, and a conservative appointments tradition worked against with-it trendiness. Instead, social anthropologists had built strength by the century's end in a few specialties: transnationalism, third-world movements, ethnic violence and medical anthropology.

But biological anthropology emerged as the most vibrant wing of the department. Additional appointments, growing links to OEB, Psychology, and a new interdisciplinary Center for Genomics, enabled it to compete successfully with other major universities. And by the cultural adaptation of allowing the biological, archeological, and social wings to admit their own students, Harvard's anthropologists avoided the fate of their Stanford colleagues, who in 1998 divided into separate departments of Social and Biological Anthropology.[36]

Sociology richly profited from the radicalism of the late sixties and early seventies, and bore the brunt of that era's more problematic effects on academic life. The department continued to attract bright graduate students and talented faculty. It persisted, too, in its administrative slackness, notable even by the undemanding standards of the University. (Some as-yet-unexplained law of social behavior appears to dictate that the inability of sociologists to engage in effective social organization is matched only by the inability of psychologists to understand each other's mind-sets or of anthropologists to tolerate each other's folkways.)

Like Anthropology, Sociology at Harvard was small and disunited. The department regained full independent status with the dissolution of Social Relations in 1972; but only three of its eleven senior professors—George Homans, Harrison White, and Daniel Bell—were full-time members. It was as deeply divided internally—between sociology-as-science and sociology-as-social-analysis—as were its other behavioral brethren. Junior faculty members complained of too much disorganization and too little consultation; graduate students objected to a lack of colleagueship and being denied a role in appointments and the curriculum.[37]

The department was weakest in those areas with the greatest prestige in the discipline: systematic analysis, survey research, organization theory. Despite the presence of Harrison White and the part-time appointment of Seymour Martin Lipset, its strength lay in the more eclectic, less quantitative approaches of George Homans, Daniel Bell, Nathan Glazer, David Riesman, and Orlando Patterson.

By the early 1980s the senior faculty was unable to "overcome strong internal divisions over younger . . . scholars," the situation made worse by "the . . . fragmentation of the field of sociology itself." It was a matter of shame to some (and of pride, perhaps, to others) that Harvard's was the only major sociology department in the country without a federal research training grant. An advisory committee of sociologists from other universities was convened to do something about the appointments logjam. It patiently worked with the department to bring in more empirical sociologists. After much huffing and puffing, and several turndowns (rumor had it that Harvard offers gave a major boost to the salaries of sociologists at Wisconsin), new appointments were made. The department became more eclectic; mathematical modelling and statistics coexisted with social theory and a substantial engagement with racial, ethnic and gender issues. Like other branches of social and natural science, sociology by the century's end had to respond to the increasing presence of members of the discipline in the professional schools and the challenge this posed to its disciplinary and pedagogical autonomy.[38]

Economics was the social science that most successfully combined a scientific persona and high public prestige. The Harvard department was not identified with a particular school of economic thought. Why not? Primarily because when, in the 1960s, it set itself the task of challenging the primacy of the Paul Samuelson-led MIT economics department, the discipline was mathematics-and-theory driven. Elegant solutions to problems set in a Peter Pan world of pure theory: that was the thing.

Meanwhile the stagflation of the seventies took the bloom off the Keynesian rose, and the collapse of the Soviet Union in the late 1980s further weakened the already shaky academic standing of central planning. But Chicago's longtime preeminence in market economics foreclosed Harvard switching from a Keynesian to a neoclassical commitment.

The radical flurry of the late 1960s and early 1970s gave a brief fillip to left-wing economics at Harvard. A covey of radical juniors won much student support. Unsurprisingly they did not get tenure (except for Stephen Marglin); unsurprisingly, their backers charged political repression. When the department's visiting committee came around for a look in the spring of 1970, a faculty member attacked that body for having "too many business men and members of the establishment, and no welfare mothers, Black Panthers, and women." The Graduate Economics Club campaigned for a course in Marxist theory, and the visiting committee responded by supporting an "objective" course in Marxian economics and "other shades of radical economic thought."[39]

The remorseless spread of impersonality in a large department posed a more substantial challenge to its culture. Graduate students were unhappy with the inaccessibility of some professors, many believing that "the senior faculty has little interest in teaching them and is not concerned with their welfare." The faculty declared that teaching would be a major requirement for appointments and set up a (short-lived) center for the improvement of economics teaching. But like the science departments it sought to emulate, Economics responded slowly if at all to calls for the appointment of women and minorities.

Harvard's economists cared most about the department's place in national rankings, getting the pick of each year's litter of graduate applicants and junior faculty, and hiring and holding senior superstars. The result: a sharp, competitive, sciencelike atmosphere, infused with the belief that they were the brightest of the bright, doing work that was hard, challenging, important. Undergraduates found the teaching very good, junior faculty found the department an attractive place despite their small promotion chances. By the mid-seventies Economics was outsized, with around 600 concentrators (peaking at almost 700 in 1981), 1,000 undergraduates flooding each year into Economics 10, the introductory course, and a staff of more than fifty regular appointees and about seventy teaching fellows.[40]

A number of the department's most conspicuous members—Edward Mason, Wassily Leontieff, Simon Kuznets, John Kenneth Galbraith—

retired in the mid-1970s. Leontieff and Galbraith, men of the Left, were bothered by the increasing presence of theorists, whose work seemed to them to have little to do with real economic life. Leontieff chastised the department for its lack of ideological variety (for example, only one Marxist) and called for more faculty "with a wide range of interests."[41]

But the lure of disciplinary top doggery was more compelling. New appointees Zvi Griliches, Kenneth Arrow, and Dale Jorgenson were theorists or econometricians, superstars engaged in dialogue with a world audience of fellow economists. Many members of the department—among them Martin Feldstein, Lawrence Summers, Thomas Schelling, and Jeffrey Sachs—were called to service by the Council of Economic Advisers, the Federal Reserve, the World Bank, the International Monetary Fund, and the Treasury Department, and as advisers to presidents and presidential candidates. (Summers would become Secretary of the Treasury and in 2001 Harvard's new president.) Gregory Mankiw, a hot young Ph.D. from MIT, got a flock of offers from leading departments, among them Princeton and Harvard. Mankiw reported to Martin Feldstein that he had been told at Princeton that if he did well there, tenure was likely. What were his prospects at Harvard? Feldstein assured him that if he did well at Harvard, he was very likely to get tenure—at Princeton. Mankiw came to Harvard, and quickly got tenure—at Harvard.

During the 1980s Feldstein and Summers became the most conspicuous figures in the department. They presided over the National Bureau of Economic Research (NBER), which had recently moved to Cambridge from its longtime Columbia berth in New York City. Under their leadership the bureau became a center of empirical, policy-oriented economic analysis. Feldstein called it a "retreat from Keynesian economics." The bureau was located halfway between Harvard and MIT, but ideologically it was much closer to—and dominated by—Harvard. In a notable reversal of its old Keynesian days, Harvard Economics became a hotbed (better: a coolbed) of high-powered neoclassical macroeconomics. The Hungarian Janos Kornai came as a comparative systems theorist, as did the ultraorthodox Robert Barro.[42]

By the end of the century, Harvard Economics was arguably the world's best, certainly the largest and most intellectually powerful of the University's social science departments. MIT had slipped compared to earlier decades. The Chicago Economics department, feisty, contentious, closely linked to its Business and Law Schools, inclined to frown on NBER-style policy-oriented research—Athens to Harvard's Sparta—did garner more Economics Nobel prizes during the 1990s.

Harvard continued to be more likely to troll the waters for big fish elsewhere than to breed its own; but then, with its wealth and prestige, it didn't have to.[43]

After 1970 as before, History was the most troubled of Harvard's social science departments. An Old Guard fought with tenacity for decades to fend off threats to the quality of what (with some reason) it regarded as one of Harvard's great departments. Historical metaphors come readily to hand: Leonidas and his band at Thermopylae; Bourbons who learned nothing and forgot nothing; perhaps most apt, Canute ordering the tide not to come in.

Recruitment difficulties began to crop up in the 1960s. History's prideful desire to get the best in the world led to recurrent failures, followed by the appointments of sure-to-accept former students. Journalist Theodore White, who chaired the History visiting committee in 1971–72, took on the recruitment problem. History was, he agreed, "famous today as a professional's department." But its senior faculty was fear-ridden "that pressure from the outside for expansion, or for symbolic appointments, may dilute the quality of scholarship of which they are so proud." That attitude increased the risk of a self-destructive "intellectual elitism." Defensively, some department members viewed White's comments as a plea for more theatrical teachers such as once-over-lightly "Frisky" Merriman, who had been White's teacher when he attended the College.

Harvard History had twenty-five tenured professors, compared to thirty-six at Yale and thirty-four at Columbia. But it showed no desire to get larger, and its assistant professors in 1972 were down to fourteen from twenty-seven the year before. One consequence was reduced course offerings, a further disincentive to a student generation not particularly drawn to history. The fact that a number of the senior faculty—Oscar Handlin, Donald Fleming, Robert Wolff, Franklin Ford, Richard Pipes—were prominent critics of student radicalism did not help.

The treatment of graduate students, previously criticized by the visiting committee as "the worst kind of Social Darwinism," improved. But their morale (as elsewhere in the humanities and the social sciences) was as low as their job prospects. The junior faculty, too, had a full plate of grievances. They had little hope of promotion and criticized the senior members for ignoring the intellectual ferment in the discipline: a broadly expanding, politically radical social history, shaped by a race-class-gender triad that had little place in the more pluralist, structural-functional approach of most of Harvard's senior historians.

The visiting committee thought that Harvard had not responded sufficiently to the new currents stirring the discipline. The department did not agree.[44]

History began to do better with undergraduates: "The bitterness and rancor of 1968–69 seems to have vanished." But students' unhappiness persisted over their favorite subject, American history. Columbia had fourteen American history lecture courses in 1971–72; Harvard had three. The number of bracketed (announced but not offered) History courses inspired a student T-shirt emblem: "[History]."

During the 1970s senior Americanists David Donald and Stephan Thernstrom strengthened that wing; fourteen junior appointees leavened the lump (though blacks and women did not yet loom large on the department oscilloscope). But each professor taught what he wanted, with little regard for curricular needs. And graduate students suffered from widespread cutbacks in jobs and fellowship aid. Unfilled senior slots remained the rule: the department continued to find it hard to identify candidates who both met its standards and wanted to come. The chairman glumly reported in 1982–83: "All in all I suppose I am suggesting a kind of tiredness among the senior members."[45]

Turf concerns helped block the appointment of distinguished Princeton French historian Robert Darnton. And the denial of tenure to popular modern American historian Alan Brinkley in 1986 stirred more than the usual flap. By now the average age of the senior Americanists was sixty-one; no new appointment had been made for more than a decade. A discouraging number of prospects turned down feelers or offers, and the department suffered from a steady trickle of departing seniors very rare in the past: William Bouwsma, David Landes (who moved to Economics), and Harold Hanham in the 1970s, John Brewer in the 1980s, Olwen Hufton and superstar Simon Schama in 1993. One consequence: a graduate student intake of declining quality as well as quantity. With dismaying frequency, top choices (especially in American history) went to other schools, Yale in particular. The yield of admitted graduate students was one of the lowest in the Faculty of Arts and Sciences. The visiting committee in 1990 saw "a department in crisis." A rating of History departments in 1995 put Harvard behind Princeton, Yale, Berkeley, Stanford, Chicago, and Michigan.[46]

The recruitment problem remained, decade after decade, larger in History than elsewhere. Why? In part because the shape of the discipline had changed dramatically: from a pyramid, in which a few outstanding scholars and departments by general agreement were at the apex, to a mesa, populated by ever more numerous historical clans, each defined by a subfield, each with its own pecking order. The department's older members, outstanding products of the pyramidal past, found it hard to adapt to the new order of things.

But even a change of personnel could not assure the alteration of what had become a well-established departmental culture. A third of the senior faculty was due to retire during the first half of the 1990s: potential for large change. Fourteen searches were under way in the fall of 1990. Promotions from below in borderlands areas—Vietnamese history, African history, Turkish history—came readily enough. But European historian and Women's Studies chair Olwen Hufton departed in 1993 after only six years in residence, which for the moment left both American and western European history without a female professor.

A younger generation struggled to escape the mortmain of the past. Search committees scoured the historical landscape; a forum in 1996 reported on who was doing what in American history. But turndowns continued to be frequent, and the repeatedly announced intention of promoting from below continued to be honored mostly in the breach. The unresolved tension between a departmental culture in which a few senior people exercised a veto power and the growing competitive strength of other schools gave special poignancy to the definition of History as a discipline whose subject matter is change.

Government, like History, was challenged during the 1960s and 1970s: most notably by Yale but also by MIT, Michigan, Chicago, and Stanford. Yet in dramatic contrast to its sister department, Government enhanced its standing during the 1980s and 1990s. This was due in part to more effective leadership and (not unrelated) to the lack of a powerful older faculty cadre standing in the way of adaptation to new academic conditions. Certainly the fact that from the 1950s on Government was readier than History to recruit senior faculty who had gone to other graduate schools made it a more cosmopolitan department.

Members of the department, as befitted students of politics, got along by going along. Government chair James Q. Wilson reported in 1972–73 that the American politics staff was nicely distributed among specialists in quantitative analysis, institutional analysis, and public policy. A comparable balance of power prevailed among the department's four major wings: American politics, comparative government, international relations, and political theory.[47]

But not all was steady and serene. Some senior members were often away on affairs of state; as Wilson observed, when the option became "adviser to Presidents or teacher of kids" it was obvious which would win out. Faculty disillusionment after the troubles of the late sixties also left its mark. Political theorist Judith Shklar observed: "The only lasting legacy of that time is a general flight from the classroom."[48]

The hoary practice of each wing of the department selecting its own faculty appointees remained the norm. When in 1982 the department had a junior position in international relations to fill, it advertised nationally. But it looked locally: at three Harvard products, able students of international relations barons Stanley Hoffmann and Samuel Huntington. The committee recommended that the position be split between a Hoffmann and a Huntington protégé. The department was asked to vote on whether or not to accept that arrangement rather than choose between the candidates. Most of the junior faculty abstained from participating in what some thought was a corrupt bargain among their superiors. There was much talk of patronage, as in the bygone days when Carl Friedrich and William Yandell Elliott carved things up between them. Indeed, old habits died hard. A leading non-Harvard political scientist, asked in 1991 for his views on a list of candidates for an American politics position, observed that each of them "has close professional relationships with one or more senior people in the Government department, which implies that each has an important internal constituency."[49]

Political Science at Yale ranked above Government at Harvard until the 1980s. Just as Economics responded to MIT two decades before, the department met the challenge by going beyond its longtime commitment to institutional analysis and into the cutting edge of the discipline: in this case, rational choice theory. Counters who counted—Morris Fiorina of Cal Tech, Kenneth Shepsle and James Alt of Washington University—came in, moving the study of American politics away from its institutional flowering under Samuel Beer, Edward Banfield, James Q. Wilson, and Richard Neustadt into a new, more mathematical and theoretical realm.

Greater sensitivity to trends in the discipline meant more appointments from outside. Shepsle in American politics and Joseph Nye in international relations politely had at each other on this subject in 1991. Harvard, Shepsle observed, was uniquely parochial in the degree to which it appointed its own graduate students to junior positions. Instead, it should do what Yale Political Science did in its glory days: export its best products to the hinterland. He wanted this to be a general rule, broken only for compelling reasons. The American politics wing had no junior appointees with a Harvard Ph.D. But international relations was 100 percent homegrown, and the comparative and theory areas were not far behind. Nye was willing to prefer outside candidates, all things being equal, but he did not want a rigid rule. International relations, with its all-Harvard chorus line, did not, Nye observed, have the lowest reputation in the department. (American politics, he implied, did.) Naughtily he asked, "Correlation, not causation?"[50]

Methodological diversity raised the potential for conflict in the department. An ongoing civil war between the new rational choice school and the old institutional and political theory people was the most conspicuous instance. Comparativists and one-country specialists also viewed the discipline through differently tinted spectacles. So, too, did conservative political theorist Harvey Mansfield, against almost all his colleagues.

The rise of regional study centers, the Center for International Affairs, and the Kennedy School of Government posed another threat to the department's cohesion. As in the case of other departments, Government wanted area specialists who were also accomplished social scientists. But it had to respond to the lures of additional positions, research money and released teaching time that these other units could offer.[51]

As elsewhere, the gulf between tenured and nontenured faculty—the academic equivalent of class difference—caused some discontent and alienation. The junior members of the department felt excluded from what looked to them like a steep status hierarchy. Graduate students decried the "Christmas party" phenomenon, named after an annual fete attended by almost none of the senior faculty. It might be noted that one of the more original—if controversial—insights emerging from the Harvard Government department in the century's closing decades was Robert Putnam's perception that Americans were "bowling alone," that is, were less and less bound by ties of voluntary association.

For reasons best explained by abnormal psychologists, members of the department during the 1970s and 1980s figured in several of the more notorious sexual harassment cases of the time. The department was hardly awash with tenured women: two out of about twenty-five in the mid-eighties, three in the mid-nineties. Nor did its racial makeup change. It had one African American professor, Martin Kilson, in 1970, and no other black professor when Kilson retired in 1998. Teaching politics, like practicing it, remained primarily a white male contact sport.

Nevertheless the quality and range of the Government department moved it to the top of its field. Of twenty-six junior offers made during the 1980s, all but one was accepted. Graduate instruction improved, as did the quality and yield of students. And it retained its popularity with undergraduates (especially those Law School bound, on their way to rule the world). The department weathered the academic storms of the late twentieth century better than did most of its social science peers. Its great time of change was during the years from 1940 to 1970. The patterns established then—a slowly growing commitment to the discipline as a quantitative, theory-generated social science (though one member quipped that Political Science was to science as Christian Science was to science); a faculty made up increasingly of members who trained and taught at schools other than Harvard—set the tone to the century's end.[52]

The most notable change in late-twentieth-century Harvard social science came not so much in substance or method as in organization: the growing prominence of area studies centers. The major academic disciplines had shaped Harvard's scholarly and instructional life during the first half of the twentieth century. Many observers thought that autonomous research centers would play a comparable role during the second half, as expressive of worldly Harvard as the departments had been of meritocratic Harvard.

Certainly America's ever larger international role, and the faculty's interest in cross-disciplinary inquiry (to say nothing of its interest in reduced teaching, fewer administrative obligations, and more sponsored research time) were powerful spurs to the rise of the centers. A Government professor equated them with alluring mistresses, tempting faculty away from the "conjugal obligations" of their departmental membership.[53]

Harvard's first important centers were in Russian (1948), Middle Eastern (1954), and East Asian (1957) areas studies and International Affairs (1958). Lesser add-ons were the Joint Center for Urban Studies (1959) and the Charles Warren Center for American History (1965). More kept coming: the Center for West European Studies (1969), renamed European Studies in 1974; the Ukrainian Research Institute (1973); the Center for Jewish Studies (1977). By the end of the century the Korean Institute, the Olin Institute for Strategic Studies, the Harvard Academy for International and Area Studies, and the well-endowed Center for Latin American Studies had been added: a panoramic representation of places, peoples, and topics.

The big centers—Russian, East Asian, West European, International Affairs—were major players in the academic game. They raised money for faculty chairs and made appointments (always in conjunction with a department); funded fellowships for graduate students, postdoctoral fellows, and visiting scholars; and served as gathering places for specialists in the Boston area, the nation, and the world.

Yet for all their resources and attractive power, as of 2000 the centers had not yet seriously challenged the departments as the primary definers of the University's curricular and intellectual life. The inflation of the 1970s badly eroded their slender endowments. Underfunded positions and fiscal indiscipline forced retrenchment in the 1980s, especially at the Center for International Affairs. Faculty of Arts and Sciences dean Michael Spence gave CFIA a million dollar bailout, at the price of more stringent controls over the numbers and financing of the faculty attached to it. Half-time appointments in the centers were cut back and control over the search for new appointees was vested firmly in the departments.

The rise and fall of the cold war and the changing relations of the United States with other nations had a more substantial impact on the centers than on the academic departments. The Russian Research Center's major funding from Ford ended in the mid-1970s. The end of the cold war further reduced the center's academic clout, though a $20 million gift from a private donor in the mid-1990s strengthened it financially. The Center for Middle Eastern Studies had ongoing difficulties stemming from the Arab-Israeli conflict. Although it was under some pressure to focus on contemporary problems, most of Harvard's Middle East scholars continued to work on the less controversial earlier history and culture of the region.[54]

The Center for International Affairs (renamed in 1998 the Weatherhead Center after a donor) was initially dependent on government and foundation support for inquiries into What's Hot. It spawned research programs, sponsored seminars and conferences, and brought senior government officials to campus for advanced study. CFIA was a target for anti-Vietnam War protesters, and Samuel Huntington, its director from 1978 to 1987, came under fire as an American triumphalist. But this hardly dampened CFIA's ambitions. An affiliated Program for Science and International Affairs flourished during the time it worked with CFIA in the 1970s. It had a seven-year, $3 million Ford Foundation grant and a cast of twenty-four researchers. Under the leadership of biochemist Paul Doty, the program provided much ammunition for the arms control movement of the time. (It transferred to the Kennedy School in 1978, the year Huntington became head of CFIA.) Under the sweeping title of Transnational Processes and Institutions, Huntington also conducted Rockefeller-financed inquiries into the oil crisis of the early 1970s, multinational corporations, and the global impact of the American media. Out of this, eventually, came his prediction of cultural conflict between major world civilizations, which set off a media buzz in the late 1990s.[55]

The Harvard Institute for International Development (HIID), which replaced CFIA's Development Advisory Service in the 1970s, epitomized the worldly University. This was the umbrella organization for Harvard-led (and foundation or government-financed) overseas aid and development programs. Controversy inevitably dogged its heels. In 1980 University of Chicago economist Arnold Harberger was chosen to head HIID. However, he had been the chief economic adviser to Chile's Pinochet regime: a major no-no in the post-1970 American university scene. Students and faculty loudly protested; Harberger pulled out. China specialist Dwight Perkins of the Economics department took the post, to general satisfaction.[56]

After the collapse of the Communist empire, eastern Europe and the former Soviet Union became prime HIID territory. Its new director, Harvard economist Jeffrey Sachs, and his staff gave effective advice in Poland. But HIID's Russian experience was more clouded. During the early and mid-1990s, Harvard economist Andrei Shleifer and legal expert Jonathan Hay ran an HIID-sponsored program, subsidized by the U.S. Agency for International Development (AID), to help the Russian government create capital markets for the privatization of state enter-prises. More than $40 million in funding went from AID to HIID and the Russian project. In the spring of 1997 AID alleged that Shleifer and Hay were using their positions for private gain and cancelled its support. Sachs removed them from the project and from HIID. Accusations of collusion between HIID and the Harvard Management Company, the University's investment instrument, to get HMC in on bargain-base-ment auctions of shares in Russian companies, added to the cloud that hung over this Harvard-in-the-world enterprise. In 1999 a faculty committee recommended that the size and scope of HIID be signifi-cantly reduced. Activities not directly related to the educational programs of the schools were to be closed down. Cleanliness, it appeared, was not necessarily next to worldliness.[57]

Despite these problems, the appeal of international and area studies remained strong. If anything, America's cultural hegemony strengthened the cause of Harvard's internationalism, much as British higher educa-tion took up remote places, people, and tongues during the apogee of the Empire. Preparing their case in the mid-1990s for the multibillion dollar Campaign for Harvard, a Committee on International Priorities took a fresh look at CFIA and the area centers. There were twelve of them, spending $10 million a year: a bit more than half from endowment, the rest from government, foundations, and private donors. They proposed to work together on a problem-centered agenda and do more comparative and theoretical studies, in tune with the trendy academic emphases of the time. The committee recommended that $32 million be earmarked for the centers in the campaign, along with $50 million already committed or to be raised in other ways: a healthy sum, though not of a scale to pose a serious challenge to the hegemony of the departments. Still, the centers clearly were there to stay. They were bound to benefit from the long-term trend of Harvard becoming a richer, more international and interdisciplinary university.

## The Humanities

The humanities in the late-twentieth-century university faced an unprepossessing present and a bleak future. Fewer than one in ten high school students taking the Preliminary Scholastic Aptitude Test expressed an interest in the field. Resolutely practical courses of study—business administration, the health professions, public administration, computer and information sciences—flourished; English, Philosophy, foreign languages, and humanities outlier History declined. In the past, thought a disconsolate humanist, students sought values and knowledge; now they sought high wages and job security.[58]

Given these conditions, what were beleaguered humanists to do? Remake themselves, that's what. The upheaval of American (and Western) culture in the 1960s and after opened the door to a postmodern approach to literature, art, and philosophy, which as it turned out met the need of the humanities for a new footing in an academic world that was rapidly devaluing them. The highly technical language and theory-drenched style of postmodern criticism enabled its practitioners to claim a command of arcane mysteries comparable to that of scientists and economists. Gnostic youths coming of age in the 1960s and after were drawn to a critical style that disdained existing authority, hierarchy, and canons. No less attractive was postmodernism's rejection of older concerns—voice, quality, values—in favor of race, class, and gender as the prime components of critical analysis. At the same time, and on a less elevated level, Cultural Studies could—and did—lay claim to all forms of human expression from Shakespeare to comic books.

But as hegemonic postmodernists plunged into a brave new world of critical understanding, they encountered indigenes: the Old Humanists. A Kulturkampf broke out between beleaguered defenders of the old and ardent advocates of the new. That widely bought (and almost as widely unread) defense of the Old Humanities, Allan Bloom's *The Closing of the American Mind* (1987), sparked numerous rebuttals. The Modern Language Association's often self-parodic convention panels and papers led to the creation of a countercountercultural Society of Literary Scholars. So fierce were the passions, so florid the rhetoric, so outsized the positions on each side, that even the media took notice.[59]

This new ancients versus moderns struggle played out at Harvard slowly, prudently: in short, in the University's time-honored way of absorbing the best that was said and done some time after it was said and done. Although Harvard did not act in a crisis mode, it was hardly immune to the crisis in the humanities. Half of the College's students chose humanities majors in the 1920s; less than a third did so in the 1970s, a fifth to a quarter by the late 1990s. Graduate students suffered from the general shortage of academic jobs and its accompanying sense of malaise.

And Harvard's humanists had reason to look with foreboding on their prospects in an institution ever more dedicated to worldliness. One of them took Bok to task for omitting culture in his vision of "an international Harvard." Another bemoaned the fact that "as we have pressed out into the world, we have seemed intent on not merely tolerating but even fostering the politicization of those few domains in which universities have a centuries-old record of success."[60]

English and American Literature, the largest and most powerful of Harvard's humanities departments, was the chief battleground of the Culture Wars between the humanities' Ancients and Moderns. Like the department of History, English suffered badly from declining student interest and Old Guard-Young Turk intergenerational conflict. But to a far greater degree it was caught up in the issues of gender, race, ideology, and disciplinary character and purpose that had come to characterize the humanities.

The English department's status and internal coherence suffered rude shocks after 1970. Tensions ran high between a senior faculty accustomed to running the store and a junior faculty with few or no future prospects at Harvard. Students criticized the paucity of modern or offbeat courses, and the visiting committee took the department to task for its "dismissive defensiveness" toward new critical theory. By common consent, deconstructionist Yale outstripped Harvard in the 1970s and 1980s as The Place to Be (though half of Yale's new literary theorists were educated at Harvard). A 1982 national ranking put Harvard's English

department behind those of Yale, Berkeley, and Virginia. A discomfiting number of outside offers were rejected in the early 1970s, and the
graduate student intake declined to about half of what it had been in the
heady days of the sixties. Average time to a degree, 7.1 years in 1975–76,
stretched out to 9.3 years by the early 1980s.[61]

On the cusp of retirement in 1982, literary biographer Walter Jackson
Bate dwelt on his beloved department's decline. He contrasted the
lucent past with the dismal present, warning of a "crisis in English studies." Seeking to escape the trammels of specialization, Bate held, English
Literature pursued "horizontal spread": women's, ethnic, and gay studies,
business English, filmography. But the theory-ridden new darlings of
the field—structuralism and poststructuralism, deconstruction—were in
fact the old philology and New Criticism in a fresh guise: different in
style and substance, similar in their reliance on insider jargon. Meanwhile, Bate thought, the importance of writers and literature as the
interpreters and mirror of life declined.[62]

Yet the English department—in many respects Bate's department—
did not avidly pursue the postmodernists. It continued to seek out
traditional scholars such as Richard Ellmann, the eminent biographer of
Joyce, who chose to stay at Oxford.

Poetry critic Helen Vendler, in 1980 the first woman proposed for a
full-time professorship in the department, was hardly *nouvelle vague*.
Her broadly cultured, close and sensitive readings of poetry were in an
old tradition. The balance of power between newcomers and old-timers
was slow to shift. One reason: the department's size and scope imposed
a constant need to appoint specialists in areas where the new sensibility
was only a faint whisper. But slowly, haltingly, the English department
edged into postmodernism. Yale cornered the pioneers; Harvard went
after, and got, some of the stars of the next wave. These often turned out
to be women. Yale-trained Marjorie Garber came from Haverford in
1981 with a reputation for teaching Shakespeare effectively to undergraduates. Energetic and quick-witted, Garber liked to engage in what
she called "intellectual cruising." She became a strong voice for literary-
turned-cultural studies and won wide public recognition with books on
toothsome topics such as cross-dressing and dogs. And she taught
Shakespeare with a scatological verve light years from the buttoned-
down felicities of her predecessors.

During the 1980s English (much like History) deadlocked over a
number of its mainstream appointments. When offers were made, more
often than not they were turned down. And in a few cases the ad hoc

committee and the president did not support the department's nominee. In 1988 an outside receivership (polite term: advisory) committee was created to break the jam. Its charge was to help the department fill six vacant slots, stretching from the novel and twentieth-century literature to feminist and cultural theory, philosophy and literature, and the New Historicism (the latest turn of the postmodernist wheel). The committee recommended and the department appointed Elaine Scarry, whose interest in the body and pain stretched the envelope of literary criticism, New Historicist doyen Stephen Greenblatt of Berkeley, traditional eighteenth-century scholar Leopold Damrosch, and very nontraditional nineteenth-century novel specialist David Miller, who came for a few years and then cruised off to Columbia.

With Garber, Barbara Johnson (recently come over from Romance Languages), Scarry and Greenblatt in place, it appeared that the new wave in literary studies had come into its own. But the road to power proved unexpectedly bumpy. Undergraduates did not necessarily thrill to the same postmodernist siren songs that enraptured their professors. The canon still rumbled from afar: courses with trendy names often had venerable reading lists. Helen Vendler showed how compelling informed textual criticism could be and was not averse to taking a swipe or two at the more exotic forms of feminist criticism.

The junior faculty remained alienated by the lack of tenure prospects. And the new facts of academic life that impeded senior appointments in other departments—the capacity of other schools to meet and surpass a Harvard offer, the deterring effect of spousal commitments, the persistence of personality conflicts and factional academic politics—worked in English as well. By the century's end, Harvard's distinctive blend of caution and clout kept it from rivaling Yale's Age of Deconstruction in the 1970s and 1980s. But it avoided anything like the takeover, sacking, and departure of a postmodernist band at Duke.[63]

English had a close though not always an easy relationship with Comparative Literature, an interdisciplinary graduate program of cutting-edge novelty and stratospheric standards under Harry Levin in the 1950s and 1960s. Levin retired in the late 1970s, to be replaced by Claudio Guillen, a solid successor unassociated with the new wave in literary theory. A stab at trendiness came in 1986 when an offer went to Columbia's Edward Said, the voice of the Third World literary sensibility; but Said stayed at Columbia. An attempt was made in the mid-nineties to merge Comp. Lit. with an undergraduate concentration in Literature, established in 1981, which had become a gathering place for students attracted by cultural studies. But Literature chair Barbara

Johnson argued that her program was for generalists, Comp. Lit. was for specialists; and she prevailed.

By the end of the 1970s there was an evident "crisis and debilitation in French Studies." Old problems—internecine conflict, neglect of graduate students and junior faculty, a less than world-class reputation—were worsened now by what critics called an "archaic" chronological approach to its subject and "a stultifying indifference to any of the new trends and developments in literary theory."[64]

A committee made up of professors from other departments was charged to recommend new appointments. One of these was Jules Brody, who became Romance Languages chair and energetically sought to get French literature at Harvard up to postmodernist snuff. Barbara Johnson arrived from Yale in 1983, a disciple of deconstructionist guru Paul de Man who had the ability to champion the new critical theory without rousing the hostility of traditional scholars. Another gifted post-modern critic was Susan Suleiman, who helped fill a yawning gap in twentieth century French literature. When Johnson switched over to the more center-stage English department, she was replaced by Alice Jardine, a controversial expositor of the ever more important feminist strain in literary criticism. That raised eyebrows, and Bok made Jardine's promotion contingent on future appointees who taught the canonical literature of earlier periods. Here was Harvard's customary response to new academic developments: best characterized (mixed-metaphorically) as getting on the bandwagon without rocking the boat.

The presence of Suleiman and Jardine led a conservative journalist to publish an exposé of Harvard's French department in *Le Figaro*. He called it a hotbed of modish feminism and political correctness, and dismissed the scholarly credentials of Suleiman and Jardine. Those ladies were not for burning. They brought suits for libel in France and eventually collected tidy sums: Harvard worldliness in yet another guise.[65]

The German and Slavic Language and Literature departments were only lightly touched by the winds of postmodernism and had a shared sense of marginality in worldly Harvard. Students might be interested in acquiring useful linguistic skills, but they had neither the time nor the taste to steep themselves in the literary cultures of other lands (or, indeed, their own). Harvard undergraduates long before had lost interest in German; now Spanish displaced French as the language of choice. Fixed staffing levels and endowment-guaranteed positions kept Harvard's language and literature departments from shrinking. But low student interest and few jobs for graduate students were persistent realities. So, too, was an appointments market made up of seemingly slim domestic pickings and attractive but hard-to-get and hard-to-keep foreigners.

During the 1970s, off-ladder language teachers (long a fixture on most American university campuses) became more common at Harvard. A faculty of research-oriented literature professors was not disposed by training or inclination to provide elementary language instruction. At the same time, language teachers became more professional, and in the late years of the century an increasingly international-minded student body began to show more interest in learning other tongues. Enrollments shot up in Chinese and Japanese, and by 2000 it was not clear whether the literature dog wagged the language tail, or vice versa.

The appetites of Harvard's more arcane language departments—East Asian and Near Eastern, Sanskrit, Celtic, Linguistics—got bigger during the Great Academic Barbecue of the 1950s and 1960s. The University's commitment to a rich and diverse humanities program, the disinclination of the faculty to abandon a subject, and most of all the duty of a worldly university to pay attention to the non-Western world protected these waifs. (Though not unqualifiedly so: in the late 1990s a proposal to add a position in Bengali to the numerically challenged Sanskrit department relied heavily on the argument that as many as 250 million people spoke the language. The entreaty of an administrator— "Isn't that enough?"—momentarily derailed further discussion.)

Current events—the Arab-Israeli conflict, the oil crisis of the 1970s— reinforced the cultural importance of Near Eastern Languages and Civilization. The problem was to stay on the academic straight and narrow in so politically and ideologically charged an area. The department had kept its academic skirts clean by emphasizing the culture of the region's deep past. As a result it faced a problem familiar in other humanities departments: trying to fill positions in arcane subjects whose best scholars were often distinguished foreigners who did not travel well, or at all. But American James Kugel in Jewish Studies proved to be an inspired teacher of the Hebrew Bible.[66]

Linguistics remained to the century's end a small and troubled department, weighed down by its strongly philological, Indo-European past, overshadowed by Chomskyan MIT nearby. With only two senior faculty members, it barely made it into the top ten American departments in the field. Recurrent efforts by the administration to get Linguistics to identify more closely with the language departments, or Psychology or Anthropology, got nowhere. The occasional stab at closing it down (as Columbia and Yale had done) fared no better; linguistics-minded faculty in other Harvard departments rallied to the support of their embattled brethren.[67]

Nowhere was the potential for big trouble in a small venue greater than in Sanskrit. By the 1990s two of its three senior members, German-born Michael Witzel and American-born Diana Eck, were at loggerheads. On one level the argument was substantive. Witzel wanted the department to teach Sanskrit in the context of Indian/South Asian studies; Eck wanted to emphasize the religious dimension of the classic Sanskrit literary texts. Administrative and personality conflict added richness to the mix. The dean of the Graduate School had to take over as chair, and graduate student discontent surpassed even the husky Harvard norm.[68]

Harvard Philosophy had a past glory comparable to English. True, a 1969 ranking put the department second to Princeton's, and it would not be easy to replace soon-to-retire major figures Willard Quine and Nelson Goodman. But John Rawls (who came in 1962) and Robert Nozick (in 1969) gave new life to the plain language philosophy that most attracted undergraduates and the public. Together with mathematical logician Hilary Putnam and philosopher of aesthetics Stanley Cavell, they kept the department at or near the top of the academic philosophy charts.

This did not grant immunity from the discontents of post-1970 university life. Undergraduates complained of inaccessible, research-obsessed faculty and of a paucity of courses in the history of philosophy and continental thinkers, subjects of declining professional but strong student interest. By 1974 undergraduate concentrators were down to twenty-five. Graduate students, also a shrinking breed, had similar grievances. Junior faculty complained that the department was badly managed, that its members had no shared goals. (A more realistic view might have been that conditions were close to normal.)[69]

When it came to new Philosophy appointments, the meritocratic standard of the past—the best minds in narrowly defined bodies of knowledge—continued to prevail. But the department found its ability to beckon, and get, much reduced. In 1971–72 a choice had to be made between logicians David Kaplan of UCLA and Saul Kripke of Rockefeller University. If the issue was mind over body—spectral smarts over defined diligence—Kripke was the winner. But a department had to be lived in, and Kripke (who, some averred, had descended to earth from the planet Kripke) might be a handful. The department chose Kaplan, and Bok supported it; Kaplan stayed where he was. A year later Kripke was approached; he, too, said no.

By the early 1980s Philosophy, like English, could look back on a decade of notable lack of success in filling its vacant senior slots. The reasons were familiar. Few met the department's exacting standards; those who did chose not to come. The appointment in 1983 of under-graduate-accessible moral philosopher Thomas Scanlon improved student relations. Gisela Striker, the department's first senior woman, came on a joint appointment in Philosophy and Classics, soon left for Oxford, soon after returned. By the end of the century she had been joined by moral philosopher Christine Korsgaard.

Philosophy maintained its stature as a source of significant discourse in a more worldly university. But it could not avoid the loss of discipli-nary edge that afflicted so many of the humanities during the closing years of the twentieth century.

The Harvard Classics department was among the best in the United States, yet it also shared in the general humanities malaise. As elsewhere, Classics graduate student applications declined, and many who came soon departed, claiming to feel "cowed or depressed." The department was criticized for continuing to emphasize the language and literature of the ancient world over history and philosophy, and was urged to embrace Medieval Latin, Byzantine Studies, and modern Greek. But the fusti-ness of Classics was part of its charm, and it continued to attract a devoted cadre of undergraduates, refugees from contemporary relevance. Its sixty-six concentrators in 1976 equaled those of the non-English European language departments combined. Of help, too, was the new scholarly ferment in archeology, linguistics, and epigraphy.[70]

John Finley, who epitomized Old Classics at Harvard, bemoaned the loss of departmental cohesion: "The old sense of community has broken down socially, intellectually, and residentially." But Classics was largely (though not entirely) spared the divisions over method and substance prominent in other humanities departments. Ad hoc committees asked for more broadly engaged and pedagogically talented nominees, but they customarily went along with the department's unexceptionable proposals.[71]

Fine Arts and Music, steeped in scholarly traditions of connoisseurship and musicology, were under greater pressure to respond to the new world of postmodern cultural and aesthetic criticism. At the same time they faced a growing student desire for active engagement in artistic creation.

The President's Committee on the Practice of the Arts addressed that need in 1972 and recommended not only that students have more opportunity to paint and sculpt, but that they get course credit for their work.

A major source of strain in Fine Arts was the tension between the connoisseurship of the Fogg Art Museum's curators and the cultural perspective of the department's younger art historians. The latter regarded the Fogg's holdings as teaching materials with which to school students; the curators saw their role as acquiring, interpreting, and displaying their wares to the public. In the past, that line had not been sharply drawn: curators taught in the department, and professors did curatorial work. But after the appointment of Daniel Robbins as director of the Fogg in 1971, relations with the department soured. Temporary relief came with the appointment of senior faculty members to head the museum after Robbins left in 1974. But the burden of administration was too much for them. Finally in 1991 Bok came up with James Cuno, a museum professional who had a Harvard Ph.D., and charged him to tend first to the department's teaching needs, then to the care and feeding of the collections, and finally to the museum-going public.[72]

The arts-conscious cultural ambience of the 1960s and after gave the Fogg a new lease on life. Funds were raised for a substantial addition to the museum, designed by British architect James Stirling (not everyone's cup of tea). But as construction costs mounted, a MATEP-burned president Bok tried to kill the project, to the deep distress of Fogg director Seymour Slive, his colleagues, and donor "friends of the Fogg." Additional funds were raised, Bok was forced to back down, and the Sackler Museum opened in the early 1980s.[73]

Despite the substantial female component of Fine Arts students, women professors were slow to arrive. In 1976 Jean Boggs, the director of the Toronto Art Museum, came to teach a Harvard curricular stepchild, twentieth century art. But after a couple of years she went off to direct the Philadelphia Museum of Art. Not until the 1990s did women figure prominently in the department lineup.[74]

Many of the leading Harvard art historians of the midcentury decades—Ernst Kitzinger, John Coolidge, Oleg Grabar, Sydney Freedberg, John Rosenfield, Seymour Slive—had retired or left by the mid-1980s. It was difficult to find comparable replacements. And the aesthetics of the field were changing, in pace with the humanities at large. Cutting-edge art criticism, like cutting-edge literary criticism, had an increasingly adversarial relationship to the traditional canon. New appointments in Indian, Islamic, Chinese, and ancient Middle Eastern art strengthened the non-Western areas. But the bulk of student course enrollments were in Western art, and turndowns perpetuated the weakness of the more traditional areas. Timothy Clark, a brilliant, flamboyantly radical interpreter of nineteenth- and twentieth-century Western art, came in 1980 only to leave for Berkeley in 1988. A divided department chose literary critic-turned-art historian Norman Bryson to replace Clark. He was a spokesman for the prevalent postmodernist view that pictures, like literature, were best seen as signifiers rather than as self-contained works of art.[75]

By the 1990s the department was in thrall to the postmodern critical sensibility. It decided that Fine Arts 13, Harvard's traditional history of Western Art survey course, should be replaced. Critics contended that the course was narrowly based on a single tradition, was more or less limited to painting and sculpture, and was dominated by formalist concerns. Instead, the department proposed a set of survey courses covering Indian, Renaissance, Modern, Japanese, African, Roman, Medieval, Chinese, and Ancient Near Eastern art, and the history of architecture. Advocates saw this as an opportunity to emphasize "multiplicities of perspectives and value systems"; opponents thought it faculty specialization and postmodern critical values run amok. Pressure for a single introductory course—from students and the faculty's Educational Policy Committee—persisted. In response the department created a new course, "Art and Visual Culture: Introduction to the Historical Study of Art and Architecture." Disdaining chronology, it focused on analytic concepts derived from the study of works "taken from all times and places." But it did not appear to win the hearts and minds of Harvard undergraduates.[76]

Chair Irene Winter favored a shift in Harvard's Fine Arts appointment policy from a "monolithic" concept of The Best "to an expanded notion of scholarship, pedagogy and citizenship that serves our many constituencies far better." In 1997 Fine Arts changed its name to the Department of the History of Art and Architecture. The older label carried unwanted hierarchical connotations, out of place in African art and other areas, and seemed to the new generation of art historians far too exclusionary. Fusty Fine Arts had become modishly mod.

Music was a small department, in which tensions between musicologists on the one hand, and composers and performers on the other—between viewers and doers—remained high. The musicologists' attitude toward the others was very like art historians' view of studio practitioners: they were perhaps necessary but marginal appendages to the department.

At the same time student interest in musical performance was grow-ing. Before 1970 the department had just one composition course, offered instruction only in piano (by Luise Vosgerchian, later the department's first female professor), and gave no credit for performance preparation. The musicologists complained that a new, student-driven emphasis on performance undercut music's academic objectives, made it more like a conservatory than an arts and sciences department. A review committee Solomonically recommended one new appointment in composition and one "bridging appointment" in theory. When these were made, tensions gradually eased. Reinhold Brinkmann came in as a musicologist who had the rare distinction of winning the approval of the composers. And in the 1990s the talented pianist and Mozart expositor Robert Levin brought a Leonard Bernstein–like flair to the department's offerings.[77]

The Department of Visual and Environmental Studies (VES), established in 1968, was the place where undergraduates could learn not only to appre-ciate but to create art. Students initially criticized VES's emphasis on architecture and design (which reflected its Graduate School of Design origins) over courses in moviemaking, painting, and sculpture. Things changed in the 1970s. By 1978 VES had 100 concentrators and 1,500 course enrollments, and was deep into studio art and moviemaking. Hands-on instruction was too attractive to the post-1960s young to be denied.

But in these later days doing art could have consequences unknown to those who merely viewed it. In 1987–88 a visiting sculptress gave a live chicken to each member of her class. They were instructed to interact with it for a day, have it killed, cook and eat it, and then make a sculpture of its bones. The purpose of this exercise was to reduce the distance between the artist and the object: as part of the student's body, the chicken would expand its host's artistic imagination and understanding. Animal rights groups and three of the seventeen students saw it differ-ently. The former protested, the latter took their chickens to an animal shelter (and an uncertain fate). But the lure of the new could not be gainsaid. As one junior observed: "It's a very interesting process to watch. It's something you don't usually see."[78]

Despite this liveliness, problems remained. A 1993 review of the work of VES found much to criticize. Studio art, film and photography, and design instruction coexisted, but were neither coordinated nor developed in sufficient depth. Distinguished artists were loath to come from New York or the West Coast, and academic salaries and schedules could not compete with successful professional careers. One solution: bring in short-termers to meet teaching needs. Turning necessity into a virtue, the well-connected New York painter Ellen Phelan came as VES chair and recruited a lively group of visiting artists. The department in 2000 could look back on steady growth, improvement, and (especially in its filmmaking program) student popularity. But with the small size of its tenured faculty, and the lingering academic bias against creative art, it was not yet fully part of the Harvard mainstream.

The contrast between VES and the Loeb Drama Center, that earlier grand gesture to the creative yearnings of undergraduates, could not have been greater. In conception and funding, the Loeb was to be the students' theatre. And their desire to act, like their desire to paint, sculpt, play music, and make movies, was strong and growing. But the Loeb was too complicated an instrument for undergraduates to use without substantial professional instruction. "They tell us," reported the visiting committee, "that they often feel like a talented group of football players asked to play big-time football with inadequate coaching." The best solution appeared to be to hire a full-time director, with the resources to provide serious instruction to student actors and the authority to mount productions of acceptable quality.[79]

In 1978 Robert Brustein, who had caused a stir in repertory theatre circles as director of the Yale Drama Center, came to run the Loeb. In order to get him, Harvard agreed to his setting up a professional repertory company as he had at Yale, besides seeing to it that interested undergraduates got professional instruction. (Brustein wanted to run a full-fledged, degree-granting drama school, but that was thought to be a bit rich for Harvard's blood.) Students protested, fearing (with some reason) that they would be crowded out. But Bok thought that Harvard would be well served by a theatre that culturally uplifted the community as well as the University. So Brustein came as director of the drama center and professor of English, with a professional repertory company—and the charge to pay "particular attention . . . to improving the quality of undergraduate drama" at Harvard.[80]

Under the initial agreement, half of the Loeb's main stage offerings were supposed to be student productions. But by 1983 these were down from seven to four a season. Much student drama was shunted to the Loeb's small experimental theater, Radcliffe's Agassiz Theater, and (as in the old days) the undergraduate houses, where it thrived. Brustein, meanwhile, set out to make his American Repertory Theatre (ART) a major national, even international, force: a worldly theater for a worldly University. His productions reflected the new stress of the modern stage on sensation and the body rather than language and ideas. Tom Stoppard's plays were conspicuous by their absence; their author was, said Brustein, "jejune." But Brustein was traditional enough to resist the view, part of the new multiculturalism, that only blacks could play or write about blacks.

His considerable gifts of showmanship won ART much critical acclaim and—that ultimate accolade for the avant-garde—much audience distaste. During ART's early years, subscribers turned over at a startling rate. But a steady stream of students and other arrivals to Harvard and Cambridge provided new customer cannon fodder: not unlike the fresh troops thrown into the Western Front in World War I. Bok's worldly University did not insist that this new tub sit on its own bottom. Instead it wrote off the Loeb's deficit as a worthwhile contribution to the community and to art. Meanwhile FAS and the central administration kept squabbling over who should bear the cost of that patronage.[81]

By the year 2000, the department of African and Afro-American Studies had morphed into a prominent player on the Harvard academic scene. How that happened says much about Harvard's adaptive capacity in the closing decades of the twentieth century. It is also an object lesson in the difference that leadership can make.

Afro was a product of the turmoil of the late sixties and early seventies. The department's early years were as tense and tumultuous as American race relations itself. Some of Afro's members regarded appointments, curriculum, and scholarship not as the traditional business of the University, but as weapons in a larger movement for African American cultural and political identity.

Not until 1975, six years after the creation of the department, did a visiting committee take a look at it. Ewart Guinier, Afro's first chairman, was still its only tenured member, and Afro students had a strong sense of second-class citizenship, of exclusion from the Harvard mainstream. In 1976 musicologist Eileen Southern came with a joint appointment in Afro and Music to replace the retiring Guinier as chair. By any reasonable measure Afro's state was parlous: frequently unsatisfactory short-term appointees; a minute number of concentrators (eighteen sophomores, juniors, and seniors in the spring of 1976); a politicized atmosphere that made life difficult for Southern. Her take-charge manner did not sit well with students or (mostly male) junior faculty accustomed to a larger voice in departmental affairs. A 1979 evaluation recommended that the department be downgraded to a committee, a live grenade that Dean Henry Rosovsky promptly doused in cold water.[82]

In 1981, at the end of Afro's first decade, *Harvard Magazine* concluded that it was "drowning in a sea of student impatience, faculty ennui, administrative impotence, and the crushing weight of its negative reputation." Ernest J. Wilson '70, who as an undergraduate played an active role in the campaign to have a department rather than a program of African American studies, wrestled with the problem in an article, "What Went Wrong." He confessed that "I sometimes feel that I helped create a Frankenstein."[83]

Afro-American historian Nathaniel Huggins, with a joint appointment in History, took over as chair in 1980. He had the qualities necessary to command the respect of his FAS colleagues: a Harvard Ph.D., solid professional standing as an historian, a calm demeanor, no administrative experience. Huggins set out to bring Afro and its subject matter into the Harvard academic mainstream. He recruited Werner Sollors, a German-born scholar of Afro-American literature who was also appointed to the English department. Sollors's appointment kicked off an Afro student protest because he was white, but Huggins would hear none of that. Together the two brought in African American economist Glenn Loury, who had a joint appointment in Economics. But this flowering was short-lived. Huggins died of cancer in 1990, and Loury moved over to the Kennedy School, leaving Sollors the department's only tenured member: back to the square one of the early seventies. As in years past, prominent black academics turned down tenure offers. Some Afro students conducted a sit-in in the president's office to protest the lack of faculty: the first such incident since 1978.

Finally in 1992 literary scholar Henry Louis ("Skip") Gates came from Duke to a joint professorship in Afro and English and the department chair. He turned out to be an effective advocate of the department-building approach that Huggins pioneered: nonadversarial, meritocratic, firmly committed to the view that African American studies had a legitimate place at the Harvard academic table.[84]

Gates's first senior appointee was philosopher Kwame Anthony Appiah, an upper class, Cambridge-educated Ghanaian philosopher. In style and perspective Gates and Appiah were at a vast remove from Afro's concentrators. But in fact the in-your-face black nationalism of the past quarter of a century was, by the 1990s, giving way to more complex and nuanced attitudes. Separatist though they were, the students wanted the department to offer more social science courses that would give them the disciplinary skills necessary to succeed in careers or be more effective activists. And they complained that the same books cropped up in too many Afro courses.

Gates was the right man at the right time. At first he pointed the department in the direction of his own primary interests: literature and culture. Then he moved into the social sciences. In 1994 he induced charismatic social commentator Cornel West to come from Princeton with a joint appointment in Afro and the Divinity School. Chicago sociologist William Julius Wilson—the sort of mainstream social scientist that Afro's students wanted—joined the department and the Kennedy School.

The media spoke histrionically of Afro's "Dream Team." By 2000 it had close links through joint appointments with other Harvard departments and schools, a thriving W. E. B. DuBois Institute for Afro-American Research, its own Ph.D. program, and in Gates one of the most politically adept members of the Harvard faculty. The department, born in activism, had at first self-defensively turned in on itself and rejected the prevailing standards of the academy. That was not the road to success in late-twentieth-century Harvard. When Afro entered more fully into the life of the worldly University of which it was a part, prosperity came in full measure.[85]

In many ways the humanities at Harvard adapted to the demands of a more worldly university. Harvard's notable capacity to absorb, temper, and even in some Hegelian way synthesize seeming irreconcilables operated in the humanities as it did elsewhere. Older departments such as Classics were well-padded with endowed chairs and maintained a hoary Harvard tradition of humanistic learning. And much of what was least admirable in Harvard's humanist past came under assault. The old appointments insiderism—if in doubt, or if not in doubt, hire your own—continued to decline. The philological tradition of graduate instruction that so tenaciously persisted in the English and foreign languages and literatures departments now finally went quietly into that good night.

New programs in cultural, women's, and African-American studies added vitality and liveliness to the Harvard humanities scene. But that scene also contained within it some of the constricting political correctness, destructive nihilism, and jejune vulgarity that seemed to be indivisible parts of the postmodernist package. How Harvard's humanities would deal with *that* remained to be seen.

## ～ 18 ～

# THE PROFESSIONAL SCHOOLS

H arvard's graduate and professional schools were where the tension between social responsibility and teaching the technical skills demanded by a complex society most fully emerged. The Graduate School of Arts and Sciences and the traditional Big Three of Law, Business, and Medicine continued to dominate the Harvard professional school scene (though the Kennedy School of Government was coming up fast). From 1940 to 1970, they and the smaller schools took on their modern configuration: meritocratic, intensely professional, intellectually ambitious. From 1970 to 2000 they faced a variety of internal challenges to that academic culture, as well as constant competition from their counterparts in other universities.

## The Graduate School of Arts and Sciences

After he became president in 1971, Derek Bok devoted his first annual report to Harvard College, his second to the Graduate School of Arts and Sciences. This was not surprising: the closely linked College and Graduate School were Harvard's traditional academic core. What, he asked, was GSAS's essential mission? Now as before, it was to train scholars and add to basic knowledge. But the Graduate School was in trouble. One problem was student attrition. Up to half of those who entered failed to get their Ph.D.s, compared to a drop-out rate of less than 5 percent in Law and Medicine. The fault, Bok thought, lay in the lack of structure in many doctoral programs, and he prodded the faculty to do something about that. Another concern was the Ph.D. job shortage. Nonscientists had to be ready to have careers in colleges, not just in research universities. That meant that the Graduate School would have to teach its students how to teach. At his urging in 1976 the Danforth

Center for Teaching and Learning (renamed the Bok Center in 1991) was set up to tend to the pedagogical instruction of graduate students.[1]

Declining academic job prospects cast the longest shadow over GSAS in the 1970s. More than 1,000 students entered in the peak year of 1966–67; by 1971–72 the number was down to 560. The humanities were particularly hard hit: the 1975–76 entering class in English Literature was 16, compared to 70 a decade before. Not only the number but, many thought, the quality of GSAS applicants fell off as the lures of law and business brightened and academic career prospects dimmed. Discouraging, too, was the time it took to get a Harvard Ph.D. Attempts at cut-backs in GSAS were inevitable. But although the national falloff in jobs and outside research support bit more deeply, and lasted longer, than anyone expected, the faculty's resistance to substantial cuts in graduate programs—for most, their primary teaching concern—was tough and tenacious.[2]

This raised problems for the University that went beyond faculty morale. Harvard had long relied more than did Yale, Princeton, or Stanford on using graduate teaching fellows for some of its undergraduate instruction. Now the staffing of science labs, of tutorials and discussion sections in the College, of resident tutorships in the houses—the pedagogical finery of an affluent university—was more difficult. Belt-tightening decisions were made to reduce financial aid and end tuition abatements for teaching fellows. No one bothered to consult the graduate students. An ephemeral graduate student union staged an unprecedented one-day work stoppage on March 28, 1972—though their "strike" was as much an expression of general angst as it was a job action.[3]

By the mid-1970s the Graduate School was a leaner place, with low-key demoralization its regnant tone. A GSAS visiting committee complained that only a few departments tried "to present a comprehensive and coherent curriculum" and plaintively declared: "Somewhere in the academic administration of the University there should be the moral authority to encourage the others to do likewise." Bok's moral suasion had at best mixed results. Neither FAS dean Henry Rosovsky nor GSAS dean Burton Dreben—both believers in the autonomy of the professor-as-scholar—were inclined to intervene.[4]

In 1984, fifteen years after its last physical, GSAS went in for another checkup. The examining committee found not a school in any meaningful sense, but a congeries of graduate programs defined by the departments that ran them. Chemistry oversaw more than $6 million in annual research grants and contracts, English had none. Economics laid claim to a large sector with 21 senior faculty and 140 graduate students; Linguistics chattered along with 3 full-time senior faculty equivalents and 12 students. Ph.D. degrees in the 1980s took an average of 5.6 years in the natural sciences, 6.5 years in the social sciences, and 8 years in the humanities. By 1995–96, the GSAS mean was 9.1 years.

Some administrative tightening did occur. The number of "ghosts"— nonregistered students working on dissertations, God knew for how long or with whom—declined from 10 to 20 percent of students to less than 4 percent. (The senior faculty of a department discussed a student in the fifteen-to-twenty-year range. What had become of him? At first, no one could recall; he had not been seen in recent years. Then one spoke up: "Oh, of course, now I remember.... [H]is adviser died two years ago, and so we do not know what he has been doing since.")[5]

Some expected better times for the faculty job market when the children of the baby boomers descended on the colleges in the late nineties. Former Princeton president William Bowen, the head of the Mellon Foundation, turned his economist's eye in 1989 on appointment prospects in the humanities and the social sciences. After examining demographic and other entrails, he predicted a "staggering" shortage of professors in those areas by the end of the century unless the Ph.D. output increased. Bowen's was a cloudy crystal ball. The depressed national academic job market persisted, sustained by financial stringency, a continuing Ph.D. surplus, and the removal of age constraints on senior faculty retirement.[6]

During the 1980s and 1990s a number of departments pulled up their graduate program socks, reforming their curricula and tightening requirements. But at the end of the century as before, the economy and the job market, intellectual developments in the disciplines, and autonomous departments, not policy handed down from above, set the tone in the Graduate School. The humanities continued to struggle, the social sciences held their own, the sciences (relatively) prospered. Typical was the 1996 Ph.D. output: half in science, a quarter each in humanities and social sciences; 78 percent male; two thirds with academic jobs, 20 percent without immediate employment. About a third of the students—mainly in science—were foreign, and the proportion of foreign applicants continued to rise.[7]

A 1995 National Research Council ranking of graduate programs (of questionable accuracy, but much noticed) reported that Harvard was among the top five in all of its offerings except Psychology, Sociology, Romance Languages and Literature, and Linguistics. As striking was the fact that a number of schools—familiar contenders Yale, Princeton,

MIT, Cal. Tech., Chicago, Columbia, Berkeley, and newer ones like Stanford and the University of California at San Diego—had sufficient strength in one discipline or another to edge past Harvard.[8]

This fact, along with the influx of money during its end of the century fund-raising campaign, stirred Harvard's competitive juices. Though the continuing job shortage tended to stretch out graduate student careers, a Mellon Foundation grant for dissertation fellowships raised hopes for a shorter journey to the doctorate. And greater financial aid helped departments bid for top students. But problems that had plagued GSAS since the 1960s—the duration of graduate training, Harvard's "special" responsibility for producing Ph.D.s, the morale of graduate students and their role in undergraduate instruction—remained unsolved, perhaps unsolvable.

And a new question arose. The prestigious Ph.D. degree, under the control of the Graduate School, had a strong appeal to other Harvard faculties by the 1990s. The School of Public Health wanted to start Ph.D. programs in its new Division of Biological Sciences. Public Health dean Harvey Fineberg pointed out that all but two of the nation's twenty-six schools of public health—Harvard and Loma Linda—awarded Ph.D.s. Dental School antennae quivered at the prospect of support from the National Institutes of Dental Research for a D.M.D./Ph.D. program. Divinity School dean Ronald Thiemann maintained that his school's Th.D. was fully comparable to the Arts and Sciences Ph.D.; the existence of separate degrees in the advanced study of religion was "an anomaly of history." He wanted a joint doctoral program in the subject, with the Divinity School a coequal partner.[9]

A large number of students had gotten Ph.D.s over the years in the venerable Medical Sciences program, run jointly by FAS and the Medical School. Now, flush with Hughes Foundation and other money, ambitious HMS dean Daniel Tosteson wanted to be able to award the degree in his own programs, with his own faculty. After all, many of them had Ph.D.s; and what they did differed little from Biology and Biochemistry in FAS.

Similar considerations led the Business School's John McArthur—like Tosteson, no shrinking violet—to the same view. Ph.D.s would make his students more competitive for teaching positions in business schools. Why, he asked in business speak, should Arts and Sciences have an exclusive "franchise"? One HBS professor put the case in more substantive terms. FAS was stuck in the mud of the traditional disciplines. But the rapidity of change in the real world made the professional schools' faculties "less apt to be satisfied with internal standards of quality that might be upheld by an obsolescing discipline.... I have colleagues who think of parts of the Economics department the way Galileo surely thought of the Vatican." The Kennedy School of Government also got into the act. Dean Albert Carnesale observed in March 1993 that its dependence on FAS was a growing problem. The bottom line: the school needed to be able to award its own Ph.D.[10]

Medical School dean Tosteson proposed that the Graduate School be removed from its FAS straitjacket and turned into a centrally directed agency, overseeing Ph.D. programs in Harvard's professional schools as well as GSAS. He called this a "modest" reorganization of the Graduate School. Graduate School dean Christolph Wolff more accurately observed that it would turn the Graduate School into an agency of the central administration, without an academic identity. Dean Jeremy Knowles of FAS worried that losing control of the Ph.D. would devalue it. As of 2000 the degree remained an FAS preserve. But new programs in Social Policy, Information Technology, and Public Health Sciences raised the number of Ph.D.s awarded jointly by FAS and other schools to twelve.

## Law

Strong in its teaching, finances, and its faculty's self-estimation, with a secure job market for its students, the Harvard Law School seemed ideally situated to weather the storms that swept over the University after 1969. But in fact it was deeply unsettled by the new social, cultural, and intellectual currents in post-sixties Harvard.

In 1982 president Derek Bok took a reformer's look at his old bailiwick. The legal profession, he warned, was in a state not unlike health care two decades before: "There is far too much law for those who can afford it and far too little for those who cannot." It was necessary to reduce the law's complexity and cost, and make it less alluringly profitable to bright young people who might better serve society as business executives, public servants, engineers, or educators.

What could the Law School do to help? Encourage research into the costs and efficiencies of the legal process. And teach students not only the adversarial approach to law but "the methods of mediation and negotiation" and "the gentler arts of reconciliation and accommodation." Bok pointed to sprouts of that agenda pushing their way through the resistant soil of the Law School: Roger Fisher's proposals for "getting to yes" without going to court, and Gary Bellows's popular Clinical Education program, which dealt with the delivery of legal services to the poor. He seemed to be proposing a paradigm shift in the curriculum from law as a social science to law as a social service. The core of the faculty's scholarly work, he suggested, should consist of practical inquiries designed to increase the law's social utility. The Law School should break out of the traditional professional school mold of "training practitioners for successful careers while failing to acquaint them with the larger problems that have aroused such concern within the society."[11]

As things turned out, HLS in the decades after 1970 was dominated by internal upheaval that echoed Bok's concerns, but hardly followed his let's-all-pull-together prescriptions. The most conspicuous challenge came from a faculty group associated with the new school of legal thought called Critical Legal Studies (CLS). Closely related to literary deconstructionism in its ideology and method, CLSers—"Crits" in Law School jargon—rejected Bok-style reform in favor of a root-and-branch assault on the very idea of the rule of law, which they saw as a capitalist tool. Reinforcing the CLS critique was a steady drumbeat of student complaints that HLS was too slow in appointing blacks, women—and then, in a triumph of synthesis, black women—to the faculty.

Critical Legal Studies found a place in other major law schools as well: Columbia, Stanford, Yale, even stereotypically conservative Chicago. But nowhere did the conflict between the Crits and the older faculty generation have the bite, or the longevity, that it had at Harvard. Bitter conflicts over appointments, admissions, and the curriculum raged from the 1970s to the end of the century. For a while, Critical Legal Studies threatened to replace Legal Realism, which had been the reigning ideology in legal education since the 1930s, much as Cultural Studies bid fair to dislodge older forms of discourse in literature and some of the social sciences. But by 2000 the Law and Economics movement—in intellectual style and political subtext the polar opposite of CLS—could claim greater intellectual standing in academic law, much as did the rational choice approach in political science, and sociobiology and its physiological-neurological offshoots in psychology and anthropology. But the question remains: why were things so sour for so long at HLS, compared to the rest of the University and law schools elsewhere?

From the days of Felix Frankfurter, members of the Harvard Law faculty sought the opportunity to serve in government. Over the decades this fostered a new order of academic values, in which time on the Boston-Washington shuttle replaced time in the Law School library as the hallmark of a modern major law professor. Meanwhile the legal system, and law school subjects, became ever more specialized. This bred faculty experts eminent not in "the law" but in their particular niche of the law. Harvard, the largest of the nation's leading law schools, had both categories—power brokers and legal technocrats—in abundance. Into this law school world swept the Crits, seeking the philosophic roots and the applicable praxis of revolutionary change in the law. It was as if a corps of left-bank Parisian intellectuals had descended on a trade school. They laid claim to an academic purity that their more workaday colleagues found difficult to challenge. The result was an ever greater loss of community, among faculty and between faculty and students. The Crits and their enemies waged aerial dogfights over legal philosophy, while grim trench warfare went on below over admissions, appointments, and curriculum. It is easy to point to the hypocrisy of students and faculty drawn to Harvard in their climb up the greasy pole of success, and then turning against the qualities that made the school what it was. But it is no less easy to understand the guilt that this could engender in the idealistic young (and the ideological old), and to see why biting the feeding hand became so much a part of life at the Law School during the 1970s and 1980s.

Somewhere between Derek Bok's beloved community of legal improvers of the human breed and the Crits' condemnation of HLS and all its works, the bulk of the school's faculty went on their middling, mainstream way. However challenged by ideological fissures, the old HLS faculty sense of being a band of brothers bound by the mysterious science of the law remained a force to be reckoned with. So, too, did affluence: the school's endowment was $36 million in 1974, $638 million in 1998.

Change came slowly in this fortress of (white male) meritocracy; but it came. Women, allowed in since 1950, still made up only 9 percent of the student body in 1970; by 2000 they were up to 44 percent. Blacks, barely a blip on the screen before the late 1960s, settled down to 7 to 10 percent of the student total during the century's late decades. Instruction changed in response to the new academic environment. The faculty in 1973–74 replaced the traditional numerical grading system with less precise letter grades. There was general agreement on the need to pay more attention to professional ethics, though whether this should be through separate courses or worked into the curriculum at large stirred much controversy.

The size, talent, and activist backgrounds of the student body assured a high level of confrontation over faculty appointments and the curriculum. The adversarial style of instruction enshrined in the book and movie

*The Paper Chase* was on its way out by the 1970s. An alumnus reminiscing years later about "Fear and Loathing" in the HLS classrooms of the 1960s assured his readers: "The Law School of this article no longer exists, its faculty and courses transformed by civil rights and feminism, consumerism, environmentalism, and their resulting cascades of revolution and reform." But what was left so grated on modern student sensibilities that an exaggerated view of the Law School as a total institution comparable to a prison, asylum, or boot camp persisted long after the fact. Women in particular chafed under the HLS regimen: a member of the Class of 1994 complained that her classroom experience consisted of "mean, twisted men in tight suits berating us into oblivion."[12]

A larger source of students' discontent was their perception of the law itself. True, most HLS graduates continued to follow well-trodden paths to Wall Street firms or their counterparts across the nation. But a substantial number wanted alternative careers and sought government or public interest jobs or dropped out of legal practice entirely. The Law School responded to these new interests. A rich menu of student public interest programs, organizations, and publications became an established part of the HLS scene. A special fund enabled graduates going into public service law to write off up to half of their student loans. In 1977 the faculty inserted a short term in January, during which female and minority visiting faculty, practitioners, and people from other disciplines could offer minicourses sanitarily separated from the regular curriculum. (But even this enterprise did not escape prevailing discontents. Black students boycotted and picketed a civil rights course because it was taught in part by Jack Greenberg, the former director of the NAACP's Legal Defense Fund, who bore the stigma of being white.)[13]

As elsewhere in the University, research-minded professors involved themselves in autonomous scholarly enterprises. Stanley Surrey's program on international tax policy, Jerome Cohen's Center for East Asian Studies, and the Center for Criminal Justice run by James Vorenberg and Lloyd Ohlin were among the most prominent of these. But the faculty found it hard to take on commitments beyond its demanding basic curriculum. Unlike FAS, reduced teaching was not highly prized. Nor was social science-inspired research always a comfortable fit with the assumptions underlying legal rules and reasoning.

The result was that, more than elsewhere, the Law School faculty had to face up to its internal ideological divisions. Faculty appointments became the most conspicuous battleground. Neither nice-guy Dean Albert Sacks (1971–81) nor Bok-like liberal Dean James Vorenberg

(1981–90) abated the hostility between the Crits and their faculty opponents. Gender, race, and ideological concerns moved from the periphery to the center of the appointment process. A committee in 1979 found a high level of personal hostility in the faculty, and no shared view of the school's educational mission. While it had been possible to make nine appointments of senior professors from other law schools in the late 1970s, internecine warfare prevented any in the early 1980s. Conservative Paul Bator resigned in protest in 1985; middle-of-the-roader Charles Nesson called for an end to "vilification, name-calling, backstabbing and character assassination."[14]

In 1981 the *Harvard Law Review* rethought its hoary practice of choosing student editors based on their class standing. The student body by now was 28 percent female and 14 percent minority. But only eleven of its eighty-nine editors were women, one was Asian American, none were African American. After much argument, the *Review's* staff agreed to let considerations of race and gender enter into the selection of eight of each year's intake of forty-eight editors. Minority applicants could submit statements describing the obstacles they had overcome; their grades had to be "close to" those of regularly chosen editors. Professor Charles Fried, whose background as a refugee from Hitler made him sensitive to this issue, warned that the new plan "attempts to confer the benefits of membership in a meritocratic organization while being dishonest about the attainment of merit."[15]

Bok's appointment of Robert Clark as dean in 1989 set off a new round of controversy. There was more than a little testing of the new boy in this: a Jesuit-trained expert in corporation and antitrust law hardly personified the New Age professoriat. In 1992 a group of students brought a suit (quickly dismissed) to the state's Supreme Judicial Court, arguing that their education was harmed by the lack of minority professors at the school. Derrick Bell, the school's first tenured African American faculty member, was a leader in this agitation. Bell announced in 1992 that he would not continue to teach at HLS until a black woman was given tenure, and moved to New York University. Yet 20 percent of the faculty consisted of minorities, and Harvard had the highest percentage of minority students among the nation's top twenty law schools.

New dean Clark was young and tough and canny, had solid scholarly standing, and presided at a time when a successful $150 million campaign helped to heal wounds. He coolly faced up to his opponents: "Conflict of viewpoints is hardly surprising in an institution such as ours." The Crits, as activists do, lost their revolutionary zeal: "This place is dead," one declared. New senior appointments were made of women and blacks, and even, in 1998, a black woman: Lani Guinier, Harvard College and Yale Law graduate, Penn Law School professor, exponent of a radical approach to race and the law, and coincidentally the daughter of Harvard's first Afro chair.

More female and minority professors, and a politic sharing of appointments between the Crits and their opponents, softened the adversarial Law School ambience. By the end of the century a new generation of faculty and students was less caught up in the old divisive issues. Clark encouraged curricular expansion—"letting a hundred legal flowers bloom"—and the study of worldwide legal systems. The proportion of foreign nationals in the student body (15 percent) was the highest of any law school. Sixty-five percent of the graduating class of 1999 went off to well-paying jobs in private firms, 25 percent to judicial clerkships; only 10 percent to public service jobs and "other pursuits, with a rising number moving directly into business ... as venture capitalists."

But some things were more resistant to change. A 1991 survey of student quality of life and educational satisfaction at 165 major law schools ranked Harvard a dispiriting 154th. In 1999 Clark commissioned his own survey, which identified the usual suspects: large classes, unrestrained competition, inaccessible faculty and unattractive living conditions.[16]

## Business

Like the Law School, the Harvard Business School was flush with money, high in standing, and readily placed its graduates in cushy jobs. But it was free of the ideological fissures that rent the Law School. Even during the troubled years of the early 1970s, Dean Lawrence Fouraker reported that his students were calm and serious about their work; the applicant pool and yield (about 80 percent) were pleasingly ample; faculty recruitment went well and retention stayed high.

In years past there had been some sentiment abroad in the University that a graduate school of business was not quite comme il faut. But that diminished as HBS built a faculty and curriculum heavy in economic theory and social science analysis, and came to boast scholarly jewels such as Alfred Chandler and Thomas McCraw, Pulitzer Prize winners in American history. By the mid-1970s there was talk of HBS evolving from a traditional business school into a center for research. The school entered into a joint program with the Kennedy School of Government to train senior public officials in policy making and the delivery of services. And with the financial incentive of a multimillion-dollar gift from financier John Shad in 1992, it turned its attention to integrating the teaching of ethics into the HBS curriculum.

Problems lurked beneath this calm-seas-and-a-prosperous-voyage exterior. By the 1980s the school's curriculum was getting long in the tooth. Go-ahead Stanford edged it out as number one in some rankings. And HBS students shared their Law School counterparts' disinterest in long-term careers at large firms. Only 95 of the 723 graduates in 1970 wound up in the nation's 1,000 largest companies. By 1995, two-thirds of the graduates of the 1960s were running businesses that they themselves had started.[17]

There was another cloud on the horizon in the late 1970s, named Derek Bok. Harvard's president had problems with the tone and substance of the HBS curriculum. It bothered him that its faculty was top-heavy with its own graduates. These "locals" tended to devote their careers to teaching and case preparation rather than scholarship. The latter was mostly the province of "cosmopolitans" who came from other schools in midcareer, usually with Arts and Sciences backgrounds. And Bok thought that the Business School did not distance itself sufficiently from the values and interests of big business. An objective view of government-business relations, the social responsibility of the corporation, and the ethics of business practices were customarily taught (if at all) in isolation from the HBS core curriculum. He quoted—with no approval—the remark of "one official from a prominent [business] school: As far as ethics are concerned, we figure that our students either have them or they don't."

What to do? HBS needed to hire young professors who wanted to be scholars as well as teachers. It should reorganize its languishing doctoral program by cooperating more closely with Arts and Sciences professors in Economics, Government, Sociology, and Psychology. And it needed to encourage its students "to master analytic techniques and conceptual material." The chief obstacle to that, Bok thought, was the school's traditional case method of instruction.[18]

This was root-and-branch criticism, not warmly received by its target. Associate Dean John McArthur gave Bok his own view of the school's problems: inconsistent appointment standards, weak or stagnant areas of instruction, and the need to develop "organizing themes that cut across the boundaries of traditional areas." He put a high priority on teaching entrepreneurship as well as ethical and moral values. And interschool programs left him cold: faculties, he said, don't work together; people do.

McArthur was the clear faculty choice to be the next dean when Lawrence Fouraker left, and in 1980 Bok appointed him. For the next fifteen years McArthur flourished as one of Harvard's most vigorous— and certainly one of its most contentious—deans. He nurtured HBS's identity as a major Harvard professional school and did not take kindly to Bok's prescriptions. Here was yet another instance of the limited ability of Harvard presidents to guide their autonomous faculties.[19]

At the same time McArthur on his own did many of the things that Bok wanted. Support for faculty research increased, more Ph.D.s joined the staff, and analytical approaches similar to those of the JFK School's Public Policy program supplemented the case method of instruction. McArthur strongly supported the work of homegrown corporation guru Michael Porter and recruited faculty superstars Robert Merton and Michael Jensen. A larger, more diverse faculty taught a larger, more diverse student body. Only a quarter of the staff had business school degrees by 1992. And the curriculum changed to reflect students' new career goals and the faculty's new scholarly aspirations. The traditional stress on the production, marketing, and finance skills needed by managers in large industrial firms gave way to New Capitalism topics: Business, Government, and the International Economy; Ethics; Management Communication; Human Resource Management. Courses became more theory-driven and quantitative. In the early 1990s the curriculum-reform pendulum swung again: to result-oriented rather than theoretical training, with emphasis on a more laid-back and participatory management style instead of the traditional take-charge ethos.[20]

The student body got larger, smarter, more focused. Entering M.B.A. candidates increased from 606 in 1948 to 950 in the late 1990s. A solid grasp of quantitative methods was a requisite for admission, as was some experience in the real world. No member of the class of 1993 came directly from college, and eight out of ten were over twenty-five years old. The number of female students slowly increased, from 11 percent in 1974, to 27 percent in 1990, to 33 percent in 2000. Blacks were pursued with growing vigor, so that by the mid-seventies it was no longer thought necessary to use a "modified quota system." By 2000 they made up 5 percent of the student body.[21]

Nevertheless Harvard kept slipping in business school rankings. McArthur thought that HBS risked becoming an also-ran unless it raised more money and improved its staff. Only a hair, he warned, separated success from "floundering mediocrity." Much of this was rhetoric designed to stir support for a large fund-raising campaign. But the school fell to an embarrassing fifth place in a *Business Week* ranking in the early 1990s. (MacArthur dismissed such ratings "as [expletive]".) More serious was the widely held view that for all its money and prestige, HBS had not kept pace with a fast-changing business world. It was compared to big, plodding General Motors, McArthur to "a conservative company man."

The school sought to renew itself by engaging in the favorite ritual dance of the academic tribe, a large-scale curriculum review. The result was *Leadership and Learning*, a detailed blueprint for change. Harvard, it said, should rely less on case studies and more on team projects, interactive computer-based learning, and other new boys on the pedagogical block. Some students with little or no work experience should be admitted to foster diversity. The faculty agreed in December 1994.[22]

When HBS engaged in a business venture of its own, the result was anything but stellar. The thought was that the case studies that the faculty churned out as teaching material, their burgeoning research, and the widely read *Harvard Business Review* could, if properly marketed, produce more revenue for the school. Toward this end, in 1990 HBS set up its own publishing firm, the Harvard Business School Publishing Corporation, and got Ruth McMullin, who had headed the publisher John Wiley and Sons, to run it.

Management problems soon abounded. The *Review* went through a clutch of editors. McMullin brought in T (no period) George Harris, a flamboyant New Age editor who had juiced up *Psychology Today* and *American Health*, to head the *Review* in late 1993. He was out in four months: "the fit between his talents and experience and our needs," said McMullin, "just wasn't right." McMullin herself was fired in March 1994. Her management style included such provocative techniques as hiring a psychologist, at $1,500 a day, to analyze staff members so that she could better manage them. From one perspective, what happened was "a culture clash between a profit center and the academy"; from another, "an object lesson in how not to run a business." The episode was a fit topic for an HBS case study: as of 2000, not yet done.[23]

In the spring of 1995, after a feisty fifteen years as dean, McArthur resigned. The *Crimson* called him "arguably Harvard's most powerful figure." During his term in office the HBS endowment went up sixfold to $600 million, its endowed professorships from fifty to eighty-one. The school added $200 million in new buildings and splendidly gussied up its campus. McArthur was a unique mix of an introvert whose forte was hands-on, skillful behind-the-scenes management—he was notably protective of his faculty and staff—with a gruff public style. Only he could have shared with the press his view of what faced incoming president Neil Rudenstine in 1991: "[We] have to understand we can't make endless demands on the poor bugger. When he came here it was like landing on Normandy beach. . . . it's this poor bastard getting swept in from Princeton and landing on the beach and he doesn't know anybody." And only he could have responded as he did when Corporation fellow Henry Rosovsky asked whether the new Business School chapel would be nonsectarian: "Of course. We'll have inscribed over the entrance: Jesus Saves; Moses Invests."[24]

Vivid, too, was McArthur's final report to the alumni. Discussing the recent HBS curriculum change, he resorted to the discomfiting analogy of a successful nursery school, "where there is a lot going on to engage the minds and energies of all those kids. . . . Conversely, when there isn't enough going on, the kids take over. Before you know it, they are crawling through the windows, clogging up the sinks, and getting into every other kind of mischief they can invent." So it was at HBS: "only here, it's the faculty that tends to wiggle out of control." Hence curriculum reform.[25]

McArthur's successor, Kim Clark, was a popular professor specializing in technology and operations with a Harvard Ph.D. in Economics and a strong research orientation: a new dean for a new age. His plans included a sizable investment in information technology, expanding the school's executive education programs, and increasing the number of foreign students. Well aware of arch rival Stanford's close ties to Silicon Valley and the e-com revolution, Clark set up a California Center in Menlo Park and put entrepreneurship at center stage in the HBS curriculum. New research centers soon sprang up in Hong Kong, Buenos Aires and Paris. These innovations reinforced more than altered a going concern. As was the case with Dean Robert Clark's Law School, Dean Kim Clark's Business School by the century's end was not in the throes of change but engaged in the preventive maintenance of a prospering institution.[26]

## The Medical Area

In most accounts (including this one), the Medical School is bracketed with Law and Business as one of Harvard's three major professional schools. Yet in key respects it is quite different, set apart in character as well as location from its sister Brobdingnagian faculties. HMS admitted about 200 students each year, far fewer than the 500 and more in the Law and Business School classes. The Medical School's complex relationship with a score of affiliated hospitals and research units, and its vastly more extensive research programs, gave it a very different faculty as well.

A core of full professors was backed by (literally) a cast of thousands—7,932 in the year 2000—of lesser full- and part-time appointees; most of them attached to the hospitals, unpaid by Harvard, doing a bit of teaching in exchange for an HMS affiliation. In contrast to other medical schools, the dean of HMS had no control over—or resources from—the affiliated hospitals, which ran their own research programs. To add to the complexity of it all, the Schools of Public Health and Dental Medicine were close—both physically and functionally—to the Medical School. This medical area was a world unto itself: part of Harvard, certainly, but of such mass and self-sufficiency that it sometimes seemed to be as distant from the central administration as Jupiter is from Old Sol.[27]

Even more than in the Law or Business Schools, the dean of the Medical School was a powerful figure because of the size and complexity of the operation he oversaw. During the troubled times of the late sixties and early seventies, HMS benefited from the emollient deanship of Robert Ebert, who readily responded to the campus spirit of the time. He was instrumental in creating the Harvard Community Health Plan, an early health maintenance organization that used Harvard's name although it was not officially connected to the University. He substantially expanded the school's clinical role and in 1970 established a well regarded joint degree program with M.I.T in Health Sciences Technology. By the end of Ebert's deanship in 1977, female HMS students had increased from 7.5 percent to 31.5 percent, minorities from 3 percent to 20 percent.

New Age medical education did not come easily to the strong-minded doctor-scientists who made up the senior faculty. In January 1976, six HMS professors complained to the Faculty Council about the "erosion" of standards, as in the case of a student who graduated despite his failure after five attempts to pass Part I of the National Board examination. And in the spring of that year professor of Microbiology and Molecular Genetics Bernard Davis wrote an article in the *New England Journal of Medicine* charging that most students admitted under racial double standards performed poorly and that the school was diluting its criteria in an effort to keep them in good standing. A storm of public criticism, and censure by the HMS faculty council, followed.[28]

When Ebert left the deanship in 1977 Bok trolled the alumni and others in the medical community for a successor. He got over 270 recommendations, met with dozens of faculty members to discuss candidates, and sought the advice of experts in government, foundations, and other medical schools. His choice was Daniel C. Tosteson, a physiologist committed more than Ebert was to basic science. Tosteson had built up an impressive administrative record at Duke and became dean of the University of Chicago School of Medicine in 1975. With his bags barely unpacked, he answered the call to Harvard in 1977 (to much distress at Chicago). This reserved and distant but intellectually energetic and persuasive man turned out (along with Henry Rosovsky of FAS and John McArthur of HBS) to be one of the major Harvard deans of the late twentieth century. He left a substantial legacy of curricular reform, effective fund-raising (endowment went from $128 million to $1.1 billion in twenty years) and growth in the size and quality of research programs.[29]

Derek Bok of course had views as to the current state and future prospects of the Medical School. It was the most remote and complicated part of his dominion, and he knew it. He concentrated not (as with Law and Business) on the discordance between the medical profession and society at large, but on the students' need to be relieved from an outdated method of instruction. That consisted of two preclinical years of lectures in basic science and another two years of unstructured practical exposure to patients through hospital rounds. Then they faced "the tyranny of the National Boards with their emphasis on rote memory and factual detail."

The result was too much passive information ingesting, too little emphasis on problem solving, and a "lack of attention to the nonscientific side of medicine"—ethics, the history of medicine, the behavioral sciences, the economics of health care—subjects that conveyed "the useful message that medicine is more than science." The prevailing view was that to "think like a doctor" meant to see sickness "as a scientific phenomenon consisting of deviations from a biomedical norm," and to downplay psychological and social-behavioral causes. Bok conceded that, given the dramatic scientific advances of recent decades, "the traditional concept has much to recommend it." But it was necessary for doctors-to-be to learn new approaches to diagnosis and treatment: "In sum, there is no substitute for doctors who can understand and integrate a range of subjects quite outside the body of bioscientific knowledge."[30]

Tosteson was well aware of the need to reform medical education, though he placed greater weight than Bok did on the primacy of scientific knowledge. His major innovation was a curriculum reform, grandiosely called The New Pathways to General Medical Education, designed to teach the art of "learning how to learn in medicine." Formal planning began in 1982, and The New Pathways became fully operational in 1989. It emphasized small group instruction, a self-directed approach to learning, and a more fully integrated mix of basic science and clinical experience. Gone were most of the large lecture classes and heavy memorization. The focus now was on learning how to gather and use medical knowledge and on greater sensitivity to patients' needs and wants.

At the same time the biological-genetic revolution, and the estimated doubling of medical knowledge every four years, could not be ignored. The New Pathways changed not only *how* HMS students were taught, but *what* they were taught. Each core science course became the responsibility of faculty drawn from several departments. And the science departments themselves underwent substantial transformation. By the time Tosteson left the deanship in 1997, Anatomy and Physiology had been merged into Cell Biology, Biological Chemistry and Pharmacology into Biological Chemistry and Molecular Pharmacology. New departments of Social Medicine and Health Care Policy responded to those now urgent medical concerns.

By most accounts The New Pathways was a resounding success. As in the Law School, the old cutthroat medical school culture gave way to a more compliant ambience. When the chosen few of a first-year HMS class arrived for orientation, they were met by a passel of eager-to-please deans, faculty, and upperclassmen who gave new meaning to the concept of medicine as a helping profession. A member of the staff observed in 1996: "This medical school is filled with students who are as happy as medical students can be."[31]

For all the importance of The New Pathways, Tosteson's deanship was dominated by the need to administer a rapidly growing research empire and by the continuing complexities of HMS relations with the affiliated hospitals. Of necessity he expanded the HMS bureaucracy. Not surprisingly, many senior faculty felt that their power was much diminished. Department of Cellular and Molecular Physiology chair Howard Green groused to Tosteson: "Is life in the hotel to be determined exclusively by the management?"

HMS had to deal, too, with the erosion of its core faculty's commitment to the institution. The model of the physician-researcher-teacher gradually gave way to that of the research scientist supported by government or foundations or industry. The clinical faculty, focused on teaching, came to feel (with reason) that they were second-class citizens. In the early 1980s an attempt was made to reduce the status gap between research and clinical appointees by applying the title of professor to both. But part-timers still were called clinical professors, and many of the full-time professors in the hospitals held appointments "of indefinite duration," not the same as University-backed tenure. The old pecking order persisted under a thin disguise.[32]

Big medical science required big money. HMS fund-raising was low-keyed when Tosteson arrived on the scene: the school had a development staff of four, devoted primarily to opening envelopes and removing the checks inside. A new source was tapped when Harvard began to license patents to biotech companies. This produced $500,000 in 1989, $3.6 million in 1993. But the Medical School's research budget continued to depend overwhelmingly on the federal government, which provided three-quarters of the total.

A few years after he arrived, Tosteson looked into fund-raising prospects. Consultants thought $40 million was all that could be expected: not enough to go ahead. He decided to seek what he wanted rather than what he was told he could get and came up with a goal of $150 million. Bok, who had some discomfort with large-scale fund-raising, was skeptical, but allowed Tosteson to make a pitch to the Corporation. The fellows, more at ease with big sums, supported a campaign to begin in 1984, and its goal was raised to $170 to $180 million. A proper development office got to work, and in due course the goal was met—indeed, exceeded. The old laboratory spaces were refurbished, and new buildings went up to help house Harvard's ever expanding medical research empire. Its appetite whetted, the Medical School raised more than $300 million in the University's multibillion dollar campaign in the 1990s.[33]

Other new sources of income beckoned. Worldliness most intrusively entered the medical area in the form of linkages between research and private drug companies. The pioneering venture was a 1975 alliance with the Monsanto Chemical Company, a long-term project that supported the cancer research work of Judah Folkman, Bert Vallee and their associates. Tosteson actively sought "industrial liaisons" to meet the rising costs of HMS research. By 1996 the Medical School had five major corporate alliances, with a combined funding of $92 million.[34]

Medical Science Partners (MSP), a $36 million venture capital fund to finance the commercial use of medical discoveries, was launched in 1988. HMS was a silent partner with a claim to 10 percent of the profits, which would be reinvested in research through a nonprofit fund. The school would screen ventures in which the fund might invest: in effect, giving it the Harvard imprimatur. (A less friendly formulation: selling the Harvard name.) By 1996, MSP had eleven companies and nine projects. And in that year the Harvard Institutes of Medicine was set up in a revamped high school. The idea was to encourage collaborative work by housing HMS and hospital scientists in the same building. But the project turned out to be merely a research condominium with no incentives for the researchers to collaborate. Top-down integration was no easier to implement at the medical school than in other parts of the University.

In 1994 the school created Harvard Medical International (HMI), a nonprofit subsidiary corporation of the University. Its purpose was to raise the quality of medical education, biomedical research, and health care around the world. The revenues generated would be "used to support HMI projects and the core academic programs of the Faculty of Medicine." By the year 2000, HMI was engaged in forty projects in eighteen countries, though a potentially lucrative deal to manage Saudi Arabian hospitals was nixed by President Neil Rudenstine and the Corporation.[35]

This two-and-half-gainer dive into worldliness called for a new conflict of interest policy: one that closely monitored academic/industrial relationships while maintaining Harvard's traditional ban on faculty profit from health-related discoveries. Faculty leaders wanted (and got) a tight restriction on outside activities, required reporting of outside income related to research, and prohibitions against support from companies in which they owned stock or were otherwise involved. At the end of the century, HMS's conflict of interest rules were among the strictest of any medical school.

Despite these links with the business world, research productivity continued to be the measure of all things. And research in the Medical School, the hospitals, and the affiliated laboratories was big, complex, often loosely supervised by senior investigators. The result: a flurry of scandal. A special vocabulary (avoided by Harvard) described the major forms of scientific research misbehavior: "cooking" (choosing the data that best supported the hypothesis), "trimming" (discarding conflicting evidence), "dry-labbing" (inventing data). There were about fifteen such instances in the medical area during the late 1970s and early 1980s. A 1981 case was especially disturbing. Thirty-two-year-old John R. Darsee, who did his work at Brigham and Women's Hospital, was "one of the most promising cardiologists in the country." Evidence emerged that he had fabricated some of his results, a number of papers had to be retracted, a $724,000 federal research project was closed down. It turned out that Darsee had gotten into similar trouble at Emory and that his nominal supervisor, Chief of Medicine Eugene Braunwald, had been too remote from Darsee's work to give it proper attention. The number of scientific misconduct cases increased substantially during the 1980s and 1990s, as the federal government required schools to set up formal review procedures.[36]

Different in character, but also a product of the new high-powered world of medical science, was the case of Bernardo Nadal-Ginard, chief cardiologist at Children's Hospital and a Harvard professor of Pediatrics, whose work was widely thought to be of Nobel Prize potential. He was accused of stealing $7.6 million from the Boston Children's Heart Foundation, which he headed. Apparently the temptation of easy pickings, a lush lifestyle, and a sense of being insufficiently remunerated were mutually reinforcing.

Yet another sort of problem was posed by HMS psychiatrist John Mack, whose causes over a long and colorful career included the nuclear threat, the Middle East, the cold war, holotropic breathwork, and the est movement. Mack's 1994 book *Abduction* took seriously reports of contact with extraterrestrial visitors, a cause of some embarrassment to his colleagues. A Medical School committee took him to task for "affirming the delusions" of patients who claimed to have been abducted.[37]

As the century neared its end, relations between HMS and its affiliated hospitals, always complicated, were made still more so by the changes rippling through those institutions. Medical research at the major hospitals had been getting increased federal support for some time, and they became less dependent on the Medical School. But they faced escalating problems of finance and administration. Their patient and research costs kept mounting, as did their debt. Hospital mergers were in the air. As things turned out, the Medical School was not a major player in that game. Not that it didn't try. Dean Tosteson struggled for months early in 1993 to implement his "vision for the future": a five-hospital federation hegemonically called the Harvard Medical Group. But the hospitals' interests were too divergent. Massachusetts General and Brigham and Women's called for time out from negotiations to see if they could get their own act together, and then suddenly announced in December 1993 that they would merge into Partners Health Care System—a decision to which neither Tosteson nor Rudenstine was privy. (Another twist of the knife: HBS dean John McArthur chaired the Brigham trustees.) Beth Israel and Deaconess hospitals subsequently joined together as Care Group. The size and complexity of the medical area's activities had come to be all but out of anyone's control.[38]

Tosteson retired from the HMS deanship in June 1997. Joseph B. Martin, his successor, had spent the past eight years as dean and then chancellor of the University of California Medical School in San Francisco. His goal, much like that of Tosteson, was for HMS to be the impresario of the Boston area's managed health care. He buoyantly hoped to entice the affiliated hospitals back into closer collaboration with HMS, as he had done (impermanently, as it turned out) with the hospital and health care networks of the University of California and Stanford medical schools. One spur was the diminishing income to the hospitals from clinical care. Martin had a reputation as a skillful manager of people, as indeed he would have to be to master the medical area labyrinth. As of 2000, the jury was still out on that one.[39]

The changing world of medical science left its mark as well on the Schools of Public Health and Dental Medicine. SPH's standing improved: public health, epidemiology, and tropical medicine fit the growing interest in health care delivery and the Third World. While Bok initially thought that the Schools of Public Health and Medicine should be merged, by the 1970s SPH had a substantial enough faculty and income base to sustain an independent existence. Dean John Snyder retired in July 1972 and, as in other Harvard Schools, was succeeded by a man appropriate to the post-1969 University. Howard Hiatt came to the SPH deanship from Beth Israel, where he had been chief of medicine. Like his counterpart Ebert in the Medical School, he was more interested in sickness and health as a public policy issue than as a medical science problem. He wanted his school to concentrate on three areas: environmental factors affecting health, American health care delivery systems, and the health problems of the Third World. Old SPH programs—"pushing condoms and spraying DDT," as one faculty member dismissed them—gave way to new ones such as an Executive Program in Health Policy Management, funded by HEW and run in conjunction with the Business and Kennedy Schools. The Center for the Analysis of Health Care Programs was set up to do what its title said it would do.

Hiatt inherited an SPH-HMS relationship in which the M.D.s at HMS looked down on the M.D.s at SPH. He found a faculty deeply divided over the school's purpose and "a lack of mutual trust and understanding among faculty and between faculty and administration." Hiatt sought to raise appointment standards at SPH in part by recruiting faculty stars from other schools, most notably statistician Frederick Mosteller and health policy expert Harvey Fineberg. Given a mandate by Bok to change SPH, Hiatt nevertheless found the going tough and soon was at odds with many of his faculty. Junior professors complained that the school was becoming a health institute composed of autonomous research programs. Old-timers denigrated the dean's effort to make SPH "Kennedy School West." In June 1978, two-thirds of the tenured faculty, led by Nobelist and professor of Tropical Medicine Thomas Weller, tried to get Bok to remove Hiatt. Not surprisingly, the president backed his dean.[40]

Things eased after Hiatt brought biochemist Elkan Blout from the Medical School to be SPH's dean of academic affairs. But tension between advocates of the social and the scientific aspects of public health remained. In a bow to the egalitarianism of the worldly university, the school abolished administrative tenure, the SPH equivalent of the Medical School's clinical appointments, in 1982 and thereafter all senior appointments carried academic tenure.

Hiatt left the deanship in 1984 to devote his energies to avoiding what he took to be the looming threat of a nuclear war with Russia. Harvey Fineberg, who followed him in the deanship, proved to be a successful fund-raiser. In 1997 the School of Public Health reached its seventy-fifth anniversary. It had much to celebrate besides sheer survival: 778 students, 11 academic departments, an established place on the Harvard (and national) medical scene. But like all of Harvard's Lilliputian faculties, it lacked the gravitas of the Law-Business-Medicine Brobdingnagians. A student summed up the SPH ambience: "People are generally p.c., non-competitive, very friendly."[41]

The School of Dental Medicine had an inconspicuous and far less contentious place in the medical area scheme of things. Applications went up fourfold, and female applications tenfold, during the early 1970s. By 1977–78 there were forty candidates for every place in the school, and a nice balance of eighty predoctoral and eighty doctoral candidates. Dean Paul Goldhaber enlarged the research component of dental education by adding a fifth (research) year to the program. And as in SPH, the delivery of care took its place alongside more traditional dental concerns.

Goldhaber stepped down in 1989 after twenty-one relatively calm years as dean, succeeded by R. Bruce Donoff and more tranquility. The only stir of substance came when students complained about the three-year clinical program that followed on their participation in the preclinical two years of the Medical School's New Pathways. In 1996 the SDM clinical program was reduced to two years, and it echoed the problem-based emphasis of its HMS counterpart.[42]

# Education, Divinity, and Design

Harvard's old mini-trinity, its schools of Education, Divinity, and Design, continued to wrestle with their old problems in the late twentieth century: persistent shortages of money and conflicts over mission. Lacking the carapace of resources and professional identity enjoyed by the larger faculties, they were more vulnerable to the financial and ideological tempests of the post-1969 years.

None of Harvard's professional schools was harder hit by the crisis of 1969, and the monetary-morale hangover that followed in the 1970s, than the Graduate School of Education. In 1972 Paul Ylvisaker, who headed the Ford Foundation's public affairs programs, succeeded Theodore Sizer as dean: GSE's more socially sensitive counterpart to Vorenberg in Law, Ebert in Medicine, and Hiatt in Public Health. He took over a school in financial and programmatic disarray. Sharp declines in foundation and government aid had reduced GSE training programs from twenty-two to ten. Ylvisaker tried to tighten things further by reducing the school's offerings to three areas: Human Development and Reading; Learning Environments (which meant children's television); and Administration, Planning, and Public Policy. This reduction still didn't leave much room for traditional bread-and-butter tasks such as the training of teachers, curriculum development, or looking into the needs of primary and secondary schools.[43]

And heavy budget weather loomed ahead. GSE's operating deficit was projected to climb to $300,000 in 1974–75. Federal research money, mother's milk to the school in the 1960s, faded fast: from a high of $4.7 million in 1968–69 to $1.2 million in 1975. Tuition produced 11 percent of the school's income in 1967–68, between 32 percent and 60 percent in the 1970s. Heavy teaching loads and thin tenure prospects for the faculty hardly brightened the picture.[44]

But this was, after all, *Harvard's* School of Education, and the state of America's public schools had become a major national concern. Ylvisaker grandly observed that when "a great University determines those professions which are essential to the well-being of the society," it "cannot simply thereafter allow priorities and quality to be set by the vagaries of contemporary economic and political markets." The school's chief concern came to be not so much survival as improvement: making the curriculum less theoretical, adding more structure and requirements, providing better student advising and placement.[45]

The upswing gained momentum in the 1980s. An effort at "self-definition" led GSE to a more active relationship with primary and secondary schools, and more midcareer instruction for teachers and administrators. New foundation grants strengthened the school's finances. And in 1982 Ylvisaker gave way as dean to former Radcliffe vice president Patricia Graham. She brought to her job the perspective of a historian of American education and the political smarts of an academic tested on the Barnard-Columbia battleground. She was aware that public school policy was determined by administrators, college-educated (and hence know-it-all) parents, and policy wonks more informed in management and analysis than in the history and philosophy of education. Somehow, she thought, GSE had to get back to first principles: as she put it, to educate professional educators committed to "nurturing and enhancing the wit and character of the young."[46]

Graham benefited from Derek Bok's strong interest in the problems of American education. His 1985–86 annual report gave the full treatment to GSE. He took note of the anomaly between billowing public concern over the state of American education and the declining influence of education schools. Bok thought that Harvard's School of Education went astray in the flush sixties when, beguiled by research money and the lure of the social sciences, it tried to become more like the Arts and Sciences departments. Then came the downturn of the 1970s. The interests of faculty turned from the public schools to trendy but essentially peripheral concerns: educational television, the instruction of prisoners, cross-cultural studies, preschool education within the family. As the faculty went galloping off in different directions, students not surprisingly became unclear as to why they were there or where they were going.

Now GSE was turning back to its proper core concern, the public schools. Teacher education and administrative training programs voted down in 1974 were resumed in 1983. A large problem remained: how to "fashion a stable marriage of teaching and research at a level of quality appropriate to a major university." Unlike the Business School, GSE had no solid financial support to compensate for its fuzzy disciplinary base. Choosing priorities was all. The public schools were where America's educational dilemmas assumed their starkest form. They were ideal guinea pigs for new tools of educational research: the cognitive sciences, program evaluation, policy analysis. What better subject matter for the education school of a worldly university?

But even if GSE knew what it was supposed to do, how, and from where, would it get the people, the students, and above all the money to do it in a proper way? The College took one out of six applicants, the Law School one of nine, the Medical School one of eighteen; GSE admitted two out of three. From time to time Bok provided modest (but critical) financial support from his discretionary funds. But beyond that he could offer only unspecific optimism: "The hope must be that over time, using its own classrooms as a laboratory, the school will succeed in making advances of genuine interest not only to itself but to other faculties as well."

Bok took another look at GSE in 1987. He approved of its new faculty experts in educational psychology, politics, and economics, and its growing emphasis on cognitive psychology, information technology, and program evaluation. Its educational mission seemed clearer now than in the past. Yet only a quarter of its 1985 graduates took school jobs, and about half of the school's Ed.M. students were in general purpose programs without requirements or direction. With 1,233 students in 1990, it was Harvard's fourth largest school, but it was ninth of ten in endowment. The School of Education still found it difficult to establish a distinctive persona as a professional graduate school. As in the past, it seemed to be trapped in a dependence on the conceptual frameworks of other disciplines and schools. Nor did the rise of postmodern psychothought do much to stiffen GSE's disciplinary backbone: "the jargon of the human potential movement" had become "the lingua franca of the ed schools."[47]

Still, by the century's end GSE was a different, and stronger, school than in the midcentury decades. Its new dean, Jerome Murphy, who took over in 1992, surfed the prosperity wave of the nineties, raising $111 million, far more than GSE or any other school of education had ever garnered. A more worldly GSE offered advanced management training programs for school principals and superintendents, college administrators, and college presidents, and embarked on a joint venture with HBS to explore new forms of educational entrepreneurship.[48]

The Harvard Divinity School was less financially troubled than Education, and its faculty had a more widely shared sense of purpose. It had the luxury in 1974 of choosing 115 new students from 800 applicants. Its biggest problem: it had fifteen tenured and only four nontenured faculty, a recipe for professorial arteriosclerosis.[49]

The school responded to the gnostic mood of the late twentieth century by reducing the size of its doctoral programs and putting more emphasis on ministerial training. Krister Stendahl, its dean from 1968 to 1978, observed in 1974: "Particularly the blacks and women who are now studying here are not letting us forget the part we play in oppression and injustice if we do not open our eyes to new sources of insight and resources that are already close at hand. We realize more and more our complicity in these evils if we do not cooperatively explore any channels open to us to help eliminate them." He wanted the school to move from the "negative, passive non-denominational attitude" of the past "toward a positive involvement in the pluralism of American religious life where outsiders [blacks, women, Hispanics] . . . with definite ideas of what they want from religious training could turn the school from its tweedy university style."

Liberation theology and gay and lesbian studies flourished. A quarter of the school's scholarship funds was reserved for black students, although it was hard to attract black ministry students when so many other avenues of expression and attainment were open to them. And in the late 1970s HDS students joined in the common complaints of the time over the lack of a coherent curriculum, faculty remoteness, and (for women especially) the difficulty of finding jobs. The faculty, as in the Education School, complained of overwork.[50]

George Rupp (whose talents led him later to be president of Rice and then of Columbia) took over as dean of HDS in 1979. He inherited a student body still overwhelmingly Protestant (though with a scattering of Jews, Buddhists, a Hare Krishna or two, and even a brief Moonie takeover scare). Rupp paid due obeisance to the fashionable curricular gods of consolidation, coherence, and the integration of academic and practical work. But the school seemed to be more tolerant of theological differences than of varying views on social issues. In 1985 Ari Goldman, an Orthodox Jew who wrote on religion for the *New York Times*, spent a year as a student at HDS and published a book about his experience, *The Search for God at Harvard*. He found plenty of group consciousness— there were African American, gay, lesbian, feminist, Catholic, and Jewish student caucuses—and a pervasive concern over social issues. What he failed to find was much religion.[51]

The Graduate School of Design was troubled not so much by the question of what it was put on earth to do as by internal unrest. In part this was a product of the ideological and aesthetic conflicts rocking the architecture and city planning professions, in part a consequence of the roll of the personnel dice. GSD's dean in 1970 was former Business School professor Maurice Kilbridge, brought in to quiet the tempests that rose in the later years of the Gropius-Sert era. He did much to restore the school's financial stability by more than doubling the student body from 293 to 622. But he could not provide the intellectual and personal leadership that GSD badly needed. The Architecture department took off after him when he observed that faculty members "generally stop learning at the age of 35." The senior City and Regional Planning professors accused Kilbridge of violating their due process rights, disrupting programs, fomenting distrust. (Corporation fellows Hugh Calkins and John Blum duly looked into the charges and dismissed them.)

More serious was the fact that after Sert retired, GSD had no star architect. The department of Architecture seemed stodgy, locked into a "modernism" now half a century old, still caught up in the aesthetics of design and an "almost meaningless production of visual variety" at a time when housing's social and environmental surround assumed new importance. Nor was City and Regional Planning getting any better. Its urban design program was sterile, with only a "tenuous connection to reality." The program was chaired by an economist; only one of its eight new members had a degree in city and regional planning; it had little contact with relevant departments and programs elsewhere at Harvard.[52]

Gund Hall, the new GSD building completed in 1972, came in for much critical comment as "the building that nobody wanted": about as big an embarrassment as could be imagined for an architecture school. Designed to emphasize studio work and easy interaction, it ill served a school deeply divided over political, contextual, and aesthetic approaches to its subject matter. A sign of the (new) times: Gund Hall studios were converted into classrooms.[53]

Design, like the other Harvard professional schools, had powers of recuperation nourished by the strength of the University of which it was a part. Brian Berry came in 1975 from Chicago to be professor of City and Regional Planning and to direct an innovative laboratory for computer graphics and spatial design. Gerald McCue arrived from Berkeley to head up Architecture in 1976, and Moshe Safdie gave that department a world-class incumbent once again when he came in 1978 to run an Urban Design program. One thing the school could not do: stanch the flow of urban planning from design to social science. In 1980 Bok approved the transfer of the department of City and Regional Planning—home to 40 percent of GSD's students—to the Kennedy School. Not coincidentally, Kilbridge, bowing to various pressures, gave up his deanship in that year, and the more generally acceptable Gerald McCue of Architecture succeeded him.[54]

McCue turned out to be an effective dean, though GSD's small endowment, the loss of tuition revenue from Planning, and the need to remodel that "albatross" Gund Hall were heavy crosses to bear. GSD approached the century's end still riven by the competing views of design as an aesthetic challenge and as an application of social policy, and by the gulf between large dreams and a small exchequer.[55]

## The Kennedy School

The Harvard academic enterprise closest to Derek Bok's heart and mind was the Kennedy School of Government (KSG). He saw in it the most likely breeding ground for the mix of scholarship and public service that fit his vision of Harvard as a more socially useful university. In the wake of the Vietnam War and Watergate, he asked what universities in general, and Harvard in particular, might do "to improve the level of public service" and "prepare students for public careers." The problems of effectiveness and legitimacy afflicted not only government, but all large American institutions (including universities). Their headlong growth in size and complexity outpaced their capacity to manage themselves. The civil service in particular suffered from a shortage of people "with the general skills required to take the work of many specialists and transform it into coherent plans and programs to deal with major public problems."

How to meet the need? By the same prescription Bok doled out to the Law, Business, Medical, and Education schools: a curriculum that gave students the analytic tools required to select proper policies and see to it that they were effectively applied. But more was required as well: an understanding of the legal and historical context of government and, most of all, a thorough grounding in ethics. In short, to know what to do, how to do it, and why it should be done.

Bok distinguished between a graduate school of public administration devoted primarily to the academic study of its subject and the training of new scholars, and a professional school of government that trained people to have careers as public servants. His "marked preference" was for the latter. Worldly Harvard "must devote ... [its] energies to educating those who will occupy positions of authority in public institutions." He foresaw KSG doing "for the public sector much of what Harvard's Business, Law and Medicine do for their respective private professions." The initiative closest to his heart was the Kennedy School's Public Policy Program, which began in 1969. Here more than anywhere else, Bok's worldly Harvard, dedicated to the marriage of expertise and ethics, of professionalism and public service, might fulfill itself.[56]

But the character of the school with whose fortunes he so strongly identified was complex and ambiguous. KSG's Institute of Politics focused on the concerns of practicing politicians, and its Program for Public Administration brought in midcareer civil servants. Then the two-year Program in Public Policy was added. Analytical, theoretical (only one of its four core courses was devoted to political analysis), it brought a welcome sense of professional autonomy to the JFK School and fostered the development of a separate faculty not beholden to Arts and Sciences.

A notable event in the evolution of the Kennedy School was the decision not to build the Kennedy Library on its projected Cambridge site. The ostensible cause was the resistance of local residents to the removal of a fine stand of sycamores to widen adjoining Memorial Drive. More basic was the desire of the locals to rid themselves of an establishment likely to draw hordes of tourists. A harbor site next to the new campus of the University of Massachusetts at Boston became the Library-Museum's permanent home. The fourteen-acre Harvard site instead came to be occupied by a seven-acre JFK Memorial Park, the Kennedy School (three acres), and four acres of tax-paying commercial development. That turned out to consist of a posh hotel, restaurants, and expensive offices and apartments. The ensemble was a splendidly iconic representation of the ecology-minded, higher-education-fixated, chic lifestyle ambience of the Kennedy years and of the school that bore his name.

Graham Allison of the Government department, who became dean of the Kennedy School in 1977, proved to be a first-order academic entrepreneur. The school had no body of well-heeled, well-disposed alumnae of the sort that stoked the boilers of Law and Business. Nor did its work of training civil servants and politicians seem likely to win the benefactor gratitude and loyalty that the other professional schools evoked. But Bok's commitment to its cause, the energy of its dean, and above all KSG's heady mix of power and good works attracted a number of donors and made it Harvard's biggest success story in the last third of the twentieth century.

The school's progress was initially slowed by the general economic downturn of the 1970s. But its Institute of Politics flourished. The institute brought a steady flow of public figures to the Harvard campus, playing a role comparable to the Oxbridge debate unions as a center for the free discussion of public issues. For undergraduates and many others, this was the most visible part of the Kennedy School at work. The institute also began to field intensive orientation sessions for newly elected mayors and congressmen: a success until 1994, when the Republican freshmen refused to attend on the ground that the Kennedy School was a wholly owned subsidiary of the Democratic Party. Not coincidentally, the next director of the institute was retired GOP Senator Alan Simpson of Wyoming, and the next executive dean of the Kennedy School was 1996 Republican presidential candidate Robert Dole's chief of staff, Sheila Burke.

From the perspective of most of the school's faculty, the Institute of Politics was marginal to the real business at hand: training aspiring and midcareer public servants. The Master of Arts in Public Administration (M.P.A.) program, a holdover from pre-Kennedy School days, attracted state and local officials with up to ten years' experience under their belts and enough clout to swing a year at Harvard. More prestigious and high-powered was the Master of Arts in Public Policy (M.P.P.) program, which by the late 1980s attracted 1,000 applicants for a class of 150. And a growing number of executive programs for public officials closely echoed the Business School's advanced management training programs.

Given Bok's—and the Kennedy School's—commitment to government as a profession, it was unsettling that only about half of its graduates went into public service jobs. Why? In part because a federal government that grew slowly if at all did not have that much to offer. And in part because the graduates were drawn off to the lobbying and consulting organizations, law firms, think tanks, and environmental and other single-cause groups that had grown up around the formal branches of government.[57]

Bok celebrated the Kennedy School's new professionalism. But he was well aware that policy making involved more than policy planning: "problems of ethics and political tactics" did not disappear when confronted by cost-benefit analysis. In an age of high and growing disillusionment with government, how could a faculty committed to theory and analysis deal with the vacuum in belief that afflicted all too many of its students? It was hard to measure how effectively KSG prepared its graduates for a profession that perhaps was not a profession at all. And the school had troubling internal tensions. One of the most persistent was between the Economics and Government professors who came to teach there, dragging their departmental/disciplinary tails behind them, and the growing number who had made a full commitment to the School. Another was the intermittent discord between Dean Graham

Allison's fund-raising efforts and post-1970 academic sensibilities. In 1979 the Charles Engelhard Foundation gave a million dollars for a public affairs library. Engelhard had South African gold-mining interests that did not sit well with students stirred up over apartheid. A student petition called on Allison not to name the library after the donor, but to keep the money; the *Crimson* fanned the flames; a speech by a Harvard senior at the library dedication stirred the crowd; finally the Engelhard name was dropped. A decade later Allison got into trouble again because he promised to appoint the husband-and-wife donors of $500,000 "to appropriate positions in the School of Government that will accord them status as Officers of the University with the privileges associated therewith." Even though not much more than a Harvard library card appeared to be at stake, there was much tut-tutting over the sale of offices.[58]

Allison left the deanship in 1988, having seen the faculty grow from 20 to 75, degree candidates from 200 to 750 a year, executive programs from 1 to 10, research centers from zero to 9, endowment from $20 to $150 million. Professor of Comparative Government Robert Putnam succeeded him, a distinguished scholar whose appointment signified the school's full emergence into academic respectability. But Putnam's appointment brought to a boil the simmering internal dispute between politics and government doers and public policy thinkers. According to a *Boston Globe* columnist, "in a wrenching demonstration of the gulf between analytic skill and political acumen that is at the root of the ever-normal Kennedy school identity crisis, Putnam crashed." In 1991 he returned to the relatively Arcadian groves of the Government department, succeeded as dean by the more nuts-and-bolts Albert Carnesale and then in 1995 by the politic (and certainly political) professor of government and national security expert Joseph Nye.

Bok thought that over the course of its first two decades the JFK School had become a self-standing entity, with a viable curriculum of policy analysis and public management. The next stage was to figure out a way to "help government officials move beyond being mere bureaucrats and technicians to become the kinds of human beings to whom we would willingly entrust decisions that affect our lives." Despite ongoing efforts to shape the curriculum to these ends, it was not clear that Harvard—or any other institution—had met this challenge. The place of money in political life and the Clinton impeachment follies of 1998–99 hardly suggested that American politics and government was undergoing a moral sea change. And despite Bok's emphasis on government service, JFK alumni by the end of the century continued to be conspicuous in the consulting firms, lobbying organizations, and public interest groups to which public policy making was being outsourced.[59]

The saga of the Kennedy School presents in pristine form a problem that increasingly afflicted Harvard and other leading American universities in the last decades of the twentieth century. To the meritocracy and affluence of the 1940s, 1950s, and 1960s was added the worldliness, the diversity, the egalitarianism of the 1970s, 1980s, and 1990s. Harvard's professional schools, like its Arts and Sciences disciplines, won world prestige of a sort rarely seen among social institutions. But at the height of the University's power, wealth and prestige, nagging issues persisted: the questions of purpose ("mission"), of connection with the larger society. Universities steadily cost more; are they worth it? Universities steadily accumulate knowledge and expertise; does their social value commensurately increase? Universities dedicate themselves to large social values—diversity, egalitarianism; do they thereby sway public opinion? Universities claim to be doing ever more good for society; does society agree?

## ~ 19 ~

## THE COLLEGE

What place did Harvard College have in the modern University, with its expansive central administration, research-driven faculty, ambitious and high-powered professional schools? A much more important one than this litany of potential threats might suggest. The College remained the most conspicuous and prestigious part of the University. It produced the most generous donors; it outclassed its rivals in attracting the most sought-after students; it exemplified Harvard in the public mind. And it shared in the worldly ambience of the late-twentieth-century University.

### Getting In and Paying for It

For decades, Harvard College admissions was a battleground over who would be accepted and on what grounds access would be granted. The admission of Jews was a touchstone issue in the conflict between the Brahmin and meritocratic impulses from the 1920s to the 1950s. Then another problem came to the fore: how to choose a freshman class from a swelling number of qualified applicants. As selection became ever more complex and arcane, the sheer size and quality of the applicant pool enabled the dean of admissions and his staff, rather than the faculty, to define the terms of entry.

The result was that classes were crafted to be outstanding in more than purely academic-intellectual terms. Intellectual superstars were a small group of near-certain admits. After that, a solid level of academic ability set an admissions floor, above which character, extracurricular activities, artistic or athletic talent, "legacy" status, and geographical diversity figured in the admissions gene pool. After the 1960s, diversity came to embrace race and gender. Chase Peterson, who was dean of admissions during the tumultuous years from 1967 to 1972, thought that during his time the criteria for selection broadened to include tenacity, perseverance, having learned something deeply and well, social generosity, intellectual openness, and strength of character. A statement on admissions desiderata in the 1990s included "honesty, fairness, compassion, altruism, leadership, and initiative" and stressed: "We place great value in a candidate's capacity to move beyond the limits of personal achievement to involvement in the life of the community at large." One of Dean of Admissions Wilbur Bender's 1950s ideal admits, a "Scandinavian farm boy who skates beautifully," had better have headed his local skating club or taught skating to inner-city youth if he hoped to get into Harvard at the century's end.[1]

The new dispensation carried with it some old biases. A 1977 Faculty Task Force on the Composition of the Student Body conceded that the stress on diversity "necessarily implies some deviation from a strictly academic admissions criterion." It warned that reliance on grades and board scores alone would yield students predominantly suburban and upper middle class, creative in the arts but not very athletic. When Admissions Dean Peterson explained to a faculty group that "the donut" was a shorthand term for the comfortable city-circling suburbs from which such applicants came, a Jewish faculty member balefully suggested that a more appropriate term would be "the bagel." Peterson's not wholly reassuring response was that "whether or not the suburban high school was part of a bagel or a Yorkshire pudding, the committee seemed to be successful in selecting applicants independent of racial considerations."[2]

As some inequities eased, others got worse: fairness, it appeared, was a zero-sum game. During the 1980s, some thought Harvard had a "middle-class problem": difficulty in attracting applicants whose families were in the $18,000 to $40,000 income range. Financial aid based on family income and assets disfavored hard-saving, debt-free middle-class families. And blue-collar applicants, never abundant, significantly declined in numbers. Only about 10 percent of the class of 1988 had noncollege family backgrounds.[3]

But the College's commitment to racial and ethnic diversity was rock solid. The dean of admissions declared: "If Harvard is to be the strongest university in the 21st century, ... [it] will be the most diverse; ... excellence and diversity are the same goal." President Neil Rudenstine devoted his 1993–95 annual report to an extended history of diversity at Harvard, seeking to show how well it had served the University. And in truth the most numerous new groups—women, Asians—raised the general academic level of Harvard applicants. SAT median scores of freshmen were in the high 500s in 1956, in the high 600s in 1979, in the low 700s in 1999.

Women were the most noticeable new presence on the Harvard College scene. During the early seventies, Derek Bok changed the prevailing male-female admissions ratio from 4 to 1 to 2.5 to 1. When, soon after, the Radcliffe and Harvard admissions offices merged, admissions became sex blind. With the help of Harvard's extensive recruitment network and superior financial aid resources, female applications increased by 60 percent between 1975 and 1984, while the number of white male applicants in 1984 was 1,000 fewer than in its peak year of 1978. By 2000, women were over 46 percent of the student body.[4]

A rising tide of academically strong Asian American applicants was another significant new feature of Harvard admissions. Korean Americans in particular had a yen for Harvard. A cram school named Harvard-Excel catered to Koreatown children in Los Angeles, Bakersfield, and Irvine. A young Los Angeles immigrant, who had left Seoul three years earlier, was admitted to Harvard, Yale, and Princeton; he told his grocer father that he wanted to go to Princeton; his father replied: "What are you talking about? You're going to Harvard."

The number of Asians on campus resurrected old fears of overrepresentation by a high-performing minority. A study found that the group had SAT scores on average 112 points higher than their white classmates. But there was no suggestion of a quota for Asian Americans, and their proportion rose from 4 percent of students in 1979 to 17 percent in 2000.[5]

Black and Hispanic admissions were more controversial. A debate arose over numbers and quotas that in its intensity resembled the earlier brouhaha over Jewish admissions, except that now the issue was not about keeping the numbers down, but raising them up. It was generally agreed that during the late 1960s and early 1970s inadequately prepared black students were admitted, to everyone's disadvantage. But entrance standards were tightened, and Harvard attracted a substantial share of the nation's highest-scoring black applicants. In 1998 the College enrolled sixty-three National Achievement Scholars (a competition limited to African American students), two to three times the number at each of the next four schools; Blacks made up 7 percent of the student body in 1979 and 8 percent in 2000. Over the same period Hispanics rose from 3.4 percent to 8 percent.

Harvard's growing commitment to racial and gender diversity coexisted with older admissions interests: greater regional variety (especially as the American population shifted to the South and West); athletes;

faculty-driven pressure to recruit the intellectually gifted; the ever strong claim of "legacies" (old prep schools and old families, the children of alumni, big donors, and faculty). A participant in the annual admissions process likened it to a commodities exchange, with specialist floor traders—in legacies, athletes, scientists, southerners, African Americans, Hispanics, you name it—touting their wares.

And then there was the massive increase in the size of the applicant pool. Harvard-Radcliffe entering classes stayed at about 1,660 during the last decades of the century. But the number who sought entry skyrocketed: from 7,000 to 8,000 a year in the 1970s to 15,000 to 20,000 in the 1990s. The quality of the pool was no less striking. The 18,691 applicants who sought admission in 2000 included nearly 2,000 with perfect 800 scores on their verbal SATs and over 2,500 with 800 math scores. About 3,000 were high school valedictorians. Only 2,035 (10.9 percent of the applicants) were admitted. And Harvard's matriculation rate was close to 80 percent, far higher than at any other school.[6]

Late-twentieth-century Harvard had become America's University, a totemic institution like professional football's Dallas Cowboys in the 1980s. Why? The dean of admissions in 1994 thought the answer lay in media hype, aggressive recruiting, need-based financial aid, the quality of the plant, and the Harvard-success connection. The superior quality of a Harvard education did not make the list. H. L. Mencken (see the Preface) would have agreed.[7]

Some questioned the wisdom of massive recruiting when only one in nine or ten applicants could hope to be successful. Dean of Admissions William Fitzsimmons responded in 1998: "No one wants to be turning down 15,000 people. But if you want to build that great class you have to do that." This reflected a deep faith in the ability of the admissions staff to engage in large-scale "social engineering" (a term they used). Whether or not the game was worth the candle was unclear, though admissions officers insisted that their outreach was effective marketing: it signaled Harvard's relentless commitment to students of top quality.[8]

The result: Harvard admissions was no business for (faculty) amateurs. In the early 1990s each of twenty-nine staff members read up to two thousand dossiers, thus in theory assuring two or three readings of each application. But as the number kept rising, it was impossible to maintain this level of review. By the end of the 1990s, more than six thousand requests for early action (an increasingly popular admissions category) had to be considered from late October to mid-December, and the rest of the applicants from late December to mid-March. Subcommittees for each of the major regions struggled with their allotments, as did staff members specializing in the "feeder" secondary schools. Hundreds of alumni (guided by a forty-three-page "Interviewers' Handbook") quizzed prospective students, adding their impressions to the grades, board scores, teacher recommendations, applicants' essays, and readers' comments flowing into admissions central. In March a thirty-one-member admissions committee (including faculty, who could make themselves felt on the margin) reviewed the subcommittee recommendations, and by April a class was born.[9]

There were measurable changes in the makeup of the Harvard College student body. Eighty percent were non-Hispanic whites in 1976, 43 percent in 2000. By the 1990s, 70 percent of Harvard's students came from public high schools. Alumni children were 20 percent of the class in 1970, 10 to 15 percent by the end of the century. The *Crimson* thought it improper that alumni children still were three times more likely to be taken than nonlegacy applicants, but the admissions office claimed that on balance they were better qualified.[10]

Humanities faculty members suspected that the science-minded fared best among the more intellectually gifted applicants. Certainly early talent in science and mathematics was more readily observable, and the scientists made sure that the most able of their breed were taken. Of the students admitted to the class of 1997, 861 listed science as their intended area of concentration, compared to 377 in the social sciences and 354 in the humanities. (How many actually majored in science was another story.) Admissions claimed that it had to dig deeper into the applicant pool to keep up the number of humanities admits.[11]

Tuition and financial aid became contentious issues in the late twentieth century. Steep tuition rises during the 1970s were defensible responses to inflation. But in the early 1980s increases began to outrun the rise in the cost of living. By 1993 the price of a Harvard education was, by one estimate, twice what it would have been if it had done no more than keep pace with inflation since 1982.[12]

From the early 1970s on, Harvard was sufficiently flush to select the applicants it wanted and then offer support packages—a mix of grants (55 percent), loans (9 percent), and jobs (10 percent)—sufficient for all of them to come. But as costs escalated (they totaled $32,164 for a year's tuition, room and board, and fees in 2000–2001) pressure grew to ease up on parental contribution, loan, and work provisions. The competition for attractive applicants led other colleges to offer merit-based scholarships in the 1990s—"sending the limo" in the jargon of the trade. A case in point: the parents of one Japanese-American applicant accepted by

Harvard and Yale in 1998 had a combined income of $100,000. They were asked by Harvard to pay more than $20,000 a year for tuition, which endangered their retirement savings. Their child went instead to Boston University, which offered a full tuition scholarship. Some black applicants also had family incomes that limited their eligibility for need-based aid. Other schools gave them aid packages without regard to their family situation, and the matriculation rate of blacks admitted to Harvard dropped for a time in the early 1990s.[13]

The progressive minded decried "scholarships for the rich" and saw in it the regnant conservatism of end-of-the-century America. Neil Rudenstine thought the rapid growth of merit-based scholarships endangered need-based aid and went beyond the bounds of good taste and common sense. But from the perspective of aspiring colleges and universities, such awards were the only way in which they could attract the better students that their faculties wanted and on which their futures depended. What was good for Harvard was not necessarily good for everyone else.[14]

In 1998 Princeton increased its aid for students from families with incomes up to $90,000. Yale, Stanford, and MIT followed. Caught unawares, Harvard in its sinuous way increased its financial aid budget and told successful applicants that if they got better offers elsewhere they "should not assume that we will not respond." Soon thereafter the college officially boosted the amount of grant money in its aid package. About 70 percent of Harvard undergraduates received some form of financial aid in 2000; the average package topped $23,000. But it was clear that competition would be the major constraint on the charge-what-the-market-will-bear tuition policy of a worldly university.[15]

## The Core and the Classroom

After the crisis of 1969, the College's General Education program came under the microscope, and then under the knife. Gen. Ed. had grown long in the tooth, its intellectual cohesion drained, its offerings increasingly eclectic, its reason for being unclear. By 1970 a fresh look at Harvard's course requirements seemed as appropriate as it did at the end of World War II. The commitment to some form of general education remained, but its substance had to be adapted to a new generation of students. And it would be taught by a much more specialized faculty, for whom large thoughts about great ideas did not come easily.

Against this background, FAS dean Henry Rosovsky launched a

reconsideration of undergraduate education in 1974. For several years a committee of six faculty and two students tried to decide what a well-educated Harvard graduate should know and how to produce such a wonder. Dozens of professors contributed to the ultimate formulation of the new Core Curriculum program adopted in 1978, though in good part it was the brainchild of political scientist James Q. Wilson with a major assist from historian Bernard Bailyn. They replaced the older Gen. Ed. program's emphasis on a shared body of knowledge with a different goal: the cultivation of diverse approaches to knowledge. The Core Curriculum eventually consisted of carefully vetted courses sorted into ten parts, covering topics in Historical Study, Foreign Cultures, Literature, Music and Art, Social Analysis, Science, and Moral Reasoning. Students had to choose courses in eight topics—the equivalent of a year's work—furthest from their concentration or major. The Core's "theory" was that exposure to how the major disciplines worked would give Harvard students intellectual perspectives that would serve them throughout their lives. In this sense the Core epitomized the triumph of the academic disciplines in the 1950s and 1960s, as General Education did the triumph of democracy and Western civilization in the 1930s and 1940s.[16]

The Core caused a stir in American higher education comparable to General Education thirty years before. Many schools adopted knockoffs; admirers admired it, critics criticized it; once again, Columbia and Chicago people vainly reminded everyone in and out of sight that they had done it all before. But for better or worse, fair or not, when Harvard talked, people listened.

Between 1981 and 1996, the Core fielded 350 courses, 80 percent of them created for the program. Some—"Matter in the Universe," "Human Behavioral Biology," "Principles of Economics," "Justice," "The Bible and Its Interpreters," "Shakespeare"—were enormously popular, drawing hundreds of students. But it sometimes was hard for students (and not only students) to see what the difference was between a Core course and a regular department offering. And undergraduates complained that there were not enough courses to choose from in some Core areas. Nor were the Core's goals of teaching "ways of thinking" and "modes of understanding" explicit in every Core course or readily comprehensible to most undergraduates.

In the mid-1990s a faculty-student review committee took a fresh look at what had been wrought two decades before. The committee, then the FAS faculty at large, overwhelmingly agreed that the Core's achievements outweighed its shortcomings. Ninety percent of Core courses were taught by senior faculty, many of whom had been content in the past to teach only students concentrating in their field. Because it built on rather than rejected disciplinary ways of thinking, the Core program kept the faculty's support. The major substantive change by the end of the century was to add required work in quantitative reasoning, reflecting the degree to which that skill had become an essential element in undergraduate education.

Harvard concentrations—majors—became more numerous over the course of the late twentieth century, in pace with the growing specialization and variety of academic disciplines. By the end of the century a Harvard student could choose from over forty of them, including traditional majors such as English, Economics, and Biology, established interdepartmental programs (History and Literature, Social Studies), and new compounds (Women's Studies, Environmental Science, and Public Policy). For those still not satisfied, the Committee on Degrees in Special Concentrations was ready to smooth the way to a customized course of study. But most students stayed on the main, well-trodden concentration paths. In 1975–76, 59 percent of them clustered in seven departments: Biochemistry, Biology, Economics, English, Government, History, and Psychology and Social Relations. The same subjects (plus no longer access-limited Social Studies) accounted for 57 percent of concentrators in 1998–99.

A 1998 survey of graduating seniors found that 85 percent were "generally satisfied" or "very satisfied" with their concentration courses. Two-thirds said the same about general faculty availability. But the curriculum was not necessarily the most significant part of the undergraduate experience. With a four course workload and a far from backbreaking calendar—eleven to thirteen weeks of classes and a two week reading period each semester—it is easy to see how Harvard students were able to engage so fully in the rich extracurricular life of the College.

## Campus Life

In the spring of 1975 FAS dean Henry Rosovsky set up a Task Force on College Life, charged in effect to look at the results of the tempestuous past decade. It found that the old style of guiding students by "gentlemanly innuendo" was gone. A heterogeneous student body required more organized, bureaucratic management. Personal contact with professors was more or less limited to those undergraduates whose talents and/or personality enabled them to surmount the barriers of a high student-faculty ratio and the faculty's absorption in its own research. These contacts occurred most frequently not in the houses, as intended originally, but in the classroom. Most of all, the task force report implied that easy generalizations could not hope to capture the experience of thousands of intelligent, energetic young people. From the perspective of 2000, it is clear that the social forces of the 1960s had a profound and lasting impact on surface aspects of Harvard student life. But it is all too easy to overlook the degree to which the culture of a college as old and strong as Harvard absorbed as well as bent before the winds of change.[17]

A big loser in the admissions transformation of the last quarter of the century was Brahmin Harvard's student core, the white Protestant graduates of New England's elite prep schools. Significant numbers of Exeter-Andover products still came to Harvard, but they were now as likely to be Jewish or African American or Asian as old family. And the eight elite undergraduate social clubs, the "Final Clubs," were definitively marginalized. Three percent of the undergraduates were members at the end of the century. The less socially exclusive Hasty Pudding and Signet Clubs admitted women after 1970; the Final Clubs resisted. Still, a third of their presidents were Jewish in 1986 and one was black. The Porcellian, the most final of them all, took an occasional Jew, and in 1983 (to the horror of some elders) admitted a black—who had gone to St. Paul's.

The greatest pressure on the clubs was to end their male-only entry rules. "This," said an administrator, "is the battle of the new Harvard against the old." It was over that issue that the University cut its remaining links with the clubs, which meant that they lost the use of low-cost, Harvard-generated steam for heat, as well as access to the school's central telephone service and alumni mailing lists. Apparently they could bear the financial and social costs of their isolation: as of 2000, none had female members.[18]

For all the increase in the racial and ethnic diversity of the Harvard student body, its class makeup changed little over the course of the twentieth century—except that the children of generally well-heeled and/or highly educated professionals switched places with the children of generally well-heeled businessmen, and the already small number of students who came from manual worker or farm families was halved.[19]

| Father's Occupation | Students | |
|---|---|---|
| | Enrolled 1903 (%) | Class of 1986 (%) |
| Professionals | 29.5 | 59.3 |
| Businessmen | 56.7 | 31.0 |
| Government | 3.0 | 4.3 |
| Manual workers | 7.8 | 5.0 |
| Farmers | 3.0 | .5 |

Diversity suffered also from the cultural homogeneity of late-twentieth-century post-adolescents. Harvard admissions standards—high board scores, preternatural extracurricular talent and/or community engagement—fostered a certain sameness of social outlook. A left-liberal political stance was as pervasive on the late-twentieth-century campus as a moderate Republicanism had been during the first half of the century. An embattled scattering of conservative ideologues and their often jejune publications eerily echoed the tone and style of the leftist handful of days past.

The dress, language, and mores of the post-1970 student culture reinforced the fact that the late sixties decisively changed the style and tone of undergraduate life at Harvard and other elite schools. Blue jeans and windbreakers or down jackets were as ubiquitous as chinos and tweed jackets had been a generation before. The backpack replaced the green bookbag as the *sac de choix*. A professor observed: "The object is to look as if you were going to Middle Tennessee College." Student dress in times past had conveyed the message: "I am well-born, and I go to Harvard"; now the pervasive dressed-down style announced: "I am of the people, although I go to Harvard."[20]

The stirring events of the sixties produced a more politically engaged and antimaterialist Harvard student body. But the end of the Vietnam War and harder economic times in the 1970s saw a revival of career enhancement: "From a conviction that 'all we need is love,' there was a shift to all we need are [top] grades." An undergraduate informed the alumni that preprofessional careerism had "replaced the bubble-blowing Harvard of 1968–1972." Only 3.8 percent of the class of 1979 sought a business career when they entered in 1975; 18.4 percent had such plans by the time they graduated. Harvard Student Agencies served as an outlet for undergraduate entrepreneurial impulses, leading to ventures such as the *Let's Go* travel guides. By the century's end start-up internet businesses blossomed in dormitory rooms. A growing number of Harvard graduates gravitated to the lucrative world of movies and television. They were producers, agents, directors, writers, composers, lawyers, managers; they had a large hand in writing scripts for *The Simpsons* and *Beavis and Butthead, Saturday Night Live* and other opiates of the masses. The *Lampoon*, Harvard's undergraduate humor magazine, became a pipeline to Hollywood jobs as was the *Crimson* to the *New York Times*. This was social activism of a sort, though hardly a body blow to the cash nexus.[21]

At the same time political concerns and involvement in good works remained a conspicuous feature of the campus scene. The embers of Vietnam were still glowing when the issue of South African apartheid caught fire. As their predecessors in the sixties focused on Harvard's complicity through ROTC, so did the new protesters concentrate on the University's investments in companies doing business in South Africa. An April 1986 rally in the Yard drew a crowd of five thousand. But when the white South African government fell in the early 1990s, and Nelson Mandela came in, that was that. Though feminism, gay rights, and other causes offered tempting opportunities for demonstrations and declamations, not since the fall of apartheid has a major international, or national, issue comparably seized the attention of undergraduates. (But Harvard administrators remember 1969: to the end of the century, the doors of University Hall were locked and campus police were posted whenever a demo went on in the Yard.)[22]

In the spring of 2001 two dozen students occupied the president's building to protest the wages of Harvard's lowest-paid service workers. The decorum of the occupiers was matched by the hands-off restraint of the authorities. After three weeks the parties came to a settlement that allowed each to claim victory. The occupiers emerged to wide acclaim, and then to the quick oblivion peculiar to an age of instant celebrity and a short public attention span.

Volunteerism has had a more consistent and substantial place in Harvard undergraduate life. Phillips Brooks House, the leading community service organization, dated back to 1900. There was some falloff in participation during the post-Vietnam backlash years of the mid-seventies, and the Task Force on College Life fielded the oxymoronic idea that there be "a required program of volunteering time to good causes during the Freshman year." Even without that spur, by the end of the century some 70 percent of undergraduates were engaged in community service in over 140 programs.[23]

When members of the class of 1971, which had been in the vortex of the heady events of 1969 and after, gathered for their twenty-fifth reunion in 1996, much note was taken of this rite of passage, not least by the members themselves. They were more politically liberal than their generational norm, and more of them regularly smoked pot (11 percent) than cigarettes (8 percent). But other facts suggest that human nature did not change all that much in April 1969. The members of the class were less radical by far than they had been a quarter of a century before; 90 percent were married; they had a respectable average of 2.6 children; most believed in God. And like the Harvard grads who came before (and no doubt, those who would come after), when they looked upon themselves, what they saw was good.[24]

More quotidian aspects of college life, such as athletics, adapted the ways of the old to the demands of the new. Student interest in intercollegiate football declined through the last decades of the century. The *Crimson* tried to stir things up by criticizing the outsized alumni support for football and hockey, compared to less favored sports. But little could be done to discourage the Varsity Club and other friends of old-style Harvard athletics. Besides, many of the more well-heeled and generous alumni cared about football and other intercollegiate sports, so these had to be kept respectable.

Much was made in the 1970s of the decrepit state of the school's athletic facilities: the worst in the Ivy League, according to the 1979 visiting committee. Harvard lagged badly behind rivals Dartmouth and Princeton in spending on intercollegiate sports. Sympathetic alumni responded warmly, and new athletic facilities (a hockey rink, an Olympic-size swimming pool, a field house) were, with the Kennedy School, among the most substantial physical additions to late-twentieth-century Harvard.

Meanwhile New Age physical fitness became a conspicuous part of the Harvard scene. In the prevailing style of empathetic discourse, the Athletics visiting committee noted that the importance of sport lay in the fact that it "teaches people to care about each other." Notable too was the rise of women's intercollegiate athletics spurred by Title IX of the 1964 Civil Rights Act, which was interpreted as a mandate to equalize funding for women's sports. The growth of women's competition meant that by the 1990s well over 10 percent of undergraduates belonged to some forty intercollegiate teams. And intramural sports strongly appealed to a student generation well schooled in nurturing their bodies. Some 4,500 of 6,000 students participated in the College sports programs in 1979. In typical Harvard make-the-most-of-it fashion, the slogan "Athletics for All" was attached to a $30 million fund drive.[25]

## Diversity and Community

The most visible problem in late-twentieth-century Harvard College life was the tension between the new ideal of racial, ethnic, and cultural diversity—being your own thing—and the old ideal of communitarian identification with the College. While the former ties that bound—the clubs, football, the houses—languished, groupings based on ethnic and sexual identity, social and intellectual interests, and political causes flourished. The College had 65 officially recognized student organizations in 1971, over 200 (including ephemera such as Stupid People at Harvard) in 1994. Between 1975 and 2000, the number of student drama groups increased from sixteen to sixty-six, orchestras from two to six, dance troupes from one to seventeen. Over 80 percent of the student body belonged to one or more of these organizations, and over half devoted more than twelve hours a week to their activities. "Diversity" embraced many forms of group affiliation. By the century's end these included, but were not limited to, blacks, Jews, Asians, Catholics, Hispanics, gays and lesbians, fundamentalist Christians, libertarians, Marxists, ecologists, and feminists.[26]

The most visible and distinctive group identity on campus was that of black undergraduates. But however alike they might appear to their white fellow students, they were in fact complexly varied. Many were upper middle class; about 75 percent went to top prep schools or predominantly white high schools. They often discovered their blackness as Harvard freshmen, influenced by the group consciousness-raising efforts of older minority students. Many (black sociologist Orlando Patterson estimated about half) had parents born outside of the United States—mainly in the Caribbean—and had grown up either in white neighborhoods or their own ethnic enclaves in black ghettos. An unknown but not small number came from interracial families. And "a number" (precise breakdowns are hard to come by) were from working class or welfare families in the inner cities and rural areas.[27]

The sudden increase in the number of black students on campus in the early 1970s, coinciding as it did with an upsurge in militant black nationalism, made for difficult race relations. Many black undergraduates were caught up in the politics of the new Afro-American Studies department, and more generally with issues and an agenda that widened the gulf between them and most white students. Race relations did not noticeably improve during the 1970s. Blacks tended to cluster in a couple of the houses and eat at separate dining tables. But it was not uncommon for black men to date white women, a source of some unhappiness for black female students (who by the 1980s outnumbered male black students three to two).[28]

In response to black students' protests over their treatment at the University, Derek Bok issued an "Open Letter on Issues of Race at Harvard" in February 1981. He reaffirmed his commitment to diversity and set up the Harvard Foundation for Intercultural and Race Relations, designed to reduce the "alienation and estrangement" of African-American undergraduates. The students had wanted a social center of their own, but under the leadership of Allen Counter, a former associate professor of Biology, the foundation alternative soon won general support. Shortly afterward, Hilda Hernandez-Gravelle was appointed to head the Office of Race Relations and Minority Affairs. (Before long she and Counter were embroiled in a turf war over who would be in charge of race relations programs in the College.)[29]

Incidents roiling black-white relations on campus continued through the 1980s and into the 1990s. In 1989 Hernandez-Gravelle of the Office of Race Relations sponsored a weeklong series of panels and workshops designed to cleanse white students of racism and ethnocentrism. Its linguistic excesses seemed to one critic "more appropriate to a war-crimes trial than for the first year of college." Sociologist Nathan Glazer in 1990 described a campus of "frustrated blacks and weary whites."[30]

Controversy swirled around the Harvard Foundation's Allen Counter as well. In 1982 the *Crimson* filed a grievance against him for referring to one of its reporters as a "militant Jew." Anti-Semitic City College of New York Afro-American Studies professor Leonard Jeffries gave an inflammatory talk at Harvard in 1992 under the sponsorship of the Black Students' Association, and Counter attacked student journalists critical of Jeffries as "*Crimson* writers active in Hillel." The *Crimson* accused Counter of anti-Semitism; Counter apologized for any "discomfort" and "misunderstanding" he might have caused; President Neil Rudenstine pronounced himself satisfied. But in 1993 when conservative Government professor Harvey Mansfield said that grade inflation grew in pace with black student recruitment in the early 1970s, the reaction was more forceful. Provost Jerry Green told the *Crimson*: "When you hear ... [things] like this you have to take account of who said them, who they're coming from." And Rudenstine asserted that he took seriously the complaints of minority student spokesmen about the climate of opinion at the University.[31]

By the end of the century a strong Afro-American Studies department, many courses dealing with "cultures of color," and decades of more than token black admissions had reduced tensions. Studies, polls, and informed impressions agreed that there was substantially more social and academic interracial student contact than the rhetoric of separatism let on. Almost 65 percent of all students chose to live in mixed race groups in the Houses, and 80 percent said that they had interracial friendships.[32]

The integration of women undergraduates was more sweeping and considerably less stressful. The full absorption of women into College housing occurred in the early 1970s, with much own-back-patting by social engineers and tut-tutting by social conservatives about the end of civilization as we know it. It may be assumed that more opportunity produced more sex. But it also appeared to be the case that coresidential living led to the rise of mixed-gender groups of college friends, who developed incest-taboo constraints on intragroup sexual relationships. Intercourse, yes; intracourse, no.[33]

At first the more luxurious and prestigious Harvard houses appealed to women, while the distant and comparatively spartan former Radcliffe dorms had little appeal to men. In 1973, when coresidence officially began, 120 men were consigned to the Radcliffe Quad—"Vermont," in student vernacular, as compared to the "New York" of the houses. But over time things evened out. The Radcliffe dorms, renovated into suites with more space than the crowded River houses, became equal partners. Here as elsewhere in the College culture of the late twentieth century, egalitarianism ruled.[34]

Harvard's undergraduates by 2000 were arguably the brightest and most talented in the University's, perhaps any university's, history. And they displayed comparably high levels of satisfaction—most of all, perhaps, over being at Harvard. Yet in the midst of this turn-of-century good feeling, certain inalienable discontents—the inescapable burdens of life, the licentiousness of liberty, the often futile pursuit of happiness—remained a part of the Harvard student (as, indeed, of the human) condition.

In the mid-1990s, the new randomization policy for housing undergraduates allowed freshman groups of eight (initially sixteen) to move together. This encouraged small group self-selection, but attracted criticism for making a larger residential community impossible. The president of the black students' association argued that minorities "feel more comfortable with people who look like you and listen to the same music, and have the same problems." A teaching fellow, noting that the tendency of minority students to take courses on their own cultural heritage was producing "separate but equal curricula," asked: "What does diversity matter if the students do not experience it?"[35]

The presence of women undergraduates made previously tolerated levels of violent male behavior unacceptable, and heightened sensitivity to the emotional problems of undergraduates in general. But recurring instances of "date rape" suggested that the new intergender life style did not mark the end of ancient urges. While drug use was down, alcohol use was up, not unrelated to the apparent rise in sexual offenses.[36]

An especially chilling indicator that diversity had its costs came in 1998, when an alienated, isolated Ethiopian undergraduate, on the verge of being abandoned by her Vietnamese-American roommate, stabbed the other girl and then hanged herself. Harvard officials treated this as an inexplicable tragedy and engaged in spin control on a Washingtonian scale. But as the story unfolded, it became in part a failure of the New Bureaucracy: a lost soul somehow overlooked by an elaborate system of agents and agencies designed to spot such students. And it became apparent, too, that the loneliness of late adolescence was heightened in this case by a cultural gap as wide as the enormous geographical and social distances that separated Ethiopia, Vietnam, and Harvard. Assiduously cultivated diversity and bureaucratized caring had striking successes. But they did not—could not—rid the Harvard student world of its discontents.[37]

# EPILOGUE

As of the year 2000, Harvard was stronger academically, financially, and in national and international reputation than ever before in its (and perhaps any university's) history. The sources of this preeminence—Harvard's iconic national and international standing; the quality of its students, faculty, libraries, laboratories, and plant; its access to the money that made it all possible—showed no signs of diminishing at the century's turn: quite the contrary. Old rivals Yale, Chicago, Columbia, Berkeley were not, by common consent, what they once had been. New challenger Stanford was something else again, but could not yet claim equal superpower status.

Harvard's is an archetypal American success story. And a number of other American universities have had comparable trajectories since World War II. That has been the record of the past. The question for the future: will the great American research universities—and in particular, Harvard—thrive in the decades to come as they have in decades past? Harvard's age, wealth, quality, and prestige may well shield it from any conceivable vicissitudes. But if history teaches anything, it is that every institution, however successful, carries within it the seeds of future trouble. Times, values, social demands change. A century ago, the leading German universities had a similarly dominant position in the world of higher education. That preeminence, to understate the matter, did not last.

## 1986

In 1986, a half century after its 1936 fete, Harvard had another special birthday to celebrate, its 350th. Sesquis are not centennials, and the 350th Celebration (that was its official name; the proper Latin title,

"Tercentennial Quinquagesimal," was a clear nonstarter) did not carry the symbolic heft of the 1936 Tercentary. Still, more than a third of a thousand years of institutional survival was nothing to sniff at. Nor was there a shortage of achievements to commemorate. The Harvard of 1936 had seemed rich and substantial at the time; who could have foreseen what it would be fifty years later? The 1936 endowment of $143 million had grown to $1.3 billion in 1986 (and would balloon to $19.2 billion in 2000). Its undergraduate student body expanded from 3,735 men to 3,839 men and 2,781 women, its alumni from 70,000 to 180,000 (and to 270,000 by 2000). The University's range of academic activities; the racial, religious, and ethnic mix of its students and faculty; its standing in America and the world were beyond the wildest imaginings of 1936.[1]

These accomplishments bolstered the decision to make Harvard's 350th anniversary not the occasion for a gathering of the world's intellectual good and the great, as in 1936, but rather "a birthday party," "a family affair." And just as the blossoming meritocratic impulse and the world crisis turned the 1936 fete into something more than was originally intended, so the 350th celebration became a showcase not only of the triumphant meritocratic University, but also of the more worldly Harvard taking form.

The Harvard faculty mounted 106 symposia, a vast academic flea market ranging from "The AIDS Epidemic" and "Tobacco, Smoking and Health Policy" to "The Universe: The Beginning, Now, and Henceforth." The policy issues taken up in many of the symposia did not relate to overriding threats to peace and to freedom as in 1936. Rather, each topic had its own reason for being, and was addressed by and to those who shared its frame of reference. In this the 1986 conclave faithfully reflected the diverse, segmented academic-intellectual life of its time, as its forerunner reflected the more grandiose, synergistic intellectual ambience of 1936.

As things turned out, the 350th fete also accurately mirrored the larger American culture of 1986, and the place of Harvard within that culture. It was a festival of sound and light as well as of words and ideas; not only an event, but a happening. "There was," said one observer, "a surprising amount of froth and glitz"; it was, said another, "part Disneyland." The eve of the celebration featured a four-and-a-half hour "floating birthday party" on the Charles, with fireworks, concerts, light shows, and a plastic rainbow of helium-filled arches spanning the river—the event depressed by a steady drizzle. An old grad grumbled: "Three hundred and fifty years is a long time to wait for something like this."[2]

"Harvard's Birthday Bash" formally began when more than 16,000 people gathered on September 3, now called "Foundation Day." The star turn was not an academic or political luminary, but an icon of another sort: Charles, Prince of Wales, clad in a gold-embroidered silk academic robe as magnificent as it was meaningless. He suffered through a forty minute prelude of prayers and songs (Harvard Hillel's rabbi offered the blessing; the African American preacher of the University oversaw the proceedings; a female minister offered the benediction), which he characterized when his time finally came as "an exquisite form of torture." In the same spirit of jocular downsizing of the occasion, Charles told his audience: "I confess that I have not addressed such a large gathering since I spoke to 40,000 Gujarati buffalo farmers in India in 1980." What followed (far less noticed) was his familiar assault on the dangers that technology posed to the human spirit.[3]

Like the prince, most of the prominent outsiders who participated in the 350th came from the worlds of celebrity and politics rather than higher education or the life of the mind: politicos Caspar Weinberger, George Schultz, "Tip" O'Neill, Eliot Richardson, and academic-turned-senator Daniel Patrick Moynihan; Saudi Arabia's Sheik Yamani; the Ford Foundation's McGeorge Bundy; liberal Supreme Court icon Justice William Brennan. And as in (but not like) 1936, the outside world imposed itself on these festivities despite the in-house emphasis of the event. Ronald Reagan was (with some reluctance) invited, as had been every president at fifty-year intervals since Andrew Jackson in 1836. Unlike his predecessors, Reagan declined: ostensibly because he was not offered an honorary degree (none were given at the celebration), possibly because his reception was likely to be unpleasantly hostile. (Some thought that the no-degree rule was crafted with him in mind.)[4]

The confrontational style of campus protest born in the late 1960s fed on this ceremonial sitting duck. Even before the fete began, the office of celebration organizer Thomas Stephenson was occupied by a dozen antiapartheid activists. On the final night of the celebration, President Derek Bok led some six hundred guests (including many of the University's prime donors) to a black-tie dinner in Memorial Hall. They found their way blocked by a small antiapartheid group; there was an extended, nasty confrontation; to avoid further trouble the dinner was called off.[5]

The climactic event was a sound and light show in Harvard Stadium before forty thousand alumni and other members of the Harvard community. It included seven hundred performers, the Boston Pops, fireworks, and king of TV newsmen Walter Cronkite as master of ceremonies. David Wolper, the impresario responsible for staging the Los Angeles Olympics in 1984 and the just completed unveiling of the Statue of Liberty in New York, was asked to work his special brand of magic on the 350th. Wolper turned things over to his lieutenant Tommy Walker, whose credits included the opening of Disneyland. Walker assured those involved that he did not intend to repeat his staging of hundreds of Elvis Presley look-alikes at the Statue of Liberty reopening. But his production still had plenty of show-biz pizzazz. Glitz isn't cheap. The spectacle cost well over a million dollars, the pain softened by income from the sale of officially licensed Harvard-inscribed T-shirts, tote bags, and coffee mugs. Nor was it a freebie: reserved seat general admission tickets went for $12.50 and $25.00, more desirable "Crimson Circle" accommodations cost $350 a pair ($300 of which was tax deductible).[6]

Harvard no longer needed to push its claim to the top of the academic pecking order. That was a given, certified time and again by the secular equivalent of a papal blessing, public opinion polls. Drowning out occasional criticisms of Harvard's arrogance and elitism were the hard, overpowering facts of its academic preeminence: libraries with over 14 million volumes, far ahead of any other university in the world; strikingly successful alumni; a proud tradition of academic freedom; a vigorous, diverse, outspoken faculty and spectacular students. Even the right-wing *National Review*, no Harvard-lover, which predictably found that "[t]here has been severe aesthetic and cultural attrition in Harvard Square and the campus generally," had to concede: "There is undoubtedly life in the old place."

If the intellectual tone of the 350th was varied, unfocused, a buzzing confusion, that too was very much part of the time. Fascism and depression wonderfully concentrated the life of the mind in 1936: on freedom and truth, and their fragility. Success, prosperity, and most of all "the democratic and demographic revolution that has transformed the university" now set a very different tone. The *New York Times* took editorial note, as it had fifty years before, of Harvard's self-celebration. This time there was no disquisition on academic freedom and the state of Western civilization, but rather an "Editorial Notebook" piece by *Times* staffer (and Harvard graduate) Jack Rosenthal. He was glad to observe that the object of celebration now, as compared to half a century ago, was not elitism, excellence, intellectual attainment, the pursuit of truth, or freedom of inquiry, but "the impulse to share." What impressed him was not the University's academic prowess, but the fact that "[s]ince the 1930s Harvard has led in the direction of diversity and hence democracy."[7]

## 2000

It is not surprising that many end-of-the-century overviews of the state of American universities in general, and of Harvard in particular, inclined toward the triumphal. In 1992 former Harvard FAS dean Henry Rosovsky asked: "Do we need to fear the future?" His answer was a resounding no. He brushed aside the jeremiads of critics right and left, dwelling instead on the invigorating intellectual climate fostered by research and disciplinary specialization. Harvard Corporation fellow Hannah Gray, who had been president of the University of Chicago, also rejected golden age nostalgia as a misguided response to "the vast extent and continuing explosion of knowledge [and] ... diversity of intellectual styles."[8]

Others, stirred by the transformation of the university from ivory tower to knowledge factory, sounded more cautionary notes. Literary scholar David Bromwich took issue with Rosovsky's buoyant view of the state of American universities. "We are," he thought, "living in a period of academic conformity as strange as any the world has seen." He worried about the tendency to identify the life of the mind with groups rather than individuals and decried the linkage of the academic and outside worlds that Rosovsky welcomed.[9]

These issues had been gathering for some years. Harvard historian Oscar Handlin, in "Peering Toward 2036," written at the time of the 350th anniversary celebration, looked back yearningly to an earlier Harvard of intellectual freedom, "rejection of market mentality," and a communal faculty. Growth—in size, money, administration, programs, students, tuition, buildings—had changed all that. The faculty was scattered physically as well as intellectually; community had given way to separate careers pursued outside the University: all at the cost of the pursuit of truth. Handlin's History colleague Bernard Bailyn had similar worries. He thought that Harvard stood in danger of becoming "a mere holding company for highly publicized, semi-independent service institutes, its original core faculty still respectable but old-fashioned, diminished, and by-passed in importance." Wistfully he hoped that the next Harvard president would oversee a shift back "toward the magnet of learning, toward disinterested stands, toward intellectual pursuits not for extrinsic purposes but for their own sakes."[10]

Even Derek Bok, midwife to worldly Harvard, sounded a cautionary note. He was aware of the danger that the faculty, caught up in the pursuit of fame and money, could slight its responsibilities to scholarship, to students, to the University. He warned, too, of the threat that political correctness posed to the free flow of ideas on campus. And too many students, he feared, found less than their soul's fulfillment in scholarship, objectivity, and disciplinary rigor.[11]

In 1991 Harvard chose a new president to succeed Bok when he resigned at the end of a twenty-year term in office. The obligatory culturally correct search preceded the selection of his successor: 258,000 letters to alumni (yielding 1,536 replies); ads in major newspapers (noting, of course, that Harvard was an equal opportunity/affirmative action employer); 763 nominees and 32 applicants. Out of this emerged 3 finalists: Chicago provost (and later Stanford president) Gerhard Caspar, Harvard economist Martin Feldstein, and the eventual choice, former Princeton provost and then Mellon Foundation executive Neil Rudenstine.

Harvard's twenty-sixth president was fifty-six years old, the oldest to take office since John Walker in 1853. He was a Princeton summa, a Rhodes Scholar, a Harvard Ph.D. in Renaissance literature. After a brief sojourn as a junior faculty member at Harvard, he returned to Princeton to teach and be dean of students. He became dean of the college and President William Bowen's provost, and then went with Bowen to the Mellon Foundation.

Rudenstine's high academic credentials were spiced by deliciously low, ethnically mixed social origins: his Jewish father was a prison guard, his Italian mother was a waitress. He called himself a "multicultural, multi-ethnic, multireligious product." His personality was no less Now: as the *Crimson* put it, "He's a 90s man, nurturing." He was an exemplar both of meritocracy and diversity: possibly "a man for all seasons," as a friend said; certainly a man for his season.

Henry Rosovsky said that he and his Corporation colleagues wanted someone who could "bring the University together." The *Crimson* took note that Rudenstine was Harvard's first "professional president," with a career as an administrator rather than a scholar or teacher. In this sense Rudenstine resembled Pusey, and indeed his relationship to Bok was not unlike that of Pusey to Conant. He added financial flesh and administrative sinew to Bok's vision of a diverse, socially engaged, internationally minded—a more worldly—Harvard.[12]

Rudenstine brought Harvard's 1990s fund drive to a triumphant $2.6 billion conclusion. His easy manner and sincerity won the trust and affection of big donors. And he was greatly helped by his wife, Angelica, a distinguished museum curator fluent in artspeak, the lingua franca of the rich. (She, too, had impeccably diverse origins: a father who was a German Jewish refugee, and a Dutch Protestant mother.)

Rudenstine fully subscribed to the prevailing higher education zeitgeist, in which ethnic, racial, and gender diversity and Harvard's engagement with social concerns mattered as much as meritocracy and ivory-tower scholarship. His first report, in the fall of 1993, looked sweepingly at "Harvard: The Years Ahead." He repeated the now fashionable Harvard mantra of educating future leaders and serving society "by helping to address the most important problems that confront the nation and the larger world." Health policy, the environment, professional ethics, public education, the economy: that was the proper agenda of the worldly University. And it should be pursued across disciplinary and school lines, "especially in those areas where it is essential for us to plan and act more as a single institution rather than as a confederation of moving parts." To bolster his push for One Harvard, Rudenstine reactivated the office of the provost—a position unfilled since Paul Buck's days in the 1940s—whom he expected to be a "cloned president."[13]

Rudenstine's biggest surprise when he came to Harvard was to find how large a gulf yawned between the president and his faculty (unlike cozy, centralized Princeton, about the size of Harvard's Faculty of Arts and Sciences). He tried to bridge the gap by conducting a hands-on presidency, staying up to all hours writing lengthy personal notes to faculty and staff. He devoted comparable time and energy to reviewing permanent faculty appointments. But even with the help of a provost the demands imposed by the sheer scale of Harvard brought him to the verge of exhaustion, and a leave of absence in 1994. Success—especially Harvard-scale success—had a price.

As he settled into his presidency, Rudenstine turned his attention to Harvard's each-tub-on-its-own-bottom culture of autonomous schools. That culture was too deeply entrenched to be challenged head-on—in any case, not his style. He sought instead "coordination and collaboration" between the center and the faculties. He created a cabinet-like advisory group made up of the deans of Harvard's ten professional schools, and solicited their advice on big ticket, all-University issues such as information technology and the expansion of Harvard's physical plant. But the utility of the group was iffy, given the disparity in size of the schools and the swirl of conflicting decanal interests. Rudenstine also set up small working groups composed of faculty and senior administrators to "think through" what Harvard should do about problems such as how to deal with intellectual property concerns and the faculty's outside activities. His larger goal was to encourage deans, faculty, and administrators alike to think and act as "citizens of the University."

More meat-and-potatoes was his effort to foster "integrated studies": research and teaching across school and disciplinary lines. By 2000 there were a dozen "interfaculty initiatives" embracing academic topics such as environmental studies; ethics and the professions; and mind, brain, and behavior, as well as more activist programs seeking not only to study but to promote the interests of children, health policy, nonprofits, and Native Americans.

James Bryant Conant had also sought "methods of counteracting the centrifugal forces which tend to separate our faculties." But at the end of his presidency he confessed that his efforts "to bring about a greater integration have for the most part failed." He had found that the only successful academic collaborations "are those that arise spontaneously by almost the accidents of the personalities in the various faculties." While the center should "help such 'grass-roots' movements ... there is little that a president can do to stimulate them."

The initiatives set in motion by Rudenstine are still in a rudimentary stage. It is by no means clear that if faculty horses are enticed to gather at center-selected waterholes, they will drink deeply. But perhaps vastly greater resources and the more worldly current bent of faculty and administrators will override the older culture of faculty autonomy and the poor track record of top-down planning. If the initiatives do work, they will be benchmarks of Harvard's evolution into a more tightly integrated University.[14]

In his 1999 Commencement address, Rudenstine singled out three "transformations" under way at Harvard. One was cross-school, cross-disciplinary initiatives. Another was Harvard's effort to take a leading role in the application of modern information technology to teaching, research, and distance learning. Finally, much progress had been made in the globalization of the University. It now had 3,000 full-time foreign students from 150 countries and 33,000 alumni living abroad. And "we are beginning to establish small-scale Harvard research centers in various parts of the world." He foresaw in Harvard's future "a far-flung empire on which the sun never sets."[15]

Rudenstine's Harvard was not to everyone's taste. That great naysayer, the *Crimson*, took the administration to task in 1998 for being "out of touch with its soul," focused on fund-raising but disinterested in the quality of undergraduate teaching: "Rudenstine knows more about the interests of Harvard's top donors than about the needs of the Harvard undergraduates." The paper looked back fondly on Bok's readiness to take on substantive academic issues: he was "an intellectual leader fit for an intellectual institution like Harvard." There was more than an echo here of the comparisons drawn half a century before between Pusey and Conant. Builders and consolidators are as essential to an institution as the visionaries whose ideas they implement, but they are more likely to be without honor in their own time.[16]

After a decade in office (the shortest Harvard presidential term since the 1860s), Rudenstine decided to retire in June 2001. He saw himself not as the inheritor of Bok's worldly university, but as the first Harvard president to confront the post-cold war world. Yet from the perspective of Harvard's history, it appears that his legacy will be that he built upon and raised the money for existing goals: internationalism, diversity through affirmative action, trying to solve social problems, creating a more centrally coordinated University.

In March 2001 the Corporation chose Lawrence Summers, former Secretary of the Treasury, to be Harvard's 27th president. Forty-six years old, Summers had a stellar career as a professor of economics at Harvard and chief economist of the World Bank before moving to the Treasury. In many ways he exemplified new academic man: a brilliant scholar turned major public servant, with powerful connections to the world of business and government and a global perspective. His academic pedigree (despite the fact that he had been rejected by Harvard College) was of a high order: an undergraduate degree from M.I.T., a Harvard Ph.D., parents who were professors of economics at the University of Pennsylvania, and two Nobelist uncles, economists Paul Samuelson of M.I.T. and Kenneth Arrow of Stanford. That Summers is a nephew of Samuelson, who experienced anti-Semitism first-hand at Harvard in the 1930s, makes his appointment an apt expression of the degree to which Harvard had transformed itself in the intervening decades.

According to the *Boston Globe*, the presidential search committee was looking for "a new face with new ideas, an agent of change" who could "think outside the higher education box." The implication is that as in the case of Eliot in 1867, Conant in 1933, and Bok in 1971, there was a sense that the time had come to strike out on a new course: not just to strengthen the existing state of things but to subject it to questioning, and perhaps to change.[17]

What possible ground can there be for a felt need for new ideas and new directions in these piping times of Harvard prestige, prosperity, and power? Yet it appears that just as Brahmin and meritocratic Harvard came to be freighted with difficulties and discontents, so does affluent, worldly Harvard face present and potential problems.

## The Faculty: Freedom and Freebooting

The Harvard faculty can lay good claim to being the world's best. Nevertheless the forces in modern academic life that erode faculty members' commitments to their institution and to scholarship have left their mark. The meritocratic University nurtured the ideal of detached, objective scholars committed to the pursuit of truth. But in many areas of the academy, a new, postmodern skepticism with regard to objectivity and truth has come into its own. Closely related is political correctness, with its deadening effect on the free exchange of ideas. True, these tendencies are less evident at Harvard than at many other universities, and some of their grosser manifestations have faded. But it is arguable that Harvard today is no more (and possibly less) open to diversity of thought than it was at the height of the cold war during the 1950s. Harvard's faculty, for all its cherished tradition of academic freedom, cannot be expected to transcend prevailing intellectual fashion now, any more than it was able to in the past.

More serious is the siren lure of the world outside. The Harvard tradition of autonomous professors, departments, and schools reinforces the faculty's readiness to be independent academic entrepreneurs. There has been a substantial rise in outside calls on its professional expertise. Harvard scientists consult, sometimes market their discoveries, and enter into commercial relationships at an unprecedented rate. Some law professors have gone beyond lucrative advising and representation to selling their legal talents in the media and on the Internet. Social scientists and humanists have been less successful in mining the richest seams of the contemporary culture's mother lode. But a few have cashed in on the large public capacity for psychobabble, race-and-gender discourse, and the more errant applications of the postmodern sensibility. The result, thought one observer, is "a diminished core and a cloud of external relationships," with the University serving "merely to accredit the quality of the activities conducted in the cloud."[18]

The constraints of a simpler age—restrictions on patenting health-related discoveries for profit, limits on the time devoted to off-campus activities—cannot readily contain these impulses. It is possible that the traditional definition of the university as a place for teaching students and pursuing truth may check the new faculty worldliness. President-elect Summers has spoken of the need to induce in the faculty a greater concern for undergraduate education. But meanwhile, the magnetic pull on the faculty of its professional involvements and the lure of the world outside, and the consequent weakening of its institutional and pedagogical commitments is, if anything, increasing.[19]

## Marketing the Brand

Endowed with one of the world's most widely recognized names, Harvard in 2000 earned $650,000 in fees for the carefully monitored use of its trademark. Nothing at Harvard, it appears, is without market value. In the spring of 2000, the vice president for corporate communications of the *New York Times* Corporation left that job to "develop the strategic plan for the business segment of [the] globalization project"—of the Center for the Study of World Religions at the Harvard Divinity School. The press reported in late 1999 that Harvard was contemplating the sale of its educational wares over the Internet, in the face of a venerable tradition of not commercially exploiting its name. The University, a consultant lamented, "is a global brand without a global distribution."

Provost Harvey Fineberg saw no conflict between quality and large-scale marketing. "Harvard," he said, "has to change. No institution remains in the forefront of its field if it does the same things in 20 years that it does today." The University's educational "products" were too valuable to be left to the disposal of individual faculty members, or even Harvard's schools. The ground rules for Harvard's entry into the Internet, concluded its general counsel, would have to be set by her office, not by the deans or the faculty: "We know that if we didn't, it will be like living at the rodeo with a lot of cowboys out there. So we need to give them some boundaries. But we won't be the architects." Education School psychologist Howard Gardner had a different fix on things: "What should Harvard not do? What line should the University not cross? What is it that you don't give away?" But worldly Harvard had already crossed many lines and showed few signs of slowing down. (Besides, who said anything about *giving* things away?)[20]

A major example of Harvard in the world's (and the market's) service is the exponential growth of fee-paying participants in "nontraditional" (that is, anyone can come) programs, ranging from the extension and summer schools to a bewildering variety of short-term executive education programs fielded by Harvard's professional faculties. As of 2000, there were fewer than 20,000 full-time degree-seeking students at the university—and more than 67,000 part-time nontraditionals, including 55,000 enrolled in special advanced programs. The Kennedy School had four-and-a-half times as many enrollees in its executive programs as it had degree students. The Business School's executive mid-career programs were especially lucrative. By 2000 they ran from three days to ten weeks, cost $4,000 to $47,000, had 5,000 enrollees (compared to about 1,750 M.B.A.s), and accounted for a quarter of the school's income.

During the last decade of the twentieth century the number of international students enrolled in degree programs rose by 34 percent. By 1999 they were 25 percent of all graduate and professional school students. According to John Dunlop, former dean of FAS, rising enrollments in executive education programs and the accelerating globalization of the student body raised questions for a new Harvard president to ponder: "What does increasing special programs do to regular educational programs? . . . Do executive programs lessen faculty attention to disciplinary research and growth?" One might also ask how globalization works in classrooms where undergraduates are often exposed to foreign-born teaching fellows whose English is seriously inadequate, or where professional school faculty struggle against the burden of teaching students who do not recognized the culture-bound references of American academic discourse.[21]

## Raising Money, Admitting Students

"[A] reduction in large gifts would not be fatal to us now. We have enough for a great university if wisely used": thus A. Lawrence Lowell in the far from affluent year of 1937. Had money raising become almost an end in itself by 2000, with only a vague relationship to institutional needs? Granted, it is expensive to run a modern university. To remain vibrant it must change and grow; old subjects (usually) should not be jettisoned to make way for new interests. But it is also the case that the in-house demand for money increases with its supply, that the relative ease with which Harvard can raise money undermines incentives for cost containment, and that the money tail can wag the dog—shape the agenda—of teaching and scholarship.

A similar caution could be raised as to the other major growth sector at Harvard, the College's application pool. There are about ten applicants for every slot. This is a tribute to Harvard's appeal to many of the nation's best and brightest young people. But it also runs the risk of fostering resentment among the rejected 90 percent, especially if the process comes to be perceived as unfair.[22]

## Seeing Like a State

Conflict between the central administration and the faculties (Arts and Sciences in particular) persists like a low but stubborn fever. We have seen how in the years after 1970 that tension erupted in issues such as the employees' union, the disposition of real estate, technology transfer, and faculty pensions. The discordance between top-down planning—"seeing like a state"—and the ground-level realities of Harvard life goes on.

In July 1999 the center took on the task of creating a University-wide administrative data system: Project ADAPT. A year later it was bogged down in a MATEP-like quagmire of technological glitches, escalating costs, and disgruntled faculty and staff complaining that they weren't consulted or listened to. Nor is it evident that the deans of the major schools accept the provost or the vice presidents as loci of authority between them and the president. Indeed, an activist successor, with a large discretionary fund and an ambitious provost and vice presidents, could well set out on a collision course with one or more of Harvard's faculty "tubs."[23]

Another potential source of trouble is Harvard's physical expansion. The University now holds 240 acres of land (140 of them owned by the Business School) in the Boston neighborhood of Allston, across the Charles River from the 206-acre Cambridge campus. An ever expanding university must have space to meet its future needs. But deciding which schools, or programs, or facilities move and which stay put will not be easy. In 1999 Neil Rudenstine asked the Law School faculty to contemplate an eventual move across the river. The all but unanimous response: not even to consider it.[24]

It seems, in sum, that a major challenge facing twenty-first-century Harvard is not unlike the one that confronted the newly independent

United States in the late 1780s: the problem of federalism. How can the necessary and legitimate tasks of central authority in a large and worldly university be exercised without jeopardizing the pedagogical and intellectual benefits of autonomous faculties?

The tentativeness and relatively circumscribed character of the red flags we have raised suggests how much our tale of Harvard's past two-thirds of a century is one of success. No institution is without its warts, and we have not sought to hide them. But the bottom line at the beginning of the twenty-first century is that this dense, complex palimpsest of a university, its original intent of serving the needs of a colonial commonwealth successively overwritten by Brahmin elitism, meritocratic striving, and worldly engagement, is one of the most illustrious institutional adornments of American life. Its capacity to adapt to intellectual, social, and cultural change has been the chief source of modern Harvard's success—and the chief source of its problems and discontents. As far as our historians' eyes can see, this is likely to remain the case.

# AFTERWORD

On an exquisitely beautiful Friday, October 12, 2001, forty-six-year-old Lawrence Summers became Harvard's twenty-seventh president. A welcoming article in the *Atlantic Monthly* called him "A Worldly Professor": a fit man to head a worldly university. His inauguration was bathed in the self-confidence one would expect from the premier university at the top of its game. Not Harvard, but the world it rather sententiously claimed to serve, seemed out of joint. The terrorist attacks of September 11 were only a month past, and on everyone's mind.

The new president took due note of Harvard's resplendent past. But he focused on its present strengths and future challenges. The Corporation urged him to make undergraduate education, science, and the new Allston campus across the Charles River his primary concerns. To these he added two themes that had been in the Harvard air for some time and echoed the more abstract rhetoric of the world of government from which he came. These were "community": "the need to come together as a university," and "globalization": Harvard's continuing on its progress from a national to an international institution.

But just as the national unity that followed 9/11 came to seem like an artifact of some remote, Arcadian time, so too did Summers's high hopes for his presidency erode under recurrent conflict with faculty and administrators. In February 2006 he announced his resignation, ending the shortest-lived Harvard presidency since the sudden death of Cornelius Felton in 1862.

## The Summers Storm

Summers's departure came after a perfect storm of clashing personalities, differences over political and academic issues, and discontent with his lack of consultation. It came down to a president schooled in the "intellectual imperialism" of Economics and the political culture of Washington confronting a faculty with little patience for either.

Summers first took on political correctness in the academy, a decision whose courage was less questionable than its prospects for success. He spoke up in support of ROTC, barred from the Harvard campus since the 1960s. Then came the news that Summers had taken iconic black University professor Cornel West to task for neglecting serious scholarship and giving too many As to his students. West responded with well-orchestrated outrage.

In the fall of 2002 Summers observed that anti-Israeli views had secured a foothold in "progressive communities." Referring to a petition, signed by some faculty members, that called on Harvard to divest its stock holdings in companies doing business with Israel, Summers warned that "serious and thoughtful people are advocating and taking actions that are anti-Semitic in their effect if not their intent." Although he asserted that "we should always respect the academic freedom of everyone to take any position," the *Harvard Crimson* and the *Boston Globe* strongly criticized him for stifling debate.

Summers's assault on political correctness came to a climax in January 2005, when he spoke at a National Bureau of Economic Research symposium on the problems of women in academic science. He had been assured that this was to be a private, no-holds-barred discussion. Summers included genetic factors among those that might explain the relative scarcity of women at the cutting edge of science. An MIT biologist in the audience famously declared that his comments made her physically ill. The press—and Summers's growing body of faculty critics—had a field day.

In what was by now a familiar pattern, Summers explained that all he wanted to do was stimulate discussion. He apologized for injured sensibilities and pledged to avoid future mishaps. His ROTC and Israel comments were minor provocations compared to the Cornel West and women-in-science incidents, and he put big money behind his penitence: large supplements to an Afro-American faculty already more than sufficient to its student market; some $50 million to further the advancement of women faculty at Harvard.

The gathering force of anti-Summers sentiment came to a head at FAS faculty meetings in February 2005. Political scientist Theda Skocpol spoke scathingly of "the pathologies of leadership that are undermining the honor, competitive effectiveness, and collegial governance of Harvard University." Leland Matory, a professor of African American Studies and

Anthropology, associated himself with Cornel West, women, and the Palestinians as a potential Summers target ("that could have been me") and offered a no-confidence motion. Skocpol proposed a more mollifying resolution that took exception to Summers's presidential style but commended him for his pledge(s) to act more collegially.

By a 218–185 vote, an unusually large turnout of faculty declared a "lack of confidence" in Summers's presidency. He promised to mend his ways, and the Corporation continued to back him. He brought in a new chief of staff (his third) and a personal press spokesman in the fall of 2005 and dropped his active role in curriculum reform.

But it did seem that character was destiny. Faculty discontent bubbled up again in early 2006: this time over matters that belonged not to the realm of political correctness but to issues of leadership, trust, and credibility. A group of Arts and Sciences department chairs, primarily from the Humanities and the Social Sciences, had begun to meet weekly in early 2005. They included some who wanted "to get Larry out, period," and some who were more concerned about governance, in particular the diminished capacity of the Dean to conduct the Faculty's business.

Criticism grew of the abrasive style with which Summers questioned the quality of proposed new appointees, of individual faculty members, and of whole departments in the humanities and the softer social sciences. His calls for a shift "from old disciplines to new" and "from old structures of governance to new" left many faculty members uneasy. And some scientists objected to what they saw as Summers's bias in favor of the more high profile life sciences.

Both Summers and Dean of Faculty William Kirby, whom he had appointed to replace chemist Jeremy Knowles, came to be widely regarded as less than effective leaders: the one for being more assertive than he should, the other for being less assertive than he should. Summers put pressure on Kirby to give up his office. But before Kirby could announce his resignation, word spread that he had been fired.

At a February 7, 2006, faculty meeting, the many strands of anti-Summers sentiment coalesced. Ill-feeling stirred by the manner of Kirby's removal was enhanced by concern over the supposed misdeeds of Economics professor Andrei Shleifer. A former student and close friend of Summers, Shleifer had led a U.S.-funded Harvard program that advised the post-Communist Russian government on privatizing state enterprises. In the course of his work he, an associate, and their wives invested in that country's developing bond market. A Federal court found Shleifer guilty of conspiracy and Harvard in breach of contract with the government. Shleifer paid $2 million and Harvard $26 million to settle the case. The story, detailed in an article anonymously distributed to some faculty members before the February 7 meeting, led to questions from the floor as to what Summers knew, and when. He claimed to have no opinion or detailed knowledge on the matter, to the manifest disbelief of many of those present.

Fifteen faculty members (including five scientists) spoke against Summers; no one defended him. A few days later Anthropology professor Peter Ellison, who had resigned as Dean of the Graduate School because of unsatisfactory dealings with Summers, criticized him for his treatment of Kirby. He also accused Summers of being less than truthful when he denied that there had been discussions about extending the authority to grant Ph.Ds to non-FAS Schools.

Criticism by prominent faculty citizens, and the prospect of a more sharply worded no-confidence vote at the next FAS faculty meeting, convinced almost all members of the Corporation that the game was up. Summers announced his resignation on February 21, blaming "rifts between me and segments of the Arts and Sciences faculty" that irrevocably blocked his agenda for Harvard's renewal.

Much of the faculty saw this as a measure of its ability to rid itself of an offending president. Much of the outside world saw it differently. Boston city officials and business leaders, who liked Summers's plans for development of the Allston campus, were unhappy. So were some donors, who supported his vision for Harvard's future. There was considerable media tut-tutting over political correctness run wild, and over faculty grandees who "wanted no part of a president who actually dared to lead." A group of anti-Summers faculty, distressed over these reactions, asked acting president Derek Bok to issue a public statement detailing the reasons why Summers was removed. Bok, Brahmin in essence if not by birth, is said to have responded: "I won't do that, because it isn't done."

The Tong war between Summers and a portion of his faculty had two notable aspects: gloves-off acrimony, and extensive media attention. In (still-short) historical perspective, these appear to have been closely related to Harvard's place as the most notable of the great, worldly American universities.

The Summers storm resonated with the recent experience of a number of the nation's major institutions, their leaders, and their critics. It resembled not so much past Harvard imbroglios (Conant and some faculty in the late 1930s, Pusey and the University Hall bust in the late 1960s) as notable public flare-ups such as the Bork and Thomas Supreme Court appointment hearings, the Clinton impeachment, and the fervid politics of the Bush II years.

Over the course of the past half-century, there has been a growing tendency to subject leaders of the nation's major political, corporate, media, religious, and academic institutions to public laundering (and dirtying). This had its roots in the 1960s and the major alterations in public consciousness that then emerged. The mindset identified with the counterculture—many of whose advocates were in, and stayed in, the universities—left its mark on later generations' views of authority and leadership. And most conspicuously in the humanities and the softer social sciences, the belief took root that the highest academic calling was to craft language and fields of inquiry that would further a new academic culture, transcending the trammels of race, gender, class, institutions, and hierarchy.

A strikingly different world view flourished in other areas of the academy, most notably the natural sciences and Economics. Here the highest goals were to discover and apply the rules—the laws—that governed nature, human nature, and social behavior. Organization, expertise, and institutions were not objects of suspicion, but essential tools for getting on with the world's work.

Conflict between these perspectives fitfully lit up the Harvard sky in the course of the late twentieth century. Clashes rose over academic content (social *v.* biogenetic analysis in the social sciences, deconstruction/postmodernism *v.* traditionalism in literature and the arts, the Crits *v. omnes* in the Law School); over political correctness; over faculty and student gender and racial diversity; over the character of general education.

Summers's appointment bid fair to heighten these tensions. In intellect, temperament, talent, and experience he embodied the purposeful, take-charge style favored by the Corporation. And his agenda—to strengthen the sciences, instill more vitality into undergraduate teaching and the curriculum, develop the new Allston campus, foster more diverse political-intellectual discourse—had many supporters in the faculty, and among the students.

But a growing body of professors were alienated by Summers's ill-concealed contempt for the softer disciplines and his attacks on icons of political correctness. They came into unlikely alliance with faculty, administrators, and members of the Governing Boards who subscribed to an older, more genteel and circumscribed Harvard leadership style. One journalist colorfully if hyperbolically observed: "When Larry Summers got to Harvard he saw lazy, leftist professors inflating grades in what looked like an outdated Yugoslav workers' co-operative. The faculty saw a bumptious boor hijacking their university." It would have taken great subtlety and forbearance on Summers's part, and great indulgence in the demands of leadership on the faculty's part, for relative tranquillity to have prevailed. Neither was in the cards.

Summers's departure was the most conspicuous Harvard event of the new century. But it is not clear that it would turn out to be the most significant one. Rather, what was happening, not happening, and likely to happen to teaching and scholarship, governance, the development of bioscience and the new Allston campus, and Harvard's ever-growing political and commercial worldliness, defined the university as it proceeded along its twenty-first-century way.

## Undergraduate Life and Learning

There were aspects of undergraduate life other than the curriculum that exercised the faculty. Student culture remained deeply altered since the 1960s: barely regulated, the sexual revolution unabated, drinking on the rise. And grade inflation continued to be a fact of modern undergraduate life. As and Bs went from 52 percent of all grades in 1950 to more than 88 percent in 2004–2005. By 2000, 91 percent of Harvard's graduating students received honors degrees, compared to 51 percent at Yale and 44 percent at Princeton (whose students couldn't be *that* inferior). In 2005 the Faculty capped honors degrees at 50 percent of the total. It remained to be seen how long this exercise in quality control would withstand the demands of an ambitious, high-achieving student body.

When Summers talked about "globalization" as a major attribute of modern, worldly Harvard, he had in mind study abroad for all Harvard undergraduates. But most of them had no desire to spend term time overseas. Of the 792 students (out of a student body of about 6,500) who "pursued significant international experiences" in 2003–2004, a modest 166 were in course-credit programs. More than 400 "sought formal study, research, internship, or service opportunities during the summer." Another 200 or so "traveled 'with purpose'."

"Significant," it seemed, was a many-faceted word. But expanding student interest in the larger world was real enough. Summer internships and study programs, and Harvard-funded research abroad, substantially increased during the Summers years. By 2006, 1,100 students participated, 900 of them during the summer break.

Why did Summers and the Corporation think that large-scale curriculum reform was so important a priority when he came into office in 2001? One source: surveys of elite university students' satisfaction with their education persistently put Harvard at the low end of the scale.

Large courses, remote senior faculty, and a limited and rigidly applied Core curriculum fed discontent. And there was a widespread belief that Harvard had lacked a sense of purpose and direction in recent years and that the existing framework of disciplines, concentrations, and requirements was too confining at a time of rapidly changing intellectual constructs and student aspirations.

Summers gave some lip service to historian Bernard Bailyn's view that the chief need was to redirect Harvard students toward learning for its own sake. But this was submerged by the rule-the-world purposefulness of much of the student body and the faculty, as well as Summers's commitment to science and public service. He wanted a big increase in faculty-student contact through freshman and junior seminars; a fresh, hard look at the Core; an overhaul of the advising system; greater weight given to science and quantitative analysis. No fewer than seven committees reviewed the whole curricular ball of wax: general education, concentrations, science and technology, pedagogy, advising and counseling, writing and speaking, the calendar.

There were some tangible results. Almost all new students were accommodated in freshman seminars, in theory a big step forward in relieving the anomie of first-year undergraduate life. Significant numbers of full-time faculty, coming from both Arts and Sciences and the professional schools, were enlisted to teach the seminars. The advising system expanded, relying on non-faculty proctors and student peers rather than an overloaded and under-motivated regular faculty.

By common agreement, the 2004 report of the committee working on general education was a failure. Thomas Ehrlich of the Carnegie Corporation called its conclusions "pitiful." Beset by tensions between scientists and humanists, the committee threw up its hands and proposed to replace the Core with a distribution requirement, a something-for-everybody of three courses each from the natural sciences, the humanities, and the social sciences. That might have seemed innovative in 1900. But it struck most observers a century later as uninspired.

This was not the result of faculty indifference to undergraduate education, but of substantial disagreement over what its character should be. (Yale came up with a similarly unsatisfactory result in 2003 after a four-year curriculum review.)

In the fall of 2006 a committee of six senior faculty took another crack at the problem. Echoing Conant's 1945 General Education scheme, they sought "to connect what students learn at Harvard to life beyond Harvard, and to help them understand and appreciate the complexities of the world and their role in it." Instead of the Core's emphasis on disciplinary modes of understanding, they proposed broad topical themes: Aesthetic and Interpretive Understanding, Culture and Belief, Empirical and Ethical Reasoning, The Life and Physical Sciences, Societies of the World, The United States in the World. It remained to be seen how this latest squaring of the general education circle would ultimately fare. But it did reflect a large—perhaps the largest—intellectual development of early twenty-first-century Harvard: the growth of teaching and scholarship that cut across traditional disciplinary boundaries.

Of comparable potential significance was the January 2007 report of a Task Force on Teaching and Career Development, chaired by ubiquitous Dean of the Graduate School Theda Skocpol. It condemned the absence of incentives for good teaching in the Faculty of Arts and Sciences and called for mandatory course evaluations and greater weight to teaching in salary and tenure decisions. But again, it was unclear how this would sit with a faculty bred to and selected for its capacity for scholarship.

## Governance

Modernizing Harvard's governance and instilling a greater sense of community were goals as attractive as improving undergraduate education. Attaining them proved to be no less difficult.

Summers did not question the growth of the central administration that began under Derek Bok in the early 1970s. The burgeoning bureaucracy by now was thoroughly professional; Old Harvard types staying on to serve Alma Mater were virtually gone. Officials with government or business backgrounds abounded. A new vice president regularly sent e-mails to an extended "special list," in which each recipient was assured in the best Harvard Business School managerial style, "I want you to be the first to know."

Under former National Institutes of Mental Health director and Harvard psychiatry professor Steven Hyman, the Office of the Provost became a more significant presence in Harvard affairs, interjected between those traditional players, the President and the Deans. It got a big boost from the substantial increase in endowment controlled by the Center, a product of Neil Rudenstine's fund-raising campaign in the 1990s. The Provost's Office swelled with vice and deputy provosts, including several professors: a new source of Center administrators. They had little or no line responsibility for academic functions, and no control over academic appointments or budgets. But as interdisciplinary and interfaculty centers and research initiatives grew, so did the potential of the Provost's Office to take a larger place in the University's academic life.

As in centuries past, the Corporation was in principle the ultimate governing body of the University. But the difficulty of knowing what was going on in so large and complex a place as Harvard substantially limited its role. The Corporation's small size and remoteness from the workings of the University made it a council of advisers more than a decision-making body. Its power to appoint (and to request the resignation of) the President, and its oversight of investments, were its most significant areas of authority.

In its makeup the Corporation of the early 2000s was a far cry from the past. As of 2006, none of its members except the President lived in the Boston–Cambridge area. That at least one Fellow have an academic background had become standard practice. In 2005 Hanna Gray, the tough-minded former president of the University of Chicago, retired to be replaced by former Duke president Nannerl Keohane, reputed to be as consultative as Gray was assertive. Attorney Conrad Harper joined the Corporation in 2000 as its first black member. He resigned five years later, in a letter to the Corporation protesting Summers's salary increase in the face of "patterns of faculty grievances." Harper's successor, black Georgetown Law professor Patricia King, and economist and Congressional Budget Office head Robert Reischauer, who joined in 2002, reduced the business-investment wing of the Corporation to James R. Houghton, Robert Rubin, and Treasurer James Rothenberg.

Washington and the academy had come to have a greater presence on Harvard's Board than Boston and the private sector. This was due in part to the University's ever-greater national character, and in part to the decline of Boston's Brahmins as movers and shakers. The degree to which this would alter the role of the Corporation in Harvard governance has yet to be seen. The same might be said of the alumni-elected Board of Overseers, changing in ways not dissimilar to the Corporation, and seeking as always to make its place in Harvard governance more substantial.

One thing remained as in the past: the looming presence of Harvard's endowment. When Summers left Harvard to go to Washington in 1991, it was a hearty $4.76 billion. When he returned as president a decade later, it was a stunning $15 billion. By 2007 it was closing in on a mind-boggling $30 billion, compared to competitor Yale's $18 billion.

Summers was prepared to raise and spend big money. Building expenditures averaged under $80 million a year in the late 1980s; they rose to $495 million a year in 2001–2005. Escalating investment returns induced the Corporation to temporarily raise endowment distribution from its customary 4-to-5 percent average to 8-to-9 percent. The additional income was to be used for student financial aid, faculty growth in the sciences, and the life sciences infrastructure planned for the new campus in Allston. The abrupt end of his term in office left Summers's initiatives up in the air. But there was little reason to think that they would be reversed, any more than that Harvard's capacity to raise large sums would be diminished.

## The Faculty of Arts and Sciences

Now as before, the Faculty of Arts and Sciences was the most conspicuous and (at least in that Faculty's estimation) the most important jewel in the Harvard diadem. It had some 700 members in 2006, closing in on its goal of about 750. Harvard's 11–1 faculty-undergraduate and 5–1 faculty-graduate student ratios were not as favorable as those of its chief competitors, so a good case could be made for expansion. But relatively small departments given to rigorous selectivity made growth difficult. Another sticking point was the junior faculty's prospects for tenure. As in the past, the nagging fear that those up for promotion were not necessarily the best that ever were or would be worked against rapid growth.

Nor did the Faculty's resistance to the reality of its aging encourage turnover. In 1991 then-Dean Henry Rosovsky contemplated the imminent end of mandatory retirement. He predicted that the lures of estate-building, collegial companionship, scientists keeping their lab space, light teaching, and the fact that "the pace and productivity of self-generated work is not—to put it gently—closely supervised or regulated," made staying on as long as possible a rational choice.

Rosovsky linked this behavior to a decline in professorial civic virtue. He confessed himself unable to say what the standard teaching "load" amounted to. Unilateral reductions by individuals and departments, team-taught courses in which each faculty participant took full course credit, absence from Cambridge during term time: all of these transgressions went on without the Dean's authorization.

Rosovsky's prediction of delayed post-mandatory retirement turned out to be all too accurate. A third of the scientists who had reached the age of seventy since 1994 had not yet retired by 2000–2001. By 2006 about a third more of the FAS faculty was over sixty than under fifty.

Almost 25 percent of the Faculty was female by 2006, 14 percent were minority: black, Hispanic, Asian. Given the relative newness of the drive to diversity, representation not surprisingly was lower in the tenured ranks: women 18.6 percent, minorities 9.3 percent. While the number of women in science tripled between 1991 and 2000, they still held only 6.8 percent of tenured science positions, compared to 21.9 percent in the humanities and 14.4 percent in the social sciences. Was this impressive, or disappointing, progress? Most vocal opinion said the latter.

Diversity was pursued with comparable vigor, and more statistical success, in the selection of undergraduates. The class that entered in the fall of 2006 was 52 percent female, 10 percent African American, 21 percent Asian American, 9.5 percent Latino, and 8 percent foreign.

But student economic and political diversity was less evident. In 2004 a Harvard Financial Aid Initiative exempted families with incomes under $40,000 from paying tuition. The exemption was later raised to $60,000, with lesser aid up to incomes of $80,000. The number of lower- and middle-income Harvard students rose, but its proportion remained small. About 75 percent of Harvard's undergraduates continued to come from the highest socioeconomic quartile, 16 percent from the bottom half. In this respect, at least, early twenty-first-century Harvard was not so different from early twentieth-century Harvard.

The announcement that Harvard would end its early admissions program in 2007 won much acclaim as another step in the University's long march toward a student body of greater economic diversity. Acting president Bok noted that early admissions programs "tend to advantage the advantaged," weighing against poorer, less sophisticated students unaware of the much higher likelihood that an early admissions applicant would be accepted.

Harvard's policy change came in the face of the general rush of colleges to an early admissions policy as a means of wooing and securing desirable applicants. But few schools chose to follow Harvard's lead. As in the case of Harvard's criticism of the merit scholarships that other schools adopted during the 1990s, its substantial lead in the admissions scramble hardly impeded its capacity to rise above crass self-interest. Besides, the new policy had a three-year cap. If it had untoward consequences, it could be dropped.

## Science, the Professional Schools, and the New Campus

The most striking new development in Harvard's academic life was arguably in the realm of the life sciences. The social significance, and intellectual power and originality, of the field, and the money that it required, made bioscience the 800-pound gorilla of the twenty-first-century university.

There was some question as to how well Arts and Sciences was responding to this challenge. A February 2005 review of the past fifteen years found that while the FAS social science faculty had grown by 18 percent, and its humanities faculty by 11.2 percent, the natural sciences faculty expanded by only 7.7 percent. Why? One explanation was limited space, which long constrained Harvard's ability to be a major player in Big Science. Not coincidentally, Harvard's scientific tradition leaned more to the theoretical than to the applied.

An attention-getting July 2006 report by a University-wide Planning Committee for Science and Engineering focused on the new Allston campus as the potential meeting ground for scientists from Arts and Sciences, the Medical School, the School of Public Health, and the affiliated hospitals. In early 2007 a new University-wide standing committee on science and engineering was established, to act as midwife to "a new era of collaborative, cross-disciplinary science initiatives." A $50 million fund would get things started. And planning got under way for a new Department of Developmental and Regenerative Biology, run by the relevant Harvard Schools and the affiliated hospitals.

This agenda for new paths in science faculty-building was the most substantial challenge yet to the primacy of Harvard's existing departments and Schools. But it raised troubling questions. Who would pay for what promised to be a massively expensive effort? What, and who, would the appointees teach—if indeed they did any teaching? How (if at all) would they fit into the established structure of academic governance?

As of 2007, things were very much in flux. The Cambridge campus had seen a considerable expansion of the FAS science and engineering plant. But new battle lines emerged as big bioscience came to twenty-first-century Harvard. The traditional pecking order of scientific primacy—FAS first, the Medical School next, the Hospitals last—had been inverted: first by the Medical School outstripping FAS in some of the life sciences, and then by the Hospitals, flush with federal money, pulling ahead of HMS. Breaking with Harvard-centric tradition, Summers set out to help raise money to support genome research at the

Broad Institute: M.I.T.-based, but in which the Harvard Medical School, the Hospitals, and FAS scientists collaborated.

A comparable dynamism was evident in Harvard's major professional schools. Large curricular reforms in Law, Business, and Medicine stood in dramatic contrast to the uncertainty attending the future of general education in Harvard College. They had strikingly common concerns, reflecting the changing character of their professions.

The destructive ideological divisions at the Law School were all but gone in the new century, under the ameliorating deanships of Robert Clark and Elena Kagan. The Law and Economics school of legal analysis, the intellectual and ideological antithesis of the Critical Legal Studies movement of the 1960s and 1970s, became more prominent. And a new generation of younger faculty, without a strong commitment to either of those schools of legal thought, adopted a pragmatic approach to the law as a tool for getting things done. The Law faculty voted unanimously in 2006 to add required first-year courses in non-judicial lawmaking (legislation and administrative law), international and comparative law, and a more holistic approach to the solving of clients' problems.

The Business School added two courses to its first-year core in 2000. One was in entrepreneurship. Most HBS students wanted not to join large corporations but to start their own firms. The other dealt with leadership and corporate accountability: the existing concern for business ethics raised to a higher pedagogical power.

With a student body more than a third "international" (defined as having a non–United States passport), and business at the core of globalization, HBS had to cast itself in a new light. Thirty percent of its trademark case studies came to be based on international enterprises, and the School set up five research centers worldwide. Its major problem appeared now to be not the traditional one of its place in the Harvard professional school pecking order, but how to find faculty willing to give up the greater pecuniary rewards of the business world. One response: bring in Ph.Ds (by 2006 only half of the faculty had a business school background) and instruct them in the mysteries of HBS pedagogy.

Like Business and Law, Medicine changed its general curricular approach in the early 2000s. It sought to adapt its instruction to the revolution in molecular medicine, add more small-group instruction, and integrate the care of patients more closely with the medical science curriculum. Like its fellow Schools, HMS put additional emphasis on the social dimension of its profession: health policy, medical ethics. And an Academic Center for Teaching and Learning, in which at least some of the HMS faculty of over 9,000 might be helped to become more effective teachers, came into being in 2006.

Under Joseph Martin, who served as Dean for a decade from 1997, the Medical School adapted to the powerful surge of genetic and biomedical research. The political appeal, cost, and need for clinical trials in this work led government and other funding agencies to favor researchers at the Harvard-affiliated hospitals over those based in the Medical School. In response Martin brought together some 800 Boston area oncologists to form the nation's largest cancer research center at the Dana-Farber Cancer Institute. Its success in attracting major government grants made it a model for other efforts in the collaborative study of disease.

The growth of Centers and joint degree programs, products of the brave new academic world of inter-disciplinary approaches and subjects, reinforced the sense that new academic currents were eroding the primacy of the traditional Arts and Sciences disciplines. By 2003 Harvard had more than a dozen "multifaculty" degree programs, and twice as many inter-faculty "initiatives." Research centers, programs, projects, and institutes spread like kudzu grass. There were more than fifty of them in the Kennedy School, some thirty in the Ed School, numerous others in FAS, Law, Medicine, and Public Health. Every bottom now had a tub, observed one wag. But many of these enterprises, particularly in the Kennedy School, were lightly funded.

Centers and institutes could respond quickly to new areas of research, and they fostered collaboration across disciplinary or School lines. But they came at a cost. It was not always clear to whom they reported, and often they lured professors from teaching and other departmental responsibilities. Dean Jeremy Knowles set up five-year reviews of the FAS Centers' funding and called on them to demonstrate their value as teaching and not just research bodies.

The most conspicuous setting for the forces defining twenty-first century Harvard was the new campus across the Charles River in Allston. Larger than the Cambridge campus, it could not be developed all at once: much of it was tied up in long-term leases and permanent easements. But that hardly removed the need for large-scale planning. An official called the development of the Allston campus a "city building" project, replete with issues of transportation, land use, and design, requiring the expenditure of billions of dollars and decades of time.

A University Physical Planning Committee wrestled with varying visions: A science park embracing scientists from Arts and Sciences, the

Medical and Public Health Schools, the Harvard-affiliated hospitals, and even outlier MIT? Or a new academic campus replicating the old one in Cambridge, with a mix of undergraduate and graduate education, museums and housing, and science research centers?

By 2007 the agreed-upon model was a mixed-use campus. Several new undergraduate Houses might eventually rise on the Allston side of the Charles (though whether or not this meant a larger student body was unclear). The Schools of Public Health and Education were likely to move there; the Law School was equally unlikely to do so.

Unsurprisingly, concrete (in both senses of the word) progress came first in the realm of the life sciences. Planning for a half-million-square-foot building to house in part a new Harvard Stem Cell Institute got under way in 2006, with another unit of equal size to follow. Construction and fundraising proceeded slowly. But the impetus behind big bioscience in Allston appeared to be unstoppable.

## Looking Ahead

Is Harvard, as one journalist put it, an institution "that needs serious renovation"? Certainly not if money, prestige, and the quality of its students and faculty are the measures. Harvard's chief problem is to adapt its extraordinary assets to the demands of a fast-changing academic environment.

The financial and organizational needs of the life sciences and the new Allston campus are likely to be the most prominent items on that agenda. That may well lead to alternatives to the traditional Harvard framework of departments encased within either the Faculty of Arts and Sciences or the professional schools.

It remains necessary to cultivate a student body attracted not only by the status that Harvard confers but by its vast intellectual resources. Yet other, competing claims—of "legacies" (faculty, alumni, and donors' children), diversity (of race, gender, income), character and talent—assure an ongoing tension between conflicting student recruitment purposes.

The worldly university's desire for a public leadership role has to come to terms with the constraints imposed by political correctness in the faculty culture. And an autonomous faculty can drift into a self-sufficiency which negates the ideal of Harvard as a community of scholars.

The University's evergreen desire for more money and prestige makes for incessant fund-raising. This can have consequences ranging from admitting the marginally competitive children of big donors to research grants with questionable strings attached.

Finally, the size and complexity of governance feeds the growth of central administration inclined to make policy from the top down instead of fostering change from the bottom up.

To general acclaim, Derek Bok, who more than three decades before had quieted an institution in turmoil from the conflict of the late 1960s, answered "a second call to calm troubled waters" by becoming acting president for the 2006–2007 academic year. The most pressing issue of the moment was the selection of Harvard's next president.

In February 2007 the choice was made: fifty-nine-year-old Drew Gilpin Faust, a historian of the American South who since 2001 had been the notably successful Dean of the Radcliffe Institute for Advanced Study. In the by-now established Harvard presidential sequence (Conant-Pusey, Pusey-Bok, Bok-Rudenstine, Rudenstine-Summers), she was most conspicuous for her contrast with her predecessor. Hers was a purely academic career: in this she was to Summers what Pusey had been to Conant. Her academic roots were planted as deeply in the pliant soil of the humanities as Summers's were in the harsher terrain of Economics. In her leadership style she promised to be as conciliatory and consensual as Summers (and Conant) were edgy and contentious. She was also, of course, Harvard's first woman president, and the first without a Harvard degree. But Pusey the first small-college president, Bok the first non-Harvard College graduate, and Summers the first Jewish president also broke new ground.

Faust faced essentially the same cluster of issues—the issues of the worldly university—that confronted her predecessors. For the foreseeable future, as in the recent past, the need remained for a leader with the vision, skills, and toughness necessary to handle the demands of rapid intellectual change, big science, a new campus, a knows-its-own-mind faculty: of a Harvard ever larger, ever more intricate.

# A NOTE ON THE NOTES

Our major archival sources were the James Bryant Conant and Nathan Marsh Pusey Presidential Papers, housed in the Harvard Archives. Each consists of some 500 boxes of presidential correspondence, incoming letters, copies of important correspondence to and from the deans and other officers, memoranda and reports, and much else besides. They provided rich and detailed access into the day-to-day, year-by year life of Harvard from 1933 to 1971.

Since Parts I and II of this book are heavily based on these manuscript collections, we have tried to make our endnote citations as compressed as possible, while enabling the curious (or skeptical) reader to track down our sources. In all cases we indicate folder names and box numbers. (The Archives now has inventory lists of the box numbers of all folders in the Conant and Pusey Presidential Papers). If—as was almost always the case—an item cited from the Conant or Pusey Presidential Papers falls within that man's time in office, we omit a reference to the collection from which it comes: that should be self-evident. We have also made use of other collections, all in the Archives.

The evidentiary base for Part III, covering Harvard's history from 1971 to 2000, is different in character. The Bok and Rudenstine presidential papers were not available to us. We were able to see internally published reports and, on occasion, to use correspondence from faculty members with their permission. Phyllis Keller was active in the administration of the Faculty of Arts and Sciences from 1973 to 1997, and we have drawn on her experience for much of our discussion. Newspapers and magazines, both on campus and off, proved to be richly helpful: a tribute in its own way to Harvard's iconic place in modern American life.

We have adopted the following abbreviations for frequently cited names and references:

| | |
|---|---|
| AAC | Arnold Arboretum Case, Harvard Archives |
| AAS | Afro-American Studies |
| ALL | Abbott Lawrence Lowell |
| ALLPP | Abbott Lawrence Lowell Presidential Papers, Harvard Archives |
| *AM* | *Atlantic Monthly* |
| *AR* | *Annual Report*, Harvard Archives |
| *BG* | *Boston Globe* |
| CFIA | Center for International Affairs |
| *CHE* | *Chronicle of Higher Education* |
| CM | Minutes of the Corporation |
| DCB | Derek C. Bok |
| DEAP | Division of Engineering and Applied Physics |
| DWB | David W. Bailey |
| FAS | Faculty of Arts and Sciences |
| FASGF | Dean of FAS, General Files—Departments 1939–84, Harvard Archives |
| FF | Franklin Ford |
| GSAS | Graduate School of Arts and Sciences |
| GSD | Graduate School of Design |
| GSE | Graduate School of Education |
| GSPA | Graduate School of Public Administration |
| *HAB* | *Harvard Alumni Bulletin* |
| *HB* | *Harvard Bulletin* |
| HBS | Harvard Business School |
| *HC* | *Harvard Crimson* |
| HDS | Harvard Divinity School |
| *HG* | *Harvard Gazette* |
| HJ | Henry James |
| HLS | Harvard Law School |
| *HM* | *Harvard Magazine* |
| HMS | Harvard Medical School |
| HR | Henry Rosovsky |

| | |
|---|---|
| int. | interview |
| JBC | James Bryant Conant |
| JBCPP | James Bryant Conant Presidential Papers, Harvard Archives |
| JDG | Jerome D. Greene |
| JBC Pers. Papers | James B. Conant Personal Papers, Harvard Archives |
| JDG Mss | Jerome D. Greene Manuscripts, Harvard Archives |
| JRR | James R. Reynolds |
| JTD | John T. Dunlop |
| KSG | Kennedy School of Government |
| McGB | McGeorge Bundy |
| MCZ | Museum of Comparative Zoology |
| mss. | Manuscripts |
| NELC | Near Eastern Languages and Cultures |
| news rel. | news release, Harvard Archives |
| NMP | Nathan Marsh Pusey |
| NMPPP | Nathan Marsh Pusey Presidential Papers, Harvard Archives |
| NR | Neil Rudenstine |
| *NYT* | *New York Times* |
| OHRO | Oral History Research Office, Columbia University |
| PB | Paul Buck |
| rec. | recommendation |
| RFK | Robert F. Kennedy |
| RRC | Russian Research Center |
| SDM | School of Dental Medicine |
| TSL | Thomas S. Lamont |
| VES | Visual and Environmental Studies |
| VC | Visiting Committee |
| WLM | William L. Marbury |
| WLM Mss | William L. Marbury manuscripts, Harvard Archives |
| WmB-S Mss | William Bentinck-Smith manuscripts, Harvard Archives |
| *WSJ* | *Wall Street Journal* |

# NOTES

*Notes to Prologue*

1. David McCord, *In Sight of Sever* (Cambridge: Harvard Univ. Press, 1963), 41; JDG to Henry C. Clark, Oct. 21, 1936, "Accounting/Ambassadors," JDG Mss. See also Harvard University, *The Tercentenary of Harvard College* (Cambridge: Harvard Univ. Press, 1937).

2. Archibald Thacher to JDG, JDG to Thacher, Oct. 23, 1936, "Minutes and Papers of the Tercentenary Commission," Henry James to Charles H. Watkins, Aug. 13, 1936, JDG Mss.

3. JDG to JBC, May 12, 1934, "Conant"; JDG to Henry James, Nov. 27, 1934, JDG Mss.

4. *Time*, 28 (Sept. 14, 1936), 53; JDG to JBC, Dec. 31, 1935; Harvard, *Tercentenary*, 9–11; *NYT*, Sept. 14, 1936, 1:63.

5. JDG to Ray Lyman Wilbur, n.d., JDG Mss; "The World's Wise Men," *BG*, July 15, 1936 ff; *NYT*, Mar. 19, 1937, 19:3.

6. *Time*, 28 (Sept. 28, 1936), 26; JDG to Rabbi Joseph S. Shubov, Apr. 21, 1936, to Judge Julian Mack, Jan. 5, 1935, to Willard Sperry, Dec. 31, 1934, Mar. 31, 1935, "Jewish Holidays," JDG Mss.

7. *BG*, July 1, 1936; *NYT*, Sept. 1, 1936, 1:2; Harvard, *Tercentenary*, passim.

8. Harvard, *Tercentenary*, 214.

9. Bernard De Voto, "A Puritan Tercentenary," *Harper's Monthly*, 173 (Sept. 1936), 445–48.

10. JBC, *AR*, 1935–36, 6; *NYT*, Sept. 14, 1936, 1:6.

11. Hermann Hagedorn to Keyes Metcalf, Jan. 18, 1939, JDG Mss.

12. *NYT*, Sept. 17, 1936, 1:3, Sept. 18, 1936, 1:16.

13. Frank G. Thomson to JBC, June 26, 1936, JDG to Thomson, July 9, 1936, "Alumni Association Meeting of Sept. 18," JDG to Henry C. Clark, Sept. 29, 1936, "Accounting/Ambassadors," JDG Mss.

14. *HAB*, 70 (Feb. 24, 1968), 18–21.

15. "Weather," JDG Mss; McCord, *In Sight of Sever*, 74; *Time*, 28 (Sept. 29, 1936), 22–26.

16. JBC to Francis R. Stoddard, Mar. 19, 1945, "Military Service: Comments on," Box 268.

17. JBC to Albert Einstein, Dec. 23, 1935, "EA-EE," Box 54; *NYT*, Sept. 4, 1936, 10:2; *Time*, 28 (Sept. 14, 1936), 50; JDG to Henry James, Aug. 13, 1936, "James, Henry," JDG Mss.

18. *Time*, 28 (Sept. 28, 1936), 22–26; Paul Hazard, "Le troisième centenaire de l'Université Harvard," *Revue des deux mondes*, ser. 8, 36 (Nov. 1, 1936), 225–29.

19. William B. Tolley in "Delegates' Reports," JDG Mss.

20. JBC, *AR* 1934–35, 5–6, *AR* 1935–36, 17.

## Chapter One

1. Phyllis Keller, *Getting at the Core* (Cambridge: Harvard Univ. Press, 1982), 1–10. See also Julie Reubin, *The Making of a Modern University* (Chicago: Univ. of Chicago Press, 1996); Henry James, *Charles W. Eliot*, 2 vols., (Boston: Houghton Mifflin, 1930); Hugh Hawkins, *Between Harvard and America: The Educational Leadership of Charles W. Eliot* (New York: Oxford Univ. Press, 1972).

2. Samuel E. Morison, *Three Centuries of Harvard* (Cambridge: Harvard Univ. Press, 1936); on Brahminism, Digby Baltzell, *Puritan Boston and Quaker Philadelphia* (Boston: Beacon Press, 1979).

3. *HAB*, 35 (1932–33), 289; ALL, *AR* 1908–9. See also Henry A. Yeomans, *Abbot Lawrence Lowell* (Cambridge: 1948), and Alex Duke, *Importing Oxbridge* (New Haven: Yale Univ. Press, 1996), ch. 4.

4. Jerome Greene to Henry James, Apr. 21, 1937, "Lowell, A. Lawrence," Box 88; Eliot quoted in Marcia G. Synnott, *The Half-Opened Door: Discrimination and Admission Policy at Harvard, Yale, and Princeton, 1900–1970* (Westport, Conn.: Greenwood Press, 1979), 26; *HAB*, 35 (July 7, 1933), 1027; for full list of buildings, *HAB*, 45 (1942–43), 221. See also Yeomans, *Lowell*, and the revealing essay by Nathan Pusey, *Lawrence Lowell and His Revolution* (Cambridge: 1980).

5. "An Account of the Year 1933," Special Subject Files, JBC Mss; JBC, *My Several Lives: Memoirs of a Social Inventor* (New York: Harper & Row, 1970), 88–90; James G. Hershberg, *James B. Conant* (New York: Knopf, 1993), 66–75; ALL to Kenneth B. Murdock, Nov. 18, 1932, Folder 521, ALL Mss; on Conant's agnosticism, JBC to William H. Cowley, Oct. 2, 1944, "Ham-Hap," Box 260.

6. ALL to JBC, June 27, 1933, Folder 990, ALL Mss.

7. JBC to Marjorie Bush-Brown, May 17, 1933, JBC Mss, Pt. II; Eliot quoted in James, *Eliot*, I:12–14, 310.

8. JBC to Donald Scott, May 10, 1934, "Pe," Box 15; *NYT Magazine*, Mar. 18, 1934, 3, 22; JBC to H. I. Brock, Mar. 5, 28, 1934, "New York Times," Box 14.

9. Ronald Story, *The Forging of an Aristocracy: Harvard and the Boston Upper Class, 1800–1870* (Middletown, Conn.: Wesleyan Univ. Press, 1980).

10. Curtis to JBC, Nov. 4, 1935, JBC to Curtis, Nov. 22, 1935, Apr. 30, 1936, "Curtis, Charles P. Jr.," Box 53; Willard van Orman Quine, *The Time of My Life: An Autobiography* (Cambridge: MIT Press, 1985), 121.

11. Henry James to JBC, Oct. 24, 1945, JBC to James, Oct. 25, "James,

Henry," Box 280; James to JBC, Apr. 6, 1945, JBC to James, Apr. 18, "James, Henry," Box 261; JBC to Willis Smith, Jan. 24, 1947, "Dr-Dz," Box 299.

12.  James to JBC, Mar. 14, Apr. 16, 1947, "James, Henry," Box 302; Clark to JBC, Mar. 4, 1947, Clark to James, Mar. 28, 1947, "Clark, Grenville," Box 298; Norman Cousins and J. Garry Clifford, eds., *Memoirs of a Man, Grenville Clark* (New York: Norton, 1975), 163.

13.  Shattuck notes, "The Marbury Case," Incoming Correspondence, JBC Mss; "Overseers: General," Box 327; Coolidge to JBC, Sept. 30, 1947, "Coolidge, Charles A.," Box 318; "Harvard Memo," May 10, 1948, "Clark, Grenville," Box 318.

14.  Memos, May 7, 10, 1948, "Clark, Grenville," Box 318; news rel., Jan. 14, 1949, "Treasurer," Box 355.

15.  JBC to Rev. Minot Simons, Nov. 14, 1933, "Overseers: General, Committees," Box 15; DWB memo to Board of Overseers, Mar. 20, 1947, "Overseers: General," Box 306; PB to JBC, Oct. 16, 1944, "Arts and Sciences: Dean of Faculty," Box 255.

16.  JBC to Robert F. Bradford, Apr. 3, June 13, 1950, Bradford to Conant, June 10, "Overseers' Committee," Box 378.

17.  JBC memo, Jan. 2, 1946, "Corporation," Box 277.

18.  Hershberg, *Conant*, ch. 1; Clement A. Norton, quoting Boston Chamber of Commerce member Ellerton J. Breough, to JBC, c. Nov. 3, 1937, "Norton, Clement A." Box 117.

19.  JBC to Adolph H. Corwin, Feb 12, 1935, "Conant, J. B.: Chemistry," Box 27.

20.  JBC to Henry Bent, Oct. 28, 1937, "Bea-Beq," Box 103.

21.  Conant, *My Several Lives*, 136; JBC to Harold W. Dodds, May 2, 1945, "Princeton University," Box 265.

22.  JBC to R. M. Hughes, Mar. 16, 1938, "National Resources Committee," Box 116; JBC, *AR* 1933–34; JBC, *AR*, 1933–34.

23.  JBC to Irvin C. Poley, Jan. 29, 1935, "Middle States Association of Colleges and Secondary Schools," Box 38; JBC to Prof. L. C. Graton, Apr. 10, 1935, "Gra-Gri", Box 11; *HAB*, 37 (1934–35), 447; JBC to Arthur Pope, Mar. 24, 1936, "Fogg Art Museum," Box 57; Tercentenary address, Harvard, *Tercentenary*, 207–16; JBC to William H. Cowley, Nov. 4, 1947, "Cowley, William H.," Box 319.

24.  JBC to L. J. Henderson, Oct. 10, 1939, "Fa," Box 155.

25.  JBC to Frederick A. Saunders, Sept. 21, 1933, "Physics Department," Box 15; JBC, *AR*, 1932–33; JBC to Julian Coolidge, Apr. 30, "American Council on Education," Box 1.

26.  JBC to Stephen H. Stackpole, July 1936, "Conant, J. B.: Personal," Box 52. See also Alfred N. Whitehead, "Harvard: The Future," *AM*, 158 (Sept. 1936), 260–70.

27.  A. W. Page to Henry James, Oct. 25, 1934, "Advisory Research: Committees," Box 21; Thomas W. Dunn to JBC, with letter from classmate T. Graydon Upton, Oct. 9, 1936, "Dr-Dz," Box 81; JBC to E. G. Stillman, Jan. 5, 1938, "Ste-Sto," Box 121.

28. Clark to JBC, June 3, 1938, JBC to Clark, June 6, 1938, "Clark, Grenville," Box 105.

29. JBC to Harvey Lehman, Mar. 28, 1938, "Law-Len," Box 137; JBC, "The Selective Principle in American Colleges," address to Association of American Colleges, *HAB*, 39 (1936–37), 472.

30. JBC to Ben D. Wood, Dec. 5, 1945, "Conant: Personal," Box 276; Carl C. Brigham to JBC, Jan. 3, 1938, JBC to Brigham, Jan. 20, 1938, "Princeton University," Box 118; Nicholas Lemann, "The Structure of Success in America," *AM*, 276 (Aug. 1995), 41–60.

31. R. M. Hughes to JBC, Apr. 2, 1935, JBC to Hughes, Apr. 12, "Hu-Hy," Box 35; JBC to Roger Lee, Nov. 20, 1939, "Honorary Degrees: Committee on," Box 157; JBC to Dodds, Nov. 20, 1939, Dodds to JBC, Jan. 3, 1940, JBC to Dodds, Jan. 8, Dodds to JBC, Jan 10, "Princeton University," Box 165.

32. JBC to Hutchins, Aug. 15, 1936, "Chicago, University of," Box 51; on bugs, Hutchins to JBC, c. Aug. 10, 1936, "Chicago, University of," Box 51; Hutchins to JBC, May 24, 1938, JBC to Hutchins, June 1, "Chicago, University of," Box 105. See also William H. McNeill, *Hutchins' University: A Memoir of the University of Chicago* (Chicago: Univ. of Chicago Press, 1991).

33. JBC to Laird Bell, June 26, 1946, "Alumni Assocn.," Box 271; Vannever Bush to JBC, n.d., "Chicago, Univ. of," Box 318; JBC to Thomas W. Lamont, June 3, 1948, "Lamont, Thomas W.," Box 323.

34. JBC to D. M. Little, 1937, "Mi-Nat," Box 87.

35. JBC to Archibald MacLeish, June 18, 1937, "Maa-MAP," Box 88.

36. JBC, "Education for a Classless Society," *AM*, 165 (May 1940), 593–602; JBC to William B. Snow, Jr., Nov. 28, 1944, "Sn-Sta," Box 267; JBC to Arthur W. Page, Aug. 5, 1941, "Pa," Box 190.

37. Conant, "Wanted: American Radicals," *AM*, 171 (May 1943), 43; JBC statement, "Time," Box 311; JBC to John P. Marquand, Nov. 4, 1946, "Mar," Box 303; JBC to Elton Mayo, Feb. 28, 1946, "Mas-Maz," Box 282.

38. JBC to Walter Lippmann, Mar. 3, Aug. 1, 1942, "Lippman, Walter," to Harvey Bundy, June 6, 1942, "Legislative Bills," Box 209; JBC to Roscoe L. West, Dec. 13, 1944, "National Education Association," Box 263.

39. JBC to Harry Hopkins, Dec 26, 1941, "Hom-Hr," Box 207; JBC to Roosevelt, Mar. 28, 1942, Roosevelt to JBC, Apr. 27, "Roosevelt, President Franklin Delano," Box 215.

40. JBC to Eric Johnston, Sept. 28, 1943, "Ja-Jom," Box 246.

41. Wyzanski to JBC, Dec. 1943, "Wim-Wy," Box 253; JBC, *AR*, 1942–43; news rel., Jan. 23, 1945; *AR*, 1944–45, Box 255.

42. Capt. Vincent N. Florack to JBC, Feb. 20, 1945, JBC to Florack, Mar. 5, "Ku-Ky," Box 261. Conant continued to hold these views into the postwar years: JBC, "Who Should Go to College?" *Ladies' Home Journal*, 65 (June 1948), 40, 106–07, 109, 111. See Richard M. Freedland, *Academia's Golden Age* (New York: 1992), 73–74.

43. JBC, "Some Aspects of Modern Harvard," *Journal of General Education*, 4 (Apr., 1950), 175–184.

44. JBC, *AR*, 1946–47; JBC to Evans Clark, Apr. 8, 1947, "Advertising Coun-

cil," Box 294; on parochial schools, "AASA Comments," Box 415; *HAB*, 54 (1951–52), 575.

45. JBC, *Diaries*, Dec. 22–23, 1952.

46. JBC, *AR*, 1952–53; *HAB*, 55 (1952–53), 335 f.

## *Chapter Two*

1. Martha G. Synott, *The Half-Opened Door* (Westport, Conn.: Greenwood Press, 1979), 40–47; Henry A. Yeomans, *Abbott Lawrence Lowell* (Cambridge: Harvard Univ. Press, 1948), 199–218.

2. Anne MacDonald, "Memorandum Concerning Admission Office, Apr. 7, 1934," "Admissions: Committee on," Box 1; *HAB*, 35 (1932–33), 235.

3. JBC to Walter D. Head, Dec. 7, 1934, "Hea-Heo," Box 34; JBC to A. C. Hanford, Mar. 6, 1934, "Scholarships General (Committee on)," Box 18; *HAB*, 40 (1937–38), 103; JBC to A. C. Hanford, Sept. 29, 1937, "Admissions," Box 100.

4. "Annual Report, Comments on," Box 1, JBCPP (1933–34); *HAB*, 36 (1933–34), 824; JBC to King Smith, Feb. 6, 1934, "Annual report—Comments on—M-Z," Box 1.

5. "The Harvard College National Scholarships: A Descriptive Report at the End of Six Years" (Cambridge, 1941), 32; *HAB*, 43 (1940–41), 507.

6. JBC to Clay Judson, Apr. 16, 1946, "Jon-Jy," Box 281; JBC to William D. Orcutt, Sept. 18, 1944, "Ol-Oz," Box 263; PB to JBC, Aug. 30, 1945, "Scholarships: Committee on," Box 290; *HAB*, 49 (1946–47), 464.

7. Paul Buck, "Who Comes to Harvard?" *HAB*, 50 (1947–48), 313–17; William J. Bender to JBC, Jan. 2, 1952, "College," Box 424.

8. Buck, "Balance in the College," *HAB*, 48 (1945–46), 406 f, Buck, "Who Comes to Harvard?" 313; PB to JBC, Dec. 9, 1947, "Arts and Sciences: Dean of Faculty," Box 315.

9. PB to JBC, Dec. 9, 1947, "Arts and Sciences: Dean of Faculty," Box 315; PB to JBC, Sept. 23, 1944, "Veterans Counsellors," Box 268; Bender in *HAB*, 49 (1946–47), 467; Bender, "The Top-One-Percent Policy," *HAB*, 64 (1961–62), 59.

10. Bender to PB, May 27, 1953, "Aa-Alk," NMPPP, Box 18; Bender to JBC, Jan. 2, 1952, "College," Box 424.

11. On commuters, E. J. Kahn, *Harvard* (New York: Norton, 1969), 77; Theodore H. White, *In Search of History: A Personal Adventure* (New York: Harper & Row, 1978), 41–44; *HAB*, 35 (1932–33), 89–90.

12. "Sn-Sta," Box 290 (1945–46); *HAB*, 36 (1933–34), 8.

13. ALL to James H. Lowell and Charles P. Curtis, Mar. 29, 1933, Folder 29, ALL Mss; *Report of the Dean of Faculty* (1932–33), 96; *HAB*, 37 (1934–35), 225; 1935 *Class Album*.

14. *HAB*, 37 (1934–35), 991; cf. "Lampoon" in "Laa-Lav," Box 36 (1934–35); *HAB*, 42 (1939–40), 674.

15. Student Council, "The Freshman and Harvard College Life," Part Four, "Student Council," Box 331; Folder 707, ALL Mss; *Class Album*, 1933, 1935;

Richard B. Buck, "Fair Harvard's Intellectual Giants of the Early 1930s," *Modern Age*, 32 (1988–89), 121.

16.  Julian Coolidge, "The Untouchables," *HAB*, 34 (Jan. 15, 1932), 446–51; "A Report on the Commuting Student Situation in Harvard College," Mar. 6, 1935, A. C. Hanford to JBC, Mar. 13, 1935, "Commuters," Box 27.

17.  Memorial Church *VC* 1933–34; Spier Whitaker to Assistant Dean William H. Cary, Jr., Sept. 25, 1937, "Wel-Wh," Box 124.

18.  PB to JBC, Feb. 27, 1952, "Department of Hygiene," Box 432; JBC to Southworth Lancaster, Mar. 18, 1942, "Law-Len," Box 208.

19.  "Political Activity in the College," *HAB*, 37 (Nov. 2, 1934), 176–177; *HAB*, 42 (1939–40), 1057; JBC to Eugene C. Sheehan, late June 1939, "Memorial Day Incident," Box 139; 1939 *Class Album*, 50 f; A. C. Hanford to JBC, Dec. 2, 1941, "Dean of Harvard College," Box 203.

20.  JBC to Willard Connely, May 13, 1944, "American University Union," Box 240; *HC*, June 5, 1995; George H. Chase to George F. Plimpton, July 12, 1943, "Pi-Po," Box 249; DWB to William Bachmann, Feb. 18, 1946, Box 272. See also "Comments of Harvard Alumni on their College Education," May 1950, "Statistics," Box 383.

21.  Francis M. Wilhoit, "Harvard Men by Act of Congress," *HAB*, 60 (1957–58), 166 f; PB to JBC, Dec. 7, 1946, "Arts and Sciences: Dean of Faculty," Box 295; "Veterans Counsellor," Box 292 (1945–46).

22.  DWB to Dean Willard Sperry, Jan. 23, 1948, "Bri-Bt," Box 318; *HAB*, 50 (1947–48), 591, 345; *HAB*, 51 (1948–49), 159.

23.  *HAB*, 52 (1949–50), 206, *HAB*, 53 (1950–51); Memorandum on Public Disturbance, June 1952, "College," Box 424.

24.  JBC to PB, Feb. 12, 1951, PB to JBC, Feb. 16, May 22, JBC to PB, May 25, "Provost," Box 409.

25.  Morris A. Bealle, *The History of Football at Harvard 1874–1942* (Washington D.C.: Columbia Publ. Co., 1948).

26.  *HAB*, 36 (1933–34), 295; James R. Angell to ALL, Oct. 24, 1930, ALL to Angell, Oct. 25, to Isidor Siegel, Apr. 11, 1931, Folder 156, ALL Mss 1930–33.

27.  "Athletics," "Princeton University," "Yale University" (1934–35); JBC to W. J. Bingham, Mar. 26, 1935, "Athletics," Box 24.

28.  PB to JBC, Nov. 24, 1944, "Athletics—3 Centuries," WmB-S Mss; *HAB*, 48 (1945–46), 244–248; news rel., Nov. 20, 1945, "Athletic Association," Box 272; JBC to PB, Nov. 17, 1950, "Provost," Box 409; "Athletics—3 Centuries," WmBS Mss; JBC to A. Whitney Griswold, Nov. 16, 1951, "Athletics Current," Box 420.

29.  Dean of Faculty, *AR* 1932–33, 81; DWB memo to JBC, Dec. 3, 1948, "Arts & Sciences: Faculty of," Box 335; *HAB*, 37 (1934–35), 1,089; *HAB*, 36 (1933–34), 535, 548–49; *HAB*, 39 (1936–37), 41.

30.  Student Council Committee on Education, *Report*, June 12, 1939, "Student Council," Box 144.

31.  Table, "Student Council," Box 121 (1937–38); *HAB*, 38 (1935–36), 111, 395; "Proposals for Broadening the Basis of Concentration for Students in the Social Sciences at Harvard College," "Arts and Sciences: Comments on Committee of 8 Report," Box 126 (1938–39); JBC, *AR* 1941–42.

32. Wilbur K. Jordan to JBC, Dec. 9, 1944, transmitting the Report of the Subcommittee on the Education of Women, "Radcliffe College," Box 266.

33. John Finley to JBC, Feb. 24, 1944, JBC to Finley, Mar. 9, "El-En," Box 244; *HAB*, 48 (1945–46), 23–30.

34. JBC to John Cowles, Sept. 19, 1945, "Coo-Coz," Box 276; Howard E. Wilson to JBC, Oct. 22, 1943, PB to JBC, Apr. 17, 1944, "Committee on Objectives," Box 245.

35. PB to JBC, May 8, 1950, "General Education: Miscellaneous," Box 370; Phyllis Keller, *Getting at the Core* (Cambridge: Harvard Univ. Press, 1982), 14–15; Jacques Barzun to JBC, Oct. 11, 1945, "Barn-Baz," Box 274; William H. McNeill, *Hutchins' University: A Memoir of the University of Chicago* (Chicago: Univ. of Chicago Press, 1991), 110, 116. Cf. Daniel Bell, *The Reforming of General Education* (New York: Columbia Univ. Press, 1966).

36. WmB-S to PB, Oct. 16, 1945, "Secretary to the Corporation: Smith," Box 267; news rel., Nov. 1, 1945; JBC to Prof. W. H. Cowley, Sept. 6, 1945, to Robert N. Yerkes, Sept. 6, to Edmund E. Day, Aug. 25, to Walter Lichtenstein, Sept. 12, "Objectives Committee Report—Comments," Box 260; Conant, "Public Education and the Structure of American Society," *Teachers' College Record*, 47 (Dec. 1945), 145–94.

37. "An Analysis of General Education at Harvard, 1952," "Student Council," Box 443.

38. Comparison of Course Offerings in the Faculty of Arts and Sciences 1907–8 and 1947–48, "Annual Report," Box 315; Wright, Memorandum on the Tutorial System and Its Future in Harvard College, "Ta-Te," Box 267; JBC to Levin Campbell, Apr. 4, 1946, "Str-Sz," Box 290; PB to Bailey, Apr. 18, 1947, "Arts and Sciences: Dean of Faculty," Box 295; PB memo to JBC, Dec. 29, 1948, "Statistics," Box 354.

## Chapter Three

1. Kim Townsend, *Manhood at Harvard: William James and Others* (New York: Norton, 1996), 92–93.

2. Marcia G. Synnott, *The Half-Opened Door* (Westport, Conn.: Greenwood Press, 1974), 44–47; Morison to WmB-S, June 18, 1975, "Correspondence with SEM," Box 1, WmB-S Mss.

3. Henry A. Yeomans, *Abbott Lawrence Lowell* (Cambridge: Harvard Univ. Press, 1948), 68; Synott, *Half-Opened Door*, 34, 60; Richard N. Smith, *The Harvard Century* (New York: Simon & Schuster, 1986), 85–89.

4. Synnott, *Half-Opened Door*, 62–63, 90–91.

5. Synnott, *Half-Opened Door*, 58–70; on 1920s data, DWB to NMP, Aug. 14, 1953, "Memorial Church," Box 19, NMPPP; JBC to ALL, Dec. 5, 1933, ALL to JBC, Dec. 6, "Lowell, A. Lawrence," Box 12.

6. Thomas W. Slocum to JBC, July 2, 1934, "Si-Sm", Box 44; Berenson to JBC, Sept. 17, 1934, JBC to Berenson, Sept. 20, "Ber-Bj," Box 24; Berenson to Harry Barnard, June 19, 1963, "Ber-Bj," Box 4, NMPPP.

7. J. W. Lowes to JBC, Jan. 21, 1937, "Dean of Harvard College," Box 80;

J. W. Lowes to JBC, May 21, 1937, "House Masters: General," Box 85; Synnott, *Half-Opened Door*, 114, 117; Coolidge to JBC, May 9, 1939, "Lowell House," Box 137.

8. On exclusion from Harvard Clubs, C. C. Burlingham letter, *HAB*, 40 (1937–38), 880; Tozzer to JBC, Jan. 12, 1938, "Anthropology," Box 101.

9. Synnott, *Half-Opened Door*, 120, 122, 112; A. C. Hanford to JBC, Nov. 24, Dec. 1, 1941, "Dean of Harvard College," Box 207.

10. On Hillel, *Harvard Crimson*, Commencement issue, June 7, 1994, B1; Nitza Rosovsky, *The Jewish Experience at Harvard and Radcliffe* (Cambridge: Harvard Univ. Press, 1986).

11. Kane to JBC, Nov. 14, 1951, Bender to JBC, Nov. 21, "Kane, R. Keith," Box 432; Bender to JBC, Jan. 2, 1952, "College," Box 424.

12. *CM*, Nov. 10, 1913, Jan. 9, 1922.

13. Lowell to Judge Frederick P. Cabot, May 23, 1922, Comstock to Lowell, Nov. 21, 1928, "Radcliffe College," Box 119 (1937–38); Paul Buck, "Notes Toward a Biography of Ada Comstock Notestein," WmB-S Mss.

14. JBC to William T. Brewster, Feb. 8, 1939, "Barn-Baz," Box 127.

15. Course list in "Radcliffe College," JBCPP 1938–39, Box 142; George H. Chase to John W. Atherton, June 13, 1941, "Bu-By," Box 174; *CM*, Mar. 8, 1937; Comstock to JBC, May 26, 1941, "Radcliffe College," Box 214.

16. "Condensed Review of Conditions, Policies, and Needs," "Radcliffe College," Box 93 (1936–37); Barbara M. Solomon, *In the Company of Educated Women* (New Haven: Yale Univ. Press, 1985), 143, 183.

17. "Notes from Library Gleanings," Mar. 26, 1981, "Radcliffe—1977 Agreement," WmB-S Mss; Comstock to JBC, Mar. 11, 1937, JBC to Comstock, Mar. 13, "Radcliffe College," Box 93.

18. JBC to Comstock, Apr. 21, Comstock to JBC, Apr. 26, JBC to Comstock, May 3, 1938, "Radcliffe College," Box 119.

19. *CM*, Sept. 25, 1933, Jan. 8, 1934; James P. Leake to JBC, Apr. 15, 1937; Mead to JBC, Nov. 4, 1936, Stackpole to Mead, Dec. 10, "Me," Box 88.

20. PB to President and Fellows, Feb. 24, 1943, "Radcliffe—1977 Agreement," WB-S Mss; cf. "Radcliffe College," Box 235 (1942–43); *CM*, Apr. 5, 1943; on tutors, Aileen Ward int.; news rel., Apr. 18, 1943, "Radcliffe College," Box 214.

21. Jacqueline Van Voris int., Folder 3, Comstock File, Mar. 31, 1971, "Radcliffe—1977 Agreement," WmB-S Mss; news rel., Oct. 21, 1947, "Radcliffe College," Box 329; "Radcliffe," Box 381 (1949–50); Dorothy Billings to JBC, Jan. 4, 1953, Willard Sperry to Billings, Nov. 6, "Criticism and Suggestions," Box 454.

22. Wilbur K. Jordan to JBC, Apr. 16, 1946, "Radcliffe College," Box 289; PB to JBC, Feb. 19, 1946; G. Wallace Woodworth to JBC, Feb. 14, 1946, PB to JBC, Feb. 12, JBC to Woodworth, Feb. 14, "Me," Box 283; Abraham Flexner to JBC, Apr. 18, 1949, JBC to Flexner, Apr. 26, "Fl-Fo," Box 341.

23. Edsall to JBC, Mar. 1, 1934, JBC to Edsall, Mar. 9, "Public Health, School of," Box 16; Cecil K. Drinker to JBC, Nov. 2, 1935, Feb. 8, 1936, "Public Health, School of," Box 67.

24. *CM*, Jan. 19, 1942, Mar. 1, 1943, June 5, 1944; GSD, *VC*, 1942–43, 1946–47.

25. *CM*, June 21, 1943; HMS, *VC*, 1943–44; Report of Committee to Consider Admission of Women, n.d. (authors' possession); JBC memo to Corporation, Apr. 24, 1944, "Medical School: General," Box 247; *HAB*, 47 (1944–45), 75, 78.

26. Pauli Murray to Thomas R. Powell, May 13, 1944, Powell to Murray, June 13, FDR to JBC, May 31, George H. Chase to FDR, June 5, "Mr-My," Box 248.

27. Powell to Murray, June 22, 1944, Murray to A. Calvert Smith, c. June 26; Edmund M. Morgan to JBC, July 6; Smith to Murray, July 12, Murray to Smith, July 20, to HLS Faculty, July 20, Smith to Murray, Aug. 8, 1944, "Mr-My," Box 248. See Pauli Murray, *Song in a Weary Throat: An American Pilgrimage* (New York: Harper & Row, 1987), 238–44.

28. Report of Committee, Apr. 15, 1949, "Law School: General," Box 344; Griswold to JBC, Oct. 15, 1949, "Law School: Dean," Box 373.

29. Norton to JBC, Mar. 21, June 16, 1936, "Norton, Clement A.," Box 65.

30. Werner Sollors, Caldwell Titcomb, and Thomas A. Underwood, eds., *Blacks at Harvard* (New York: New York Univ. Press, 1993), pp. xxiii, 1–7; Robert C. Weaver to WmB-S, Mar. 15, 1966, "Was-Wek," Box 29.

31. Lowell to DuBois, June 26, 1931, Folder 504, ALL Mss 1933–34; Buell to Conant, Apr. 11, Hocking to Harper Woodward, Apr. 17, Conant to Buell, Apr. 13, 1935, "Philosophy," Box 41.

32. DWB to W. I. Gibson, Apr. 1, 1947, "AA-Alk," Box 294, DWB to Stuart E. Grummon, Mar. 7, 1947, "Gro-Gy," Box 301.

33. DWB to W. I. Gibson, Apr. 1, 1947, "AA-Alk", Box 294; W. B. Donham to Doxey Wilkerson (ed., *The Negro in America*), Apr. 22, Dental School Dean Leroy Miner to George H. Chase, May 2, 1940, "Na-Ne," Box 162.

34. *HAB*, 43 (1940–41), 824; JDG to Leonore Shalit, Oct. 16, 1942, "Athletic Association," Box 200; "Memorandum re Annapolis Incident," JBC to Russell Willson, May 9, 1941, "U.S. Naval Academy," Box 195.

35. Agnes Meyer to JBC, June 24, JBC to Meyer, July 10, 1944, "Me," Box 262; William Neilson to JBC, July 29, 1943, "Na-Ne," Box 248.

36. "Ros-Rz," Box 251 (1943–44); JBC to Deans, Apr. 30, May 16, 1945, "Na-Ne," Box 263; Francis C. Gray to JBC, Jan. 19, JBC to Gray, Jan. 31, 1945, "Ki-Kl," Box 261.

37. JBC to Mrs. Henry L. Corbett, May 16, 1945, "Coo-Cox," Box 257; Mrs. Joseph E. Goodbar to JBC, Apr. 14, 1952, "Ch-Chi," Box 423.

38. PB to DWB, Feb. 13, 1952, "Government," Box 430. On Elliott, Paul Samuelson, "Pastiches from an Earlier Politically-Incorrect Age" (typescript in authors' possession).

39. DWB to Paul J. Braisted, Mar. 17, 1952, "Har-Haz," Box 430.

*Chapter Four*

1. Keppel in *HAB*, 37 (1934–35), 394; JBC, *AR*, 1933–34; Seymour Martin Lipset and David Riesman, *Education and Politics at Harvard* (New York: McGraw-Hill, 1975), 153.

2. Murdock to JBC, Apr. 1, 1935, "Arts and Sciences: Dean," Box 23; on Birkhoff, *Science*, 102 (Dec. 7, 1945), 578–80.

3. JBC to Harvard Club of Boston, in JBC to Harold H. Burbank, Dec. 6, 1933, "Economics," Box 5.

4. JBC to Henry M. Wriston, Feb. 10, 1937, "Bri-Bt," Box 77; *HAB*, 36 (1933–34), 1,073.

5. John L. Taylor to John W. Lowes, Apr. 25, 1935, "James, Henry," Box 35; "Personnel and Promotion at Harvard," *HAB*, 42 (Nov. 3, 1939), 180–86; Roger Geiger, *To Advance Knowledge: The Growth of American Research Universities, 1900–1940* (New York: Oxford Univ. Press, 1986), 308; Table of Positions Filled, "Appointment Office," Box 102 (1937–38); JBC to Henry M. Wriston, Oct. 5, 1938, "Bri-Bt," Box 128. See also Granville Hicks, "Harvard and the Interest Rate," *New Republic*, 99 (June 14, 1939), 153–54.

6. JBC to Alfred C. Redfield, Feb. 10, 1938, "Biology," Box 103.

7. JBC to Garrett Birkhoff, Mar. 17, 1936, "Economics," Box 54; JBC to Murdock, Nov. 1, 1936, "Walsh-Sweezy Case, Box 24, WmB-S Mss.

8. JBC to Lippmann, Apr. 13, May 5, 1937, "Lippmann, Walter," Box 88; Report on the Terminating Appointments of Dr. J. R. Walsh and Dr. A. R. Sweezy by The Special Committee Appointed by the President of Harvard University (1938), in "Walsh-Sweezy: Committee Report," Box 123 (1937–38).

9. *HAB*, 39 (1936–37), 874; Clark to JBC, June 30, Feb. 26, 1938, "Clark, Grenville," Box 105; Murdock, Memorandum to Members of the Corporation, Charles Coolidge to JBC, Apr. 27, 1937, F. O. Matthiessen and D. W. Prell to JBC, June 3, 1938, "Walsh-Sweezy Case," Box 24, WmB-S Mss; Sweezy to JBC, Dec. 16, 1937, J. Raymond Walsh to JBC, July 5, 1937, "Economics," Box 107; JBC to William A. Lockwood, Jan. 22, 1945, "Century Club of New York," Box 256. See also *HB*, 40 (1937–38), 1,050.

10. "Walsh-Sweezy: Committee Report: Comments on" folder, JBC to Ralph B. Perry, June 17, 1938, "Walsh-Sweezy Committee," Box 123.

11. "Report on Some Problems of Personnel in the Faculty of Arts and Sciences" (Cambridge: Harvard Univ. Press, 1939); Confidential Report to the Corporation from the President of the University, Sept. 11, 1944, "Corporation," Box 257. See also "Personnel and Promotion at Harvard," *HAB*, 42 (Nov. 3, 1939), 180–86; M. H. Stone, "Harvard's New Appointment Policy," *Nation*, 149 (Dec. 2, 1939), 606–607.

12. Frankfurter to JBC, Apr. 4, 1939, "Committee of Eight: Comments on Report," JBC to Ralph B. Perry, Mar. 30, May 5, 1939, Shapley to JBC, June 5, 1939, "Committee of Eight," Box 130.

13. Hicks, "Harvard and the Interest Rate," 154; JBC, *My Several Lives: Memoirs of a Social Inventor* (New York: Harper & Row, 1970), 162 f.

14. Memo on tenure, Nov. 7, 1940, "Tenure, etc.," WmB-S Mss.

15. *HAB*, 49 (1946–47), 342; E. Y. Hartshorne, "Growth and Metabolism at Harvard," *Harvard Educational Review*, 12 (Mar. 1942), 143–64; FAS *VC* 1949–50; Johnson to JBC, Sept. 26, 1945, "Ad hoc Committee: Sociology," Box 270.

16. *HAB*, 41 (1938–39), 598; David Rockefeller to JBC, Feb. 15, 1941, "Roa-Ror," Box 192.

17.  PB to Dr. F. L. W. Richardson, Jr., May 27, 1948, "Provost," Box 329; PB to JBC, Oct. 31, 1952, "Provost," Box 467.

18.  PB to JBC, Nov. 20, 1952, "Provost," Box 467; *HAB*, 46 (1943–44), 362; Crane Brinton to JBC, Apr. 5, 1950, "Society of Fellows," Box 383.

19.  PB rec., Feb. 25, 1948, "Radcliffe College," Box 329; PB to JBC, Jan. 28, 1952, "Arts and Sciences, Faculty of," Box 419; JBC, *AR* 1951–52, 8–9.

20.  Whitehead to JBC, Dec. 28, 1934; JBC to Whitehead, Jan. 4, 1935; "Advisory Research Committee: Humanities," Box 21.

21.  Kim Townsend, *Manhood at Harvard: William James and Others* (New York: Norton, 1996), 178; Bruce Kuklick, *The Rise of American Philosophy: Cambridge, Massachusetts, 1860–1930* (New Haven: Yale Univ. Press, 1977), pts. 2, 3; Samuel E. Morison, ed., *The Development of Harvard University* (Cambridge: Harvard Univ. Press, 1930), 3–32; on Wolfson, George H. Williams, "At Home and Homeless at Harvard," "Divinity—Three Centuries," WmB-S Mss.

22.  Philosophy *VC* 1946–47; Philosophy *AR*, 1934–35; Hocking to JBC, Oct. 30, 1935, JBC to Hocking, Nov. 6, "Philosophy," Box 66; PB rec., "Pf-Ph," Box 263 (1945–46).

23.  Willard van Orman Quine int.; PB rec., Feb. 17, 1948, "Pf-Ph," Box 329; Willard van Orman Quine, *The Time of My Life: An Autobiography* (Cambridge: MIT Press, 1985).

24.  Isaiah Berlin to JBC, Jan. 18, 1950, PB to JBC, Jan. 24, 1950, JBC to PB, Jan. 26, "Ad hoc: Philosophy," Box 357; JBC to PB, April 27, 1949, "Ad hoc: Philosophy," Box 334; Oppenheimer to C. I. Lewis and Donald C. Williams, May 24, 1949, "Pf-Ph," Box 351.

25.  Quine int.; PB to JBC, May 22, 1952, "Philosophy 150," Box 440.

26.  Quine and Burton Dreben ints.; Putnam, "Half Century," 176–77.

27.  Glenn Bowersock int., Apr. 22, 1996.

28.  Morison, ed., *Development*, 33–64; JBC to William B. Munro, Dec. 21, 1940, "Classics," Box 176; on Bloch, Sterling Dow to Arthur S. Pease, Apr. 30, 1946, "Ad hoc Committees," Box 294.

29.  Morison, ed., *Development*, 74–81; Walter Jackson Bate int.; Sean O'Faolain, "The Philological Syndicate at Harvard," *HAB*, 67 (1964–65), 112 f; M. H. Abrams, "The Transformation of English Studies: 1930–1945," *Daedalus*, 126 (Winter 1997), 106; Neilson quoted in Walter J. Bate, "The Crisis in English Studies," *HM*, 85 (Sept.-Oct. 1982), 46–53.

30.  Morison, ed., *Development*, 101; James B. Munn to JBC, Feb. 5, 1936, "English: Jones," Box 56.

31.  Chart: English, JBC to Munn, Sept. 5, 1939, JBC to Spencer, Jan. 15, 1940, "English," Box 155; English *VC* 1948–49; Bliss Perry to William S. Ferguson, Oct. 14, 1941, "History and Literature," Box 206, faintly praised Mathiessen's *American Renaissance*.

32.  Robert Frost to JBC, Sept. 21, 1939, "Fr-Fy," Box 155.

33.  Harry Levin to JBC, Nov. 3, 1946, JBC to Levin, Nov. 16, "Princeton Lecture: Comments on," Box 288.

34. PB to JBC, June 4, 1951, JBC to Grayson Kirk, June 6, "Ad hoc: English," Box 387.

35. Germanic Languages *VC* 1934–35, 1939–40, *AR* 1934–35.

36. Morison, ed., *Development*, 85–90; PB rec., "Romance Languages and Literatures," 1943–44, Box 251; PB rec., Sept. 27, 1945, Louis Solano to Arthur Whittem, Aug. 31, 1945, "Romance Languages and Literatures," Box 289.

37. PB to JBC, July 3, 1952, "Provost," Box 468; PB to JBC, Oct. 28, 1952, "Romance Languages: General," Box 479.

38. PB rec. of Poggioli, "Slavic," Box 310; PB rec. of Jakobson, Jan. 25, 1949, "Sl-Sm," Box 354; Levin to PB, Dec. 18, 1951, "Slavic," Box 443.

39. Clark to JBC, Mar. 1, 1945, "Ki-Kl," Box 261.

40. PB to JBC, Sept. 20, 1947, "Mr-My," Box 305; PB to JBC, Jan. 15, 1951, "Provost," Box 409.

41. Morison, ed., *Development*, 130–45; *HAB*, 43 (1940–41), 768–73, 1024; Marjorie Cohn, "The Heavenly Twins" (essay prepared for Fogg Centennial, 1995, authors' possession.)

42. *HAB*, 47 (1944–45), 185; JBC to Paul J. Sachs, May 18, 1948, "Retirements," Box 329; PB to JBC, June 26, 1947, "Fogg Art Museum," Box 300; JBC to PB, May 20, 1952, "Fl-Fo," Box 429.

43. Deknatel to PB, May 23, 1947, William B. Dinsmore to JBC, Dec. 21, 1947, PB to JBC, Jan. 27, 1948, acting chair Charles L. Kuhn to PB, Jan. 22, 1948, JBC to PB, May 12, 1948, "Ad hoc Committee: Fine Arts," Box 313.

44. Howard W. Odum, ed., *American Masters of Social Science* (Port Washington, N.Y.: Kennekat Press, 1927), is a compendium in which the only Harvard faculty member was past-his-prime Frederick Jackson Turner; see also Dorothy Ross, *The Origins of American Social Science* (Cambridge, U.K.: Cambridge Univ. Press, 1991). JBC to Sydnor H. Walker, May 2, 1935, Walker to JBC, Apr. 25, "Social Science," Box 44; Jeffrey L. Cruikshank, *A Delicate Experiment: The Harvard Business School* (Boston: Harvard Business School Press, 1987), 165–67; Bureau for Street Traffic Research, *AR 1935–36*; JBC to Miller McClintock, June 16, 1936, "Bureau of Traffic Research," Box 50.

45. JBC to Wallace B. Donham, June 20, 1936, "Business School: Dean," Box 50; JBC to Francis T. Spaulding et al., Feb. 13, 1941, "Coordination of Studies, Committee on," Box 177; JBC statement, 1937–38, "Social Sciences: Committee of Research on," Box 121; Minutes, Oct. 3, 1934, "Advisory Research Committee: Social Sciences," Box 21.

46. JBC to Lawrence J. Henderson, Oct. 24, 1938, "De-Dm," Box 131; Oliver P. Field to JBC, Feb. 16, 1938, JBC to Field, Mar. 12, "Minnesota, University of," Box 115; JBC to Lippmann, Apr. 24, 1936, "Walter Lippmann," Box 62. See also Carl Schorske, "The New Rigorism in the Human Sciences, 1940–1960," *Daedalus*, 126 (Winter 1997), 295–96; Daniel Bell, *The Social Sciences since the Second World War* (New Brunswick: Transaction Press, 1982).

47. Robert Solow, "How Did Economics Get That Way and What Way Did It Get?" *Dadelaus*, 126 (Winter 1997), 39; Edward S. Mason, "The Harvard Department of Economics from the Beginning to World War II," *Quarterly Journal of Economics*, 97 (Aug. 1982), 383–433; JBC to Edwin F. Gay, Oct. 13, 1933,

"Economics," Box 5; JBC to Mitchell, Nov. 5, 1938, "University Professorship, Suggestions for," Box 145.

48.  Kenneth B. Murdock to JBC, May 24, 1934, Clark to JBC, June 1, 1934, Dwight P. Robinson to JBC, June 4, JBC to Wolman, June 22, Gay to Murdock, May 23, JBC to Gay, June 18, Gay to JBC, June 20, Lippmann to JBC, May 24, "Economics: Wolman, Leo," Box 6.

49.  JBC to Walter Lippmann, Jan. 17, 1935; *HAB*, 38 (1935–36), 1,103; memo of conversation with Mitchell, "Economics," Box 54 (1935–36).

50.  Paul Samuelson int.

51.  "Confidential Report on Long-Range Plans for the Department of Economics (rev. ed.)," Feb. 25, 1948, Burbank to PB, Mar. 10, 1948, "Ad hoc Committee: Economics," Box 313.

52.  Haberler, Hansen, and Harris to JBC, Apr. 6, 1948, PB to JBC, Apr. 15, 1948, "Ad hoc Committee: Economics," Box 313.

53.  Haberler to JBC, Nov. 5, 1951, "Economics Department," Box 427; Samuelson, Galbraith ints.; Wolfgang F. Stolper, *Joseph Alois Schumpeter: The Public Life of a Private Man* (Princeton: Princeton Univ. Press, 1994), 12–13; Paul Samuelson, "Pastiches from an Earlier Politically-Incorrect Age" (typescript, authors' possession).

54.  PB rec. to President and Fellows, Feb. 7, 1949, "Economics: Budget 1949–50," Box 340; PB to JBC, Apr. 15, 1949, JBC to Randall, May 12, 1949, "Alumni Association," Box 335; Robert Bradford to President and Board of Overseers, Nov. 21, 1949, "Overseers Committee," Box 378; proposed statement, July 7, "Corporation," Box 338; statement of President, Oct. 25, 1949, news rel., Nov. 22, 1949, Galbraith to JBC, Nov. 22, JBC to Galbraith, Nov. 23, "Economics: Galbraith," Box 367. See also Henry Rosovsky, "The Most Famous Professor at Harvard," in Samuel Bowles, Richard Edwards, and William G. Shepherd, eds., *Unconventional Wisdom: Essays in Honor of John Kenneth Galbraith* (Boston: Houghton Mifflin, 1989), 327–46.

55.  Rockefeller to Randall, Jan. 25, 1951, Lamont to JBC, Feb. 20, Randall to JBC, Jan. 26, Feb. 12, 1951, "Economics Department," Box 397.

56.  JBC to John V. Lintner, Jr., Mar. 1, 1951, Lintner to JBC, Mar. 13, JBC to Lintner, Mar. 19, Box 397.

57.  Randall to JBC, Dec. 15, 1949, Apr. 13, 1950, "Overseers Committee," Box 378; Randall to JBC, Sept. 14, Dec. 1, 1950, "Economics Department," Box 397; Economics *VC* 1950–51; JBC to Randall, Feb. 4, 1952, Randall to JBC, Feb. 29, JBC to Arthur Smithies, June 10, Randall to JBC, Oct. 17, 1952, "Economics: Budget," Box 455.

58.  History *VC* 1933–34, 1937–38; Murdock to JBC, Dec. 18, 1933, "History," Box 9.

59.  PB to JBC, Nov. 2, 1945, "Ad hoc Committee: History," Box 270; PB rec. of Schlesinger, Jr., Feb. 8, 1946, "History," Box 280.

60.  PB to JBC, Apr. 14, 1944, "History," Box 245; PB rec., Feb. 16, 1945, "Sn-Sta," Box 267; David Owen to PB, Feb. 23, 1949, JBC to PB, Mar. 18, 1949, "Ad hoc: History," Box 334; PB memo, June 3, 1953, "History," Box 447.

61. Government *VC* 1937–38; Samuel Beer, "Encounters with Modernity, or How I Became a Political Scientist," typescript, Woodrow Wilson Center; Beer int.

62. PB rec. of Beer, Dec. 5, 1945, "Gli-Go," Box 279, of Hartz, Jan. 20, 1947, "Government," Box 301; JBC to PB, May 3, 1949, "Ad hoc: Government," Box 334; on Bunche, JBC to PB, Jan. 5, 1950, "Ad hoc: Government," Box 357; Ralph Bunche to President and Fellows, Feb. 8, 1952, "Bu-By," Box 422. See also Charles E. Lindblom, "Political Science in the 1940s and 1950s," *Daedalus*, 126 (Winter 1997), 225–52.

63. Morison, ed., *Development*, 202–15; Anthropology/Peabody *VC* 1939–40; Edwin B. Wilson to JBC, Feb. 27, 1935, Kroeber int., Jan. 18, 1936, "Anthropology," Box 22.

64. "Anthropology" (1940–41), Box 173; Anthropology *AR* 1946–47; *HAB*, 54 (1951–52), 108; *Crimson*, Mar. 18, 1995, 3.

65. On Coon, PB to JBC, Mar. 29, 1948, "An-Az," Box 315; JBC to PB, Jan. 10, 1950, "Ad hoc: Anthropology," Box 357; PB to JBC, Feb. 24, 1953, "Social Relations," Box 470.

66. Jerome D. Greene to Edwin G. Boring, Mar. 19, 1941, Boring to Greene, Mar. 24, Secretary to Boring, Mar. 25, "Psychology Department: General," Box 191; Boring to Dean George H. Chase, Feb. 4, 1942, "Hom-Hr," Box 207.

67. Morison, ed., *Development*, 216–22; Psychology *AR*, 1934–35, 1935–36; Henry A. Murray, "The Harvard Psychological Clinic," *HAB*, 38 (1935–36), 142–49; JBC to Boring, Mar. 22, 1937, JBC to Lashley, Apr. 5, 1937, "Psychology," Box 92; JBC to Boring, Feb. 11, 1937, "Psychology," Box 92. See also Forrest G. Robinson, *Love's Story Told: A Life of Henry A. Murray* (Cambridge: Harvard Univ. Press, 1992), ch. 9; Edwin G. Boring, *A History of Psychology in Autobiography* (Worcester, Mass.: Clark Univ. Press, 1952), 27–52.

68. JBC to Leonard Carmichel et al., May 2, JBC to Gregg, June 11, 1945, "Psychology: Commission on," Box 288.

69. *Report of the University Commission to Advise on the Future of Psychology at Harvard*, Boring to JBC, May 26, 1947, PB note attached, JBC to Allan Gregg, Apr. 14, 1947, "Psychology: Commission on," Box 308.

70. PB to JBC, Apr. 5, 1946, "Arts and Sciences: Dean of Faculty," Box 272; PB to JBC, Dec. 10, 1946, "Psychology: Commission on," Box 308; Robinson, *Love's Story Told*, 291 f.

71. Morison, ed., *Development*, 223–30; "Sociology," Box 144 (1938–39); Barry V. Johnston, *Pitirim V. Sorokin: An Intellectual Biography* (Lawrence: University Press of Kansas, 1995); on Ford, George D. Birkhoff memo, Sept. 26, 1935, "Sociology," Box 69.

72. Johnston, *Sorokin*, 125 f; Parsons to JBC, Feb. 8, 1942, "Sociology," Box 216.

73. Johnston, *Sorokin*, 154; PB int., Carnegie Project, OHRO 1968. See also Gordon Allport and Edwin Boring, "Psychology and Social Relations at Harvard University," *American Psychologist*, 1 (Apr. 1946), 119–122.

74. Parsons to PB, Feb. 20, Sorokin to Buck, Sept. 15, JBC memo to PB, Oct. 30, 1945, "Ad hoc Committee: Sociology," Box 270; PB memo to JBC, Sept. 1, 1946, "Arts and Sciences: Dean of Faculty," Box 272; PB rec. of Stouffer, Jan. 5, Sorokin to JBC, Jan. 16, 1946, "Sociology," Box 290; Johnston, *Sorokin*, 156, 162.

75. Johnston, *Sorokin*, 166 ff; JBC to Sorokin, Oct. 11, 1944, "Social Science," JBCPP 1944–45; Bailey to PB, Oct. 8, 1952, "Re," Box 469.

76. JBC to Robert T. Crane, May 26, 1945, "Social Science" in "Sr-Sta," Box 267; Stouffer to JBC, Oct. 25, JBC to Stouffer, Oct. 30, 1947, "Social Relations," Box 331.

77. PB, Talcott Parsons ints., Carnegie Project, OHRO, 1968; JBC to PB, Jan. 29, 1946, "Arts and Sciences: Dean of Faculty," Box 272; JBC to Josephs, Sept. 25, Josephs to JBC, Oct. 9, 1947, Robert M. Lester to JBC, Oct. 17, 1947, "Carnegie Corporation," Box 318.

78. Robert M. Lester to JBC, May 21, 1948, "Carnegie Corporation," Box 318; PB int., OHRO, 30, 37–41, 58; PB to JBC, May 6, 1948, "Provost," Box 329; PB rec. of Hughes, May 7, 1948, "History, Box 322. See also interviews with David Riesman and Talcott Parsons, OHRO.

79. JBC to PB, Dec. 19, 1949, PB to JBC, Jan. 16, 1950, "Provost," Box 380; JBC to PB, Feb. 23, Mar. 19, 1951, "Russian Research Center," Box 410.

80. *Report of the Reviewing Committee of the Russian Research Center*, June 6, 1952, "Russian Research Center," Box 442.

81. David A Hollinger, *Science, Jews, and Secular Culture: Studies in Mid-Twentieth Century American Intellectual History* (Princeton: Princeton Univ. Press, 1996), 97 f.

82. JBC to Hugh S. Taylor et al., Jan. 30, 1935, "Chemistry," Box 46.

83. Frank Westheimer, "Chemistry at Harvard," Nov. 1, 1995, typescript in authors' possession; Chemistry *VC* 1935–36; Saul Cohen int.

84. JBC to Nathan Hayward, Feb. 7, 1944, "Overseers: General," Box 249; Informal Record draft, Sept. 10, 1945, JBC to Prof. W. K. Lewis, etc., Sept. 10, 1945, "Ad hoc Committee: Chemistry," Box 270; JBC to PB, Aug. 14, 1945, "Chemistry," Box 276.

85. Warren Weaver to JBC, May 21, 1951, "Rockefeller Foundation," Box 410; news rel., Sept. 2, 1951, "Th-Ti," Box 444.

86. Gerald Holton int.; Van Vleck to PB, Mar. 25, 1947, "Physics," Box 307; Katherine R. Sopka, "Physics at Harvard during the Past Half-Century: A Brief Departmental History" (June 1978), mss. in possession of Gerald Holton.

87. Frederick Saunders to JBC, Jan. 23, JBC to Saunders, Jan. 28, 1935, "Physics," Box 41.

88. JBC to H. R. Mimno, May 13, 1936, "Physics," Box 66; JBC to E. O. Lawrence, Oct. 26, 1938, "California," Box 129," to Vannevar Bush, Nov. 22, 1938, June 17, 1939, "Carn-Ce," Box 129; JBC to E. T. Stannard, Dec 10, 1936, "Physics," Box 91. See also "Physics: Cyclotron," Box 66 (1935–36).

89. Edwin Kemble to JBC, Feb. 27, Apr. 4, JBC to Kemble, Mar. 3, 1942, "Physics," Box 213.

90. PB to JBC, Jan. 17, 1946, "Physical Sciences Panel," Box 287; JBC to PB, Feb. 9, 1946, "Provost," Box 288; *HAB*, 48 (1945–46), 115; Physics *AR*, 1946–47; PB recs., Jan. 21, May 29, 1947, "Physics," Box 307.

91. PB to JBC, Feb. 5, 1946, JBC to R. Lee, Apr. 7, 1947, "Retirements," Box 308.

92. Redfield to JBC, Mar. 16, 1936, "Biology," Box 49; Redfield to JBC., Oct.

26, 1938, "Biology," Box 128; Redfield to JBC, Mar. 4, Apr. 26, 1938, "Biology," Box 103.

93. "The Case of Assistant Professor Edward S. Castle," "Biology: Castle, E. S.," Box 150 (1939–40).

94. Biology *VC* 1946–47; JBC to PB, Feb. 4, 1942, "Biology," Box 199; JBC to PB, Jan. 24, 1950, "Ad hoc: Biology," Box 357.

95. JBC memo, June 1, 1951, JBC to PB, June 13, 1951, "Ad hoc: Biology," Box 387; PB rec. of Lederberg, Dec. 20, 1943, "Biology," Box 241; PB to JBC, Mar. 18, May 12, 1952, "Ad hoc: Genetics," Box 416.

96. Ernst Mayr int.; PB to DWB, Mar. 28, 1946, "Museum of Comparative Zoology," Box 284; *HM*, 88 (July-Aug. 1986), 34–38.

97. PB to JBC, Feb. 11, 1946, Romer to Henry Lee Shattuck, Jan. 18, 1951, "Museum of Comparative Zoology," Box 405; "Confidential Report to the Corporation, Sept. 11, 1944, "Corporation," Box 257; Biology *VC* 1943–44.

98. "Harvard's Botanical Empire," *HAB*, 46 (1943–44), 129 ff; Roger Lee to NMP, May 3, 1954, "Lee, Roger I.," Box 17, NMPPP; Arnold Arboretum *VC* 1931–32; *HAB*, 38 (1935–36), 465–71.

99. Clark to JBC, Nov. 14, 1950, "Grenville Clark—Correspondence/ Dodge Opinion," *AAC*, Box 4; JBC to Corporation, Oct. 15, 1952, "Arnold Arboretum," Box 449; Coolidge to WLM, Oct. 13, 1953, enclosing Clark to Bishop Lawrence, Oct. 8, Coolidge memo to NMP, Dec. 22, Coolidge to Welles V. Moot, Jan. 12, 1955, "Arnold Arboretum—General (1953–54)," *AAC*, Box 1.

100. JBC to E. P. Kohler, Dec. 23, 1933, "Chemistry," Box 3; JBC to Hans Clarke, June 6, 14, to H. D. Dakin, Sept. 18, June 6, 1935, "Medical School: Faculty Appointments," Box 38; JBC to PB, Apr. 27, 1948, "Arts and Sciences: Dean of," Box 315; JBC *Diaries*, Apr. 7, 1951, Oct. 20, Dec. 31, 1952.

101. PB to JBC, Jan. 28, 1951, "Biology," Box 421; Kistiakowsky to JBC, May 21, 1952, "Biophysical Chemistry," Box 421.

102. JBC memo to Corporation, Mar. 8, 1934, "Engineering School: General," Box 6; JBC to E. O. Lawrence, Feb. 10, Lawrence to JBC, Mar. 2, 12, JBC to Lawrence, Mar. 5, 1936, "Engineering School: Faculty Appointments," Box 55.

103. "Memorandum on the Future of Research and Instruction in Engineering and the Physical Sciences at Harvard University," Nov. 12, 1945; Minutes of Meeting on Physical Science, Dec. 17, 1945, "Physical Science Panel," Box 287; Gordon M. Fair to JBC, Nov. 10, Buck memo to JBC, Nov. 12, 1948, "Engineering School: Dean," Box 340.

104. PB to JBC, Jan. 5, 1949, "Arts & Sciences: Faculty of," Box 335; news rel., Nov. 4, 1949, "Engineering School: McKay Trust, Box 368; JBC to Vannevar Bush, Apr. 18, "Engineering: McKay Trust," Box 340; JBC to VB, Sept. 24, 1949, Jan. 16, 1950, "Engineering School: McKay Trust," Box 368; "Report of the Panel on the McKay Bequest" (1950), 8.

105. PB to JBC, Nov. 24, 1950, Jan. 15, June 16, 1951, "Applied Science," Box 390.

106. Mathematics *VC* 1949–50; PB to JBC, Oct 15, 1945, "Mas-Maz," Box 282.

107. *HAB*, 41 (1938–39), 881; "I.B.M.—Calculator Acceptance Ceremonies,"

Aug. 1944, Box 261; *HAB*, 47 (1944–45), 14–16. See also I. Bernard Cohen, *Howard Aiken: Portrait of a Computer Pioneer* (Cambridge: MIT Press, 1999).

108. Memo re meeting of Nov. 7, 1944, Harlow Shapley to JBC, Oct. 31, Nov. 11, 1944, "Conant, James B.—Memorandums A. C. Smith," Box 257.

109. Morison, ed., *Development*, 292–95; *HAB*, 40 (1937–38), 481.

110. Committee Report, June 18, 1952, "Observatory—Harvard College," Box 438; JBC to Oppenheimer, Jan. 7, 1953, "Observatory—Harvard College," Box 465; JBC to PB, July 29, 1952, PB to JBC, July 30, Shapley to JBC, July 22, "Astronomy," Box 449; on Menzel, McGB rec., Dec. 29, 1953, Observatory-Harvard College," Box 348.

111. PB to JBC, May 26, 1945, "Geology: General," Box 279; JBC to Donald McLaughlin, Apr. 14, 1950, "Engineering School: McKay Trust," Box 368.

112. Neil Smith, " 'Academic War Over the Field of Geography': The Elimination of Geography at Harvard, 1947–1951," *Annals of the Association of American Geography*, 77 (1987), 155–72; JBC to PB, Jan. 13, 1948, "Ad hoc Committee: Geography," Box 313.

113. "Geographical Exploration: Institute of," Box 57; J. C. Greene to JBC, Oct. 6, 1939, "Institute of Geographical Exploration," Box 158; *HAB*, 34 (Feb. 26, 1932), 643–49; *HAB*, 54 (Oct. 13, 1951), 59–61; PB to JBC, Aug. 28, 1942, "Gen-Gle," Box 206; A. H. Rice to JBC, Sept. 15, O. M. Shaw to JBC, Sept. 24, 1951, "Geographical Exploration, Institute of," Box 430.

114. Sarton to JBC, Sept. 13, 1934, "Advisory Research Committee: Humanities," Box 21; JBC to Sarton, Jan. 7, 1935, "History of Science," Box 34; JBC to A. V. Kidder, Oct. 10, 1933, "History of Science," Box 9; JBC to Harold Laski, Mar. 26, 1938, "Laa-Lav," Box 112; JBC to Sarton, Sept. 17, 1941, "History of Science," Box 183.

115. JBC to Crane Brinton, rec. Kuhn for Society of Fellows, Jan. 3, 1948, "Society of Fellows," Box 331.

*Chapter 5*

1. Samuel E. Morison, ed., *The Development of Harvard University* (Cambridge: Harvard Univ. Press, 1930), 451–62; JBC to John W. Lowes, Nov. 20, 1934, "Graduate Students: House for," Box 31.

2. "Table of Positions Filled," "Appointment Office," Box 102 (1937–38); *HAB*, 40 (1937–38), 10–11; Arthur M. Schlesinger to JBC, Nov. 25, 1941, JBC to Schlesinger, Dec. 1, "Arts and Sciences: Committee to Study Graduate Education," Box 199.

3. "Review of the Activities of the Office of the Graduate Dean," July-Aug. 1943, Howard M. Jones memo to PB and JBC, c. Dec. 8, 1943; Dorothy Priest report, "Arts and Sciences: Graduate School," Box 241.

4. "Preliminary Report of the Graduate School of Arts and Sciences," Apr. 13, 1944, Jones to JBC, May 24, 1944, JBC to Jones, May 27, Jones to JBC, May 29, JBC to Jones, June 6, "Arts and Sciences: Graduate School," Box 241.

5. JBC memo to Corporation, Mar. 16, 1948, "Corporation," Box 319; Keith

Kane to JBC, Apr. 6, 1951, "Foundation for Advanced Study and Research," Box 398; *HAB*, 53 (1950–51), 59.

6. Morison, ed., *Development*, 472–507; Arthur Sutherland, *The Law at Harvard* (Cambridge: Harvard Univ. Press, 1967); Laura Kalman, *Abe Fortas* (New Haven: Yale Univ. Press, 1990), 16.

7. *HAB*, 39 (1936–37), 528; *HAB*, 41 (1938–39), 669; Mrs. Amasa Walker to JBC, Jan. 29, 1934, JBC to Mrs. Walker, Feb. 6, "Waa-War," Box 19.

8. George K. Gardner to JBC, Oct. 16, 1933, "Law School: General," Box 11; JBC to Grenville Clark, Oct. 13, 1933, "Law School: General," Box 11. See also David Wigdor, *Roscoe Pound* (Westport, Conn.: Greenwood Press, 1974); James F. Clark, "The Harvard Law School Deanship of Roscoe Pound, 1916–1936," HLS student essay, 1999.

9. Clark to JBC, Feb. 15, 1936, "Law School: Recommendations for Deanship," Box 87; Frankfurter to JBC, Oct. 5, "Law School: Biklé," Box 61; George C. Cutler to JBC, May 19, "Law School: Recommendations for Deanship," Box 87.

10. JBC to Biklé, Mar. 14, 1936, Biklé, "Comments on Draft Report Concerning Harvard Law School," Mar. 25, 1936, "Law School: Biklé, Box 61; on heart trouble, Charles C. Burlingham to JBC, July 6, 1946, "Bu-By," Box 296; Biklé to JBC, June 11, 1936, to William James, June 12, "Law School: Biklé," Box 61.

11. McLaughlin to JBC, Jan. 21, 1936, "Law School: Dean," Box 61; Clark to JBC, Mar. 11, 1937, JBC to Clark, Mar. 13, Clark to JBC, Mar. 15, "Law School: Recommendations for Deanship," Box 87; Landis to JBC, Feb. 15, 1940, "Law School: Dean," Box 158.

12. HLS *VC*, 1942–43; Greene to Theodore Miller, Apr. 23, 1942, "Mia-Mil," Box 210; W. Barton Leach to JBC, July 10, 1944, "Law School: Ad hoc Committee," Box 261.

13. JBC to Edmund M. Morgan, July 22, 1944, "List of A Men at HLS," "Law School: Ad hoc Committee," Box 261; Charles Wyzanski to JBC, Feb. 26, 1945, "Wim-Wy," Box 269; Landis to JBC, Mar. 10, 1945, "Law School: Budget," Box 261.

14. Erwin Griswold to JBC, Nov. 1, 1946, "Law School: Budget," Box 302.

15. Coolidge to JBC, May 4, 1945, JBC to Coolidge, May 8, "Coo-Coz," Box 257; Thomas K. McCraw, *Prophets of Regulation* (Cambridge: Harvard Univ. Press, 1984), 205.

16. Landis to JBC, Apr. 29, 1946, Harrison Tweed to JBC, May 25, "Law School: Recommendation for Dean," Box 281.

17. Griswold to JBC, July 11, 1950, "Law School: Dean," Box 402; news rel., Sept. 11, Nov. 13, 1952, "Law School: Dean," Box 460; "Law School: Dean," Box 323 (1947–48).

18. Griswold to JBC, Dec. 8, 1949, JBC to Griswold, Dec. 12, Griswold to JBC, Dec. 14, "Law School: Dean," Box 373.

19. JBC to Alan Gregg, Jan. 11. 1947, "Rockefeller Foundation," Box 309; Morison, ed., *Development*, 555–94.

20. Robert H. Ebert int., Aug. 20, 1974, "Medical–3 Centuries," WmB-S Mss; JBC to Burwell, Mar. 1, 1935, "Medical School: Dean," Box 38; JBC *Diaries*, June 14, 1940.

21. "Summary of the Statement of the President to the Committee on Resources and Organization," "Medical School: Committee on Resources," Box 325 (1947–48); Henry Meadow int., "Medical School," WmB-S Mss; JBC memo to Corporation, Nov. 9, 1948, "Corporation," Box 338.

22. JBC to Burwell, Nov. 24, 1948, "Medical School: Berry," Box 346; "Preliminary Statement of Policy," June 1, 1948, "Harvard Medical School—Hospitals," Box 326; JBC to Harvie Branscomb, Oct. 9, 1947, "V," Box 332; Keith Kane memo to JBC, Feb. 17, 1948, "Medical School: Committee on Resources," JBC to Burwell, Mar. 18, 1948, "Medical School: Dean," Box 325.

23. JBC to Edward D. Churchill, Jan. 7, 1949, "Medical School: Suggestions for Dean," Box 347; Meadow, Ebert ints in "Medicine—3 Centuries," WmB-S Mss; JBC to George P. Berry, Mar. 15, 1949, "Medical School: Berry," Box 346; JBC memo, Mar. 9, 1949, JBC memo to Burwell, Dec. 2, 1948, "Medical School: Hospitals," Box 346; JBC to Leonard Scheele, Feb. 14, 1951, Scheele to JBC, Mar. 2, "Medical School: Research & Development," Box 405.

24. HBS *VC* 1936–37; *HAB*, 41 (1938–39), 676.

25. JBC to Walter Lippmann, Apr. 24, 1936, "Walter Lippmann," Box 62; Jeffrey L. Cruikshank, *A Delicate Experiment: The Harvard Business School, 1908–1945* (Boston: Harvard Business School Press, 1987), 191, 165–66, 253; *HAB*, 37 (1934–35), 156–57; "Business School: Committee on Government and Business," Box 25 (1934–35).

26. JBC to Hillman, Dec. 22, 1941, "Oa-Ok," Box 212; Donham to JBC, Sept. 26, 1941, "Business School: Dean," Box 201.

27. HBS *VC* 1942–43; Cruikshank, *Delicate Experiment*, ch. 5; news rel., Oct. 8, 1945, "Business School: General," Box 275; Donald K. David int., Oct. 4, 1976, "Business—3 Centuries," WmB-S Mss; on surplus, Claflin to David, Oct. 29, 1945, "Treasurer," Box 291; Deborah Shapley, *Promise and Power: The Life and Times of Robert McNamara* (New York: Little, Brown, 1993), 28 f.

28. David to JBC, Sept. 1, 1944, "Business School: Dean"; "Report of the Transition Committee," Nov. 28, 1944, "Business School: General," Box 256; Cruikshank, *Delicate Experiment*, 270 f.

29. JBC to E. D. Starbuck, Jan. 12, 1946, "Sn-Sta," Box 290; Cruikshank, *Delicate Experiment*, 273; David to Robert Moses, Oct. 21, 1946, "Mo," Box 305; news rel., June 10, 1949, "Roa-Ror," Box 353.

30. Greer Williams, "Schools of Public Health: Their Doing and Undoing," typescript in "Public Health—Three Centuries," WmB-S Mss; Jean A. Curran, *Founders of the Harvard School of Public Health* (New York: Josiah Macy, Jr., Foundation, 1970), pt. I.

31. Typescript, "Report of the School of Public Health Committee," "Public Health: School of," Box 250; Curran, *Founders*, 131.

32. "Confidential Report to the Corporation from the President of the University," Sept. 11, 1944, Box 257; Burwell to JBC, Aug. 31, 1943, Report of SPH Committee, "Public Health: School of," Box 250.

33. "Confidential Report to the Corporation from the President of the University," Sept. 11, 1944, Box 257; JBC to Philip Drinker, June 8, 1944, JBC to Burwell, Apr. 9, 1945, Burwell to JBC, Apr. 14, 1945, Corporation, Informal

Record, June 20, 1945, Acting Dean Edward G. Huber and Burwell to JBC, June 20, 1945, "Public Health: School of," Box 265; news rel., Jan. 10, 1946, "Public Health: School of," Box 288.

34. Henry L. Shattuck to JBC, Oct. 22, 1946, Simmons to JBC, Nov. 15, 1946, Cecil Drinker to JBC, Dec. 4, 1946, "Public Health: School of," Box 308.

35. Booz, Hamilton report, Jan. 27, 1949, "Public Health School," Box 351; Simmons to President and Fellows, Apr. 15, 1952, "Public Health School: Budget," Box 441.

36. JBC to Dr. Maurice E. Peters, May 2, 1939, "Dental School: Comments," Box 132; JBC to Miner, Oct. 3, 1939, "Dental School: Dean," Box 153; JBC to Junius S. Morgan, Sept. 21, to Alan Gregg, Sept. 22, 1939, to Dr. Lawrence N. Baker, Jan. 5, 1940, "Dental School Endowment," Box 153; *HAB*, 42 (1939–40), 1244–45.

37. Miner to JBC, Oct. 8, 1940, "Dental School: Dean," Box 178; JBC memo to A. Calvert Smith, Nov. 25, 1940, "Annual Report," Box 173.

38. Sidney Burwell to JBC, May 28, 1942, "Dental School: Dean," Box 204; JBC to L. M. S. Miner, Apr. 4, 1944, "Dental School," Box 243; JBC report, "Corporation," Box 277 (1945–46); SDM *VC*, 1948–49; JBC to Arthur H. Merritt, Dec. 7, 1952, "Me," Box 461; James M. Dunning to George P. Berry, Feb. 28, 1951, "Rockefeller Foundation," Box 410.

39. JBC to Willard B. Sperry, Feb. 7, 1940, "Divinity School," Box 154.

40. JBC to Lloyd K. Garrison, Jan. 8, May 16, July 1, 1940, "Overseers: Committees," Box 163.

41. JBC to Lloyd K. Garrison, Jan. 8, May 16, July 1, 1940, "Overseers: Committees," Box 163; JBC to Niebuhr, Sept. 23, 1941, Niebuhr to Sperry, Oct. 7, 1942, Sperry to Niebuhr, Oct. 15, Niebuhr to JBC, Oct. 17, "Niebuhr, Reinhold," Box 232; Sperry to JBC, May 21, Aug. 22, 1942, "Divinity School," Box 204. See also Richard W. Fox, *Reinhold Niebuhr* (New York: Pantheon, 1985), 211–212.

42. "Confidential Report to the Corporation from the President," Sept. 11, 1944, Box 257; JBC to John D. Rockefeller, Jr., Oct. 25, 1944, to John W. Nason, Dec. 9, "Divinity School," Box 258; JBC to O'Brian, Sept. 20, 1945, to Commission members, Nov. 15, 1945, "Divinity School," Box 277; James G. Hershberg, *James B. Conant* (New York: Knopf, 1993), 579–80.

43. "Report of the Commission to Study and Make Recommendations with Respect to the Harvard Divinity School," "Divinity School," Box 319 (1947–48); JBC to Charles W. Gilkey, Apr. 6, 1948, John D. Rockefeller, Jr., to JBC, Oct. 16, 1947, "Divinity School," Box 319; JBC to John Nicholas Brown, Sept. 27, 1948, "Divinity School: Commission on," Box 339.

44. JBC to William E. Stevenson, Jan. 16, 1950, "Oberlin College," Box 378; JBC to Stevenson, Sept. 8, 1950, "Divinity School," Box 396; JBC to Stevenson, Oct. 4, 1950, "Oa-Ok," Box 407; Neibuhr to JBC, Sept. 20, 1950, "Corporation," Box 395.

45. JBC to H. V. Chase, Apr. 1, 1939, "Annual Report: Comments on," Box 125; JBC to Francis T. Spaulding, Oct. 17, 1939, "Education, Graduate School of: Dean," Box 154; *HAB*, 38 (1935–36), 833; JBC to Howard M. Jones, Dec. 12,

1938, "English," Box 133. See also JBC, *MSL*, 180–84, 417 f, and Arthur G. Powell, *The Uncertain Profession: Harvard and the Search for Educational Authority* (Cambridge: Harvard Univ. Press, 1980).

46.  JBC confidential memo to Corporation, Apr. 11, 1939, "Corporation," Box 131.

47.  Spaulding to JBC, Apr. 7, 9, 1942, Spaulding memo to Faculty, Jan. 13, 1942, "Education: Graduate School of: General," Box 204; George H. Chase to P. M. Palmer, Nov. 16, 1944, "Law-Len," Box 261.

48.  "Memorandum to the Corporation Concerning the Future of the School of Education," July 20, 1945, "Corporation," Box 277.

49.  JBC to Francis H. Spaulding, June 27, 1945, "Education: School of: Dean," Box 258; Spaulding to JBC, Sept. 2, 1945, "Education: School of: Dean," Box 278; JBC memo to Clark, James, and Shattuck, Apr. 10, 1946, "Education: School of: General," Box 278.

50.  JBC memo to GSE Faculty, June 27, 1946, "Education: School of: General," Box 299; JBC to Devereaux Josephs, May 11, 1948, "Carnegie Corporation," Box 318.

51.  Powell, *Uncertain Profession*, 245, ch. 10; Keppel to JBC, Nov. 4, Dec. 29, 1952, "Education: Fund Raising," Box 456; GSE *VC* 1946–47.

52.  GSD *VC* (1934–35); Walter F. Bogner, "The Education of Architects," *HAB*, 36 (Jan. 19, 1934), 429 f.

53.  JBC to Joseph Hudnut, June 7, 1935, "Architecture: Dean," Box 23; GSD *VC* 1937–38.

54.  Hudnut to JBC, Apr. 16, 1946, Jan. 26, 1945, "Design: School of," Box 277; Hudnut memo to Faculty, Apr. 25, 1949, JBC memo to Corporation, "Concerning an Emergency Situation in the School of Design," May 24, 1950; Hudnut to JBC, Jan. 9, 1950, JBC to Hudnut, Jan. 16, "Design School: General," Box 366.

55.  JBC *Diaries*, June 18, 1952; Gropius to JBC, Dec. 4, 1951, "Design: School of," Box 427; JBC memos to Corporation, Oct. 6, Dec. 20, 1952; news rel., Jan. 14, 1953, "Design School: General," Box 454.

56.  "Public Administration—Three Centuries," WmB-S Mss; "Memorandum Regarding the Establishment of an Institute of Public Administration in Harvard University," Mar. 15, 1934, "Government," Box 8; JBC to Carl L. Friedrich, Nov. 20, 1934, "Government: Institute of Public Administration," Box 31; JBC to Morris R. Lambie, May 16, 1935, "University Training for Government Service: Committee on," Box 46.

57.  Littauer to JBC, Nov. 13, 1935, "Public Administration: Littauer," Box 67; JBC to ALL, Dec. 3, 1935, "Lowell, A. Lawrence," Box 62; JBC to Leonard D. White, Dec. 2, 1935, Frankfurter, "Some Observations," "Public Administration: Commission on," Box 67.

58.  JBC to Robert M. Hutchins, Mar. 17, 1936, Hutchins to JBC, Mar. 27, JBC to Hutchins, Apr. 8, Hutchins to JBC, Apr. 16, "Chicago, University of," Box 51.

59.  JBC to Dodds, Jan. 4, 1936, Hutchins to JBC, c. July 1, 1936, White cables to JBC, June 27, June 28, 1936, "Public Administration: Commission on," Box 67; JBC to Dodds, June 16, "Chicago, University of," Box 51; Littauer to JBC, June

30, 1936, "Public Administration: Lucius N. Littauer Foundation for," Box 67; Littauer to JBC, Nov. 25, 1936, JBC to Littauer, Nov. 28, "Public Administration: Littauer," Box 93.

60. JBC to John H. Williams, Feb. 6, 1940, "Public Administration: Graduate School of," Box 165; Williams to JBC, Feb. 21, 1947, "Public Administration: School of," Box 308; Hart to Williams, Oct. 9. 1941, Griswold and Hart to Conant, Apr. 30, 1942, JBC to Hart and Griswold, May 19, "Public Administration: Graduate School of," Box 213.

61. "Public Administration—3 Centuries," WmB-S Mss; SPA *VC* 1940; *CM*, Feb. 28, 1938.

62. Claflin to JBC, May 12, 1944, "Treasurer," Box 252; Wyzanski to JBC, Nov. 12, 1943, JBC to Wyzanski, Dec. 6, 1943, "Overseers: General," Box 249.

63. Williams memo to GSPA, Jan. 8, 1947, "Public Administration: School of," Box 308.

64. News rel., Apr. 16, 1947, "Public Administration: School of," Box 328; JBC to Murray Seasongood, Jan. 23, 1953, "Schu-Sef," Box 469; GSPA *VC*, 1953–54; JBC, *AR*, 1951–52.

## Chapter 6

1. JBC, *AR* 1951–52; DWB to Colin English, Feb. 4, 1949, "Fl-Fo," Box 341, to Oscar A. Silverman, June 26, 1947, "Bu-By," Box 296, to Richard Harper, July 18, 1950, "Information in re Harvard," Box 402. See also Treasurer, *Statutes and History of Government of Harvard University*; E. J. Kahn, Jr., *Harvard* (New York: Norton, 1969), 343.

2. *HAB*, 39 (1936–37), 499; *HAB*, 36 (1933–34), 57; *CM*, Sept. 26, 1938; JBC to Lowes, Aug. 20, Oct. 2, 1941, "Financial Vice-President," Box 180; *CM*, Dec. 19, 1938; *HAB*, 41 (1938–39), 441; JBC, *AR* 1951–52, 13 ff; Chase to Hermon D. Smith, Jan. 31, 1940, Harvard Clubs: Miscellaneous," Box 156.

3. Lowes file memorandum, Oct. 31, 1940, "Dean of the University," Box 177; William H. Claflin to JBC, Apr. 28, 1941, "Treasurer," Box 195.

4. A. Calvert Smith to Wells, July 22, 1942, "Treasurer," Box 195; *HAB*, 42 (1939–40), 7; JBC to Eric A. McCouch, May 26, 1941, "Harvard Clubs, Associated," Box 182.

5. JBC, *Diaries*, Nov. 28, 1940.

6. Memo on University Mail Service, Jan. 30, 1945, Smith memo to JBC, Dec. 1, 1944, "U," Box 268; JBC to William Emerson, Oct. 23, 1945, "El-En," Box 278; JBC, *My Several Lives: Memoirs of a Social Inventor* (New York: Harper & Row, 1970), 298; JBC memo, Jan. 2, 1946, "Corporation," Box 277; JBC to Roger Lee, Jan. 22, 1946, "Law-Len," Box 281; Philip Cronin, "Provost Buck: Consistent Freedom," *HC*, Jan. 18, 1953, M6. See also WmB-S, "He Carried the Load," *HM*, 76 (July-Aug. 1974), 44–49, 60.

7. Crozier to John C. Baker, Sept. 8, 1941, Smith memo to JBC, Sept. 16, 1941, "Purchasing Agent," Box 214.

8. Gladys McCafferty to JBC, July 1, 1941, Conant to McCafferty, July 2, "Personnel Relations Office," Box 190.

9. Coolidge to JBC, Feb. 7, 1946, "Coo-Coz," Box 276; PB to JBC, June 15, 1950, "Arts and Sciences, Faculty of," Box 360.

10. JBC to Clark, Jan. 13, 1938, "Clark, Grenville," Box 105; McCafferty to Conant, Nov. 19, 1941, Durant to William A. Boyle, Dec. 4, "Harvard University Employees' Representative Association," Box 206.

11. Edward Reynolds to JBC, Oct. 17, 1947, "Administrative Vice-President," Box 314.

12. *HAB*, 52 (1949–50), 655; *CM*, Dec. 21, 1935, Mar. 22, 1937; DWB to Clarence N. Callender, Nov. 20, 1950, "Information in re Harvard," Box 402; Claflin to JBC, Feb. 1, 1945, "Treasurer," Box 267; "Pensions," Box 379 (1949–50).

13. JBC to Dean A. N. Johnson, Feb. 12, 1935, "Annual Report: Comments on," Box 22; A. Calvert Smith to Roger P. McCutcheon, Dec. 15, 1944, "Ta-Te," Box 267; Edwin J. Cohn to JBC, Jan. 5, 1945, "Pa," Box 263; Burwell to Jerome Greene, Dec. 29, 1941, in "Dr. Cohn's Patents," Box 22, NMPPP 1953–54.

14. News rel., May 7, 1944; statements of Professors Lamb and Baxter, Paul Buck, and Calvert Smith; Edwin Land to JBC, May 3, 1944, Roger Ernst to Calvert Smith, May 12, 1944, "Polaroid Corporation," Box 249.

15. Paul Buck to JBC, Dec. 26, 1944, "Arts and Sciences: Dean of Faculty," Box 255.

16. Claflin to Irwin Stewart, Nov. 17, 1943, Stewart to Claflin, Nov. 25, Jan. 14, 1944, "Treasurer," Box 252; Kane memo to JBC, Dec. 27, 1948, "Special Advisor to the President," Box 354; Roger W. Hickman memo to PB, Jan. 10, 1952, "Arts and Sciences: Faculty of," Box 419.

17. Samuel E. Morison, ed., *The Development of Harvard University* (Cambridge: Harvard Univ. Press, 1930), 608–31; *HAB*, 47 (1944–45), 345.

18. JBC to George W. McClelland, Dec. 9, 1940, "Pe," Box 190.

19. PB to JBC, Jan. 14, 1952, JBC to Metcalf, Jan. 21, JBC to N.Y. Public Library board chairman Morris Hadley, Mar. 1, "Library," Box 433.

20. Max Hall, *Harvard University Press: A History* (Cambridge: Harvard Univ. Press, 1986), ch. 3; JBC to Charles P. Curtis, Jr., Mar. 29, 1934, to Allston Burr, June 4, 1935, "Personnel Report," Box 41; JBC to Francis P. Miller, June 27, 1942, "Wia-Wil," Box 219; "Report"; Hall, *Harvard University Press*, ch. 4.

21. Scaife to JBC, July 9, 1942, "Press, Harvard University," Box 213; Claflin to JBC, July 21, 1942, "Treasurer," Box 217; Malone to JBC, July 17, 1943, JBC to H. James, Dec. 8, 1943, "Press: Harvard University," Box 250; Hall, *Harvard University Press*, ch. 6.

22. "Press: Harvard University" (1946–47), Box 307; JBC to Wilson, Oct. 25, 1951, "Press: Harvard University," Box 440.

23. ALL to Willard Connelly, June 22, 1931, ALL Mss, Folder 339.

24. *HAB*, 39 (1936–37), 961; chart in "Treasurer," Box 195 (1940–41); *HAB*, 36 (1933–34), 317; *CM*, Oct. 21, 1935; "Report to the Overseers' Committee of Administration and Accounts," "Overseers: General," Box 40.

25. *HAB*, 41 (1938–39), 598; *HAB*, 44 (1941–42), 89 ff; *HAB*, 45 (1942–43),

114; A. Calvert Smith memo to JBC, Feb. 16, 1944, "Secretary to the Corporation," Box 251.

26. William H. Claflin to JBC, July 22, 1942, John C. Baker to Claflin, Aug. 12, 1942, "Treasurer," Box 217; Claflin to JBC, July 27, 1944, "Treasurer," Box 267.

27. *HAB*, 49 (1946–47), 217; PB to President and Fellows, Jan. 28, 1953, "Arts and Sciences, Faculty of," Box 449.

28. JBC, *AR* 1951–52; *HAB*, 53 (1950–51), 161.

29. Keith Kane to JBC, Dec. 14, 1950, "Kane, R. Keith," Box 402; Paul Cabot to W. J. Brockelbank, Mar. 17, 1952, "Schu-Sef," Box 469. See also George Putnam, Jr., "Investing Harvard Money," *HAB* 53 (1950–51), 628–34, and "Sound Investing," *HAB* 55 (1952–53), 628–30; Seymour E. Harris, *The Economics of Harvard* (New York: McGraw-Hill, 1970).

30. *HAB*, 36 (1933–34), 898–905; *HAB*, 38 (1935–36), 1149; *HAB*, 39 (1936–37), 52–53; John R. Tunis, "Twenty-Fifth Reunion," *Scribner's Magazine*, 99 (June 1936), 321–326.

31. John Price Jones to JBC, Mar. 5, 1934, "Jon-Jy," Box 11; *HAB*, 54 (1951–52), 622; Memo to Corporation, "Financial Vice-President," Box 180 (1940–41); *CM*, Sept. 24, 1934; JBC, *AR* 1951–52.

32. *CM*, June 19, 1935; JBC "Proposal" and "A Tentative Estimate of the Needs of the University Tercentenary Fund," Box 45 (1933–34); JBC, *MSL*, 120–26; Report of the Committee on Special Research, Apr. 6, 1934, "Three Hundredth Anniversary Fund," Box 19; JBC to Henry James, Sept. 28, 1934, "James, Henry," Box 35; JBC to Frederick P. Keppel, Sept. 24, 1935, "Carnegie Corporation," Box 51.

33. JBC to Corporation, to Grenville Clark, Nov. 18, 1933, "David, Donald K.," Box 5; JBC to Clark, Sept. 28, 1934, "Clark, Grenville," Box 26; JBC to Paul Sachs, Nov. 20, 1935, "Fogg Art Museum," Box 57; *HAB*, 38 (1935–36), 294–300; JBC Memorandum, Feb. 1, 1935, "Harvard Clubs: Miscellaneous," Box 58; "Tercentenary Fund: Alumni Committee-Critical Letters," Box 71.

34. JBC to C. H. Wolfe, Nov. 29, 1935, "Tercentenary Fund: Alumni Comm.," Box 71; Henry James to JBC, June 26, 1936, Grenville Clark to JBC, June 22, 1936, "Terc Fund: Special Gifts Comm," Box 71.

35. JBC to Learned Hand, Sept. 2, 1936, "Alumni Association," Box 47; Jeffrey L. Cruikshank, *A Delicate Experiment: The Harvard Business School, 1908–1945* (Boston: Harvard Business School Press, 1981), 196; JDG to ALL, Jan. 5, 1937, "Lowell, A. Lawrence," Box 88; JBC, *My Several Lives*, 126.

36. "Memorandum," Aug. 25, 1936, "Corporation," Box 53; *HAB*, 39 (1936–37), 32; "Approximate Status of the Tercentenary Fund," Dec. 11, 1936, "Tercentenary Fund: Special Gifts Committee," Box 71; JBC to Hale G. Knight, Feb. 7, 1934, "Rackham Trustees," Box 17; JBC to Harper Woodward, Nov. 5, 1940, "Win-Wy," Box 196; Arthur W. Page to JBC, May 8, 1940, JBC memo to Corporation, May 21, "Corporation," Box 152; JBC to Page, May 1, July 10, 1940, "Page, Arthur W.," Box 163.

37. Annielouise Bliss Warren to JBC, Dec. 1, 1940, to A. Calvert Smith, Dec. 11, "Waa-War," Box 196.

38. MacLeish to JBC, Sept. 6, 1939, "MacLeish, Archibald," Box 159; MacLeish, "The Next Harvard," *AM*, 167 (May 1941), 582 f; JBC to MacLeish, Sept. 7, 1939, "MacLeish, Archibald: The Next Harvard," Box 185; JBC to C. F. Adams, Oct. 30, 1940, "Overseers: General," Box 189.

39. Virginia Proctor memo to JBC, Sept. 27, 1946, "Gen-Gle," Box 300; Lamont to JBC, Jan. 7, 1948, news rel., Feb. 11, 1948, "Lamont, Thomas W.," Box 323.

40. JBC to Rockefeller Foundation, Mar. 21, 1945, Rockefeller Foundation to JBC, May 25, "Rockefeller Foundation," Box 266; grants list, 1947–48, "Rockefeller Foundation," Box 330; JBC to Coolidge, Nov. 10, 1947, Coolidge to JBC, Nov. 21, "Coolidge, Charles A.," Box 318; Coolidge to JBC, Nov. 14, 1947, "XYZ Foundation," Box 333; memo for Paul Hoffman, May 24, 1951, "Ford Foundation," Box 398.

41. James M. Dunning to JBC, Jan. 8, 1951, "Ford Foundation," Box 398; JBC memo to Deans, Apr. 10, 1951, "Deans: Committee on," Box 396; Berry to JBC, July 28, 1952, "Medical School: General," Box 462.

42. JBC memo, Jan. 2, 1946, "Corporation," Box 277; "New Resources of University; Committee on," Box 248; A. Calvert Smith memo to JBC, Dec. 19, 1944, "Conant, James B.—Memorandums—AC Smith," Box 257; Claflin note, Dec. 18, 1946, "Princeton University," Box 307; cf. also Yale Treasurer Laurence G. Tighe to Claflin, Sept. 20, 1947, "XYZ Foundation," Box 333; JBC to T. W. J. Taylor, May 18, 1949, "Str-Sz," Box 354.

43. JBC to Grenville Clark, May 25, 1946, "Clark, Grenville," Box 276; JBC to Alex I. Henderson, Dec. 28, 1946, "Hea-Heo," Box 301; JBC to Keith Kane, June 14, 1947, "Ka-Kel," Box 302; Kane memo to JBC, Nov. 18, 1947, "Col-Con," Box 318.

44. Reports in "New Resources of University: Committee on," JBC to Carl S. Ell, Feb. 16, 1948, "Ni-Ny," Box 327; JBC *AR*/news rel., Jan. 21, 1948; JBC memo to PB, Nov. 29, 1948, "Provost," Box 351.

45. Keith Kane memo to JBC, Oct. 1, 1950, "University Programs: Progress and Perspectives," Box 398; on Korean War, JBC open letter, Apr. 1951, "Fund Council," Box 399; "Progress Report," Nov. 25, 1951, "Assistant to the President," Box 449.

46. JBC to Keith Kane, Sept. 20, 1947, Kane memo to JBC, May 10, 1948, "Special Advisor to President," Box 331; "Assistant to the President," Box 360 (1949–50); Kane to JBC, Apr. 11, 1949, "Overseers: Committee on Resources," Box 350; series of letters to JBC from Kane on functions of his office, in "Special Advisor to the President," Box 354.

47. Kane memo to JBC, Apr. 27, 1949, "Special Advisor to the President," Box 354; Coolidge to Kane, May 19, 1949, "Coolidge, Charles A.," Box 338; JBC to John W. Nason, Dec. 20, 1948, "Str-Sz," Box 354.

48. Dana Doten to JRR, Sept. 29, Oct. 4, 1950, "Assistant to the President," Box 390; JRR to NMP, Nov. 9, 1953, "Asst. to the Pres-: JRR," Box 4, NMPPP. See also "A Perspective on the Growth of American College and University Endowments from 1900 to 1950," "John-Jy," Box 402.

*Chapter 7*

1. *HAB*, 35 (1932–33), 924; 36 (1933–34), 453; JBC to Malcolm M. Willey, Jan. 20, 1936, "All-Am," Box 47; economist quoted in Harvard, *Tercentenary*, 52. See also Stephen Stackpole to George D. Riley, May 16, 1938, "Was-Wek," Box 124; *HAB*, 37 (1934–35), 171.

2. JBC to Kirtley Mather, June 28, 1934, "Summer School," Box 19; JBC, *MSL*, 117; JBC *Diaries*, Jan. 29, 1935; JBC to Alan J. Lowery, May 11, 1934, "Lor-Lz," Box 55; George H. McCaffrey to JBC, Dec. 30, 1935, JBC to McCaffrey, Jan. 11, 1936, "Me," Box 63.

3. Greene to Charles C. Burlingham, June 1, 1935, "Commencement—1935," Box 27; JBC to Elliot C. Cutler, June 10, 1935, Greene to Barrett Wendell, Jr., July 10, "Honorary Degree, Henry Wallace: Comments on," Box 34; *HAB*, 36 (1933–34), 894–97.

4. Everett R. Clinchy to ALL, June 8, 19, 1933, Lowell to Clinchy, June 26, Folder 999, ALL Mss, 1933–34.

5. Harlow Shapley to Henry L. Shattuck, Aug. 1, 1933, Shattuck to Shapley, Aug. 3, JBC to S. P. Duggan, Oct. 30, 1933, Laski to JBC, Oct. 7, 1933, JBC to Laski, Nov. 3, "German Scholars."

6. Clark to JBC, Oct. 26, 1933, JBC to Clark, Nov. 14, "German Scholars."

7. E. Keyse Bolton to JBC, Sept. 8, 1933, JBC to Bolton, Sept. 13, JBC to Clarke, Sept. 22, 1933, Clarke to JBC, Dec. 21, "German Scholars"; Robert E. Kohler, *From Medical Chemistry to Biochemistry* (Cambridge, U.K.: Cambridge Univ. Press, 1982), 270–71.

8. Bessie Z. Jones, "To the Rescue of the Learneds: The Asylum Fellowship Plan at Harvard, 1938–1940," *Harvard Library Bulletin*, 32 (Summer 1984), 205–38; Julian Mack to Roscoe Pound, Sept. 18, 1934, "Maa-Map," Box 37; *Boston Transcript*, Sept. 17, 1934; Charles Beard, "Germany Up to Her Old Tricks," *New Republic*, 80 (Oct. 18, 1934), 299; *HAB*, 37 (1934–35), 65, 84; *HC*, Nov. 23, 1934.

9. JBC to Charles Singer, Apr. 24, June 23, 1936, "Heidelberg University," Box 59; JBC to Hallowell, Mar. 19, 1936, "Haa-Hal," Box 58.

10. Butler to JBC, Apr. 15, 1936, JBC to Butler, Apr. 23, 27, May 12, "Heidelberg University," Box 59.

11. Angell to JBC, Aug. 13, 1936, Birkhoff to JBC, July 1, JBC to Angell, Aug. 17, "Heidelberg University," Box 59; see also *HAB*, 38 (Apr. 10, 1936), 812–18.

12. Dodd to Conant, Mar. 18, 1937, JBC to Dodd, Mar. 23, JBC to JDG, May 28, JDG to JBC, June 1, 1937, "Goettingen University: Comments," 1936–37, Box 83; Clark to JBC, Apr. 26, 1937, WmB-S Mss; *HAB*, 39 (1936–37), 901.

13. JBC to Erich Brandeis, Nov. 26, 1938, "Bov-Bre," Box 128; *CM*, Nov. 28, 1938, May 15, 1939; *HAB*, 41 (1938–39), 320, 331, 357, 363, 578; *HAB*, 42 (1939–40), 60; Hanford to JBC, July 28, 1944, "Dean of Harvard College," Box 258.

14. *CM*, Dec. 1938; on policy, John M. Russell to James M. Landis, Aug. 8, 1940, "Law School: Dean," Box 158; JBC to F. Gowland Hopkins, Jan. 22, 1941,

"Hom-Hr," Box 183; Karl S. Cate to JBC, May 12, 1938, George F. Plimpton to Cate, June 8, "Carn-Ce," Box 104.

15. *HAB*, 38 (1935–36), 123–26.

16. JBC to Edward B. Starbuck, Feb. 12, 1935, "Sn-Sta," Box 44; Thomas Lamont to Charles H. Ingersoll, Apr. 9, 1936, "Lamont, Thomas W.," Box 61.

17. JDG to Hanford, Jan. 9, 1935, Hanford to JDG, Jan. 11, "Dean of Harvard College," Box 28.

18. *CM*, Nov. 13, Dec. 11, 1939; Clark to JBC, Nov. 24, 1939, "Browder, Earl," Box 150; Baldwin to JBC, Nov. 17, 1939, JBC to Baldwin, Nov. 24, "Reed, John, Society," Box 166.

19. *NYT*, Oct. 12, 1940; Patrick O'Dea to JDG, Oct. 13, 1939, Dean Arthur C. Hanford to Greene, Oct. 23, 1939, "Academic Freedom," Box 146.

20. JBC to Arthur W. Page, Apr. 17, 1940, JBC memo to Corporation, Apr. 24, "Russell, Bertrand, Case of," Box 167.

21. John T. Bethell, "Harvard and the Arts of War," *HM* (Sept.-Oct. 1995), 32–48.

22. W. R. T. Metzner to JBC, Jan. 11, 1942, JBC to Metzner, Jan. 20, "Me," Box 209; JBC to Daniel L. Marsh, Oct. 5, 1939, "Arms Embargo," Box 147; JBC to Henry L. Shattuck, Oct. 11, 1940, "Seg-Sha," Box 193.

23. "Harvard Views the War," Class Album, 1941; *HAB*, 42–44 (1939–40 to 1941–42), passim.

24. JBC to Carlton P. Fuller, July 16, 1940, "Conant, J. B.: Personal," Box 152; James G. Hershberg, *James B. Conant* (New York: Knopf, 1993), ch. 7, 177–78; JBC to A. Calvert Smith, Sept. 8, 1940, "Secretary to the President: Smith," Box 193; JBC letter to Governing Boards, c. Aug. 25, 1945, "Deans: Committee on," Box 277; see also "National Defense Research Committee," Box 285; Henry James to JBC, Jan. 6, 1942, "James, Henry," Box 208.

25. Henry L. Shattuck to JBC, Dec. 16, 1943, "Seg-Sha," Box 251; PB to JBC, Aug. 30, 1945, "Governing Boards," Box 279.

26. William McNeill, *Hutchins' University: A Memoir of the University of Chicago* (Chicago: Univ. of Chicago Press, 1991), 102–7; Hershberg, *Conant*, 396; JBC memo to A. Calvert Smith, June 16, 1941, "Do," Box 178; Donald C. McKay to Smith, Aug. 22, 1941, WW II Papers, Box 6; JBC to Stanley King, Sept. 30, 1941, "All-Am," Box 198.

27. PB to NMP, Jan. 5, 1954, "Arts and Sciences: P. H. Buck," Box 3, NMPPP; press rel., Nov. 10, 1951; Len Wright to A. Calvert Smith, Sept. 10, 1945, "Secretary to the Corporation: Smith," Box 290. See also V. R. Cardozier, *Colleges and Universities in World War II* (Westport, Conn.: Praeger, 1993), 186–87.

28. George H. Chase to Bryan Rust, Sept. 28, 1942, "Ros-Rz," Box 215; *HAB*, 45 (1942–43), 39, 81; memo for Overseers, July 12, 1943, "Overseers: General," Box 249.

29. *HAB*, 44 (1941–42), 209; JBC, "Special Report to the President and Fellows of Harvard College," Jan. 5, 1942, DR [Document of Record] No. 38.

30. News rel., Dec. 19, 1941, Box 197; JBC to Claflin, Aug. 5, 1942, "Treasurer," Box 217; History and Literature *AR* 1944–45.

31. Report on discussion, June 26–27, 1943, "Deans' Committee," Box 225; JBC to A. Calvert Smith, Nov. 22, 1943, "Secretary to the Corporation," Box 251.

32. "Confidential Report to the Corporation from the President of the University," Sept. 11, 1944, Box 257; news rel., Sept. 13, 1946, "Statistics," Box 310.

33. *HAB*, 48 (1945–46), 400; DWB to Hollis P. Allen, May 21, 1948, "Bri-Bt," Box 318; Hershberg, *Conant*, 397–98.

34. JBC quoted in Hershberg, *Conant*, 394; Louis G. Smith to JBC, Apr. 8, 1947, "Sl-Sm," Box 310; JBC to David E. Lilienthal, March 29, 1947, "Leo-Lim," Box 303.

35. Roger Baldwin to JBC, Feb. 14, 1948, "Barnes bill," Box 316; address in "Baa-Barm," Box 316; news rel., Jan. 21, 1948, "Annual Report," Box 315; PB to Mason Hammond, May 4, 1949, "Commencement," Box 338.

36. JBC to Seymour Harris, Nov. 6, 1947, "Marshall Plan, Committee on," Box 324; on the Committee on the Present Danger, JBC, *Diaries*, Jan. 2, 1951; DWB to Louise K. Klement, Apr. 14, 1948, Matthiessen to JBC, Apr. 6, "Ch-Ci," Box 318.

37. JBC to Frank B. Jewett, Apr. 6, 1948, "Ja-Jom," Box 323; Hershberg, *Conant*, 391–92, 456.

38. *Life*, May 5, 1941, 89–99; *HAB*, 49 (1946–47), 17; FDR to JBC, Feb. 17, 1944, "Honorary Degree: Winston Churchill," Box 246; MacArthur telegram to JBC, Apr. 17, 1946, "Honorary Degrees: Committee on," Box 280.

39. George C. Marshall to JBC, May 28, 1947, "Commencement 1947," Box 298.

*Chapter 8*

1. *HAB*, 55 (1952–53), 699 ff; Richard N. Smith, *The Harvard Century* (New York: Simon & Schuster, 1986), 197 f.

2. "Pusey, Nathan M.," WmB-S Mss; "Pusey: Letters Supporting Appointment," Box 468, JBCPP 1952–53.

3. "President," Box 468, JBCPP 1952–53; JBC *Diaries*, Jan. 18, 1953; Burton Dreben, Franklin Ford ints.

4. Roger Lee to A. J. Janata, Nov. 18, 1953, "Universities and Colleges," Box 28; Joseph C. Grew to NMP, July 24, 1953, "Pusey: Congratulations," Box 24; Keith Kane to DWB, May 28, 1953, "President," Box 468, JBCPP 1952–53; TSL to NMP, May 27, 1953, "Lamont, Thomas," Box 17.

5. *NYT Magazine*, Sept. 27, 1953, 11 f; *Time*, 63 (Mar. 1, 1954), 58 f; Marbury quoted in Pusey int.

6. WmB-S to Mrs. Deborah Calkins, June 28, 1955, "Eo-Ez," Box 1; NMP int.

7. DWB to NMP, June 4, 1954, "President," Box 23; John D. Rockefeller, Jr., to NMP, Dec. 23, 1953, "Roa-Ror," Box 25.

8. NMP to Gabriel Hauge, Sept. 29, 1953, "Freshman Address (Comments)," Box 14; NMP to Nathan Adler, Dec. 15, 1953, "Divinity Address (Comments) A-E," Box 11; NMP to Andreas F. Lowenfeld, Jan. 14, 1954, "Lor-Lz," Box 17.

9. Elizabeth Stouffer to NMP, June 8, 1971, Sperry to Harold L. Schwab, Mar. 29, 1953, "Memorial Church," Box 19.

10. *HC*, Mar. 26, Apr. 9–11, 18, 23, 1958; WmB-S memo, Apr. 1958, "Memorial Church Controversy," NMP to George H. Williams, Apr. 17, Faculty protest letter, Apr. 24, "Memorial Church," Box 128; news rel., Apr. 23, 1958. See also NMP memo, June 9, 1971, "Memorial Church," Box 19.

11. NMP note, "American Council on Education," Box 87 (1956–57); NMP int.; NMP remarks at Tillich luncheon seminar, Nov. 3, 1993.

12. E. J. Kahn, Jr., *Harvard: Through Change and Through Storm* (New York: Norton, 1969), 274; NMP to Jane Sehmann, Jan. 26, 1960, "To-Ty," Box 191.

13. Kahn, *Harvard*, 278; WmB-S to NMP, May 23, 1963, "Pusey, Nathan M.," WmB-S Mss; NMP int.

14. NMP to Thomas J. Wilson, Jan. 25, 1963, "Press, Harvard University," Box 22; *HAB*, 61 (1958–59), 66 f; NMP int. See also NMP, "A Decade of Harvard University," *School and Society* 93 (Feb. 20, 1965), 115–120.

15. JRR to NMP, Nov. 9, 1953, "Assistant to the President: JRR," Box 4; *HAB*, 61 (1958–59), 415; JRR memo to NMP, Sept. 23, 1953, "Overseers Committee on Resources," Box 21; on Harvard Fund, Osgood Nichols to WmB-S, May 18, 1955, "Ni-Ny," Box 51. See also Roger L. Geiger, *Research and Relevant Knowledge: American Research Universities since World War II* (New York: Oxford Univ. Press, 1993).

16. JRR to Gaylord P. Harnwell, May 2, 1956, "Pa-Ph," Box 80.

17. *HAB*, 64 (1962–63), 59, 68; NMP to H. Rowan Gaither, Mar. 8, 1954, "Ford Foundation," Box 13; NMP draft letter to Milton Katz, n.d., 1961–62, "Ford Foundation," Box 12; DWB memo to NMP, Mar. 12, 1958, "Ford Foundation," Box 121.

18. *HAB*, 62 (1959–60), 459 ff.

19. George Berry to NMP, Sept. 15, Nov. 19, 1955, "Medical School: Dean," Box 77; McGB to DWB, Apr. 8, 1954, "Overseers: General," Box 21; McGB memo to NMP, Sept. 10, 1954, "Arts and Sciences: Dean of," Box 33; TSL to NMP, Nov. 29, 1955, "Lamont, Thomas," Box 74; McGB to NMP, Oct. 11, 1956, "Arts and Sciences: Faculty of," Box 88.

20. Minutes of the University Resources Committee, Jan. 16, 1956, William F. Kurtz to NMP, Feb. 17, "Overseers Committees," Box 80; Lamont to WmB-S, Feb. 4, 1957, "Program for Harvard College," WmB-S Mss; Pusey in *HAB*, 59 (1956–57), 383.

21. McGB to Douglas Dillon, June 25, 1957, "De-Dm," Box 93; McGB to WmB-S, June 3, 1957, "Arts and Sciences: Dean of Faculty," Box 88.

22. "An-Az," 1957–58, Box 113; memo, Oct. 25, 1957, "AA-Barm," Box 114; "Program for Harvard College: General," Box 132.

23. Robert Saudek to NMP, Nov. 11, 1955, "Ford Foundation," Box 70; Laurence Pratt to WmB-S, Jan. 28, 1959, "Program: General," Box 159.

24. NMP to Erwin R. Griswold, Feb. 24, 1959, "Law School: Dean," Box 153; on White, WmB-S to NMP, July 2, 1958, "Assistant to the President: WmB-S," Box 142; NMP int.; news rel., Nov. 24, 1958, "Program: General," Box 159.

25. Harold Vanderbilt to Irving Pratt, Jan. 6, 1960, "V," Box 192.

26.  Report on PHC, "Pr-Py," Box 24 (1964–65); DWB memo, Jan. 14, 1959, "Corporation," Box 146.

27.  TSL memo to NMP and Corporation, Sept. 29, 1958, "Fund Council," Box 150; Roy Larsen to University Resources Committee, Sept. 10, 1962, "Overseers: Committee on Resources," Box 21; *HAB*, 66 (1963–64), 59.

28.  JRR memo to NMP, Sept. 9, 1959, "Assistant to the President: J. R. R.," Box 168; George P. Berry to NMP, July 15, 1963, "Medical School: Dean," Box 20; *NYT*, May 8, 1963, 41; Thomas Cabot to NMP, Feb. 18, 1963, "Overseers: General," Box 21.

29.  "Summary of Gifts 1954–1965" and "Five Year Summary," "Statistics," Box 27; Kahn, *Harvard*, 327; William Pinkerton to Paul Cabot, etc., Oct. 13, to JRR, Oct. 27, 1964, "To-Ty," Box 28.

30.  *HAB*, 64 (1962–63), 59, 68; Griswold to Paul Cabot, July 8, 1964, "Law School: Dean," Box 18; "Assistants to the President," NMPPP 1969–70, Box 3.

31.  *HAB*, 69 (Feb. 11, 1967), 11; NMP *AR*, 1965–66.

32.  *HAB*, 70 (Nov. 25, 1967), 8.

33.  *HAB*, 67 (1964–65), 575; *HAB*, 59 (1956–57), 107; Paul Cabot, "Chasing the Budget: My Twelve Years as Treasurer," *HAB*, 65 (1962–63), 634 f; *HAB*, 52 (1959–60), 107.

34.  Coolidge to NMP, Aug. 13, 1953, "Coo-Coz," Box 9; WmB-S to Boyd N. Everett, Dec. 18, 1957, "Eo-Ez," Box 120.

35.  *HAB*, 57 (1954–55), 160–63, 66 (1963–64), 155; McGB to Edward Reynolds, May 21, 1958, "Arts and Sciences: Dean of," Box 113.

36.  Paul Cabot to Sherwin C. Badger, Feb. 15, 1957, "Criticisms and Suggestions," Box 92; Cabot, "Should Harvard Borrow? The Treasurer Thinks No," Cooper, "On the Other Hand," *HAB*, 63 (1960–61), 65–67; Bundy memo to NMP, June 28, 1957, "Houses," Box 98.

37.  *HAB*, 69 (Oct. 29, 1966), 15; *HAB*, 67 (1964–65), 107.

38.  Corporation meeting notes, Mar. 15, 1954, "Dr. Cohn's Patents," Box 22; Edward R. Reynolds to Charles Coolidge, May 18, 1954, "Administrative Vice President," Box 2.

39.  NMP to Council of Deans, Sept. 28, 1965, "Deans: Committee of," Box 10; Harvey Brooks to FF, Oct. 6, 1965, FF to NMP, Nov. 4, "Patents," Box 24; Harvey Brooks to NMP, April 15, 1971, NMP memo to Daniel Steiner, Apr. 23, "Pa," Box 20.

40.  L. Gard Wiggins, "Outside Support of University Research," "Medical School: Committee on Research and Development," 1955–56, Box 77.

41.  William Pinkerton to McGB, Nov. 23, 1953, "Contracts," Box 9; NMP notes, "Research Contracts," Box 24, NMPPP 1960–61; "Comparison with Other Universities of the Relationship of US Government-Sponsored Research to Total Income 1958–59," "Contracts," Box 172.

42.  Edward Reynolds to NMP, Nov. 13, 1956, "Carnegie Foundation," Box 91.

43.  *HAB*, 65 (1962–63), 543; Office of Governmental Relations to Council of Deans, Apr. 8, 1965, "I," Box 17; NMP to Department Chairs, etc., "Ea-Ek," Box 11; memo to Department Chairs, etc., June 28, 1966, "Cost-Sharing," Box 9.

44.  George W. Mackey to FF, Apr. 8, 1966, Brooks to NMP, Apr. 18, "Cost-Sharing," Box 9; Charles P. Whitlock memo to NMP, Sept. 22, 1966, Dec. 6, "Ea-Ek," Box 11.

*Chapter 9*

1.  William H. Bond, "William Bentinck-Smith," *Proceedings of the Massachusetts Historical Society* 105 (1993), 165–68.

2.  JBC to Edmund E. Day, May 3, 1945, "Coo-Coz," Box 257, JBCPP; Roger Lee to NMP, July 8, 1953, "President," Box 23; NMP int.; Kai Bird, *The Color of Truth: McGeorge Bundy and William Bundy: Brothers in Arms* (New York: Simon & Schuster, 1998), ch. 7.

3.  On Burr, NMP int.; WLM to NMP, Nov. 3, 1959, "Marbury, William L.," Box 181; WLM to NMP, Aug. 7, 1964, "Marbury, William L.," Box 18.

4.  TSL memo to NMP and Francis H. Burr, Mar. 24, 1964, "Treasurer," Box 28.

5.  On Nickerson, NMP int.; "Corporation: New Member," 1967–68, Box 11; McNamara to NMP, Apr. 19, 1968, Gardner to NMP, May 13, news rel., May 14, 1968, "Corporation," Box 11.

6.  WLM to NMP, Apr. 19, 1962, "Mar," Box 19; TSL memorandum, Sept. 13, 1966, "Lamont, Thomas S., Box 18; NMP notes on "The Kane-Lamont Memos," "Corporation," (1966–67), Box 9; Burr to NMP, Nov. 4, 1966, "Bu-By," Box 6.

7.  NMP memo, May 11, 1954, "Corporation," Box 9; "Corporation," Box 9 (1964–65).

8.  DWB to Frank Keppel, Jan. 16, 1956, "Education, School of," Box 69.

9.  McGB to NMP, Sept. 8, 1953, "Arts and Sciences: Dean of Faculty," Box 4; *HAB*, 66 (1963–64), 343; Lamont to George P. Baker, May 13, 1964, Baker to Lamont, May 13, "Lamont, Thomas S.," Box 18.

10.  "General Summary of Officers," "Pr-Py," Box 52; Virginia Proctor to NMP, June 1, 1955, "Massachusetts," Box 48; "Proposal for the Redistribution of Office Space in Massachusetts Hall," May 27, 1965, "Buildings," Box 6.

11.  O. M. Shaw to NMP, Sept. 30, 1966, "Ropes & Gray," Box 24; NMP to President and Fellows, June 24, 1958, "Appointments, Administrative and Miscellaneous," Box 142.

12.  Harvey Brooks to FF, Dec. 21, 1966, "Arts and Sciences: Dean of Faculty," Box 4.

13.  News rel., Jan. 23, 1962, "Holyoke Center," Box 16; John W. Teele to L. Gard Wiggins, July 20, 1961, "Personnel Office," Box 24; *HAB*, 66 (1963–64), 156–57.

14.  "Report of Committee to Review the Department of Hygiene," Jan. 20, 1954, "Department of Hygiene," Box 16; Charles A. Coolidge to NMP, Sept. 21, 1955, "Coolidge, Charles A.," Box 66; Ebert memo to NMP, June 16, 1970,

"Medical School: Dean," Box 22. See Michael J. Gross and Jeffrey L. Cruikshank, *A Laboratory for Change* (Cambridge: Harvard Univ. Press, 1998).

15.   Bundy to NMP, May 2, 1955, "Library," Box 47, McGB to NMP, Sept. 7, 1954, "Arts and Sciences: Dean of," Box 33; Howard M. Jones to Charles A. Coolidge, Jan. 28, 1954, "Library Committee," Box 17; notes, May 17, 1951, "Library," Box 403, JBCPP; McGB to NMP, May 2, 1955, Sept 27, 1954, NMP notes, Sept. 8, "Library," Box 47; NMP to DWB, Apr. 3, 1964, "University Professors," Box 30.

16.   PB cover letter to 1961–62 report, "Library," Box 17, NMPPP 1962–63; NMP notes, "Library," Box 19, JBCPP 1965–66; *HAB*, 70 (Mar. 30, 1968), 17 ff.

17.   Max Hall, *Harvard University Press: A History* (Cambridge: Harvard Univ. Press, 1986), 125 f.

18.   Francis Crick to NMP, Apr. 13, 1967, WmB-S memo to NMP, Apr. 18, NMP notes, May 17, Shaw to NMP, May 12, NMP to Thomas J. Wilson, May 23, "Press, Harvard University," Box 23; Hall, *Harvard University Press*, 165–68.

19.   William M. Pinkerton memo, 1953–54, "News Office," Box 21; TSL to NMP, Mar. 29, 1956, "Lamont, Thomas," Box 74.

20.   Francis H. Burr to NMP, Sept. 22, 1964, "Bu-By," Box 6; *HAB*, 67 (1964–65), 155; Douglas Lawson to NMP, Dec. 8, 1962, "Classes," Box 7.

21.   NMP to DWB, Apr. 3, 1964, "University Professors," Box 30; McGB to NMP, Nov. 6, 1956, "Honorary Degrees," Box 97; Faulkner to JBC, Mar. 20, 1952, "Honorary Degrees," Box 431, JBCPP; Purcell to NMP, Feb. 12, 1956, "Honorary Degrees," Box 73.

22.   Keith Kane memo, Nov. 6, 1963, Charles Coolidge memo, "Honorary Degrees," Box 16.

23.   Galbraith to NMP, Nov. 23, 1959, NMP to Galbraith, Nov. 25, "Honorary Degrees," Box 177; on Stevenson, Charles A. Coolidge to Neil McElroy, Oct. 25, 1963, "Honorary Degrees," Box 16.

24.   *HAB*, 53 (1950–51), 68.

25.   Denison B. Hull to JBC, Apr. 16, 1951, "Hu-Hy," Box 401, JBCPP; WmB-S memo to NMP, May 23, 1963, "Pusey, Nathan M.," WmB-S Mss.

26.   NMP to Alfred Carpenter, March 28, 1961, "Carn-Ce," Box 200; *HAB*, 65 (1962–63), 383; on William James, "Behavioral Sciences Center," 1961–62, Box 4; NMP to Harry Levin, June 28, 1961, "Baa-Barm," Box 197; "Buildings," WmB-S Mss; *HAB*, 60 (1957–58), 251; WmB-S memo to NMP, Apr. 16, 1964, "Science Center," Box 27; Harvey Brooks to FF, Apr. 10, 1968, "Administrative Vice President," Box 3. See also Robert Campbell, "In Praise of Redness," *HM*, 89 (Sept.-Oct. 1986), 107–14; *Building Harvard: Architecture of Three Centuries* (Harvard University Information Center, 1975); Bainbridge Bunting, *Harvard: An Architectural History* (Cambridge: Harvard Univ. Press, 1985).

27.   *HAB*, 59 (1956–57), 390; NMP to Salvatore Costa, Dec. 5, 1956, "Coo-Coz," Box 92; DWB to John W. Teele, Mar. 30, 1959, "Me," Box 154; Ott Shaw to Edward Reynolds, July 18, 1957, "Memorial Hall," Box 129.

28.   Arthur M. Schlesinger, Jr., to NMP, May 18, 1955, "Shady Hill," Box 54.

29.   *HAB*, 63 (1960–61), 463; Ott Shaw memo, Aug. 28, 1962, L. Gard Wiggins memos, Aug. 14, 1962, Mar. 22, 1963, "Real Estate," Box 24.

30.   On Vellucci, Charles P. Whitlock memo to NMP, Jan. 26, 1965,

"Cambridge," Box 7; NMP to Mrs. William H. Wainwright, Nov. 21, 1955, "Wa-Wd," Box 85; James Killian to NMP, Nov. 22, 1955, "Massachusetts Institute of Technology," Box 75; Whitlock to NMP, Mar. 25, 1960, "Cambridge: Citizens Advisory Committee," Box 170; on roads, NMP to Harry Della Russo, Feb. 6, 1964, "Massachusetts: Commonwealth of," Box 19.

31. Whitlock memo to NMP, June 29, 1961, "Hom-Hr," Box 15, to NMP, Oct. 6, 1960, "Assistant to the President: C. P. W.," Box 197, to NMP, Oct. 11, 1963, Apr. 10, 1964, "Cambridge, City of," Box 8.

32. Ellen Schrecker, *No Ivory Tower: McCarthyism and the Universities* (New York: Oxford Univ. Press, 1986); Sigmund Diamond, *Compromised Campus: The Collaboration of Universities with the Intelligence Community, 1945–1955* (New York: Oxford Univ. Press, 1992); on Chafee and Sutherland, see Schrecker, *No Ivory Tower*, 183–86.

33. Marbury statement for Corporation, Mar. 23, 1953, TSL memo to DWB, Mar. 5, "Congressional Investigation: Furry," Box 453, JBCPP; WLM, "Harvard and the Cold War, 1948–1960," WLM Mss, Box 2, Harvard Archives; Schrecker, *No Ivory Tower*, ch. vii.

34. DWB memos to NMP, Dec. 2, 28, 1954, McGB memo to NMP, Oct. 11, 1954, "Communism," Box 37; NMP memo to Board of Overseers, July 1, 1962, "Col-Con," Box 8.

35. NMP to Howard S. Bunn, Nov. 16, 1953, "Bu-By," Box 5; NMP to Mrs. Eugene Meyer, Nov. 12, 1953, "Meyer, (Mrs.) Eugene," Box 19.

36. On McCarthy, news rel., Nov. 9, 1953, "Congressional Investigations," Box 8; NMP to Griswold, Mar. 16, 1954, "Law School: Dean," Box 17; Richard N. Smith, *The Harvard Century* (New York: Simon & Schuster, 1986), 206–8.

37. NMP notes, June 10, 1955, "Bea-Beq," Box 34; NMP to McGB, May 16, 1955, "Sn-Sta," Box 55; Parsons memo to Faculty Committee, May 23, 1955, Corporation vote, June 6, 1955, "Communism," Box 37; McGB to NMP, June 21, 1956, "Arts and Sciences: Faculty of," Box 60; exchanges among Diamond, Bellah, Bundy, and others in *New York Review of Books*, Apr. 28, May 26, June 9, July 14, 1977; Diamond, *Compromised Campus*, ch. 2; McGB to NMP, Sept. 21, 1953, "Lor-Laz," Box 17.

38. Charles Wyzanski to Barry Wood, Jan. 12, 1954, "Overseers Committees," Box 21; NMP notes, Oct. 29, 1953, "Fox, John," Box 14.

39. DWB memo to NMP, Sept. 30, 1957, "Overseers: General," Box 131; "Veritas Foundation," Box 28, NMPPP 1960–61.

40. "Legislative Bills," Box 47, NMPPP 1954–55; WmB-S memo to NMP, Feb. 2, 1956, "Legislative Bills," Box 75; McGB to NMP, Oct. 3, 1955, "James Lectures," Box 74, "Fund Council," Box 70, NMPPP 1955–56.

41. FF memo, Apr. 24, 1963, William Preston to FF, Apr. 30, DWB to FF, May 17, "Russian (and Satellite) Scholars," Box 25.

42. "National Defense Education Act," Box 157, JBCPP 1958–59; NMP to JFK, Sept. 28, 1959, "United States Government," Box 191; NMP to L. G. Derthick, Nov. 12, 1959, "United States Government: Health, Education, and Welfare," Box 192.

43. JFK to NMP, Oct. 26, 1959, Richard M. Nixon to NMP, Feb. 27, 1960,

"National Defense Education Act: June to January," Box 185; Charles P. Whitlock memo, Oct. 16, 1962, "National Defense Education Act," Box 20.

44. DWB to NMP, Apr. 25, 1962, "AA-Alk," Box 1; on Riesman, WmB-S to NMP, Sept. 15, 1964, "Ste-Sto," Box 26; WmB-S memo ("very confidential") to NMP, May 11, 1961, "Cuba," Box 9.

45. *HC*, May 4, 1961; "Schu-Sef," Box 25; NMP to TSL, June 9, 1962, "Lamont, Thomas S.," Box 18.

46. NMP notes, "Library," Box 75, NMPPP 1955–56; Metcalf-Fischer correspondence, Ruth Fischer Papers, Houghton Library, vol. 582.

47. DWB memo to NMP, May 4, 1956, "Ch-Cn," Box 64.

48. NMP to Corporation, Mar. 21, 1960, "Appointments," Box 168; "The Impact of Federal Programs on Harvard University," July 1961, "Government-University Relations Text," Box 13; NMP to Carl Elliott, July 13, 1964, "United States Government: General," Box 29.

49. WmB-S memo to NMP, Dec. 20, 1957, "Military Science and Tactics," Box 129; Bundy to Hugh M. Milton II, Aug. 11, 1955, "Military Science and Tactics," Box 78.

50. Cushing to NMP, May 25, 1956, NMP to Cushing, May 29, "Cr-Cz," Box 66; WmB-S to Horace M. Gray, Apr. 26, 1962, "Gra-Gri," Box 14.

51. List, "AA-Alk," Box 1, NMPPP 1962–63; John K. Galbraith to NMP, Feb. 9, 1961, "Absence, Leave of," Box 194; cartoons, *HAB*, 63 (1960–61), cover, 385; JFK int. with WHRB reporter, "Overseers: General," Box 22; Arthur M. Schlesinger, Jr., to WmB-S, June 23, 1961, WmB-S to Schlesinger, June 27, "United States Government: General," Box 27.

52. Bundy to NMP, Feb. 4, 1961, "Public Administration," Box 23; Bundy to NMP, May 31, 1963, "Overseers: General," Box 21; JFK to DWB, Nov. 29, 1960, "Overseers; General," Box 22; JFK to NMP, Mar. 7, 1963, "Overseers: General," Box 21.

*Chapter 10*

1. HAB, 57 (1954–55), 343; *HAB*, 59 (1956–57), 669; WmB-S memo to NMP, Dec. 16, 1954, "Arts and Sciences: Faculty of," Box 33; McGB to TSL, Dec. 12, 1957, "Lamont, Thomas S.," Box 124. See memo on growth of faculty and intellectual resources, 1931–56, DWB to NMP, June 7, 1956, "Statistics," Box 83.

2. McGB to NMP, Sept. 14, 1954, "Arts and Sciences: Dean of," Box 33.

3. *HAB*, 34 (1953), 58; "Endowed Professorships," Box 149; *HAB*, 66 (1963–64), 343; DWB memo to NMP, Nov. 10, 1959, "Pi-Po," Box 188; *HAB*, 68 (1965–66), 155; Barton Leach to NMP, Apr. 6, 1955, NMP to Leach, Apr. 27, "Law School: General," Box 47.

4. PB rec., Feb. 25, 1948, "Radcliffe College," Box 329; *HAB*, 62 (1959–60), 69.

5. DWB to Ott Shaw, Jan. 23, 1964, to NMP, May 22, 1964, "University Professors," Box 30; *HB*, 73 (Dec. 7, 1970), 16; "Report of the Committee on Appointments, Promotions, and Retirements," Mar. 14, 1956, 11.

6. Seymour Harris to NMP, Oct. 21, 1954, "Arts and Sciences; Faculty of,"

Box 33; FAS, *Report of the Committee on Compensation*, Feb. 10, 1956; Bundy to NMP, Nov. 23, 1960, "Arts and Sciences: Dean of Faculty," Box 197.

7.  McGB to NMP, Dec. 27, 1954, "Retirements," Box 53; DWB memo to NMP, Apr. 22, 1965, "Retirements," Box 25; McGB to NMP, Feb. 3, 1960, "Retirements," Box 190.

8.  L. Gard Wiggins memo to NMP, Jan. 2, 1962, "Pensions: General," Box 23.

9.  DWB memo to NMP, Feb. 3, 1959, "Absence, Leaves of: General," Box 139.

10.  DWB memo to NMP, Jan. 20, 1958, "Bea-Beq," Box 114; McGB to DWB, Apr. 25, 1960, McGB to NMP, Feb. 12, 1959, "Absence, Leave of," Box 165; McGB to NMP, Mar. 16, 1959, "Arts and Sciences: Dean of Faculty," Box 142.

11.  Spencer Klaw, "The Affluent Professors," *Reporter*, June 23, 1960, 16 ff; McGB letter, *Reporter*, Sept. 1, 1960, 12.

12.  DWB memo to NMP, Nov. 14, 1961, "Salaries," Box 26; Charles Coolidge to NMP, Jan. 22, 1962, Lamont to Coolidge, Nov. 22, 1961, "Col-Con," Box 8; WmB-S to NMP, Feb. 5, 13, 1958, "Corporation," Box 118; FF to NMP, Apr. 14, 1965, NMP to Ott Shaw, Apr. 2, "Conflicts of Interest," Box 9.

13.  McGB to Edward Reynolds, May 10, 1960, "Arts and Sciences: Faculty of," Box 168; NMP to Treasurer and Fellows, May 23, 1961; NMP to Corporation, May 28, 1961, "Arts and Sciences: Faculty of," Box 197.

14.  Arthur D. Trottenberg to NMP, Sept. 6, 1961, FF to NMP, May 14, 1962, NMP to Corporation, May 21, "Arts and Sciences: Dean of Faculty," Box 197.

15.  FF to NMP, Sept. 20, 1965, "Arts and Sciences: Dean of Faculty," Box 44; FF to Marbury, July 7, 1965, "Marbury, William L.," Box 10; FF to NMP, Feb. 23, 1966, WmB-S memo to NMP, Dec. 14, 1965, "To-Ty," Box 10.

16.  NMP to JTD, Apr. 6, 1967, "Col-Con," Box 8; *HAB*, 70 (June 8, 1969), 6–7; FAS, *Report of the Committee on Recruitment and Retention of Faculty*, May 1, 1968.

17.  FF to TSL, Sept. 2, 1964, TSL to FF, Jan. 27, to NMP, Jan. 28, 1965, NMP to TSL, Feb. 4, "Lamont, Thomas S.," Box 17.

18.  Arthur Schlesinger, Jr., int.; FF to Galbraith, Feb. 2, 1966, Galbraith to FF, Feb. 8, FF to Galbraith, Feb. 9, "Gli-Go," Box 15; FF to Galbraith, Apr. 24, 1967, "Ea-Ek," Box 11.

19.  *The Behavioral Sciences at Harvard* (June 1954); *HAB*, 59 (1956–57), 394 f; George P. Berry to NMP, Mar. 25, 1955, McGB to NMP, Apr. 6, "Bea-Beq," Box 34; McGB to Edward Reynolds, Apr. 14, 1960, "Cognitive Studies Center," Box 171; Psychology AR 1961–62.

20.  McGB rec. of Wylie, Feb. 27, 1959, "Social Relations," Box 161; Boring to McGB, May 19, 1955, NMP to McGB, June 3, NMP notes, "Ad hoc: Social Relations," Box 31; Vogt ad hoc, "Ad hoc: Social Relations," Box 2; McGB rec., Sept. 16, 1959, "Social Relations," Box 191.

21.  Social Relations *AR*, 1966–67, 1960–61, 1967–68, 1969–70.

22.  George C. Homans to JTD, May 28, 1971, JTD to NMP, Dec. 29, 1970, NMP to JTD, Dec. 30, "Arts and Sciences: Dean of Faculty," Box 2.

23.  Psychology *AR* 1965–66; NMP notes, Feb. 23, 1961, "Psychology," Box 23; NMP notes, Feb. 23, 1961, Edwin G. Boring to NMP, Apr. 19, 1962, S. S.

Stevens to NMP, May 14, McClelland to NMP, June 4, "Psychology," Box 23; *HAB*, 66 (1963–64), 163 f.

24. NMP note, Oct. 17, 1962, Boring to NMP, Oct. 24, NMP memo, Oct. 26, Boring to NMP, Dec. 15, NMP to Boring, Dec. 16 (?), "Psychology," Box 23.

25. Anthropology *AR* 1963–64, 1966–67.

26. Francis Boyer to NMP, Mar. 22, 1960, "Overseers: General," Box 187; NMP to file, Mar. 22, 1966, Hugh Hencken to NMP, Mar. 29, "Peabody Museum," Box 24; NMP notes, Apr. 14, 1967, memo for file, Apr. 17, notes, Apr. 20, "Peabody Museum," Box 22; William R. Bullard, Jr., to NMP, Aug. 31, 1967, NMP notes, Sept. 13, Oct. 4, 17, 20, "Peabody Museum," Box 27.

27. Watson Smith to NMP, Dec. 17, 1967, Sargent Kennedy memo to NMP, Apr. 16, 1969, Ad hoc Committee report in Minutes of 116th Meeting of Faculty, "Peabody Museum," Box 27; Charles Y. Wadsworth to Ott Shaw, Apr. 15, 1969, "Roa-Ror," Box 17; Williams to Ernst Mayr, May 7, 1969, "Pe," Box 15.

28. G. Harold Duling to NMP, Nov. 22, 1954, McGB to NMP, Dec. 6, "Leo-Lim," Box 47; Social Relations *AR* 1954–55.

29. McGB to NMP, Apr. 1, 1960, "A&S: Dean of Faculty," Box 168.

30. McGB rec., Nov. 5, 1959, "Social Relations," Box 191; Leary to Robert F. Bales, Nov. 28, 1962, WmB-S to NMP, Feb. 1963, "Social Relations: General," Box 25; *Time*, Mar. 29, 1973, 72 f; *CM*, May 6, 1963; Leary to NMP, c. Apr. 15, 1966, "Law-Len," Box 19; *HAB*, 65 (1962–63), 304–05, 71 (Oct. 21, 1968), 16 f.

31. McGB to Pusey, Oct. 22, 1953, "Economics," Box 12; Arthur Smithies to McGB, Oct. 26, 1953, NMP to McGB, Dec. 17, "Ad hoc: Economics," Box 1; McGB rec. of Kaysen, Dec. 23, 1953, "Economics: Budget 1955–56," Box 12.

32. DWB memo to NMP, Jan. 6, 1958, "Overseers: General," Box 131; McGB rec. of Galbraith, Dec. 31, 1958, "Economics: Budget 1959–60," Box 148.

33. McGB rec. of Kuznets, Dec. 4, 1959, rec. of Otto Eckstein and Henry Houthakker, Mar. 2, 1960, "Economics," Box 174; Economics *AR* 1964, 1965–66, 1967–68, 1968–69.

34. McGB to NMP, Apr. 16, 1959, "Economics: Budget 1959–60," Box 148; Department statement, "Economics: Budget," Box 10; David Rockefeller to NMP, June 24, 1966, "Overseers: Committees," Box 23; Summary, 1968–69, "Overseers: Committees," Box 15.

35. PB rec., June 22, 1953, "History," Box 15; on Ford, NMP to McGB, June 7, 1955, "Ad hoc: History," Box 30; on Bailyn and Pipes, McGB recs., Feb. 27, 1958, "History," Box 123.

36. Bernard Bailyn int.; Oscar Handlin to David Owen, Nov. 4, 1954, to McGB, Dec. 11, "History," Box 30.

37. McGB to NMP, Apr. 29, 1958, "Carn-Ce," Box 116; Proposal, Feb. 24, 1965, "Him-Hol," Box 15; History *AR* 1965–66.

38. FF rec. of Landes, Apr. 14, 1964, "History: Budget," Box 16; on Bouwsma, Bailyn to JTD, Feb. 25, 1971, to NMP, Apr. 8, "Him-Hol," Box 14.

39. Henry Friendly to Donald Fleming, May 11, 1967, "Overseers: Committees," Box 22; History *AR* 1967–68 f.

40. Samuel Huntington, "The Changing Culture of Harvard," *HB*, 72 (Sept. 15, 1969), 51.

41. Government *AR* 1958–59; McGB rec. of Kissinger, Mar. 30, 1959, "Government: Budget 1959–60," Box 151.

42. William Y. Elliott to NMP, Nov. 20, 1962, "Retirements," Box 24.

43. James Q. Wilson and Stanley Hoffman ints.; Government *AR* 1967–68, 1966–67; Government *AR* 1965–66; FF rec. of Deutsch, Sept. 27, 1966, "Government," Box 15; rec. of Shklar, Feb. 25, 1963, "Government: Budget," Box 13; Judith N. Shklar, "A Life of Learning," American Council of Learned Societies occasional paper, (no. 9), 125–26.

44. McGB to NMP, Nov. 16, 1959, "Arts and Sciences: Dean of Faculty," Box 168; DWB memo to NMP, May 10, 1962, "Overseers: General," Box 22.

45. Joseph Alsop to F.A.O. Schwarz, Jan. 1961, NMP to Schwarz, Jan. 27, Fairbank to NMP, Feb. 3, Merle Fainsod to Joseph Alsop, Feb. 16, "Far Eastern Languages," Box 11.

46. News rel., Mar. 4, 1959; Dorothy W. Bernstein to NMP, Mar. 13, 1959, "Urban Studies, Joint Center for," Box 163; NMP note, June 23, 1965, James Q. Wilson to NMP, July 23, 1965, "Urban Studies, Joint Center for," Boxes 28–29.

47. McGB to NMP, May 19, 1960, "Arts and Sciences: Dean of Faculty," Box 168; proposal, Apr. 1960, "International Studies," Box 178; NMP to Deans, Sept. 27, 1960, "Deans, Committee of," Box 9; McGB to NMP, Oct. 4, 1960, "Arts and Sciences: Dean of Faculty," Box 197; FF to NMP, Sept. 9, 1964, "Ford Foundation," Box 13.

48. CFIA *AR* 1967–68; Edward S. Mason to NMP, Nov. 30, 1961, Don Price to NMP, Jan. 15, Feb. 16, 1962, NMP memo, Jan. 29, NMP to Robert R. Bowie, Feb. 26, "International Affairs, Center for," Box 17.

49. Edwin C. Kemble to NMP, Dec. 13, 1961, Bruner to Kemble, Feb. 14, "Gen-Gle," Box 13.

50. DWB memo to NMP, Mar. 4, 1954, "Higgins Trust," Box 15; McGB to Paul Cabot, Oct. 5, 1954, "Higgins Trust," Box 44; NMP to Grayson Kirk, Sept. 25, 1957, "Higgins Trust," Box 123; DWB memo to NMP, Jan. 21, 1965, "Higgins Fund," Box 16.

51. FF to NMP, Mar. 29, 1967, "Maa-Map," Box 19; FF to NMP, Oct. 26, 1966, "Arts and Sciences: Dean of Faculty," Box 4; Alfred S. Romer to Carroll Williams, Mar. 20, 1961, McGB to NMP, Oct. 5, 1960, "National," Box 20; NMP to Sargent Kennedy, Nov. 4, 1965, "Natl. Science Foundation," Box 21.

52. FF to NMP, Feb. 3, 1966, "Arts and Sciences: Dean of Faculty," Box 4; William L. Marbury to NMP, May 27, 1964, "Corporation," Box 9; FF to NMP, Aug. 26, 1964, "Schu-Sef," Box 26.

53. DWB to NMP, Oct. 6, 1960, "Overseers: Committees," Box 21; Chemistry *AR* 1959–60, 1963–64; Frank Westheimer, "Chemistry at Harvard," Nov. 1, 1995 (authors' possession); Jeremy Knowles int.

54. William N. Lipscomb to FF, May 5, 1964, "Arts and Sciences: Faculty of," Box 5; Chemistry *AR* 1959–60; McGB rec. of Corey, June 1, 1959, "Chemistry," Box 145.

55. Chemistry *AR* 1961–62, 1962–63, 1955–56, 1963–64, 1970–71; Westheimer, "Chemistry."

56. Paul Martin, Gerald Holton ints.; Katherine Sopka, "Physics at Harvard

During the Past Half-Century: A Brief Departmental History" (1978) (ms. in possession of Gerald Holton); NMP to McGB, May 18, 1956, "Ad hoc: Physics," Box 59; rec. of Gell-Mann, Feb. 13, 1964, "Physics: Budget," Box 24; NMP to McGB, Apr. 14, 1955, "Ad hoc: Physics," Box 30.

57. FF to NMP, Mar. 24, 1964, "Cambridge Electron Accelerator," Box 8; Francis Pipkin int., Sopka File.

58. NMP to Edward S. Mason, Apr. 30, 1969, "Pf-Ph," Box 15; Pipkin int., Sopka File; Informal *VC* Report, May 4, 1970, "Physics," FASGF, Box 6. See also Peter Galison and Bruce Hevly, eds., *Big Science: The Growth of Large-Scale Research* (Stanford, Calif.: Stanford Univ. Press, 1992).

59. Informal Report of Visiting Committee, May 4, 1970, "Overseers: Committee," Box 10; Physics *AR* 1969–70; Paul Martin int., Sopka File.

60. NMP to McGB, Mar. 21, 1955, "Ad hoc: MCZ," Box 30; McGB to Alfred S. Romer, Dec. 19, 1955, "MCZ," Box 78; NMP to McGB, Mar. 12, 1956, "MCZ," Box 58.

61. JBC to McGB, Dec. 31, 1958, "MCZ," Box 156; Ernst Mayr, "The Museum of Comparative Zoology and Its Role in the Harvard Community," Apr. 1969.

62. McGB rec. of E. O. Wilson, Apr. 30, 1958, rec. of James D. Watson, May 14, "Biology: Budget," Box 114. See also E. O. Wilson, *Naturalist* (Washington, D.C.: Island Press/Shearwater Books, 1994).

63. Wilson, *Naturalist*, 219, 222–29.

64. McGB rec. of Watson, Dec. 28, 1960, "Biology," Box 198; McGB rec. of Meselson, May 11, 1960, "Biology Budget," Box 169; FF recs. of Meselson and Wilson, Feb. 27, 1964, "Biology," Box 6.

65. Alfred Romer to NMP, Sept. 17, 1968, Carroll Williams to NMP, Sept. 29, "Ber-Bj," Box 4; Mayr to NMP, May 22, 1968, "MCZ," Box 25; Keith R. Porter to NMP, June 23, 1967, "Biology," Box 5.

66. Biochemistry *AR* 1962–63; Biology *AR* 1966–67.

67. FF to NMP, Nov. 13, 1964, Paul Doty to FF, Nov. 5, 1965, FF memo to NMP, Nov. 5, "Arts & Sciences: Dean of Faculty," Box 4.

68. Biology *VC*, Oct. 14, 1968, "Overseers: Committee," Box 25; Biology *AR* 1967–68, 1970–71.

69. DAS *AR* 1956–57; Thomas D. Cabot to Harold Hazen, Oct. 15, 1954, "Applied Sciences: General," Box 33.

70. W. F. Ryan to NMP, Sept. 5, 1956, "Engineering and Applied Physics," Box 94; Bundy to NMP, Nov. 1, 1954, Karl Terzaghi to NMP, May 31, 1955, NMP note to DWB, Dec. 1954, "Applied Sciences: General," Box 33; Thomas Cabot to NMP, Jan. 5, 1955, "Engineering and Applied Physics," Box 94.

71. Harvey Brooks, "From Crystals to Computers," *HAB*, 64 (1961–62), 637–42; DEAP *AR* 1953–54; *HAB*, 59 (1956–57), 543; Anthony Oettinger, "The Status of Plans for the Harvard Computing Center," Feb. 28, 1961, "Computation Laboratory," Box 201; news rel., Aug. 4, 1954, "Col-Con," Box 37; Ford to NMP, Oct. 19, 1965, NMP to L. Gard Wiggins, Dec. 1, Arthur Trottenberg to Ford, Jan. 31, 1966, "Computing Center," Box 9.

72. Harvey Brooks to NMP, Dec. 12, 20, 1968, "El-En," Box 9; George P. Baker to NMP, Mar. 20, 1969, "Computing Center," Box 7; "Computing at

Harvard: A Report of the Ad Hoc Committee on Computing Services," Jan. 1970, "Computing Services, Committee on," Box 10; *VC* Report, Mar. 26, 1970, "Overseers: Committee," Box 25.

73. Oscar Zariski to Schlomo Sternberg, Jan. 7, 1959 (authors' possession).

74. Mathematics *VC*, May 7, 1958, "Overseers: Committees," Box 131; Mathematics *AR* 1961–62; McGB rec. of Bott, Mar. 5, 1959, "Mas-Maz," Box 154.

75. McGB to Menzel, June 7, 1961, "Observatory: Harvard College," Box 21; NMP to Menzel, May 3, 1966, Menzel to NMP, May 16, "Observatory," Box 22.

76. JBC to PB, July 29, 1952; DWB note to NMP, "Observatory," Box 21; McGB to NMP, Jan. 26, Mar. 17, 1955, Menzel to McGB, Jan. 24, news rel., May 10, "Observatory; Harvard College," Box 51.

77. NMP to Donald Menzel, Jan. 26, 1961, "Observatory: Harvard College," Box 21; Donald Menzel to NMP, Jan. 11, 1962, NMP memo, Feb. 27, "Observatory: Harvard College," Menzel to NMP, Dec. 21, 1964, "Observatory," Box 22; L. Gard Wiggins to NMP, July 23, 1970; Leo Goldberg to John Dunlop, July 23, "Observatory, Harvard College," Box 20.

78. Menzel to NMP, Nov. 16, 1962, Charles Coolidge to NMP, Jan. 2, 1963, "National Aeronautics and Space Administration," Box 20; McGB rec. of Goldberg, Feb. 2, 1960, "Astronomy," Box 168; Leo Goldberg to NMP, Oct. 28, 1970, Dunlop to NMP, Nov. 17, ad hoc committee report, Feb. 1971, NMP notes, May 17, "Observatory: Harvard College," Box 20.

79. English *AR* 1957–58; Lee Grove, "Forget the Plots, Remember the Posies," *Boston Magazine* (Sept. 1974); English *AR* 1959–60, 1960–61, 1967–68.

80. DWB memo to NMP, Oct. 3, 1962, "Overseers: General," Box 21; Bate int.

81. McGB rec., Mar. 30, 1956, "English," Box 58.

82. English *AR* 1964–65, 1966–67; recs., spring 1965, "English," Box 12; English *VC*, Oct. 14, 1968, "Overseers: Committee," Box 25; History and Literature *AR* 1969–70.

83. Helen Vendler int. See also Fumi Takano, "Harvard-Radcliffe: Education in Humility," *HAB*, 64 (1961–62), 460 f.

84. McGB recs., Mar. 4, 1955, "Classics," Box 37; NMP to McGB, Mar. 9, 1955, "Ad hoc: Classics," Box 30.

85. Glenn Bowersock, Zeph Stewart ints.

86. Willard van Orman Quine, *The Time of My Life: An Autobiography* (Cambridge: MIT Press, 1985), 229, 261–62, 307; Morton White to McGB, Oct. 7, 14, 1955, "Philosophy," FASGF, Box 6; McGB recs. of Dreben, Oct. 28, 1955, Albritton, May 3, 1956, "Philosophy," Box 80.

87. McGB rec. of Albritton, Apr. 22, 1960, "Pf-Ph," Box 188; McGB rec. of Dreben, Jan. 10, 1961, Alonzo Church to McGB, Dec. 28, 1960, "Philosophy," Box 23; Burton Dreben int.

88. Burton Dreben int.; on Wild, McGB to NMP, Apr. 22, 1960, "Pf-Ph," Box 188, Philosophy *AR* 1960–61; NMP note, Dec. 16, 1963, "Pf-Ph," Box 24. See also Morton White, "Harvard's Philosophical Heritage," *HAB* 60 (1957–58), 161 f.

89. Rogers in Romance Languages *AR* 1962–63, 1965–66; Frank M. Chambers to NMP, Apr. 17, 1957, NMP to Chambers, Apr. 18, "Chi-Ci," Box 91.

90. McGB to Harry Levin, July 11, 1955, "Mo-Mz," Box 78; McGB rec., Feb. 29, 1956, "Romance Languages: General," Box 82; NMP to McGB, Feb. 13, 1956, "Romance Languages," Box 59; McGB to Seznec, Feb. 19, 1958, "Ol-Oz," Box 130; McGB rec., Apr. 2, 1958, "Romance Languages," Box 135.

91. Frohock to Marcel Françon, Mar. 20, 1958, "Roa-Ror," Box 135, Dec. 9, 1959, "Romance Languages," Box 190; McGB to NMP, Nov. 3, 1960, "Romance Languages: Budget 1961–62," Box 25; Solano to NMP, Apr. 29, 1968, "Roa-Ror," Box 30.

92. McGB rec. of Marichal, Dec. 28, 1960, "Romance Languages: Budget 1961–62," Box 25; McGB rec. of Benichou, Feb. 12, 1959, "Romance Languages," Box 161; Romance Languages *AR* 1958–59; McGB to NMP, Feb. 15, 1971, "Pusey: Retirement," Box 23.

93. FF to Thomas Eliot, Apr. 3, 1969, "Overseers: Committees," Box 15; NMP to Wade McCree, Jr., Mar. 31, 1971, "Overseers: Committees," Box 20.

94. McGB to NMP, Apr. 29, 1959, "Ja-Jom," Box 153; Jakobson to McGB, Mar. 5, 1960, McGB to Jakobson, Mar. 7, "Slavic Languages and Literatures," Box 190.

95. Comparative Literature *AR* 1965–66, 1969–70.

96. Comparative Philology *AR* 1935–36; *HAB*, 63 (1960–61), 62; Linguistics *AR* 1959–60; committee report, Nov. 29, 1960, "Linguistics," Box 17; Linguistics *AR* 1957–58.

97. Lincoln Kirstein to William E. Hutton, Sept. 15, 1954, "Classes," Box 37; John Coolidge to NMP memo, Dec. 1953, "Fogg Art Museum," Box 13.

98. Fine Arts *AR* 1961–62; Fred B. Deknatel to McGB, Dec. 15, 1953, "Fine Arts," Box 1; Meyer Schapiro to NMP, May 6, 1965, "Pi-Po," Box 23; McGB rec. of Freedberg, Feb. 1, 1954, "Fine Arts," Box 13, McGB rec. of Ackerman, Feb. 16, 1959, "Fine Arts," Box 149; Slive rec., Dec. 28, 1960, "Fine Arts," Box 11.

99. John Coolidge to NMP, Oct. 3, 1962, "Ros-Raz," Box 25; TSL note, 1963–64, "Lamont, Thomas S.," Box 18.

100. News rel., Apr. 9, 1956, McGB to NMP, Sept. 12, 1955, "Visual Arts," Box 84; McGB memo to NMP, Apr. 25, 1957, "Fogg Art Museum," Box 95; VES *AR* 1965–66, 1970–71; Fine Arts *AR* 1967–68.

101. *HB*, 73 (Mar. 1971), 41; McGB to NMP, Nov. 30, 1954, "Music Department: General," Box 50; DWB memo to NMP, Oct. 31, 1957, McGB to Randall Thompson, Aug. 29, "Mr-My," Box 129; McGB rec., Apr. 30, 1958, "Music Department: General," Box 129.

102. "Preliminary Statement of Purposes," Oct. 14, 1957, "Theater," Box 136.

103. Confidential Report, Oct. 1962, "Loeb Drama Center," Box 17; *HAB*, 61 (1958–59), 498; *HAB*, 57 (1954–55), 620, *HAB*, 63 (1960–61), 107; *HAB*, 66 (1963–64), 386–87; Loeb to McGB, July 8, 1959, "Th-Ti," Box 162.

104. Theater *AR* 1960–61, 1965–66, 1966–67, 1969–70, 1971–72.

105. "Dumbarton Oaks," Box 12; McGB to NMP, Dec. 16, 1954, "Dumbarton Oaks," Box 40; McGB to NMP, June 30, 1954, "Dumbarton Oaks," Box 12; notes, 1960–61, "Dumbarton Oaks," Box 10.

106. "Old Dominion Foundation," 1959–60, Box 187; "Hellenic Studies, Center for," 1960–61, Box 14.

107. Report, Mar. 3, 1960, "I Tatti," Box 179; on Cabot, FF int.; WmB-S to NMP, Nov. 4, 1960, "I Tatti," Box 16; on McGB, WmB-S memo to NMP, Mar. 30, 1964, "I Tatti," Box 17; John Walker to Lawrence Berenson, Apr. 17, 1963, Waa-War," Box 27; JRR to NMP, July 29, 1963, "Assistants to the President," Box 5.

## Chapter 11

1. JRR to NMP, Mar. 20, 1962, "Foundation for Advanced Study and Research," Box 12; see "Foundation for Advanced Study and Research," Box 14, NMPPP, 1963–64; Notes of Wyzanski talk, Jan. 16, 1954, "Alumni Association," Box 2.

2. NMP to Hugh Taylor, Mar. 5, 1959, "Woodrow Wilson National Fellowship Program," Box 164; E. S. memo to NMP, Feb. 21, 1961, "Wilson National Fellowship Program," Box 28; Elder to Chairs, Apr. 17, 1967, "Arts and Sciences: Graduate School," Box 4; on ratings, Charles J. Anderson to NMP, Nov. 6, 1970, "American Council on Education," Box 2; *HAB*, 69 (Jan. 14, 1967), 11: *HAB*, 71 (Apr. 7, 1969), 12–13.

3. Griswold to NMP, Sept. 4, 1968, "Law School," Box 12; Donald K. David int., Oct. 4, 1974, in "Business—3 Centuries," WmB-S Mss.

4. Griswold memo to NMP, Nov. 4, 1953, Law School: General," Box 17; Louis Loss to WLM, Feb. 11, 1966, "Marbury, Wm. L." Box 20; Erwin Griswold to NMP, Oct. 25, 1954, Mar. 1, 1955, "Law School," Box 30.

5. Griswold to NMP, Dec. 1, 1955, "Law School: Dean," Box 75; Griswold to NMP, Dec. 14, 1965, "Law School: Dean," Box 10; Henry J. Friendly to NMP, Nov. 14, 1967, "Law—3 Centuries," WmB-S Mss; Griswold to NMP, Nov. 1, 1960, "Law School: Dean," Box 17; Griswold to NMP, Sept. 10, 1964, NMP to Griswold, Oct. 6, Griswold to NMP, Oct. 8, "Law School: Budget," Box 18.

6. Griswold to NMP, Jan. 4, 1963, "Law School: Dean," Box 17; Griswold memo to Faculty, Feb. 17, 1961, "Law School: General," Box 17; Charles Wyzanski to NMP, May 25, 1965, "Wim-Wy," Box 29; Griswold to NMP, Jan. 7, 1960, Fuller memo, "Law School: Dean," Box 180.

7. Law School *VC* June 11, 1969; Robert Amory, Jr., to NMP, Nov. 20, 1967, "Law—3 Centuries," WmB-S Mss.

8. NMP note, Dec. 26, 1967, "Law School: New Dean (Suggestions from Faculty)," Box 21; "Law—3 Centuries," WmB-S Mss; NMP to Corporation, Jan. 22, 1968, "Law School:" Appointments," Box 21.

9. DCB to NMP, Nov. 2, "Law School: New Dean," Box 21; *HB*, 71 (Oct. 21, 1968), 10; HLS *VC*, June 11, 1969; Steven Jacobson to NMP, May 12, 1971, "Law School: Dean," Box 16. See also John J. Osborn, *The Paper Chase* (Boston: Houghton Mifflin, 1971); Scott Turow, *One L* (New York: Putnam, 1977).

10. James Vorenberg int.; WLM to NMP, Mar. 16, 1971, Charles Wyzanski to NMP, Mar. 15, Henry Friendly to NMP, Mar. 23, Richard Brodsky and James Montgomery to NMP, Feb. 24, "Law School: New Dean," Box 16.

11. Jeffrey L. Cruikshank, *A Delicate Experiment: The Harvard Business School,*

*1908–1945* (Boston: Harvard Business School Press, 1987), 283–84; TSL to NMP, Dec. 31, 1954, May 6, June 2, 1955, NMP notes, June 14, "Business School: New Dean," Box 35; Donald K. David int., Oct. 4, 1971, in "Business— 3 Centuries," WmB-S Mss; TSL to NMP, April 25, "Business School: Budget," Box 5; Cruikshank, *Delicate Experiment*, 285.

12.  NMP to Donald David, Apr. 26, 1955, "Trade Union Program," Box 55; Emery Bacon to NMP, July 18, 1960, "United," Box 27; DWB memo to NMP, Oct. 25, 1962, "Trade Union Program," Box 26; 1965 Report, "Trade Union Program," Box 28; on women, news rel., May 13, 1959, "Business School: General," Box 144; committee memo to faculty, Dec. 3, 1962, "Business School: Dean," Box 6; *HAB*, 65 (1962–63), 385.

13.  Cruikshank, *Delicate Experiment*, 283–84; Teele to WmB-S, June 4, 1957, "Business School: Dean," Box 90; WmB-S memo to NMP, Oct. 31, 1958, "Business School: General," Box 144; WmB-S memo to NMP, Jan. 28, 1959, "Law-Len," Box 153.

14.  John MacArthur int.; George P. Baker to NMP, Feb. 28, 1966, "Business School: Dean," Box 7; meeting of Executive Council of Deans, Dec. 3, 1963, "Deans: Committee of," Box 10; TSL to NMP, etc., Jan. 23, 1959, "'Business School: General," Box 144.

15.  *HAB*, 70 (Oct. 14, 1967), 5; Don L. Harmon to NMP, May 2, 1969, "Business School: New Dean," Box 5.

16.  JBC to George Berry, May 13, 1955, "Medical School: Dean," Box 49; Greer Williams, "How Doctors Are Made," *Saturday Evening Post* (Jan. 25, 1958), 24–25, 83–86; Berry to NMP, Mar. 16, 1954, "Medical School: Dean," Box 19.

17.  Williams, "How Doctors Are Made"; George P. Berry, "Financing the Harvard Medical School," *Harvard Medical Alumni Bulletin*, Apr. 1955, 7–16; Berry to Francis H. Burr, etc., May 6, 1955, "Medical School: Dean," Box 49; NMP to Berry, Jan. 16, "Medical School: General," Box 77; Williams, "How Doctors Are Made," 24–25.

18.  Berry to Lester J. Evans, Dec. 30, 1954, "Medical School: Dean," Box 49; Berry memo, Mar. 10, 1964, "Statistics," Box 28.

19.  Berry to NMP, Jan. 12, 1956, NMP to Berry, Jan. 16, "Medical School: General," Box 77; Berry to WmB-S, Mar. 14, 1958, "Medical School: Dean," Box 127; Berry to NMP, Oct. 13, 1962, "Medical School: Dean," Box 19; Robert H. Ebert int., Aug. 20, 1974, in "Medical—3 Centuries," WmB-S Mss.

20.  NMP to Robert Ebert, Aug. 4, 1965, "Medical School (Term Appointments)," Box 21; NMP notes, Dec. 13, 1963, "Medical School: New Dean," Box 21; NMP int.; Davis, etc., letters in "Medical School File" notes, "Medical—3 Centuries", WmB-S Mss.

21.  NMP to DWB, Feb. 8, 1965. "Medical School: Budget," Box 19; Ebert int., Aug. 20, 1974, "Medical—3 Centuries," Henry Meadows int., Oct. 30, 1974, "Medical School," WmB-S Mss; NMP notes, Mar. 31, 1965, "AA-Alk," Box 1; Report of Subcommittee on Curriculum Planning, May 1966, "Medical School Faculty Meetings," Box 21; HMS and SDM *VC*, Oct. 31, 1969.

22.  Ebert to NMP, Nov. 9, 1970, Coons to Paul Densen, June 29, "Medical School: Ad hoc Committees," Box 17.

23. "Medical School: Faculty Meetings," Box 18, NMPPP, 1970–71.

24. John C. Snyder and Hugh R. Leavell to NMP, NMP notes, May 12, 1954, "Public Health: Dean," Box 24, John C. Snyder to NMP, Aug. 7, 1954, NMP to DWB, Oct. 4, 1954, "Public Health: Dean," Box 53.

25. News rel., Jan. 6, 1956, "Ham-Hd," Box 71; Snyder to NMP, Jan. 28, 1960, "Public Health: Dean," Box 189.

26. Snyder to NMP, May 27, 1964, "Public Health: Budget," Box 25; Weller to NMP, June 9, 1958, "Public Health: General," Box 134.

27. Ebert to NMP, Apr. 27, 1971, notes of Overseers Committee meeting; NMP to Roger L. Nichols, Apr. 16, "Public Health: General," Box 22.

28. Berry to NMP, May 9, 1955, "Dental Medicine, School of," Box 38; Curtis Prout to Francis H. Burr, Oct. 5, 1959, "Burr, Francis H.," Box 170; Oliver Cope to NMP, Feb. 3, 1954, "Medical School: General," Box 49.

29. Ebert to NMP, Mar. 11, 1968, "Dental Medicine, School of," Box 12; NMP to Dean Paul Goldhaber, Mar. 19, 1969, "Dental Medicine, School of," Box 8.

30. Frank Keppel to NMP, Jan. 19, 1955, "Education: Dean," Box 40; DWB to NMP, Jan. 17, 1956, "He-Hn," Box 72; GSE *VC* Report 1957, "Education—3 Centuries," WmB-S Mss.

31. GSE *VC* 1961; DWB to NMP, Jan. 16, 1958, "Education: Dean," Box 120.

32. Keppel to NMP, Jan. 28, 1959, NMP notes, Mar. 13, "Education: Dean," Box 149; WmB-S memo to NMP, May 24, 1963, "Education: General," Box 11; *CM*, Oct. 7, 1963.

33. NMP notes, Jan. 27, 1961, "Education: Dean," Box 10; Keppel to NMP, Aug. 3, 1961, "Education: Dean," Box 11; Theodore Sizer to NMP, Dec. 26, 1962, David W. Tiedeman to NMP, Dec. 12, Ralph Tyler to NMP, Feb. 6, 1963, "Education: New Dean," Box 11.

34. NMP to Corporation, Apr. 15, 1963, "Education: Budget," Box 10; DWB to Corporation, Feb. 11, 1964, "Education: Budget," Box 12.

35. *HAB*, 68 (1965–66), 59–60; Sizer to NMP, Feb. 12, 1964, "Education: Budget," Feb. 1, 1965, "Education School: Budget," Box 12; *HAB*, 72 (Mar. 23, 1970), 15; GSE *VC* 1969–70.

36. *HAB*, 72 (Mar. 23, 1970), 14–15; Sizer to NMP, Jan. 15, 1970, "Education: Dean," Box 16; Sizer to NMP, Jan. 16, 1969, "Education: Dean," Box 8a; Pusey to Sizer, Jan. 6, 1971, "Education: Dean," Box 11.

37. Reports of Dean to President, 1969–70, "Education—3 Centuries," WmB-S Mss; Sizer to NMP, Nov. 2, 1966, "Education: Dean," Box 11; Sizer to Edward J. Meade, Jr., Oct. 31, 1968, "Education: Dean," Box 8a.

38. Sizer to NMP, Mar. 3, 1969, "Education: Dean," Box 8a; NMP to Sizer, Aug. 13, 1969, "Education: Dean," Box 16; GSE *VC* 1969–70; Informal report of *VC*, 1970–71, "Overseers: Committee," Box 20; Report of *VC*, Dec. 1969, "Overseers: Committee," Box 25.

39. WmB-S memo to NMP, Jan. 15, 1954, "Divinity School: General," Box 12; NMP to Corporation, Apr. 6, 1959, "Divinity School: Budget 1959–60," Box 147.

40. News rel., Jan. 18, 1956, "Divinity School: Dean," Box 67; HDS *VC* 1972, "Divinity—3 Centuries," WmB-S Mss.

41.  John Lord O'Brian to NMP, Jan. 18, 1955, Gordon Huggins to NMP, Jan. 25, NMP to O'Brian, Jan. 27, "Divinity School: Endowment Fund," Box 38.

42.  NMP to David A. Horgan, June 20, 1956, "Ca-Cg," Box 63; Horton to NMP, Mar. 14, 26, 1958, "Divinity School: Budget," Box 119.

43.  HDS *VC*, 1961–62, 1964–65; McGB to NMP, Mar. 20, 1958, "Ham-Hap," Box 122.

44.  HDS *VC*, 1972–73.

45.  Proposal, Mar. 4, 1965, "Divinity School: General," Box 11; Miller to L. Gard Wiggins, Mar. 1, 1963, "Divinity School: Budget," Box 9; proposal, Feb. 21, 1969, "Divinity School: Dean," Box 8; Stendahl to NMP, Apr. 24, 1968, "Divinity School: Dean," Box 13; O'Brian to NMP, June 24, 1969, NMP to O'Brian, June 30, "Divinity School: Dean," Box 8.

46.  McGB draft statement, 1953–54, "Arts and Sciences: Dean of Faculty," Box 4; GSD *VC* Report, June 17, 1954, "Design School: General," Box 11.

47.  Sert to DWB, May 15, 1956, "Design, School of," Box 67; Sert to NMP, Apr. 14, 1959, "Design, School of," Box 147; Stanley Marcus to NMP, June 30, 1960, "Overseers: Committees," Box 187; Marcus to NMP, June 13, 1961, "Overseers: Committees," Box 21; GSD *VC* 1963–64.

48.  Sert memo, Dec. 15, 1959, "Design, School of," Box 173; Martin Meyerson memo to Sert, Feb. 14, 1964, "Design, School of," Box 11; GSD Development Program, May 13, 1965, NMP to US Office of Education, Mar. 19, "Design, Graduate School of," Box 10; Sert to Alumni, Nov. 8, 1968, "Design, School of," Box 8.

49.  Walter Bogner to NMP, Nov. 23, 1968, Louis Bakanowsky to NMP, Dec. 21, Sert to NMP, Mar. 9, 16, "Design, School of," Box 11; William A. Doebele int.; Bainbridge Bunting, *Harvard: An Architectural History* (Cambridge: Harvard Univ. Press, 1985), 238–39.

50.  Students to NMP, Mar. 22, 1968, Sert to NMP, May 8, "Design, School of," Box 12; on MIT, R. Stephen Browning to NMP, Aug. 1, 1969, "Design, School of," Box 14; Maurice Kilbridge to John Blum and Hugh Calkins, Nov. 9, 1970, "Design: Dean," Box 10.

51.  NMP notes, Nov. 8, 1968, "Design, School of," Box 8; Kilbridge to NMP, Sept. 22, 1969, Apr. 23, June 8, 12, "Design, School of: Dean," Box 15.

52.  William A. Doebele to NMP, Dec. 9, 1969, NMP to Frederick E. Smith, Dec. 2, "Design, School of: New Dean," Box 10; Kilbridge to NMP, Nov. 20, 1970, "Design: Dean," Box 10; chairmen to NMP, Martin Meyerson, Dec. 29, 1969, "Design, School of," Box 14;

53.  GSPA *AR* 1958–59; news rel., Apr. 19, 1954, "Public Administration School," Box 23; Edward S. Mason to McGB, Apr. 18, 1956, "Public Administration," Box 81.

54.  *CM*, Mar. 17, 1958; GSPA *AR* 1958–59. See also Paul M. Herzog, "A Study of the Graduate School of Public Administration," Jan. 1957, "GSPA," Box 6.

55.  GSPA *VC*, 1960–61, "Public Administration—3 Centuries," WmB-S Mss.

56.  GSPA *AR*, 1962–63; GSPA *VC*, 1960–61; on Hirschman, Price to NMP, Jan. 29, 1964, "Public Administration: Budget," Box 24; Don K. Price to NMP,

Aug. 12, 1963, "Public Administration," Box 25; Price to McNamara, June 28, 1963, "Gli-Go," Box 10.

57.  NMP note, June 23, 1961, "Kem-Kez," Box 16; "Kennedy Library," 1961–62, NMP notes, June 18, 1964, "Kennedy Library," Box 18.

58.  WmB-S to NMP, May 1, 1964, TSL to NMP, May 29, FF to NMP, June 15, NMP notes on meeting, June 18, "Kennedy Library," Box 18; Price memo, July 23, 1964, NMP to Robert F. Kennedy, Sept. 22, Arthur Maass to FF, Oct. 22, 1964, NMP note for file, Nov. 10, "Kennedy Library," Box 17.

59.  NMP notes, Jan. 12, 1965, "Institute of Politics," Box 16, Dec. 15, 1966, "Kennedy School of Government," Box 18.

60.  Don K. Price to NMP, Sept. 30, 1966, "Public Administration," Box 23; Richard Neustadt to NMP, July 26, 1966, Ott Shaw to NMP, Oct. 1, 1965, "Kennedy Library," Box 18, Shaw to NMP, July 28, 1966, "Kennedy Institute," Box 17.

61.  WmB-S memo to NMP, May 25, 1966, NMP to RFK (draft), June 22, "Kennedy Library," Box 18; RFK to NMP, Mar. 12, 1968, NMP to RFK, May 9, Edward F. Kennedy memo to NMP, Jan. 21, 1970, Don Price memo to NMP, etc., June 2, May 13, 1970, "Kennedy," Box 20; NMP memo to Corporation, Jan. 9, 1969, "Kennedy," Box 12.

62.  Don Price to NMP, Sept. 25, 1967, NMP notes, "Kennedy Library," Box 21; WmB-S memo to Corporation, June 11, 1971, Corporation vote June 16, 1971, Richard Leahy draft memo to NMP, etc., Dec. 7, 1970, "Kennedy," Box 16.

63.  Jacqueline Kennedy to NMP, Oct. 20, 1966, "Kennedy Institute," Box 17.

64.  Price memo to NMP, Oct. 14, 1968, "Kennedy," Box 12.

65.  Ted Kennedy to Neustadt, Apr. 16, 1969, Neustadt to Kennedy, Apr. 23, "Kennedy," Box 12; NMP int., June 21, 1967, "Kennedy," Box 20; KSG *AR* 1971–72, 406.

66.  Price, "Some Notes for Discussion," Mar. 6, 1971, "Kennedy School of Government: Dean," Box 16.


*Chapter 12*

1.  1956–57 Statistics, "Annual Report," Box 88.

2.  WmB-S memo to NMP, Dec. 9, 1954, "Na-Ne," Box 50; McGB memo to NMP, Oct. 2, 1957, "Arts & Sciences: Dean of Faculty," Box 113.

3.  "Catholics at Harvard," *Current*, Spring 1963.

4.  Eileen Ellis to NMP, June 1, 1955, "Q-Ra," Box 53; NMP to Terry Ferrer, Sept. 9, 1957, "Na-Ne," Box 129; NMP to Judy Mendels, June 13, "Me-Mn," Box 76; *HAB*, 62 (1959–60), 69.

5.  John W. Teele memo, Jan. 16, 1955, "Personnel Relations," Box 52; DWB memo to NMP, Nov 29. 1963, "Overseers: General," Box 23.

6.  *HAB*, 58 (1955–56), 585–86; Jill Ker Conway, *True North: A Memoir* (New York: Knopf, 1994), ch. 2.

7.  Archibald MacLeish to NMP, Feb. 16, 1955, NMP to MacLeish, May 26, "Maa-Map," Box 48; "Men and Women Holding Regular Faculty Appointments,"

1959–60, "Statistics," Box 191; Catherine Clinton, "Women and Harvard: The First 350 Years," *HM*, 89 (Sept.-Oct. 1986), 123–28.

8. Rec. of Tilly Edinger, Mar. 30, 1954, "Museum of Comparative Zoology," Box 20.

9. Keith Kane memo to Corporation, Jan. 19, 1955, NMP to Paul Cabot, etc., Dec. 21, 1954, Corporation Informal Record, Dec. 7, 1955, "Honorary Degrees: Committee on," Box 44; Charles C. Burlingham to NMP, June 17, 1955, "Bu-By," Box 34.

10. News rel., Oct. 2, 1955, "Memorial Church," Box 78; Sperry memo, Sept. 19, 1953, "Memorial Church," Box 19; draft news rel., Sept. 20, 1959, "News Office," Box 186.

11. Bailey memo to NMP, Dec. 29, 1960, "Absences, Leaves of: General," Box 194; David W. Bailey memo to WmB-S, July 6, 1961, "Absence, Leaves of," Box 1.

12. DWB to President and Fellows, May 12, 1955, "Corporation," Box 38; Bailey memo to NMP, May 9, 1957, "Appointments, Administrative and Miscellaneous," Box 88; Bailey memo to NMP, Jan. 13, 1959, "Appointments, Admin. and Miscellaneous," Box 142.

13. McGB to NMP, June 8, 1960; Helen Gilbert to NMP, Jan. 25, 1960, "Radcliffe," Box 189; McGB to NMP, June 30, 1958, "Arts and Sciences: Faculty of," Box 142; McGB rec. of Bunting, Nov. 12, 1959, "Biology," Box 169; *HAB*, 63 (1960–61), 303.

14. NMP to Frank H. Canaday, Mar. 12, 1963, "Canaday, Frank H.," Box 7; news rel., Nov. 21, 1957, "College: Dean of," Box 117; *HAB*, 60 (1957–58), 159, 207; *HAB*, 62, (1959–60), 418–19; Merle Fainsod to FF, Dec. 1, 1966, "Library," Box 19; Karen M. Nelson to NMP, Nov. 12, 1969, NMP to Nelson, Nov. 18, news rel., Jan. 5, 1970, "Radcliffe," Box 27.

15. Bunting cited in *HAB*, 71 (Mar. 17, 1969), 9; NMP to Bruce Chalmers and Jerome Bruner, Dec. 17, "Houses," Box 10; *CM*, Dec. 15, 1969; Committee report, Mar. 30, 1970, "College: Dean of," Box 8; *HAB*, 67 (1964–65), 343; "Houses," 1965–66, Box 17; *HB*, 73 (Nov. 16, 1970), 16.

16. NMP to Bunting, Apr. 7, 1971, "Radcliffe," Box 24; Bunting to NMP, July 20, NMP notes, Aug. 13, 1965, "Radcliffe," Box 26; Bunting to NMP, Sept. 12, 1965, "Radcliffe," Box 26.

17. Bunting to NMP, Nov. 29, 1965, NMP to Bunting, Dec. 10, "Radcliffe," Box 26; Bunting to NMP, Nov. 17, 1966, "Radcliffe," Box 24; *HAB*, 71 (Mar. 17, 1969), 9; Draft Memorandum of Understanding, 1968–69, "Radcliffe," Box 16.

18. Robert Shenton to NMP, Apr. 28, 1969, "Arts & Sciences, Faculty of," Box 3; *Time* (Mar. 14, 1969), 57; Bunting and Helen Gilbert Memorandum #2, Jan. 23, 1970, "Radcliffe," Box 27; *Crimson*, Aug. 25, 1969; NMP int.

19. Wolff to Bunting, Sept. 26, 1969, Bunting to Wolff, Sept. 30, 1969, Memorandum #2, "Radcliffe," Box 27; *HAB*, 72 (1969–70), 18.

20. Shattuck to NMP, Feb. 9, 1970, NMP to Shattuck, Feb. 10; Chase Peterson to NMP, Jan. 30, "Radcliffe," Box 27; *HAB*, 72 (1969–70), 11; Helen Gilbert

to Hugh Calkins, Aug. 14, 1970, "Radcliffe Merger," Box 24; Report of Committee, Nov. 12, 1970, "Caa-Carm," Box 7.

21.  Graduate women's letter, Apr. 29, 1970, "Radcliffe," Box 27; Joan Goodyear, Anne Micholini, and Maria Tymoczco, "Whatever Happened to the Radcliffe Merger?" *HB* 73 (Oct. 26, 1970), 17–22; *HB*, 73 (Mar. 1, 1971), 12; news rel., Mar. 8, 1971.

22.  DWB to Betty G. Riddle, Feb. 16, 1955, John W. Davis to NMP, June 17, WmB-S to McGB, June 22, "Na-Ne," Box 50; Catherine T. Johnson to NMP, June 25, 1956, "Ca-Cq," Box 63; Charles Whitlock memo to NMP, Jan. 5, 1962, "Assistant to the President: C.P.W.," Box 4.

23.  Eric Cutler to Charles C. Lund, June 10, 1954, WmB-S to NMP, June 11, "Harvard Club of Boston," Box 15; NMP to William Brantley, Oct. 11, 1957, "*Meet the Press*," Box 128.

24.  Charles Whitlock memo to L. Gard Wiggins, Mar. 28, 1961, "Personnel Office," Box 23; L. Gard Wiggins to George P. Berry, June 8, 1962, "Administrative Vice President," Box 2; John Monro to Earl McGrath, May 12, 1964, "Col-Con," Box 9; Louis A. Toepfer to WmB-S, Apr. 23, 1964, "Statistics," Box 28; Griswold memo for files, Jan. 14, 1965, "Law School: Dean," Box 18.

25.  *HAB*, 65 (1962–63), 632–33; William M. Brewer to NMP, July 16, 1963, John Monro to Brewer, July 23, "AA-Alk," Box 1.

26.  George F. Bennett to WmB-S, Jan. 21, 1965, NMP form letter, "Middle South Utilities," Box 20; Richard Wilson to NMP, Apr. 15, 1968, NMP to Wilson, Apr. 18, "Wia-Wil," Box 24.

27.  E. J. Kahn, *Harvard: Through Change and Through Storm* (New York: Norton, 1969), 111; Joseph Strickland memo to Dunlop, etc., May 19, 1970, "Arts & Sciences: Dean of Faculty," Box 3.

28.  Hooks Burr to NMP, Mar. 6, 1969; Daniel M. Fox to NMP, Apr. 23, "Aa-Alk," Box 1; Charles A. Whitney essay, Apr. 29, 1969, "An-Az," Box 3. See also *HAB*, 71 (May 19, 1970), 15–16.

29.  News rel. Oct. 17, 1969; students to Richard Musgrave, Sept. 22, 1969, "African-African-American," Box 1.

30.  Philip Lee to Archibald Cox, Nov. 24, 1969, Cox to Lee, Nov. 30, news rel., Dec. 5, 13, 15, "Black Unity, Organization of," Box 5.

31.  Statement of Steering Committee, NMP to Derrick Bell, Dec. 13, 1969, Association to NMP, June 4, 1970, NMP to Bell, June 5, "Black," Box 5; NMP to Deans, Jan. 21, 1970, news rel., Feb. 10, "Affirmative Action program," Box 1; NMP to Deans, Feb. 13, 1970, "U.S. Govt.-HEW-Equal Employment Opportunity," Box 29.

32.  Elizabeth Kuehl memo to NMP, May 25, 1971, "AA-Alk," Box 1; Hayward Henry, Jr., to JTD, Mar. 1, 1971, JTD to Henry, Mar. 26, JTD to NMP, Sept. 22, 1970, "Afro-American," Box 1 Harold Amos to NMP, May 10, 1971, "Arts and Sciences: Dean of Faculty," Box 2; Orlando Patterson int.; Sylvester Monroe, "Guest in a Strange House: A Black at Harvard," *Saturday Review of Education* (Feb. 1973), 45.

*Chapter 13*

1. *HAB*, 59 (1956–57), 307, 350, 383, 671; *HAB*, 57 (1954–55), 63 f; *HAB*, 59 (1956–57), 383.

2. *HAB*, 63 (1960–61), 639–40; *HAB*, 65 (1962–63), 17.

3. David Boroff, "Imperial Harvard," *Harper's Magazine*, 217 (Oct. 1958), 30; "Religion at Harvard," Feb. 1956, "St-Sz," Box 83; Nick Carrera to NMP, Apr. 11, 1957, "Carn-Ce," Box 91.

4. NMP to Sydney James, June 27, 1956, "Sk-Ss," Box 82; DWB to Bradford A. Booth, June 27, 1956, "Ca-Cg," Box 63; McGB to NMP, Jan. 14, 1954, "Athletics: Ivy Group," Box 4; Bolles to NMP, Dec. 26, 1956, McGB to NMP, Jan. 4, 1957; Athletics," Box 89.

5. *Harvard Independent*, Nov. 17–23, 1977; news rel., Jan. 13, 1954, "Houses & College Dormitories," Box 16; *HAB*, 58 (1955–56), 67.

6. Boroff, "Imperial Harvard," 29.

7. WmB-S memo to NMP, Sept. 20, 1966, "Houses," Box 16; WmB-S memo to NMP, Oct. 17, 1957, McGB to NMP, Nov. 8, news rel., Feb. 18, 1959, "Houses," Box 152; McGB to NMP, Dec. 12, 1960, "Arts and Sciences: Dean of Faculty," Box 197.

8. *HAB*, 60 (1957–58), 8; *HAB*, 61 (1958–59), 11; *HAB*, 64 (1961–62), 633; Harvard College, *Admission and Scholarship Newsletter*, 5, no. 2, "Admisssions & Financial Aids, Dean of," Box 87.

9. Bender to TSL, Jan. 25, 1957, "Admissions & Financial Aids, Dean of," Box 87.

10. McGB to TSL, Apr. 3, 1956, "College," Box 64.

11. Bender to NMP, Jan. 12, May 5, 1955, "Admissions & Financial Aids," Box 31.

12. *HAB*, 59 (1956–57), 110; WmB-S to NMP, May 26, 1959, "Admissions & Financial Aids, Dean of," Box 140; *New Yorker*, "How an Ivy League College (Yale) Decides on Admission," Sept. 10, 1960, 178.

13. On Bender, TSL to NMP, Mar. 14, 1960, "Lamont, Thomas S.," Box 180; McGB to NMP, Oct. 14, 1959, "Admissions & Financial Aids, Dean of," Box 166; Wilbur J. Bender, "The Top One-Percent Policy," *HAB*, 64 (1961–62), 21f.

14. *HAB*, 60 (1957–58), 8; Fred Glimp and Dean Whitla, "Admission and Performance in the College," *HAB*, 66 (1963–64), 304–9; Glimp to TSL, Aug. 2, 1965, "Admissions & Financial Aids," Box 2; Glimp to Myron Rindberg, Nov. 28, 1966, "Admissions & Financial Aids," Box 3.

15. Chase Peterson, "Undergraduate Scholarship Policy Choices," Nov. 4, 1970, "Admissions & Financial Aids," Box 1; Fred Glimp to TSL, July 12, 1966, "Lamont, Thomas S.," Box 18.

16. Fred Glimp to Charles Zukofski, Jr., July 21, 1966, "X-Y-Z," Box 30; William Penick to Peter Gunness, Apr. 17, 1968, WmB-S memo to NMP, Apr. 22, "Admissions & Financial Aids," Box 3.

17. Fred Glimp to NMP, FF, Aug. 23, 1963, news rel. Jan. 12, 1964, "Admissions & Financial Aids," Box 3.

18.  Admissions *AR* 1960–67; Alexander W. Astin to NMP, Dec. 3, 1968, "American Council on Education," Box 2.

19.  WmB-S memo to NMP, Jan. 14, 1963, "University Health Services," Box 26; Robert McCarley, *Walk Around the Yard: A Study of the Freshman Year at Harvard* (Harvard Senior Thesis, 1959); *HAB*, 63 (1960–61), 14–15, *HAB*, 68 (1965–66), 720; Study of Class of 1962, 1962–63, "Gra-Gri," Box 14. See also Stanley H. King, *Five Lives at Harvard: Personality Change During College* (Cambridge: 1973).

20.  *HAB*, 64 (1961–62), 300 f; *HAB*, 61 (1958–59), 340, 380; Report, 1963–64, "Council for Undergraduate Affairs," Box 10; on Brinton, *HAB*, 70 (Feb. 24, 1968), 26–28.

21.  *HAB*, 62 (1959–60), 108–9; William G. Perry, Jr., and Charles P. Whitlock, "Of Study and the Man," *HAB*, 60 (1957–58), 350–54.

22.  John Monro to NMP, Dec. 30, 1964, "College: Dean of," Box 8; WmB-S memo to NMP, Dec. 2, 1964, "Leo-Lim," Box 18; John Rauch to NMP, Jan. 11, 1965, "Q-Ra," Box 25.

23.  DWB memo to NMP, Jan. 17, 1955, "Arts & Sciences: Faculty of," Box 33; General Education *AR* 1957–58, 1960–61; *HAB*, 66 (1963–64), 692–93; *HAB*, 67 (1964–65), 16–18; *HAB*, 68 (1965–66), 203.

24.  *Time*, 73 (June 22, 1959), 56 f; *HAB*, 65 (1962–63), 17.

25.  John Monro to NMP, Dec. 30, 1964, "College: Dean of," Box 8. See also Noah Gordon, "The Hallucinogenic Drug Cult," *Reporter*, 29 (Aug. 15, 1963), 35 f; "Getting Alienated with the Right Crowd at Harvard," *Esquire*, 60 (Sept. 1963), 73.

26.  Boroff, "Imperial Harvard," 34; *HAB*, 61 (1958–59), 11; Richard Day to NMP, Feb. 8, 1961, NMP to Day, Feb. 15, "Annual Report: Comments on," Box 196.

27.  Boroff, "Imperial Harvard," 31; WmB-S to NMP, Mar. 22, 1961, "Crimson," Box 21.

28.  *HC*, Apr. 23–28, 1962; *HAB*, 64 (1961–62), 678; *Time*, 79 (May 25, 1962), 52; *Newsweek*, 59 (May 28, 1962), 58–59; JFK to NMP, May 22, 1962, "United States Government," Box 28.

29.  Michael Rice to Dean Robert Watson, June 6, 1962, Monro to Rice, July 18, "Radio & Television," Box 24.

30.  *HAB*, 59 (1956–57), 306; *HAB*, 61 (1958–59), 340–41; Leaflet, 1959–60, "Classes," Box 146; *HAB*, 62 (1959–60), 160.

31.  *HC*, Oct. 1, 9, Nov. 6, 1963; Monro to Lamont, Nov. 29, 1963, "College: Dean of," Box 9; Marbury to NMP, Nov. 1, 1963, "Marbury, Wm. L.," Box 19; NMP to Dean Caswell, Dec. 19, 1963, "Carn-Ce," Box 8.

32.  FF to NMP, Oct. 3, 1963, "Houses," Box 16; Monro to NMP, Nov. 15, "Parietals," Box 24.

33.  *HAB*, 66 (1963–64), 110–11, 160–61, 179, 223, 292; NMP to Benjamin Ginzburg, Nov. 13, 1963, Responses, Nov. 1963, "Parietals," Box 24; Report, Feb. 1964, "Council for Undergraduate Affairs," Box 10.

34.  Monro statement, Fall 1966, "College: Dean of," Box 9; Dean's Committee

on Parietals Report, May 8, 1968, "Pa," Box 27; Paul Perkins, Jr., to NMP, Nov. 29, 1968, "Pa," Box 15.

35. *HAB*, 57 (1954–55), 716; *HAB*, 61 (1958–59), 111; *HAB*, 67 (1964–65), 158–59.

36. *HAB*, 61 (1958–59), 579; *HAB*, 65 (1962–63), 548; NMP to Marshall Ganz, May 18, 1964, "Ch-Ci," Box 8; John Monro to NMP, Dec. 29, 1964, NMP to Monro, Jan. 5, "Him-Hol," Box 16.

37. *HAB*, 63 (1960–61), 112, 304; *HAB*, 64 (1961–62), 419; Michael Schwartz, "Harvard Politics: The Careless Young Men," *HC* Ten Year Supplement, Sept. 1963.

38. *HAB*, 67 (1964–65), 298; Robert Watson memo to WmB-S, Dec. 7, 1964, WmB-S to NMP, Feb. 25, 1965, "College: Dean of," Box 8.

39. Monro to FF, May 20, 1966, "College: Dean of," Box 9; NMP to Monro, Oct. 28, 1966, "Str-Sz," Box 26; FF to TSL, Dec. 30, 1966, "Lamont, Thomas S.," Box 18.

40. Warren Pierson to NMP, Jan. 23, 1967, Clark Kerr to NMP, Apr. 17, "Kem-Kez," Box 17; WmB-S to Archie Epps, Apr. 15, 1965, *Chicago Tribune*, Mar. 12, WmB-S to Charles Muscatine, July 14, "California, University of," Box 7; Henry Friendly to NMP, Jan. 29, 1965, NMP to Friendly, Feb. 3, "Overseers," Box 22.

41. FF to TSL, Dec. 30, 1966, "Lamont, Thomas S.," Box 18; Monro to Howard Whiteside, May 6, 1967, NMP to George Beadle, Sept. 8, 1966, "Ch-Ci," Box 8.

## Chapter 14

1. *HAB*, 66 (1963–64), 632–33; WmB-S memo to NMP, Apr. 6, 1965, "V," Box 28; *HAB*, 69 (July 8, 1967), 13.

2. NMP to Robert McNamara, Nov. 10, 1966, McNamara to NMP, Nov. 15, "McNamara Incident," Box 19; *HAB*, 69 (Nov. 30, 1966), 11; Lawrence E. Eichel et al., *The Harvard Strike* (Boston: Houghton Mifflin, 1970), 31–33.

3. Monro to NMP, Feb. 16, 1967, NMP to Goldberg, Feb. 21, Goldberg to NMP, Mar. 15, "Gli-Go," Box 15; Wiener quoted in *Public Interest*, 8 (summer 1967), 143.

4. *HAB*, 69 (July 8, 1967), 12 f; fliers in "Str-Sz," Box 22; *HAB*, 70 (Oct. 28, 1967), 6.

5. *HAB*, 70 (Nov. 25, 1967), 9 ff; Marbury to WmB-S, Nov. 3, 1967, "Marbury, Wm. L.," Box 23.

6. Samuel Beer to NMP, Oct. 26, 1967, "Dow Incident," Box 13; Minutes of Special Faculty Meeting, Oct. 31, 1967, "Arts and Sciences, Faculty of," Box 5; *HAB*, 70 (Nov. 11, 1967), 5, 17; *HAB*, 18, (Jan. 13, 1968), 3; Eichel et al., *Harvard Strike*, 37–39.

7. *HAB*, 70 (May 25, 1968), 10; *Crisis at Columbia* (New York: Vintage, 1968), 194; on David Rockefeller, memo to NMP, May 1, 1968, "Overseers: General," Box 27; minutes of May 7, 1968 meeting, "Deans: Committee of," Box 12.

8. *HAB*, 70 (Feb. 3, 1968, 6; (Mar. 16), 5–7; (Mar. 30), 11; WmB-S memo to NMP, Feb. 23, 1968, NMP to Bright Wilson, Mar. 19, "V," Box 33.

9. NMP *AR* 1966–67; *HC*, Jan. 24, 1968; *HAB*, 70 (July 1, 1968), 11; Roger Baldwin to NMP, June 20, 1968, "Honorary Degrees," Box 19.

10. Steven H. Armstrong, "Why Harvard Fails," Robert J. Samuelson, "Instant Insurrection," Richard D. Paisner, "A Continent in Trouble," *HAB*, 71 (Sept. 30, 1968), 22–24, 26–31, 35–36.

11. FF to WLM, July 19, 1968, "Mar," Box 13; NMP to David B. Stone, Dec. 9, 1968, "Ste-Sto," Box 18; Eichel et al., *Harvard Strike*, 75.

12. Seymour Martin Lipset and David Riesman, *Education and Politics at Harvard* (New York: McGraw-Hill, 1975), 230.

13. NMP to Carl J. Friedrich, Jan. 21, 1969, "Arts & Sciences: Faculty of," Box 3; Roger Rosenblatt, *Coming Apart* (Boston: Little, Brown, 1997), 57.

14. NMP to FF, Sept. 23, 1968, "Arts & Sciences: Dean of Faculty," Box 3; FF to Roger Brown, Sept. 30, 1968, Brown to Mrs. Benjamin F. Deford, Jr., Dec. 24, 1968, "Sn-Sta," Box 18.

15. *HAB*, 71 (Apr. 7, 1969); *HAB*, 11, (Dec. 2, 1968), 7; Eichel et al., *Harvard Strike*, 72.

16. *HC*, June 12, 1969 ff; "Ea-Eak," Box 8a; *HAB*, 71 (July 7, 1969), 19.

17. *HAB*, 71 (Oct. 21, 1968), 7; Minutes in WmB-S Mss; *HAB*, 71 (Jan. 13, 1969), 9, *HAB*, 71 (Feb. 3), 11; Eichel et al., *Harvard Strike*, 51 ff.

18. *HC*, Feb. 3, 1969; *HAB*, 71 (Feb. 24, 1969), 7; FF to NMP, Feb. 11, 1969, "Arts & Sciences: Dean of Faculty," Box 3; NMP to FF, Feb. 18, 1969, "ROTC: Official," Box 18.

19. Eichel et al., *Harvard Strike*, 79 ff; Ansara reported in George Keitt to NMP, Apr. 28, 1969, "Str-Sz," Box 18; Archie C. Epps III, "The Harvard Student Rebellion: Through Change and Through Storm," *Proceedings of the Massachusetts Historical Society* 107 (1995), 6; Chase Peterson to Daryl Pearson, June 10, 1969, "Admissions & Financial Aids," Box 2; E. J. Kahn, *Harvard: Through Change and Through Storm* (New York: Norton, 1969), 140.

20. FF to NMP, Apr. 14, 1969, "Arts and Sciences: Dean of Faculty," Box 3; on Eliot's desk, Kahn, *Harvard*, 80.

21. NMP notes, Apr. 10, 1969, "Caa-Carm," Box 5; Eichel et al., *Harvard Strike*, 104; Rosenblatt, *Coming Apart*, 104–17; *HB*, 71 (June 9, 1969), 4; Galbraith, Wilson, Pusey ints.

22. NMP, Fred Glimp, Derek Box ints.; Eichel et al., *Harvard Strike*, 129; NMP to local police chiefs, May 2, 1969, "Administrative Vice President," Box 2.

23. Paul Cabot to George Bennett, Apr. 28, 1969, "Caa-Carm," Box 5; Keith Kane to NMP, Dec. 23, 1968, "Ka-Kel," Box 12; Morison to WmB-S, July 24, 1975, "Three Centuries," WmB-S Mss.

24. Robert Lee Wolff to NMP, May 7, 1969, NMP to Wolff, May 12, "Him-Hol," Box 11.

25. File memo, June 20, 1969, WmB-S memo to Livingston Hall, June 19, "Committee of Five," Box 7.

26. FF to NMP, Apr. 14, 1969, FF to Ruth Maupin, May 14, 1970, "Arts & Sciences: Dean of Faculty," Box 3; Eichel et al., *Harvard Strike*, 185.

27.  *HAB*, 71 (Apr. 28, 1969), 18 ff; NMP, Stanley Hoffman ints.; Rosenblatt, *Coming Apart*, 215.

28.  *HAB*, 71 (May 19, 1969), 12; JBC to Don Price, Nov. 23, 1970, "Kennedy School of Government: Dean," Box 16.

29.  Glazer in *HB*, 73 (Sept. 21, 1970), 23–30, (Jan. 4, 1971), 14.

30.  Beer to NMP, Sept. 27, 1969, "Gli-Go," Box 27.

31.  Eichel et al., *Harvard Strike* (Boston: Houghton Mifflin, 1970), 133 f, 156; Roger Rosenblatt, *Coming Apart* (Boston: Little, Brown, 1997), 43; Lorna Slocombe to NMP, June 27, 1969, "Arts & Sciences: Faculty of," Box 3.

32.  Rosenblatt, *Coming Apart*, 52; Wald to NMP, Sept. 25, 1969, "Bea-Beq," Box 5.

33.  Rosenblatt, *Coming Apart*, 123; Galbraith to Wolff, Dec. 9, 1969, Wolff to Galbraith, Dec. 12, "Him-Hol," Box 18.

34.  Eichel et al., *Harvard Strike*, 158 f; *HAB*, 71 (Apr. 28, 1969), 43 f.

35.  Rosenblatt, *Coming Apart*, 107 f; *HAB*, 71 (Aug. 11, 1969), 12; Committee of Fifteen, "Interim Report on the Causes of the Recent Crisis," June 9, 1969.

36.  Committee of Five to NMP, June 10, 1969, Kenneth Arrow to NMP, May 22, "Committee of Five," Box 7; Eichel et al., *Harvard Strike*, 304–5; *HB*, 72 (Sept. 15, 1969), 20; WLM to NMP, Aug. 15, 29, 1969, "Committee of the Faculty and Fellows, Joint," Box 9; NMP to John Dunlop, Jan. 8, 1970, Roger Brown to FF, Dec. 8, "Arts & Sciences: Dean of," Box 3.

37.  James Q. Wilson to FF, July 15, 1969, HR to FF, July 22, FF to NMP, Sept. 15, 1969, "Arts & Sciences: Dean of Faculty," Box 3; HR to FF, Sept. 15, 1969, "Ea-Ek," Box 16; NMP to FF, Sept. 19, 1969, "Shadow Cases," Box 29.

38.  *HB*, 72 (Oct. 27, 1969), 11–14.

39.  "Report of the Committee on the Organization of the Faculty of Arts & Sciences," Minutes, "Arts & Sciences: Faculty Meeting," 1970–71, Box 3; "Moratorium, Correspondence re," 1970–71, Box 23.

40.  James Q. Wilson to NMP, n.d., "Gli-Go," Box 17; May 2, 1969, letter, "Arts & Sciences: Faculty of," Box 3; *HAB*, 71 (June 9, 1969), 11–12; *HB*, 72 (Mar. 23, 1970), 21; Ulam, "The University Should Mind Its Own Business," Hughes, "The Need Now Is to De-Politicize the University," *HB*, 72 (Sept. 15, 1969), 29–34, 35–38; *Harvard Independent*, Nov. 17, 1977.

41.  *HAB*, 71 (Mar. 17, 1969), 13; *HAB*, 69 (May 13, 1967), 24–27. See also Marshall W. Meyer, "After the Bust: Student Politics at Harvard, 1969–1972," in David Riesman and Verne A. Stadtman, eds., *Academic Transformation* (New York: McGraw-Hill, 1973), 153; news rel., Mar. 2, 1971, "College: General," Box 8.

42.  Rosenblatt, *Coming Apart*, 88–89; *HAB*, 71 (Dec. 23, 1968), 19; 72 (Nov. 17, 1969), 16; *HB*, 73 (May 3, 1971), 11, 21 f; Craig Ulman to F. Skiddy von Stade, June 21, 1970, May to NMP, Dec. 21, "Overseers: General," Box 20.

43.  *HB*, 73 (Apr. 12, 1971), 19 f, *HB*, May 13, 1971, 13; *HC*, Mar. 22, 1970; *HB*, 73 (Mar. 22, 1971), 22, 14.

44.  *HB*, 73 (Dec. 7, 1970), 14, 18 f; *HB*, (Mar. 22, 1971), 27.

45.  *HB*, 73 (May 24, 1971), 12.

46.  *HAB*, 71 (May 19, 1969), 12–14; Eichel et al., *Harvard Strike*, 240–59.

47. *HB*, 72 (Oct. 6, 1969), 9; Edmunds to NMP, June 25, 1970, NMP to Edmunds, July 8, "Ea-Ek," Box 11.

48. William G. Anderson to NMP, May 14, 1969, "Commencement," Box 7; WmB-S to Loren F. Attwood, July 9, 1969, "Commencement," Box 7; Allen in *25th Anniversary of the Class of 1969*; *HAB*, 71 (June 9), 11 (July 7, 1969), 15 ff, 32 f; Eichel et al., *Harvard Strike*, 318–21.

49. *HAB*, 71 (Aug. 11, 1969), 17; Ford to Robert Bowie, June 27, 1969, "International Affairs, Center for," Box 11.

50. *HB*, 72 (May 25, 1970), 11; *HB*, (June 6, 1970), 11.

51. FF to NMP, Nov. 28, 1969, NMP to Sargent Kennedy, Apr. 1, 1970, "Arts & Sciences: Dean of Faculty," Box 3; *AR* 1968–69; *HB*, 72 (March 23, 1970), 15.

52. NMP to J. Lawrence Pool, June 16, 1970, "Commencement," Box 8; *HB*, 72 (July 6, 1970), 19–24.

53. Council Minutes, Sept. 10, 1970, "Deans, Council," Box 10; *HB*, 73 (Sept. 21, 1970), 17; *HB*, 73 (Oct. 26), 9; *HB*, 73 (Apr. 12, 1971), 11; JPD letter to FAS, "Arts and Sciences: Dean of Faculty," Box 2, NMPPP 1970–71; summary, June 4, 1971, "Rights & Responsibilities, Committee on," Box 24.

54. Dr. and Mrs. Seymour Rothschild to DCB, June 20, 1971, "Ros-Sz," Box 24.

55. NMP notes, "Corporation: New Members," Box 14; Charles A. Coolidge to NMP, Sept. 17, 1969, "Corporation Elections of 1969–709—Notebook No. 1," Box 11; NMP to George C. Homans, Jan. 15, 1970, "General Letter to Faculties," Box 13; Homans to NMP, Jan. 16, 1970, "Sn-Sta," Box 29.

56. Theodore H. White to Dillon, Sept. 3, 1969, "Overseers: General," Box 25; Dillon to NMP, Mar. 12, 1969, "Overseers: General," Box 15; Dillon to Sargent Kennedy, Sept. 16, 1969, Amory Houghton to NMP, Nov. 25, 1969, NMP to Houghton, Nov. 28, White to Dillon, Sept. 3, 1969, "Overseers: General," Box 25.

57. Keith Kane memo to Corporation, July 24, 1969, NMP to Henry Friendly, Sept. 1, "Overseers: Long-Range Study Committee," Box 25; Nickerson to NMP, July 2, 1969, "Ni-Ny," Box 24.

58. Daniel P. Moynihan to Friendly, July 28, Hugh Calkins to Friendly, Sept. 10, "Overseers: Long-Range Study Committee," Box 25; news rel., Sept. 19, 1969, "Committee on Governance," Box 9; *HB*, 72 (Oct. 16, 1969), 9.

59. *HB*, 73 (Oct. 26, 1970), 9; Schuyler Hollingsworth to NMP, Richard Metz to Richard Heath, Oct. 28, 1970, "Fr-Fy," Box 12.

60. Minutes, Dec. 2, 1969, meeting, "Deans, Council of," Box 14; *HB*, 73 (Nov. 16, 1970), 15; *HB*, 73 (Jan. 4, 1971), 4; JTD to NMP, Sept. 25, 1970, "Arts & Sciences: Dean of Faculty," Box 2; news rel., Feb. 7, 1971, "Development Office," Box 11; *HB*, 73 (Mar. 1, 1971), *HB*, 11, (July 5, 1971), 14.

61. Cox to NMP, Mar. 17, 1970, "Law School: General," Box 21; John McArthur and M. Colyer Crum to NMP, Apr. 6, 1970, Calkins to NMP, Apr. 15, 1970, NMP to Paul Cabot, Apr. 27, "General Motors Stock," Box 17; "Report of the Committee on University Relations with Corporate Enterprise" (Jan. 1971); news rel. May 18, 1971, "Gen-Gli," Box 13; news rel., Mar. 5, 1971, "An-Az," Box 1; Fortas to John Loeb, Mar. 24, 1971, NMP to Loeb, April 1, "University Relations with Corporate Enterprise, Committee on—General Correspondence," Box 25.

62. James Q. Wilson to NMP, Oct. 16, 1968, Daniel P. Moynihan to Friendly,

July 28, 1969, "U," Box 19; "Overseers: Long-Range Study Committee," 1969–70, Box 25.

63.  John K. Galbraith, "The Modern University: Three Steps Toward Today"; Kane to Corporation, June 19, 1967, "Ka-Kel," Box 17; Galbraith, "The Case for Constitutional Reform," *HAB*, 71 (Dec. 23, 1968), 11–13; NMP memo for file, June 29, 1971, in "Ga-Gem," Box 10; Coolidge in *HAB*, 71 (Feb. 24, 1969), 14 f, 21 f.

64.  Charles Coolidge to Francis Burr, Jan. 27, 1969, "Bu-By," Box 5.

65.  *HAB*, 73 (May 3, 1971), 12; *HAB*, 73 (Nov. 16, 1970), 16; Albert Nickerson to NMP, Jan. 16, 1969, to Corporation, June 25, 1969, "Ni-Ny," Box 15.

66.  Douglas Dillon to George Putnam, Dec. 10, 1969, "Overseers: General," Box 25; DCB to NMP, Feb. 24, 1969, "Law School: Dean," Box 12.

67.  Sargent Kennedy to Albert Nickerson, Sept. 17, 1969, news rel. Oct. 21, "McKinsey Study," Box 22; "Meeting the Challenges of the 1970s," Feb. 16, 1970, "McKinsey Study," Box 17; NMP to McGB, Feb. 18, 1971, "Pusey: Retirement," Box 23.

68.  Blum to NMP, Jan. 15, 1971, Moynihan to NMP, Feb. 26, Riesman to NMP, Mar. 2, Bok to NMP, Mar. 1, "Pusey: Retirement," Box 23; JBC to NMP, Feb. 20, 1970, NMP to JBC, Mar. 2, "Coo-Coz," Box 10.

69.  McGB, "Were Those the Days," *Daedalus*, 99 (Summer 1970), 531–567.

70.  Joseph Alsop to Douglas Dillon, Nov. 4, 1970, "Pusey: Governing Boards Dinner," Box 23; *HB*, 73 (June 14, 1971), 14.

71.  NMP talk, Sept. 24, 1970, "College: General," Box 8; news rel. June 17, 1971, "Ka-Kel," Box 14.

*Chapter 15*

1.  Calkins quoted in *HAB*, 74 (June 1972), 20.

2.  "President: New," NMPPP, 1969–70, Box 21.

3.  DCB chapter, "History," 24, WmB-S Mss.

4.  Committee on Governance, "Discussion Memorandum Concerning the Choice of a New President," Apr. 1970; DCB int.; *NYT*, Jan. 12, 1971, 24; *NYT*, Jan. 17, 1971, sec. 4, 11.

5.  *HM*, 89 (Oct. 1986), 207.

6.  Minutes of Special Faculty Meeting, Sept. 28, 1971; Burton Dreben, DCB ints.

7.  Bok int.; Derek Bok, "The Crisis in South Africa: One University's Response," March, 1986; *HM*, 93, (July-Aug., 1991), 28; Derek Bok, *Beyond the Ivory Tower: Social Responsibilities of the Modern University* (Cambridge: Harvard Univ. Press, 1982), 243–60.

8.  DCB, "Open Letter on Issues of Race at Harvard," Feb. 1981.

9.  DCB, *AR*, 1986–87.

10.  DCB quoted in Peter David, "The Knowledge Factory," *Economist*, Oct. 4, 1997, 53; DCB int. See DCB, *Higher Learning* (Cambridge: Harvard Univ. Press, 1986) for an extended critique of undergraduate and professional education.

11.  In 1999, Harvard ranked second among universities in percentage of

foreign students enrolled and tenth in absolute number. *CHE Almanac*, 46 (Aug. 27, 1999), 29.

12. DCB, *AR* 1988–89, 1989–90; DCB, "The Social Responsibilities of American Universities," *HG*, June 14, 1991, 17; Bernard Bailyn, "Fixing the Turnips," *HM*, 93 (Mar.-Apr. 1991), 75–78; *Christian Science Monitor*, Oct. 10, 1970, 7.

13. Richard M. Huber, *How Professors Play the Cat Guarding the Cream* (Fairfax, Va.: George Mason Univ. Press, 1992), 32–33.

14. *NYT*, Oct. 31, 1980, 21.

15. *HM*, 91 (Jan.-Feb. 1989), 63; *HC*, Mar. 24, 1993.

16. *HM*, 78 (July-Aug. 1976), 125–29. *HM*, 80 (Jan.-Feb. 1978), 75–76; Derek Bok and William Bowen, *The Shape of the River: Long-Term Consequences of Considering Race in College and University Admissions* (Princeton: Princeton Univ. Press, 1998).

17. HM, 86 (Jan.-Feb. 1984), 78–79; *NYT*, July 7, 1985, 24; Committee on the Status of Women, "Report on Women in the Sciences at Harvard," Feb. 1991.

18. Radcliffe Class of 1960, "Report" (Mar. 1996).

19. *BG*, June 27, 1997, C2; "The Final Touch," *HC*, June 4, 1998.

20. *BG*, Apr. 21, 1999, 5; *HC*, June 10, 1999.

21. *HC*, Oct. 13, 1995.

22. "Have the Culture Wars Ended?" *CHE*, Mar. 6, 1998, B4, B6.

23. James Q. Wilson, "Liberalism versus Liberal Education," *Commentary* (June 1972), 51.

24. Richard Herrnstein, "I.Q.," *Atlantic Monthly*, 228 (Sept. 1971), 43–64; *HC*, Oct. 18, 1980, 23. See also Robert Klitgaard, *Choosing Elites* (New York: Basic Books, 1985), 157–65.

25. Seymour Martin Lipset, "The Sources of Political Correctness on American Campuses," author's possession; FAS, *Free Speech Guidelines;* Randall Kennedy, "Should Private Universities Voluntarily Bind Themselves to the First Amendment? No!" *CHE*, Sept. 21, 1994, B1–2.

26. *HM*, 101 (July-Aug. 1999), 82; Jon Levenson quoted in Jane Tassel, "The Thirty Years' War," *HM*, 102 (Sept.-Oct. 1999), 61.

27. "International Studies in The Faculty of Arts and Sciences," July, 1993; *CHE*, Dec. 12, 1998, A69.

28. Roderick McFarquhar int.; *BG*, June 1, 1998, A1; Janine R. Wedel, *Collision and Collusion: The Strange Case of Western Aid to Eastern Europe, 1989–1998* (New York: St. Martin's Press, 1998), 121–182.

29. *Newsweek*, Apr. 29, 1996), 56 f; *NYT*, Dec. 7, 1980, 98.

30. Charles Clotfelter, *Buying the Best: Cost Escalation in Elite Higher Education* (Princeton: Princeton Univ. Press, 1996), 26–30.

31. Christopher Rathbone, "The Problems of Reaching the Top of the Ivy League ... and Staying There," *Times Higher Education Supplement*, Aug. 2, 1980, 10–11.

32. Huber, *Professors*, 40; *HG*, June 14, 1991, 17. See also Martin Anderson, *Imposters in the Temple* (New York: Simon and Schuster, 1992).

33. *Economist* (June 3, 1995), 28.

*Chapter 16*

1. Andrew Heiskell, *Outsider, Insider* (New York: Marian-Darien Press, 1998), 230.

2. HR, McGB ints.

3. Heiskell, *Outsider, Insider*, 227; Committee on the Structure and Function of the Board of Overseers Concerning Harvard's Governmental Structure, "Report" (Dec. 1978), 11.

4. *HAB*, 74 (Apr. 1972), 60–61.

5. Heiskell, *Outsider, Insider*, 227.

6. JTD int.

7. Committee on Governance, "Organization and Structure of the Governing Boards and the President's Office" (Mar. 1971).

8. John Morton Blum, Jack Reardon ints.

9. Administrative Services *VC*, 1974–75; Max Hall, *Harvard University Press, A History* (Cambridge: Harvard Univ. Press, 1986), 195–99.

10. Charles Daly, Daniel Steiner ints.

11. "Robin Schmidt, Memorandum to Charles Daly," quoted in *HC*, Jan, 6, 1975.

12. Daniel Steiner int., Committee on Governance, "A Memorandum on Issues and Choices, Harvard and Money" (Cambridge; Harvard, 1970), 6.

13. Governance, "Harvard and Money" 13; *HAB*, 75 (Oct. 1972), 18–19, *HAB*, 75 (July 1973), 34; *HM*, 76 (Nov. 1973), 14.

14. *HM*, 77 (Feb. 1975), 12c-d; *NYT*, Nov. 25, 1975, 25; "Financial Report to the Board of Overseers," 1973–74, 60.

15. Carl A. Vigeland, *Great Good Fortune* (Boston: Houghton, Mifflin, 1986), 154, 159; Robert Lenzner and Stephen S. Johnson, "Harvard Is Knee-Deep in Derivatives," *Forbes* (Nov. 20, 1995), 106–12.

16. Henry Hansmann, "Why Do Universities Have Endowments?" *Journal of Legal Studies* (Jan. 1990), 3–42; "Financial Report," 1998–1999.

17. *WSJ*, Oct. 13, 1998, C1.

18. "Harvard and Money," 31–32.

19. Hale Champion and Thomas O'Brien ints.; "Financial Report," 1995–96.

20. Susan Feagin int.; Bayley Mason to John T. Dunlop, Jan. 8, 1971.

21. Fred Glimp, HR ints.

22. Fred Glimp, Thomas Reardon, and Susan Feagin ints.

23. Robert Frost, "Build Soil—A Political Pastoral," in *Complete Poems of Robert Frost* (New York: Holt, Rinehart & Winston, 1964), 430; *NYT*, Mar. 15, 1995, B11; Thomas Reardon int.

24. John T. Bethell, "How Does It Feel to Have a 73-Megawatt Headache?," *HM*, 82 (July-Aug. 1980), 19–29; Hale Champion and Thomas O'Brien ints.; Vigeland, *Great Good Fortune*, 25–27.

25. Daniel Steiner, Hale Champion ints.

26. Heiskell, *Outsider, Insider*, 23.

27. Thomas O'Brien int.

28. Putnam quoted in BG, June 1, 1980; John Bethell, "How Does it Feel to Have a 73-Megawatt Headache?" *HM*, 82 (July-Aug. 1980), 19–29; Hooks Burr int.; on DCB, private source.

29. John Hoerr, *We Can't Eat Prestige* (Philadelphia: Temple Univ. Press, 1997), 59–62, 192.

30. Taylor quoted in ibid., 211; Kristine Rondeau, Anne Taylor, Peter McKinney ints.

31. JTD int.; Theodore Barnett, "Exempt Employees at Harvard University, 1973–1988" (typescript); Office of Financial Systems, "Tabulation of Salaried Staff," Nov. 2, 1993, Oct. 29, 1999, a/p; *HM*, 102 (May-June 2000), 71.

32. "Statement of Policy in Regard to Patents and Copyrights as adopted by the President and Fellows on November 3, 1975."

33. Joyce Brinton int.; James H. Snider, "Harvard's Gene Splicing Affair: A New Relationship Between the University and Industry" (Senior Thesis, Harvard College, Mar. 1981); "Memorandum to the Harvard Corporation from the Ad Hoc Committee on DNA Technology," May 6, 1980, quoted in Snider, "Gene Splicing Affair."

34. David Landes int.; typescript of remarks at faculty meeting, May 2, 1995; A. Michael Spence int.

35. Daniel Steiner int., Benefits Process Review Committee, "Report to the Dean," Nov. 7, 1994; "Statement by Harvard Corporation Regarding Benefits Issues," Apr. 27, 1995.

36. Landes remarks, May 2, 1995; David Landes int.

*Chapter 17*

1. Henry Meadow int., Oct. 1974, WmB-S Mss.

2. Dean of FAS, *AR*, 1984–85, 1985–86, 1986–87; A. Michael Spence int.

3. *HM*, 92 (May-June 1990), 67; *HC*, Sept. 29, 1989, Apr. 2, 1990.

4. Dean of FAS, *Letter to Faculty*, Feb. 9, 1994; Dean of FAS, *AR* 1995, 1996.

5. Dean of FAS, *AR*, 1979–80.

6. FAS Standing Committee on the Status of Women, "Report on Women in the Sciences at Harvard" (1991).

7. *HM*, 84 (Sept.-Oct., 1981) 82–83; Dean of FAS, *AR*, 1980–81; *BG*, May 20, 1997, B1, 4.

8. Sidney Verba int.; Sidney Verba to Phyllis Keller, Sept. 9, 1981.

9. *BG*, May 20, 1998, B1, 4.

10. *Washington Post*, Dec. 25, 1994, 1; *Science*, 270 (Oct. 6, 1995), 121 ff; *NYT*, Sept. 13, 1995, B7; Paul C. Martin and George M. Whitesides, "Science and Engineering at Harvard," for FAS meeting Apr. 9, 1991. Note the nonpresence of Harvard in Peter Galison and Bruce Hevly, eds., *Big Science: The Growth of Large-Scale Research* (Stanford: Stanford University Press, 1992).

11. Stephen S. Hall, "Lethal Chemistry at Harvard," *NYT Magazine* (Nov. 29, 1998), 120–28; *BG*, Jan. 2, 2001, D1, 6.

12.  Philip J. Hilts, "The Science Mob," *New Republic* (May 18, 1992), 24–31; *HM*, 85 (July-Aug. 1983), 22–28; *HM*, 77 (Jan. 1975), 12a-b. See also Daniel Kevles, *The Baltimore Case: A Trial of Politics, Science and Character* (New York: Norton, 1998).

13.  *Christian Science Monitor*, May 30, 1995; *HG*, Jan. 5, 1995; *CHE*, Mar. 17, 1993, A33, Mar. 24, A26; Joyce Brinton int.

14.  Biochemistry and Molecular Biology *VC* 1981–82; Committee on Research Policy Minutes, Dec. 19, 1994; Paul Martin memo to Jeremy Knowles, Mar. 18, 1995.

15.  Richard C. Lewontin, "Women versus the Biologists," *New York Review of Books* (Apr. 7, 1994), 31–35. See also Paul R. Gross and Norman Levitt, *Higher Superstition* (Baltimore: Johns Hopkins Press, 1994); Alan Sokol and Jean Bricmont, *Fashionable Nonsense* (New York: Picador, 1998).

16.  *HM*, 79 (Oct. 1976), 30–33. See also Stephen J. Gould, *The Mismeasure of Man* (New York: Norton, 1981); Richard C. Lewontin, Steven Rose, and Leon J. Kamin, *Not in Our Genes* (New York: Pantheon, 1984).

17.  *Science*, 267 (Jan. 6, 1995), 29; *Science*, 266 (Oct. 21, 1994), 367.

18.  Frank Westheimer, Paul Martin ints.; Chemistry *VC* 1975–76, 1977–78.

19.  *HM*, 76 (Feb. 1974), 22–26; Physics *VC* 1971–72, 1973–74, Physics *AR* 1972–73.

20.  Physics *VC* 1975–76.

21.  David Nelson remarks, History of Science symposium, Harvard, May 15, 1992; *NYT*, Sept. 22, 1998, D1, 5, Jan. 19, 1999, D3; Alan Lightman, "One Stuff," *HM* (July-Aug. 1999), 25 f.

22.  Arnold Arboretum *VC* 1974–75, 1975–76; 1977–78; 1980–81; Max Hall, "The Coming Rejuvenation of Botany," *HM*, 93 (Sept.-Oct. 1990), 38–45.

23.  Ernst Mayr int.; Biology *VC* 1975–76, MCZ *VC* 1974–75, 1978–79; on Mayr, *NYT*, Apr. 15, 1997, C4.

24.  Biology *VC* 1978–79; OEB *VC* 1982–83.

25.  Biology *VC* 1971–72, 1973–74, 1975–76; *HM*, 83 (Oct. 1980), 23–28.

26.  Biochemistry *VC* 1975–76, 1978–79; *HM*, 85 (Jan.-Feb. 1983), 61–69.

27.  Edward O. Wilson, "The Molecular Wars," *HM*, 97 (May-June 1995), 42–49; Wilson, "The Coming Pluralization of Biology and the Stewardship of Systematics," *BioScience*, 39 (Apr. 1989), 242–45.

28.  Mathematics *VC* 1974–75, 1983–84; Benedict Gross int.

29.  Geology *VC* 1975–76, 1976–77, 1983–84.

30.  Astronomy *VC* 1982–83, 1994–55.

31.  Center for Earth and Planetary Physics *AR* 1971–72; Astronomy *VC* 1974–75, 1975–76, 1977–78.

32.  Committee to Review the Division of Engineering and Applied Science, *Report* (July 1975); DEAP *VC* 1973–74, 1975–76; Paul Martin int.

33.  Paul Martin int.

34.  Psychology/Social Relations *VC* 1973–74, 1975–76; Psychology *VC* 1983–84; Brendan Maher int.

35.  Anthropology *VC* 1974–75, 1976–77, 1978–79, 1980–81.

36. Anthropology *VC* 1980–81, 1983–84; David Pilbeam int.; on Stanford, *CHE*, May 29, 1998, A51.

37. Sociology *VC* 1971–72; Daniel Bell, Theda Skocpol, Nathan Glazer ints.

38. Sociology *VC* 1973–74, 1975–76, 1980–81; Peter Marsden int.

39. Economics *VC* 1971–72.

40. Economics *VC* 1969–70, 1970–71, 1971–72, 1973–74, 1975–76.

41. Economics *VC* 1973–74, 1975–76; *NYT*, Feb. 9, 1975, 1.

42. *BG*, Aug. 31, 1986, 78 f.

43. Economics *VC* 1979–80; *BG*, Jan. 9, 1994, 53 f; *Economist*, Mar. 30, 1996.

44. History *VC* 1971–72.

45. History *VC* 1973–74; David Landes, Bernard Bailyn ints.; History *VC* 1982–83.

46. *HC*, Oct. 2, 1986, *NYT*, Oct. 5, 1986, 54; History *VC* 1989–90; *U.S. News & World Report*, Mar. 20, 1995, 108.

47. Government *AR* 1971–72, 1972–73, 1975–76.

48. Government *VC* 1975–76, 1976–77; Judith N. Shklar, "A Life of Learning," *American Council of Learned Societies Occasional Papers*, 9 (1989), 6; James Q. Wilson int.

49. Walter D. Burnham to Chair, 1991; permission of the writer.

50. Kenneth Shepsle, James Q. Wilson ints.

51. Government *VC* 1982–83, 1984–85.

52. Government *VC* 1994–95; Sidney Verba int.

53. Sidney Verba int., quoting Adam Ulam.

54. RRC *VC* 1973–74 f. See also Robert Klitgaard, "On Renewing International Studies," *Journal of Higher Education*, 52 (Mar.-Apr. 1981), 124–42.

55. CFIA *VC* 1973–74, 1975–76, 1981–82 f.

56. *BG*, Jan. 12, 1997, G1.

57. *WSJ*, May 27, 1997, A14, Aug. 13, 1997, A1; *BG*, May 25, 1997, A1, A30; *HC*, June 4, 1998; Janine R. Wedel, *Collision and Collusion* (New York: St. Martin's Press, 1998).

58. James Engell and Anthony Dangerfield, "Humanities in the Age of Money," *HM* (May-June 1998), 48–55, 111.

59. Allan Bloom, *The Closing of the American Mind* (New York; Simon and Schuster, 1987); Alston Chase, *Group Memory: A Guide to College and Student Survival in the 1980s* (Boston: Atlantic Monthly, 1980).

60. Oleg Grabar to DCB, July 15, 1987, Jan Ziolkowski to Jeremy Knowles, May 6, 1992; permission of the writers.

61. Walter J. Bate, "As Rich and Varied as Life Itself . . . ," *HM*, 94 (Nov.-Dec. 1991), 12 f; English *VC* 1973–74, 1975–76, 1982–83.

62. Walter J. Bate, "The Crisis in English Studies," *HM*, 85 (Oct. 1982), 46–53.

63. *HC*, Oct. 9, 1992, 3; Helen Vendler, "Feminism and Literature," *New York Review of Books*, May 31, 1990.

64. Romance Languages *VC* 1974–75, 1978–79.

65. Susan Suleiman int.; Susan R. Suleiman, "Big Bad Wolf: A Short Chapter in the Long Story of Franco-American Relations," *Sites*, 4 (Spring 2000), 145–51.

66. NELC *VC* 1978–79.

67. *HM*, 96 (Jan.-Feb. 1994), 63–64; Linguistics *VC* 1982–83.

68. *HC*, June 7, 1995, 1, 3.

69. Philosophy *VC* 1971–72, 1973–74, 1983–84; Willard van Orman Quine int.

70. Zeph Stewart int.; Zeph Stewart to Phyllis Keller, Oct. 29, 1995; Classics *VC* 1979–80, 1982–83, 1976–77.

71. Classics *VC* 1976–77, 1983–83; *HM*, 76 (Feb. 1974), 38–44; *HM*, 76 (Mar. 1974), 36–42.

72. *HM*, 76 (Oct. 1973), 73–76; Fine Arts and Museums *VC* 1971–72; Seymour Slive, Neil Levine, James Cuno ints.

73. Fine Art and Museums *VC* 1977–78, 1980–81; Seymour Slive int.

74. *HM*, 80 (July-Aug. 1978), 52–54.

75. Fine Arts *VC* 1983–84.

76. Neil Levine, James Cuno, Irene Winter ints.

77. Music *VC* 1975, 1977–78; *HB*, 73 (Apr. 1971), 50.

78. VES *VC* 1975–76, 1977–78; *NYT*, Nov. 7, 1987, 8.

79. Loeb Drama Center *VC* 1971–72, 1973–74.

80. Final Memorandum of Agreement with Robert Brustein (1978); news rel., Dec. 11, 1978.

81. Loeb Drama Center *VC* 1982–83.

82. Orlando Patterson int.; David Riesman to Phyllis Keller, Feb. 17, Apr. 19, 1976; AAS *VC* 1975, 1982–83.

83. *HM*, 84 (Sept.-Oct. 1981, 38–46; Ernest J. Wilson, "AAS at Harvard: What Went Wrong," *HM*, 84 (Sept.-Oct), 40–41.

84. *HM*, 84 (Sept.-Oct., 1981), 38–46, 62. *HM*, 93 (Jan.-Feb. 1991), 54; *HC*, Oct. 23, 1990; *HM*, 95 (Sept.-Oct. 1992), 118.

85. Tom Scoccca, "Stranger in a Strange . . . ," *Boston Phoenix*, May 2, 1978; Peter Applebome, "Can Harvard's Powerhouse Alter the Course of Black Studies?" *NYT*, Nov. 3, 1996, Education section, 24 f.

*Chapter 18*

1. DCB, *AR* 1972–73.

2. GSAS *VC* 1971–72; DCB, *AR* 1972–73, 9; DCB in *HM*, 76 (Mar. 1974), 9–10.

3. Kathleen Holden, "A History of the Graduate School of Arts and Sciences," *HG*, June 2, 1989, 23 f; *HB*, 74 (Apr., 1972), 13.

4. GSAS *VC* 1975–76, 1976–77.

5. Committee to Study the Graduate School, *Report* (Apr. 1985); Brendan Maher int.; GSAS, Degree Candidacy Statistics, 1996; Brendan Maher, *The View from Room Seventeen* (privately printed, 1992), 15.

6. William G. Bowen, *Prospects for Faculty in the Arts and Sciences* (Princeton:

Princeton Univ. Press, 1989). See also William G. Bowen and Neil Rudenstine, *In Pursuit of the Ph.D.* (Princeton: Princeton Univ. Press, 1992).

7. Office of Career Services, "Report on Ph.D. Recipients 1995–96."

8. *NYT*, Sept. 13, 1995, B7.

9. *HC*, Apr. 3, 1995.

10. Joseph Bower to Christolph Wolff, Mar. 12, 1993 (with permission of the writer).

11. *HC*, Apr. 3, 1995.

12. NMP, Charles Fried, James Vorenberg ints.; Michael Levin, "Fear and Loathing at Harvard Law School," *HM*, 97 (Mar.-Apr. 1995), 49; *Washington Post*, Nov. 26, 1994, A21.

13. *NYT*, Aug. 28, 1981, 5; *NYT*, Nov. 26, 1982, 17; James Vorenberg int.

14. *HM*, 88 (Mar.-Apr. 1986), 66.

15. *WSJ*, Nov. 18, 1992, A17; *Time* (Feb. 15, 1982), 54.

16. James Vorenberg int.; *WSJ*, Mar. 25, 1992, A13; Dean Robert Clark to Alumnae, Nov. 1992; *HC*, Apr. 29, 1991, 2, Brock Brower, "The Law School and the Law," *HM*, (Jan.-Feb, 2000), 43–51.

17. *U.S. News & World Report*, Mar. 23, 1992, 64; *U.S. News & World Report*, Mar. 27, 1995, 62; John McArthur int.; *NYT*, Mar. 19, 1995, F14.

18. DCB, *AR* 1977–78.

19. Thomas K. McCraw and Jeffrey L. Cruikshank, eds., *The Intellectual Venture Capitalist: John H. McArthur and the Work of the Harvard Business School, 1980–1995* (Boston: Harvard Business School Press, 1998), 9–13.

20. John McArthur int.; Board of Directors, Associates of the HBS, *The Success of a Strategy* (Dec. 1979); *HC*, Apr. 7, 1982.

21. HBS, "Leadership & Learning Initiative."

22. *WSJ*, Oct. 27, 1993, A3; *BG*, Nov. 2, 1993.

23. *BG*, Jan. 9, 1993, 19; *WSJ*, Jan. 11, 1993, B1, B3; *WSJ*, Mar. 25, 1994, B1, B3; *NYT*, Oct. 30, 1994, F5.

24. *HC*, Mar. 11, 1995; John McArthur int.

25. *HBS Bulletin*, Oct. 1995, 41–56.

26. *Economist* (Oct. 7, 1995), 69; *Business Week* (Mar. 20, 1995), 32; *BG*, Mar. 12, 1995, 75; *NYT*, June 18, 2000, sec. 3, 1, 16; Thomas McCraw int. For an eccentric criticism of HBS, see Kenton W. Elderkin, *Mutiny on the Harvard Bounty: The Harvard Business School and the Decline of the Nation* (Privately printed, 1996).

27. David Bray, Eleanor Shore ints.; Henry Meadow int. in WmBS Mss.

28. Robert Ebert int., Aug. 20, 1974, in "Medical—3 Centuries," WmB-S Mss; *HM*, 78 (July-Aug. 1976), 12g-h, *NYT*, May 13, 1976; *HC*, May 14, 1976.

29. David Bray, Daniel Tosteson ints.

30. DCB, AR 1982–83, 7, 9, 1, 32; Eleanor Shore int.

31. Daniel C. Tosteson, S. James Adelstein, and Susan T. Carver, eds., *New Pathways to Medical Education* (Cambridge: Harvard Univ. Press, 1994); Tosteson int.; *BG*, May 19, 1996, 73; John Langone, *Harvard Med* (New York: Crown, 1995), ch. 1.

32.  Howard Green to Subcommittee of Professors, Feb. 25, 1992 (with permission of writer); Thomas P. Stossel, "Between Service & Scholarship" (typescript), authors' possession.; Eleanor Shore, Barbara Ford Ebert ints.

33.  David Bray int.

34.  Edgar Haber, "Industry and the University," *Nature Biotechnology*, 14 (Apr. 1996), 441–42.

35.  *HM*, 91 (Nov.-Dec. 1988), 78; Susannah Hunnewell, "The Medical-Industrial Complex," *HM*, 96 (Jan.-Feb. 1994), 34–37; Jerry Green int.

36.  *WSJ*, Mar. 12, 1990, A1; Faculty of Medicine, *Faculty Policies on Integrity in Science* (Nov. 1997); "Scientific Misconduct," *HM*, 85 (July-Aug. 1985), 22–28, 54.

37.  *BG*, Aug. 3, 1995, 1.

38.  Elkan Blout and Eleanor Shore ints; *BG*, Dec. 16, 1993, 37.

39.  *HM*, 98 (July-Aug. 1996), 85; *BG*, Oct. 30, 1997, C1; *BG*, Dec. 29, 1997, C1, C4.

40.  Howard Hiatt, "Prospects and Challenges for the School of Public Health," in "Public Health—3 Centuries," WmB-S Mss; *HC*, Apr. 7, 1982, 1, 3.

41.  SPH *VC* 1981–82; *HC*, Apr. 22, 1997, 3.

42.  *HM*, 92 (Nov.-Dec. 1989), 87; *HM*, 98 (July-Aug., 1996), 86–87.

43.  GSE *AR* 1972–73; "Education—3 Centuries," WmB-S Mss.

44.  Arthur G. Powell, *The Uncertain Profession: Harvard and the Search for Educational Authority* (Cambridge: 1980), 280; GSE *VC* 1973–74, 1974–75.

45.  GSE *VC* 1975–76, 1978–79.

46.  Patricia Graham, "Schools: Cacophony About Practice, Silence About Purpose," *Daedalus*, 113 (Fall 1984), 29–57.

47.  DCB, *AR* 1985–86, 9, 36; DCB, "The Challenge to Schools of Education," *HM*, 89 (May-June 1987), 47–57, 79–80; HM, 94 (Sept.-Oct. 1991), 49; Diane Ravitch, review of *Ed School Follies*, by Rita Kramer, *WSJ*, Oct. 28, 1991, A14.

48.  *HG*, June 8, 2000, 1, 3.

49.  HDS *VC* 1973–74.

50.  "Divinity—3 Centuries," WmB-S Mss; HDS *AR* 1973–74; HDS *VC* 1975–76, 1976–77, 1977–78.

51.  HDS *VC* 1981–82; Ari L. Goldman, *The Search for God at Harvard* (New York: Times Books, 1991).

52.  HB, 74 (Sept. 1971), 15–16; *HB*, 74 (Feb. 1972), 13–14; Klaus Herdeg, *The Decentered Diagram: Harvard Architecture and the Failure of the Bauhaus Legacy* (Cambridge: MIT Press, 1983); GSD *VC* 1973–74, 1974–75, 1975–76; Eduard Sekler, William Doebele ints.

53.  *HC*, Sept. 22, 1975; GSD *VC* 1978–79.

54.  *HG*, Nov. 30, 1979; *BG*, Feb. 24, 1980, A3.

55.  *HM*, 93 (Sept.-Oct. 1990), 71; McCue discussion paper, senior faculty comments, Dec. 12, 1991.

56.  DCB, *AR* 1973–74.

57.  KSG *VC* 1966–67, 1970–71, 1981–82.

58.  *HM*, 81 (Jan.-Feb. 1979), 46–51; *NYT*, May 29, 1979, 7; *HM*, 90 (Jan.-Feb. 1988), 65–66; *HM*, 90, (May-June 1988), 97; *HC*, Nov. 12, 1987.

59.  *BG*, Nov. 20, 1991, 24; *HM*, 91 (Sept.-Oct. 1988), 87.


*Chapter 19*

1.  *HB*, 75 (Apr. 1973), 11–13; New England Association of Schools and Colleges, *Evaluation* (Nov. 1997), 15.

2.  Faculty Task Force on the Composition of the Student Body, "Report" (Mar. 1977), 33; Director of Admissions, "Report, 1967–72," 22.

3.  Task Force, "Report," 43; Director of Admissions, *AR*, 1980–81; *HM*, 98 (Nov.-Dec. 1995), 47–51.

4.  L. Fred Jewett, "Issues in Harvard and Radcliffe Admissions 1975–1984"; NR *AR* 1993–95; Office of Budget and Financial Planning, "Fact Book 2000–2001" (Cambridge, 2001).

5.  *San Francisco Examiner*, Feb. 22, 1989; *Los Angeles Times*, Sept. 25, 1966, 1; *HM*, 93 (Jan.-Feb. 1991), 55.

6.  *HG*, Apr. 6, 2000, 1.

7.  Director of Admissions, *AR*, 1993–94.

8.  *BG*, June 13, 1998, 12.

9.  *HM*, 93 (Jan.-Feb. 1991), 24–25; L. Fred Jewett int.

10.  John Larew, "Why Are Droves of Unqualified, Unprepared Kids Getting Into Our Top Colleges?" *Washington Monthly* (June 1991), 10–14; *HM*, 80 (Sept.-Oct. 1977), 83–84. See also John D. Lamb, "The Real Affirmative Action Babies: Legacy Preferences at Harvard and Yale," *Columbia Journal of Law and Social Problems*, 26 (1993), 491–521.

11.  Lawrence Buell to Marlyn Lewis, Sept. 29, 1993, Lewis to James Hankins, June 2, 1994, permission of the authors.

12.  *Washington Post*, Mar. 21, 1995, 1; *BG*, Feb. 21, 1998, 1; Charles T. Clotfelter, *Buying the Best: Cost Escalation in Elite Higher Education* (Princeton: Princeton Univ. Press, 1996).

13.  *NYT*, Dec. 17, 1978, 87; *CHE* (Mar. 6, 1998), A43; *WSJ*, Sept. 5, 1989, A1, 6.

14.  Andrew Delbanco, "Scholarships for the Rich," *NYT Magazine* (Sept. 2, 1996), 36–39.

15.  *WSJ*, Sept. 5, 1989, 1, 26; *NYT*, Sept. 3, 1992, 1; *Economist* (Dec. 5, 1998), 71; Jeremy Knowles, "Letter to the Faculty of Arts and Sciences," Jan. 28, 2000.

16.  Phyllis Keller, *Getting at the Core: Curricular Reform at Harvard* (Cambridge: Harvard Univ. Press, 1982).

17.  Task Force on College Life, *Report* (Oct. 1976).

18.  Archie Epps int.; *NYT*, Dec. 22, 1984, II:14, Nov. 24, 1987, I:8, Oct. 9, 1993, 9; *BG*, Oct. 30, 1993, 20.

19.  Harvard University, *Facts and Figures '95*, 36, 38; Stephan Thernstrom, "Poor But Hopeful Scholars," *HM*, 89 (Sept.-Oct. 1986), 115–20.

20. Richard Eder, "A Diversity of Independence," *NYT*, Dec. 4, 1979, B16.

21. *HM*, 77 (Mar. 1975), 12f-g; Office of Career Services charts; Report on the Class of 1979, Summary; *HM*, 90 (Sept.-Oct. 1987), 42; "Go to Harvard. Write Jokes. Make \$\$\$," *Newsweek* (Oct. 11, 1993), 52.

22. *HC*, Sept. 27, 1993, 1, 3.

23. Task Force on College Life, "Report," 73; *BG*, June 3, 1998, 13.

24. Frank Rich, "Class of '71," *NYT Magazine* (June 5, 1996), 21; *BG*, June 5, 1996, 1.

25. Athletics *VC* 1976–77, 1977–78, 1979–80; *HC*, Dec. 14, 1992; *HM*, 80 (Nov.-Dec. 1977), 81–82.

26. *BG*, Oct. 7, 1993, 74; *WSJ*, Aug. 25, 2000, W16; "Structure of Harvard College," (typescript), authors' possession. 34.

27. Mary C. Waters, "Some Thoughts on Race Relations at Harvard" (typescript), authors' possession; Fred Jewett, Archie Epps, Orlando Patterson ints.

28. Martin Kilson, "The Black Experience at Harvard," *NYT Magazine* (Sept. 2, 1973), 13 f; *NYT Magazine* (Oct. 14), 16 f, (Nov. 11), 191 f; Archie Epps, "A Study of Race Relations at Harvard" (1980); *BG*, Oct. 1, 1990, 1; Archie Epps int.

29. *HM*, 84 (Nov.-Dec. 1981), 84–85, *HM*, 86 (July-Aug. 1984), 77–78.

30. Robert F. Detlefsen, "White Like Me," *New Republic* (Apr. 10, 1989), 18–21; *WSJ*, Sept. 29, 1992, A16; Nathan Glazer, "Frustrated Blacks and Weary Whites," *Times Higher Education Supplement* (June 30, 1990), 15.

31. *HC*, Apr. 14, 16, 17, 27, 1992; *HC*, Mar. 18, 20, 1993; "A Year of Racial Tension," *HM*, 94 (July-Aug. 1992), 60 f.

32. Office of the Dean of Students, "Handbook on Race Relations and the Common Pursuit" (1998 ed.); Archie Epps int.; *HC*, Mar. 27, 1998; *BG*, Dec. 31, 1997, A1, 13, Apr. 6, 1999, D1, 6; Fred Jewett int.

33. *BG*, Jan. 6, 1998, D1, 6.

34. *HM*, 76 (Dec. 1973), 46–52.

35. *HC*, June 4, 1998, B8; *HM*, 98 (Mar.-Apr. 1996), 79–81; *HM*, 99 (July-Aug. 1997), 65.

36. Fred Jewett int.

37. Melanie Thernstrom, *Halfway Heaven* (New York: Doubleday, 1997).

*Epilogue*

1. Charles S. Maier, "Harvard Grows Up," *New Republic*, 195 (Sept. 8, 1986), 15–17.

2. Fred Glimp, Thomas Stevenson ints; "Birthday Bash at Harvard," *U.S. News & World Report*, 101 (Sept. 15, 1968), 3; "Charles on the Charles," *Economist* (Sept. 6, 1986), 25.

3. *NYT*, Sept. 4, 1986, sec.I, 1; Martin Peretz, "Festival Rights," *New Republic* (Sept. 29, 1986), 43; "Birthday Bash," 8.

4. Harvard 350th planners Fred Glimp and Thomas Stevenson hold that the first and not the second was the true reason for Reagan's nonappearance.

5. *NYT*, Sept. 22, 1986, 22.

6. *NYT*, Aug. 31, 1986, 34; Fred Glimp and Thomas Stevenson interviews; "Charles on the Charles," 25.

7. "Harvard at 350," *National Review*, Sept. 26, 1986, 18; Peretz, "Festival Rites," 43; *NYT*, Sept. 8, 1986, 22.

8. Henry Rosovsky, "Do We Need to Fear the Future? A Report from America" (Sir Robert Menzies Oration on Higher Education, University of Melbourne, 1992); Hanna H. Gray, "The Leaning Tower of Academe" (typescript, American Association for the Advancement of Science lecture, Oct. 21, 1995).

9. David Bromwich, reply to Rosovsky, Trilling Seminar, Columbia University (typescript). See also Alvin Kernan, *In Plato's Cave* (New Haven: Yale Univ. Press, 1999).

10. Oscar Handlin, "Peering Toward 2036," *HM*, 89 (Sept.-Oct. 1986), 139–42; Bernard Bailyn, "Fixing the Turnips," *HM*, 93 (Mar.-Apr.(Mar.-Apr. 1991), 78.

11. DCB, "Worrying About the Future," *HM*, 93 (May-June, 1991), 37–47.

12. Craig Lambert, "Renaissance President," *HM*, 93 (May-June, 1991), 29–36; *HC*, Apr. 8, 1991, 2; Henry Rosovsky int.

13. *Diversity and Learning*, NR, *AR* 1993–95; Rudenstine, "The Uses of Diversity," *HM*, 98 (April 1996), 49–62.

14. JBC, *AR* 1951–52, 22; NR, Dennis Thompson ints.

15. *HG*, June 17, 1999, 3–4.

16. *HC*, June 4, 1998, A12.

17. *BG*, March 18, 2001, 1, A22

18. Peter David, "The Knowledge Factory," *Economist* (Oct. 4, 1997), S3.

19. *WSJ*, Nov. 22, 1999, A1, 10.

20. *NYT*, April 4, 2000, C16. *BG*, Sept. 19, 1999, A1, A21.

21. *WSJ*, Sept. 12, 2000, B1; John Dunlop, "The Professional and Global University," *HM*, 103 (Jan.-Feb. 2001), 57.

22. Bruce Weber, "Inside the Meritocracy Machine," *NYT Magazine* (Apr. 28, 1996), 44 f.

23. *HC*, Mar. 21, 2000.

24. NR, Denis Thompson ints. *BG*, Aug. 22, 1999, B1, 6.

# ACKNOWLEDGMENTS

In telling this tale we have relied heavily on the generosity of both friends and strangers. We are especially grateful for the research support of the Spencer Foundation. Without the act of faith of that exemplary institution, our book could not have been written. We owe a large debt as well to Brandeis University for its support. And we offer special thanks, too, to the Harvard Corporation for making archival materials available to us, as well as to the Rockefeller Foundation for a term as Resident Scholars at its Bellagio Center.

The staff of the Harvard Archives—in particular, University Archivist Harley Holden and Reference Archivist Brian Sullivan—were endlessly helpful. So, too, were our research assistants, Michael Fein and Darra Mulderry, whose intelligent assiduity made it possible for us to absorb the contents of 1,000 manuscript boxes. Jacob Gertzog and Greg Renoff did a fine job of checking footnotes, and Mr. Gertzog ably helped us to gather the book's illustrations.

We greatly benefited from the knowledge of Bernard Bailyn and Stephan Thernstrom of the Harvard History department, and longtime *Daedalus* editor Stephen Graubard, who took time out from busy careers to read our manuscript in its entirety and give us their detailed and insightful reactions. We owe much as well to the good judgment of our Oxford editor, Peter Ginna, and our agent, John Wright.

Scores of people, both in and out of Harvard, responded candidly to our interviews and questions, and/or read parts of our text or helped us in other ways. These coadjutors greatly enhanced our understanding of the complex institution that is the subject of this book. If errors of fact and understanding remain in our account (and we have little doubt that they do), that is our doing (or not-doing), not theirs. We thank them all:

Daniel Aaron, James Adelstein, Walter Jackson Bate, Fran Beane, Sam Beer, Daniel Bell, Ann Berman, Elkan Blout, John Blum, Derek Bok,

Glen Bowersock, David Bray, Joyce Brinton, McGeorge Bundy, Francis Burr, Ann Carter, Hale Champion, Catherine Clinton, I. Bernard Cohen, Saul Cohen, Heather Cole, Daniel Coquillette, James Cuno, Charles Daley, William Doebele, John Dowling, Burton Dreben, John Dunlop, Henry Ehrenreich, Archie Epps, Susan Feagin, David Fischer, Franklin Ford, John Fox, Charles Fried, John K. Galbraith, Fred Glimp, Warren Goldfarb, Patricia Graham, Jerry Green, Stephen Greenblatt, Benedict Gross, Oscar Handlin, Stephen Harrison, Stanley Hoffmann, Gerald Holton, Fred Jewett, Jane Kamensky, James Kloppenberg, Jeremy Knowles, David Landes, Marlyn Lewis, Neil Levine, Roderick MacFarquhar, Brendan Maher, Peter Marsden, Paul Martin, Ernst Mayr, John McArthur, Joseph McCarthy, Thomas McCraw, Peter McKinney, David Nathan, Richard Neustadt, Thomas O'Brien, Orlando Patterson, David Pilbeam, Richard Pipes, Lorraine Powers, Nathan Pusey, Willard Quine, Jack Reardon, Thomas Reardon, David Riesman, Henry Rosovsky, Neil Rudenstine, Paul Samuelson, Arthur Schlesinger, Eduard Sekler, Robert Shenton, Kenneth Shepsle, Eleanor Shore, Theda Skocpol, Seymour Slive, A. Michael Spence, Daniel Steiner, Zeph Stewart, Edith Stokey, Susan Suleiman, Ann Taylor, Carol Thompson, Dennis Thompson, Daniel Tosteson, Toni Turano, Helen Vendler, Sidney Verba, James Vorenberg, Frank Westheimer, Dean K. Whitla, Edward Wilson, James Q. Wilson, Irene Winter, Jeffrey Wolcowitz, Betty Woodward, Richard Zeckhauser, Sally Zeckhauser.

# INDEX